The Felt Community

The Felt Community

Commonalty and Mentality before the Emergence of Indian Nationalism

Rajat Kanta Ray

OXFORD

UNIVERSITY PRESS

YMCA Library Building, Jai Singh Road, New Delhi 110 001

Oxford University Press is a department of the University of Oxford. It furthers the
University's objective of excellence in research, scholarship, and education
by publishing worldwide in

Oxford   New York

Auckland   Bangkok   Buenos Aires   Cape Town   Chennai
Dar es Salaam   Delhi   Hong Kong   Istanbul   Karachi   Kolkata
Kuala Lumpur   Madrid   Melbourne   Mexico City   Mumbai   Nairobi
São Paulo   Shanghai   Taipei   Tokyo   Toronto

Oxford is a registered trademark of Oxford University Press
in the UK and in certain other countries

Published in India
By Oxford University Press, New Delhi

© Oxford University Press, 2003

The moral rights of the author have been asserted
Database right Oxford University Press (maker)

First published 2003

ISBN 0 19 565863 9

Typeset by Le Studio Graphique, New Delhi 110 017
Printed at Roopak Printers, New Delhi 110 032
Published by Manzar Khan, Oxford University Press
YMCA Library Building, Jai Singh Road, New Delhi 110 001

Contents

Part I
Ambiguous Encounters At Close Quarters

Part II
Storm Across The Ganges

Preface

This book addresses a knotty old question: what were nations like before nationalism? To this question there is a knotty current answer: there were no nations before nationalism. The great Max Weber himself seemed to come close to saying this, but he then spoke of communities of sentiment which preceded nations. I wish to explore the basis of commonalty and the nature of mentality before the emergence of nationalism.

A nation is born when it perceives itself as such. For all the objective factors that may assist it in this self-perception, this is, in the last resort, a mental process. Its roots are to be found in the history of mentality. Mentality, of course, consists of both ideas and emotions. It is a barren history that tells the story of a national movement in terms of intellectual outlook alone, although that is by no means to discount its crucial importance. Nationalism is above all an idea: the modern idea of the sovereign national state. However, emotion is equally important. You may try and engineer a nation by propagating an idea. You may 'invent' a tradition, 'construct' an identity, 'imagine' a nation, but however much you print or propagate, the 'project' will not be successful until you hit upon some real emotional bond.

Furthermore, it may be possible to invent the idea, but it is not as easy to engineer the emotion. You may discover the emotion if it exists, and harness it to your idea. Ideas have been known to be manufactured, but would you also say you can manufacture an emotion? Yes, an emotion may be triggered. But there are limits to this: it cannot be done against the grain. Only if power is built upon an existing passion will there be a tangible achievement, not otherwise. An emotion, a passion, is triggered by mechanisms. Manipulate the mechanism, and perhaps you may detach the emotion from an older idea and forge it into a newer one. The emotions are the building blocks. One may construct structures of widely divergent shapes with the blocks. One may build a united India, a separate Pakistan, a liberated Bangladesh, an independent Kashmir, a sovereign Khalistan. Much will depend on the specific developments and historical circumstances, on the chain of events. Nonetheless, the general principle is still valid: ideas and emotions are equally important in the political processes of forging a nation.

In the mental history of the *Homo sapiens*, nationalist ideas are only a product of recent history. Patriotic emotions are older in origin. Patriot and nationalist: the same individual is both today. There was, however, a time when a patriot would not and could not have been a nationalist. The modern nationalist has acquired by virtue of his ideology a universal hold which the patriot of the past could not derive from emotion alone. Intermittent as the emotion was, it lacked the uniformity of a creed and the power of an organization. Nor did it have the potential for oppression which it has today, as for instance when one nation appropriates a territory inhabited by other, submerged nationalities.

The transformation of a civilization into nationhood in the Indo-Pak–Bangla subcontinent between 1858 and 1971 was a triumph which was at the same time a tragedy—for Pakhtoons and Kashmiris, Chakmas and Nagas, Mohajirs and Andamanese. The triumph and tragedy of nationalism lies in the break-up of the old, sometimes oppressive, civilizations of the past. The Europe of the Holy Roman Empire, the Caliphate of the Ottomans, the Celestial Empire of China, the India of the Great Mughals are such instances. As free nations emerged out of sprawling civilizations, other submerged nationalities and communities of sentiment were suppressed in the process. There is no escape from this until nationhood learns to transform itself into confederate inter-nationalism of the kind that the Association of South East Asian Nations (ASEAN) and the European Union appear to promise. If the South Asian Association for Regional Cooperation (SAARC), and the world at large, follow suit, the patriot of an ever-widening community of emotion might yet have his day, and the nationalist of the suppressed nationality might find a way out of his predicament.

Nehruvian India was secure in the notions of democracy, secularism, and socialism. Not all the notions of the time worked out. The India of my childhood was nonetheless an emotionally safe place, and nationalism appeared to promise a just and rational way of life. In my youth the study of Indian nationalism in the context of Bengal offered me intellectual sustenance.

After a while I wanted to move on to a new area. So when Professor Irfan Habib asked me to write again on the nationalist movement for an issue of *The Indian Historical Review* devoted to the topic, I chose instead to explore the initial resistance to the British in the Mughal *suba* of Bengal. The question at the back of my mind was: how did this initial resistance relate to modern Indian nationalism? I could not see much of a connection at the time.

Later I was induced by my friend Mushirul Hasan to write in memory of the late Professor Eric Stokes for whom I had always felt a deep affection. I wrote on his subject, the 'Mutiny'. Even before this I had begun exploring the possibility of a history of emotions, as distinct from intellectual history. I was not certain then that emotions might have a history. Thoughts, notions, concepts, yes, but emotions, sentiments, impulses? It struck me that conscious sentiments and felt emotions might interact in new ways with changing ideas and altered notions of life, even while remaining what they always were. As I wrote on the Mutiny, the outlines of a mentality became clearer. I saw raw impulses, inchoate ideas, and keen sentiments intertwined in a mass upsurge that lay outside the sphere of the modern nationalist agitation that had just begun to manifest itself in Bengal, away from Hindustan.

Even then I did not have a book in mind. On the night of 6 December 1992, millions of people in India, Pakistan, and Bangladesh experienced trauma as the BBC displayed the domes of the Babri Masjid collapsing under the blows of hate-inspired, demented crowds. In the riots that followed, shouts of *'Musalmanon ka do sthan, Pakistan aur Kabristan'* were accompanied by the horrifying act of small children being thrown out of a moving train because they belonged to the community named in the chilling slogan. Lal Krishna Advani sought to justify what had happened in the pages of *The Telegraph*. Swapan Dasgupta, the editor and a friend of Advani, was fair minded enough to let me rebut all that the politician had written. The hate mail in response convinced me more than ever that there is no deliverance for us except within a loose confederation of the nation states of the subcontinent. For such a confederation to work, it must draw sustenance from the felt community which is evident in history.

I began to trace the identities dubbed Hindu, Muslim, and India in our history. As I did so, the connections with my earlier work on the Mutiny and the initial Mughal resistance to the British conquest became evident. I then rewrote these earlier themes along with the theme of the emergence of 'Musalmanan', 'Hunud', and 'Hindian' in our past. I had encountered the expression 'Hindus and Musalmans of Hindustan' in the Mutiny proclamation earlier in my research. I now traced the evolution of Hindu, Musalman, and Hindustan in the civilization and mentality of the subcontinent, and tied this up with the attempt of the Mutineers to restore the Mughal *Padshahi*. The earlier effort to defend the Mughal sovereign against the East India Company fell into place naturally in this historical scheme. This book is the result.

I feel my adolescent faith in reason, modernity, nationalism, secularism, and democracy from my days in Presidency College as strongly as ever. The circle of reason will expand in the longer run and will incorporate the citizens of Pakistan, India, and Bangladesh in an extended civil society, but I have no hope that I will see this in my lifetime.

Acknowledgements

The bulk of this book has not been published in any earlier form. Some sections, however, are based on what I have published earlier in rather different form in 'Colonial Penetration and the Initial Resistance: the Mughal Ruling Class, the English East India Company and the Struggle for Bengal 1756–1800', *Indian Historical Review*, July 1985–January 1986, vol. XII, nos. 1–2 (copyright: Indian Council of Historical Research); 'Calcutta or Alinagar: Contending Conceptions in the Mughal–English Confrontation of 1756–1757', in Indu Banga (ed.), *Ports and Their Hinterlands in India (1700–1950)*, Manohar, New Delhi, 1992 (sponsored jointly by the Urban History Association of India, the Nehru Memorial Museum and Library, and the Indian Institute of Advanced Study); 'Race, Religion and Realm: The Political Theory of "the Reigning Indian Crusade", 1857', in Mushirul Hasan and Narayani Gupta (eds.), *India's Colonial Encounter: Essays in Memory of Eric Stokes*, Manohar, New Delhi, 1993 (copyright: Mushirul Hasan and Narayani Gupta). I rewrote all this earlier material for this book and I express grateful acknowledgements to the editors, copyright holders, and sponsors. Individuals to whom I am deeply indebted include, among others, Irfan Habib, Iqbal Hussain, Moin-ul-Haq, Nupur Chaudhuri, Asad-uz-Zaman, Gautam Bhadra, Dhruba Gupta, Rukun Advani, Shireen Maswood, Lakshmi Subramanian, and Deep Kanta Lahiri Chaudhuri.

Calcutta
May 2002

RAJAT KANTA RAY

Part One

Ambiguous Encounters
At Close Quarters

1

Nationalism and Patriotism

Modern nationalism was born out of civil society. Civil society, a society of individuals which runs implicitly counter to descent groups, was the product of the intellectual and political transformation of the Atlantic world in the seventeenth and eighteenth centuries. The Glorious Revolution, the American War of Independence, and the French Revolution, were the signposts to this wider process. In India an adolescent civil society manifested itself in the Indian National Congress in the late nineteenth century. However, everywhere in the nineteenth-century world, national movements, ethnic stirrings, and communal mobilizations appeared to emphasize the reification of descent groups, with roots in earlier histories of mentalities and emotions. The extensions of print culture and public educational systems with a strong emphasis on standardized school syllabi stimulated the growth of civil society in India and abroad. At the same time, the process helped in the articulation of ethnic or religious groups with strong emotional appeals inherited from a remembered patriotic past. The emergence of the modern world system of sovereign nation-states is therefore a complex story, with intertwined intellectual and emotional components. Nationalism, civil society, and the sovereignty of the people are but manifestations of the same process: a modern intellectual and political development that extended from Western Europe outwards to the Americas and the Indian Ocean. This is intellectual history; it is a history of modern times. Patriotism and the drives and collective emotions underlying ethnic and religious attachments have a psychic and emotional history that stretches back to antiquity. The emergence of the modern world has, therefore, to be viewed in terms of the history of a mentality. Such a history will incorporate emerging ideas, rooted emotions, and shifting identities into a single complex psychic weave.

Soon after the Chinese Revolution of 1911, Max Weber wrote:

> Only fifteen years ago, men knowing the Far East, still denied that the
> Chinese qualified as a 'nation'; they held them to be only a 'race'. Yet
> today, not only the Chinese political leaders but also the very same
> observers would judge differently. Thus it seemed that a group of people
> under certain conditions may attain the quality of a nation through specific
> behaviour, or they may claim this quality as an 'attainment'—and within
> very short spans of time at that.[1]

What is this 'specific behaviour' which Weber spoke of? Slightly
later, he defined it as the disposition of a people to manifest themselves
in a sovereign national state. 'One might well define the concept of a
nation in the following way: a nation is a *community of sentiment* which
would adequately manifest itself in a state of its own; hence a nation is
a community which normally tends to produce a state of its own.'[2]

In the case of Japan, the idiom of the modern national state manifested itself earlier than in China, during the Meiji Restoration of 1867.
In India, this might perhaps be dated to the formation of the Indian
National Congress in 1885, if not earlier. With regard to the possibility
of an earlier date, the question might here be asked: had the Indians
shown the will to become a sovereign national state in the uprising of
1857? If not, why not? Also, why had they not behaved in the manner
specified by Weber during the wars of resistance of the rise of the
English East India Company in the eighteenth century? The most
obvious answer would be that the behaviour alluded to expresses itself
through a new idiom. This is the language of the modern national state.
The rebels of 1857 and the warriors opposed to the East India Company's
rise to power did not command this idiom. Weber however did not
speak only of 'specific behaviour'; he also mentioned 'community of
sentiment'. In his formulation, the latter necessarily precedes the former.
Nationalism has, then, a prehistory, a history of sentiment; it is bound
up with the evolution of a mentality, of which the idea of the sovereign
national state is only the latest element, preceded by emotions and
sentiments spanning an extended period of time.

In his autobiography, Surendranath Banerjea spoke of his heady
sense of participation in 'a nation in making'.[3] The time he referred to
was the last quarter of the nineteenth century. Barely fifty years earlier
Ram Mohun Roy, impelled by a sense of the multiplicity of the
population of the subcontinent, had spoken in London of 'the nations
of Hindoostan'.[4] He did not speak of a single Indian nation then. When

two generations later Banerjea sensed its emergence, he still would not speak of it as already 'made'. Nationalism, i.e. the ideology of the sovereign national state, was a new thing in India, and indeed in the world. National movements crystallized in Europe no earlier than the romantic plots against the Restoration of 1815. This was ethnic nationalism, astir in the multinational Habsburg dominions governed by Prince Metternich. Civic nationalism was slightly older: the Declaration of Independence by the United States of America (1776) and the defence of the first French Republic by the nation in arms (1792–3) are early examples. Ethnic nationalism may or may not have been rooted in civil society; civic nationalism, by definition, is so rooted.

Indian nationalism derived from the idea of civil society imported from Europe. However, as in Europe and elsewhere, the sentiments behind it derived from a longer history, rooted, as these emotions were, in a culture of great antiquity. As emotions are as strong as, if not stronger than, ideas, the history of nationalism in India must begin with its prehistory. Formally, the inception of the Indian nationalist movement may be dated to the Indian National Congress of 1885, or perhaps a little earlier to the provincial political associations that agitated for constitutional rights. But that is the history of the idea brought from Europe. Political science, which itself arose from the idea of the modern national state, has rendered the history of nationalism in terms of the history of this idea. Intellectual history ought not to be read in isolation from emotional history, where large masses of people are concerned, and least of all in India, the graveyard of countless nationalities and the cradle of unsuspected nationalisms.

The prehistory of every national movement lies in emotions, identities, and notions. These constitute the mentality and culture of the body of people who are or have been seized by the idea of becoming a sovereign national state. That idea may be new, but the mentality and emotions are rooted in the past. In India, the Mutiny of 1857 gives us a glimpse of the emotions and identities that constituted the indigenous political mentality of the people untouched as yet by the imported idea of nationalism. The aspirations then defeated somehow led to the subsequent birth of a nationalist movement. The Mutiny, the earlier wars which resulted in the replacement of Mughal suzerainty by English sovereignty, and indeed the whole evolution of identities in the subcontinent over a millennium, transmitted emotions that had a bearing upon the struggle(s) for freedom in late colonial India.

Nationalism

Weber's understanding of the nation as a chemical compound comprising the sovereign state and the pre-existing community which felt itself to be one was not a wholly new definition. The felt community which he called the 'community of sentiment' was earlier referred to by Hegel by the ancient term 'nation', which at one time was interchangeable with race or tribe or community. 'Nations', said Hegel, 'may have had a long history before they finally reach their destination—that of forming themselves into states'. More recently, a growing band of political and social scientists have rejected the notion that nations existed at all before their fusion with the state resulted in nationalism. 'It is nationalism which engenders nations, and not the other way round.'[5]

In this view of the matter, nationalism is not the awakening of an old, dormant force; it is, on the contrary, a new form of social organization.

> Nations as a natural, God-given way of classifying men, as an inherent though long-delayed political destiny, are a myth; nationalism, which sometimes takes pre-existing cultures and turns them into nations, sometimes invents them, and often obliterates the pre-existing cultures: that is a reality, for better or worse, and in general an inescapable one.[6]

Before the age of nationalism, which produced the present international system of sovereign national states, there was therefore no nation, at least not in the sense understood by these scholars. The very possibility of imagining the nation arose only with the rise of script languages, organized states, and a modern view of the cosmos.[7]

For Benedict Anderson, the modern nation is an artefact, 'an imagined political community'. The institution that fostered it was 'print capitalism'.[8] Ernest Gellner, from another angle, finds the critical factor in the uniform school syllabi which modern educational systems propagate through standardized languages.[9] Whatever the factor that makes it possible to imagine the nation, there is in the concept of the nation a constructed or invented element.

> And just because so much of what subjectively makes up the modern 'nation' consists of such constructs and is associated with appropriate and, in general, fairly recent symbols or suitably tailored discourse (such as 'national history'), the national phenomenon cannot be adequately investigated without careful attention to 'the invention of traditions'.[10]

Crawford Young, who takes a roughly similar position with regard to the nations of Africa, maintains that there occurred critical transformations of the metaphor of commonalty under colonial rule. In Rwanda and Burundi, for instance, the Belgians extended their rule over the unprivileged Hutu majority, as well as the dominant Tutsi minority, and in the process 'made these concepts much more systematic and extensive classifications of the subject populace'. He is, however, constrained to admit, 'Tutsi and Hutu were not colonial innovations'.[11] And well he might. It would be no consolation to the Tutsi and the Hutu, who have massacred one another in the bloodiest pogroms of post-colonial Africa, to learn that they are the figments of Belgian imagination, with no call to dwell on the bloodshed as there is no knowing who spills whose blood.

Shorn of the exaggerated stress on the invented, imagined, or constructed element of the nation, however, there is much to recommend the view that the nation, as redefined by nationalism, is a novel phenomenon in history; and nowhere more so than in India. Nationalism is indeed an integral part of the modern vocabulary. In India it was part of English vocabulary. The earliest use of the word 'nation' cited in the *Oxford English Dictionary* dates back to 1300 CE. The dictionary, however, cites no earlier use of the word 'nationalism' than *Fraser's Magazine* in 1844: 'nationalism is another word for egotism'.[12] Johnson's *Dictionary* of 1755 has no entry on nationalism, but does dwell on the word 'nation'.[13]

The early use of the term nationalism was theological: the doctrine that certain nations (as contrasted with individuals) were the object of divine election. Thus, we have G.S. Faber (1836): 'The several doctrinal systems, usually denominated Arminianism, Nationalism and Calvinism ...' Later the same term acquired the meaning of 'devotion to one's nation; national aspiration; a policy of national independence'.[14] Political science gave it a more defined meaning; and in that sense, the word could not have come into use before a relationship was established between three modern developments: (1) the sovereign state with its exclusive territory over which it claims a legitimate monopoly of the means of violence; (2) the doctrine of popular sovereignty; (3) a civil society[15] in which the rule of law detaches the individual from communal bonds and treats him as a subject/citizen equal in the eye of the law. These developments, combined with the older sense of ethnic or historical identity, created nationalism.[16] In India, all these developments, setting aside the question of historical identity for the moment, were colonial developments.

In 1883, at the height of the controversy over the Ilbert Bill which generated much ill will between 'Europeans' and 'natives', a body was formed under the leadership of Surendranath Banerjea called the Indian National Conference, which claimed to represent a new political constituency named 'the Indian nation'. Two years later, yet another body called the Indian National Congress assembled in Bombay under the retired English Civilian Alan Octavian Hume, and claimed the same constituency more successfully. The following year, the two bodies merged. After 1886, the Indian National Congress acquired an uncontested right to speak for the novel constituency implicit in its name. In the years to come, the Indian nation coalesced around this body. A split in the Congress in 1907, far from endangering the emerging nation, intensified its emotional existence.

The Indian nation was a new political category: just a generation before the Ilbert Bill, the Mutiny in upper India had claimed no such constituency for itself. Although the idea of the nation was even then not altogether unknown among the English-educated Indians in the Presidency towns of Calcutta, Bombay, and Madras, the Mutineers did not speak in that language. Their war against the infidels (*nisara*) and the Europeans (*firangi*) was conducted in the name of the Mughal Emperor and on behalf of 'the Hindus and Musalmans of Hindustan'. They strove to restore the realm (*mulk*) of an emperor (*padshah*) who derived his title from a vanished supremacy created in the sixteenth century by Emperor Akbar and his ancestors. The category 'Hindus and Musalmans of Hindustan' was, however, a coinage of the sepoys and rebel princes themselves. It was, in that respect, no less novel than the category 'Indian nation'.

And yet what a gulf lay between these two categories as far as political and social ideas are concerned! One looks forward to a 'modern' world; the other looks back to a 'medieval' past. The idea of nationalism, a phenomenon of which the intellectual antecedents can be dated back no earlier than the movement led by Ram Mohun Roy and his contemporaries for the constitutional rights of the Indians, is fairly well documented. The phrase 'Hindus and Musalmans of Hindustan' coined by the leaders of the Mutiny is more elusive in its descent. It contains three distinct elements: 'Hindustan', 'Hindu', and 'Musalman'. Severally, these categories were much older, and the relationship between the three elements, hinted at in the phrase, was also the product of a long historical evolution. Furthermore, indigenous equivalents of the foreign term 'Indians'—'Hindustanis', 'Hindis' (Hindian) 'Ahl-e-Hind'— were well known in medieval times. In antiquity, the Puranas had spoken of the 'Bhārati' (sons of King Bharata) as one people sprung from a common ancestor. The complex evolution of identities, which threw up over the course of time categories such as Bhāratavarsha, Al-Hind, Hindustan, Hindus, Muslims, and Hindis, offered a range of terms from which the phrase 'Hindus and Musalmans of Hindustan' was chosen in 1857.

The term 'Indian nation' was by contrast a foreign coinage. But this too, despite its newness and its strong link with the British colonial state, was unavoidably connected with the historical evolution of identities in India. Colonialism and nationalism were linked political phenomena in nineteenth- and twentieth-century Asia and Africa, but nations in the older ethnic and cultural sense of the term had existed long before the political phenomenon of nationalism.

Nation

The sphere in which Weber located the community of sentiment is culture. When a cultural community assumes definite shape in a state, it becomes, in his perception, a nation: henceforth, its sphere, by contrast, is politics.[17] Historically and psychologically, the cultural community does, however, often underpin the nation-state. Indeed, if a community of emotion, in the process of becoming a nation-state, incorporates more than one cultural community, the structure may, in certain conditions, fragment. The 'nation' and the 'fragment' have been juxtaposed in some recent accounts of colonial and post-colonial Indian politics. Warm as the advocacy of the 'fragment' has been, the terms have trapped its advocates into defining the part in relation to the whole.[18] In a subcontinent as diverse as South Asia, the nation is culturally and emotionally far more difficult to track than the fragment, but the psychic bond that unites the whole is not therefore less important than that which distinguishes the part. Several cultural communities can and do fuse into an overarching community of emotion: India, both as a civilization in the past and as a nation at present, is an example.

The cultural and emotional distinctiveness of Indian civilization and its modern transformation into the nation-state has often constituted an identifiable historical theme.[19] The theme in no way leads to any denial of the nationality of the various cultural communities that have made up the civilization and the nation(s). To describe these distinct cultural communities as fragments does not go far enough; it is historically closer to reality to treat these various communities of sentiment as nationalities coexisting in a civilization underpinned by a common mentality, i.e. a broader community of emotion. 'Nationality', like 'nationalism', is a modern term. It indicates those ethnic, language or cultural groups, or even religious communities, which have not manifested themselves in states, but might do so through national liberation movements.[20] The term has been applied felicitously in the Indian context by a leading historian of Indian nationalism: 'In so shapeless, so jumbled a bundle of societies, there were not two nations, there was not one nation, there was no nation at all. What was India?— a graveyard of old nationalities and the mother of new nationalisms struggling to be born.'[21]

The term 'nation', unlike the more recent 'nationality', is older than 'nationalism'. Before the age of nationalism, it was close to the ethnic sense in which the term nationality is used today.[22] It might or might not include the factor of common government.[23] The political sense is obviously not in the mind of the Jewish moneylender Shylock as he contemplates his hated antagonist Antonio: 'he hates our sacred nation ... Cursed be my tribe if I forgive him.'[24] The Jew's dislike for the Christian—'I hate him for he is a Christian'—is here a national dislike. Even before the American and French Revolutions, however, the concept of nation did not altogether exclude territory and government. Illustrating the sense of the term, Johnson's *Dictionary* cites Temple: 'A *nation* properly signifies a great number of families derived from the same blood, born in the same country, and living under the same government.'[25] In Latin, the word *natio* meant 'A breed, stock, kind, species, race ... Also in a contemptuous sense, a race, tribe, set ... In a more restricted sense, a race of people, nation, people'. The historian Pliny refers to 'Ad Nationes', the name of a portico in Rome, built by Augustus, where the images of all known nations were created.[26]

In Persian, the terms *natio* and nation had a fairly close equivalent in the word *qaum*. *Qaum* might mean what Pliny understood by *natio*, and Shakespeare by nation: '... people, nation; tribe, family, kindred; a sect.' *Qaumi* Musa would mean, as Shylock would understand it, 'the people of Moses, the Israelites'.[27] From Persian, the word entered the

Hindwi language, and it had the same malleable quality: 'A people, nation; a tribe, race, family; sect, caste.'[28] It is in that same ethnic and religious sense that the medieval sant Dadu wrote of the distinction between 'Hindu' and 'Turk', and sought to cancel it at the philosophical plane:

> There is no difference between
> Allah and Ram, Hindu and Turk
> My mistake is dispelled
> I see you in all.[29]

The community of emotion here included both the Turks who had settled in India and the Hindus, a term which still retained its earlier ethnic connotation in Dadu's time. These were nations, *qaums*: nationalities within a civilization, drawing gradually closer to form a broader community of emotion; but not 'two nations', nor yet 'one nation'. Dadu himself, what was he?: a low born Indian Muslim of the Dhuni caste. He was not, then, a Turk, which, however, in his time, also meant a Musalman. Was he, then, a Hindu? Perhaps, if we take the older Arabic sense of the term, implying a native of Al-Hind; but not in the religious sense, for the religious connotation of the term Hindu was in the process of being established during his lifetime. What, then, was Dadu? If we use a term coming into use by that generation, he was a 'Hindi', i.e. Indian. Today, however, he is remembered as a Hindu sant. These were multiple identities, shifting communities of emotion; but it will not do to ignore them in any long-term historical and psychological perspective of the nations that inhabit the Indian subcontinent fifty years after Independence.

Emperor Jahangir records that the fourteenth century Sufi saint, Shaikh Nizamuddin Auliya, was so struck by the diversity of faith among the nationalities inhabiting Delhi, that he exclaimed, 'Every people have their way' (*Har qaum rast rahay*).The biographer of Sher Shah spoke of the Afghans as one nationality in their war with the Mughals of Humayun.[30] Sixteenth- and seventeenth-century European travellers to India spoke of both the European 'nations' trading to India and the 'nations' inhabiting the subcontinent. Purchas wrote at second hand of Cambay, Deccan, and 'the neighbouring nations'. The Portuguese visitor Linschoten found his compatriots living in Goa 'among all sorts of Nations, as *Indians*, *Heathens*, *Moores*, *Jewes*, *Armenians*, *Gusartes* (Gujaratis), *Benianes* (Banias), *Bramenes* (Brahmans) and of all Indian Nations and people'.[31] Bernier observed: 'The empire of the Great Mogol comprehends several nations, over which he is not absolute master.'[32] John Fryer observed that the Deccanis were 'a Warlike and Troublesome Nation ... of all Religions'. He could see at the same time that the people of Madras (Tamil Nadu) were 'of the same nation' as those of Masulipatam (Andhra Pradesh), an important observation stressing the commonalty of the people of different regions. Elsewhere, speaking of the Fakirs as 'the pest of the Nation they live in', he appeared to convey a sense of the common nationality of the Indians. Along with this, he enumerated 'Three Nations, English, French and Dutch', coming in ships to trade in Surat.[33]

Qaum, ahl, nation were all terms well established in Indian, Islamic, and European usage in the medieval world. The meaning, which might shift according to the specific context, would include: the people of a province; a race, tribe, or caste; a community of faith; a people, a nationality, a community of descent, custom, and government. In the last sense, the term came quite close to modern usage. The Latin terms *natio* (pl. *nationes*), *gens* (*gentes*), *populus* (*populi*), used interchangeably in the medieval period, were closer to the meaning of the modern sense of the nation than historians stressing the novelty of nationalism would feel comfortable with. As Susan Reynolds has observed in her study of community and kingship in medieval Europe:

> There is no foundation at all for the belief, common among students of modern nationalism, that the word *natio* was seldom used in the middle age except to describe the *nationes* into which university students were divided. It was used much more widely than that, and often as a synonym for *gens* ... *Populus* ... was yet another synonym for *gens*. Like a *gens* or *natio*, a *populus* was thought of as a community of custom, descent, and government—a people.[34]

The study of medieval texts made it plain to Marc Bloch that 'so far as France and Germany were concerned this national consciousness was already highly developed about the year 1100'.[35] Such national consciousness, when we look at the Persian usage of the term *qaum*, might spring up on the basis of religion; and it might then need a government to flourish, or it might not. The Qaum-i-Musa, the ancient nation of Israel, survived over a millennium without a country or a government. On the other hand, the Qaum-i-Sikkan, or the nation of Sikhs, suddenly developed an urge to form a government of its own, and so it converted the Punjab into a confederate republic in the late eighteenth century.

The extent to which national consciousness developed in the medieval world varied in different parts of Eurasia. It was highly developed in Japan. India was more like Europe, a civilization of several nationalities. The fifteenth century saw Europe, much in the fashion of India during the invasion of Timur Lang, united in opposition to the Turks.[36] However, the European identity, unlike the common identity of the population of the Indian subcontinent, coexisted with a fuller articulation of its nationalities. In the opinion of Johan Huizinga, 'French patriotism' was in full flower in the fourteenth and fifteenth centuries. Addressing France, the poet Eustache Deschamps achieved touching accents of love of the fatherland:

> You have endured and will, no doubt, endure
> So long as reason will be loved by you,
> Not otherwise, so hold the balance
> Of justice to yourself, and let it be well kept.[37]

As an English writer on nationalism commented, 'if the Hundred Years' War [1337–1453] between France and England is as far as possible from being a national war in its origins, yet towards its close genuine nationality appears, splendid and triumphant, with Jeanne d'Arc'.[38] In Japan something similar happened, long before the Meiji Restoration. In 1669 the Japanese scholar Yamaga Soko wrote a book entitled *Actual Facts about the Central Realm*, expressing in it a clear sense of the association of nationality with people and government: 'The body of the nation is made up of the people. When the people suffer the nation declines; when the people are at ease the nation flourishes ... The people are the foundation of the state.'[39] National learning (*kokugaku*), a reaction against Chinese classics and philosophy, led to the exploration of the Japanese classics. There was a movement to establish that the Way of Japan was the Way of the Gods. This movement introduced the word '*shinsu*' (Land of the Gods) into common use. Hirata Atsutane (1773–1843), son of a Samurai of Sataki-han, summed up the sentiment underlying this phenomenon when he proclaimed: 'This, our glorious land, is the land in which the gods have their origin, and we are one and all descended from them.'[40]

Honour (*kokutai*) was to Yoshida Shoin (1830–59), the one thing that must be preserved even if there should occur a war impossible to win: 'Kokutai, as it is the essence of one country, may be called unique.' Shocked by the acceptance of Commodore Perry's demands in 1853, this samurai of the Choshu-han blamed the loss of honour on the unwillingness of the Bakufu and the samurai 'to die loyally for the sake of the country'. If the spirit had been there, 'then what do we have to fear from Russia or America?'[41] The doctrine of 'revere the Emperor' (*son-no*) had usually been taken in Tokugawa Japan to imply advocacy of 'a closed country' against the barbarians. The scholars of the Mito-han pointed out, however, that a closed country was not a traditional imperial policy. Reverence for the emperor need not therefore be automatically associated with mere isolation. What the Mito-han proposed as an alternative to closing the country was *jo-i*. This term came into use in the 1830s, meaning 'repel the barbarian'.[42] The slogan, 'revere the Emperor, repel the barbarian' culminated in the Meiji Restoration.

This strong national reaction to the arrival of armed foreigners distinguished Japan from India and China, and implied the existence of a stronger national identity there. In Japan, Vietnam, and to some extent China, love of the land was linked to ethnicity, and ethnicity in turn was linked to the imperial idea: the emperor was the embodiment of the race, its life symbol, the sign of its existence. This embodiment suffered a setback in China with the Manchu conquest,[43] and it never existed in India in the first place. In India, the identity of the people was rooted in a mixed, plural culture, and not in political institutions. Identity, moreover, was not merely ethnic, it was also religious: and there were multiple ethnic and religious identities. National identity was much less evident. Europeans, prior to the age of colonialism, perceived 'nations' in India, whereas the Japanese, Chinese, and Vietnamese appeared to them to constitute individual nations. Nor did 'the Indians' resemble the Europeans. The latter were becoming organized into several contending nations, more clearly differentiated than the various ethnic, regional, and religious groups in India. An overarching cultural unity had invested the land in India with emotional values derived from notions of sacred space. This was a civilization of many nationalities capable of developing into one, two, or more nation-states, but what was durable was the civilization itself, however many the nations that might develop within it.

Nations have existed long before nationalism; and civilizations have endured where nations have disappeared. India as a civilization persisted, while the Scythians, Huns, and other nationalities which were assimilated in it, disappeared altogether in the end. In much the same way the German tribes, and the barbarian kingdoms founded by them, merged into European civilization, to form the characteristic medieval oecumene articulated through the Empire and the Papacy. The subsequent development of the nations took Europe along a different trajectory of growth. India, where this did not happen, retained the option of developing into a confederate nation. In all these examples, the common feature is the prior existence of the emotional community in a variety of interrelationships: one among many, and many amidst one. One community of sentiment might develop into many contending nation-states (Europe); several such communities might form into one nation-state (China). However, the emergence of the modern world community of sovereign national states is inconceivable without the prior existence of these emotional collectivities. 'Modern history' is but a small part of history.

Patriotism

What collective emotions did these felt communities, described at the time as '*qaums*' or 'nations', feel, identify, articulate? Nationalism, with its well known and well publicized sentiments, was yet to be born, so how does one describe these earlier and not so publicized emotions? The European vocabulary had already, even prior to the democratic–nationalist revolutions in America and France (1776–89), developed a word from its stock of Latin: 'Patriotism'. It was sometimes used to sneer at individuals. 'Patriotism is the last refuge of a scoundrel,' said Johnson in 1775. More ponderously, Berkeley pronounced in 1750: 'Being loud and vehement against a court, or for a court, is no proof of patriotism.' In 1605, admiration was expressed in England for 'such as were known patriots, sound lovers of their country'. A patriot was defined in Johnson's *Dictionary* as 'one whose ruling passion is the love of his country'.[44] Literally, patriotism was love of the fatherland.

The Sanskrit adage, 'The mother, and the motherland, too, are greater than heaven',[45] expressed a similar sentiment. Though the gender of the land of birth was different here, love of it/him/her was the same. Robert Clive resorted to an ingenious use of the term patriot when he sought to persuade the banker Jagat Seth to arrange a peace between the English and Nawab Sirajuddaulah: 'In so doing you will get the name of a patriot and prevent the country from being made a scene of ruin and plunder.'[46] Sirajuddaulah's notion of the love of his land was naturally altogether different: '... I will expel them totally out of my country.'⁴⁷ As the country fell, instead, into the power of Englishmen, Nawab Mir Qasim wrote passionately to Englishmen about the ruin which their trade was bringing to his land: 'So my country is to go to ruin and I am not to say a word.'⁴⁸ It was 'such behaviour in the country' that drove him to war with the English: 'I will turn them out.'⁴⁹

The spontaneous love of the land, as distinguished from the modern ideology of nationalism, is as old as 'history' itself, if by that term we designate the first work of history, namely, the *Histories* of Herodotus. Love of the land was focused in the first place upon the Polis ('Was any Lacedaemonian willing to give his life for Sparta?'). This felt community, however, extended at the same time to embrace all of Hellas (The Lacedaemonians 'will never accept thy terms, which would reduce Greece to slavery').⁵⁰ Representatives of the city states 'who were well affected to the Grecian cause' met at a conference to exchange mutual guarantees against the invasion of Xerxes and the first thing done was to compose the feuds going on amongst them: 'Their wish was to unite, if possible, the entire Greek name in one, and so to bring all to join in the same plan of defence, inasmuch as the approaching dangers threatened all alike.'⁵¹ In pursuit of the plan, envoys were sent out to obtain the powerful aid of the Hellenic ruler of Syracuse, with the following plea:

> We have been sent hither by the Lacedaemonians and Athenians, with their respective allies, to ask thee to join us against the barbarian. Doubtless thou has heard of his invasion, and art aware that a Persian is about to throw a bridge over the Hellespont, and, bringing with him out of Asia all the forces of the East, to carry war into Greece, professing indeed that he only seeks to attack Athens, but really bent on bringing all the Greeks into subjection. Do thou, therefore, we beseech thee, aid those who would maintain the freedom of Greece, and thyself assist to free her; since the power thou wieldest is great, and thy portion in Greece, as Lord of Sicily, is no small one. For if all Greece join together in one, there will be a mighty host collected, and we shall be a match for our assailants; but if some turn traitors, and others refuse their aid, and only a small part of the whole body remains sound, then there is reason to fear all Greece may perish.⁵²

As the Lacedaemonians and Athenians would not yield to Syracuse the supreme command of 'the Grecian forces during the war with the barbarian', the Greeks of the mainland had to face Xerxes on their own. The dispute over command showed that there were contending *nationes* within the confederate *natio*; emotional communities within the felt community. The Greek colonists of Syracuse, for their part, had to face an attack from Carthage with no aid from Greece precisely around the time when Xerxes launched his assault. This notwithstanding, the Hellenic world prevailed against both Persia and Carthage, but only because the defenders were moved by strong emotion and were prepared to pay the supreme price. On the pass at Thermopylae, the little band under Leonidas defended themselves to the last, an event which Hellas commemorated in inscriptions on pillars set up on the spot.

> Here did four thousand men from Pelops' land
> Against three hundred myriads bravely stand.

The sentiment that stirred Leonidas and his men was thus put into their own mouths on the pillar:

> Go, stranger, and to Lacedaemon tell
> That here, obeying her behests, we fell.[53]

Was the emotion here—i.e. the psychic response—so different from the sentiment of a modern nationalist? If we leave aside the question of ideas for the moment, then indeed it would be difficult to detect any difference between the classical patriot and the contemporary nationalist in this instance. Both belong to communities that felt a tug at their heart-strings and a lump in their throats.

The trial of Jeanne d'Arc and her replies in cross-examination give us a closer personal view of the notion of a patriot. What is more, the evidence is contemporary (Herodotus wrote his history a generation after the war), and the emotion described is by herself and her witnesses. Born in a locality between Burgundy and Lorraine called Domremy, the shepherdess Jeannette, called Jeanne in France, heard voices and therefore, in her own words, 'came to France', by which she meant the realm of the king of France, as an opponent of 'the Burgundian's side', a power aiding the English in the siege of Orleans. To quote from the trial record:

> *Question*: In your extreme youth had you great wish to go out against the Burgundians?
> *Joan*: I had a great will and desire that my king have his kingdom ...

Dynastic loyalties were mixed with patriotic emotions, as were religious sentiments. She told her judges that she went to the King of France from God, and Virgin Mary, and the Saints in paradise.

Question: What doctrines did he [the Angel St Michael whose voice she heard] teach you?
Joan: ... he told me to come to the help of the King of France ... And the angel told me the pity [pitiful state] that was in the Kingdom of France.[54]

In 1429 Jeanne d'Arc broke the siege of Orleans by the English. In her letter of summons to the English before the delivery of Orleans (22 March 1429), she called upon them to quit the good towns that they had violated: '... I am here sent by God, the King of Heaven, body for body, to drive you out of all France'. In her third and final summons, the political sentiment shone clearly through the religious rhetoric: 'You, Englishmen, who have no right in this Kingdom of France, the King of Heaven orders and commands you through me, Joan the Maid, that you quit your fortresses and return to your own country, or if not I shall make you such *babay* that the memory of it will be perpetual.'[55] And then the miracle happened: as the Bastard of Orleans wrote after the delivery, the victorious Maid entered the city to the rejoicing of the clergy and the people who thanked God 'for the very great succours and victories which He had given them against the English, ancient enemies of this Kingdom'.[56] Christine de Pisan was moved to write a poem commemorating the delivery:

> Then the people saw this happen
> Which, truly, was unthinkable
> France, which one and all considered ruined
> By divine providence
> From its misery was restored to prosperity
> So will it ever be remembered
> That God did ordain that a tender maid
> Would cause these events to happen and
> Thus release on France such a wonderful grace.[57]

During her imprisonment Jeanne d'Arc declared fearlessly before the earls of Warwick and Stafford: 'I know that these Englishmen would put me to death, because they think, after my death, to win the Kingdom of France. But were they a hundred thousand godons [i.e. goddams, the nickname for English soldiers] more than they are now, they will not have the Kingdom.' Angered, the Earl of Stafford half drew his dagger to strike her, but was prevented from doing so by the Earl of Warwick. She was put on trial.

La Fontaine: Does God hate the English?

Joan: Of the love or hate which God has for the English, I know nothing; but I know that they will be driven out of France, excepting those who will die there, and that God will send victory to the French over the English.[58]

This was patriotic sentiment coloured by strong religious emotion. Indeed, the two were indistinguishable in the mentality of the Maid. As the usher Jean Massieu testified, Jeanne d'Arc at the stake, while in flames, asked him to hold the cross before her eyes until she died: 'Being in flames she ceased not until the end to proclaim and confess aloud the holy name of Jesus, imploring and invoking without cease the help of the saints in paradise.' Sentenced to death for heresy, she uttered the name of Jesus with her last breath.[59] It was not until the rise of nationalism that religious devotion and patriotic fervour were split in France and elsewhere. In the lands of Islam and in India, the split was even then not complete.

Were the peoples of the East capable only of religious emotion and not of patriotic sentiment? By no means. Iran's national epic, the *Shahnama* of Firdausi (1010 CE), puts into the mouth of its hero a sentiment for which there is no other word but patriotic. Rustam writes to his brother: '*Chū Irān nabāshad tan-i-man mabād*'. [60] As early as the eleventh century, then, a literary character is capable of expressing the undying sentiment: 'If Iran not be, let this body of mine cease.' Even in the central lands of Islam, patriotic national sentiment strongly underlay the onrush of universal religious brotherhood.

Vietnam, where the patriotic tradition also stretched a long way back into the past, is historically rich in the articulation of the sentiment. When Ho Chi Minh appealed to the Vietnamese people in his 'Letter from Abroad' (1941) to overthrow the Japanese and the French, he prefaced this modern nationalist and revolutionary appeal by a reference to the invasion of Vietnam by the Mongol army of Kublai Khan from Peking and his defeat by General Tran Hung Dao whose temple at Kiep Bac was still the site of annual pilgrimage during the feast. Ho recalled how the elders had on that occasion 'called on their sons and daughters throughout the country to stand up as one man to kill the enemy', and then went on to draw a modern lesson from the past: 'National salvation is the cause of our entire people. Every Vietnamese must take part in it.'[61] Commemorating Tran Hung Dao's victory over

Mongols in 1288, a Tran poem expressed a more ancient sentiment: 'The barbarians no longer pollute our country—peace reigns for ever.'[62]

Ho was not the first among the modern nationalist revolutionaries to recall this ancient sentiment. Nguyen An Ninh, a journalist educated in France, said at a demonstration in Saigon in 1926: 'The French have nothing more to do here. Let them give us back the land of our ancestors ... Our country has given birth to innumerable heroes, men who know how to die for their land. Our race is not yet extinguished.' The nationalist struggle against the French sought inspiration in the earlier Vietnamese wars against the armies of China. A generation ago, the leaders of the resistance to the French colonization of Vietnam did the same. Its last great leader, Phan Dinh Phung (1847–96), a man popularly remembered because 'his loyalty to the king ranked above all else',[63] appealed from the heart of the jungle to the historical memory of his people:

> Now, upon reflection, I have concluded that, if our country has survived these past thousand years when its territory was not large, its army not strong, its wealth not great, it was because the relationship between king and subjects, fathers and children, have always been regulated by the five moral obligations ... Ah, if even China, which shares a common border with our country and is a thousand times more powerful than Vietnam, could not rely upon its strength to swallow us, it was surely because the destiny of our country was willed by Heaven itself.[64]

These patriotic sentiments came into play as soon as the French imposed a protectorate. Vietnamese governor and mandarin Nguyen Quang Bich (1830–90) responded to a French appeal for surrender in 1888: 'If now another country, stronger than yours, came to control your own country, would you then obey that invader? Or would your heart bear resentment and anger appear in your face? We are certain that you would respond to such an invasion in the same manner in which we now respond to you.'[65] What he articulated was an emotion, and one that was rooted in earlier struggles against the Chinese. These sentiments underscore the well known fact that the modern anti-colonial movement after 1925 was preceded by the birth, development, and eventual defeat of the great movement of patriotic resistance known as loyalty to the king (*can vuong*). The latter in turn was rooted in folk memories of considerable antiquity: in 1076, during the repulsion of the Sung army from China, a Vietnamese officer who had concealed himself in a temple impersonated the river genie and terrified the Chinese at night by reciting in sepulchral tones, 'How, barbarians, do you dare invade our soil?'[66]

Tran Hung Dao, on whose altars Ho Chi Minh saw people lay offerings, issued the famous proclamation Hich tuong si (1284) during the Mongol invasion. He warned the officers and soldiers, 'military leaders of an independent nation', what misery it would be if they gave in, and accepted 'the dishonour of the fatherland' without the least shame.

> Not only would I lose my fief but your privileges and properties would pass into other hands. Not only would my family be scattered, but your wives and children would be captured by the enemy. Not only would the tombs built by my ancestors be trampled by foreigners, but the temples of your ancestors would also be profaned. Not only would I undergo, while still living, unmentionable humiliations and after death perpetual dishonour, but the reputation of your families would be tarnished by defeat.[67]

This was patriotism; an old ethnic Vietnamese patriotism. It fashioned a felt community which the revolutionary nationalism of Ho inherited.

Vietnamese folk sentiments against the first Chinese occupation, at the dawn of Vietnam's emergence, is preserved in folk songs. Two sisters went to war: one of them, who had lost her husband in the war, swore before she fell in battle: 'I swear first, to avenge the nation: Second, to restore the Hung's [Hung dynasty] former position;/Third, to have revenge for my husband;/Fourth, to carry through to the end our common task.'[68] The defeat of the Trung sisters led to the first effective Chinese occupation (43 CE). In 248 CE yet another young Vietnamese woman, Trung Thi Trinh (19), led a revolt:

> I want to ride the storm, tread the dangerous waves, kill the fierce sharks in the ocean, wipe out the Ngo, win back the Fatherland and destroy the yoke of slavery. I do not want to bow down my head working as a simple housewife.

At the age of 23 years, this maiden committed suicide, but the words attributed to her were ingrained in folk memory through centuries of Chinese occupation. Vietnam, apparently an extinct nationality, emerged again, its identity rooted in 'our dynastic temples and to gods of the land and the harvests'.[69] Ancestor worship was the religion here: thus religious sentiment itself fostered a well-marked ethnic community in Vietnam. By contrast, numerous nationalities were housed, arrayed, and absorbed during these centuries by the assimilative civilization of India. What happened in the subcontinent may be likened to the steady accretions of a honeycomb consisting of innumerable cells. The social and political system was made up of multiple communities of ethnic, linguistic, regional, religious, and caste sentiment forming one intangible felt community.

Islam, with its ideal of a universal community of religious senti-ment, was also somewhat uneasily absorbed into the cellular structure of Indian society, a process culminating in the Mughal empire of Akbar. This process and structure, a cultural and mental phenomenon largely beyond the sphere of politics, was inimical to the development of the kind of patriotism seen in Japan and Vietnam. India was far too large an entity for that sort of development. Her imperial tradition, too, was intermittent in comparison to that of China and lacked the ethnic and xenophobic strength of the latter.

Patriot and Nationalist

Nevertheless there is now a growing recognition that an externally recognized and internally felt community of Indians entertained sentiments that did not exclude the 'patriotic'.[70] As we will see, Timur Lang and Nadir Shah both brought the emotion into play by their violence against the 'Hindis'. However profound the distinction between Hindus and Muslims may have been, the common 'Hindi' sentiment was evident to both invaders. This sentiment incorporated the 'Hindus' and the 'Muslims' as the communities constituting the Hindian empire of Akbar and his successors, and informed the Mughal resistance to the East India Company from Plassey to Buxar and, after the Mughal defeat, fostered the Indian confederacy that taxed all of Warren Hastings's skill and resources. The same sentiment charged the mass that formed itself into 'the Hindus and Musalmans of Hindustan' in the 'Reigning Indian Crusade' of 1857, and still later brought into being the Indian National Congress in the wake of the Ilbert Bill controversy of 1883. However, the path of transition from patriotism to nationalism, i.e. the transfor-mation of the felt community into the nation, was a more complex and less continuous process here than in Japan, Vietnam, or even China. Various patriotic, regional, religious, and clan loyalties existed in perfect confusion and the transformation of the civilization into nationhood was capable of several alternative forms.

Recently, C.A. Bayly has argued that while regional and community patriotism supplied materials for Indian nationalism, broader loyalties existed in India and provided the basis of a plan for the 'alliance of all turban-wearers against all hat-wearers'. Bayly speaks of 'a specifically Indian imperial patriotism' fostered by Akbar, and he equates this Mughal patriotism with the 'subtle sense of Hindustani patriotism' in the couplets of the late Mughal poet Ghalib. He concludes that resistance to the East India Company and early revolts against it constituted 'a series of patriotic rebellions which linked together many nobles and artisans and plebeians'[71] in common attachment to land, historical memory, and institutions.

Mughal legitimism, originally fostered by Akbar's pan-Indian imperial cause, appeared indeed as a Hindustani patriotism when two centuries later, the governors and subjects of the Mughal realm, joined in resisting the Company. The Hindustani sentiment shines in Nawab Siraj-ud-Daulah's refusal to hand over the defeated French officer Jean Law to the victorious Robert Clive:

> As to what you have wrote regarding Mr. Law, that it was very improper to set him at liberty, and that they should join with my enemies against me, therefore your forces would follow them, and you desired that they might meet with no opposition from me, it is not the custom of Hindostan to bind or deliver up to their enemies the weak or those who have begged their protection.[72]

The patriotic Mughal cause is tied here to the honour of Hindustan; the same honour is manifest also in Mir Qasim's rejection of the demand of Englishmen that they should pay no duties but that their Indian competitors must do so: 'I can never approve of my people and merchants being distressed, my countrymen oppressed, myself despised and subjected to daily insult, and my servants and officers ill-treated.'[73]

The Mughal historian Ghulam Husain Khan was profoundly convinced that under the Mughal rulers down to the time of Shah Jahan, 'everything in Hindustan was quietness, love and harmony'. He perceived indeed that the Empire was in decline 'these sixty years past', when every Governor ruled independently of the Emperor, but yet, as none of them departed 'from those rules and maxims of government by which the Empire had hitherto flourished', their subjects lived 'easy and contented'. The danger in his eyes arose from the fact that provincial independence induced the Europeans to 'the conquest of India'. As the new English rulers were 'quite alien to this country, both in customs and manners', evils and miseries were 'unworthily heaped over the heads of the poor Hindustanies', until the sobs and groans of the oppressed reached the very canopy of heaven: 'O God, come to the assistance of your afflicted people, and set open some door through which they may escape from oppression.'

While from one angle, the Hindus and Muslims appeared to Ghulam Husain Khan to be two different nationalities, at the same time he clearly saw from another perspective that Indians and Europeans were two different 'nations' and 'governments' in almost every institution and custom. In this late Mughal historical narrative, three circles are in constant overlap: the community of Muslim sentiment, the community of Hindu sentiment, and the community of anti-British Indian sentiment.[74] The tangled Indian situation appears to evoke the human condition in all its complex ethnicity. A broad question arises out of this Indian testimony: what is in general the nature of the felt community? There is only one criterion: it is a community knit by love of its collective self. As Weber recognized, there is no objective criterion: even a common language is not indispensable, nor sufficient in itself. 'One may state that there is a specific Swiss national sentiment in spite of the lack of common language; and, in spite of a common language, the Irish have no common national sentiments with the British.'[75] What is essential for the felt community to come into being is, after all, the communication of the feeling, and this has on occasion been effected without a national language. In medieval India, the constant interchange of ideas between the vernacular languages, the emergence of Hindustani as a link language understood by the common people in the camp and the bazaar, the development of a variety of Indian music and dance, appreciated by all, the popularity of the saints irrespective of their religious affiliation, the values attached to the land—these and other factors ensured the communication of sentiments which the absence of a single language is supposed to hinder.

Speaking in general, nationality implies a felt community moved by patriotic sentiment. However, patriotism, unlike nationalism, is not a specific historical category associated with a particular stage of the evolution of human society: it is too indeterminate for that. In all of recorded history from 500 BC to 1800 CE patriotic responses have brought a variety of felt communities into play. The confederacy of Hellas tapped this indeterminate emotional energy in the war against Persia; so did the heroines and heroes of old Vietnam against repeated Chinese incursions. Robert Bruce and Jeanne d'Arc responded to the same intangible emotion in their struggle against English intruders in Scotland and France. Patriotism existed long before the modern state, the doctrine of popular sovereignty, print capitalism, standardized national languages, and mass school syllabi.

The novelty of nationalism becomes more subtly evident when we bear in mind this variety of antique political sentiments. Nations as the predominant mode of human political organization is a modern phenomenon. Of course, nationalities were in existence prior to nationalism. Such entities were rising and disappearing all the time. What didn't happen was the permanent organization of humanity into nation-states. That was the outcome of nationalism. Prior to that, nationality was not the most important, nót to say exclusive, human bond. There were many others, of which the national tie was only one. Its rise to predominance is the characteristic of modern societies.

If the sovereign national state is the product of modern history, then the felt community belongs to history as such (i.e. since Herodotus). The two together have constituted the modern nation. A study of both components, the community of sentiment and the ideology of national-ism, is necessary to understand the historical process that has produced the modern world community of nation-states. The phenomenon of nationalism is organizationally and ideologically a uniform thing; insofar as it exhibits variations, these differences derive from the prior element of patriotism which has gone into its making. Modern history cannot be understood apart from history. There have been many felt communities in the past. The only common element among them is that they felt themselves as communities. This community of sentiment is an emotional collectivity, in the sense that it is moved by a common emotion. When the community of patriotic emotion combines with the ideology and organization of nationalism, it becomes a modern nation.

Communalism

In addition to 'nationalism', another category is frequently used in modern Indian history: religious strife in politics is referred to as 'communalism'. This phenomenon is sometimes essentialized and is thought to be characteristic of Indian social evolution since the coming of Islam. Both terms were, however, colonial in origin, and in some ways, one was as novel as the other. Communalism, in Indo-British usage, was a loaded term, set in apposition to nationalism, and in the political vocabulary of the Indian National Congress, Muslim communalism was set against Indian nationalism. Congressmen, including Muslim members, were 'nationalists'; Muslims opposing the Congress were, by implication, 'communalists'. Hindus opposing the Congress in the name of a specific Hindu nationalism were also included in the category of communalists.

The use of a pejorative term, to hierarchize the contending political and social ideologies of the late colonial period, traps today's historians into the confrontations of the past. It is best to leave the term 'communalism' alone. Indian anti-colonial nationalism had to contend with a more specific Muslim nationalism, and in this struggle it inclined, on certain occasions, towards an equally specific Hindu nationalism. The rise of contending nationalisms in the subcontinent reflected the plurality of identities and loyalties in this old graveyard of nationalities. Even so, the mixture of cultures and the shared experience of subjection to alien rule provided a common emotional basis to the struggle(s) for freedom. Freedom in the subcontinent was in that sense one and many at the same time: Indian, Pakistani, Kashmiri, and so on. To abandon the term communalism is not to express a general approval of all splinters, fragments, and secessions. Nor is it to deny the validity of Indian anti-colonial patriotism, an emotion shared by all the nationalities fighting for freedom, and all the nations struggling to be born.

Communalism, in the unique Indian sense of the term, is, according to one description, a 'construction'; to be more exact, however, the term arose from a real historical process in late colonial India. Initially the colonial rulers, and later, nationalist leaders, used the term in the pejorative sense of sectarian strife in the political sphere.[76] In European vocabulary, communalism meant something quite different: it would refer, in the dictionary sense of the term, to the theory of government by local autonomy, and might mean, in the hands of a Dutch economist writing on Indonesia, 'original organic social bonds' as distinct from the individualistic relations of a capitalist society.[77] As late as 1938, the *Concise Oxford Dictionary of Current English* ignored the peculiar Indian sense of the term: it defined 'communal' as 'of a commune; of the Paris Commune; of the commonalty, of or for the community, for the common use (esp. c. kitchens in the great war)'. During the Second World War, the dictionary dropped the reference to communal kitchens in the First World War, but added to the rest an interesting new clause:

'(India) of the antagonistic religious and racial communities in a district ('voting, elections, disturbances, etc.)'.[78]

An Anglo-Indian expression in origin, colonial officialdom meant by it the phenomenon of separate sects in India, essentialized for all time in history, and their endemic hostility to one another. Indian nationalists adopted the term and made it serve another political purpose: communalism was the type of loyalty to a religious community which detracted from the common purpose of the nation; in other words, communalists were those who were opposing the nationalists on the ground of a specific sectarian interest. In the 1930s, the Indian National Congress deployed the binary opposition between secular nationalism and religious communalism in the propaganda war with the Muslim League, the Hindu Mahasabha, and other political opponents. It was in order to defeat this ideological offensive that the Muslim League articulated the theory of two nations in 1940: being Muslim above everything else was no longer being minority communalist; on the contrary, it was being nationalist.[79]

The official accounts of political unrest often narrated the events in terms of collective actions by Hindus, Muslims, and Sikhs, as if these were monolithic blocs. The narration would do away with the many distinctions within each bloc: smaller categories which were sometimes more real than the broader aggregates.[80] Yet the official narratives might not have been without a real basis: parties articulated political programmes on the basis of these blocs, and violent crowds carried out the bloody pogroms of 1946–7 by deploying these very categories. The use of 'communal' categories might have been loaded, but were not entirely fictitious. A growing number of academics are beginning to use the term 'communitarian' in order to avoid the negative implications of the term 'communal'.[81] Where, however, does 'communitarian' end and 'communal' begin in such a close association of ideas? The same historians have, therefore, found it more convenient to substitute the term 'religiously-based majoritarian nationalism' for 'communalism'.[82]

The conscious effort to avoid the term communal may not adequately serve the purpose, but it is a step in the right direction. Ayesha Jalal has recently attacked the utility of the term altogether: under the 'secularist' leadership of the Indian National Congress, the Hindu majority's interests were often unconsciously identified with the emerging Indian nation, and then the self-defence of the Muslim

minority was consciously dubbed as communalism. Her recommen-
dation that we should abandon the binary opposition between secular
nationalism and religious communalism is a distinct advance towards a
more catholic historical analysis.[83] There was a time, specifically the
year 1920 which witnessed Gandhi and Mohammad Ali calling jointly
for Ram Raj and Khilafat, when Hindu nationalism, Muslim nationalism, and Indian anti-colonial nationalism[84] coexisted in one synthetic
discourse and did not threaten one another.

It may be objected on the basis of the European experience that
nationalities are categories based on ethnicity while these are based on
religion. Even in Europe, however, in the wake of the disintegration of
the Soviet Bloc and Yugoslavia, the nationalities that have emerged
include, besides submerged ethnic groups, persecuted religious communities too. If the Slovaks are a nationality, so are the Muslims of Bosnia.
In Asia, the terms 'ethnic' and 'religious' form a continuum which is
not easy to separate: it ranges through Malayan/Chinese, Sindhi/
Mohajir, Buddhist Sinhalese/Hindu Tamil, Bangladeshi Muslim/
Chakma Buddhist, Hindu/Sikh, Kashmiri Muslim/Kashmiri Pandit.
Such is the confusion that there is no hard answer in the history of the
subcontinent, to the question whether the Parsees, for instance, are a
race or a religious community. They are both, and might as well be
designated a 'nation' in old usage, or a 'nationality' in modern
terminology. Bearing in mind Weber's 'specific behaviour' which could
cause a race to become a nation, the question occurs in this context
whether a religious community might become a nation by adopting
the same specific behaviour. Logically, the answer would have to be
yes, if the religious community acquires or struggles persistently to
acquire a sovereign state of its own. If Weber saw the Chinese, a race,
become a nation in his lifetime, so did the Jews, a religious community,
become one when they founded the state of Israel nearly thirty years
after his death. In the same sense, the Muslims of Bosnia became a
nation when they claimed statehood against the invading Serbian army.

Furthermore, a religious community, like a race, might sometimes
be a sort of nationality in the world of yore. In the older sense of the
term nation, for which *qaum* was the corresponding word in eighteenth-
century India, the Sikhs were as much a nation as were the Marathas,
though the former did not have the sort of ethnic basis that the latter
might claim. Yet, in the Persian chronicles of the period, the Sikh sect
was no less a *qaum*, a nationality, than the Maratha people. Both are

depicted as troublesome nationalities, habitually in rebellion against the Mughal sovereign of Hind.[85]

On a broader plane and longer time span, Muslim and Hindu sentiments were forces to reckon with in pre-colonial Indian politics, not least of all in the eighteenth and early nineteenth centuries which witnessed a series of riots: in Ahmedabad, between Banias and Muslims in 1713; in Delhi, Agra, and Kashmir, during the festivals of Holi, Muharram, and Id in the 1720s; in Surat, by Muslim weavers against Parsee and Bania contractors in 1788 and 1795; in Delhi, by Muslim crowds against Hindu bankers in 1807; and in Banaras, between Hindus and Muslims over a disputed shrine in 1809.[86] The fact that these pre-colonial and early colonial riots differed in scale and nature from the Hindu–Muslim riots of the late nineteenth and twentieth centuries furnishes no valid reason for the historian to avoid coming to grips with the long-term psychic continuities in history. The so-called colonial construction of communalism is certainly not a valid argument in this context. Recent research suggests that a pre-existing religious tension dating back to the later Mughals linked up with the disturbance of the economic and political balance between Bania capital and Muslim crowds during the ascendancy of the East India Company at the turn of the nineteenth century. The specificity of the confrontations between the Bania allies of the Company and its Muslim opponents combined, according to Lakshmi Subramanian, with the pre-existing tension to produce the Surat riot of 1795 and that in Delhi in 1807.[87]

On a longer view of history, this religious tension is of even earlier origin. Cynthia Talbot, while not denying that modernization has led to a sharper articulation of identities encompassing broad communities, points out that the broader religious identities of colonial India did not spring fully fashioned out of nowhere. In her opinion, 'supra-local identities did indeed exist in pre-colonial India' and 'these identities were themselves historically constructed and hence constantly in flux'. Rejecting the primordialist view that postulates the inherent and natural roots of national and ethnic identity, she nonetheless maintains that the modern leaders of Hindu and Muslim mobilization employed myths and symbols of earlier forms of identity which formed 'incipient cores of ethnicity' as early as the fourteenth century and as far south as Andhra. The Vilasa grant of Prolaya Nayaka in the fourteenth century, for instance, recounted how he 'purified the lands of the Andhras which were contaminated by sin because the Turks had passed through them':

he re-established Brahman villages, revived Vedic sacrifices, and restricted himself to the lawful portion of the peasants' crops in revenue. Talbot concludes:

> Although the emergence of a sense of Hindu identity cannot be attributed solely to the stimulus of an opposing Muslim community, it is widely recognized that prolonged confrontation between different groups intensifies self-identities. While I believe that the Brahmanical tradition had a degree of self-awareness before the presence of Muslims, it seems that a broader, more inclusive, Indic identity began to develop after the Muslim polities were founded in South Asia. One sign of this is the non-Muslim writers' adoption of the designation Hindu, which begins to figure in Andhra inscriptions from 1352 CE onward, in the title Sultan among Hindu kings (Hindu-raya-suratrana) assumed by several kings of the Vijayanagara empire. To the best of my knowledge this is the earliest dated usage of the term Hindu in any Indian language source.[88]

The broader Indian identity which Talbot visualizes as a reaction to the coming of the Turks was in fact well established in antiquity. It was expanded and transformed by the inclusion of the Muslims as the foreign element became indigenous. At the same time, the Muslim identity emerged as a hard new distinction even as the foreign identity disappeared. The foreign and local Muslims came to constitute communities which, even as they came to share the broader Indian identity, remained distinct from the rest of the population. The Turks had disappeared in the vast Indian population by the time of Babar's invasion of 1526. Nor did the predominantly foreign Mughal nobility of his grandson Akbar retain their separate race rule in the India of Muhammad Shah and Shah Alam. All racial distinctions were blurred by the eighteenth century. The 'Mughal' cavaliers still prided themselves on their 'Turani' and 'Irani' origin, but these were mere pretensions. The high-born Muslims of Delhi and Agra and their peers in Hyderabad and Arcot become yet another cell in the cellular structure of Indian society. In the process, the various immigrant Muslim groups and the Indian converts to Islam hardened into an Indo-Muslim community. The racial divide was replaced by a religious distinction. The Muslims were themselves divided into many groups. Yet at the same time, a broad Indo-Muslim identity had emerged within the even broader Indian identity, and this time there was no assimilation on the earlier pattern of Indian history. In the reshaped cellular structure, the Hindus and Muslims were perceived 'opposites', each a *qaum* of all-India scope, and quite unlike the various local castes, tribes, and sects that had otherwise constituted society in the subcontinent.

A *qaum*, as we have seen, is a malleable category. It can mean a people, a race, a religious community, a tribe, a linguistic group, a regional group, a nation: in short, a people, however constituted. The course of Indian history is littered with the debris of *qaums*, nationalities, communities—interchangeable terms—which rose and disappeared. However, two categories are broader and more enduring: Hindus and Muslims. These are not immutable categories. As we will see, they evolved out of historical processes, as did the identity dubbed 'India'/ 'Hind', associated with 'Indians'/'Hindis'. India represented an even older and broader category denoting an entire civilization: the culture of a subcontinent. The 'Hindi-s' (Hindian) too, were a *qaum*, perceived as such by Indo-Muslim writers over several centuries; and long before that, the Greeks had perceived the Indians as one people, a people apart.

To say this is not to take an 'essentialist' position. It is to recognize that the instrumentalist position is inadequate. Nationalities, people, *qaums*, to use the apt phrase of Surendranath Banerjea, are constantly 'in the making'. That is a better and truer description than nations being 'constructed', 'imagined', 'invented'. They arise out of processes, sometimes abrupt and explosive, at other times of longer duration. They may upon certain occasions be engineered. However, for the achievement to be durable, the engineers must latch on to pre-existing emotional/mental processes. As the nation exists by definition in self-perception, the mentality in which it is embedded is the critical factor, and mentalities are not formed in a day.

Mentality

The instrumentalists have virtually invented the 'primordialists' as their other. In their view the primordialists are wrong in assuming that there are distinctive cultures which have persisted from time out of mind. This explanation of ethnicity (an 'invented' explanation, let it be added) is dismissed in favour of the theory that élite groups manipulate the cultural symbols to create political identities. New cultural groups are manufactured for purposes of economic and political domination. Paul Brass, a self professed instrumentalist, poses the following question while seeking the origins of a separate Muslim political identity in north India: 'Given the existence in a multi-ethnic society of an array of cultural distinctions among peoples and of actual and potential cultural conflicts among them, what factors are critical in determining which of these distinctions, if any, will be used to build political identities?'[89] His answer is that the ideology of Muslim separateness flowed not so much out of objective differences between Hindus and Muslims as out of the manipulation of those differences through a conscious political choice of symbols.

This view of the matter has been rejected by Francis Robinson who sees a deeper connection between Islamic thought and political separatism.[90] The instrumentalists have met with opponents persistently refusing to conform to the primordial other of their imagination. To maintain that the Hindu/Muslim or Hutu/Tutsi divides are pre-colonial distinctions rooted in ancient memories of real and imagined violence is not to seek a primordial explanation of the greatest massacres in post-colonial history. It is no more than a simple recognition that such felt communities are historically conditioned by psychic responses to stimuli that spasmodically triggered violence during the colonial period, and, to some extent, even earlier than that. They therefore are not the constructs of any colonial, nationalist, bourgeois, or modern 'discourse'.

Given multiple identities in a society, several alternative group formations are indeed possible in nationalist or communitarian politics. Groups have arisen and disappeared in history, not due to any organic biological formation/elimination, but by a social and cultural process. Many cultures may be embedded in the same political space, not all may develop the urge to be nations. When an internal necessity develops within a culture urging it to become a nation, it is only then that élites may successfully manipulate symbols to create a constituency for their rise to power. There are definite limits to instrumentality. More often than not, intellectuals and élites are the products of these impersonal processes; are not so much instrumental as instrumented. It is not by appealing to fictitious entities that one can appeal to imagination successfully and durably. Manipulating élites set a high price on success. Such men will choose those symbols that will sell, select those bonds that will hold; foster those entities that will truly appeal. Even the most cynical politicians have to search around within the mind, explore the mentality of possible followers, and locate the communities of emotion that will bring them durable power. Generally, however, the cause finds the leader rather than the reverse.

The imagined primordialists and the professed instrumentalists both have a clue, but they do not have the key. Mentality, culture, and history: these constitute the key to the study of felt communities. The essentialists are right in recognizing that a people is already there, even if they may be mistaken in assuming that this people has always been there. The instrumentalists are right in pointing to the innovators who engineer this people's claim to be a state, but they are wrong in imagining the entire process to be engineered. The felt community, long established in history and with a specific culture and mentality, is reinvented as the nation when the state positions itself in this community of emotion. As a culture evolves, the community becomes rooted in its own mentality. When this community of sentiment links up with the sovereign national state, it tags on to a genuinely new concept produced and universalized by the intellectual and political evolution of the modern world. It is then that a nation, in the modern sense of the term, is born. This entire process is a long-term mental and intellectual one. In the course of it, the emotion called patriotism is generated in the first instance. Subsequently, the emotion links up with the organized concept of nationalism and provides the means for constructing the state.

A cultural and evolutionary view of group formation must place equal emphasis on the long-term formation of mentalities and their modern transformation. Specialization in modern history to the detriment of knowledge of the more remote past and the professional urge to propound novel theses regarding the period selected for research tend to produce a distorted perspective in which the smallest recent changes in the human condition loom large and the critical transformations of culture and mentality earlier and over the longer time span either recede into the background or are deliberately played down to heighten the impression of novelty. Historians of the modern age then begin to act as if modern history stands on its own, quite apart from ancient (and, where it is posited, medieval) history. Modernity as an idea—reason, democracy, nationalism—did indeed set apart an age quite distinct from the rest of history, Even so, the compartmentalization of time into ancient, medieval, and modern, while useful in tracking permutation in organization and ideas, is only an artificial superimposition over the flow of what is after all a continuous stream of emotions and identities.

How amenable is the human psychic response at its most basic level to these compartmentalizations? Purely on the emotional plane, leaving aside the very diverse ideas that are of course also involved in the mental process, periodization is very hazardous indeed. Can we locate a palpable difference between what the patriot felt in antiquity and what the nationalist feels in the modern age? Did the emotions that evoked the anger, the pride, the attachment that moved these communities of sentiment in history differ? Are they not all of them felt communities that experienced in themselves the leap of the heart, and the rush of the blood? Such feelings are not amenable to definition. What is telling is the instant recognition of these emotions across time, though the ideas and notions that motivated those communities are difficult enough to grasp at this distance.

Identities are not 'created' all of a sudden, nor are communities 'imagined' overnight. As it is not possible to grasp an identity without exploring the mentality in which it is rooted, and the culture in which it has grown, it is evident that there is nothing given about it from the start. There is one exception to this: an identity that is biologically 'given', that is represented by the collective Unconscious of *Homo sapiens*. The human psyche cuts across races, cultures, and continents; it comprises 'primitive' tribes and 'civilized' nations. The fundamental bio-psychic structure of the human being was formed at the time when the naked ape emerged from the forest. All other identities in human society are culturally constructed. Nations, religious communities, even tribes, are fashioned by history. This group attachment with the associated emotion of loyalty is psychologically specific to *Homo sapiens*. Culture and history are unique components of the process through which men and women organize themselves into groups around selected identities. The same ancestry, the same territory, the same religion, the same ethnic core (real or imagined), the same political and social institutions, provide complementary or alternative rallying points. The attachment to a religious creed is a variant of the same psychic response that might manifest itself elsewhere in attachment to a *patrie*. The most intense sentiments in history have been generated by jihad/crusade and patriotic war/national upsurge. These bonds differ in outward form. But their inner psychic content is that intense feeling of loyalty of which mankind is mentally capable. Such bonds evolve and differentiate, and they have a history.

The raw unfashioned feelings of the multitude would appear to be the same in both old patriotism and new nationalism. However, the notions and ideas that also form part of the collective mentality do not reflect the same outlook in these instances. The changing historical forms of outlook fashion the raw feeling into widely divergent dispositions. The political and religious patriotisms of Indian antiquity and the nationalisms of the modernizing societies of the subcontinent drew upon the same emotions but shaped them into different articulate sentiments.

This brings us to the realization that there are two distinct historical elements in the formation of the mentality behind nationalism: there is the felt community, the old community of emotion and patriotic sentiment; and there is the modern ideology of the sovereign national state. The felt community of history was transformed by its interaction with the modern state system into the nation of the nationalist age. Emotionally and psychologically, the community might have remained identical in both situations; but the leadership and organization and sense of purpose of the community become profoundly different with the rise of the nationalist ideology.

In what follows, three episodes will be explored. They illustrate the history and mentality of a felt community before the rise of nationalism. The first of these episodes is the formation of the broader identities (Indian, Hindu, and Muslim) in the Indian subcontinent over the longer term (c.302 BC[91]–1800 CE); the second is the Mughal struggle against the usurpation of the East India Company (1756[92]–1803[93]); the third is the revolt of 1857. These episodes are psychically and ideologically related. The Mutiny, or Great Rebellion, was ideologically an attempt to restore the legitimate sovereignty of the Mughal emperor, and thereby to release 'the Hindus and Musalmans of Hindustan' from the domination of the Company. In this ideology it differed from the nationalist movement led by the Indian National Congress (1885–1947). I wish to explore the political mentality that moved Indian society before the rise of nationalism. The attempt of the rebels of 1857 to restore the Mughal sovereign had a century-old precedent in the Mughal struggle to preserve the Emperor's sovereignty against the Company; and the body that articulated itself in 1857 as the Hindus and Musalmans of Hindustan was derived from the longer evolution of three different identities: Hindustan, Hindu, and Muslim. The historical establishment of an association between these three entities formed the necessary psychic background to later political events: these events were the initial Indian resistance to colonial penetration, the Mutiny, and eventually the freedom struggle (including the Pakistan movement).

A word about the interweaving of mentalities in the subcontinent. Mentality is understood here as a commonalty of shared emotions and notions. I have a series of related points to make about the psychic community that existed in the subcontinent before the emergence of Indian nationalism. There is a view that the Muslims belong to too many diverse linguistic and regional backgrounds to form one community of sentiment. The same is said to be true of the Hindu community too. I believe, however, that just as one might encounter a Bengali mentality and a Sindhi mentality, while travelling from Karachi to Dacca, so might one encounter a Hindu mentality and a Muslim mentality, in Sind, in Bengal, and indeed everywhere in the subcontinent. It does not reveal enough about a person's identity to say that s/he is a Bengali or a Sindhi. To say that she is a Bengali Muslim, and he a Sindhi Hindu, would clarify matters. That, however, is not sufficient, for if it were so, we would be left with an insensible mass of confused, tangled separations. One might catch a sight of the mass itself if one observes it from a certain perspective. Stand back and you will see that she and he both have something in common. Both are in some sense Indian (or Pakistani, or Bangladeshi). There is, then, a Hind-i or Hindwi mentality, and within the Hindi mentality, a Muslim mentality and a Hindu mentality, and, furthermore, within the Muslim/Hindu mentality, a Bengali and a Sindhi mentality.

What I wish to stress here is the interlocking of identities which gave rise to broader communities of sentiment: Muslim, Hindu, and Hindi. The existence of diverse regions and languages has been seen by most historians of the subcontinent to be consistent with an overall Indian identity ('unity in diversity'). If this is so, then the same diversity is no less capable of coexisting with the broader subcontinental communities of Hindu sentiment and Muslim sentiment, and of course, the Hindu and Muslim identities are capable of coexisting with an even broader Hindi identity (*'Hindi hain ham'*—Mohammad Iqbal). A woman may be a Bengali, a Muslim, an Indian/Pakistani/Bangladeshi, and at the same time, as far as a Tajik or Turkoman is concerned, a woman of Hind, a Hindi. Such are the complexities of mentality in the subcontinent.

An expanding civil society that guarantees personal rights irrespective of ethnicity and religion, is capable of incorporating all these identities in one commonwealth, and of merging it in due course with humanity at large. For this, civic nationalism, and not ethnic or religious nationalism, constitutes the signpost. The patriotism of antiquity is the ethnic nationalism of today. Civic nationalism, which ultimately knows no ethnic boundaries, is the patriotism of the future. Since the French Revolution and the Napoleonic empire, humanity has known a type of civic patriotism that is capable of extension everywhere. The population of the subcontinent had experienced patriotic sentiments and a variety of ethnic and religious loyalties in the past. With the emergence of the Indian National Congress, it also came to experience civic nationalism. The future of the subcontinent lies in the extension of civil society, and in the development of civic, eventually humanistic, patriotism. It is this new form of patriotism that Raja Rammohun Roy advocated in a letter to his friend J.S. Buckingham in which he expressed dismay at the suppression of dissenters in Bourbon Naples by Austrian troops. His sympathy lay entirely with the rebels who had asked for a constitution, equality among all classes, and democratic rights:

> From the late unhappy news, I am obliged to conclude that I shall not see liberty universally restored to the nations of Europe, and Asiatic nations, especially those that are European colonies possessed of a greater degree of the same blessing than they now enjoy.
>
> Under the circumstances I consider the cause of the Neapolitans as my own, and their enemies as ours. Enemies to liberty and friends of despotism have never been and never will be ultimately successful.[94]

If Rammohun Roy saw the transition from the Mughal to the British government to be a transition to a 'milder, more enlightened and more liberal' regime, it is because the latter guaranteed 'the enjoyment of civil and religious liberty' and upheld 'those civil and religious rights that had been so often violated' by the old rulers of India. Even so, he saw that 'the more valuable privileges of the English law, and the rights which it bestows were confined to the ruling class, to Europeans', and voiced a demand for 'an equality of privileges' for 'Hindoos and Mohamedans', so as 'to protect Mohamedans and Hindoos from the operation of Christian prejudices'.[95] This was civic patriotism, not ethnic/religious nationalism. Rooted in civil society and capable of expanding into universal humanism, it did not threaten minorities within or nationalities abroad, and in this was quite unlike ethnic exclusivity or religious majoritarianism.

The Europe which Rammohun Roy watched with such interest was a felt community developing then into several nation-states, but capable, as the Concert of Europe had underscored by its very unity in oppression, of becoming one multinational confederation in the longer run. In this, India strongly resembled Europe: here, too, was a felt community comprising several communities of sentiment, all of which might claim nationhood in course of time, or federate into one composite nation. Several routes of historical development lay open. The generation that belonged to Rammohun Roy's grandsons construed one idea of nationality: a united Indian nation. The idea was propounded by Surendranath Banerjea's Indian National Conference. Behind the fragile construal lay a persistent community of emotion: the 'Hindian'. Two generations elapsed before the Muslim League of Muhammad Ali Jinnah came up with yet another theoretical construction: Pakistan. Behind it lay a similarly ancient felt community: the Muslims of Hind. Other construals have followed, based upon various tangled communities of sentiment: the Bengali Muslims of East Pakistan have become a nation dubbed Bangladesh; and in India, an effort is on to make yet another nation based on the felt community of the Hindus. The problem with these identifications, with the exception of a confederation based on the Hindian, is that they are all communities of emotion based on the principle of exclusion. Hindiyat, unlike Hindutva, represents the principle of inclusion and not exclusion, and is therefore a less oppressive basis for building a state; one that Rammohun Roy would have approved.

In all these instances, however, the construed nation emerges from the pre-existing emotion, and not the other way round. Which particular emotion would be chosen in this tangled situation to realize the idea of the nation-state is the critical issue: an inclusive emotion or an exclusive one? On it depends the promotion of a civil society, and a civilized way of life. The two were identical in Adam Ferguson's *History of Civil Society* (1767). An inclusive emotion fosters an ever-widening idea, such as Europe, or Hind. An exclusive emotion produces an ever more narrowly focused idea, such as a Bosnia subject to still further contrary pulls by Croats, Serbs, and Muslims. A similar instance in South Asia would be a Kashmir split up into Jammu, Kashmir, Ladakh, Hunza, Gilgit, Baltistan, and the homeless Pandits.

Civil society guarantees the identity of each nationality, and inter-mixes them in an ever wider felt community, until all distinctions merge in the original species of *Homo sapiens*. When Rabindranath Tagore, Rammohun Roy's intellectual heir, sang of 'the sea of humanity on the shores of India' (*ei Bhārater mahāmānaber sāgara tire*), it is this ideal he held up before the world at large. It will not escape the discerning historian's eye that the keenness of the poet's sentiment derived from the ambiguities of the encounter between India and the West, and between Islam and Al-Hind.[96] The instrumentalist might contend that Hume invented India, and that Jinnah imagined Pakistan. If in some sense they did, they could do so only because of an internal necessity. The efficacy of an idea depended in this tense situation on the strength of the emotion.

Civil society is not naturally born. It is put together. The nation-state and civil society are part of an ideologically engineered modern world. To put it in terms intelligible to the instrumentalists, civil society is a modern construction. However, construals have had an older role in history.

Historians sometimes write histories of the Jews, Iran, Rome, Byzantium, Islam, Hindus, Franks, Tibet, England, as if these are objects merely awaiting a narrative display. To assume their prior existence is to adopt a shallow approach. It does not go to the roots of the entity to be examined. The very denominations are construed by historical processes. The changing terms by which the entities articulate themselves in history need to be scrutinized all the time. That is what history is about.

Notes and References

1. From, *Wirtschaft und Geselleschaft* (posth. 1921), extracted in H.H. Gerth and C. Wright Mills (trans.), *From Max Weber: Essays in Sociology* (London, 1967), p. 174. Weber started writing the essay in 1910 and wrote most of it before 1914.

2. *Gesammelte Augsaetze zur Soziologie and Sozialpolitik* (posth. 1924), in *From Max Weber*, p. 176. Emphasis mine.

3. Surendranath Banerjea, *A Nation in Making* (London, 1963).

4. 'His Majesty [Shah Alam], at the period of the first British conquest of the Western provinces ... was still regarded by the nations of Hindoostan as the only legitimate fountain of either honour or dominion.' Ram Mohun Roy to the Chairman and Deputy Chairman of the East India Company, 25 June 1831, *The Correspondence of Raja Rammohun Roy*, vol. 1 (1809–1831), ed. Dilip Kumar Biswas (Calcutta, 1992), p. 596.

5. Ernest Gellner, *Nations and Nationalism* (Oxford, 1983), extracted in John Hutchinson and Anthony D. Smith (eds.), *Nationalism* (Oxford Readers, New York, 1994), p. 64.

6. Ibid., pp. 63–4.

7. Benedict Anderson, *Imagined Communities* (London, 1991), in Hutchinson and Smith (eds.), *Nationalism*, p. 89.

8. Ibid.

9. Gellner, *Nations and Nationalism*, in Hutchinson and Smith (eds.), *Nationalism*, p. 64.

10. Eric Hobsbawm, 'Introduction', in Eric Hobsbawm and Terence Ranger (eds.), *The Invention of Tradition* (Cambridge, 1983), extracted in Hutchinson and Smith (eds.), *Nationalism*, p. 76.

11. Crawford Young, 'The Colonial Construction of African Nation', in Hutchinson and Smith (eds.), *Nationalism*, p. 227.

12. 2nd edn., Clarendon Press, Oxford 1989, prepared by J.A. Simpson and E.S.C. Weiner.

13. 'Nation [Fr. Nation, Latin *natio*] a people distinguished from another people; generally by their language, original or government.' Samuel Johnson, *A Dictionary of the English Language* (1st pub. 1755, rpt. New York, 1967).

14. *Oxford English Dictionary* (OED).

15. Adam Ferguson in 1767 used the term civil society to mean a society in which the rule of the law guarantees the personal rights of every individual. *An Essay on the History of Civil Society*, ed. Fania Oz-Salzberger (Cambridge, 1995), pp. 149–151, 251, 260.

16. A similar line of argument, but with a somewhat different emphasis has appeared in the most recent critique of the Gellner–Anderson–Hobsbawm School: Adrian Hastings, *The Construction of Nationhood. Ethnicity, Religion and Nationalism* (Cambridge, 1997). Hastings emphasizes the rise of the vernacular languages behind the rise of the European nations. I emphasize the common Indian mentality cutting across the vernacular languages.

17. 'In so far as there is at all a common object lying behind the obviously ambiguous term "nation", it is apparently located in the field of politics.' The nation should not, therefore, be conceived as 'a culture community': its sphere is power, politics, the state. *From Max Weber*, p. 176.

18. Partha Chatterjee, *The Nation and Its Fragments* (New Delhi, 1993); Gyanendra Pandey, 'In Defence of the Fragment: Writing about 'Hindu–Muslim Riots in India Today', *Representations*, vol. 37, Winter, 1992.

19. The theme has, for instance, been so identified in Ravinder Kumar, 'India: a "Nation-State" or a "Civilization State"', Occasional Papers on Perspectives in Indian Development, No. VIII, Nehru Memorial Museum and Library, May 1989.

20. In Lewis Namier's vision of the history of nineteenth century Europe, a crucial part related to the submerged nationalities of Eastern Europe. See his *Vanished Supremacies: Essays in European History 1812–1918* (London, 1958).

21. Anil Seal, *The Emergence of Indian Nationalism: Competition and Collaboration in the Later Nineteenth Century* (Cambridge, 1971), p. 339.

22. 'In early examples the racial idea is usually stronger than the political; in recent use the notion of political unity and independence is more prominent.' *Oxford English Dictionary*, 2nd edn., 'Nation'.

23. E.J. Hobsbawm contends that originally the concept of nation implied nothing but origin and descent, and it was not until the late nineteenth century that government was specifically linked to the concept of nation. *Nations and Nationalism since 1780: Programme, Myth, Reality* (Cambridge, 1992), pp. 14–15.

24. William Shakespeare, *Merchant of Venice* (1596), Act I, Scene III.

25. Samuel Johnson, *A Dictionary*, 'nation'.

26. Charleton T. Lewis, *A Latin Dictionary* (1st edn., Oxford 1879, this edn. New York 1987), 'natio'.

27. F. Steingass, *A Comprehensive Persian–English Dictionary* (rpt., New Delhi 1992), 'qaum'.

28. John T. Platts, *A Dictionary of Urdu, Classical Hindi and English* (Oxford, 1884, Indian rpt 1977), 'qaum'.

29. '*Alaha Rāma bhrama chhutā morā / Hindu Turak bheda kuchh nahi dekhau darshan torā.*' Kshitimohan Sen, *Dadu* (in Bengali) (Santiniketan, BS 1342), p. 92.

30. The courtiers of Sher Shah told their sovereign: 'By your blessing dissent has been banished from among the Afghan nation ...' *Tarikh-i-Sher Shahi* of Abbas Khan, in H.M. Elliot and John Dowson, *The History of India as Told by Its Own Historians: The Muhammadan Period*, vol. IV (rpt. Allahabad, n.d.), p. 374.

31. J. Tallboys Wheeler (ed.), *Early Travels in India* (*16th and 17th centuries*) (rpt. Delhi, 1974), pp. 80, 168.

32. François Bernier, *Travels in the Mogul Empire AD 1658–1668*, trans and ed. Archibald Constable (rpt. New Delhi, 1972), p. 205.

33. John Fryer, *A New Account of East India and Persia: Being Nine Years' Travels 1672–1681*, ed. William Crooke, 3 vols. (rpt. New Delhi, 1992), vol. I, pp. 111, 210, 241; vol. II, p. 67.

34. Susan Reynolds, *Kingdoms and Communities in Western Europe 900–1300* (Oxford, 1984), pp. 251–4; extracted in Hutchinson and Smith (eds.), *Nationalism*, p. 140.

35. Marc Bloch, *The Feudal Society*, trans. A.L. Manyon (Chicago, 1964), p. 436.

36. When the Turks invaded Europe, a new order of Chivalry was formed, that of the Passion, to remedy all the evils of the century. Its aim was to unite Christendom in a common effort to expel the Turks, and burgesses and villeins were to find a place in it besides the noblemen. J. Huizinga, *The Waning of the Middle Ages. A Study of the Forms of Life, Thought, and Art in France and the Netherlands in the Fourteenth and Fifteenth Centuries*, trans. F. Hopman (rpt. London, 1990), pp. 84–5.

37. Ibid., p. 102.

38. Sydney Hobart, *Nationality and its Problems* (New York, 1919), p. 67 ff. Cited in Walker Conner, 'When is a Nation?', extracted in Hutchinson and Smith (eds.), *Nationalism*, pp. 154–9.

39. David Magarey Earl, *Emperor and Nation in Japan: Political Thinkers of the Tokugawa Period* (Seattle, 1964), p. 50.

40. Ibid., pp. 68, 80.

41. Ibid., pp. 162, 164, 170.

42. Ibid., p. 90.

43. When loyalty to Ming became treachery to Ch'ing, many Chinese ethnic patriots fled to Chinese colonies in South-east Asia; in the mainland a sort of imperial patriotism aiming at a combination of Manchu and Chinese became the official creed, in the same fashion as the Mughals propagated the imperial idea embracing Hindus and Muslims. A restriction was placed on voyages so that the Ming loyalists of South-east Asia might not infiltrate China.

44. These examples are cited in *OED*, 'patriot', 'patriotism'.

45. '*Janani janmabhūmish-cha svargād-api gariayasi.*' The term '*janma–bhūmi*' is literally 'place of birth', used here in the feminine gender. A pre-colonial tract by an eighteenth century Bengali fakir thus celebrates the birthplace (*janma–bhūmi*): 'One should not cease to love one's birth place (*janma–bhūmi prem*). I shall sing her glory elsewhere.' *Jnana Sagar* by Ali Raza alias Kanu Fakir, ed. Abdul Karim (Calcutta, BS 1324), p. 36.

46. Clive to Seth Mahtab Rai and Maharaja Swarupchand, 21 January 1757, in S.C. Hill (ed.), *Bengal in 1756–57* (Delhi, 1985), vol. II, p. 125.

47. Nawab to Coja Wajid, 28 May 1756, Hill vol. I, p. 4.

48. Nabob Mir Qasim to Governor Vansittart, 5 March 1763, *Original Papers Relative to the Disturbances in Bengal Containing every Material Transaction from 1759 to 1764*, 2 vols. (London MDCCLXV), vol. II, p. 113.

49. Henry Vansittart, *A Narrative of the Transactions in Bengal 1760–1764* (Calcutta, 1976), p. 250.

50. *The Histories of Herodotus*, trans. George Rawlinson (rpt. London 1964), vol. II, pp. 157, 169.

51. Ibid., pp. 174–5; Herodotus, *The Histories*, trans. Aubrey de Selincourt (Harmondsworth, Middlesex, 1960), p. 463.

52. *The Histories*, trans. Rawlinson, pp. 180–1.

53. Ibid., p. 209.

54. Regine Pernoud, *Joan of Arc by Herself and Her Witnesses*, trans. Edward Hyams (London, 1964), pp. 20, 31.

55. Ibid., pp. 70, 87.

56. Ibid., p. 93.

57. Ibid., p. 94. trans. from the French by Nupur Chaudhuri.

58. Ibid., p. 175.

59. Ibid., p. 232.

60. Harendrachandra Pal, *Parasya Sahityer Itihas* (in Bengali, Calcutta, 1954), p. 48.

61. Thomas Hodgkin, *Vietnam, The Revolutionary Past* (London, 1981), p. 304.

62. Ibid., p. 49.

63. 'Poem on True Heroism', composed 5 years after his death. Ibid., p. 167.

64. Reply to fellow villager collaborating with the French, rejecting the latter's appeal for surrender (1895). Ibid., p. 166.

65. Ibid., p. 166.

66. Ibid., p. 38.

67. Ibid., p. 46.

68. Ibid., p. 21.

69. Tran Hung Dao. Ibid., p. 45.

70. An instance of this recognition is the Radhakrishnan Lectures delivered by C.A. Bayly at Oxford, 1996, now published in C.A. Bayly, *The Origins of Nationality in South Asia: Patriotism and Ethical Government in the Making of Modern India* (Delhi, 1998).

71. Ibid., pp. 38, 39, 42, 63.

72. Nawab to Clive, 26 April 1757, Hill vol. II, p. 359.

73. Bisheswar Prasad, *Bondage and Freedom*, vol. I (Allahabad, 1977), p. 66.

74. Seid-Gholam Hossein-Khan, *The Seir Mutaqherin*, trans. Nota-Manus (rpt New Delhi, 1986), vol. III, pp. 158–210.

75. *From Max Weber*, pp. 177–8.

76. Gyanendra Pandey, *The Construction of Communalism in Colonial North India* (Delhi, 1990), pp. 1–22. Pandey, claiming a 'subaltern' historian's magisterial distance from what he terms 'colonial' and 'nationalist' historical writings, has discovered positive popular elements in the phenomenon. He thereby construes positively a term that these two (constructed) types of historians construed so negatively.

77. J.H. Boeke, *Economics and Economic Policy of Dual Societies as Exemplified by Indonesia* (New York, 1953), pp. 12–14.

78. *The Shorter Oxford Dictionary*, 3rd edn., 1994, also referred to this sense of the term as it then prevailed in India. For growing use of the term in the Indian press and political debates in the late 1920s and early 1930s, see Ayesha Jalal, *Self and Sovereignty: Individual and the Community in South Asian Islam since 1850* (New Delhi, 2001), pp. 267, 309, 327, 346.

79. Ayesha Jalal, *The Sole Spokesman: Jinnah, the Muslim League and the Demand for Pakistan* (Cambridge, 1985), p. 57 and passim; Farzana Shaikh, *Community and Consensus in Islam: Muslim Representation in Colonial India* 1862–1941 (Cambridge, 1989), p. 230 and passim.

80. Mushirul Hasan (ed.), *India's Partition: Process, Strategy and Mobilization* (Delhi, 1993), 'Introduction', pp. 33–6.

81. Sugata Bose and Ayesha Jalal (eds.), *Nationalism, Democracy and Development: State and Politics in India* (Delhi, 1997), 'Introduction', p. 8. See also Jalal, *Self and Sovereignty*, p. 44.

82. Ibid. I do not, however, recommend wholesale abandonment of the term 'communalism'. It is a term for the condemnation of the religious strife and intolerance that is prevalent in South Asia. Patriarchal gender systems constantly feed communal exclusiveness and aggression in India, Pakistan, and Bangladesh. On the other hand, it is not historically valid to describe Jinnah's Pakistan movement as an instance of communalism. Jinnah was a secular man. He constituted a new nationalist movement aimed at a homeland for the Muslims of India, preferably within a confederation with its centre in New Delhi.

83. Ayesha Jalal, 'Exploding Communalism: The Politics of Muslim Identity in South Asia', in ibid., pp. 85, 89.

84. The Pakistani scholar Shahnaz Rouse, uses this term in 'Gender, Nationalism(s) and Cultural Identity', in Kumari Jayawardena and Malathi de Alwis (eds.), *Embodied Violence: Communalising Women's Sexuality in South Asia* (New Delhi, 1996), p. 49.

85. Compare, for instance, Saiyid Ghulam Hussain Khan's description of the Sikhs with his narration of the doings of the Marathas. *Seir*, vol. I, pp. 81–91 (Sikhs), pp. 107–113 (Marathas) and passim.

86. C.A. Bayly, 'The Pre-history of "Communalism"? Religious Conflict in India, 1700–1860', *Modern Asian Studies*, vol. 19, No. 2, 1985; Pandey, *Construction of Communalism*, pp. 23–65; Lakshmi Subramanian, *Indigenous Capital and Imperial Expansion: Bombay, Surat and the West Coast* (Delhi, 1996), pp. 206–38.

87. Ibid.

88. Cynthia Talbot, 'Inscribing the Other, Inscribing the Self: Hindu–Muslim Identities in Pre-colonial India', *Comparative Studies in Society and History*, vol. 37, 4 Oct. 1995, pp. 694, 700, 703.

89. Paul R. Brass, 'Élite Competition and Nation Formation', in Hutchinson and Smith (eds.), *Nationalism*, pp. 85–9.

90. Francis Robinson, 'Nation Formation: the Brass Thesis and Muslim Separatism', and reply by Paul R. Brass, *Journal of Commonwealth and Comparative Politics*, vol. 15, No. 3, 1977, pp. 215–34.

91. Megasthenes becomes ambassador to Pataliputra, the capital of 'Indoi'.

92. The beginning of the Mughal–English confrontation: the year of Siraj-ud-Daulah's attack on Calcutta.

93. The occupation of the Red Fort by the Company troops.

94. Rammohun Roy to J.S. Buckingham, 11 Aug. 1821, in Dilip Kumar Biswas (ed.), *The Correspondence of Raja Rammohun Roy*, vol. I (Calcutta, 1992), pp. 60–1.

95. Petition to Parliament on Jury Act, Nov. 1826, ibid., pp. 363, 367, 372–3.

96. Hark, my heart, awake at the pilgrimage
To the sea of humanity on the shores of India.
Hordes have merged here in one surging mass
Aryan, non-Aryan, Dravid and Chin
Scythian and Hun, Mughal and Pathan.
The West has opened its doors today
And has brought from there a range of gifts,
They will give and take, mingle and merge

And no one will go away
From the sea of humanity on the shores of India.

Government of West Bengal, *Rabindra Rachanavali* (new edn.), vol. 4
(Calcutta, 1987), song no. 756 dated 18 Asharh BS 1317 (1910), p. 320.

2

Communities of Sentiment: Muslims, Hindus, and Hindis in History

In human societies, identities are hardly ever given from the start. They arise from a process that we call history. A bond that is born can also dissolve, unlike the unborn and immutable soul posited by the *Bhagavad Gita* (*ajo nityah shāsvatoyaṁ purāno*). The country that is called 'India' in history (since 1971 consisting of Bangladesh, Pakistan, and the Indian Union) was no 'unborn, immutable, eternal, ageless' entity. The 'people of India' (a term occurring in the Preamble to the Constitution of India and earlier encountered in the *Travels* of Ibn Battuta which mentions *'ahl-e-Hind'*[1]) arose out of a historical process. So did the two communities that form the principal components of the population of India, Pakistan, and Bangladesh today, namely the Hindus and the Muslims.

The beginning of civilization in the subcontinent is lost in the dim and distant past. The identities marked 'India', 'Hindu', and 'Muslim' are of more recent origin. They are not, however, as a current intellectual fashion would have us believe, so recent as the nineteenth century. Some historians have sought to demonstrate that such terms as India, Hindu, and Muslim are relatively novel constructions that arose out of the new political and religious discourse of the colonial period. Not just the Indian people, but the communities of the subcontinent, too, are dubbed 'imagined communities'—one scholar would go so far as to say 'imaginary communities'.[2]

Psychological realities that go back over generations cannot be wished away so easily. If we are to believe these historians, the Indian people, the Hindu community and the Muslim community, 'invented' themselves under Western eyes, 'constructed' their identities anew, 'imagined' themselves into existence. They did these things, we are told, no earlier than during the reign of Queen Victoria. However, are psychic realities produced so suddenly, and at one particular moment in history? Can such things be so triumphantly exposed, by the latter-day instrumentalists, as the mere fantasies of the imagination? The emotions that form the raw materials of a people's history, and the symbols and categories of the mind through which such impulses work themselves out, are embedded too deep in the unconscious to be amenable to such ready-made deconstructions of colonial or anti-colonial 'discourses'.

Etymology, shorn of the exaggerations of deconstruction, is a useful tool for historians in this field. The emergence of the terms India, Hindu, and Muslim can be dated with a fair degree of accuracy. India, in the sense of a single civilization covering the entire subcontinent, emerges in definite outline from the inscriptions of Asoka, in which the country is referred to as 'Jambudvipa'.[3] Just a generation before him, the Greek envoy Megasthenes used the term 'Indoi' for the entire country from Pataliputra ('Palibothra') to Pandya ('Pandaia').[4] This was in 302 BC. The use of the terms 'Hindu' and 'Muslim' came much later than the coining of the term India (Sindhu [Sanskrit] > Hindush [Iranian] > Indoi [Greek] > India [Latin]). The two former terms can be pushed no further back than the coming of the Arabs in the eighth and ninth centuries. The Arab geographers, who knew the land by the name Al-Hind (Sindhu > Hindush > Hind), invented the term 'Hindu' for its inhabitants. The people whom they identified as the Hindus had of course existed before, but the term implied a redefinition made all the sharper by the juxtaposition of the new term 'Muslim', a label applied to the Arab, Ghaznavi, and Ghori conquerors alike by the Persian chroniclers who emerged in the thirteenth century.

The identities 'India', 'Hindu', and 'Muslim', as they currently exist, are basically concepts produced or reproduced in the middle ages. Even so, they are old enough, and these identities were not made in a day. To construe them as new colonial entities of the nineteenth century is to delete a thousand years of history. It is to forget the clear distinction drawn between Hindus and Muslims as communities in the old ballads and chronicles, and to ignore the concept of India as a country which was no less clearly articulated in those medieval narratives. As with all identities in history, the labels used in the ballads and chronicles, too, arose out of a process, and were in that sense construals. However, some

identities have been around with us for too long to be labelled
'imaginary'. There are dangers in stressing the novelty of the impassioned
mass identities of the subcontinent today. If such 'novel' categories as
Hindus and Muslims could have been persuaded that they did not in
fact exist,[5] how much simpler things would have been. Unfortunately,
life is not so simple, nor is history.[6]

As historians of ancient and medieval India are well aware, the roots
of our categories of existence go far back into the past, through a ceaseless
series of transmutations. An identity arising out of history, rooted in
the past, undergoing many transformations in course of time, may
remain all the same an identity recognized across the generations.
Historians seeking to uncover the mentalities embedded in the oldest
surviving civilization of the world must be prepared to delve deep in
order to grasp the spontaneous and virtually unconscious identifications
made by the milling crowds in the public spaces of the subcontinent.

All serious historians will recognize that 'nationalism' and
'communalism', as political programmes, were fostered by India's
colonial encounter, and that this happened no earlier than the nineteenth
century. However, historians capable of taking the longer view would
be no less aware of the old sentiments that went into the making of
these programmes. These emotions were embedded in a collective
unconscious formed many centuries prior to the experience of colonial
subjection. As psychical phenomena, the current political emotions of
the subcontinent cannot be delinked from the earlier and no less
important encounter between Al-Hind and Islam: an encounter that
differentiated Hindus[7] and Muslims,[8] and at the same time produced
the composite identity dubbed Ahl-e-Hind, that very identity which
spelt itself out, in course of its modern transformation, as 'We, the
people of India'. Were we to assume that imagined communities require
no core of affinities to coalesce around, then we must also admit that
they would be liable to dissolve as quickly as they are formed.
Imagination requires the stuff of real and familiar sentiments to work
upon when it constructs communities that prove to be as tenacious as
those that occupy the political space in the subcontinent today.

A subcontinent sustaining, over the centuries, a distinct civilization;
a mindset visible beneath the highly differentiated texture of that culture;
an emotional space that retains its basic design while the political space
has been fragmented into three nations since 1971; a political space
which, before the invention of so novel a thing as the nation-state, was

divided into countless realms for two and a half millennia of recorded history—such a thing is difficult to describe. However, historians who would dismiss it as 'imaginary' would do so at their peril. A passage into its psychological realities is afforded by the specific terms and expressions used by the denizens and visitors to categorize the land and the people. The terminology, along with the contemporary narratives and descriptions, open a window into the soul: not unborn, immutable, eternal, and ageless, but all the same a mentality identifiable across the vast spaces of the subcontinent, and across the long span of the middle ages linking antiquity to modernity. That which the Christian missionary J.N. Farquhar in an inspired moment called 'the common heart of Hindustan'[9], recalling the life and songs through which a weaver named Kabir articulated its mysterious and elusive beat.

Identity and Subcontinent

Twelve hundred years ago, when the youthful world of Islam confronted the newborn realm of the Franks across the Pyrenees, China and India, separated by the high Himalayas, were the only civilizations to survive from prehistory. Known to each other as 'Maha Chin'[10] and 'In-tu'[11], the two ancient societies had well-formed, markedly different characteristics. As both civilizations fell, a thousand years later, under the domination of the now more advanced 'Franks' ('*firangees*'),[12] their respective characteristics persisted, as sharply distinct as ever. One was politically integrated by the persistent re-creation of the 'Middle Kingdom', the other depended on the geographical design of a 'subcontinent' for the no less persistent articulation of its culture.

In the meanwhile, about six centuries before the consolidation of the European ascendancy on the Indian subcontinent, the militant, proselytizing creed of Islam, carried by the Turks to the valley of the Ganges, established a new government over India. Islam, however, did not achieve here the wholesale religious conversion that it had previously effected in the ancient Aryan-speaking land of Iran. The tense, close interaction that followed had no parallel in the history of civilization. In consequence, an unusual experiment in acculturation and commonalty took place on the subcontinent. Nowhere else did two world religions coexist for so long in the same enclosed space. The Caliphate established Islam in the conquered lands of the Sassanid and Byzantine empires. Latin Christendom, in turn, stamped Islam out of

Western Europe in the process of recovering Spain and Sicily. Commonalty in medieval India, by contrast, accommodated duality. The imperial ruling class was Muslim; the subject population, and their native chiefs, were Hindu.[13] The event shaped the subsequent course of history. The land emerged as a cultural space in which the encounter between the two alien civilizations would reach its inconclusive, and uncertain, denouement.

The cultural identity that evolved in India over the centuries did not, as in China, depend upon a framework of political solidarity. As Irfan Habib has pointed out, the listing of the sixteen *mahajanapadas* of the sixth century BC itself suggested, for the first time, the notion of a country to which all these principalities belonged.[14] Kautilya's *Artha Shastra* did, indeed, express the idea of a universal dominion from the Himalayas to the Ocean (*himavat-samudra-antaram chakravarti-kshetram*).[15] The idea, however, had no hard substance. A system of balanced rivalries between competing princes is the reality that is glimpsed in the Sanskrit inscriptions. Ashoka was, perhaps, the only monarch of ancient India, to lay effective claim to universal dominion, though in the far south he had to reckon with 'the people of the uncon-quered territories lying beyond the borders of my dominions'.[16] The Sultans of Delhi, and after them the Mughal Emperors, laid claim to the same universal dominion. However, while their conquests imparted a certain solidarity to 'Hindustan' (understood in the narrower sense as the Gangetic plain)[17], the 'Dakkan', apart from brief interludes, escaped their dominion. It fell to the British East India Company, a foreign corporation, to acquire paramountcy in 1803. The British retained this paramount power till 1947. Upon their departure the land was divided once again, this time into two states, and subsequently into three. The shared culture, however, still distinguishes the subcontinent from Myanmar to the east, Tibet to the north, and Afghanistan to the west.

The Term 'India'

India, then, was no given entity from the outset. It emerged, as stated, out of a historical process. Its very nomenclature reveals this. A long time would elapse before a process of acculturation would convert the physical space between the Himalayas and the Indian Ocean into an identifiable cultural space. There was no common name for the land until over a thousand years after the composition of the *Rik Samhita* (c.1500 BC), which may be regarded as the first literary expression of civilization on the subcontinent. What made the acculturation possible was the lie of the land. It was this that defined the imaginary space of the universal king (*Chakravarti Kshetra*). No continental zone was better defined in early history. Australia, a late discovery by Captain Cook, was somewhat better defined on account of the sea that surrounded it on all sides, but India was only a little less well defined.

As Abul Fazl pointed out in the sixteenth century, India was surrounded on three sides by the ocean, and even to the north the lofty range of mountains and the intermediate range of countries separating it from the vast frontiers of China might be 'likened to another ocean'.[18] The very vastness of the space, however, implied a prolonged time span for its acculturation. A common name did not begin to be applied to the land until over a thousand years had elapsed since the composition of the first Vedic hymns in Punjab, for it is not until the end of the fourth century BC that the first dated proof of the exploration of the Indian peninsula to its tip is forthcoming . The first dated and historically ascertained evidence of this is Megasthenes's reference to the 'Pandaian realm' of the matriarchal tribe of 'Pandae' who occupied 'that portion of India which lies to the southward and extends to the sea'.[19]

It is no accident of history that a territorial name which had earlier denoted the Indus valley expanded its connotation at this time to cover the entire subcontinent. This was the term India. In the process, the term itself underwent a linguistic transfer as it passed from native to foreign usage. The early Aryans of the Indus Valley referred to their land as 'Sapta Sindhava'. The 'Hapta Hindu' of the *Avesta* was coterminous with 'Sapta Sindhava' of the *Rig Veda*, the Iranians replacing the 's' by 'h' and 'dh' by 'd'. The Achaemenid emperors, whose empire included the territory on the west bank of the Indus, referred to it in the Persepolis and Naksh-i-Rustam inscriptions by the name 'Hi[n]du'. The same name became ' Índoı' (= India) in Greek, the 'h' being absent in that language. The 'h' was indicated by a sign of aspiration over the first vowel in the early Greek texts, but as the sign disappeared from later Latin writings in Roman characters, the name was transformed into 'India'.[20]

Herodotus in his *History* (fifth century BC) referred to ' Índoı' as the twentieth satrapy of the Achaemenid empire under Darius I (522– 486 BC). The province stretched along the banks of the Indus to the sea, bounded by a desert to the east (now known as the Thar desert of

Rajasthan). The Indoi of Herodotus, and of the earlier Ionian logographer Hecateus of Miletus, was apparently located in Sind. As the Greeks led by Alexander reached the banks of the Indus, they became aware of the vast territories rolling away from the opposite bank of the river down to the delta of the Ganges, where a formidable people named the Gangaridai were said to be arming against them. The name Indoi was extended from Sind to the Gangetic Valley as the Greeks become more familiar with the land.[21] Arrian, basing himself on the evidence of Alexander's general Nearchos and the Greek ambassador Megasthenes, chose to call the country on the opposite bank 'India proper'.[22] The lower Indus Valley, which was the original 'India', thus merged in nomenclature with the vaguely perceived Indo-Gangetic plains at the time of Alexander's invasion of 'India' in 327 BC. A quarter of a century later, Megasthenes, posted as ambassador at Pataliputra, perceived Indoi as a vast quadrilateral stretching down from the Mauryan capital to Pandaea in the south. He could also see that Sandrokottos (Chandragupta Maurya), at whose court he was ambassador, was 'the king of the Indians'.[23] Here at length was a historical monarch with a genuine claim to be the sovereign overlord (Chakravarti Raja) of myth. The distinct space involved in the notion of the universal dominion (*chakravarti kshetra*) was also in evidence, for as the Indians told the Greeks, 'a sense of justice', which probably meant a sense of the unclean nature of the lands beyond the pale, 'prevented any Indian king from attempting conquest beyond the limits of India'.[24]

The situation was ripe for the invention of an indigenous name for the subcontinent as distinct from the Greek appellation 'Indoi', or the Chinese term 'Yin-tu'. The original Chinese terms, 'Shentu' and 'Hsien-tou', were derived, like 'Indoi', from Sindhu. The later term 'Yin-tu' which appeared during Tang, applied, as Hiuen Tsang's account would make it clear, to the subcontinent as a whole, and not just Sind.[25] In India, on the other hand, neither 'Sapta Sindhava', the original settlements of the Indo-Aryans in the Indus valley, nor the later and broader northern Indian appellation of Aryavarta with its centre at 'Madhya Desha' (central land) on the upper reaches of the Doab, meant anything beyond the specific original connotations. In the meanwhile, the Brahmanical–Sanskritic norms and the protestant sects of Buddhism and Jainism had spread to the east and the south. The far-flung rock edicts of Chandragupta Maurya's grandson, Ashoka (272–232 BC), were the first chronologically ascertainable manifestation of the common culture which the land had just then acquired; and it was in those same rock edicts that we encounter the first indigenous appellation of the subcontinent, 'Jambudipa'.[26]

Ashoka referred to his universal dominion as both 'Pathavi' (*prithvi*, i.e. the earth) and 'Jambudipa'. Jambudipa (Jambudvipa) was the extensive region over which his power ('Pakama', or *parakrama*), exerted itself in the promotion of the sacred moral law (*dharma*).[27] Since his association with the Buddha's *sangha*, he said, his 'subjects in Jambudipa, who had been unmingled with the gods, were made by him mingled with them'.[28] The Chinese traveller I-Tsing later referred to the dominions of Ashoka as 'Jambudvipa' and distinguished it from China on the north and from Fu-nan or Poh-nan (Siam and part of Cambodia) which lay to its south.[29] Ashoka was acutely aware of the people of the unconquered territories lying beyond the borders of his dominions, namely, the Cholas, Pandyas, Satyaputra, and Keralaputra as far as Tamraparni (Sri Lanka) to the south, and the Yonas (Greeks) to the west.[30] At the same time, he drew a distinction between the foreigners and the indigenous population: 'Excepting the country of the yavanas, there is no country where these two classes, viz. the Brahmanas and the Shramanas, do not exist.'[31] He evidently had in mind a territory and a population over which the Brahman priests and the Buddhist monks held moral sway. This would include the people beyond the southern borders of his dominions. We find here an unmistakable notion of the Indian moral and social order. Almost unconsciously, Ashoka identified a culture, a civilization, of which he was the champion.

In the period of the Puranas, in the early centuries of the Christian era, the term Jambudvipa acquired a wider cosmic connotation, including lands far away from India. Brahmanical cosmology then invented another term, Bharata Varsha, which had a more restricted sense, to denote the Indian subcontinent. In Bana's romance, for instance, we hear Mahashweta thus address her friend: 'Dear Kadambari, there is a king named Tarapida in the continent of Bhārata (*Bhārate Varshe rājā ... Tārāpida nāma*), whose subjects are protected by the four oceans (*chatuh samudra*).'[32] The earliest epigraphic reference to the name occurs in the Hathigumpha inscription of Khāravela, who ruled in Kalinga in the latter half of the first century BC. The *Vishnu Purana* describes it as follows:

Uttaram yat samudrasya Himādreshchaiva dakshinam
Varsham tad Bhāratam nāma Bhāratī yatra santatih.

The *Vayu Purana* describes it in practically the same terms:

Uttaraṁ yat samudrasya Himavaddakshinañcha yat
Varshaṁ tad Bhāratam nāma yatreyaṁ Bhāratī prajā.³³

North of the sea and south of the Himadri or Himavat range lies the country of Bhārata, and its offspring are the Bhāratī. The Bhāratī prajā or the Bhāratī *santati*, 'Indians' to use Arrian's term, appear to have derived their name from the ancient Bharata tribe of the *Rig Veda*, later described in the Buddhist texts as the 'seven Bhāratas' enjoying dominion over most of the land. The Mahabharata is named after the tribe. The legend is that king Bharata, son of Dushyanta, was a Chakravarti Raja.³⁴

Another name that occurs in the Puranas is 'Kumāra Dvipa'. This land had the Kiratas (a Mongoloid tribe) to the east, the Yavanas (Greeks) to the west, and the four Varnas (Brahman, Kshatriya, Vaishya, and Shudra) in the middle.³⁵ Here the concept of India becomes the fourfold social order of 'Hinduism'.

The Hindus did not call themselves 'Hindu' in antiquity. If and when they thought of themselves in the collective sense, they referred to the four varnas together; and they distinguished them collectively from the impure races living beyond the land in which the Brahmanical system prevailed. 'Tradition', Hiuen Tsang tells us, 'has so hallowed the name of this tribe [Brahmans] that there is no question as to difference of place, but the people generally speak of India as the country of the Brahmans (Po-lo-men).'³⁶ Muslim travellers and warriors from abroad coined the term 'Hindu' to denote the natives of Hindustan, associating with that category the 'Shamaniyya' (Buddhist), too.³⁷ An early piece of evidence of a Hindu king naming himself as such occurs in the inscription of Rana Kumbha of Mewar who claimed to have 'received the title of Hiṁdu-Suratrāna by defeating the sultans of Dhilli and Gurjaratra'.³⁸ The Muslim influence is evident in the linguistic derivation of his description of himself as Hindu and Suratrāna (sultan).

The name Hindustan is Iranian in origin, and was later adopted by the Muslims upon their occupation of the Sassanid empire. An inscription of the Sassanid Emperor Shapur I, datable to 262 CE, refers to Hindustan, 'land of the Sindhu', probably referring thereby to the lower Indus country.³⁹ The early Muslim writers spoke of Sind and Hind, distinguishing one from the other perhaps on the ground that

Sind, since its conquest by Muhammad bin Qasim, had been incorporated in the Caliphate. Al Biruni was aware of the distinction, but he spoke of Hindustan as an entire subcontinent.[40] Timur Lang's officers before setting out on the expedition to India, declared: 'Praise be to God that we are at this time Shahinshah of Iran and Turan, and it would be a pity that we should not be supreme over the country of Hindustan.'[41] His descendant Jahangir was to write later in his Memoirs: 'Notwithstanding that I grew up in Hindustan, I am not ignorant of Turki speech and writing.'[42]

Abul Fazl's Gazetteer of the Mughal empire and its *suba*s brought into focus the fact that Hindustan was a concept both wider and older than the Mughal empire. Akbar's sovereign dominion had newly given the country a certain solidarity. Having described the *suba*s in which his master had divided the empire, Abu Fazl proceeded to describe 'the general conditions of this vast country', together with an analysis of its ancient civilization.[43] He prefaced this account with the remark:

> Hindustan is described as enclosed on the east, west and south by the ocean, but Ceylon, Achin, the Moluccas, Malacca and a considerable number of islands are accounted with its extent. To the north is a lofty range of mountains, part of which stretches along the uttermost limits of Hindustan, and its other extremity passes into Turkestan and Persia. An intermediate region lies between this and the vast frontiers of China, inhabited by various races, such as Kashmir, Great and Little Tibet, Kishtawar and others. This quarter may therefore be likened to another ocean. With all its magnitude of extent and the mightiness of its empire it is unequalled in its climate, its rapid succession of harvests and the equable temperament of its people.[44]

Muhammad Sharif Hanafi, an officer from the Deccan, provided another interesting description at the beginning of Shah Jahan's reign from a southern point of view. He begins by equating 'the whole country of Hindustan', which formed 'one fourth of the inhabited world', with the fourteen *suba*s in which the empire was divided: Delhi, Agra, Lahore, Kabul, Deccan (Ahmadnagar), Khandesh and Birar, Malwa, Gujarat, Bihar, Oudh, Ajmir, Allahabad, Sind, and Bengal. However, as he goes on to describe 'the whole territory of the Dakhin', it is at once evident that part of the peninsula lies beyond Mughal dominion. The Dakhin, he specifies, consisted of five provinces: the Mughal *suba* of Dakhin or Ahmadnagar, the joint Mughal province of Khandesh and Birar, the independent sultanates of Bijapur and Golkunda, and last of all, Karnatik, 'a large territory extending as far as Setband

Rameshwar'. During a journey with his father through the Karnatik, he perceived a distinct culture, brought home to him by a scene which he witnessed as a child in the town of Madurai. The ruler died, and, in the words of the author, 'went to the lowest hell', his 700 wives throwing themselves into the fire after him. The author then underlines the strangeness of the land: 'All the people of this territory are idolators, and eat all the wild animals of the forest. There is not a single Musulman here. Occasionally a Musulman may visit the country, deputed by Nizam Shah, Adil Shah or Kutb Shah, but the natives are all infidels.' All the same, the tip of the peninsula was linked in the author's mind to the rest of the country by the fact that routes of Hindu and Muslim pilgrimage ran from the north to the extremity of the peninsula, and onwards to Sri Lanka.[45]

It would seem that the Dravidian culture of the place impressed itself on the author's mind (he was a child at the time of his visit to Madurai) with a sense of strangeness. However, for centuries both before and after Christ, the extreme point of the peninsula had been a sacred spot of the subcontinent. As early as 80 CE, we find 'the Cape of Comari', with its shrine of Kanya Kumari, mentioned in *The Periplus of the Erythraean Sea*: 'hither come those men who wish to consecrate themselves for the rest of their lives, and bathe and dwell in celibacy; and women also do the same; for it is told that a goddess once dwelt here and bathed'.[46] The virgin goddess still looks out towards the ocean, in the direction of the rising sun; but her consort, lord Shiva, has his abode on Mount Kailash, up and behind 'the cold, impenetrable regions where', in the words of Al Biruni, 'the snow never melts nor disappears'.[47]

The Land and the People

The land stood out sharply in the consciousness of both the inhabitants of, and visitors to, the subcontinent. A man who had been to Tibet and claimed to have seen both India and China from 'the top of the highest peak' told the somewhat bemused Al Biruni: 'From the height of this mountain [20 *farsakh*!] India appears as a black expanse below the mist, the mountains lying below this peak like small hills, and Tibet and China appear as red.'[48]

Through the centuries, what struck the Greek, Chinese, and Arab travellers about the physical appearance of the country was the 'level plain', which, as the more perceptive among them surmised correctly, had been 'formed from the alluvial deposits of the river'.[49] Fa-hien, who braved 'winds, rain, snow, drifting sand and gravel stones' while crossing the Ts'ung-ling mountain, saw a strikingly different sight when he reached the Indus: from there to the Southern Sea of south India, he puts it on record, 'the land is level throughout, without great mountains or valleys, but still there are rivers'.[50] Al Biruni, who was struck by the same sight, tells us: 'But if you have seen the soil of India with your own eyes and meditate on its nature ... you could scarcely help thinking that India has once been a sea which by degrees has been filled up by the alluvium of the streams.'[51] The Kushan conquerer Kanishka's dominions (78 CE) which stretched from the steppes and ranges of Central Asia into the Gangetic plains, served only to underline the distinctiveness of India in Chinese eyes. His highland China hostages, says Hiuen Tsang, had separate establishments for the cold and hot weather: 'during the cold they resided in India and its different parts, in the summer they came back to Kapisha'[52] (Kanishka's capital in northern Afghanistan).

Because of 'the many vast plains of great fertility', all alike 'intersected by a multitude of great rivers', India was, as early as the fourth century BC, a nation of husbandmen, who appeared to Megasthenes to be far more numerous than any other class of the population.[53] The monotonous regularity of the intensive cultivation through the centuries is attested to by Hiuen Tsang's comments nine centuries later. The seasons, he said, were particularly hot, the land, well watered and humid, and the valleys and plains, well cultivated, fruitful, and productive.[54] As the population grew amidst the heat and the humidity, the annual revenues and the accumulated treasures increased too. 'The whole of this country', wrote a Persian chronicler of Shah Jahan's time, 'is very fertile, and the productions of Iran, Turan and other climates are not equal to those of even one province of Hindustan.'[55]

The horsemen of the steppes of Central Asia eyed the lie of the land with avid interest. Timur's purported autobiography provides us with an interesting glimpse of how the land, which offered no real obstacle once the plains were reached, was appraised by a master strategist.[56] Before the expedition started out, his officers identified four defences in the country, and were of the opinion that he who could break down these four defences would be master of Hindustan. The defences were the five large rivers that could not be crossed without boats, and bridges; the woods and forests and trees which, with branch interwoven with branch, made it difficult to penetrate into the country; the zamindars, rajas and their levies who inhabited fastnesses in those forests and lived there like wild beasts; and the elephants, which were trained to lift horse and rider up with their trunks and dash both to the ground. Such were the difficulties facing the march of an army, but such tactical obstacles were no barrier to the spread of a culture over the generations. The plains, as Fa-hien saw, rolled away continually along the river valleys of Aryavarta and Dakshinapatha. For the Brahmanical and Buddhist values and notions, there were no barriers to overcome, only distances to traverse.

The gradual diffusion of the Brahmana–Shramana culture along the Sindhu–Ganga–Brahmaputra plain brought the *terra incognita* at the eastern extremity under the beaten track by the seventh century. That explains how Hiuen Tsang came to trudge across the entire breadth of that plain to reach the eastern march of Kamrup, no more than two months away from the Chinese province of Szechwan which lay on the other side of the mountain. 'But', the traveller learnt when he explored the prospect of getting straight across to his native land, 'the mountains and rivers present obstacles, and the pestilential air, the poisonous vapours, the fatal snakes, the destructive vegetation, all these causes of death prevail.' Such topographical features put the Indian plain apart from what lay beyond the Himalayan range, and this obliged the intrepid traveller to retrace his steps. On the way back he saw herds of wild elephants roaming about in numbers.[57]

The rains, the rivers, the forms of wildlife, could not but leave a deep impression on the human consciousness moulded in that environment. The rain and the clouds influenced the collective unconscious in countless unseen ways. A children's rhyme in Bengali hinting at the suicide of a married girl runs as follows:[58]

> 'Clouds have darkened the horizon on the other bank. Red chillies gleam on this side of the river. The rain pours ceaselessly. O brother, my heart is full of anguish.'
> 'But hang on for a month somehow, my dear sister.
> I will get a decorated palanquin to take you away next month.'
>
> 'The fibres of my body have twisted into strings, the very marrow of my bones sizzles in the frying pan.
> May the current swell up from the river, and let me jump into the flood.'

Strangers were awestruck by the strength of the floods, and by the size of the rivers. The Greeks were aware of the Sindhu and the Ganga, but not of the Brahmaputra, and they judged that both were greater than the Egyptian Nile and the Scythian Ister, 'even if their streams were united into one'.[59] Bakhtiyar Khalji's band of adventurers were thunderstruck when they arrived at the Brahmaputra, which, in length, breadth, and depth seemed to them to be three times greater than the Ganges. It was a fateful sight, this first glimpse, for the majority of them were destined to be drowned in it during the retreat from Tibet.[60] On an earlier occasion the army of Alexander of Macedon was obliged to beat a retreat in midsummer when the plains were flooded by the Indus.[61]

The Macedonian conqueror abandoned the expedition to the Gangetic valley as hopeless when he learned that the Gangaridai had four thousand elephants trained and equipped for war.[62] Nearchos, who saw the skin of a tiger, was informed by the Indians that the tiger, when it encountered an elephant, would leap upon its head and kill it.[63] As if this were not enough, there were crocodiles in the river,[64] and Nearchos had to be cautious about the snakes, which were 'nimble in their movements',[65] and for whose bite the Greek physicians had no cure.[66] Indian proverbs, too, illustrate the distinctive character of the fauna. An old Bengali proverb defines a dilemma as 'the crocodile in the water and the tiger on the land', and an even older proverb, cited by the poet Jnanadas, compares a dangerous foe with 'stepping on the snake's tail'.[67] Yet another proverb stresses that a dead elephant is worth a lakh of rupees. This is curiously reminiscent of Arrian's notion that 'Indian women, if possessed of uncommon discretion, would not stray from virtue for any reward short of an elephant'. He was, however, given to understand that on receiving this 'a lady let the giver enjoy her person'. The animals fostered a certain amount of mythicizing of the land; indeed, some of the encounters were strange enough. Al Biruni, for instance, saw a young rhinoceros attack an elephant and throw it down on its face.[68]

In contrast with 'Libya', as the Greeks knew Africa of the elephants,[69] the striking forms of wildlife in India flourished amidst large human settlements multiplying all the time. Shrub, jungle, and forests were interspersed through an old, intensely cultivated civilization, reflected in the curious children's rhyme, 'The tiger ate the bullock of the plough, so the ant draws the ladder across the field'.[70] Megasthenes noted mingling of land and forest: 'The greater part of the soil, moreover, is under irrigation and consequently bears two crops in the course of the year. It teems at the same time with animals of all sorts,—beasts of the field and fowls of the air,—of all different degrees of strength and size.'[71] In Abul Fazl's time, when the same land was sown each year, and in many places 'three harvests and more' were taken 'in a single twelve-month', the stretches of cultivation were virtually continuous throughout Hindustan: 'Notwithstanding its vaste size, it is cultivated throughout. You cannot accomplish a stage nor indeed travel a *kos* without meeting with populous towns and flourishing villages, nor without being gladdened by the sight of sweet waters, delightful verdure and enchanting downs'.[72] The continuous expansion of 'culture', in both its material and moral forms, implied the constant incorporation of wild tribes (the 'Andhras' and 'Pulindas' of Ashoka's rock edicts and the 'Atabikas' of Samudragupta's Allahabad pillar inscription) and the gradual emergence of caste society. Megasthenes's confused description of seven castes based on certain broad occupations is illustrative of an early form of that society.[73] Nine centuries later, the system, governed by the laws of Manu, had taken a harder shape as seen by Hiuen Tsang.[74]

The elements of the wild, woven into the texture of the civilization, reflected a process of constant interpenetration of nature and culture, each affecting the other. Visually, the plains and the rains were the two predominant features of the 'natural' setting of the culture. Abul Fazl's account of the 'Seasons, Natural Beauty and Crops' dwells on the green plains and the trees in foliage from autumn through the depth of winter, and 'the elasticity of the atmosphere' during the rainy season, 'enough to transport the most dispirited and lend the vigour of youth to old age'. The perception here is indigenous and not foreign (Abul Fazl was born and brought up in a family settled in Nagore for many generations), reminiscent of Kalidasa's *Meghadutam*. The monsoon and the green cultivated plain, were the two most important factors in the ecology of Indian civilization. It was the secret of the dense, ever-increasing population.[75]

Insular and self contained from early times, the Indian population had a distinct identity in the eyes of foreigners. Megasthenes, as quoted by Arrian, expressed this somewhat inaccurately when he said that 'the Indians neither invade other men, nor do other men invade the Indians'.[76] The latter was certainly not true. His remark that 'India neither received a colony from abroad, nor sent out a colony to any other nation', might have been a hint at the restrictions placed upon foreign travel and sea voyage by Baudhayana and Manu,[77] an objection later articulated by the East India Company's sepoys in their refusal to cross 'black waters' (*kala pani*). There would, in that event, be some

sense in his supposition that 'India, being of enormous size when taken
as a whole, is peopled by races both numerous and diverse, of which ...
all were evidently indigenous'. By his time, of course, the Austric,
Dravidian, and Aryan-speaking population had been settled on the
subcontinent from time immemorial.[78] Later, as the Brahmanical code
and its insular character grew rigid, 'the Hindus', seen by Al Biruni,
were convinced that there was 'no country but theirs, no nation like
theirs, no kings like theirs, no religion like theirs, no science like theirs'.
Interested scholars from abroad felt an invisible mental barrier here:
'Their haughtiness is such that, if you tell them of any science or scholar
in Khurasan and Persis, they will think you to be both an ignoramus
and a liar. If they travelled and mixed with other nations, they would
soon change their mind, for their ancestors were not as narrow-minded
as the present generation is.'[79]

Perhaps as much because of their dress as because of their
physiognomy, the population appeared all alike to aliens, whether Greek,
Chinese, or Turk. 'Now the countries to the east of the Indus,' wrote
Arrian, 'I take to be India Proper, and the people who inhabit them to
be Indians.'[80] Arrian had not seen any Indians, but he had before him
the now lost texts of Nearchos and Megasthenes who had both closely
observed the 'race'. Based on these two authorities, he wrote: 'With
regard to the inhabitants, there is no great difference in type of figure
between the Indians and the Ethiopians though the southern Indians
bear a somewhat closer appearance to the Ethiopians, being of black
complexion and black haired, though they are not so snub-nosed nor
have the hair so curly; while the Indians who live further to the north
are in person like the Egyptians.'[81]

The reference to black complexion and black hair, with an implied
admission of a somewhat lighter colour up north, makes it virtually
certain that as early as the fourth century BC the Indian population
looked pretty much as it does now, far removed from the racial conception of the fair Indo-European, Aryan appearance of the nineteenth
century imagination. Nearchos, who tells us that the clothes worn by
Indians were made of cotton, reflects: 'This cotton is either of a brighter
white colour than any cotton found elsewhere, or the darkness of the
Indian complexion makes their apparel look so much the whiter.'[82]
They looked all the same to Nearchos except that 'such Indians ... as
are thought anything of, use parasols as a screen from the heat'.[83]

Nearchos described the manner of their apparel in virtually identical terms as Hiuen Tsang nearly a thousand years later, but the Chinese pilgrim's observations are more knowledgeable: 'Their clothing is not cut or fashioned; they mostly affect fresh-white garments; they esteem little those of mixed colour or ornamented.'[84] The light-skinned Turks from Khurasan, a conquering race, were contemptuous of the colour of the subject population of Hindusthan. 'They call Hind black,' wrote Amir Khusrau.[85] The attire and appearance noted by the Greek admiral, the Chinese pilgrim, and the Khurasani conqueror is exactly that painted by the British artists of early nineteenth century India. Over the centuries, the inhabitants of modern India, Pakistan, and Bangladesh, appeared different (as they do even now in the streets of London) from the Europeans (black against white), the Negroes (straighter nose and hair as against snub nose and curly hair), and the Mongoloid races.

It is implied in the narrative of Bakhtiyar Khalji's expedition, how distinct, in language and appearance, 'the infidel Hindus'[86] appeared to the Turkish conquerors of Hindustan and Bengal. The 'Hindus' meant to them all the native inhabitants of Hindustan, irrespective of the Brahmanical, Buddhist, and other faiths; indeed, the Turks did not perceive these distinctions at the time, and when they put the monks of the Buddhist *vihara*s in Bihar to death, they thought them to be Brahmans with shaven heads. They also took the monastery to be a fort and only discovered after sacking it that the place was in fact an institution of learning (madrasa), and that the word '*vihar*' meant a college in 'the Hindi language'.[87] By Hindi they meant the language of Hind, apparently the Apabhramsa tongue of the common people who did not speak Sanskrit (modern Hindi or Hindustani did not exist then). As far as the Turks were concerned, the language, the appearance, and the faith of the Hindus was the same right down from the Ganges to the Brahmaputra.[88] However, as soon as Bhaktiyar Khalji's band of adventurers left the plains of Kamrup to conquer Tibet, they perceived a visible difference. Among the hills lying between Tibet and the plains they saw Mongoloid races, looking more like themselves than the people of the plains: 'They all have Turki features and speak different languages, something between the language of Hind and that of Tibet.'[89]

The formidable Brahmaputra river, which the Turks crossed in order to get into the hills, brought home to them where one country ended and another began. 'When it enters the country of Hindustan,' comments the narrator of the expedition, 'it receives in the Hindi language the name of Samundar' (sea).[90] Hiuen Tsang, it would be recalled, had turned back from this same mountain range though his country lay temptingly on the other side. In attempting to penetrate it, Bakhtiyar Khalji brought about the annihilation of the Turks. The disastrous retreat from Tibet was a consequence of going beyond the sphere understood by the Indian powers, and a warning to the Turks not to ignore the home grown notions of political space. The final blow, the attack upon the defeated Turks desperately swimming across the Brahmaputra river, was the work of 'the Hindus of Kamrup', who were clearly seen to be distinct in race and culture from the 'brave Turks' of Tibet professing the Buddhist religion (Din-i-Tarsai), and no less hostile to 'the soldiers of Islam'.[91]

The coming of the Turks coincided with a development that proved to be as important as the encounter between Islam and the Hindus: this was the growth of the regional vernacular languages which form the basis of the linguistic provinces of Pakistan and India today, and the basis too of Bangladesh. These languages were just branching off from one another out of the parental stock of Apabhramsa dialects when the Turkish occupation was effected in northern India.[92] Around 1030 CE Al Biruni noted the distinction between Sanskrit and the vernacular language. Apparently the latter had not yet visibly differentiated itself into the regional languages of Abul Fazl's time. This is apparent from Al Biruni's remark: 'Further, the language is divided into a neglected vernacular one, only in use among the common people, and a classical one, only in use among the upper and educated classes, which is much cultivated, and subject to the rules of grammatical inflection and etymology, and to all the niceties of grammar and rhetoric.'[93]

The poet Amir Khusrau (1253–1325) noted in old age, 'There is at this time in every province a language peculiar to itself, and not borrowed from any other—Sindi, Lahori, Kashmiri, the language of Dugar [Dogri], Dhur Samundar, Tilang, Gujarat, Ma'bar, Gaur, Bengal, Oudh, Delhi and its environs.' This is a somewhat confused list, but it does represent an important change of perception from the time of the early Turkish conquerors who could only perceive an undifferentiated vernacular language of Hind which they indiscriminately called 'Hindui' or 'Hind-i'.[94] Unlike Amir Khusrau later on, they were not acquainted at the time with the Dravidian languages of the south—Tamil (Amir Khusrau's Ma'bar), Telugu (Khusrau's Tilang), Kannada (Khusrau's Dhur Samundar or Dwara Samudra), and Malayalam (not known to Khusrau as the Sultanate armies did not reach Malabar). The southern tongues had articulated themselves a long time before the coming of the Turks. However, such Indo-Aryan vernacular languages as Punjabi (Lahori), Bengali (Gaur, Bengal), and Hindustani or Hindi (Oudh, Dehli) were yet to find full articulation at the time when the Turks came. A century later Amir Khusrau noted them in a midway state of differentiation, all of them 'languages of Hind, which from ancient times have been applied in every way to the common purposes of life', and distinct from 'another language more select than the others, which all the Brahmans use'. The latter, he specified, was 'Sahaskrit', an old language the common people knew nothing of, with even Brahmani women not understanding a word of it.[95]

The vernacular languages assumed hard shape, each with a literature of its own, in the fourteen and fifteenth centuries. The completion of the process of differentiation is reflected in Abul Fazl's observations regarding the linguistic diversity of Hindustan in the late sixteenth century. He found that certain languages were mutually comprehensible, but others were not. It is a pity he did not list the languages that had preserved 'a common inter-intelligibility'. All he said was that the diversity of even these were 'innumerable'. He was however good enough to catalogue the 'forms of speech which are not understood of one another'. These, as he noted, were the dialects of Delhi, Bengal, Multan, Marwar, Gujarat, Telinganah, Marhatta, Karnatik, Sind, Afghan of Shal (between Sind, Kabul, and Qandahar), Beluchistan, and Kashmir.[96]

The common Dravidian origin of the languages of the south, the common Indo-Aryan origin of the rest, and the interpenetration of ideas between the two language groups under the predominant influence of the Sanskritic tradition and the Sufi–Bhakti movement, bound the languages together, and justified the concept of the common Hindwi, Hindui, or Hindi language of Hindustan. This meant, not modern Hindi, but a common vernacular language stock of India; a concept we find clearly articulated in Amir Khusrau's *Ashika* and *Nuh Sipihr*. While speaking of 'the merits of Hindi', he asserted: '... You will not find the Hindi words [i.e. the language of India] inferior to the Farsi.'[97] The fact that this great Persian poet spoke so consciously of 'the Hindi language' despite his awareness of a language peculiar to every province reflects a certain sense of community of language.

So strong was this sense of shared language and mentality that it penetrated across the 'Hindu' and 'Muslim' divide as early as the first century of the Turkish conquest, occasioning the proud declaration by the poet: 'I was born in Hind.' The sense of shared identity was reflected in the alternate meanings of the word 'Hindi'. In Amir Khusrau's hands, it meant not only the Hindwi language, but those 'born in Hind'. Thus, we find him critical of 'the Khurasani who considers every Hindi a fool'.[98] Here 'Hindi' means a man born in Hind, who might be a Muslim. The word had become necessary, for a Muslim born in Hind, such as Amir Khusrau, could not be referred to as a Hindu. What the two shared was not just the land, but its language too, as well as the thought expressed in it. In putting in a word about 'the languages of Hind',[99] Amir Khusrau was deeply conscious of their basic unity.

The roots and inspiration of the languages that had emerged in the thirteenth century were much the same, and the mental climate in which they were destined to evolve subsequently was similar. Even the languages of south India, with their different origins, grew up in similar conditions; so much so that men as discerning as Amir Khusrau and Abul Fazl could not distinguish between Tamil, Kannada, and Malayalam, and spoke vaguely of the language of 'Dorasamudra' and 'Karnatik'. Amir Khusrau observed that all the tongues listed by him differed from one another, and each had some peculiar merit of its own. The fact, noted by him, that every one, good or bad, learnt Farsi in Hind, 'while all the other languages which existed never moved from their bounds',[100] was a factor that promoted the absorption of Persian words by the regional languages. This, added to the common stock of Sanskrit words, enhanced the 'inter-intelligibility' which Abul Fazl found among some of the vernacular languages in the sixteenth century. The same factor was destined, in the eighteenth century, to foster the literary Hindustani language, initially known as Urdu-e-Mualla. As Jawaharlal Nehru said after Independence, each and every language was not merely the language of a part of India, but was essentially a language of India, representing the thought and culture and development of the country in its manifold forms.[101] What he said is applicable to Pakistan and Bangladesh too. The languages of the subcontinent are even today linked together by a shared mentality, evolving out of the continuity of its civilization. In Al-Hind there was no break of the kind that occurred in Islamized Egypt or rechristianized Spain, nor the sort that occurred in the vanished civilization of Byzantium when it fell to the Ottomans.

'Hind', 'Hindustan', 'India'

The antiquated expression 'Jambudvipa' continued to be used occasionally in the vernacular poetry of medieval India.[102] More familiar to the population was the Puranic term 'Bharat',[103] which was still current, but more so among Hindus than Muslims. The Arab term for the subcontinent, 'Al-Hind', together with the early literary expression 'Hind and Sind', reflected an approach from outside, with more systematic attention to geographical location. Ibn Haukal, a native of Baghdad, drew up 'a map of the world' in 976 CE, together with a separate diagram for 'every country of Islam'. There were twenty diagrams in all in his *Ashkalul Bilad*, each with a text. The twelfth chart was a map of Sind, and on this map 'Sind' and 'Hind' were located from the perspective of the Persian Gulf (Sea of Fars).[104] The accompanying text reads: 'I have placed the country of Sind and its dependencies in one map, which exhibits the entire country of Sind, part of Hind ...' (see map on next page).

It was, however, the Persian term 'Hindustan', originally an ancient Iranian expression denoting the land of the Sindhu,[105] which passed into universal use, initially amongst Muslims, then among Hindus. Tilak, a Hindu general who served Sultan Mahmud in his headquarters at Ghazni, is reported by a contemporary Persian chronicler to have reassured his master when a sudden rebellion broke out in Lahore: '... I am a native of Hindustan, the weather is hot, and I can travel in that country with greater ease.'[106] Geographically as well as historically, the term 'Hindustan' was well defined in the Persian chronicles, as, for instance, in Zia-ud-Din Barani's *Tarikh-i-Firuz Shahi*: 'Fear and respect for the Sultan had spread through Khurasan and Hindustan, and all the countries of Hind and Sind ...'[107]

'Hindustan' occurs in the Persian chronicles in two senses: the subcontinent of India and the Jamuna–Ganga valley to the border of Bengal. Muhammad Qasim Firishta means the latter when he speaks of 'a custom which prevails in the Deccan, but not in Hindoostan', and the former when he declares Ahmadabad to be 'the handsomest city in Hindoostan, and perhaps in the world'.[108] The wider sense in which Hindustan was understood prevails, too, in the terms in which the orthodox *mulla* Badauni speaks of a Sufi whom he particularly disliked:[109]

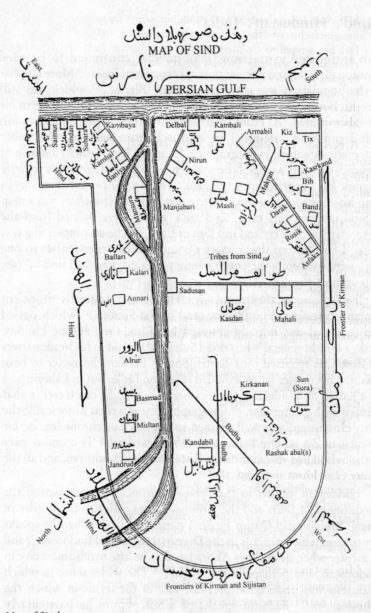

Map of Sind
Source: MSS. of *Ashkalul Bilad* by Ibn Haukal of Baghdad, 976 CE. Uri Bodl. Codd. MSS., Cat., p. 209.

In his wanderings he came to the Dak'hin, where from his want of self-restraint he betrayed the filthiness of his disposition, and the rulers of the Dak'hin wished to cleanse the tablet of existence of his image, but eventually he was only set on a donkey and shown about the city in disgrace. But since Hindustan is a wide place, where there is an open field for all licentiousness, and no one interferes with another's business, so that every one can do just as he pleases, at this time he made his way to Malwah ...

A petition to Akbar by his courtier Faizi in which Badauni was recommended to the Emperor mentions Hindustan incidentally, and in the wider sense: 'Mulla Abdu-'l Qadir has much aptitude, and he has studied what the *mulla*s of Hindustan usually study in the ordinary branches of learning.'[110] The petition was dated 1592. By this time, the use of the term Hindustan was no longer confined to the world of Persian learning alone, but had passed into wider vernacular circulation in the outlying *suba*s of the Mughal empire. Thus the following lines occur in the Bengali epic *Nabi Vamsa* by Saiyid Sultan: 'The sinner conquered Sam-desh [Syria] and Turk-sthan [Turkistan], and became a chief by conquering Hindustan.'[111] In court circles, the sense of distinction between Hindustan and other countries was also quite sharp. Emperor Aurangzeb is said to have asked his old tutor ironically:[112]

But what was the knowledge I derived under your tution? You told me that the whole of Franguistan [Europe] was no more than some inconsiderable island, of which the most powerful Monarch was formerly the King of Portugal, then he of Holland, and afterwards the King of England. In regard to the other sovereigns of Franguistan, such as the King of France and him of Andalusia, you told me they resemble our petty Rajas, and that the potentates of Hindoustan eclipsed the glory of all other kings; that they alone were Humayons, Ekbars, Jehan-Guyres, or Chah-Jehans; the Happy, the Great, the Conquerors of the World, and the Kings of the World; and that Persia, Usbec, Kashguer, Tartary, and Catay, Pegu, Siam, China and Matchine, trembled at the name of the Kings of the Indies. Admirable geographer! deeply read historian! was it not incumbent upon my preceptor to make me acquainted with the distinguishing features of every nation of the earth ... ?

Hindustan, despite the existence of many 'petty Rajas', emerges from the reported remarks of the Emperor as one entity, rather like Europe. There is here a sense of one space. That space was originally Hindu. A Sanskrit inscription in honour of the early Turkish ruler Balban[113] waxes lyrical on the happiness of his subjects 'from Gaur to

Ghazni and [upwards] from the Dravida settlements and Rameshwar Setubandha' (*ā Gaudād–Gajjanānta–Janapadāt–Setubandhāt*).[114] His soldiers are said to have 'rushed for bathing every day from the Ganga-Sagar confluence in the east to the confluence of the Indus with the sea in the west'.[115] We are further informed that whenever Balban set out on an expedition, 'the Gaudas lost all glory, the Andhras pressed into their holes, the Keralas ceased to play for fear of life, the Karnatas took shelter in their caves, the Mahrashtras fell from their places, the Gurjaras were bereft of their strength and the Latas paled with fear (cit., became like the Kiratas).'[116] Now, most of these places and peoples were not under Balban's rule at all. If the poet still felt the urge to mention them all in one breath, it was because they were associated in his mind as part of a whole. Curiously, he had no name for the whole, no denomination for India, and this was in line with the inscribed Sanskrit panegyrics of the past, which would catalogue the conquests of the patrons from one end to the other without naming the country.

The Arab geographers, looking at the land from outside, were more aware of its outline. The coming of Islam led to a new emphasis on the distinction of India, as against the innumerable distinctions within the land. The denomination of the country as Al-Hind indicates this. We have on record the observations of the merchant Sulaiman in this connection:[117]

> The inhabitants of China and India agree that there are four great or principal kings in the world. They place the king of the Arabs [Khalifa of Baghdad] at the head of these, for it is admitted without dispute that he is the greatest of kings ...
> The king of China reckons himself the next after the king of the Arabs. After him comes the king of the Greeks [Rum], and lastly the Balhara, prince of the men who have their ears pierced.
> ... The princes of India do not recognize the supremacy of any one sovereign. Each one is his own master. Still the Balhara has the title of 'king of kings'.
> The Chinese are men of pleasure; but the Indians condemn pleasure, and abstain from it. They do not take wine, nor do they take vinegar which is made of wine.

Zahiruddin Muhammad Babar, too, had an outsider's perspective of India, the land sharply defined in his vision as one among other countries on the periphery of the Islamic world. This was not the undefined Hindu perspective in which the land constituted a universe in itself, everything else being beyond the pale. Babar noted in his memoirs: 'Just as the Arabs call every place outside 'Arab (Arabia), 'Ajam, so Hindustanis call every place outside Hindustan, Khurasan. There are two trade marts on the land route between Hindustan and Khurasan: one is Kabul, the other Qandahar.'[118] This was a perspective from Central Asia in which India lay at one end of the world of Islam. Islam was instrumental, by virtue of its world perspective, in giving India a sharper focus.

The fact that the new ruling class was substantially of foreign origin served to bring the land and its population into sharper focus. Afanasy Nikitin, the Russian visitor to the Deccan in the fifteenth century, had a vague sense of this. 'All the Indian princes come of Khorassan', said he, 'and so do all the boyars. And all the people of Hindustan ... fight mounted on elephants, sending footmen forward, while the Khorassanis fight on horseback, both they and their horses clad in armour.'[119] The land lying to the west of India, far from being beyond the pale, was now a dominant presence. Both as a religion and as a political force, Islam defined the space that was formerly the universe of the Hindus, denominated it as Hindustan, and vigorously moulded its identity.

Like Hinduism, Islam conceived the land as one religious space, but unlike Hinduism, it invariably designated that space by a name. So sharp a denomination of the common space occurs rarely in the sacred Brahmanical literature. The *Vishnu Purana* on one occasion and the *Vayu Purana* on another, name as Bhārata the country (*Varshaṁ tad Bhāratam nāma*) that lies north of the sea (*uttaram yat samudrasya*) and south of the Himalayas (*Himādreshchaiva dakshinam* [*Vishnu Purana*]/*Himavad-dakshinañcha yat* [*Vayu Purana*]). Such specific references are rare in the Hindu scriptures.[120] Because it originated elsewhere, Islam referred to the land by name. A hagiographical Sufi work written during the reign of Jahangir defines the religious space in these terms:[121]

> ... Khwaja Mu'inu-d-din, of Chisht, was walking round the Ka'ba, when a voice reached him from the other world, directing him to go to Medina. Upon his arrival the Prophet (the peace of God, and rest be upon him!) appeared to him, and said, 'The Almighty has entrusted the country of India to thee. Go thither and settle in Ajmir. By God's help, the faith of Islam shall, by thy piety and that of thy followers, be spread in that land.'
> ... Khwaja Mu'inu-d-din, of Chisht, through the powerful assistance of his prayers, brought the whole country of India into the hands of Kutb-ud-din Aibak.

The authority which Shaikh Muinuddin acquired over the newly defined spiritual space is thus described in the *Siyar-al-Aqtab*:[122] 'Through his coming to Hindustan the way (*tariqa*) of Islam was established there ... For this reason Muin al-din is called Nabi al-Hind (the prophet of India).' The Chistiyya notion of the succession to the spiritual sovereignty of Hindustan traces a line of descent from Shaikh Muinuddin Chishti of Ajmer (known as Garib Nawaz) to his ascetic disciple Baba Farid of Ajodhan (Pak Pattan in Pakistan today), and from Baba Farid in turn to Shaikh Nizamuddin Auliya of Delhi. Baba Farid is said to have told Hazrat Nizamuddin: 'I have given you the spiritual empire of Hindustan. Go and take it.'[123]

Politically, too, no less than spiritually, Islam brought India into sharper focus. Thus Babar declared in his Memoirs: 'From the time of the revered Prophet down till now three men from that side [Transmontana n. of Hindu-kush] have conquered and ruled Hindustan. St Mahmud Ghazi [Mahmud of Ghazni] was the first ... St Shihabu'd-din of Ghur was the second ... I am the third.'[124] Babar places India in the political perspective of Islam, and does so self-consciously, as it were placing himself in history.

The political space which he refers to here took firm shape with the Turkish occupation of northern India in the thirteenth century. This was followed by the Mongol conquests which soon afterwards destroyed the political power of Islam in its central lands. This left India as the one safe haven of the creed from its Shamanist opponents. Minhaj-us-Siraj's *Tabaqat i Nasiri*, the first major Muslim chronicle of India, is in fact a narration of how these two events occurred. The story is built around the triple notions of 'Islam', 'Hindustan', and 'the infidel Mughals' (i.e. the Shamanist Mongol conquerors of Ajam). The *Tabaqat*, as the author himself spelt out, dealt with those early sultans of Hind 'who, in the empire of Hindustan, sat upon the throne of sovereignty ... and through whose sway the signs of the lights of the Muhammadan faith remained on the records of the different parts and tracts of Hindustan ...'.[125] The account of the Turkish occupation of Hindustan is preceded by an introductory sketch of the early history of Islam. This leads him to his main subject, the deeds of the reigning princes and noblemen of the Sultanat of Delhi, down to the time of Balban. Having dealt with Islam in its early phase and its expansion in Hindustan, the author ends up with a narrative of the eruption of the Mongols and the devastation of the world of Islam down to 1259 CE. The preface to the last section of the chronicle drew a clear distinction between the triumph of the 'Infidel Mughals' in the central lands of Islam and the survival and consolidation of the true faith in Hindustan:

> Notwithstanding that, by the will of the Almighty, and the Decrees of Destiny, the turn of sovereignty passed into the Chingiz Khan, the Accursed, and his descendants, after the kings of I-ran and Turan, that the whole of the land of Turan and the East fell under the sway of the Mughals, and that the authority of the Muhammadan religion departed from those regions, which became the seat of paganism, the kingdom of Hindustan, by the grace of Almighty God, and the favour of fortune, under the shadow of the guardianship of the Shamsi race, and the shadow of the protection of the I-yal-timishi dynasty, became the focus of the people of Islam, and the orbit of the possessors of religion; and as far as the extremity of the territories of Chin, Turkistan, Mawar-un-Nahr, Tukharistan, Zawul, Ghur, Kabul, Ghaznin, Iraq, Aran, Azerbaijan, the Jazirah, Anbar, Sijistan, Mukran, Kirman, Fars, Khuzistan, the Diyar-i-Bakr, and Mausil, as far as the boundaries of Rum and Sham, fell into the hands of the infidel Mughals, and not a trace of the Muhammadan Maliks and Sultans of Islam remained in these countries ...[126]

Hindustan, as a distinct political entity, consolidated itself against the Mongol menace, and when, towards the end of the century, Sultan Alauddin Khalji proposed in an inebriated state to leave a viceroy in India and, like Alexander the Great, set out upon the conquest of the world, the Kotwal of Delhi soberly drew his attention to two undertakings that pressed more urgently: 'The first is, the conquest of the southern kingdoms of Hindoostan, such as Runtumbhore, Chittoor, Jalwar, and Chundery; and the second, the reduction of the south-eastern provinces, as far as the sea, and on the north-west, as far as Lumghan and Kabul, so as to form a barrier to protect India from the invasions of the Mughals.'[127] The Kotwal's words reflected an awareness of Hindustan as a unit of the world of Islam. The concept was brought into fresh focus when, in the earlier part of the fourteenth century, Muhammad Tughlaq wrote to the Caliph asking for a letter of investiture appointing him 'his deputy in Hind and Sind'. In response to this, the Caliph 'wrote in his own handwriting a letter investing the emperor with powers to rule over India on his behalf'.[128]

The arrival of Vasco da Gama at Calicut in 1498, preceded by Afanasy Nikitin's voyage to the Deccan (1466–72), brought India into a European, as distinct from the Islamic, perspective. 'And that', Nikitin informed his Christian brothers of Rus, 'is where the land of India lies, and where everyone goes naked ... The men and women are all dark.

Wherever I went I was followed by many people who wondered at a white man.'[129] As trade contacts were regularized in the seventeenth century, the Russian government grew curious about India. The Tsar had a series of questions to be answered:

> In India find out what is the religion of Shah Jahan and who are his near and dear ones and do the subjects profess the same faith as Shah Jahan? Or do they have a different faith? ... If there are kingdoms of other rulers under Shah Jahan, find out whether they are of the same faith? ... Does he have many soldiers, and numerous cavalry?'[130]

Indian traders in the Russian mart of Astrakhan were regularly interviewed by the Russian government for information regarding India. Their replies reflected an awareness of their own country seen from afar, all the more distinct because seen through an altered perspective. An Indian trader named Marwari Barayev, summoned urgently from Astrakhan, deposed on 15 February 1735; 'In India the capital city is called Delhi, where the Moghul lives. There are four routes from that city.'[131] He then gave details of the routes from Delhi to Astrakhan: (1) Delhi–Kandahar–Gilan–Caspian Sea–Astrakhan; (2) Delhi–Kabul–Badakshan–Bukharan territory–Khiva–Astrakhan, (3) Delhi–Thatta–Persian Gulf–Ispahan–Gilan–Astrakhan; and (4) Delhi–Kalat–Kerman–Kashan–Ispahan–Gilan–Astrakhan. 'In Indian territory,' the Indian merchant informed the Russian authorities, 'there is never any winter or snow; two crops are harvested every year; there are various flowers and grass never disappears'. He then detailed the products of India, taking care to mention that Indian silk, though as good as the Chinese, was not available in great quantities, whereas cotton textiles abounded. He concluded his deposition with the remark: 'The place is warm and the people move about in dresses made of cotton or silk, grown there.' It was as if the Indian merchant looked at his country through the Russian prism and saw it in a form he would not otherwise have realized.

Characterizing the Country

A spy dispatched to the desert confines of Hind on the orders of Caliph Usman reported Islam's first encounter with India in the following terms: 'Water is scarce, the fruits are poor, and the robbers are bold; if few troops are sent there they will be slain, if many, they will starve.'[132] Did the man speak in fancy, the Caliph wondered, or were these hard facts?

These, the spy maintained respectfully, were hard facts. He was of course unaware at the time of a vast subcontinent watered by perennial rivers. For the time being, the Caliph decided not to send an expedition there. This was early in the seventh century. Another seven centuries elapsed before Islam as a political power reached the Ganges delta in the east and far off Madurai to the south. As a more exact sense of the space was acquired, the borders of the land stood out,[133] and its centre was located. Muhammad bin Tughlaq, considering Daulatabad 'so much more centrical than Dehly',[134] made it his capital, abortively as it proved.

For strangers, the land was full of deadly perils. The first embassy from Tibet, consisting of 7 young officers sent by the Tibetan king to learn the art of reading and writing, proceeded no further than the borders of India, where they turned back for fear of three kinds of demons, namely evil spirits, deadly fevers, and wild animals, especially the poisonous snakes that abounded there. Later, the Tibetan monastery of Thoding, founded at Tholin in 1025 CE, sent 21 monks to India to obtain the services of Indian pundits. Of them, 19 died of heat, fever, snakebite, and other causes. The celebrated pundit, Atisha Dipankara, when requested by a third embassy from Tibet to visit the country, initially refused to do so, whereupon the head of the mission, weeping bitterly, explained that he had come from the far country of Himavat, suffering the loss of many of his companions, who had died of fever, heat, and snakebite.[135] Atisha was then persuaded to go on a mission to 'Himavat', never to return to his own country. The Tibetan monks who took him away had no doubt in their minds that *'arya-desha'*,[136] his native land, constituted one country. Like the learned men of Islam (*ulama*) who followed shortly afterwards, they, too, perceived here a single space: but rather than conceiving it as the land of the 'infidels' they looked upon it as the country where the 'true doctrine'[137] had originated.

The sense of distinct space was fostered among strangers by the colourful peculiarities they observed while wandering through the land: for instance, the various species of trees with their unique fruits—listed by the curious traveller Ibn Battuta (and in greater detail by Babar), 'none of which exists in our or any other country';[138] 'the wild animals peculiar to Hindustan',[139] some of which, now confined to narrow sanctuaries, roamed all over the country at the time;[140] the tame elephants, covered in armour and immune to arrows and swords, which, to the invader Timur-i-Lang, appeared to resemble nothing so much as small mountains;[141] tigers and monkeys eyeing each other narrowly;[142] the ubiquitous ants which would crawl in thousands over every piece of bread or every article of clothing unless carefully stored in a country-made chest or cupboard constructed upon four wooden pillars set into stone cisterns full of water;[143] the sight of crows sitting upon buffaloes, so familiar to natives, yet so strange to visitors, one of whom went so far as to speculate that the buffalo preferred to stand in water up to its neck because otherwise it would never be rid of the crows;[144] fourteen feet long snakes which, before the horrified eyes of a Russian horse dealer, crawled along the streets of the stone built capital of Bidar, a sight to which, presumably, even the natives could not have been altogether indifferent;[145] a party of fakirs with a tame lion which squatted and dined with them and did no harm to the gazelle which was part of the picturesque company;[146] snake charmers, with snakes in their baskets, which danced to the tune of a peculiarly shaped musical instrument;[147] a Dasnami Naga sannyasi who would, if asked, suspend his breath for three hours, bring milk out of his veins, cut bones with a hair, and put bones into a narrow mouthed bottle without breaking it;[148] the altogether more charming scene of women, even 'the Finest of the Gentues', carrying water on their heads, 'with sometimes two or three Earthen Pots over one another for Household service'; or 'whole Droves of all Sexes and Ages coming to wash in the river, which is done twice a day'.[149]

Equally striking is the miraculous story relating how Babar ventured upon his conquest of India, the more so as the narrative is of indigenous origin. Babar, relates an old servant of the Sur monarchs, once prayed at a garden in Kabul at break of dawn: 'O God! if the government of Hindustan is destined to be given to me and mine, let these productions of Hind be presently brought before me, betel leaves and mangoes, and I shall accept them as an omen.' Precisely at that hour an Afghan nobleman of Delhi who was plotting against the Lodi monarch appeared before him with an offering of half ripe mangoes preserved in pots of honey, and betel leaves. When Babar's eyes fell on the fruit, he rose from the throne and prostrated himself before the Almighty, in the belief that He had granted him 'the sovereignty of Hind'.[150] The paan leaf and the mango fruits, characteristic products of India and not to be encountered elsewhere, obviously stood in the old Afghan's eyes as symbols of the space over which the sovereign of India was supposed to hold sway.

Babar himself left a description of India which has not been excelled by any professional geographer.[151] 'Compared with our countries,' he noted with the keen eye of a naturalist, 'it is a different world; its mountains, rivers, jungles and deserts, its towns, its cultivated lands, its animals and plants, its people and their tongues, its rains, and its winds, are all different.' Once the traveller from Kabul crossed the River Indus, everything was 'in the Hindustan way',[152] land, water, tree, rock, people, and customs.

The discerning eyes of this master strategist identified certain essential features of the lie of the land. The mountain range, which in Kabul was known as the Hindu Kush, moved into Hindustan, with, as Babar saw, a slight inclination to the south. The 'Hindustanat',[153] i.e. the countries of Hindustan, all lay to the south of it, locally known as the Sawalak Parbat, while Tibet was on the other side of the range. The snow on these mountains never lessened, and in consequence several large rivers issuing from the range flowed through Hindustan, no less than six rising north of Sirhind and all meeting near Multan, to flow westwards through the Thatta country to the sea. Several other rivers, also issuing from the Sawalak Parbat, moved in the other direction, all uniting with the Gang Darya, flowing east under its name, and passing through the Bengal country to fall into the great ocean. There was a second group of mountains within Hindustan, on which there was no snow whatever, from which arose certain non-perennial rivers, such as the Chambal, the Banas, the Betwa, and the Son, which also joined the Gang Darya.

The greater part of the Hindustan country was situated on level land, 'a dead level plain', which distressed Babar because it nowhere exhibited running water (aqar-sular),[154] by which he meant small streams and artificially constructed channels that might bring water into gardens and residences. There were, indeed, occasional areas of standing waters and of course the phenomenal rivers. Worn into deep channels by the monsoon rains, these rivers and torrents were difficult to cross at any point. Even where, as in the case of some towns, it was practicable to convey water by digging channels, Babar saw that this was not done, as canal water was not considered a necessity in cultivating crops or orchards. 'Autumn crops', Babar noted, 'grow by the downpour of the rains themselves; and strange it is that spring crops grow even when no rain falls.'[155] As there was little 'running water', the towns and villages subsisted on the water of wells, or on such as collected in tanks during the rains; while the crops were all rain grown. Certainly there was no lack of moisture, for many parts of the plains were overgrown with thorny jungle, 'behind the good defence of which the people of the pargana become stubbornly rebellious and pay no taxes.'[156]

Another feature that struck Babar was the population, which even then seemed unlimited. 'As far as Bengal, as far indeed as the shore of the great ocean, the peoples are without a break.'[157] One of the pleasant things about the country was that it had masses of gold and silver, but this did not mean that the people were rich. Peasants and people of low standing went about 'naked',[158] except for a decency clout (*languta*), which hung two spans below the navel and was passed between the thighs and fastened behind. Women were also dressed in a like manner, with a cloth round the waist, except that one half of it was thrown over the head.

Muhammad Qasim Firishta, who came from the distant shores of the Caspian Sea to the Deccan as a child, had more of an insider's view of the country, but he, too, concurred with Babar as regards the uniqueness of India. 'This country', he wrote at the end of his monumental history, 'is quite peculiar, and the manners of its inhabitants are very remarkable.'[159] The towns bore little resemblance to those of other countries, being 'filthy and uncleanly', with houses 'built like prisons'.[160] On the other hand, the land abounded with 'extensive wildernesses, full of all sorts of trees'—wastes which, Firishta agreed with Babar, offered 'inducements, both to rajas and subjects, to revolt from the government'. Firishta noted, too, the teeming population which had so impressed Babar:[161]

> The original population, and the abundance of cattle, in this country, exceed that of all others; but its depopulation and desolation are sudden and rapid beyond conception. This is owing principally to the inhabitants building their houses of thatch, and having their domestic utensils of earthen-work, both of which they relinquish without remorse, so that by taking their cattle with them, and departing to some other spot, they easily construct houses like those they have deserted, and after obtaining a few earthen vessels, they again apply themselves to husbandry.

Climate, with which Islamic science associated the colour of different ethnic groups, occasioned comparative observations of the sort usual in medieval times. The world was divided into seven parts, each with a climate peculiar to the latitude. Seven different climates were said to prevail in seven belts constituted by the parallels reckoned upwards from the equator, and in each 'climate', the colour of the human species was said to differ—1st climate (equator): 'black in colour'; 2nd climate: 'between black and wheat colour'; 3rd climate: 'generally of a wheat colour'; 4th climate: 'a wheat colour and a fair skin'; 5th climate: colour 'fair'; 6th climate: colour of inhabitants 'fair inclining to tawny and with tawny hair'; 7th climate: colour of inhabitants 'ruddy and white'.[162] Babar reckoned that Hindustan was 'in the first climate, the second climate and the third climate'. Of the fourth climate, he thought 'it had none'.[163] Abul Fazl corrected him on this point, locating Kashmir in the fourth climate, parallel to Kabul, but below Babar's native Farghana which lay with Samarkhand in the fifth climate.[164] India, in Abul Fazl's reckoning, was 'an aggregate of the first, second, third, and fourth climates'—1st climate: Mabar, Quilon; 2nd climate: Debal in Sind, Makran coast, Somnath, Ahmedabad, Nahrwala (Patan), Mandu, Ujjain, Surat, Banaras, Mathura, Agra, Sonargaon, Pandua in Bengal, Kalinjar, Ayodhya; 3rd climate: Multan, Lahore, Delhi, Peshawar, Hardwar; 4th climate: Kashmir, source of the Mihran (Indus).[165]

More exact than these pseudo-scientific speculations were the observations, by natives and aliens alike, of the weather, especially the dramatic variations through the seasons, which had inspired through the centuries two unique brands of vernacular poetry, the erotic sports of the six seasons (*shar ritu*) and the bereavements and sufferings of the twelve months (*bara masya*).[166] The Hindu calendar, which the Indian born Muslims had adopted, divided the year into six seasons and twelve months.[167] Babar, seeing things from a comparative perspective born of his Central Asian outlook, simplified and reduced these to three seasons of four months each: 'Again: whereas there are four seasons in those countries (outside India), there are three in Hindustan, namely four months are summer; four are the rains; four are winter.'[168] The features of the Indian weather which impressed him, as indeed they struck virtually every foreigner, were the rains and the hot season:[169]

Its air in the Rains is very fine. Sometimes it rains 10, 15 or 20 times a day; torrents pour down all at once and rivers flow where no water had been ... The fault is that the air becomes very soft and damp ... Not only in the Rains but also in the cold and hot seasons, the airs are excellent; at these times however the north-west wind constantly gets laden with dust and earth. It gets up in great strength every year in the heats ... so strong and carrying so much dust and earth that there is no seeing one another. People call this wind Darkener of the Sky [H. *andhi*]. The weather is hot under the Bull and Twins, but not intolerably so, not so hot as in Balkh and Qandahar and not half so long.

Bernier, coming from a colder climate, and not inured by a stint at Qandahar to the heat, found it insupportable: 'not a cloud to be seen nor a breath of air to be felt'.[170] During the night he found the absence of wind to increase the heat almost to suffocation. The heat was so intense in Hindustan, he wrote to a French nobleman in the month of July, that no one, not even the king, wore stockings. The only cover for the feet were slippers, while the head was protected by turbans woven from fine and delicate fabrics. The other garments were proportionately light. In summer, one could scarcely touch the wall of an apartment, or put one's head on a pillow. 'For more than six successive months,' he wrote, 'everybody lies in the open air without covering—the common people in the streets, the merchants and persons of condition sometimes in their courts or gardens, and sometimes on their terraces, which are first carefully watered.'[171] As a physician he speculated that 'the feebleness and languor both of body and mind', which attacked all persons here indiscriminately, was a species of unremitting malady consequent upon the excessive heat.[172]

More discerning, perhaps, was his observation of the connections between the heat and the coming of the rains. He saw that the rains began to fall in the month of July, when the heat was most intense. The rain cooled the air and rendered the earth productive. Without fully grasping the scientific laws underlying the phenomenon of the monsoon, he was led to believe that the heat of the earth and the rarefaction of the air were the principal causes of the rains: 'the atmosphere of the circumjacent seas being colder, more condensed, and thicker, is filled with clouds drawn from the water by the great heat of the summer, and which, driven and agitated by the winds, discharge themselves naturally upon the land, where the atmosphere is more rarefied, lighter, and less resisting than on the sea ...'[173] He was of the opinion that according as the heat came early or late, or was more intense or less, so the discharge, too, would vary, a principle by which he sought to explain the failure of the rains for two successive years during his stay, and the extraordinary drought and widespread famine which he witnessed.[174]

The intimate connection, in this country, between the weather and the crops was a phenomenon that could not escape the attention of any visitor,[175] and was deeply impressed upon the consciousness of every inhabitant. Firishta, whose lifelong experience was derived from the Deccan, had this to say:[176]

The autumnal crops are produced in the months when the sun is in Cancer, Leo, Virgo, and Libra, and are brought forward by the rain of the monsoon; while the spring crops, which grow during the months when the sun is in Scorpio, Sagittarius, Capricornus, and Aquarius, require no rain, nor the air of streams or wells, but are brought to great perfection by the dews and the cool nights at that season of the year, a fact which has always surprised me.

As early as the third century BC, Megasthenes had observed on his embassy to Patna that 'since there is a double rainfall in the course of each year—one in the winter season when the sowing of wheat takes place as in other countries, and the second at the time of the summer solstice, which is the proper season for sowing rice and bosporum, as well as sesamum and millet—the inhabitants of India almost always gather in two harvests annually'.[177] Ibn Battuta, who travelled through the north, the far south and Bengal in the fourteenth century, observed that the Indians derived two crops from the same soil: the corns, millets, peas, and beans of the autumn crop and the wheat, barley, and lentils of the spring crop. As for rice, however, he noted that they sowed it three times a year, so fertile was the soil.[178] Abul Fazl, at the end of the sixteenth century, observed a still further stage in the growth of intensive agriculture: 'The soil is for the most part arable and of such productive power that the same land is sown each year and in many places three harvests and more are taken in a single twelve-month and the vine bears fruit in its first year.'[179]

From remote antiquity, Indian society had an economic outline, imparted to it by the weather and the soil. It could not be mistaken for any other economy. As far back as written accounts go, this was a land of peasants. India appeared to Megasthenes to consist of 'many vast plains of great fertility ... all alike intersected by a multitude of rivers;',[180] and of its numerous population, the caste of husbandmen seemed to him to be 'far more numerous than the others'.[181] They, the second of the seven castes in which he divided the population, were said to enjoy a well understood dispensation that ensured the tradition of unbroken agriculture, 'for whereas among other nations it is usual, in the contests of war, to ravage the soil, and thus to reduce it to an uncultivated waste, among the Indians, on the contrary, by whom husbandmen are regarded as a class that is sacred and inviolable, the tillers of the soil, even when battle is raging in their neighbourhood, are undisturbed by any sense of danger, for the combatants on either side in waging the conflict make carnage of each other, but allow those engaged in husbandry to remain quite unmolested'.[182]

The convention, founded on the notion of a common political space in which a multiplicity of potentates might contend with one another, without endangering the food supply of the entire community,[183] was interrupted by the bloody carnages that accompanied the wars of the '*hammira*' (a Sanskrit expression denoting the Muslim amir or nobleman) and the '*rai*' (a Persian distortion of the title of *raya* denoting the Hindu prince or chief).[184] The notion, however, did not die out; and after a generation of warfare between the Shah of Bahmani and the Raya of Vijaynagar, in which both sides massacred men, women, and children without compunction,[185] a treaty was eventually made between the two sovereigns 'not to slaughter the helpless and unarmed inhabitants in future battles'.[186] Concluded in or after 1366, the convention was renewed in the following generation by another treaty in 1399 laying down that one party should not molest the subjects of the other.[187] 'From that time to this', says Firishta (1612), 'it has been the general custom in the Deccan to spare the lives of prisoners of war, and not to shed the blood of an enemy's unarmed subjects.'[188]

So essential was the supply of grain, no less for the contending armies than for the population at large, that yet another convention had been evolved as regards warfare: the caravans of the Banjaras, a gypsy tribe who carried grain over vast distances, enjoyed a right of transit through all territories and were regarded as neutral in all wars.[189] The links in the economy were strengthened over time as communications improved substantially due to the investments made by the Delhi Sultans for the strategic control of their far flung territories. The Khalji sovereigns of Delhi opened a chain of posts as far south as Dwara Samudra early in the fourteenth century;[190] and the Sur rulers who briefly enjoyed sovereignty during the second quarter of the sixteenth century built a caravanserai, with a well, a temple, and a kitchen, 'for the use of travellers, both Hindu and Musalman'[191] at every mile along the 2000 mile Grand Trunk Road from Sonargaon to the bank of the Indus. The road was planted all the way with rows of fruit trees, and was equipped with horse posts established at proper distances for the transmission of quick intelligence to the government. An incidental benefit was the facilitation of trade and correspondence.[192] The roads that linked the extensive Mughal dominion and the kingdoms of Bijapur and Golkunda, were well established in the seventeenth century, and a common economic space was visible which made it possible for the

French traveller Tavernier to write a chapter in his *Travels* 'concerning the Customs, the Money, the Exchange, the Weights, and the Measures of India'.[193]

Babar's shrewd eyes had detected two special features of this extensive exchange economy: the intensive specialization in a wide range of artisan products and the availability of large stocks of gold and silver in the country. Besides the 'masses of gold and silver' which struck him as one of the pleasant things of Hindustan, another good thing about Hindustan that impressed him was its 'unnumbered and endless workmen of every kind'. He saw that its basis lay in an institution unique to the country: 'There is a fixed caste (jam'i) for every sort of work and for everything, which has done that work or that thing from father to son till now.'[194] Specialization through caste, a formidable competitive advantage before the rise of the large-scale industrial unit known as the factory, made India the world's leading exporter of textiles and, by virtue of this and other advantages, the world's leading importer of gold and silver. 'It should not escape notice', wrote Bernier to the envious mercantilist statesman Colbert, 'that gold and silver, after circulating in every other quarter of the globe, come at length to be swallowed up, lost in some measure, in Hindustan.'[195] The alluvial plain, the large population, the intensive patches of double cropping, the wide range of competitive artisan products, the accumulated stocks of gold and silver—all features noted with interest by Babar—enabled his grandson Akbar to build an integrated agrarian bureaucratic state. Foreshadowed by the Delhi Sultanat, and constructed on principles of Muslim statecraft imported from Ajam, this state, like its predecessor, was demonstrably superior to the indigenous powers in its methods of management of cavalry. Even as the sea passed into the naval control of the Christian Europeans, the new state absorbed the continent[196] by imposing military and financial control over it.[197]

Surat, the Blessed Port of the Great Mughals, was 'the most frequented port in India,'[198] emerging in the seventeenth century (much like Bombay in the twentieth) as the financial capital of the subcontinent. Shroffs were active here and elsewhere in the exchange between the Mughal empire and Golkunda; and throughout the dominions of Akbar and his successors, letters of exchange were given on the provincial treasuries by the officers.[199] It was, however, the private banker's instrument, called *hundi*, which truly operated throughout India and across the borders of the Mughal Empire into Bijapur and Golkunda. An extensive *hundi* network, with its headquarters at Surat, assisted movement of money at well understood rates through Agra to Lahore and Dacca, and southwards to Goa, Bijapur, and Golkunda.[200] The integration of this economic space made 'India' a distinct financial unit in the maritime world of the Indian Ocean, for it was 'the principal trade of the nobles of India', as also of the private bankers and merchants who granted *hundi*s beyond India, 'to place their money in vessels in speculations for Hormuz, Bussora, and Mocha, and even for Bantam, Achin and the Philippines'.[201] Physically, the space manifested itself in the bazaar where, for every shop that displayed silks, fine cloths and brocades, there were 'at least five-and-twenty' where nothing was seen but necessaries of life imported from large distances: 'pots of oil or butter, piles of baskets filled with rice, barley, chick-peas, wheat, and an endless variety of other grain and pulse, the ordinary aliment not only of the Gentiles, who never eat meat, but of the lower class of Mahometans, and a considerable portion of the military'.[202]

'Hindu' and 'Muslim'

Bernier's 'Gentiles' and 'Mahometans', or the English traveller John Fryer's 'Gentues' and 'Moors', were terms derived from the older Portuguese expression 'Gentios' and 'Mouros'.[203] The corresponding expression used in India, 'Hindu and Muslim', runs through the body of the Arabic and Persian literature relating to Hind. The distinction involved in this duality is central to the construction put upon the history of the country by the medieval chronicles of Hindustan. This is not the conceptualization of the Persian chroniclers of noble origin alone, but a matter of popular perception too from at least the fourteenth century onwards. A fourteenth century Agarwal merchant family, two brothers named Khetala and Paitala, conceived the history of Delhi in terms of a clear divide between its pre-Muslim princes and the Turkish conquerors who had seized the town five generations ago and had ruled from there ever since.

> There is a country (*desha*) named Hariyana which is like heaven. There the Tomaras built a town named Dhillikā. After [the passing of] the Tomaras, the Chahamana kings, who cherished their subjects, made the kingdom free of all thorns. Then, the Mlechchha Sahavadina, whose might was like a fire that burnt down a forest of enemy clans, took the city by force. Ever since then, the Turashkas, down to this day, have enjoyed [the

lordship of] that [town]. At present Shri Mahammad Sahi, the lord of the earth, protects it.[204]

It is evident from the Sanskrit inscription of the two brothers dated 1328, that the natives of the country at this time referred to the invaders who had displaced the indigenous dynasty as Mlechchhas and Turashkas. The terms 'Hindu' and 'Muslim' became current among them somewhat later than this, and were evidently borrowed from the conquerors. At this time, at any rate, the natives did not refer to their former ruling clans as 'Hindu'. The sense of an abrupt divide is there, but the denominations are not well defined as yet: It is not until 1352 that we find a Hindu prince, Bukka I of Vijaynagar, referring to himself as Hindu in an inscription.[205] Later, Rana Kumbha of Mewar and Krishna Deva Raya of Vijayanagar assumed the same title, Hindu Emperor, for themselves in 1438 and 1513 respectively.[206] References in the vernacular literature to the term 'Hindu' would appear to have occurred in the late fourteenth century, and notwithstanding the uncertainty of dating such works, not much before that.[207] At the time of the Turkish occupation of Delhi, the Hindus had no name for themselves. As for the Muslims, the native inhabitants of the land designated them, in an unbroken tradition of perceiving the barbarian as the other from a remote antiquity, as Mlechchas, Shakas, Yavanas, Turashkas, Turaks, Turakkas, Parasikkas, Mungals, and Tatars.[208] These terms implied that they were impure aliens. As Brajadulal Chattopadhyaya has pointed out, they were rarely referred to as Muslims.[209] However, one thirteenth century Sanskrit inscription took note of the formation of a Muslim congregation (*Musalamāna–jamātha or jamā' at* of the Musalmans) in a Gujarati town.[210]

The equation of Hindu with native, and of Muslim with newcomer, is implicit in the early Muslim literature in Arabic and Persian. That is how the distinction embedded in the dual formula 'Hindu-and-Muslim' arose in the first place. Only gradually did the meaning of the formula shift from the distinction between native and alien to a recognition of two separate religious communities living in India. The process—the rise of the formula and the shift of its meaning—signified important and long-term redefinitions in Indian society.

Around 1030, when Al Biruni elucidated 'the barriers' which in his view separated 'Muslims and Hindus',[211] the former of the two already interlocked categories was still foreign to India. He located the source of the antagonism in the traditional antipathy of the Indians (the term he employed was 'the Hindus') towards all foreigners. 'But then', as he described the process, 'came Islam; ... and the repugnance of the Hindus against foreigners increased more and more when the Muslims began to make inroads into their country ...'[212] His master's exploits, the terrible raids of Mahmud of Ghazni, scattered the Hindus 'like atoms of dust' in all directions.

> Their scattered remains cherish, of course, the most inveterate aversion towards all Muslims. That is the reason, too, why Hindu sciences have retired far away from those parts of the country conquered by us, and have fled to places which our hands cannot yet reach, to Kashmir, Benaras, and other places. And there the antagonism between them and all foreigners receives more and more nourishment from both political and religious sources.[213]

It is a point worth noting that right from the beginning of Islam's encounter with 'Al-Hind', 'us' is unambiguously designated as 'Muslim', while 'they' are 'Hindu', the pagans of another land. The same antagonistic point of view obtains the other way round. In this early period of India's encounter with Islam, the inhabitants of the land, dubbed 'Hindu' by the invaders, look upon the outsiders, as Al Biruni himself informs us, as '*mleccha*', which means both 'alien' and 'impure'.[214] The Indus valley, newly converted into a province of the Ghaznavi empire, is referred to in the early Apabhramsa work, *Sandesh Rasak*, as the land of the impure aliens (michchhadesha), a description the more curious because the author, Abdur Rahman, is an Indian-born Muslim hailing from that region, and a weaver by origin.[215]

With the occupation of Delhi by the Turks, yet another shift takes place in the antagonism within the 'Hindu-and-Muslim' interlock: it is no longer a political and religious confrontation between Khurasan and Hindustan, but an encounter between the newcomers and the natives within the land itself. Nonetheless the formula through which the interaction is defined remains the same: the two-in-one formula 'Hindu-and-Muslim'. Page after page in the Persian chronicles narrate transactions between 'Hindus and Muslims'. The usurpation of Khusrau with the help of some Hindus, a brief interregnum between the Khalji and Tughlaq dynasties, is described by the historian Zia-ud-Din Barani with a shudder: 'In those dreadful days, the rites of the Hindus were highly exalted ... and through all the territories of Islam the Hindus rejoiced greatly, boasting that Delhi had once more come under Hindu rule, and that the Musalmans had been driven away and dispersed.'[216]

The Friday on which Ghiasuddin Tughlaq's victory ended the usurpation is welcomed by the pious chronicler as 'a day of joy and victory to the Musalmans, but of woe to the Hindus and infidels.'[217]

In the discourse of the sultans, the Hindus and Muslims were established categories, all the subjects being mentally classified by them into these two. Ghiyasuddin Balban, who made a calculated display of his pomp and dignity in order to impress the royal majesty upon both categories of subjects, had the satisfaction that 'Musalmans and Hindus would come from distances of one or two hundred kos to see the splendour of his equipage'.[218] In the absence of dynastic authority, he reflected, 'The Hindus become recalcitrant and the Muslims become heretics ...'[219] The courtiers and hagiographers adopted, of course, the same language. During the preceding reign of Nasiruddin Mahmud, we are told by the court poet Amir Khusrau, 'The Musalmans were powerful, the Hindus peaceful, and no one even knew the name of Mughal'.[220] Conversely, the indolence and liberality of Alauddin Khalji's weak son and successor is the reason, we are told by Barani, why 'licentiousness spread among the Musalmans, and disaffection and rebellion appeared among the Hindus'.[221] The dual formula became an established part of the military narratives of the Persian chronicles: 'The Hindoos fought bravely hand to hand with the Mahommedans, from daylight till sunset,' relates Firishta in connection with a skirmish in the Deccan between the Bahamani Sultan and a local Hindu Zamindar.[222] Nor did Persian poetry escape the pervasive influence of the formula:

> To borrow from Hindus at four hundred per cent
> Is better than receiving gifts from these Musalmans.[223]

So implicit was the notion of the Hindus-and-Musalmans of India in both the popular and official consciousness that the two-in-one formula slipped in almost unnoticed in so mundane a matter as customs revenue. Kafi Khan's text relating to certain customs regulations of Emperor Aurangzeb manifest the three related notions, Musalman, Hindu, and Hindustan, as administrative categories for the purpose of taxation:[224]

> An order was promulgated exempting the commercial goods of Musulmans for tax throughout the dominions of Hindustan. But after a short time, upon the reports of the revenue officers, and by recommendation of good and experienced persons, an order was issued that every

article belonging to Musulmans, the price of which was not large, should
pass free; but that goods of value should pay duty ... The revenue officers
then reported that Musulmans had adopted the practice of dividing their
goods into small parcels in order to avoid the duty, and that they passed
the goods of Hindus in their names, and thus the payment of the *zakat*
prescribed by the Law was avoided. So an order was given that, according
to the Law, two and a half per cent, should be taken from Musulmans and
five per cent from Hindus.

The vernacular literature began, in course of time, to use similar,
though not quite the same, terms of reference. The *Prithviraja Rasau*, a
Hindi ballad narrating the encounter between Prithviraj Chauhan and
Muhammad Ghori at a distance of about two centuries after the event,
recounts how 'Hindus and Turaks played a [bloody] game of Holi'
(*Hindu Turaka kheli Hori*)[225] on the fatal field of Tarain. The *Kirtilata*,
composed by the Maithili poet Vidyapati in 1380, contains an often-
quoted verse inspired by the notion of the two-in-one:

> As Hindu and Turk settled down together
> One made fun of the faith of the other
> Many a word and what a lot of scripture
> So many divisions yet such admixture.[226]

There is, curiously, no departure from the wording 'Hindu/Turuk'
in Malik Muhammad Jayasi's ballad of the last stand of Chitore against
Alauddin Khalji. The Muslim poet sticks to the word Turuk and puts
into the mouth of his Hindu protagonist, Rana Ratansen of Chitore,
the following words: 'Chitore is the refuge of the Hindus. Our enemy,
the Turks, have marched out with fell intent' (*Chitaur Hinduna kara
asthānā. Satru Turuka hathi kinha payānā*). The prince sends this
express message to all places 'where the name of the Hindu fraternity
prevails' (*Hindu nāma jahān lagi Jāti*).[227] What we have here is a
reproduction of the Hindus as one clan, a ' Jāti' that is no longer just a
loose assortment of various castes (*jātis*). From around the last quarter
of the fourteenth century, to judge by the evidence of the Hindi literature
of the period, the Hindus begin, for the first time, to refer to themselves
as 'Hindu'. Hitherto lacking a name, the Hindus at long last denominate
themselves by adopting the name given to them by the Muslims.

The arrival at this self-definition took a long time. Over five
centuries had elapsed since the Muslim geographers of the Arab world
had, so to speak, 'created' the Hindus by identifying them as the ethnic
population of India. As early as the tenth century, it had occurred to Al

Masudi: 'The Hindus are different from all other black people, as the Zanjis, the Damadams, and others, in point of intellect, government, philosophy, strength of constitution, and purity of colour.'[228] Hasan Nizami, a native of Khurasan who migrated to Delhi during the time of Muhammad Ghori, reflected on his own perilous journey through the hot jungle of India: '... will the boat of his life ever reach the shore of safety?—The crow-like Hindus had intercepted the roads, and in the rapidity of their movements exceeded the wild ass and the deer, you might say they were demons in human form, and covered with blackness'.[229] Islam, as these early accounts convey, defined the Hindus as an ethnic and religious category. They were its target as it penetrated India. A target is a definite object: much later we find it narrated of a Bahmani sultan that 'he made twenty-four campaigns against the Hindoos'.[230]

By then, however, the Hindus had undergone a subtle transformation in Muslim eyes. They are no longer the native population of Hind, as such, for many Muslims are also natives: they are now perceived, in the light of experience, as one among several communities living in the land. 'From Ghazni to the shore of the ocean,' says Amir Khusrau,

> You see all under the dominion of Islam. Cawing crows [i.e. Hindus] see no arrows pointed at them; nor is the *Tarsa* (Christian) there, who does not fear (*Taras*) to render the servant equal with God; nor the Jew who dares to exalt the Pentateuch to a level with the Kuran; nor the *Magh* [Zoroastrian, i.e. Parsee] who is delighted with the worship of fire, but of whom the fire complains with a hundred tongues. The four sects of the Musulmans are at amity, and the very fish are Sunnis.'[231]

As the Hindus emerge, in this new context, in clearer outline, and as their Brahmanical rituals stand out in the light of more certain knowledge, they are distinguished too from the animistic tribes of aboriginals who do not cherish those rituals. The Gonds, we are informed by Firishta, believe, 'like the Hindoos', in the transmigration of the soul, but all the same they are, in his eyes, a distinct race.[232]

During his travels in the Deccan, Afanasy Nikitin fell in with some Hindus, and was allowed to accompany them on a pilgrimage when he explained that he was 'a Christian and not a Muslim'.[233] He drew a vivid picture of the Hindus from this experience, setting them off against the Muslims as 'Indians':[234]

> The Indians eat no flesh at all—no beef, mutton, fowl, fish, or pork, although they have a great many pigs ... They do not eat or drink with

Moslems. Their food is poor and they do not eat or drink with one
another, not even with their wives ... And they eat everything with their
right hand, never touching any food with the left; they never use a knife,
and have no spoons. When journeying, each carries a pot to boil food in.
And they hide from the Moslems lest they should look into the pot or at
the food. And should a Moslem look at the food, the Indian will not eat
it. When eating, some cover themselves with a shawl, so that no one may
see them.

And they pray facing eastwards, in the Russian manner; they raise high
both hands and put them on their crown, and lie face downwards on the
ground and stretch out on it—that is how they worship. And when they
sit down to take a meal, some wash their hands and feet, and also rinse
their mouths. Their *butkhanahs* [temples] have no doors, and face
eastwards: the *buts* [idols], too, stand facing eastwards. And when someone
dies, they burn him and scatter the ashes over water.

... The Indians call the ox 'father' and the cow, 'mother'; they use the
dung as fuel to bake food and cook food and smear their faces, foreheads,
and bodies with the ashes.

While in the Deccan, Nikitin heard that the Bahmani Prime
Minister Mahmud Gawan, had been fighting 'kafirs' for 20 years, beating
them—the Hindu princes of Vijayanagar—more often than being
beaten.[235] The categories could not be more sharply drawn. One defined
the other. Defining the other, whether 'mlechchha' or 'kafir', was an
exercise promoting self-awareness. In this process of interaction, in which
the parties mutually defined each other, the original impulse derived
from the alien: the 'Khorassani' of Nikitin as against his 'Indian'.
Without the Muslims, there would be no 'Hindus';[236] at any rate not
ones who would have come to profess themselves as such. The formation
of a Muslim community imparted, therefore, a new shape and
denomination to the Hindu social structure.

A proselytizing religion, one that is bent upon converting the
followers of the other, is by implication endowed with a prior definition
of the self. The Muslims in India were aware of themselves as part of a
world community centred on Mecca. As a proverb quoted warmly by
Badauni put the matter, 'All the world is but a village, that [city of
Mecca] is the central point [of Islam].'[237] In the Indian context, 'Islam
and the Muslims' were reshaped by the otherness of 'the infidels and
plural-worshippers'. The Hindus, as 'the enemies of religion and the
state', imparted this renewed and reiterated identity to the Muslims.
Islam, no less than its idolatrous opposite, was a religion emphatic upon
the essential rituals. Such rituals marked the Muslims out from the rest

of the population. The most intimate of habits—sexual practices even—were counter-posed to those of the Hindus. Circumcision was often invoked in folk songs as one of these distinguishing marks.[238] Practices leaving such obvious marks of identification could not but rivet the attention of foreigners as well. Fryer's description of the Muslims at Surat, while nowhere near as powerful as Nikitin's description of the Hindus of the Deccan, brings out certain points of comparison:[239]

> These Eat highly of all Flesh Dumpoked,[240] which is baked with spice in butter; Pullow, a Stew or Rice and Butter, with Flesh, Fowl, or Fish; Fruits, Achars, or Pickles, and Sweetmeats ... They drink no Wine Publickly, but Privately will be good Fellows, not content with such little Glasses as we drink out of ...
>
> They are strict observers of the Hours of Prayer, when they strip off all their Gorgeous Habiliments to their shift, and after Washing Hands and Feet, Prostrate themselves during the time of Devotion ...
>
> They circumcise the Foreskin of the Male, which is performed by a Barber, at Eight years of Age; with feasting, and carrying the Boy about in pomp, with Musick and great Expressions of Joy. Of the Girls they make small account, they being instructed within doors how to pray.
>
> ... At Funerals, the Mullahs or Priests, make Orations or Sermons, after a lesson read out of the Alchoran, and lay them North and South, as we do East and West when they are Inhumed, expecting from that quarter the appearance of their Prophet ... They never Enshrine any in their Moschs, but in the places adjoining them; where they build Tombs, and leave Stipends for Mullahs to offer Petitions up for them.
>
> The Duty of the Mullah, Besides these, is to call from the Steeples of their Moschs every Pore, that is, once in three hours stopping their Ears with their Fingers: ... God is Great, I profess, there is no Deity but God, and confess that Mahomet is the Prophet of God. Their Priests say Prayers five times a day, and expound the Alchoran once a week, and that on Friday, which day they are not to lye with their Women, setting it apart for the Service of God.

The institution of the Haj at Surat provided the members of this world community with an annual renewal of the contact with 'the central point'. Emperor Akbar organized every year the departure of 'a caravan from India', with the port of Surat as the base of the fleet. He furnished too, the means to the needy to perform the pilgrimage to Mecca. All sorts of Indian Muslims were brought together under the command of the newly appointed Mir Haji, the Leader of the Pilgrims of Hindustan.[241] A popular dimension was added thereby to the official institutionalization of Islam in India. The formal appointment of a

Shaikh-ul-Islam by Iltutmish in the early years of the Sultanat of Delhi[242] had earlier implied the official affirmation of the existence of a Muslim community in India. From the appointment of a Suhrawardi Sufi as the Shaikh-ul-Islam in the thirteenth century to the institution of a Mir Haji at Surat in the sixteenth, the community of Indian Muslims multiplied to a point at which there were perhaps as many Muslims as Hindus in some parts. Such pockets might be found around 1600 in the Indus valley, the vale of Kashmir, the delta of the Ganges, the twin capitals of Delhi and Agra, the country surrounding the Muslim town of Bidar in the Deccan, and a stretch of the Malabar coast in the far south.[243] That the local followers of the Prophet of Arabia were a substantial section of the population by the sixteenth and seventeenth centuries is reflected in the composition by Muslim poets and poetesses of an increasing body of verse in the vernacular languages of Hindi, Dakhni, Bengali, Sindhi, Kashmiri and so on. The need was felt at that stage to reconstruct for this community a legendary and historical past. This placed them in the stream of time with specific reference to the land.[244]

The reconstruction of the past by means of legends and history, was a problematic exercise. The Creation myths in Islam differed from those in India, and little if anything was known at the time of the history of the land before Islam. The most puzzling of the chronological problems that had to be solved was how long Creation and mankind had been in existence. Poets and historians, devout men as they were, had implicit faith in the Islamic tradition: they reckoned that from the birth of Adam, the first man on earth and the earliest receiver of the divine message (Nabi), to the coming of the last of the Nabis, the Prophet Muhammad, no more than 8000 years had elapsed.[245] And yet, according to the sacred lore of the Hindus, there had been no Adam. Furthermore, four ages, Satya, Treta, Dwapar, and Kali, had elapsed in the Hindu reckoning since Creation, of which the last alone, the present Kali Yuga, was reckoned at more than 4,00,000 years. One could, of course, dismiss this as 'mere talk and sound',[246] but the problem remained how to place mankind in general and the Hindus and Muslims in particular in the flowing stream of time. One means of resolving the apparent contradictions was the supposition that there might have been other species of mankind, made of fire or air and not of earth, before Adam, which the Hindu legends might allude to.[247]

The most monumental work of myths and legends compiled for the Muslim community in India, the sixteenth century Bengali epic

Nabi Vamsa by Saiyid Sultan, twisted, moulded, and combined Hindu and Muslim myths to construct a wonderful history of the world down to the life of Prophet Muhammad. Comparable in its sweep to the various vernacular *Mahabharata* versions current at the time, it was inspired in its design by the Bengali *Mahabharata* commissioned by Paragal Khan. The problem of chronology was solved in one stroke by placing the four ages of the Hindus and their various gods, goddesses and incarnations among mankind (avatars), before the fall of Adam and Hāwā (Eve) to Earth 9086 years ago, which marked the initiation of the present species of mankind. In the beginning, there was nothing. Niranjan, the One and Alone, became aware of Himself in an unconscionable time. He obtained His eternal companion, Nur Muhammad, out of the light (*nur*) in which he perceived himself. He then created the universe of the four ages, and placed there a man and a woman made of fire whom the Hindus call Isvara and Parvati. They were the parents of Brahma and Vishnu. The gods and demons of the Hindus perished in their mutual wars. Then an early species of mankind, which was blessed by such incarnations as Rama and Sita (but not Krishna), peopled the earth. Though they obtained from Niranjan the four Vedas, which predicted the coming of Muhammad to earth, they fell upon sinful ways.[248]

Finally the Lord created Adam and the present species of mankind out of earth (rather than fire). They were blessed with a succession of recorded as well as unrecorded Nabis. The text dwells especially upon the following Nabis: first Adam, then Nuh (Noah), then Ibrahim (Abraham), then Hari (Krishna), then Musa (Moses), then Isa (Jesus), and finally the last and greatest of them all, Muhammad. Krishna is said to have been guilty of adultery. He repented what he had done and he commanded mankind, in the name of the Lord, not to worship his image in future.[249]

Curiously, the historicity of Krishna is accepted by the Persian chroniclers, even by so critical a man as Firishta. Among the kings of Hindustan before the coming of Islam, he mentions especially Vikramaditya, along with a host of other fictitious monarchs, all acknowledging the superior might of the legendary pre-Islamic heroes of Iran and Turan. Like the other branches of mankind, the Hindus, too, are said to have descended from the sons of Noah after the Flood, but they are represented as being submissive to those descendants of Noah that settled in Iran and Turan—Afrasiyab, Rustam, et al., a chain of fictitious chronological correspondences being invented to illustrate the subordination of the imagined princes of Hind to the mythical heroes of Iran and Turan before the coming of Islam.[250]

The mythological and historical reconstructions that juxtaposed the Hindus and Muslims in terms of space and time reflected an effort to come to terms with what is one of the most profoundly ambiguous encounters in history. At the very first encounter,[251] before the Turks settled in the country, Al Biruni was moved to explain:

> ... the Hindus entirely differ from us in every respect ... they totally differ from us in religion, as we believe in nothing in which they believe, and *vice versa* ... in all manners and usages they differ from us to such a degree as to frighten their children with us, with our dress, and our ways and customs, and as to declare us to be devil's breed, and our doings as the very opposite of all that is good and proper.[252]

The clash, he saw, was inherent in the fundamentals of the two religions: Hindu religious practice was based on the worship of idols, whereas Muslim tenets uncompromisingly prohibited even the making of a picture of the prophet.[253] The Hindus discriminated among themselves on the basis of caste, and did not sit, eat, or drink with the Muslims because they thought they would be polluted thereby.[254] 'We Muslims, of course', Al Biruni took care to point out, 'stand entirely on the other side of the question, considering all men as equal ...'[255]

Three and a half centuries later, Vidyapati described the same encounter, but from the other side of the divide. His verse depicted the encounter at a point when it had grown more ambiguous and more complex than before, with Turk and Hindu living cheek by jowl in every town:[256]

> As Hindu and Turak settled down together, one made fun of the faith of the other. So much admixture, yet so many ruptures: calls to prayer mingle with recitals from the Vedas; a witch-doctor serves the one, a eunuch the other; one observes the fast of Nakta, the other the fast of roja; so many vessels of copper and so many of clay; Namaz on the one hand, Puja on the other. The Turak rider seizes the man on the road, to make him work without pay. Brahman or Bania, he pulls them all in, placing on each head the rump of a cow, licking the sacred dot off each forehead, tearing off from every tonsured head the top-knot. And then he wants them to have a ride on his horse—this distiller of liquor from washed rice. He breaks the temple to build the mosque. The earth is so crowded with graves and sirloins of beef that one can hardly step anywhere. 'Get out, you Hindu', he says. However low he might be, the Turuka strikes his blow hard.

Because the acquaintance is closer, the portrait is also somewhat more realistic than the picture of foreign devils with which parents used to frighten children earlier, but the images are suffused with dislike:[257]

> The Turak rider goes to market, moving around to collect tolls. He glances out of the corner of his eye, sports a beard, spits out of the mouth. When the Saiyid passes the Shirni round, each eats what the other has left over. The dervish begs around chanting the Doa, and if he gets nothing, he goes away cursing.

The symbols were so contrary in the two religions, and the sensibilities were so opposed, that a clash of fundamentals could not be avoided. The Muslims of India prayed facing west, in the direction of Mecca; Hindus prayed facing east, in the direction of the rising sun.[258] Muslims buried their dead; Hindus burned theirs.[259] The two communities also differed on what happened after death: Muslims did not accept the Hindu notion of reincarnation, insisting that, under divine judgment, one either rose up to heaven or sank down to hell.[260] These were matters of belief in which, as Vidyapati put it, one might laugh at the other. Touch was, however, a more sensitive matter. Ibn Battuta records his experience in Hindu Malabar thus:[261]

> The road runs completely in the shade of trees and at every half-mile there stands a wooden house in which there are benches on which the wayfarers, infidels as well as Muslims, sit. Near each of these houses there is a well from which drinking water is taken and which is entrusted to the supervision of an infidel. He gives the infidels water in vessels, and if one happens to be a Muslim he pours water into his hands and leaves off when the latter makes him a sign or withdraws. It is the custom among the heathens in the Malabar country that no Muslim should enter their houses or use their vessels for eating purposes. If a Muslim is fed out of their vessels, they either break the vessels or give them away to the Musalmans. When a Muslim enters a place in this country in which there is absolutely no house of the Musalmans, the heathens cook his food for him, place it for him on the banana leaves and pour the soup on it; what remains over is eaten by the dogs and birds. In all the resting places along this road there are houses of Muslims with whom the Muslim travellers lodge; from them they buy everything they need. These also cook the food for the Muslim travellers. If it were not for them no Muslim could have travelled in this country.

Conversely, we have the anecdote of a lone Afghan officer of a Lodi Sultan who never ate in a Hindu house; and yet another who, on Friday night, from the time of the evening prayer, would turn out any Hindu from his assembly, and 'would not even look on the face of a Hindu during that night'.[262] It is also related of the Sultan of Ahmadnagar that, during a visit which he paid to Rama Raya of Vijayanagar in his tent, the latter took him by the hand, whereupon the Sultan called for a basin and ewer, and washed his hands, as if they had been polluted by the touch. Rama Raya muttered in his own language, 'If he were not my guest I would cut off his hands and hang them round his neck'; then calling for water, he, too, washed his hands.[263] Equally curious is the story of a Mughal officer, then serving as Governor of Lahore, who was mortified that, mistaking a Hindu for a Muslim because of his beard, he had stood up to greet him. An order was issued to the effect that Hindus should wear a coloured patch (*tukri*) on their shoulders, which earned for the Governor the nickname of Patcher (*Tukriya*),[264] Yet his master, Akbar, neither wore a beard nor ate beef.[265]

When Islam, in its transition from Arabia to India, substituted the cow for the sheep as the victim of sacrificial slaughter,[266] an explosive issue set Hindu against Muslim. The usurper Khusrau, who occupied the throne of Alauddin Khalji with the help of the Hindus, banned cowslaughter to please his retainers. The Muslims were so antagonized by this that he was soon everthrown.[267] Slaughter of the cow was absolutely forbidden wherever Hindu princes retained their independence. Abdul Razzak reports of fifteenth century Calicut: '... every thing is procurable in that port, with this sole exception, that you cannot kill cows and eat their flesh. Should any one be known to have killed a cow, his life would invariably be sacrificed. The cow is held in such respect, that they rub the ashes of its dung upon their forehead,—the curse of God upon them'.[268]

The violations involved were both physical and spiritual. How such violations might affect sensibilities is glimpsed vividly in the Sanskrit inscription of the local Andhra chief Prolaya Nayaka (*c*.1330 CE). Turushka/Parasika outrages are perceived by the chieftain here in a historical frame emphasizing three closely related sentiments: the sanctity of the ancient land of Bhārata-varsha, the purity of its moral and social order symbolized by the Brahmanical rituals, and the regional patriotic fervour centred on the province (*pradesha*) of Andhra in that land.

In the beginning, the universe was submerged in water. The god Narayana created all the worlds, in the midst of which was Earth adorned by the Golden Mountain and surrounded by the islands and seas. In the centre of the earth, encircled by the salt seas, lies Jambudvipa. It consists of nine continents, of which one is 'the part of Earth called Bharata-varsha where all works done bear fruit' (*bhāgam bhuvo Bhāratavarsham–āhuh phalanti karmāni kritāni yatra*).[269] It is a variegated land, 'divided by language and custom into many distinct countries' (*bhāshā samāchāra–bhida vibhinnair–deshair–anekair–bahudhā vibhakte*). 'In that continent, there is a beautiful country named Tilanga' (*varshe cha tasmin kamanīya Tilanga nāmāsa chakāsti deshah*). Many holy rivers flow through the province; the towns are rich, the mountains beautiful, the lakes deep, and the forts impregnable.[270]

King Prataparudra ruled this country with truth and justice, until bitter hostility arose between him and Āhammada Suratrāna (Muhammad bin Tughlaq). The Sultan, who was the God of Death (Yama) to the kings, stamped out the remnants of the royal families who had been overlooked by the sage-warrior Parashuram of yore. Though the king repelled the Sultan and his 90,000 horse no less than seven times, he was at last defeated, for the good fortunes of the people of the earth had decreased. On the way to Delhi as a prisoner of the Turushkas, he breathed his last on the bank of the river Narmada. As the sun that was the king betook itself to another world (*Pratāparudra–tigamāmshau lokāntara–tirohite*), 'the blinding darkness of the Turushkas overtook the whole world' (*Turushkāndha–tamisrena samākrāntam mahītalam*).[271]

The evil (*adharma*) he had so long repressed now sprouted in conditions favourable to its growth. The sinners subjected the rich to torture for the sake of their wealth. Many of the victims died of terror at the very sight of the Pārasikas.

The Brahmans were compelled to forsake the ties of sacred duty (*dvijātayas–tyājita–karma–bandhā*). The images of the gods were all broken (*bhagnāsh–cha–deva– pratimās–samastāh*). The Agrahara lands perpetually enjoyed by the learned were confiscated (*Vidvad– varishthaish–chira–kāla–bhuktās–sarve- pi–apāhārishat–agrahārāh*). The tillers were forcibly deprived of the profits of tillage by the sinful Yavanas, and their families were ruined (*atte karshana–lābhe pāpair– yavanair– balātkārāt dīn–adīna–kutumbah krishīvalalā nāsham–āpannāh*). In this calamity, no one dared think of any substance upon earth as belonging to oneself, wealth, wives, or whatever might belong to men (*dhana–dārādike nrinām kasmimshchid–api vastuni svāyattatā–matir–nābhud bhūvi tasyām mahāpadi*). To those low Yavanas, wine was the drink, beef the food, and slaying Brahmans the sport (*peya surā go–pishitam bhojyam lilā–vihāro dvija ghātanam cha*).[272]

The 'Tailinga' land enslaved by the Yavana soldiers, was burning like a wood consumed by wild fire (*santepe vanam–iva dāvavahni jushṭam*).[273] Then arose chief Prola of the Musumuri family of the Shudra caste. Unable to resist his might, the Yavanas abandoned their forts and fled to unknown places. The very people who had suffered under the Yavanas turned against them and put them to death. He restored the *agrahara* lands to the Brahmans and revived the performance of Vedic sacrifices. 'He cleansed the Andhra Pradesha of the pollution caused by the movements of the Turushkas by means of the butter smoke arising out of the sacrificial fire pits' (*yagñām havir–dhūma–paramparābhih Turushka–sanchārana– jāta– pāpān–Andhrān–Pradeshān–ānaghnām– akārshit*).[274] With the lawful sixth of the produce paid by the tillers of their own volition, he set his hand to the task of repairing the damage caused by the Pārasikas.

The Telengas of Prolaya Nayaka, and the Dravidas of Prince Kampan of Vijaynagar, though not yet described as 'Hindus', were part of a moral order identified with the sacred land called Bharatvarsha. The religious and patriotic fervour expressed on these occasions focused on the threat to this moral order posed by the 'Turushka' invaders who were perceived as ethnic and religious outsiders.[275] Ganga Devi, consort of Kumara Kampana of the house of Vijayanagar, had this to say of the outrages that occurred in Madurai during the brief interlude of the independent Muslim Sultanat of Ma'bar:[276]

> Villages (Agraharams) once filled with the scent of the sacrificial smoke and the music of the hymns now stink of meat and resound with the roars of the drunken Turks (Tulushkas). Alas! Look at the gardens of Madurai! The coconut trees have been cut down and rows of iron spikes have sprung up, hung with strings of human skulls. Where one used to hear the tinkle of the maiden's anklet, the noise of the chain on the Brahman's feet dragging along the road splits one's ears. The fair Tamraparni, which once gleamed with the sandal paste from the breasts of young women, flows red with the blood of cows slaughtered by the killers. My heart aches at the sight of the tearful faces of the Dravidians (Drabhidas), their lips parched, their hair ruffled.

That this might not be poetic exaggeration would be suggested by the gory details which Ibn Battuta recorded from what he saw of the operations of the Sultan of Ma'bar:[277]

All the enemies (Kuffar) whom the troopers found in the jungle were taken prisoner; and making stakes sharpened at both ends, they placed these on the prisoners' shoulders so that they might carry the same, each prisoner being accompanied by his wife and children, if any; in this way they were all brought into the camp ... And each prisoner was fixed on the sharpened stake which pierced through his body. This done, their women were slain along with their children, their hair being tied to the stakes; they were left there in the same condition.

Fortunes were soon reversed. As Gangadevi records, her consort, prince Kampana of Vijayanagar, killed the Sultan and rescued the Dravidas. It was then the turn of the soldiery of Vijayanagar to resort to the same physical and spiritual violence. The Vijayanagar armies invading the Muslim territories to the north resorted to every transgression, violating the honour of Muslim women, destroying the mosques, and killing women, children, and old men on more than one occasion.[278] Violence on such a scale transcended the physical and became spiritual. Transgressions were intended to hit as much at the enemy's mind as his body. The opponent's wife or daughter emerged from this confrontation as one of the objects of transgression. Ibn Battuta's description of the Delhi Durbar at Id provides a glimpse of what happened to the enemy's women after war:[279]

On the day of the 'Id the whole palace is hung with tapestry and magnificently decorated ... As soon as he [the Sultan] ascends the throne, the chamberlains and the palace officers call out 'Bismullah' with a loud voice ... The greetings being over, dinner is served to all according to their ranks ... Then enter the musicians, the first batch being the daughters of the infidel rajas—Hindus—captured in war that year. They sing and dance, and the Sultan gives them away to the amirs and a'izza. Then come the other daughters of the infidels who sing and dance; and the Sultan gives them away to his brothers, his relations, his brothers-in-law and the maliks' sons.

Notions of pollution, conceptions of honour, and the recurrent pattern of religious and sexual transgressions shaped the Indian custom of *jauhar*, charging the ambiguous interaction between the Rajput and Muslim powers with currents of cosmic violence. The capture of the Rajput fort of Champaner by Sultan Mahmud Begada of Gujarat provides an occasion for Firishta to describe the practice in matter-of-fact terms:[280]

> The Rajpoots seeing no chance of escape and finding that the King rejected all overtures for surrender, made a funeral pile within the walls, and having brought their property, their wives, and their children, set fire to it, and consumed them to ashes; after which they resolutely awaited the storm ... The Hindoos, thus situated, collected in a body, and running to some water near the spot, bathed, with their naked swords and spears in their hands, and then rushed on the Mahomedans. The Rajpoots were for the most part killed in the assault.

Violation of women was equally a matter of dishonour from the Muslim point of view. Medini Rai of Chanderi, Rana Sanga of Mewar, and Puran Mal of Raisen were known to have carried off Muslim women of high birth to their respective seraglios.[281] Sher Shah's declaration of war against Puran Mal defined this as the *casus belli*: '... Puran Mal, who has enslaved the families of Musalmans in Chanderi and has made dancing girls of their daughters, and did not accompany my son Kutb Khan—him I will so punish that he may be a warning to others, that hereafter no unbelievers in Hind may oppress and injure the families of Musalmans.'[282] Puran Mal moved out of the fort on being given a solemn assurance of safe conduct for himself, his women and his family. But the Muslim widows cried out to Sher Shah:[283]

> We have suffered from this inhuman and malignant infidel all kinds of tyranny and oppression. He has slain our husbands, and our daughters he has enslaved, and has made dancing girls of them, and has seized our lands, and all our worldly goods, for a long time past.

The *ulama* ruled that it was not necessary to maintain faith with an infidel who had committed so many inhuman deeds with regard to the wives and families of Musalmans. Puran Mal and his party were slain, and his daughter was given 'to some itinerant minstrels (bazigaran), that they might make her dance in the bazars'.[284]

One other form of violence that left a deep and bitter deposit in folk memory was the desecration of temples and mosques. In a cultural context, where the affirmation of authority following upon a conquest required the performance of certain symbolic religious actions, the enemy's religious symbols were obvious targets. Firishta's description of the Bahmani conquest of Condapilly brings out all the symbolic actions deemed to be essential on such occasions. Only one of these actions was deemed unnecessary: the inauspicious killing of a few

Brahmans which was identified in the popular imagination as the cause of the subsequent fall of the dynasty.[285]

> The King having gone to view the fort, broke down the idolatrous temple, and killed some Bramins, who officiated at it, with his own hands, as a point of religion. He then gave orders for a mosque to be erected on the foundation of the temple, and ascending a pulpit, repeated a few prayers, distributed alms, and commanded the Khootba to be read in his name.

Conversely, mosques were the target of Hindu armies operating in Muslim territories:

> The Hindoos of Beejanuggur committed the most outrageous devastations, burning and rasing the buildings, putting up their horses in the mosques, and performing the abominable idolatrous worship in the holy places.[286]

Medini Rai of Chanderi turned mosques into cattle sheds;[287] Shivaji converted tombs into granaries.[288] The motive here was not the discharge of sacred obligation; it was the vengeful impulse of retaliation,[289] arising out of an accumulated sense of outrage feeding perhaps upon fears experienced generations ago and ancient memories of loss. From a Sanskrit inscription[290] we learn of a Brahman who buried an image of Durga out of fear soon after the defeat of Jaychand of Kanauj at the hands of Muhammad Ghori. 'I am senseless', said he, 'out of fear of the Mlechchas.' With great sorrow, touching the image with his head, he placed it into a concealed pit, hoping that the god of war would turn their glory into dust. 'When ill fate will meet the Yavanas,' he hoped, 'she will appear again.'

The materials are too fragmentary for a psycho-history of the impact of the mutual outrages of war. Nonetheless, the same points were at issue in one confrontation after another. Constructions of community identity established linkages between memories of the past and the actions of the present. As these issues arose repeatedly folk memories reinforced the sense of community across the generations. The issues that polarized the two communities so many times and through centuries of living together reappeared as late as the Rathor rebellion in the declining days of the Mughal dynasty. After the death of Aurangzeb, Raja Ajit Singh of Marwar had 'again showed his disobedience and rebellion by oppressing Musulmans, forbidding the killing of cows, preventing the summons to prayer, razing the mosques which had been built after the destruction of the idol-temples in the late reign, and repairing and building anew idol-temples'. As soon as Emperor Bahadur

Shah marched out to punish 'this rebel and his tribe', they patched matters up by agreeing 'to rebuild the mosques, destroy the idol-temples, enforce the provisions of the law about the summons to prayer and the killing of cows, to appoint magistrates and to commission officers to collect the jiziya'.[291]

Mutual violence, it should be stressed here by way of caution, was *not* the established pattern of Hindu–Muslim interactions. The outrages occurred during war. Such transgressions as occurred were the work of the powers, not of the population at large, and only during hostilities were the soldiery urged to commit such excesses. Even the most intolerant of rulers, whether Hindu or Muslim, allowed subjects of all persuasions to practise their faith, subject to certain understood laws: no cow might be sacrificed in Hindu territory, and no new and unauthorized temples might be built in Muslim territory. The Vijayanagar soldiers might show disrespect to the Quran and destroy mosques in enemy territory, but the king erected a mosque in the capital for his Muslim subjects and showed marked respect to their holy book.[292] Similarly, even in the orthodox reign of Aurangzeb, who ordered demolition of all new and unauthorized temples, the Hindu population was allowed, according to Bernier, 'free exercise of its religion'.[293] The contemporary observations of Manucci and Tavernier made it evident that the Kumbh Mela at Allahabad and the pilgrimages to Mathura, Banaras, Puri, and Tirupati were not interrupted by the Emperor.[294]

Hinduism Emerges: Islam Arrives

Clashes of symbols are believed to arise from fundamental, unavoidable differences. It should not be too readily assumed, however, that this particular clash over symbols was predestined. There were several twists and turns in history before the symbols assumed that particular shape which would put them on a collision course. The Khutba, the Friday mosque, and the spired temple—the triple juxtaposition that lay behind so many violent deeds of the Middle Ages—were innovations that arose in the period immediately preceding the confrontation. It would not be an exaggeration to say that the symbols assumed a concrete shape from the confrontation itself.

It was no earlier than the irreversible decline of the Abbasid Caliphate that Muslim law evolved the practice whereby an independent Sultan might be mentioned as the sovereign during the delivery of the sermon (Khutba) at the Friday congregational mosque. The practice had not come into evidence during the Arab occupation of Sind;[295] but it had certainly done so by the time of the Ghaznavi and Ghori expeditions to India. When the forces of Muhammad Ghori occupied Ajmer and Delhi, an immediate need was felt for a Friday congregational mosque on the spot, so that the Khutba might be read and sovereignty might be declared. Thus evolved the Jami Masjid, a building specific to Islam in India in its early phase.

However, building a Jami Masjid would require time. The immediate need to have the Khutba read could only be met by converting an existing building into the Friday congregational mosque. Attention was drawn inevitably to the pillared hall of the enemy's spired temple which dominated the landscape for miles around. It could be hastily converted into a makeshift public mosque: an affair of two and a half days (*addhai din ka jhonpra*). And yet the spired Hindu temple too was a recent arrival in history: when Muhammad bin Qasim conquered Sind at the turn of the eighth century, neither the curvilinear Nagara temple nor the stepped Dravida temple had evolved out of the somewhat squat sanctum which represented at the time the new cults of Shiva, Shakti, and Vishnu. It was in the fifty years before and after the destruction of the Somnath temple by Mahmud of Ghazni that the classic temples of India, which draw crowds of tourists today, were built.[296]

Vedic cults, which had revolved around fire and sacrifice, had known no temple. The transition from sacrifice (*yajna*) to worship (*puja*) fostered the need for a house of worship. The temple appeared first as a low building with a small spire around the time when Arabia was preparing for its prophet and Rome had fallen to the barbarians. The new houses of worship, devoted to a novel puranic pantheon dominated by Shiva and Vishnu, would develop into towering monuments in the centuries to come, but at the time of the Arab occupation of Sind, the spires had not reached the sky and the temple (*budd*), such as it was, had the solemn guarantee of not being touched by the conquerer.[297] Only in the eleventh century did the Nagara style temples of the north throw up those gigantic curvilinear towers which caught Sultan Mahmud's avid eye. Such buildings were ready-made objects for spoliation, destruction, or—with the coming of the Ghoris—conversion into Friday congregational mosques. The juxtaposition of the Friday sermon, the congregational mosque, and the towering pillared temple was an outcome of recent history, and one full of potential for future conflict.

As disputes over the political space generated contentions over the religious symbols, Hinduism and Islam were locked into a pattern of interaction in which they redefined each other. A rebellious clan would stop the slaughter of cows, the sovereign state would enforce the sacrifice; the clan—the Rathors—would stop the call to public prayer at the Friday Mosque, the state—the Mughals—would send in officials and ulama to reinstitute the Khutba. Where, moreover, the enforcement of sovereignty required not just the mention of the prince during the Friday sermon, but also the collection of a poll tax (*jiziya*) from the population at large, the actions of the state could not but have a lasting impact on the life and thinking of the community. That is not to say that the symbols in dispute dictated an implicit, predetermined collision, for the symbols that one party targeted when attacking the other were not 'given' from the start, but were shaped by the interaction.

The dispute arose from a process: the fact, on the one hand, that 'Hinduism', with its particular symbols, was but a recent and still forming set of beliefs and practices when Islam arrived; and the development, on the other, that Islam, in its transition to a new land, restated some of its priorities, as for instance when the sacrifice of the cow at Bakr Id became a matter of honour. The fact is that two cosmic schemes were being formed, or, to be more exact, reassembled, in an enclosed space. This was not a conflict between the Vedic religion of antiquity which had nothing against the sacrifice of cows, and the original Islam of Arabia, which did not require it. Rather, it was an encounter between two parties defined by the confrontation itself: an interface between Hinduism, newly denominated by Islam, and the latter, recontextualized by the former. The two systems of belief evolved in juxtaposition and by interaction, rejecting, accommodating, disliking, influencing each other.

What the Muslims came to define as the Hindu religion, and which its own adherents knew as the nameless, eternal law (*Sanatana Dharma*), was but the third and last phase of a proto-historic cult. The cult evolved from Vedic to Brahmanical, and from Brahmanical to Hindu. A millenium (1500–500 BC) elapsed before the original Vedic cult of the sacrificial fire evolved into the orthodox Brahmanical rituals against which the Buddha organized his sect (*sangha*) in protest. It took another millenium and a half for this Brahmanical orthodoxy to assume, through the missions of Shankara (*c.*788–820) and Ramanuja (eleventh century), the shape of religion which Al Biruni defined as Hindu. The *Sanatana Dharma*, gradually assuming the new form of Hinduism, was again remoulded as the religion of the *sants* by interaction with Islam. Only then did it assume the contours which the enlightened Parsi author of the *Dabistan-i-Mazahib* found in the seventeenth century, and which the well-known orientalist H.H. Wilson delineated at the beginning of the nineteenth century.[298]

If we compare Al Biruni's description of Hinduism (1030) with that of the *Dabistan* (1654–7), we find that devotionalism (*bhakti*) had wrought a visible transformation in the intervening period. It is not that Islamic mysticism (*tasawwuf*) fostered medieval Hindu devotionalism; nor of course did *bhakti* foster *tasawwuf*. Each developed independently of the other; but yoga, *tasawwuf* and *bhakti* interacted subtly with one another to produce the intangible religious atmosphere of the Middle Ages. With the hard monism (Advaita) of Shankara and the qualified monism (Vishishtadvaita) of Ramanuja, the speculative metaphysics of the Upanishads reached a culminating point. However, as the Shaiva and Vaishnava devotees of the middle ages traced their idolatrous cults back to the orders founded by Shankara and Ramanuja respectively, it is also evident that the two philosophers initiated a new course for Hinduism, pointing towards the emotional Bhakti cult of the future. In the centuries to come, the Sufis and Bhaktas created an erotic spiritualism that may be considered India's peculiar contribution to the civilization of the medieval world. Muinuddin Chisti, Baba Farid, Nizamuddin Auliya, Amir Khusrau, Malik Muhammad Jayasi, and the elusive Shah Madar, on the one hand, and Ramanand, Kabir, Shri Chaitanya, Mirabai, Guru Nanak, and Tulsidas, on the other, were figures inhabiting the same mental universe.

The arrival of Islam in India—a process which may be reckoned to stretch from the first Arab settlement on the west coast in the time of Hajjaj bin Yusuf (c.661–714) to the campaigns of Malik Kafur to the far south (1310–11)—coincided with the emergence of what the Muslims called Hinduism. Both events, moreover, were contemporaneous with other momentous developments in Indian society: the full articulation of the caste system, in which the conventional number of '36 jatis' was tagged on in every town to the original '4 varnas';[299] the rise of the Rajputs, Marathas, Jats, Banias, and other castes which came to dominate Hindu society in the centuries to follow;[300] the growth of the vernacular languages;[301] and the emergence of the regional cultures and provincial identities which form the basis of the political systems of the subcontinent today.[302] There emerged a complex mosaic of interwoven ethnic, religious, regional, and ritual divisions which amazed and confused the Portuguese when they arrived on the west coast at the end of the fifteenth century.[303] Samual Purchas expressed this succinctly when he said: 'It is common in India that each trade and tribe distinguish a new sect.'[304]

Hinduism, as the author of the *Dabistan* and H.H. Wilson found it, was a relatively recent development, both Bhakti and the institution of the Guru (who challenged the monopoly of the Brahman), being 'an invention, and apparently a modern one, of the institutors of the existing sects'.[305] The 'existing' religious foundations, too, emerged no earlier than the coming of Shankara, Ramanuja, Gorakhnath, Ramanand, and Kabir. The author of the *Dabistan* distinguished, from the mass of ordinary Hindus believing in the ten avatars and following the observances and ceremonies of the Shastras,[306] certain specific sects, which appeared in late antiquity and the early medieval period: the Sannyasis of Shankaracharya;[307] the Yogis of Gorakhnath;[308] the 'Saktian' who followed the esoteric Tantrik practice of drinking out of skulls and copulating with female 'Saktis';[309] the 'Vichnuian Sect' (Vaishnavas) or Vairagis, among whom he distinguished in particular the Ramanandis, Haribayantis, Radhavallabhis, and the followers of Kabir;[310] the Maha Atmas, a sect of dervishes whom he characterized as Hindu Sufis;[311] 'the Nanac Panthian', who were known as 'the nation of the Sikhs';[312] and miscellaneous Bhakti cults preached by various medieval Gurus. Of these, the best known were the Sannyasis, the Jogis, and the Vairagis.[313]

With the exception of the foundations of Shankara and Ramanuja, all of these orders subscribed to cults posterior to the Vedas and which derived their sanction from unorthodox Yoga texts and Puranas and Tantras of late composition (*Hatha Yoga Pradipika*, *Brahma Vaivarta Purana*, *Kularnava Tantra*, etc). Such texts, which were oblivious of the Vedic deities, divided all Hindus into three categories—the worshippers of Shiva, Vishnu, and Shakti—but even as regards this not so ancient trinity, it is evident from the *Dabistan* and from Wilson's *Sketch* that there were medieval deviations. Krishna, Rama, and the Linga were virtually the only forms in which Vishnu and Shiva were worshipped in the medieval period.[314] As for the worship of Shakti, or the primal energy emanating from the Yoni, it flourished in close 'circles' of heterodox Tantrik devotees and their women according to rites absolutely opposed to the patriarchal Vedic norms.[315]

The first wave of Arabs do not seem to have seen or grasped what the Turks encountered three centuries later: interlocked stone representations of the Linga and Yoni, emblems especially calculated to shock Muslim sensibilities.[316] The idol which Sultan Mahmud destroyed at the temple of Somnath was in fact nothing but a Linga, a polished block of stone five cubits in height and of proportionate thickness.[317] This does not exhaust the list of the modifications of Hinduism, due whether to 'the course of time' or to 'the presence of foreign rulers',[318] which in Wilson's analysis coincided with the Muslim conquest. The earliest life of Shankara does not so much as mention the Jogis in the list of the heresies which he suppressed,[319] though these unconventional ascetics of the 'pierced ear' (*kan-phata*) were common enough when Ibn Battuta visited India.[320] Nor does the mission of Shankara seem to have encountered Radha and Krishna or Rama and Sita, the two cults destined to be most popular in the medieval age.[321] Emotional devotion to Krishna was popularized soon after the passing of Shankara by the *Bhāgavata Purāna* , a south Indian Sanskrit text of the ninth century.[322] However, the love of the older milkmaid Radha for the young cowherd Krishna was conceived no earlier than the coming of the Turks, being first delineated in the medieval eastern Indian text *Brahma Vaivarta Purana*. Subsequently, the Hindi poet Tulsidas celebrated, in preference to the illicit affair of Radha and Krishna, the altogether more respectable married union of Rama and Sita; he popularized the cult of their monkey devotee Hanuman no earlier than the reign of Akbar.[323]

As the orthodox Brahmanical Hinduism of Shankara and Ramanuja yielded to the development of popular Hinduism, the Jogis of Goraknath welcomed all and sundry into their ranks as against the more fastidious Dasnami Gosains of Shankara. A broader basis was thereby given to the worship of Shiva.[324] The Vaishnava cult experienced a popular breakthrough at the very time when the Ramanandis, addressing their devotion specifically to Rama, branched off from the Brahmanical sect of Ramanuja.[325] The Guru, that influential figure presiding over medieval Hindu devotionalism, appeared when Ramanand led the breakaway.[326] Shankara and Ramanuja wrote commentaries on the Vedanta in Sanskrit for the Brahmans. Ramanand preached devotion and imparted the Mantra in vernacular to all castes.[327] The Guru, apparently, need not be a Brahman: though Ramanand was a Brahman himself, he was said to have disciples belonging to other castes—Kabir the weaver, Pipa the Rajput, Raidas the cobbler, Dhanna the Jat—who in turn became Gurus.[328] The calm monistic contemplation of the formula 'Atman = Brahman' by Shankara and its equally logical modification by Ramanuja

now yielded to the passionate, erotic, emotional Krishna Bhakti of
Chaitanya and Mirabai:

> Thunder clouds came and went, but no message from Hari,
> Frog, peacock, partridge and cuckoo started to call.
> Lightning flashed in deep darkness, but I was alone,
> Trembling in the fragrant wind and pelting rain.
> Loneliness burnt and stung like a jet black cobra,
> And Mira's heart overflowed with love for the Lord.[329]

How far were these developments in Hinduism influenced by Islam?
The Kirtan of the Bhaktas certainly owed something to the Sama of the
Sufis.[330] Bhakti might have owed something to the example of *tasawwuf*.
The predominance of Guru and Viraha in Bhakti and of Pir and Ishq in
tasawwuf suggests parallels too strong to be dismissed as coincidence.
That is not to say that one was the product of the other. Indian society
had experienced erotic, emotional devotionalism before it encountered
Islamic mysticism. As a form of Yoga or concentration of the mind, the
technical term Bhakti occurs in the *Bhagavad Gita*, but there it is a
contemplative, intellectual devotion without the components of erotic
attachment and emotional longing (Viraha). The *Vishnu Purana* is the
last Sanskrit text to illustrate intellectual Bhakti before emotional Bhakti
makes its first appearance in the *Bhagavata Purana*. This South Indian
Sanskrit text derived its Viraha-Bhakti from the devotional Tamil poetry
of the Alvars. As early as the seventh century, Nammalvar speaks of
the temple of Krishna in these terms:

> It is the abode of Him
>   who one day in former times
> in the shadow of a screw-pine with flowers
> sucked by bees
> made my heart overflow with love and desire
>   —and then abandoned me.[331]

In Alvar hagiography, the girl Andal, a real Tamil poetess who
lived and wrote in the ninth century, exhibited the perfect form of
Viraha-Bhakti. She got married to her deity Ranganath and was then
absorbed into his image, thus ending her Viraha or suffering.[332] Bhakti,
issuing in its intense emotional form from seventh century Tamil poetry
(Nammalvar, and later Andal), transited through a ninth century
Sanskrit treatise (*Bhagavata Purana*) to the vernacular songs of the north
(Kabir, Mirabai) in the fifteenth century. At that stage, the presence of
Islamic mysticism, backed by the tradition of the Persian poetry of

Iran and Hindustan in which the elusive Beloved was identified with God, became a factor to reckon with. The notion of Viraha, in the form we encounter it in Kabir, bears a generic resemblance to the Sufi notion of love (Ishq). So does the Gaudiya Vaishnava notion of love (Prem), in which Radha–Krishna corresponds to Ashiq–Mashuq.[333] Shaikh Nizamuddin Auliya, keeping awake at night with a solitary lamp as his companion, would extinguish it with his sighs, and then make it burn brighter with the fire of his soul, till at dawn a verse might enter his mind:

> The garment by Thy separation torn
> Living, once more, once more, re-knit I must.
> And if I die, accept my frank excuse,
> Alas, the hopes that crumble into dust.[334]

As the missionaries of Islam arrived behind its soldiers, or the soldiers of Islam behind its missionaries, a context arose that was as novel for the Hindus to adjust to as it was for the Muslims—a process of interpenetration which in scale and ambiguity has scarcely a parallel in world history before Europe's expansion into Asia. The encounter between the two world civilizations—Brahmanical and Islamic—differed from one part of the subcontinent to the other, depending on the manner in which Islam came to India. In particular, the way in which Islam interacted with Hindu society at the tip of the subcontinent on both sides of the peninsula, that is to say, Malabar and the Coromandel coast, differed radically from the encounter that occurred on the Indo-Gangetic plains and the Deccan plateau. This was so because Islam came to India by two entirely different modes: by sea and by land; in the former instance, on the basis of quiet, peaceful settlement on the coastal stretches of the deep south facing the Arabian Sea and the Bay of Bengal; and in the latter instance, by sudden, purposeful expansion in Hindustan and the Deccan. In consequence, the Mappila Muslims of Malabar and the Marakkaiyar Muslims of Coromandel were peacefully absorbed into the Indian social system in much the same way as the Jews and Syrian Christians had been accommodated earlier in Kerala, and the Parsis in Gujarat. However, in Hindustan, Bengal, and the Deccan by contrast, the system of self-contained communities, unable to accommodate the power and influence of the Sultans and Sufis in quite the same manner, experienced violent disjunctures.

At the heart of the Indian social system as it had evolved at the time of the arrival of Islam lay ancient notions of purity and pollution.[335]

As early as the seventh century, the Chinese pilgrim I-tsing had noted: 'Now the first and chief difference between India of the five regions and other nations is the peculiar distinction between purity and impurity.'[336] A system was built on these notions, segregating the population sexually, occupationally, and ritually into self-contained communities. Segregation, in terms of marriage, occupation, and rituals, implied social autonomy. Such a system was capable of incorporating not merely the Hindu castes but also the animistic tribes and the Jewish, Christian (St Thomas), and Parsi sects as self-governing units of the population. The social structure that had so evolved into this form had its origin in the caste system of the Hindus but was wider in its scope.

The hierarchical and segregational notions of purity and pollution, originating in the age before Islam, affected in the course of time large parts of the surface of society. Abul Fazl recorded in detail 'unclean things', such as 'wine, blood, semen, excrement, urine, excretions from the mouth, nose, ears and eyes ... a woman in her courses, and one newly delivered ... any dead animal, forbidden food, a sinner guilty of the five great sins, or whoever touches such ... the smoke from a burnt corpse, a washerman, a hunter, a tanner, a carrier, and an oilman'.[337] As opposed to these polluted substances defined by Hinduism, he also listed in the *Ain-i-Akbari* the 'purifiers': 'austerity, suspension of breath (prānāyama), religious exercises of the Sandhya ... fire, water, air, earth, ashes ... milk, butter milk, clarified butter, and the dung and urine of a cow.'[338] The *Ain*'s explanation of the system of pollution and purification reflected a detailed awareness and perhaps a politic and detached acceptance of what it obviously perceived to be an irrational system:[339]

> If he be defiled with spirituous liquor, semen, blood, catamenia, (the touch of) a lying-in woman, ordure or urine, he must wash with water and scour with earth, and again wash with water if the defilement be above the navel; if it extend below, after the second washing he must rub himself with butter from a cow and then with its milk, and afterwards with its butter-milk, and next smear himself with cowdung and wash in its urine, and finally drink three handfuls of water from the river.

Under the system, all human beings were susceptible to pollution, but some were considered more polluted than others. Accordingly, the population was graded some centuries before the onset of the Turkish expeditions from Ghazni and Ghor, along a hierarchy of ritual purity, with the Brahmans at the top and the 'degraded outcastes' at the bottom.[340]

By then, colonies of Arab traders had sprung up on both sides of the peninsula. Thus, the process began whereby the Malayalam-speaking Mappila community emerged in Malabar as yet another community. The Tamil-speaking Maraikkayar community emerged at the same time as a sort of caste in Coromandel.

Despite the fact that notions of pollution went further in Malabar than in any other part of India, to the degree that untouchability turned into death penalty for any outcaste Pulayan who dared touch a high caste Nayar woman 'with his hand or with a stone',[341] the formation of a large and expanding Muslim community which professed an altogether different faith caused no social disjuncture there.[342] The Mappilas were placed, along with the Syrian Christians and Jews, below the Nambudri Brahmans and Nayars, and well above the 'untouchable' groups. On the opposite side of the peninsula, Tamil-speaking Muslim traders and ship-owners claiming Arab descent won recognition as the Maraikkayar caste, and the rest of the Muslim population—native fishermen, pearl divers, weavers, artisans, petty traders, leather-sellers, and other occupational groups engaged in 'polluting' activities—formed the lower-ranking Labbai caste.[343]

The peaceful assimilation of the descendants and converts of the Arabs in South Indian society was facilitated by its beehive formation, more cells being added to the cellular structure without altering the basic formation. This particular manner of accommodation, however, presupposed the continued power which the Zamorins and Nayakas enjoyed in Malabar and Coromandel, far from the reach of the Muslim powers to the north. As Islam penetrated Hindustan and the Deccan by expansion rather than settlement, carrying with it a democratic and unitary model of state and society, the beehive structure which was the central characteristic of the Indian social formation came under the most profound strain. Once the conquests were done, however, the cellular social formation slowly reasserted itself in the valleys of the Ganges and the Godavari.

There were, however, evident disjunctures. If an imaginary line is drawn across peninsular India from Cannanore on the west coast to the Kaveri delta facing the Bay of Bengal, it will at once be apparent that Islam came to markedly different terms with Indian society north and south of the line. Southwards, Arab immigration from the Gulfs by way of overseas traffic constituted the mode of Islam's arrival; northwards, the mode was Turko–Persian expansion overland, all the way from Ghazni and Ghor to Golkonda and Arcot. A simple fact reflects the distinction between these movements: the Mappilas and Maraikkayar of the deep south belong to the Shafi School of Islamic law which was once popular in Arabia; the Urdu, Bengali, and Dakhni-speaking Muslims to the north of the line belong to the Hanafi school of law which had prevailed in the Perso–Turkic area of Khurasan at one time.[344] The division coincides with the Arab–Ajam divide in the central lands of Islam. Arab immigration to the tip of the Indian peninsula began as early as the eighth and ninth centuries.[345] Turkish campaigns to the Ganges basin from the Khurasan area of Ajam got underway no earlier than the eleventh and twelfth centuries. Subsequently, the two colonizations proceeded along divergent paths, and with differential consequences: so much so, that the soldiery of the Sultanat of Delhi did not hesitate to attack and plunder the Muslim merchant community of the deep south during the brief occupation of the Hindu principality of Mabar. Khusrau, the usurper of Alauddin Khalji's throne, seized the treasure of a Muslim subject of the Pandya Raja of Madurai, and put the merchant to death despite the common expectation that his Islamic faith would protect him.[346]

This could not have happened but for the fact that the usurper and the merchant had been thrown up by two separate colonizations of Islam in India, one pushing down by land and bearing the marks of Ajam and Hanafi, the other seaborne and inspired by Arab and Shafi. The latter originated earlier, had no associations of conquest and dislocation, and fitted harmoniously into the existing society. Arab–Shafi colonization at the tip of the peninsula did no more than add a couple of cells to the cellular formation of society: a new community in Malabar and a new caste in Coromandel. There emerged in consequence a unique Hindu–Muslim symbiosis in Malabar which led to a united front against the encroachments of the Portuguese.[347] Shaikh Zainuddin al-Mabari, who chronicled the brave fight put up by the Zamorin of Calicut and his Muslim subjects against the Portuguese monopolization of pepper, had this to say regarding the background:

> Now it is a well-known fact that Allah, glory be to Him and Exalted be He, made the faith of Islam spread in most of the inhabited regions of the earth; in most countries by means of sword and force and in some by exhortation to accept Islam. But Allah has been gracious to the people of Malibar in Hind in making them accept the faith of Islam spontaneously and willingly, and not out of fear or compulsion.[348]

The Mappila Muslims were an integral part of the matrilineal society of Malabar, their property descending, as in the case of the Nayars, through the children of their sisters.[349] The people who lost their caste embraced Islam or joined the St Thomas Christians, or became Jogis.[350] The rulers, who belonged to the Nayar caste, did not punish such of their countrymen who embraced Islam.[351] On the contrary, they showed 'respect and regard for the Muslims', so that trade prospered and the towns multiplied. Muslims were assisted by the Hindu princes in the observation of the Friday prayers and the celebration of Id. Allowances were fixed by the state for *qazis* and *muazzins*, who were entrusted with the duty of carrying out the laws of the Shariat. Zainuddin wrote in praise of the rulers: 'No one is permitted to neglect the prayers on Fridays. In greater part of Malibar, whoever neglects it, is punished or made to pay a fine.'[352] In short, the Muslims of Malabar 'lived a happy and prosperous life on account of the benevolence of their rulers', until Allah, in His wrath over their transgressions, set on them 'the people of Purtukal, who were Christians'. The Portuguese scoffed at the Muslims, plundered their properties, seized their ships, burnt down their cities and mosques, trod down the Quran, seized them on their pilgrimage to Mecca, all in an attempt to monopolize pepper, ginger and other spices.[353] However, the Muslims were not without allies in their counter-attack on the infidels:

> It is well-known that the Muslims of Malibar have no Amir who possesses power and can exercise authority over them and be mindful of their welfare. On the contrary, all of them are subjects of rulers who are unbelievers. Notwithstanding this fact, the Muslims engaged themselves in hostilities against the unbelievers (the Portuguese) and spent their wealth to the extent of their means with the assistance of that friend of the Muslims, the Samuri, who also expended money on their behalf from the beginning.[354]

Zainuddin was conscious of the fact that the Zamorin and the Portuguese were both unbelievers, but he drew a theoretical distinction between the two: 'know then: There are two sets of unbelievers. One is the group that permanently dwells in their countries. War against them does not become an imperative duty of all Muslims ... The other set of unbelievers are those who invade the territories of Muslims ... The 'war against such unbelievers is an obligatory duty imposed upon every Muslim.'[355] Furthermore, the Muslims and their trade prospered because of the regard shown to them by the Hindu rulers of Malabar. The Zamorin of Calicut, in particular, sent his own Nayar troops in the just war of the Muslims against the Portuguese attempt to establish a monopoly over the spice trade:

> The Muslims and the Nayar soldiers of the Šamuri besieged the Portuguese. The Muslims from the various towns went to Kalikut in great numbers for the holy war in the way of Allah ... By that time the Portuguese had exhausted their food supply ... Therefore they decided to go out to their ships ... and escaped, set sail in their ships and went away.[356]

In the end, however, the Zamorin and the Muslims were both weakened by the unequal struggle against the Portuguese navy. Zainuddin was bitterly aware that the Muslim Sultans and Amirs who had been approached did not come to the aid of the Zamorin in the holy war.[357] The political equations which he sketched—the alliance of the Zamorin and the Muslims against the infidel Christians of Portugal— were rooted, in his view, in the manner of the coming of Islam to Malabar. The myth which he related regarding the origins of Islam in Kerala reflects the peaceful absorption of the new religion in indigenous society.

> It happened thus: A party of Jews and Christians, with their family in a big ship, entered one of the sea ports of Malabar, named Kodungallur [Cranganore] where its king resided. They received from the king grants of lands, gardens, and houses and settled there.
>
> Some years later, there arrived at Kodungallur, a party of Muslim faqirs with a Shaykh, intent on a pilgrimage to the Footprint of our Father Adam. When the king heard about their arrival he sent for them, entertained them, and made kind inquiries about them. Their Shaykh informed him of our Prophet Muhammad, the tenets of the religion of Islam, and the miracles of the splitting of the Moon. Allah, glory be to Him, and exalted be He; had caused to enter in his mind the truth of the mission of the Prophet, and the king believed in him.[358]

On the completion of their pilgrimage to Adam's peak in Sri Lanka, the party returned to the king by his request, and he embarked with the Shaikh and the fakirs for Arabia secretly at night, never to return home. The king died abroad a Muslim, but sent a mission to Kerala before his death for the propagation of the faith of Islam. The king's successor gave the newcomers plots of land and gardens. They settled there and erected a mosque in 822 CE.

Zainuddin's account corresponds closely to the indigenous myth recorded in 'Keralopatti'. The last Cheruman Perumal is remembered as having become a Muslim in his old age, and to have gone on pilgrimage

to Mecca after dividing Kerala among friends and relations.[359] Tome
Pires and Duarte Barbosa mentioned the same story before Zainuddin
recounted it at greater length, and Firishta gave a shorter version
afterwards.[360] But two centuries earlier Ibn Battuta recorded an earlier
and rather strikingly different version of the myth. He came across a
congregational mosque and a stepped well at 'Dahfattan' in the Kingdom
of a Malabar prince named Kuwayl. Near the mosque stood a green
tree which the people called 'the tree of testimony'.

> I was informed that a leaf falls from this tree every year in autumn after
> its colour has turned first to yellow and then to red, and that on this leaf
> there stands written with the pen of nature— Lā Ilāhā Ilallāh
> Muhammad-ur Rasūl Ullāh . The jurist Husain and many a reliable man
> told me that they had seen the leaf and read the inscription on it. Further,
> I was told that as the time of dropping of the leaf approached, reliable
> Muslims and infidels would seat themselves under the tree. As soon as
> the leaf fell Muslims would take one half of it, while the other half was
> deposited in the treasury of the heathen ruler (sultan). The natives consider
> it a cure for the sick. This tree was the cause of the conversion of Kuwayl's
> ancestor who had built the mosque and the bā'in; he embraced Islam
> and became a good Muslim. His story is well known and current among
> the inhabitants. The jurist Husain told me that one of the sons of that
> ruler went back to infidelity after the father's death, and became so
> perverse as to order the uprooting of that tree and it was uprooted and no
> trace of it was left. But, later on, it sprang up again and appeared better
> than before and the said infidel perished before long.[361]

The tree had obviously disappeared by the sixteenth century, for
Tome Pires, Duarte Barbosa, and Zainuddin al-Mabari recorded a
considerably altered version of the myth in which the red leaf had no
place. However, the legend of the Moor Zamorin still preserved the
memory of the peaceful absorption of Islam by Malabar society.
Northern India, by contrast, remembered the coming of Islam in terms
of a legendary conquest that preceded the historical conquest. The legend
is built around a mythical (?) fakir named Salar Masud, to whom both
Ibn Battuta and Firishta (and earlier on Amir Khusrau), made passing
references.[362] Here we have quite a different memory of how Islam
reached the foothills of the Himalayas at the other end of the country.
The myth is of considerable antiquity, for the fakir's tomb at Bahraich
was a well-known shrine during the reign of Muhammad bin Tughlaq.
The latter, according to Firishta, 'proceeded to Bhyraich, to pay his
devotions at the shrine of Salar Musaood Ghazy, one of the descendants

of Sooltan Mahmood of Ghizny, who had been killed there by the Hindoos, in the year 557 (AD 1162)'.[363]

The legend of Salar Mas'ud is built around an unresolved contradiction between 'Islam' and 'the Hindus', overlaid by the common worship of the saint by crowds of Muslim and Hindu pilgrims alike to the shrine at Bahraich. The *Mir'at-i-Masudi* of Abdur Rahman Chishti, which recorded the legend at length during the reign of Jahangir, cast it in the form of a mythical jihad. This was the myth of an earlier Islamic conquest that failed for the moment, to be succeeded by the more permanent military and spiritual conquests of Muhammad Ghori and Muinuddin Chishti. India, according to the legend, was conquered for Sultan Mahmud of Ghazni by his young nephew, Salar Mas'ud, and 'the idol of Somnath was broken in pieces by his sole advice'.[364] The warrior–saint, who came upon Bahraich in course of a hunting expedition, was determined 'to convert unbelievers to the one God and the Musulman faith', by force if necessary: 'if they adopt our creed, well and good; if not, we put them to the sword.'[365]

The Hindu chiefs of the country assembled from all quarters and attacked his seat at Bahraich. Here he had laid out a garden around a Mahua tree by the side of a bathing ghat where the Hindus used to worship an idol of the sun. He was slain by a hill Raja and laid out under the tree. Idolatry 'again reigned over the land of India' and things remained in this state for 200 years until Khwaja Muinuddin of Chisht received God's commandment to go and settle in Ajmer during the reign of Rai Pithaura. The latter was slain shortly afterwards by Sultan Muhammad of Ghor, who placed Qutbuddin Aibak on the throne of Delhi. 'Khwaja Muinu-d-din, of Chisht, through the powerful assistance of his prayers, brought the whole country of India into the hands of Kutbu-d-din Aibak.'[366]

This is how a follower of the Chishtiyya order perceived the role of the warrior–saint of Bahraich in the history of Islam and its conquest of India. In course of time the cult of Salar Mas'ud assumed the character of a popular heterodox cult, men and women, Hindus and Muslims, flocking to Bahraich from different parts of India. Legend had it that soon after Ghazi Miyan's death a Hindu milkman named Jasu Ahir, whose barren wife was blessed with a son upon praying at the shrine, rebuilt the grave with pure cow's milk and costly lime. Lepers came from all over the country in search of a cure, indicating a popular belief in the medicinal properties of the shrine. This folk superstition might explain its popularity among both Hindus and Muslims. Despite its presentation as the story of a crusade against the idolaters, the legend was thus transformed into a syncretic popular cult, drawing Hindus and Muslims together under the displeased eyes of the orthodox ulama. The long processions from various parts of the Delhi Sultanat carrying spears to the shrine at Bahraich acquired so disreputable a character that the orthodox Sultan, Sikandar Lodi, banned the festivities during his reign. The processions sprang up once again after his death, and Emperor Akbar himself is said to have seen one off from Agra in disguise.[367]

At the time of Ibn Battuta's visit to Delhi and onwards to Sylhet (1333–1346 CE), historical memories of the expansion of Islam across the vast plains stretching from the Indus to the Brahmaputra displayed both Sultans and Sufis at work, and a complex interweaving of clashes and reconciliations. While in Delhi, the redoubtable traveller from the Maghrib paid a visit to the Quwwat-ul-Islam mosque at the foot of the Qutb Minar. He had been told by the chief justice (*qazi-ul-quzzat*) of the Sultanat that Delhi 'was conquered from the hands of the infidels in 584 AH'. He deciphered the same date, erroneously, on the arch of the great congregational mosque (actually the inscription reads 589 AH/ 1193 CE or 587 AH/1191 CE).[368] Near the eastern gate of the mosque he noticed two idols of copper connected together by stones: 'Every one who comes in and goes out of the mosque treads over them.' He learnt that there had once been, on the site of the mosque, an idol house (*bud khana*), which, upon the conquest of Delhi, had been turned into a mosque.

The impressions that he subsequently recorded when he visited the Sufi saint Shah Jalal in Sylhet (East Bengal), stand in sharp contrast to the sights which he had earlier seen around the tower of victory in Delhi. The saint, whom he visited in 1346, was already something of a living legend, an impression heightened by his hoary age, and by the eyewitness account which the Moroccan traveller obtained from him of the slaying of the Abbasid Caliph at Baghdad by the Mongol general Hulagu 88 years earlier.[369] He lived in a cave outside which a hospice had been built by his disciples. 'The inhabitants of these mountains,' Ibn Battuta learnt from them, 'had embraced Islam at his hands, and for this reason he stayed amidst them.'[370] Apart from the hospice, there was no habitation in the vicinity of the cave. Ibn Battuta saw that the inhabitants of the locality, 'Musalmans as well as Hindus', came to him with gifts which the fakirs and the guests consumed, the Shaikh himself being possessed of nothing but a cow with whose milk he broke his fast of ten consecutive days.[371] Battuta's impression of Shaikh Jalaluddin of Tabriz was that of a kindly and pacific old man with many miracles to his credit. There is no hint here of the warrior–saint he was subsequently made out to be by the Muslim population of Sylhet.

The congregational mosque in the Qutb complex and the shrine at Bahraich reveal two different aspects of the spread of Islam in the Gangetic plains. One is the power of orthodox Islam represented by the Sultanat and the ulama, the other is the influence of popular Pirism built around shrines and fakirs. While the ulama might frown upon deviations from the forms which they supposed to be prevalent in Arab and Ajam, the Pirs were more responsive to the home-grown iconistic requirements of the population of Hind. The distinction between the maulvis and the fakirs, 'the learned men' on the one hand and 'the holy men' on the other,[372] were well established in the common perception. The two distinct classes of religious leadership, the ulama and the Shaikhs,[373] were assigned separate quarters in the Ibadat Khana of Emperor Akbar.[374]

The ulama represented the Islamic aspect of the state. It is on record that one day the leading scholars of the age went and saw Iltutmish and asked the Sultan to confront the Hindus with the choice of 'death or Islam'. On behalf of the Sultan, the Wazir reminded the ulama that the Muslims were as yet so few as to resemble a bit of salt in a dish piled with food. 'If the above orders,' the king's minister explained to the legalists, 'are to be applied to the Hindus, it is possible that they might combine and a general confusion may ensue and the Muslims would be too few in number to suppress the general confusion.' The ulama had to be content with the Wazir's assurance that after a few years the troops might be large enough and the Muslims sufficiently established in the capital and the small towns for the Hindus to be confronted with the choice of death or Islam.[375] The day never arrived; the gap between 'law' and 'expediency' proved too wide to bridge.

The law, in any case, offered a more enlightened third alternative: to admit the Hindus as protected subjects (*zimmis*) on payment of a poll-tax (*jiziya*). As Qazi Mughisuddin of Bayana regretfully explained to Sultan Alauddin, the Hanafi school of law, which applied to the Sultanat, admitted this alternative, other schools allowing no choice except death or Islam. The good *qazi* explained further that the due subordination of the *zimmi* was displayed in the humble manner in which he paid the revenue (*kharaj*) and by the throwing of dirt into his mouth by the revenue officer.[376] Alauddin, who, for reasons of state, decided to reduce the headmen and chiefs of the Hindus to subordination by imposing heavy revenue assessments, was amused to learn that it was 'all in accordance with law that the Hindus should be reduced to the most abject obedience',[377] but he decreed only what he thought 'to be for the good of the State' and did not care much whether it was 'lawful or unlawful'.[378] If Amir Khusrau is to be believed, three conditions were presented to the Hindus by Alauddin's generals during one of the expeditions to Warangal: 'First, that they should make profession of our faith, in order that its saving tidings may be proclaimed throughout the world; second, that, in the event of refusal, a capitation tax should be levied; the third is, if compliance with these demands be refused, to place their heads under the sword.'[379]

The reduction of the Hindu rajas of the country to the position of subordinate landholders within the Sultanat was not achieved without violent collisions. Alauddin's sack of Chitore was a climactic event, garbled memories of which subsequently caught the tragic fancy of the bards and poets. Curiously, the Muslim poet, Malik Muhammad Jayasi, emotionally identified with the Rana of Chitore, rather than with the Sultan of Delhi, whose treachery he condemned in the ballad of Rani Padmini.[380] The depiction of her *jauhar* by the devout Sufi poet reflects a brooding sense of loss. The sultan derives no pleasure from the triumph:

> He took up a fistful of ash and threw it up in the air
> The Shah thought to himself, 'The world is a vanity fair',
> The women committed Jauhar, the men fell in war
> The Badshah broke the fort, Islam claimed Chitaur.[381]

Three centuries elapsed before Sufi allegory[382] effected out of the clash a sort of resolution. The Sufi recluse who lived on virtually nothing within a cave,[383] or wandered barefoot in the desert amidst wild animals,[384] blended naturally with the religious landscape of India, making a deeper impression on the mind of its population than any man in power could.[385]

Shaikh Muhammad Ghaus of Gwalior, who wrote the first treatise by an Indian Muslim on Yoga,[386] was known to have practised 'the most severe austerities, having his dwelling in caves and subsisting on the leaves of trees'.[387] Shaikh Daud of Chati, a contemporary of Akbar, spent twenty years wandering over the plains and deserts before he settled at Shergarh in the Punjab. 'Few days passed on which Hindus, to the number of fifty or a hundred, more or less (on each day), did not come with their families and kindred to pay their respects to that holy man, receiving the high honour of conversion to Islam, and obtaining instruction in the faith.'[388] A more peaceful process of penetration was at work here, more surely turning the region around Lahore into a Muslim-majority area than the bloody clashes that had led to the occupation by the Turks. Down south, too, at the shrine of Bandanawaz Gisudaraz in Gulbarga, Abbé Carre found the road 'full of processions of fakirs and Hindus' at the time of the Urs celebration of the saint in 1673.[389] Folk songs attributed to Bandanawaz Gisudaraz were sung by village women as they ground corn or spun threads.[390]

As Islam assumed an indigenous form, it acquired a growing popular dimension, imparted to it by the regular Sufi orders, heterodox bands of Madaris and Qalandars, and the wandering dervishes attached to no particular order.[391] Shrines sprang up in all parts of India, drawing thousands of pilgrims and fakirs at the feast of Urs. The shrines of Muinuddin Chishti at Ajmer, Baba Farid at Ajodhan (Pak Patan in Punjab), and Nizamuddin Auliya in Delhi emerged in the thirteenth and fourteenth centuries, and there were many more in distant corners of the country by the fifteenth century. An early description of one such shrine, located near Bidar, was penned by Afanasy Nikitin in the mid-fifteenth century.[392]

> There is a place—the tomb of Sheik Ala-uddin at Alland, where a fair is held once a year, and whither people from all the Indian country come to trade for 10 days. It is 12 kos from Bidar. Horses are brought thither for sale, as many as 20,000 head, and all kinds of other goods, too. It is the best fair in the land of Hindustan; all wares are sold or bought there in the memory of Sheikh Ala-uddin, during the Russian Feast of the Intercession of the Holy Mother of God [1 October] ... spring came with the Feast of the Intercession of the Holy Mother of God; it is in spring, a fortnight after Intercession, that an eight-day feast is kept to honour the memory of Sheik Ala-uddin.

In the sixteenth and seventeenth centuries, when the population around such towns as Lahore, Dacca, and Bidar would appear to have been as much Muslim as Hindu, a process of peaceful absorption of the new community was under way, accompanied by visible signs of acculturation between Islam and the Hindus. Crowds of fakirs appeared at every shrine during the feast of Urs. 'The Gentils', said one European traveller, 'pay so great a Respect to these Penitents, that they think themselves happy, who can Prostitute Daughters, Sisters or Kins-women to their leudness, which they believe lawful in them; and for this Reason there are so many Thousands of Vagabond *Fakirs* throughout *India*'.[393] Yet another European traveller, horrified by these 'bold, lusty, and ... drunken Beggars, of the Musslemen Cast', noted that 'these commonly like evil spirits, have their Habitations among the Tombs', and warned that they could be 'hardly restrained from running a Muck[394] (which is to kill whoever they meet, till they be slain themselves) especially if they have been at Hodge,[395] a Pilgrimage of *Mecca*'.[396]

The Sufis of the four orders most prevalent in India, Chishti, Suhrawardi, Qadiri, and Shattari, were at the top of the world of fakirs. The wandering Madaris, Qalandars, Malangs, and other heterodox (*be-shara*) fakirs were not so highly regarded and were vulnerable to the occasional wrath of the Sultans and the ulama.[397] The Madaris were by far the most highly visible and organized among these lowly mendicants. They belonged to an order or pedigree (*silsilah*) going back to Shah Madar, supposedly a converted Jew from Aleppo who learnt the esoteric lore from Imam Mahdi of Najaf. Buried in Makhanpur near Cawnpur, he is said to have departed from the world in 1050, when Delhi was still under the Hindu rulers.[398] The characteristic performance of the Madari fakirs, who wandered all over India in large bands with strange animals as far as the footprints of Adam in Sri Lanka every year, was to walk over fire crying '*Dam Madar*'. Captain G. Sydenham observed in 1811:[399]

> All those who lead about tigers and monkies are of this sect, the followers of which are perhaps the most dissolute and vagabond of all Muhammadans. Shah Madar is buried at Makanpur, and a host of pilgrims annually resort to his tomb from all parts of Hindoostan. The Makanpur-ca-Mela, as it is called, is perhaps the most numerous and most celebrated of all pilgrimages or rather fairs, in Hindoostan.

That the peculiar ceremony of the Madariyya Silsilah has a long ancestry is beyond dispute, for Ibn Battuta saw fire-walking fakirs[400] near the Himalaya in 1336. He saw them again in the Maldive Islands: a party of Arab and Persian fakirs returning from a pilgrimage to Adam Peak. They sang and danced, trampling on the fire with their feet, and some of them ate live coals in front of the astounded traveller.[401]

The Madaris and the Qalandars were associated in the popular mind with the Yogis. 'They say,' records the author of the *Dabistan*, 'when Badieddin Madar came to Hindostan, he became a yogi ...'[402] The sect was curious enough for him to comment on it at some length:

... the Madarian, who, like the Sanyasi Avadhuts, wear their hair entangled, and the ashes which they and the Sanyasis rub upon their bodies is called bhasma; besides, they carry iron chains on their heads and necks, and have black flags and black turbans; they know neither prayers nor fasts, they are always sitting at a fire; they drink a great deal of bang; and the most perfect among them go without any dress, in severe cold, in Kabul and Kachmir, and such places ... When they sit together, they relate, that in the night, when the prophet ascended through the seven stages of heaven, he received the command of God to wander through the heavens. When he arrived at the door of paradise, he found the entrance as narrow as the eye of a needle; the porter made him a sign to enter; the prophet said: 'With this body how shall I enter through this passage?' Jabril replied: 'Say: *dam madar*' ('the breath of Madar', a particular ejaculation of this sect). The prophet said so, upon which the narrow door opened and he entered heaven.[403]

Breath control exercises were common to the Yogis and the Sufis, as was the trance which such exercises produced.[404] Badauni's description of a Sufi saint with whom he spent a night bears a certain resemblance to the well known image of the tightly disciplined Yogi. This Shaikh, too, had subjected himself to severe discipline. For fifty years, Shaikh Burhan of Kalpi had abstained from meat. At the end of his life he abstained from drinking water also, 'so that to outward appearance he was an incorporeal spiritual form, supernaturally illuminated'.[405] He, too, used to retain his breath. Sitting continually in a small dark cell, he spent his time in meditation.[406]

In the hands of these Sufis, Islam gradually assumed a local shape which made it attractive to the native population. The psychical profile that emerges from Badauni's glimpse of yet another Sufi is very much in the living tradition of the Indian satyagrahi. Shaikh Azizullah's life was governed by 'the rules of poverty, indigence, and humility'.[407] A champion of the poor and helpless who came to him with their complaints, he would, although he had entered at the time into a forty days' retreat, travel long distances on foot, not hesitant in the least 'to visit the house of one who was without the pale of faith to gain his object'. After successfully obtaining redress for his protégé, he would once again return to the cell of retirement, resuming his religious exercises as though no break had occurred.

And it would sometimes happen that an unbeliever or an oppressor would pay no heed to his intercession on the first occasion, or, (knowing that the Shaikh was without), would purposefully remain within doors, and the Shaikh would sit the livelong day expectant at his door, without being able to see his face. But on successive days the Shaikh would go again and again to his door and would sit in silence, nor would this slighting treatment produce on the clear mirror of his heart, which reflected the hidden knowledge of God, the rust of resentment. He would thus sit until the person to whom the intercession was to be made fell, shamed and remorseful, at his feet, and promptly and obediently fulfilled the desire of the beggar.[408]

Like Shaikh Nizamuddin Auliya, who had been a vegetarian, this medieval Sufi satyagrahi, too, was an adherent of non-violence. Hazrat Nizamuddin used often to recite this verse: 'He who is not my friend— may God be his friend! And he who bears ill-will against me, let his joys increase.'[409] The Shaikh had once told his audience: 'If there is a strife between two persons—say, between me and some other person, its solution is thus: I should, on my part, cleanse my heart of the ideas of revenge. If I succeed in doing that, the enemy's desire to do some harm to me would also be lessened.'[410] It was out of such strong convictions that the Sufis effected, after the initial clash, the reconciliation between Islam and India; so much so, that the community of Muslims and their saints became an integral part of Indian civilization by the time Emperor Akbar adopted Sulh-i-Kul, or peace with everyone, as the spiritual object of his regime.[411]

By then, the Khurasani Turks, who in their first rush had turned the temples of the country upside down from Delhi to Banaras,[412] were assimilated within its population. As Akbar and his band of Turki-speaking Mughal soldiers drove the Pathans before them as far as Orissa, the original Turks were nowhere in sight. 'It is impossible', writes Muhammad Habib, 'to find a Turk anywhere in India today. Our census ignores them ... The Turks or Turushkas have shared the fate of Yavanas, Hunas, Sakas and other conquering settlers in India, and are not to be found anywhere. And nobody knows for certain when they vanished.'[413]

A sure sign of the process of acculturation which resulted in the absorption of the Khurasani immigrants was the replacement of Turki by Urdu as the spoken language of the camp, and the penetration of the new mixed Indo–Muslim language to the south in the form of Dakhni.[414] The spread of this common Indian language through the mechanisms of the camp (*urdu*) and the market (*bazaar*) was an index of the gradual disappearance of the Turushka conquerors amidst the population of India. The process was at work silently from the thirteenth to the fifteenth century.[415] There were other signs, as early as the visit of Ibn Battuta in the mid-fourteenth century, of the mingling that was then taking place: Muslims taking lessons from the Jogis;[416] Brahmans ministering to a mosque in a town without resident Muslims;[417] a fasting fakir served by both Hindus and Muslims;[418] a lone silent Jogi in a temple who eagerly accepted Battuta's rosary, pointing one finger to heaven to indicate the one and only God and again westwards in the direction of Mecca;[419] a Shaikh who prepared his food with his own hands as he regarded the male as well as female servants as unclean.[420] The fakirs were governed by the infectious touch complex which prevailed as early as the fourteenth century at the shrine of Baba Farid at Ajodhan. This reflected the psychic process of Islam's absorption in India.[421]

At the time of Afanasy Nikitin's visit to the Bahmani Sultanat of the Deccan in the following century, the Khurasani ruling class was still visibly apart from the subject population.[422] However, already the Bahmani Sultan had erected at the capital an infirmary for the poor, with both Muslim and Hindu physicians.[423] In the neighbouring Hindu kingdom of Vijayanagar, a Saiyid divine was venerated by both Muslims and Hindus, 'and in that country his sayings were regarded as oracles, for no one dared to refuse obedience to his precepts'.[424] This, it is worth pointing out, was in the midst of the bitter wars that raged between Bahmani and Vijayanagar through the fifteenth century. The counting of beads was done by both Hindus and Muslims.[425] The washing of hands and feet before prayer was as important to the Muslims as was the washing and purifying of the idol for worship to the Hindus.[426] In a climate ruled by notions of pollution, it is not surprising that Muslims, too, regarded women as unclean at childbirth.[427]

Furthermore, the all-pervasive iconistic and idolatrous notions of the country constantly threatened to engulf Islam. In the last quarter of the fourteenth century, the threat galvanized Sultan Firuz Tughlaq and his ulama into repressive measures against the Brahmans. The decision was taken for the first time to levy the *jiziya* from them (something not done by the earlier Sultans of Delhi) on the ground that they were 'the very keys to the chamber of idolatry'.[428] Shams-i-Siraj Afif's account of the affair brings home exactly why the Sultan and the ulama felt vulnerable:

A report was brought to the Sultan that there was in Delhi an old Brahman (*zunar'dar*), who persisted in publicly performing the worship of idols in his house; and that the people of the city, both Musulmans and Hindus, used to resort to his house to worship the idol. This Brahman had constructed a wooden tablet (*muhrak*), which was covered within and without with paintings of demons and other objects. On days appointed, the infidels went to his house and worshipped the idol, without the fact becoming known to the public officers. The Sultan was informed that this Brahman had perverted Muhammadan women, and had led them to become infidels.[429]

The Brahman was summoned to court and the matter was referred to the judges and doctors of the law. They told the Sultan that 'the provisions of the Law were clear: the Brahman must either become a Musulman or be burned'. As the Brahman refused to embrace Islam, he was cast into the fire along with the tablet. However, the danger lay within, in the shrines springing up over the graves of departed dervishes all over the country. Sultan Sikandar Lodi forbade women from going on pilgrimage to tombs,[430] but to judge from the scrape which Badauni got into for making advances to a woman at the shrine of Shah Madar,[431] the prohibition could not have been long in force after the Sultan's death in 1517. Shah Waliullah, in the eighteenth century, attributed the popular Muslim 'worship of their living shaikhs, or their shrines if they are dead', to the foolish example of 'Hindu infidels who worship idols'.[432] The *Al-Balagh Al-Mubin*, attributed to Shah Waliullah by some historians and thought to be a nineteenth century 'Wahabi' tract by others, also stressed the strong parallel between the Hindu worship of idols and the Muslim worship of *pirs*: 'The idol-worshippers dress the idols with silk and brocade. Similarly, the saint worshippers spread silken covers on the tombs of their saints.'[433]

Fear of the loss of identity in so profoundly idolatrous an environment actuated Shah Waliuallah to emphasize the Arabic origin and pure form of Islam. 'We are Arab people', he wrote, 'whose fathers have fallen in exile (*ghurba*) in the country of Hindustan and Arabic genealogy and Arabic language is our pride.'[434] His conception of the Muslims of India as a people with a distinct political identity was revealed in the invitation he extended to Ahmad Shah Abdali to come to the aid of the Muslims when the Marathas and Sikhs overran Mughal territory.[435]

The Beehive Formation and the Unitary Community

The cellular formation of Indian society ever since its inception, and the new Islamic model of the unitary state and community, were two ideas that were profoundly at odds with each other. Each was of world significance, all-embracing in its sweep, and apparently capable of swallowing up the other. The Indian idea provided for the hierarchical existence of every group of human beings in its autonomous cell; the Islamic idea urged a fusion of all humanity with the true faith of Islam, and of the state with the egalitarian community of the faithful. These were diametrically opposed social systems, based on radically different ideologies. The strong potential of each to penetrate the other posed internal dangers to both. However, the process of mutual inter-penetration kept open the possibility of hitherto untried modes of conflict resolution amongst mankind. These were ambiguous encounters at close quarters.

The first chronologically datable exposition of the Indian doctrine of mutual coexistence of separate sects is the Shahbazgarhi rock edict of Ashoka:[436] 'Truly if a person extols his own sect and disparages other sects owing merely to his attachment to it, he injures his own sect very severely by acting in that way. Therefore restraint (alt. Concord) in regard to speech is commendable, because people should learn and respect the fundamentals of one another's Dharma.' The *Bhagavad Gita* shaped this into the characteristic Indian maxim: 'It is better to die in one's own faith for another one's faith is full of dread' (*Svadharme nidhanam sreyah, paradharmo bhayavahah, Gita* III, 35). To put it in the words of Hazrat Nizamuddin, every community has its own way.

This was not simply an abstract doctrine. Notwithstanding some prominent instances of intolerance in ancient India, freedom of worship was a well understood standard of public life. The beehive formation of Indian society was apparent to visitors from abroad. Mis'ar bin Mulhalhil, an early Arab traveller to India and China (c.942 CE), saw it in operation in Saimur, an Indian port on the west coast:[437]

> The people are very beautiful and handsome, from being born of Turk and Indian parents. There are Musalmans, Christians, Jews, and Fire-worshippers there ... The temple of Saimur is an idol temple, on the summit of a high eminence, under the charge of keepers. There are idols in it of turquoise and baijadak,[438] which are highly venerated. In the city there are mosques, Christian churches, synagogues, and Fire temples.

The ethnic mix and sectarian diversity of the population reflected the early immigration of self-contained groups. The Jews, who had come to Cochin as early as the first century of the Christian era, were found by Ibn Battuta to have their own chief at Quilon.[439] The Syrian Christians followed. They traced their origin to Saint Thomas who was said to have been martyred and buried at San Thome. His sepulchre was held in 'devout estimation, both of the Moors, Gentiles, Christians, each pretending the right of his owne Religion to the Church, where this Saint lieth interred'. We are informed by Samuel Purchas that a Moor had the keeping of the church where a light was kept continually burning.[440] The sixteenth century Portuguese traveller Tome Pires noted 15,000 Christians of Saint Thomas in Malabar and distinguished these early Christians, who were 'privileged' and were allowed to touch the Nayars, from 'those who are now being converted every day, and who are numerous'.[441] One other group, 'who were made free Denizens by the *Indians* before the *Moors* were Masters', was the fire-worshipping sect of the Parsees. They were mentioned by Fryer as having escaped in boats from the Muslim conquerors of Iran. Entertained and allowed to live among the Hindus on the condition that they were not to kill cows, they conformed to 'many of the Gentue Ceremonies', and enjoyed the same rights.[442]

Of the major immigrant religions, Islam was the last to arrive. This is how Firishta, looking back nearly a millenium later, perceived its coming. Prior to the propagation of Islam, Christians and Jews had established themselves in Malabar, till at length some vessels from Arabia bearing Muslims on pilgrimage to Adam's foot in Ceylon arrived in the country of the Zamorin. This prince, who converted to Islam and went to Mecca, sent instructions home 'to receive the Mohammedans in future with hospitality, and permit them to settle and build musjids'.[443] Early Arab evidence confirms the impression that Islam was peacefully received and assimilated all along the west coast in its initial phase. The geographer Al-Idrisi, speaking of the Hindu principality of Anhilwara Patan, tells us: 'The town of Nahrwara is frequented by large numbers of Musalman traders who go there on business. They are honourably received by the king and his ministers and find protection and safety.'[444]

An incident related by Muhammad Ufi shows the stern application, in late antiquity, of the old Ashokan maxim of mutual forbearance inscribed on the rock of Shahbazgarhi.[445] In the town of Cambay, under the Hindu king of Anhilwara Patan, there lived a body of fire-worshippers as well as a congregation of Muslims. There was a mosque in town, and a minaret from which the summons to prayer was cried. The Parsees instigated the Hindus to attack the Muslims. The mosque was burnt, the minaret was destroyed, and eighty Muslims were killed. The pious Muslim who delivered the sermon at the mosque fled to the capital of the kingdom. The courtiers, anxious to protect members of their own faith, refused to help him. The man was able to meet the king while the latter was out on a hunting expedition. The Balhara prince of Anhilwara Patan went in person to Cambay in the guise of a tradesman as he could not trust his courtiers in a case involving difference of religion. Having investigated the man's complaint, the king of Gujarat came back to the capital, put his courtiers to shame, and proclaimed it his duty 'to see that all his subjects were afforded such protection as would enable them to live in peace'. The leading men of the Brahmans and the Parsees were punished, and the mosque and minaret were rebuilt at the Balhara's expense.

On his visit to Malabar, Ibn Battuta found the Muslims controlling their own affairs in pretty much the same way as the self-administering Jews. Ibn Battuta, and later Abdul Razzaq, found the Muslims being tried according to their own law by their own judge (*qazi*) under the Hindu prince of Calicut.[446] The ancient principle of accommodating every faith was observed by the kings of Vijayanagar under the distinctly more stressful conditions generated by the war with the Muslim powers to the north. As Duarte Barbosa saw, '... the king allows such freedom that every man may come and go and live according to his own creed, without suffering any annoyance and without enquiry whether he is a Christian, "Jew", Moor or heathen. Great justice and equity is observed to all, not only by the rulers, but by the people to one another.'[447]

The peaceful assimilation of the Muslim community in the cellular structure of Indian society was predicated on the continuing power of the Zamorin of Calicut, the Balhara of Anhilwara Patan, and the Raya of Vijayanagar. Where Islam captured state power, the cellular structure was strained by confrontation with a unitary and democratic model of state and society. Still, the departure from the Ashokan principle of 'concord' was at first not so evident in Muslim public policy. In comparison to the Christian prince Charlemagne who converted the Saxons by fire and sword, the Arab conqueror of Sind was the epitome of magnanimity. While the Frankish (Firangi) emperor of Latin Christendom offered no alternative to the rigid policy of 'kill or convert', Muhammad bin Qasim decided to offer protection to the Brahmans and Buddhists of Sind on the same basis as Islamic law afforded protection to the People of the Book. 'The temples', he said, 'shall be unto us, like the churches of the Christians, the synagogues of the Jews, and the fire temples of the Magians.'[448] He imposed, indeed, a tribute (*jiziya*) upon the inhabitants, but then, as Ibn Battuta saw, so did the Hindu prince receive protection tribute (*jiziya*) from the autonomous

Jews of Quilon.[449] The Governor of Iraq, Hajjaj, instructed his deputy in Sind regarding the conquered inhabitants:

> As they have made submission, and have agreed to pay taxes to the Khalifa, nothing more can be properly required from them. They have been taken under our protection, and we cannot in any way stretch out our hands upon their lives or property. Permission is given to them to worship their gods. Nobody must be forbidden or prevented from following his own religion. They may live in their houses in whatever manner they like.[450]

The first onrush of Islam was lost quickly in the sands of Sind. The Arabs, who took wives from amongst the women of Sind, were absorbed by the population in a few generations. Sind reverted to the rule of the various Hindu clans. When the soldiers of Mahmud of Ghazni came down the Indus, they found 'only a very few' of the old Arab settlers who still held posts of honour. While tracing the fate of the Arab dominion of Sind, English travellers and scholars of the early nineteenth century could not help being struck by the absence of all visible record of their occupation.[451] The Arab conquest of Sind was a passing episode: yet another instance of the cellular structure of Indian society successfully absorbing strangers with a different religion.

The Turkish invasions from Ghazni and Ghor were quite another matter. The Sultanat of Delhi in which these eruptions from Ajam culminated, represented a profoundly altered framework of power, and a deep disruption of the society over which it was imposed. The Turks, too, were destined, like the Arabs, to disappear in the population of the subcontinent, but not before testing the cellular structure of Indian society as never before in history. The learned doctors (ulama) appointed to propound the law to the Muslim court of Delhi represented an orthodox Islamic ideology which they pressed unremittingly upon the Sultan and his officers. Saiyid Nur-ud-Din Mubarak Ghaznavi of the Suhrawardi line, upon his appointment as Shaikh-ul-Islam by Iltutmish, said in a sermon to the Sultan:[452]

> Kings will not be able to discharge their duty of protecting the Faith unless they overthrow and uproot *Kufr* and *Kafiri* (infidelity), *shirk* (setting partners to God), and worship of idols, all for the sake of God and inspired by a sense of honour for protecting the *din* of the prophet of God. But if total extirpation of idolatry is not possible owing to the firm roots of *kufr* and the large number of *Kafirs* and *mushriks*, the kings should at least try to disgrace, dishonour and defame the *mushrik* and idol-worshipping Hindus, who are the worst enemies of God and His Prophet.

This was an uncompromising challenge to the Indian doctrine that one man should not adopt another man's faith. There was not a chance this time that the Muslims would disappear, as in Sind, or be absorbed as yet another caste, as in Malabar. The Turks represented not just themselves, but a dynamic world community which shortly afterwards withstood the greatest menace in history, namely the Mongols. The Kotwal of Delhi, looking back with a sense of pride, told Sultan Alauddin Khalji: 'Your Majesty knows what rivers of blood Changiz Khan made to flow in Muhammadan cities, but he never was able to establish the Mughal religion or institutions among the Muhammadans. Many Mughals have turned Musulmans, but no Musulman has ever become a Mughal.'[453] If the Mongols became proselytes to the religion they sought so violently to destroy,[454] the Hindus living under the political domination of that faith were assuredly faced with a challenge that was penetrating in its appeal and disruptive in its force.

As the first shock passed, there was an attempt to accommodate yet another faith. The seers and saints restated the Indian belief that there was truth in every religion. The ulama argued in turn that this doctrine was opposed to the one truth vouchsafed by Allah upon humanity through His last Nabi. In the reign of Sikandar Lodi some Muslims heard a Brahman argue 'that the religion of Islam was true, but that his own religion was also true'. When this was reported to the doctors of law, they informed the Sultan. The Sultan, who was uncommonly fond of religious and legal questions and theological controversies, summoned the learned fraternity from various quarters and sought their opinion on what the Brahman had declared. The ulama gave it as their opinion that he must either embrace Islam or be put to death. The Brahman refused to adopt another faith and died in his own.[455] Theoretically, the positions taken by the Brahman and the ulama were irreconcilable. Yet an insidious interpenetration effected a sort of reconciliation. An incident narrated by Saiyid Ghulam Husain Khan from the life of the late Mughal statesman, Raja Shitab Rai of Patna, goes to the root of the doctrinal clash. One day a Brahman said to the *naib nazim* of Bihar:[456]

> 'My Lord, we have made a choice of a name for you, according to your horoscope; accept it and use it in telling your beads over'. *I have, answered Shytab-ray, made my choice already, and it is one from the thousand and one names of God; and that is enough for me.*
>
> Pray what is it, added the Brahman?

The Radja would not disclose it; The Brahman became urgent; and he was answered, that it was God's holy name, it is *Rahim* (merciful). On this the Brahman, guessing at his meaning, and desirous to soothe his mind, replied, 'My Lord, *Ram*, as well as *Rahim*, are equally the name of the same eternal one.' *I ask your pardon*, replied the Radja, *there is a difference betwixt them*; and on the Brahman's enquiry, the Radja answered, that the *word Ram always reminded him of Dusrut, his father, whereas the name of Allah, implied neither filiation nor paternity.*

Saiyid Ghulam Husain Khan speculates that the Raja's belief was not consonant with the tenets of the Hindus, and that at heart he was a Muslim. But this, he wrote, is known only to Him, who sees the innermost secrets of a man's heart. What is evident from his rendering of the episode is not just the clash of the two doctrines, but the assimilation that had developed in the minds of men.

It was not so much intellectual conviction as political necessity that initially impelled the Sultans of Delhi to put up with their Hindu subjects. 'Fool!' said Sultan Jalauddin Khalji to a courtier who urged the reduction of the rajas. 'Do you not see that the Hindus pass every day by my palace blowing their conches and beating their drums on their way to worship their idols by the bank of the Jumna? ... If I were a true Muslim king, would I let them eat their betels, wear their clean clothes and count themselves among the Mussalmans with a fearless heart? Shame on me and my kingdom!'[457] But gradually sentiment put a gloss over expediency as the Indian environment insensibly influenced popular Muslim sensibilities. Some Qawwal singers of Delhi happened to sing a curious verse as the refrain of their song before Emperor Jahangir:

Each nation has its right road of faith and its shrine.
I've set up my shrine on the path of him with the cocked cap.

When Jahangir asked the meaning of this, an old courtier explained that the poet Amir Khusrau had composed this by putting together a dialogue he had enjoyed with his Pir. One day Shaikh Nizamuddin Auliya had put his cap on the side of his head, and was sitting on a terraced roof by the bank of the Jumna, watching the devotions of the Hindus. Turning to his disciple who had just arrived, the saint asked, 'Do you see this crowd?' Then he recited the line: 'Each race has its right road of faith and its shrine' (*Har qaum rast rahay, dinay wa qiblighay*). The poet replied immediately, 'I've set my shrine in the direction of him with the cocked cap' (*man qibla rast qardam bar simt-i kaj kulahay*). This was the origin of the popular rhyme that impressed Akbar's son and successor three centuries later.[458]

During these three centuries, the saint's utterance, *har qaum rast rahay* (every community has its own way), so curiously reminiscent of Lord Krishna's exhortation of Arjuna on the battlefield of Kurukshetra (*svadharme nidhanam sreya h, paradharmo bhayavaha h*), became the refrain of the emerging choral symphony of India and Islam. Between 1300 and 1600, a succession of Sufis and Shahs, going against the ulama's monolithic version of truth, stated their conviction that every community has its appointed faith, and that all paths lead to truth. Ibrahim Adil Shah of Bijapur asked a celebrated divine from Persia which was the best of all the various sects of Islam. Maulana Ghiasuddin replied, 'Suppose a great monarch to be seated in a palace, with many gates leading to it, and through whichever you enter you see the King, and can obtain admission to his presence,—your business is with the Prince, and not with those at his gate.' The Shah again asked the Maulana which, in his opinion, was the best of all faiths. The best of every faith followed the best faith, replied the Maulana.[459] This syncretistic trend found its culmination in Akbar's conviction that 'there are wise men to be found in all religions'. The Truth, he would say, is an inhabitant of every place. Consequently, 'how could it be right to consider it as confined to one religion or creed, and that, one which had only recently made its appearance and had not as yet endured a thousand years?' The orthodox mulla Badauni, upset by the observation that Islam was not even a thousand years old, said indignantly that the Emperor picked and chose his beliefs from 'any one except a Muslim'.[460]

The Portuguese, who captured Goa by a series of raids in and after 1510, were certainly a lot less tolerant of non-Christians than the Muslim powers of Hindustan and the Deccan were by now of other faiths. The Archbishop of Goa forbade Hindus, Muslims, Jews, and Armenians open performance of their religious ceremonies, such as cremation, marriage, and 'other superstitions and devilish institutions' so as to 'avoid all occasions of dislike that might be given to Christians'. By contrast, as the Portuguese traveller Van Linschoten saw, the Moors and Jews were free in the exercise of their religion wherever they lived among 'Indians', 'wherein they use all ceremonies according to their Law: but in the places where the *Portugals* inhabite and gouerne, it is not permitted vnto them to vse them openly, neither to any *Indian ...*'

But Indian society, as irresistible for the Portuguese Christians as for the Khurasani Muslims, exacted its revenge: Van Linschoten found the converted native Christians of Goa indistinguishable from the other heathens, for 'they can hardly leaue their Heathenish superstitions.'[461]

Nothing could stand in sharper contrast to the intolerant bigotry seen by Van Linschoten in Portuguese Goa than the freedom of worship that prevailed at the time throughout Mughal India. In Akbar's capital, the Ibadat Khana accommodated free debates between learned men of every belief on Friday nights. Sufis, ulama, Sunnis, Shias, Brahmans, Jains, Buddhists, Christians, Jews, Zoroastrians, and even the materialist followers of Charvak's atheistic creed gathered together in the royal assembly, and the arguments and counter-arguments were long and heated. Remembering his father with pride, Jahangir wrote how the professors of every faith found room in the broad expanse of his father's dominion. This was different, as he observed, from the practice in other realms: 'for in Persia there is room for Shias only, and in Turkey, India, and Turan there is room for Sunnis only'.[462]

The fact that the Shias and Sunnis were accommodated along with members of every other faith made the Mughal empire a uniquely tolerant realm at a time when Christian Europe was torn by wars of religion and the contending Catholic and Protestant persecutions and burnings. This intellectual trend towards synthesis led Prince Dara Shikoh to systematically trace the parallels between the mysticism of the Vedantic Pandits of India and 'the same doctrine which is held by the sect of Soufys and the greater part of the learned men of Persia at the present day'.[463] Drawing upon the Sanskrit Upanishads, the *Mystic Rose Garden* (*Gulshan Raz*), and other Sufi texts from Persia, Akbar's great-grandson composed the aptly named *Mingling of the Two Oceans* (*Majma-ul-Bahrain*), in which the Prince demonstrated that the doctrines of the Hindus of antiquity and the Sufis of the Islamic world were the very same as regards the godhead. The Supreme Being was the life-giving principle of which human beings and all other living beings were so many parts, apparently differentiated but not really so.

Evolving a Plural Identity

The Sufis, as they moved into India, encountered everywhere the wandering Yogis of Gorakhnath, a ubiquitous sect in thirteenth and fourteenth century India. Conversions from amongst them led to the formation of the Muslim weaver caste in which the Julaha named Kabir was born. The Sufis were ambivalent about the Yogis (as was Kabir), but they translated a thirteenth century Yoga text named *Amrita Kunda* (*The Water of Eternal Life*) into several Arabic and Persian versions.[464] This and other texts circulated among the Sufis over the next four or five centuries as esoteric manuals for transmitting Yogic techniques. Saiyid Sultan's *Jnana Pradip* and Ali Raja's *Jnana Sagar*, Bengali texts of the seventeenth and eighteenth centuries respectively, were written under the Indian notion that the Yogic–Tantrik exercises for breath control and semen retention would ensure eternal life for the proper practitioner.[465] The Bauls of rural Bengal, drawn from both Muslims and Hindus, shared the same notion. The best known among them was a long-lived Muslim fakir named Lalan (1774–1890). He was an outcast Hindu Kayastha adopted by a band of devoted Julahas. Lalan and other Bauls linked their notions of life and love to the materialism of the ancient 'Char-baks', the popular Sufism of the Marfati fakirs, and the secret Sahajiya Vaishnavism of the medieval Bengali Hindus.[466] At the same time, folk idolatry began to cut across the communal divide: so much so that a fictitious Muslim princess of Delhi refused to accept the Muslim saint of the water, Pir Badar, until he appeared to her as Rama and Krishna.[467]

At the higher level of religious thought, however, it was recognized from the time of Al Biruni onwards that Vedantic Hinduism rejected idols and was as free as Islam of worshipping 'anything but God alone'.[468] Baba Farid of Ajodhan, Kabir of the weavers, and following them the Sikh Guru Nanak, all sought to convince Hindus and Muslims that 'the only essential parts of their respective creeds, were common to both'.[469] A published interview of the Punjabi Hindu Guru Baba Lal by Prince Dara Shikoh in 1649 attests to the mingling of Vedantic and Sufi notions. The Prince asked the Guru: 'How do the *Paramatma* (supreme soul) and *Jivatma* (living soul) differ?' The Guru replied: 'They do not differ, and pleasure and pain ascribable to the latter, arises from its imprisonment in the body—the water of the Ganges is the same whether it run in the river's bed or be shut up in a decanter.' 'What difference should that occasion?', asked the Prince. The Guru replied: 'Great—a drop of wine added to the water in the decanter will impart its flavour to the whole, but it would be lost in the river. The *Paramatma*, therefore, is beyond accident, but the *Jivatma* is afflicted by sense and passion.' When the Prince asked, 'which is the best religion', the Guru quoted a Persian verse from Hafiz which declared that the object of all religions was alike, and that all men sought their beloved. As all the world is love's dwelling, why talk of a mosque or a church?[470]

Baba Farid, as quoted in the *Guru Granth Sahib* of the Sikhs, is said to have declared:

The Lord dwells in every heart
I'm not Hindu, nor am I Turk.[471]

Whether the author of the verse is indeed Shaikh Farid Ganj-i-Shakar of the thirteenth century is not certain, but the verse marks a turning point in the medieval tradition. From this point, one may trace the growth of an identity transcending the divide between Hindu and Muslim. This idea did not strive, at the time, towards a national Indian identity. Rather, it pointed in the direction of an all-embracing concept of humanity and indeed of all forms of life. Characteristic of the civilization of the subcontinent, the idea culminated in the life and legend of the fifteenth century saint Kabir. The legend of Kabir, which expressed the spirit of a whole civilization, is in fact more important than his life, the details of which are not certain.

The medieval Bhakti tradition traces itself back to Ramanand and represents Kabir as one of his twelve disciples. The Brahman Guru and the Muslim Julaha are linked together in this tradition by the involuntary transmission of the mantra 'Ram'. The Guru, according to the *Dabistan-i-Mazalib*, stumbled over the weaver who had deliberately laid himself down on his path before daybreak. The former involuntarily cried out, 'Ram, Ram!'[472]

We have it on the authority of the *Bhaktamal* of Nabhaji (*c*.1600) that Kabir refused to acknowledge caste distinctions and gave instruction impartially to Hindus and Turks alike.[473] The *Bijak*, which contains his verses in the archaic form, exhibits an iconoclastic tendency: the Veda and the Quran are both declared 'worthless', for 'neither Hindu nor Turk ever grasped that mystery'.[474]

The Jogi cries:
'Gorakh, Gorakh!'
The Hindu utters
the name of Ram,
The Mussalman repeats
'God is One!'
But the Lord of Kabir
pervades all.[475]

Abul Fazl informs us: 'He was revered by both Hindus and Muhammadens for his catholicity of doctrine and the illumination of his mind, and when he died the Brahmans wanted to burn his body and the Muhammadens to bury it.'[476] The author of the *Dabistan*, recounting the legend in greater detail, introduces a fakir to resolve the dispute. 'Kabir', the fakir is said to have told the contenders, 'was a holy man, independent of both religions; but having during his life satisfied you, he will also after death meet with your approbation.' They then opened the door on his instruction, and did not find Kabir's body.[477] In the still later version of the legend recorded by H.H. Wilson, the resurrected saint himself appeared among his contentious disciples and asked them to look under the cloth covering his mortal remains. They did so, and found nothing but a heap of flowers, one half of which was burnt, and the other buried.'[478]

Kabir was one of the few persons who transcended the distinction between Hindu and Muslim and succeeded in projecting an Indian identity embracing all of life and humanity. He was not, however, the only one. Baba Farid of myth had preceded Kabir of the legend in the medieval tradition. In judging the psychical impact of such heavily mythicized persons upon a civilization, it is the growth of the legend that counts, not the factual biographical details. Just a few persons were so transformed in legend. The legendary figure then emerged as neither Hindu nor Muslim. Kabir was one such figure, but we do encounter one or two after Kabir.

Emperor Akbar was one person whose figure even in his own lifetime underwent such mythicization. Not only his subjects, but foreigners too, found themselves asking the questions whether he was a Hindu or a Muslim. 'It is uncertaine', wrote Purchas, 'what Religion hee is of, some affirming him to bee a *Moore*, some a *Gentile*, some a *Christian*, some a fourth Sect, and of none of the former.' It was rumoured that he had kept thirty children under observation, allowing neither nurse nor anyone else to teach them any religion. The object of this was that he would attach himself to the religion which the children should prefer, this being detected by means of the language the infants should speak. However, 'as they spake no certain Language, so is not he settled in any certain Religion'.[479]

Bulhe Shah of Qasur (1680–1758) declared, echoing the mythologized Baba Farid of Ajodhan, that he was neither a Hindu nor a Turk.[480] Shiva Narayan, a Rajput Guru of village Chandawan near

Ghazipur during the reign of Muhammad Shah, admitted proselytes from both Hindus and Muslims, but professed a unitarianism which paid no regard to the rites of either faith.[481] His contemporary, Majnun Nanak Shahi of Delhi, is described by a Muslim visitor from Hyderabad during the occupation of Nadir Shah as a man whose 'emaciated frame befits his name'. Dargah Quli Khan, who was on a visit to Delhi, saw a large number of Hindus and Muslims calling on him with great respect and reverence. 'Wealthy Hindus make rich offerings to him and in their false belief regard him as the Nanak of this age.'[482] None of these fakirs and gurus could perhaps be pronounced to have entirely transcended their identity as either Hindu or Muslim; yet Kabir earlier and Lalan later on did transcend both identities.

At the same time, remnants of the ancient materialists (Charvakas or Nastikas) were still to be encountered here and there, as for instance, the sect of Shunyabadis patronized by Dayaram, the Raja of Hatras, at the beginning of the nineteenth century. 'Whatever I behold is vacuity', believed these native Nihilists. On this view there is 'no difference between this and that—look into yourself and not into another, for in yourself that other will be found—there is no other but myself, and I talk of another from ignorance'. Accordingly, Bakhtawar, a disciple of Dayaram, declared in a work entitled *The Essence of Emptiness* (*Shunyasar*):[483]

> Hindus and Musselmans are of the same nature, two leaves of one tree— these call their teachers *Mullas*, those term them *Pandits*; two pitchers of one clay: one performs *Numaz*, the other offers *Puja*: where is the difference? I know of no dissimilarity—they are both followers of the doctrine of Duality—they have the same bone, the same flesh, the same blood and the same marrow. One cuts off the foreskin, the other puts on a sacrificial thread. Ask them the difference, enquire the importance of these distinctions, and they will quarrel with you: dispute not, but know them to be both the same, avoid all idle wrangling and strife, and adhere to the truth, the doctrine of Dayaram.

This was an uncompromising search for unity in variety. The *sants*, both theistic and atheistic, represented a long-term and persistent pursuit characterizing the civilization of the subcontinent. Amidst all the differentiated forms of existence, the advocates of the doctrine of vacuity saw the emptiness (*shunya*), while the Sufis and the Bhaktas saw the one pervading all. What all these groups had in common was an inward-looking disposition, a quietist non-violent attitude, and indifference to the rituals of Brahmanism and Islam in their quest for truth:

Hari dwells in the East, they say
  And Allah resides in the west
Search for Him in your heart, in the heart of your heart
    There he dwells, Rahim–Ram![484]

Behind this anguished search lay an all-pervasive experience of separation. A civilization so ridden by the touch complex was riven as a matter of course by innumerable distinctions in inter-dining. The pain inherent in this was virtually unavoidable in a hot country, for any offer of water for drinking would immediately bring the distinction into play. The points at which these distinctions were cast aside revealed a persistent underlying quest for a common human identity. Indeed, these points in time and space were invested with a special symbolic significance. The open kitchen of the Sufi hospice (*khanqah*) stood in contrast to the Hindu prohibition of inter-dining between different castes. The fact that a share was fixed in the free food (*langar*) at the shrine of Shaikh Muinuddin Chishti for the Bairagis and the general body of Hindus represented a symbolic cancellation of the distinction in a place recognized by both Hindus and Muslims as one of special sanctity.[485] The distribution of free food (*prasad*) at the temple of Jagannath again spread wide the notion that 'at this place all castes of Hindus eat together'.[486] A Persian chronicle of the eighteenth century reported:

> It is said that when the Hindus reach Parsutam, where Jagannath is, in order to worship Jagannath, first they shave their heads like Musalmans, and at the first door of the house of Shaikh Kabir ... they eat and drink his food and water, which is called in the language of the country, *tarani*. After having done so, they proceed to worship their God Jagannath. At Parsutam, Hindus unlike their practice elsewhere, eat together with Musalmans and other races. And all sorts of cooked food sell in the *bazar*, and Hindus and Muslims eat together and drink together.[487]

It is difficult to say how much of this was reality and how much wishful thinking. There is no doubt, however, that the innumerable distinctions of Indian society produced pain in every individual and fostered an inchoate desire to overcome the separation wherever symbolic acts permitted this. Acceptance of the distinctions and a yearning to meet across the divide were both part of the psychic make-up of Indian civilization. So riven a culture could not fail to produce an anguished psyche. It may not be an easy matter to track the mentality behind so complex and so tortured a civilization, but however elusive, observers from outside were convinced that there was such a thing as the soul of India. While delineating 'this huge Giantly Body of the Mogol Empire', Purchas remarked at the same time that the 'Soule or Religion thereof is more inuisible'.[488]

The Common Heart of Hindustan

A constant preoccupation with sex, love, and death; a heavy compound of eroticism and religion which became keener and sharper as it evolved; sorrow—sorrow at the transience of all existence and the suffering caused by partings in love (*viraha*); a search for life and love for ever in the hereafter: these were the distinguishing features of the culture of India as it evolved in the middle ages under the impact of the development of vernacular literature and the Muslim presence. While some of these features went back to antiquity, the other traits were specific to the mentality evolving out of the interaction between India and Islam.

'Death,' noted Megasthenes as early as the third century BC,[489] 'is with them a very frequent subject of discourse.' All existence, he was told, was 'a dream-like illusion', and death, 'a birth into a real and happy life for the votaries of philosophy'. The wise woman of the Upanishads, Maitreyi, asked her sage husband, 'Of what use to me are things which will not make me immortal' (*yenāham nāmritā syām, tenāham kim kuryām*)? This, in a way the central question of Indian civilization, was linked to the concern for life, the doctrine of non-violence, and the vegetarian diet advocated in the early Jain text *Archaranga Sutra*: 'For nothing is inaccessible to death, and all beings are fond of themselves, they love pleasure and hate pain, they shun destruction and cling to life. They long to live. To all things life is dear.'[490] Of the major civilizations of the world, India alone was a predominantly vegetarian one. No Indian religion escaped the influence of the doctrine of non-violence. Guru Nanak of the Sikhs preached the liberation of the spirit from the delusive deceits of Maya and its purification by acts of clemency and self-denial:

> Saints, Prophets, and Seers have all passed in death,
> Nanak, destroy not life for the preservation of the body.[491]

The Sufi saints and poets entertained remarkably similar feelings against the killing of living things. Malik Muhammad Jayasi, the same poet who declared through the mouth of the disappointed Sultan Alauddin that 'the world is a delusion' (*pirthimee jhuthee*), described

the Emperor's banquet with revulsion: 'Goats and sheep both large
and small were seized and brought in, so many of them as were fat ...
When the knife was laid to their throat the blood dripped like tears.
[They said] "why do you nourish your own body feeding on the flesh
of others?"'[492] Akbar's injunction against the killing of animals, while
not as extensive as Ashoka's, reflected the same feeling, and was partly
designed 'to please the Hindus'.[493] Fryer, on his visit to Bombay, noted
that not just the Hindus, but the Muslims too, were more dependent
on a vegetarian diet than the Europeans;[494] and Bernier, speaking of the
temperance of the Indians and the simple nature of their diet in
connection with the food consumption of the predominantly Muslim
cavalry of the Mughals, calculated that less than a tenth of the one
hundred thousand troopers ate animal food, most of them being satisfied
'with their kichery, a mess of rice and other vegetables, over which,
when cooked, they pour boiled butter'.[495]

For the Sufi poet Jayasi, the fish caught from the lake for Sultan
Alauddin's banquet were part of the Indian allegory of life in the world:
a great illusion (maya). The mind, like the fish, falls into the net and
cannot avoid sorrow. 'All have been nourished only to be slain: what
deliverance is there for those who have been thrown into this lake?'[496]
While Islam in its initial phase was a dynamic social creed, it subsequently acquired a mystical dimension. The development of Sufism in
Iran and India fitted in very well with the other-worldly perspective of
the older culture of the subcontinent. 'The soul is one thing, matter
another—that is the quintessence of truth,' a Jain monk had declared in
the fourth century.[497] The Sufi poet of the seventeenth century said
something rather similar: 'He joineth the body and the spirit: when
He slays them he makes two divisions. The body, weeping, falls to
earth: the spirit departs to the universe.'[498] Baba Farid, as represented in
the *Guru Granth* of the Sikhs, reacts thus to the constant presence of
death in the midst of life:

> Farid, revile not dust:
>   there is nothing like it—
> When we are alive, it's under our feet,
>   when we are dead, it's over our head;[499]

The epitaph on the grave of a Bahmani sultan of the Deccan who
died in 1375 read: 'All is vanity.'[500] The historian Firishta, who recorded
this, commented elsewhere in his chronicle: 'Alas! there is no stability
in fortune; for endless is the circle of her revolution. Expect not thou to

be free from the encroachments of time. For there is quarter to no one from his cruel sword.'[501] The petty jeweller Banarsidas, in a less exalted station of life, witnessed a death, a childbirth, and a marriage, all on the same day, and drew the moral that the world was a mockery.[502] His father's death was a hard blow:

> Kharagsen has gone to heaven
> So men spread the word
> Whither he went who knows
> These were mere words.
> Banarsi grieved for days
> His eyes full of tears
> Steeling himself he thought,
> 'No one lives for ever.'[503]

This realization, that no one survives in the world beyond a certain time (*jiyau no jaga main koi*), was an old motif of Indian civilization, reminiscent of the grieving mother who asked the Buddha to revive her dead child. She, too, realized her error: the Buddha asked her to get a handful of mustard from a family in which no one had died. In vain she went from house to house, until she realized the inevitability of death and sorrow, and became a nun.[504] This realization, and the search for life ever after, acquired a new dimension in the medieval *tasawwuf—* Bhakti tradition. The *Guru Granth Sahib* of the Sikhs contains the following conversation across the generations. Baba Farid, Guru Nanak, and Guru Ramdas speak to one another over death's barrier. Baba Farid says:

> My body is oven hot
> my bones burn like firewood:
> If my feet fail me, I'll walk on my head
> to meet my Beloved.

Guru Nanak replies across two centuries:

> Don't heat your body oven-hot,
> burn not your body like firewood,
> What harm have your head and feet done?
> Rather behold the Beloved within your soul!

Then Guru Ramdas speaks four generations later:

> I keep searching for my spouse
> but my Spouse is within me:
> *Nanak*, the Unknowable can't be seen
> but the Guru can make him seen.[505]

The conceptualization of God as the lover (*sajan*) is a relatively new construction in the age-old immortality. It may be traced back on the one hand to the Tamil poetry of the Alvars, and on the other to the Persian poetry of the Sufis. The erotic spiritualism accompanying the rise of vernacular literature and the coming of Islam marked a striking transformation in the conceptualization of love in Indian culture. The sharp theoretical distinction between libido (*kama*) and love (*prema*) which we encounter in the age of Sri Chaitanya, and the particular emphasis on the sufferings of love (*viraha*) in the medieval vernacular literature, represented important departures from Sanskrit poetics and the Brahmanical definition of the householder's aims in life. Together, these departures constituted a milestone in the evolution of Indian civilization, marking out the emotional world of the medieval epoch from the mental universe of antiquity in several important respects. A new Indian emotional identity was being forged as the interaction deepened between Jambudvipa and Islam.

Antiquity, too, had celebrated love, but in a visibly different way. In Sufi and Vaishnava love poetry, the keynote was the sublimation of loss. This was not so in Sanskrit literature, in which the convention was a happy ending however much the hero (*nayaka*) and the heroine (*nayika*) might suffer before their final union. Sanskrit poetics ruled out the unhappy ending to a play, and drama was necessarily comedy. The occasional break-away from this pattern, especially in old Prakrit literature which drew upon the folk experience, reveals to us sexual rupture and heartbreak, an ending far removed from the medieval conception of attaining salvation through suffering:

> Last night with scorn the lady gave the wanderer
>   straw for his bed
> This morning she gathers it together,
>   weeping.[506]

This is not *viraha*, which has in it an element of anticipation. Fulfilment of desire or the heartrending loss of a happiness already enjoyed are the alternate endings of eros (*kama*) conceived in antiquity. *Viraha* would of course occur in this erotic conception, but as a subordinate phase, anterior to the happy union, and an expected accompaniment of the prolonged and torrential rains.[507] In Vaishnava poetry, on the contrary, as early as the phase of the Alvars of Tamil country, *viraha* is no longer subordinate, it is given a central place and invested with a spiritual value. Andal, the ninth century Tamil poetess, declared: 'In the sole desire to unite with Him my breasts grew large and jumped with joy. [Now] they make my life melt away, and cause such agony.'[508] Such capacity for suffering had its reward in legend: she was absorbed in her Lord's image and to this day she remains part of it in the temple of Ranganatha at Srirangam.

The eroticism of this Viraha–Bhakti is not quite concealed by the spiritual gloss put upon it. The same physicality is unmistakable in the last Sanskrit Bhakti poem of pre-Islamic India. The *Gita Govinda* of Jayadeva, a twelfth century love poem which is still sung as part of the evening service at the temple of Jagannath, is explicit: 'She locks him in her arms, presses her breasts down upon him, digs her nails in his flesh, sinks her teeth in his lips, hits him hard with her hips, makes him senseless by drinking the nectar of his mouth, yet he is pleased, so strange are the ways of Kama.'[509] He is Krishna and she is Radha, but however divine this erotic sport, the text is specific in the mention of *kama*. Later on, the term *prema* is introduced as a gloss upon *kama* in the medieval Sanskrit commentary of the devotee Chaitanya Das upon Jayadeva's 'sacred' text.

The word *prema*, Sanskrit in origin, had been used earlier by the classical poets in the secular sense of love between man and woman with no religious connotation.[510] At the centre of the erotic conception of antiquity lay *kama*, recognized by the lawgivers as one of the four aims of life (*purushartha*): Dharma (the merit to be acquired by performance of the rites enjoined by the sacred law); Artha (wealth, power); Kama (pleasure, specifically erotic pleasure); and Moksha (liberation of the soul from bondage).[511] To these, the medieval Vaishnava theoreticians added a fifth aim of life, superior to all the other aims of man: *prema* (love), or *bhakti* (devotion). Thus the *Bhaktamal*: 'The fifth aim of man is love of Krishna' (*Pancham purushartha Krishna prem prayojan*); and *Chaitanya Charitamrita*: 'Devotion to God is the ultimate aim of man' (*Bhagavane bhakti param purushartha hay*).[512]

The sages of antiquity who wrote upon the third aim of the householder would argue on occasion that it was his ultimate aim, because Kama was the end product of both Dharma and Artha (*kamah phala-bhutash-cha dharmarthayoh—Kama Sutra* of Vatsyayana). Erotic conception had not split sex and love, nor had it represented *prema* as the sublimation of *kama*. On the contrary, love was conceived as an integral part of eros.[513] The components of erotic conception emerged more distinctly after the coming of Islam. It is not that the poets abandoned erotic desire as a theme of their composition: the heavy physicality of the *viraha* of their heroines shows a strong continuity with the past.[514] However, the poets were now aware of the conceptual distinction drawn between Kama and Prema by the Vaishnava theorists. Chandidas, foremost of the Vaishnava poets of Bengal and the legendary lover of the washerwoman Rami, is supposed to have declared: 'Love (*prem*) of the washerwoman, who is the very image of the young girl, her beauty untouched by any desire (*kam*), is pure gold.'[515] The theory on which this distinction is based was spelt out by the biographer of Sri Chaitanya in the form of an often quoted formula:

> The desire to please one's own senses is Kama
> The desire to please Krishna's senses is Prema.[516]

The emergence of Radha, who exemplified this ultimate devotion to Krishna, was an event of momentous importance. As Krishna's illicit lover, but his true and divine consort, she appeared in late antiquity, clothed in the explicit eroticism of Sanskrit poetry by the unknown author of the *Brahma-Vaivarta Purana* and by Jayadeva.[517] Between the departure of Jayadeva (twelfth century) and the appearance of Sri Chaitanya (1485–1527), a critical development took place in the delineation of her character: her desire to please Krishna's senses now predominated over her desire to please her own.

Sri Chaitanya's mission stimulated the growth of a whole cycle of legends around this illicit affair of the heart. Her hundred year pining (*viraha*) for him after he left Vrindaban for Mathura and her union with him in spirit (*bhava sammilana*) which finally substituted her desire to see him in the flesh were the principal episodes in the delineation of love by the medieval Vaishnava poets. The fact that she was his uncle's wife and would never be permitted to unite with him in the world produced a distinction within the concept of love (*prema*) itself: love of one's own spouse (*svakiya prema*) and love of another man's spouse (*parakiya prema*). Theoretical disputes between '*svakiya*' and '*parakiya*' resulted in the triumph of the Parakiya doctrine in Bengal, registered by a decree of the Mughal Governor of the *suba*.[518] In the meanwhile, there was subtle shift from the physical to the emotional component of *viraha*, and from the erotic to the spiritual constituent of Bhakti, though all the elements remained important in poetry.

These developments were internal to Hinduism, but the parallel spread of the Sufi notion of Ishq led to a growing emotional interaction between Islam and Hinduism. The imaginary dialogue between Baba

Farid and Guru Nanak across two centuries which we find in the *Guru Granth Sahib* points to a subtle Muslim influence. The parallel is strong, too, between the Sufi *nafs* (the soul as a longing woman) and the Hindu *virahini*, and it points to the possibility of mutual reinforcement of similar ideas. The concept of the loving woman/soul who is separated from the spouse/God was common to both religions. *Nafs* in Arabia originally meant the base instinct; its transformation in Indian Sufism as the parted wife or mistress reflected the influence of a new environment.[519]

All the same, the Sufi idea of love was Arabian and Persian in its origin and it had already taken firm shape when it was brought to India. The love stories which the Sufi saint Sharafuddin Ibn Yahya Maneri constantly referred to in *The Hundred Letters* (1346-7) were the West Asian stories relating to Laila and Majnun, and Yusuf and Zulaikha.[520] It is the same West Asian ideas which flowed through his pen when he wrote to the magistrate: 'Hence it is that spiritual guides have said that, although the verses sung before them might smack of the tavern, yet when they hear the word *union*, they think of the vision of God, just as the word *separation* connotes a veil between them and the Lord and the word *eyes*, the glance of the Lord.'[521] Yet his treatment of the story of Zulaikha's illicit passion for her servant Yusuf runs parallel to the story of Radha's unlawful love for Krishna, her shame and her suffering. He speaks of 'lovers who tread the path of reprobation', and of 'seekers who suffer for their unconventional behaviour', and then cites a Persian verse:

> We are not fellow travellers! Take your own road and go!
> May your way be full of peace and ours full of shame![522]

The first Muslim poetical treatment of *viraha* which we encounter in an Indian language indicates the facility with which this emotional construct was employed by the converted members of the new faith. Abdur Rahman's Prakrit poem *Sandesh Rasak* is the lament of a wife separated from her husband. An unmistakable Indian physicality pervades the lament, mixed with heartfelt pain:

> Then not even my necklace barred us
>   as we coupled in close embrace,
> Mountain and ocean have since distanced us
>   and fort and forest are bars in place.[523]

This was written on the eve of the Turkish occupation of Delhi, in Punjab under the rule of the Sultans of Ghazni and Ghor. In the centuries that followed, as the Muslim component of Indian culture gained greater influence, there was a shift from the erotic physicality of this *viraha* to spiritual and emotional longing for one's beloved. This shift of emphasis is perceptible in Jayasi's *Padmavati* (1540). The images of the Sufi poet are altogether more ascetic: The ochre-robed Yogini, for instance, wandering in search of her lost lover;[524] and the celebrated last prayer of Padmini and Nagmoti as they ascend their husband Rana Ratansen's funeral pyre. They circle seven times around the flames, as they did on the happier occasion of the marriage ceremony, and the two wives pray together:

> There was one kind of ring made at our bridal:
> now there is another when we go on to accompany you.
> In life, our beloved, you caressed us: in death,
> lord, let your embrace not be dissolved. That knot
> which you, our lover tied, let it never be unfastened
> from beginning to end. What is this world in which
> there is no reality? We and you, lord, will be together
> in both worlds.[525]

In no other culture would grief and longing express itself precisely in these words. Yet, in the three and a half centuries gone since Abdur Rahman wrote the sensuous lament of the separated wife, the Sufi notion of *ishq* has mingled with the Hindu notions of *māyā* and *sati*, and has effectively transformed that erotic expression of grief.

Muslim mysticism in India drew upon folk-tales of parted love—the tale of Susui and Punhun in Sind and Hir and Ranjha in Punjab—and invested these tales with a spiritual meaning. The Vaishnava movement in turn classified the emotion of Bhakti into five distinct sentiments (*rasa*)—quiet contemplation (*shanta*), willing servitude (*dasya*), friendship for the deity (*sakhya*), maternal affection for the divine child (*vatsalya*), and love of one's divine spouse (*madhurya*)[526]—and gave the highest place to the fifth sentiment, i.e. passionate love, with *viraha* at its core.

In both *tasawwuf* and Bhakti, human love was the prelude to divine love, separation and longing being seen as the essential means for the transformation of the profane into the sacred. Shaikh Piyara of Bengal, 'a man distracted with the grief of longing after God',[527] had in his youth conceived an erotic passion for an unattainable Hindu woman.

It is related that when he first came to Bandanawaz Gisudaraz's hospice in Delhi, the old man asked him: 'Dervish, have you ever been in love?' The hesitant initiate replied, 'I have come to you to learn about love; what could I know about it?' The Shaikh prodded him gently, 'My object is to examine your condition and understand your temperament and aptitude. If any incident has occurred, speak out and do not conceal it.' Reassured by this, the younger man confessed, 'Once I saw a Hindu woman. I could think of no means of (satisfying myself with) looking at her, so I put on the sacred thread, dressed in a *dhoti*, and went to the temple where she used to go for worship.' The saint embraced the initiate and told him, 'You are a man of great courage; where could I find one like you to guide on the path to God. What you have done is an act of lofty courage. People love their religion more than anything else, but you have sacrificed it for the sake of love. Come, I shall now teach you the way of real love.'[528] Shaikh Piyara in turn became the Pir of Shaikh Muhammad Maladah, a lover and a devotee, who is reported to have been tormented with longing and brought to the verge of death when he heard a song of separation from the beloved. The story goes that no sooner did the Sama performers switch to a song of union with the beloved than he was observed to have revived to a new life.

With the arrival of Kabir, *viraha*, a spiritual and emotional longing shorn of its original eroticism, becomes the keynote of medieval Indian poetry; a note infinitely sad from the beginning to the end. His favourite image, the young *virahin* wife, condemned to waiting all her life before she can hope to set her eyes on her husband, focuses upon suffering as the one means by which the wife–soul would finally reach the divine spouse ever present within:

> Clad in motley array, I circled the sacred Fire,
> > the knot was tied, true to my father's pledge:
> Without a Bridegroom, I entered wedlock—
> > on the marriage-square I stood as a widow
> > > by my lord's side.
> My husband's face, I've never seen,
> > yet people urge me to be a perfect wife.
> Says Kabir, I'll raise a pyre and I'll die on it:
> > clinging to my Spouse, I'll cross over,
> > > playing the trumpet of Victory![529]

In the following century, the pain of rupture found expression through the life, legend, and verse of Mira Bai, the Hindu princess of Mewar, and Habbah Khatun, the Muslim queen of Kashmir. The erotic element, refined but not entirely pushed out of sight, runs through their songs: with Mira a boldly extramarital (*parakiya*) love directed at her deity Ranchhor, as opposed to her resentful husband, the Rana, and in Habbah Khatun's case a more legitimate passion directed apparently at her banished husband, the last independent ruler of Kashmir overthrown by Emperor Akbar, but passing equally well for the soul burning with the desire of union with God.

Legend has it that Mira drank unharmed from a cup of poison sent by the Rana and went off to Dwarka. When the Rana's messengers came to fetch her, she entered the temple for one last vision of her true Lord. 'I have abandoned my love, my possessions, my principality, my husband. Mira, thy servant, comes to thee for refuge, oh, take her wholly to thee.'[530] Upon this the image parted to receive her, and she disappeared within. Habbah Khatun's grief as the childless wife and the deserted queen waiting in vain for the return of her banished husband was recorded in songs still sung by the folk of Kashmir:

> He glanced at me through my door—
> Who told him where I lived?
> Why has he left me in such anguish?
> I, hapless one, am filled with longing for him.[531]

It is apparent that the same sentiments run through the poetry of both the communities, revealing a collective psychic-emotional structure upholding the whole culture. What was the objective environment that could foster the articulation of such a psyche? The historian of the medieval mentality would find it instructive to explore a curious love affair related by Badauni. Badauni obtained the details from a man deeply implicated in the affair. This man was the lover's brother, a supportive sibling, who later recalled the sad affair in Persian verse and allowed Badauni to quote from it. The details are as follows.[532]

On the eve of Akbar's departure from Agra to invest the fort of Ranthambhor (1598), a Saiyid named Musa came from Kalpi to do homage to the emperor. There was a fair young woman in town named Mohini, wife of a Hindu goldsmith, whose glance smote Saiyid Musa's heart. The lady reciprocated her Muslim lover's sentiments, and when the expedition set out for Ranthambhor, Musa contrived to stay back. He took a house inside the fort in order to be near his beloved on the banks of the river Jumna. The lovers contented themselves with a glance now and then from afar, till one night Musa, at a hint from Mohini, threw a rope over the roof of her house, and climbed into her room.

They spent the night together in what the chronicler describes as 'chaste affection', citing the poem of the lover's brother Saiyid Shahi as evidence:

However much the desire of the heart was boiling,
Modesty made a proclamation: Be silent:
Before his eyes the water of life,
But not for a moment the power to drink it.
Their hearts from extreme of thirstiness fevered,
But their lips were sealed through modesty.
One place of retirement, and two persons in love,
Their hearts united, their bodies apart
They remained two heart-inflaming wounded ones,
In the game of 'united yet apart' till morning.[533]

In his interesting commentary on the notions that guided the lovers, Saiyid Shahi set 'desire' and 'love' in contradistinction. This was a medieval distinction, contrasting sharply with the theme of the Sanskrit poem *Chaura Panchashika* (eleventh to twelfth centuries) by Bilhana which dealt with the love of a daring housebreaker and a princess taken by him in her own house. Bilhana's stanzas dwell boldly on the thief's remembrance of sensuous nights:

Even today I can see her, her slender arms encircling my neck,
    my breast held tight against her two breasts
her playful eyes half-closed in ecstasy,
    her dear face drinking mine in a kiss.[534]

A contradistinction between *kama* and *prema* would have made no sense to the poet Bilhana. For Saiyid Shahi, however, the distinction between love and desire was based on the life experience of his unfortunate brother:

This is true love in my opinion
which has driven out of the heart all thought of desire.

Love, to him, was 'the friend of the sorrowful', a notion distinguishing the austere night of the Saiyid and the goldsmith's wife from the sensual nights of the princess and the thief. Such a notion could not, of course, be wholly lived up to in real life, and as dawn broke, Mohini shook Musa awake: 'Rise that we may show a care for ourselves ... While it is not yet known, we may steal away before morning.' The desperate pair climbed down and hid themselves in a friend's house for three days, while a hue and cry in town climaxed with Mohini's relatives surrounding Musa's house and bringing up claims and litigation against him and his brother. Concerned for her lover's safety, the lady returned home, with a concocted tale of having been whisked away by a god of bewitching beauty to some heavenly town. 'The silly Hindus', says Badauni, 'believed this beautiful deception', but the fact that the woman's relatives put her in chains belies this judgement. Musa showed every sign of frenzied grief and madness, and alarmed by the suspicions this generated, Mohini sent him a message that he should go away from Agra, and leave behind a confidential friend through whom she could keep in touch with him. Musa, responding to this entreaty, took leave of her (not explained how), and set off to Ranthambhor to pay his respects to the emperor.

The lovers did not quite appreciate the full strength of the political and social forces ranged against their affair. Akbar had forbidden intermarriages because they provoked religious strife. 'If a Hindu woman fall in love with a Muslim and changed her religion, she should be taken from him by force and given back to her family'; 'but so should a Musalman woman, who had fallen in love with a Hindu, be prevented from joining Hinduism'.[535] After a while Mohini fled from home to join her lover, but she was apprehended by the police magistrate on the way and handed over to her relatives. Saiyid Musa returned with the victorious imperial army to town, but however much he strove he was unable to catch a glimpse of his beloved Mohini who was being closely guarded by her kinsmen. Even so, the young woman broke out of her confinement in one last desperate flight to join her lover, but her horse was stuck in the mud by the river and her kinsmen caught up with her with the help of the citizens of Agra who were interested spectators of the girl's despair. She sent a message to him to the effect that she had made every effort, but fate had put it out of her power to join him. The heartbroken lover shut himself up in his house within the fort of Agra and his soul went forth in flight, while with his mouth he uttered thrice these last words:

> From the Beloved my heart has found a thousand lives
> A friend better than that it is impossible to find.

They bore his bier under the window of the lady who was kept a prisoner with a chain round her feet. She uttered a cry, and threw herself just as she was from the roof, and the chain broke from her foot. 'Like a mad person, with arms and feet naked she ran to the resting place of that traveller, who never tasted the joy of union ... Then making the pronouncement of the name of Sayyid Musa the practice of her lips and the amulet of her life, in the presence of the pious Mir Sayyid Jalal, who was the religious leader of the day, she recited the confession of Islam, and cast herself on the dust of her pure lover, and surrendered her soul to her beloved.' In remembrance of this sad end, the brother of the dead man wrote:

> Those two spiritual companions
> Went away from this transitory world
> From the pain and grief of separation they were freed,
> Concealed from all they sat together,
> O Sayyid why dost thou weep?
> Why dost give up thy heart to mourning?

The union of spirit spoken of in this Persian verse bears a striking resemblance to the *bhava sammilana* of Vaishnava poetry, revealing a common mental structure underlying the culture of the age. This was not just a tale: it happened. In no other culture might events have taken the course they did in this affair. Here was a culture moulded by the folk story of Sasui and Punhoon, the Vaishnava tale of Radha and Krishna, and the Arabian legend of Laila and Mujnun. The medieval men learnt to downgrade erotic desire in a manner the ancients had not thought of. They gave to the spiritual suffering of 'love' an unwonted supremacy over the natural joy of 'sex'. This was a culturally produced split; one that would have been quite unfamiliar, perhaps even incomprehensible, to Bilhana and Jayadeva five centuries earlier.

The recurrent theme of illicit love, the sadness of the erotic experience, the constant emphasis on partings and sufferings, the notion of an everlasting union in spirit, were all reflections of a sad social reality. The orthodox codes of Hinduism and Islam both imposed rigid controls over the natural play of the impulses of men and women, and sought to confine the erotic instinct to permitted areas. This was a common patriarchal structure in which the power of men over women was conjoined to the equally deadly power of the elders over the young: a system in which the girl was for the parents to dispose of as they pleased, and the young man's marriage and sex life a matter entirely for his elders to negotiate. Brahmanical and Islamic orthodoxy strengthened each other: each admired those features of the other which strengthened the patriarchal control mechanisms. Again, each condemned those features of the other which tended to relax the hold over women and youth. Thus, the two codes insensibly interacted with each other, strengthening the orthodox values of society at large.

Neither the pre-Islamic gender system of Al-Hind, nor the gender system of the Muslims of Arabia and Ajam, were so unjust to the female sex and to youth as the system that evolved in India out of the interaction between Hindus and Muslims. Al Biruni, who analysed the Hindu gender system on the eve of the Muslim occupation of northern India, was perceptive enough to understand that the social system fostered by every major religion was consciously designed to control the sexuality of men and women.[536] He also keenly observed the difference between the Hindu and Muslim systems of sexual control. What he was in no position to observe yet was the interaction between two systems and the resultant gender structure of medieval Indian society. He did, however, observe the beginning of the process which, rather than liberalizing the structure, let each orthodoxy impinge upon the other.[537]

The coming of Islam coincided with the extension of purdah. The evidence of the tenth century Arab geographer Abu Zaid is explicit that Indian women, even in the elevated circle of the royal court, were not confined in the strict system of purdah imposed over women of the lands of Islam.[538] The Muslim community, as it formed in Al-Hind, was psychologically conditioned by the prevailing attitudes in Arabia and Ajam with regard to the female body. 'The Moors,' observed the English surgeon John Fryer in the port of Masulipatam in 1673, 'are by Nature plagued by jealousy, cloistering their Wives up, and sequestring them the sight of any besides the *Capon* that watches them. When they go abroad, they are carried in close *Palenkeens*, which if a Man offer to unveil it is present death: the meanest of them not permitting their Women to stir out uncovered of whom they are allowed as many as they can keep.'[539] Although Fryer added that the Hindus did not observe so strict a purdah, it is evident that the custom was prevalent to a greater or lesser degree among all families with pretensions to gentility, not only among the Hindus but even among the converted Christian families of Portuguese Goa.[540]

The imported custom of 'sequestring' and 'cloistering' women was supplemented by indigenous sexual control mechanisms in which the natives in due course became the instructors to the newcomers. Of these, the most ubiquitous was the increasingly rigorous caste system. To this was added enforced widowhood. Yet another custom, designed to weigh the social balance in favour of the elders against the young, was early marriage, arranged by the parents before puberty. In these respects the Islamic law was more liberal than the code of Manu, but unhappily for women and the young, it was not the Hindus who learnt from the Muslims, but the other way round. Far from being influenced by the more enlightened provisions of Islam, the Hindus on the contrary influenced the attitude of the Muslims born in India. The Hindu marriage system was described with a strange detachment by Al Biruni about 1030:

Every nation has particular customs of marriage, and especially those who claim to have a religion and law of divine origin. The Hindus marry at a very young age; therefore the parents arrange the marriage of their sons ... Husband and wife can only be separated by death, as they have no divorce.

A man may marry one to four wives ...[541]

If a wife loses her husband by death she cannot marry another man. She has only to choose between two things—either to remain a widow as long as she lives or to burn herself; and the latter eventually is considered the preferable, because as a widow she is ill-treated as long as she lives. As regards the wives of the kings, they are in the habit of burning them, whether they wish it or not, by which they desire to prevent any of them by chance committing something unworthy of their husband ...

... Every man of a caste may marry a woman of his own caste or one of the castes or caste below his. But nobody is allowed to marry a woman of a caste superior to his own.

... In our time, however, the Brahmans, although it is allowed to them, never marry any woman except one of their own caste.[542]

The caste restrictions became even more rigid after Al Biruni's time, and in due course influenced the Muslim community as well, especially Indian-born Muslims. Marrying outside the caste became virtually impossible. Bernier wrote from Delhi in July 1663: 'No one marries but in his own trade or profession; and this custom is observed almost as rigidly by *Mahometans* as by the *Gentiles*, to whom it is expressly enjoined by their law.'[543] The Indian aversion to widow marriage and the Hindu custom of marrying children off before puberty affected Muslim attitudes: so much so, that Akbar was induced to try and reform these socially harmful customs. 'Boys', he laid down, 'were not to marry before the age of sixteen, nor girls before fourteen, because the offspring of early marriages is weakly.'[544] He further issued the injunction: 'If widows liked to remarry, they should not be prevented.'[545] However, imperial decrees were hardly likely to modify deeply ingrained popular prejudices. A curious case was referred to the Qazi at Mecca two centuries after Akbar's attempt to reform Muslim social customs in India. An Indian Muslim had come to Mecca on pilgrimage. He struck up a

friendship with an Arab, but no sooner did the latter arrange his widowed
mother's marriage than the Indian turned round upon the Arab. It was
then the Arab's turn to be surprised. When the matter came up before
the Qazi the Indian contended that he had rightly condemned his
erstwhile friend. 'Now I am about 40. I never heard of such an act in
India.' When he was told that there was nothing wrong with this under
Islamic law, he vehemently maintained that, if this was so, then all
Indian Muslims were infidels, and that was unthinkable. It simply could
not be that they were Muslims in name alone and not proper adherents
of the Shariat.[546]

The Sati–Asati polarity, with no middle ground between the true
wife and the adulteress was rooted so deeply in the Indian tradition as
to mould the psyche of a whole society. A story related of the founder
of the Sadhna Panthi sect is typical in this respect. Sadhna, butcher and
saint, was on a pilgrimage when the wife of a Brahman made advances
to him. The butcher, referring to his profession, said jocularly that a
throat must be cut before he would comply. To his horror, the woman
cut off her husband's head. When she saw his reaction, she rounded
upon him and accused him of the crime. His hands were cut off, but
they were restored to him by his deity Jagannath. The murderess resolved
to commit *sati*. When the *sant* saw her mount her husband's funeral
pyre, he exclaimed: 'No one knows the ways of women, she kills her
husband, and becomes a Sati.'[547] This became a popular saying. Whether
the story is true or not, the proverb certainly indicates a unique mental
make-up. Muslims, too, fell under its spell as early as the thirteenth and
fourteenth centuries. While on a visit to Baba Farid's shrine at Ajodhan,
Ibn Battuta saw people hurrying out of the camp with some of his
comrades to see a wife burn herself on the funeral pyre of her husband.
'After this, I used to see in India a woman from among the infidel
Hindus adorned and seated on a horseback and people following her—
Muslims as well as infidels—and drums and bugles playing before her
and the Brahmins, who are the great ones among the Hindus,
accompanying her.'[548]

The occasional voices of protest exposed the underlying injustice
of the whole social system. Firishta relates the story of a Muslim woman
of the Bahmani kingdom in the reign of Mahmud Sah I (d.1397) who
was brought to court on a charge of adultery. When the *qazi* asked her
how she came to be guilty of so heinous a crime, the woman replied
artlessly: 'How could I think, O judge! that the act was unlawful? Seeing
that one man may have four wives, why might not I, also, indulge with

equal propriety in four husbands?' The *qazi*, much perplexed by this unexpected repartee, let the woman off with a mild reproof on her undertaking not to repeat the offence.[549] The fact that certain castes in Malabar still lived under a matrilineal system, and that the institution of the Sambandham allowed Nayar women more than one sexual partner, served only to underline the patriarchal structure of the rest of Indian society. The lurid imagination of that patriarchal society conjured up, in connection with this curious exception, visions of a world turned upside down. Fryer, on his visit to Malabar,[550] was given to understand that the women of this coast were 'the most professedly Lewd of any; being said to instruct the Men to be patients, while they act the Masculine Part in their Lascivious Twines'.[551] Credulous visitors to the coast carried back tales that the more lovers a Nayar woman had, the greater was her honour.[552]

Such comments reveal a pervasive uniformity of patriarchal values in Indian society. In a society hedged in with so many sexual restrictions, 'desire' seeks resolution perforce in the acceptance of deprivation and reconstructs itself as 'love'. The dichotomy between *kam* and *prem* was the product of a particular culture: one that arose from the interaction of India with Islam. At the heart of the new medieval concept of eternal union with the beloved in an extra-sensory realm lay socially produced sexual rupture. It gave the long term quest for immortality in Indian civilization a more distinct medieval form: the search for salvation through the sufferings of separation. Between the 'release'-seeker Maitreyi and the 'love'-lorn Mira lies the gulf of the ages for, during the intervening period, the age-old goal of Moksha had found a contender in yet another ultimate aim of mankind: Prema. Love (*ishq, prem*), as linked to devotionalism (*tasawwuf, bhakti*), was said to be a better state of 'annihilation' than release from bondage (*moksha*). It was the new key to immortality. It is not just that Mira is inconceivable without Muhammad; it is also true that Maitreyi, conceived ages before the slave girl Rabiya,[553] could not have belonged to their world.

The world produced by the interaction of the institutions of Manu and Muhammad had well-marked psychological characteristics. Accentuation of the spiritualism of Hindu and Muslim societies, had many consequences. There was the reinforcement of the other-worldly values inherent in both systems. The mutual adoption of each other's mechanisms for the control of the libido; the social design of enhancing the powers of the elderly and the male over the young and the female; the extension of arrangements for diverting the erotic instincts of youth;

the more thoroughgoing repression of the sexuality of women; the rise of erotic spiritualism; the pervasive notion of the unattainable beloved who must be internalized in view of the impossibility of real satisfaction of the erotic urge; the perpetual longing produced by the sadness of the experience; the ever present emotion called *viraha*, or the woe of severance; the splitting of the soul from the body and of love from desire; the whole social design of substituting satisfaction in an imperfect world—these were the features of the mentality produced by the interaction of Hinduism and Islam over six centuries. The traits of this mentality imparted to medieval Indian civilization its specific character, distinguishing the period of 1200–1800 from other phases in the evolution of the culture of the subcontinent. Psychically and emotionally, the world inhabited by Baba Farid and Sri Chaitanya, Mira Bai and Habbah Khatun, the Sufis and the Bhaktas, was one world, however wide the gulf that separated them socially and institutionally. The influence of the incoming Sufis, the indigenous inspiration of folk ballads (Sasui and Punhoon, Hir and Ranjha, etc.) with their accent on the genuine emotions and sufferings of the ordinary men and women, and above all the restrictions imposed by rigid sexual controls which banished freedom of love from their lives, gave rise to a new experience summed up in the term *viraha*. The culture of love rooted in that experience expressed anew 'the common heart of Hindustan'.

Sacred Space into Universal Dominion

This culture stamped itself on a space that expanded, contracted, and shifted over the centuries. The link between the two, however, stood the test of time. The Arab geographers knew of Kabul as an Indian town,[554] and Java as a part of India.[555] To Ibn Battuta, Lanka was still an Indian island in the fourteenth century.[556] There was some uncertainty about the exact boundaries of the land, but not much doubt about the land itself. This was sacred space, defined by the impure lands beyond.

There was conversely a time in the past when India was an impure land to Islam, but still sacred to Buddhists beyond India. For the Tibetan lama Taranatha, Islam's land of infidels was the land from which the true doctrine of Buddhism originated.[557] For 'Hindus', or Indians, at the time in question, it was pollution to travel beyond the country. Hindu slaves in Muslim countries escaping and returning to India had to go through purging by means of cow dung and milk.[558]

The sacred space of the Hindus was defined by the seven rivers (Ganga, Yamuna, Godavari, Saraswati, Narmada, Sindhu, and Kaveri) named in the Puranic prayer of bathing Brahmins. In late antiquity this space came to be dotted by the ten luminous organs (*jyotirlingas*) of Shiva and the fifty two fragments of Sati's corpse which fell all over the country.[559] At this point, the sage Shankaracharya (?788–820) consciously placed the most meritorious pilgrimages at the four extreme corners of the country—Badari-Kedarnath in the north, Rameshwar in the south, Dwarka in the west, and Jagannath in the east—so that the whole enclosed space might be held sacred.[560] The four convents (*maths*) that he set up—Jyotirmath (north), Sringeri (south), Sarada math (west), and Govardhana math (east)—established orthodox Brahmanical Hinduism on a pan-Indian basis. A Nambudri Brahman from Malabar, he established his own seat at Sringeri on the Western Ghats near the sources of the Tungabhadra, travelled all the way to Kashmir, sat there on the throne of Saraswati (the Goddess of Learning), and died at the age of thirty-two at Kedarnath on the high Himalaya.[561]

The pan-Indian shape which Hinduism acquired through Shankara's mission persisted after his death. On the eve of Mahmud Ghaznavi's sack of Somnath, the idol there, the foremost of the ten Jyotirlingas, attracted over a hundred thousand pilgrims, who assembled there 'from all parts of Hindustan'. Located on the seashore of Kathiawad, the idol was washed by fresh water brought every day from the Ganges 1000 miles away.[562] During Mahmud's campaigns, the centres of pilgrimage shifted to the safer and more distant east, especially to Banaras. Anchorites and pilgrims wandered from 'farre countries' to Banaras to end their lives there.[563] By the time of the Great Mughals, however, the Jagannath temple at Puri had emerged as the most important centre of pilgrimage. The temple was visited by the largest and most 'incredible concourse of people' 'from all quarters'.[564] According to Tavernier, all the Hindu subjects of the Great Mughal made a pilgrimage at least once in their lives to one of the four most celebrated pagodas of the day: Jagannath, Banaras, Mathura, and Tirupati. These pilgrimages were not made, as in Europe, 'one by one, or two by two', on the contrary, 'the population of a town or of several villages' assembled in order to 'travel together in company'.[565]

The soil itself was sacred, and not just to the Hindus, but, as time passed, to adherents of exogenous religions as well. A popular Hindu legend was that Baba Lal, a Vaishnava saint of Punjab born in Jahangir's time, brought the sacred soil of Dwarka to his Guru at Lahore in less than an hour, and in turn became a Guru.[566] The sepulchre of the martyr St Thomas was similarly sacred to Indian Christians during the reign of Jahangir. Those who went on pilgrimage there on the first day of July, carried back with them 'a little of that earth for a great Relique'. Curiously, the church, which Purchas described as 'built after our fashion', was at the time in charge of a Muslim who 'begged of the commers for the maintenance of it, and of a light continually burning therein'.[567]

Islam, entering India later than the Christianity of St Thomas, regarded the land initially as a dark continent in which 'Satanism' had prevailed 'since the time of the jinns'. However, in the eyes of Amir Khusrau and his generation, 'these impurities of infidelity' were cleansed, by 'the flame of Islam'.[568] A Mahua tree by the bathing *ghat* at Bahraich, where the shrine of the martyr Salar Masud was established, provided in Muslim legend the first holy spot of Islam in India.[569] Next in line were the Chishtiyya shrines, stretching down from the *dargah* of Shaikh Muin-ud-Din Chishti at Ajmer all the way to the grave of Bandanawaz Gisudaraz in the Deccan. The shrines of Muinuddin and Gisudaraz attracted Hindu pilgrims too.[570] Deccanis, noted Firishta, had no doubt in their minds that 'although the Prophet was undoubtedly a great man, yet Syud Mahomed Geesoo-duraz was a far superior order of being'.[571]

None of the early Chishti Shaikhs ever performed the Haj.[572] All their holy places lay within India. One spot was considered very holy by wandering pilgrims and fakirs. This was the peak in Lanka said to be impressed with Adam's foot. Many Muslims believed that Adam and Eve on their expulsion from heaven fell upon Lanka and Jidda respectively. A Shaikh from Persia showed the way to Adam's foot around 929, and the pilgrimage was well established at the time of Ibn Battuta's visit. He saw both Muslim fakirs and Hindu Jogis during his pilgrimage to the peak. A well known route of pilgrimage led Madari Malangs and Jogis from the Gangetic valley through Madurai country to Ceylon.[573] The growth of tomb-worship at various spots so disturbed the theologian Shah Waliullah that he denounced pilgrimages to the shrines of Muinuddin Chishti, Salar Masud, and Shah Madar as a sin worse than murder or adultery.[574] Islam had assumed too Indian a shape for some purists by the mid-eighteenth century. On the eve of Nadir Shah's invasion, Muslim social life in Delhi included a well established weekly round of *dargahs* around the capital.[575] The soil was by now sacred to the Muslims, and the water too.

Even before the establishment of Muslim power in the Gangetic valley, visiting Muslims were deeply impressed by the veneration accorded to the water of the Ganges by the Hindus. Al Biruni noted the Hindu custom of throwing the burned ashes of dead bodies into the Ganges in the expectation that the dead would thereby avoid hell.[576] From as far as Cambay on the opposite coast of the subcontinent, no less than four thousand pilgrims might arrive at the mouth of the Ganges in the Bay of Bengal during the Gangasagar fair in winter; and in remote Malabar the king of Calicut and other princes observed a feast every twelve years in honour of the river, commemorating the legendary appearance of the deity Ganga in a river of their own country when its waters rose and ran backward on the last day of February.[577] The popular Muslim cult of the Pirs sought to come to terms with these rooted beliefs by establishing a legendary connection between the river Ganga and Pir Badar who is regarded as the presiding deity of the water by the Muslim mariners of Bengal. A mosque at Triveni on the lower Ganges commemorates the belief that the river Ganga accepted Pir Badar as her elder brother and assisted him in building the mosque by fetching holy stones from Setubandha–Rameswar.[578]

'The principal reason', Tavernier recorded in the seventeenth century, 'why this water of the Ganges is so highly esteemed, is, that it never becomes bad, and engenders no vermin; but I do not know whether we should believe what is said about this, taking into consideration the number of bodies which are constantly being thrown into the Ganges.'[579] But neither the people nor the princes, of whatever religious persuasion, had any doubts on the score. We have it on the authority of Ibn Battuta that when Muhammad bin Tughlaq set up his capital at Daulatabad, water was carried there for the Sultan's use all the way from the Ganges.[580] This royal usage was transmitted to the Mughal court where the courtiers loaded their camels with clay pots of Ganges water whenever the court moved out of the capital.[581] Hindu traders, too, who believed 'it will never stinke, how long soeuver it bee kept',[582] carried the water for hundreds of miles for their devotions. Tavernier met professional Brahman water carriers who carried the water of the Ganges at Banaras in round clay pots hung on a pole. They would travel 300 or 400 leagues to sell it, or to make a present of it to rich persons from whom they expected a liberal reward.[583]

The religious space was at the same time the universal dominion. The network of pilgrimages defined the space in which warfare and diplomacy were conducted. Shiva, who roamed the world with Sati's body over his shoulders, did not step out of India in the course of his demented wanderings. The fragments, as they fell from her body, marked the boundaries of the political space. For Sultan Alauddin no less than Raja Ashoka, the claim of universal dominion might imply bringing other Indian princes to subordination, but would not involve campaigns of conquest outside the country. The world of Islam was of course wider than the universe of the Hindus, and extended much further beyond India. Therefore, Firishta, who designated himself as 'the historian of the rise of the Mohammedan power in India',[584] spelt out that his task was to compile 'a history of the conquests of Islam in Hind', and to give 'some account of the holy personages who have flourished in this country'.[585] Evidently he had in mind a space which was both political and religious, and his account makes it clear that the military and political transactions narrated by him belonged to a system contained within that space. In other words, this was a self-contained political system, its distinction within the world of Islam well understood by Muslim poets and historians. Thus we have Amir Khusrau's encomium on Hindustan:[586]

> Happy Hindustan, the splendour of Religion, where the Law finds perfect honour and security. In learning Delhi can now compete with Bokhara, for Islam has been made manifest by its kings. The whole country, by means of the sword of our holy warriors, has become like a forest denuded of its thorns by fire. The land has become saturated with the water of the sword, and the vapours of infidelity have been dispersed. The strong men of Hind have been trodden under foot, and all are ready to pay tribute. Islam is trumphant, idolatry is subdued. Had not the law granted exemption from death by the payment of poll-tax, the very name of Hind, root and branch, would have been extinguished. From Ghazni to the shore of the ocean you see all under the dominion of Islam.

The Kautilyan model of rivalries and alliances between competing states of the same system, with intermittent realizations of the sphere of the universal king, now gave way to a new theoretical model: the empire of Islam in Hindustan. Governed from Delhi, it was supposed to be the political embodiment of Islam in India. The empire of Hindustan was a well understood concept: Sher Shah, for instance, referred to it on his safe and victorious return from a near disastrous campaign against a Rajput chief of the desert: 'I have sold the empire of the whole of Hindustan for a handful of millet.'[587]

The idea persisted even when the empire did not exist. As the Delhi Sultanat broke up after the sack of the capital by Timur, a derisive couplet gained currency: 'The Empire of the King of the Earth extends from Delhi to Palam.'[588] However, although the city of Delhi, with a very small tract of country,[589] alone belonged to the sovereign, the imperial idea was alive. Moreover, the political system, with all its divisions, was one. Babar perceived this clearly at the time of his expedition from Kabul to Delhi. As he put it himself, 'At the time of my conquest of Hindustan it was governed by five Musalman rulers (padshah) and two pagans (kafir). These were the respected and independent rulers, but there were also, in the hills and jungles, many rais and rajas, held in little esteem (kichik karim).' He named the five Muslim rulers as the Afghans 'who had possession of Dihli, the capital'; the ruler of Gujarat; the Bahmanis of the Dakkan, defied by their great Begs who had laid hands on the whole country; the ruler of Malwa; and Nasrat Shah of Bengal. Besides the 'great Musalman rulers, honoured in Hindustan', there were two Hindu rulers, the Raja of Vijaynagar and Rana Sanga of Mewar. In addition, there were 'very many rais and rajas on all sides and quarters of Hindustan, some obedient to Islam, some, because of their remoteness or because their places are fastnesses, not subject to Musalman rule'.[590] Babar seized this central Muslim realm of Hindustan, which existed as an idea if not in reality, in 1526. That it remained distinct in his eyes from his earlier possessions around Kabul is evident from the verse that he addressed the following year to those of his fellow adventurers who returned to Kabul:

> Ah you who have gone from this country of Hind,
> Aware for yourselves of its woe and its pain,
> With longing desire for Kabul's fine air,
> You went hot-foot out of Hind.[591]

The Mughals were careful to retain hold of Kabul as a means of defence against their rivals in Central Asia, but henceforth their universal dominion was in essence the subcontinent of India. For a time, after the flight of Humayun and the death of Sher Shah, the subcontinent reverted to its system of warring states. On the eve of Humayun's return 'three different khutbas were read in the empire of Hindustan, and money was coined in the names of three monarchs, when before there had been only one khutba and one person's name on the money'.[592] This was not, however, a reversion to Kautilya's model of rival states and alliances, for the idea of the central Muslim realm was now very much more active, and it was only a matter of time before Emperor Akbar would put 'the empire of Hindustan' on a more permanent footing. Firishta, with his long view of the rise of the Muslim power in India and his more recent experience of Akbar's life work, summed up the medieval political notion in these terms:

> Let it not remain concealed from those persons who pursue history in general, that the central portion of Hind has been subjected to the arms of the kings of Islam, (may God perpetuate their good works!) while the territories of the confines are still in the possession of several great Hindoo princes; who having submitted to pay tribute are permitted to retain their countries, which they thus preserve from foreign invasion.[593]

The central Muslim empire of Hindustan became an Indian empire under Akbar,[594] rooted in the loyalty of the Indian population. He and his dynasty fostered a new commonalty in Hindustan. Henceforward, a link was established between Mughal sovereignty and Indian political identity which survived as late as 1857 after practically a century of British colonial rule. In reminiscences of those times, portents of this momentous development appeared even before the decisive encounter at Panipat in 1556. The Afghan ruler opposing the boy emperor is said to have been told by a professional soothsayer:

> 'This I have learned from the revolutions of the heavens and the changes of day and night,—that after Humayun, his son, who is seated on the Imperial throne, will be entrusted with the entire government of Hind, and the rulers of all countries will place their foreheads in the dust before his throne, and no one will vanquish him. The land of Hindustan, from Kandahar to the sea of the south, and from Kambhayit (Cambay) to the sea of Bengal, will own his sway.'[595]

The prediction was substantially fulfilled, and this too became part of the historical memory of the population. As reports of these developments reached the distant shores of England, an assiduous collector of traveller's tales recorded[596] the definite establishment of the new empire:

> The Mogors speake the Turkish language. The Empire of this Mogor is exceeding great, contayning the countries of Bengala, Cambaya, Mendao [Mandu], and others, comprehended by some vnder the name of Industan ... Agra and Fatipore are two Cities in his Dominion, great, and full of people, much exceeding London; and the whole space, betweene, is as a continuall populous Market. Many kings he hath conquered, and many haue submitted themselves and their States voluntarily to his subjection. Twenty Gentile kings are numbered in his Court, which attend him,

equalling the King of Calecut in power. Many others pay him tribute ...
Eleuen great riuers run through his Dominions ... The whole Mouarchie
enuironeth nine hundred leagues.

These reports also contained a hint of how the imperial system
functioned: 'King *Echebar* hath many Lords; each of which is to
maintayne eight, ten, twelve or fourteene thousand Horse ... To those
Lords he alloweth certaine Prouinces, for such military seruice: for hee
is Lord of all nor hath any else possession of any thing, but at the will
of the King.' This was a clear allusion to the centralized administrative-
military service of the Mansabdars, or the ranking commanders of
imperial horse, and the interlinked system of *jagir*s, or assignments of
revenue, whereby the imperial commanders kept the Mughal troopers
and their horses in readiness.

The Red Fort at Akbarabad (Agra), which gave architectural
expression to the unity of Akbar's empire, was complemented, at the
height of Mughal power under Shah Jahan, by an even more glittering
Red Fort at Shahjahanabad (Delhi), embodying Mughal sovereignty
over India in no uncertain terms. Shah Jahan, who like his predecessors
paid close attention to maintaining the symbols of Mughal sovereignty
throughout his dominions, reacted to the defiance of his authority by
the Portuguese at Hugli by driving them from that port, so that 'the
coinage might always bear the stamp of the glorious dynasty, and the
pulpit might be graced with its khutba'.[597] Tavernier was visibly
impressed: 'The Great Mogul is certainly the most powerful and richest
monarch of Asia ... this grand King of India, whose territories are so
rich, fertile and populous, has no power near him equal to his own.'[598]
Aurangzeb, who made good the claim that 'in his reign only one
Mahomedan sovereign issued his mandates throughout all India',[599] drew
the following eulogy from a Bengali poet:

> Shah Aurangzeb, Emperor of Delhi, is a man of mighty intellect
> He is the master of horses and elephants, and of men and ships.
> More than a thousand men hold the umbrella over his head
> And throughout the world this mighty man is worshipped.
> To the south is the shore of the sea, to the north the Himal
> Of all this he, the mighty prince, is the sole owner.
> His greatness is manifest through the seven islands and nine parts
> By his mighty arm he has destroyed a host of enemies.[600]

The idea of the sovereign Mughal realm persisted in the period
after Aurangzeb's death as the centralized imperial system disintegrated.

During the reign of his son and successor Bahadur Shah, Mughal sovereignty was still cloaked in a religious garb, and officers were sent into rebellious Marwar to rebuild the destroyed mosques. The Mughal army enforced the provisions of the law about the summons to prayer; and restored the ceremonious slaughter of cows at Id. *Qazis* were appointed on the occasion for administering the law, and collectors were sent in to levy the *jiziya*.[601] However, the poll-tax on the Hindus was subsequently abolished by the Saiyid brothers in an attempt to rebuild the empire on new foundations, and a compromise was worked out with the Marathas to end the wasting war in the Deccan which had taxed all Aurangzeb's resources. The Marathas, having acknowledged the sovereignty of the Mughal emperor, were formally invested with a quarter (*chauth*) and a tithe (*sardeshmukhi*) of the Mughal revenues in their capacity as *sardeshmukh* or chief landlord. The Nizam of Hyderabad, who was now the hereditary Mughal Viceroy of the Deccan, reached a compact with the Peshwa after his defeat at Kharda. On the basis of this, the Mughals and the Marathas agreed not to demolish mosques and temples, and the slaughter of cows was banned. Later, the Maratha chieftain Mahadji Sindia induced Emperor Shah Alam to proclaim the abolition of cowslaughter in the Mughal dominions.[602] De jure imperial sovereignty was thus based on a new understanding between the Mughal rulers and the Hindu chiefs. The sovereign Mughal realm, no longer a hard reality but all the same a powerful idea, embodied the commonalty of Hind and the Hindis.

When the Kachchwaha Rajput ruler of Amer, Jai Singh II, set out to build a series of astronomical observatories, he did not confine the buildings to his new capital at Jaipur alone, but distributed them throughout the territories of his imperial master Muhammad Shah. This common set of observatories built in Delhi, Jaipur, Mathura, Ujjain, and Banaras reflected the prevalent notion of Hindustan as one country in the eighteenth century. It also reflected an interesting attempt to meet the religious and cultural needs of both the Hindus and Muslims under the aegis of Mughal sovereignty which was still recognized throughout the land despite the disintegration of the empire.

Jai Singh II constructed a set of astronomical tables in a work which he entitled, in honour of his master, the *Zeej Muhammad Shahi*. It consisted of both tables of the sun for the Hindus and tables of the moon adapted to the Arabian lunar year. In the preface to his work, he addressed the reigning Mughal sovereign and dwelt on how erroneous the tables in common use appeared to be when compared to actual observation:

> Seeing that very important affairs both regarding religion and the administration of the empire depend upon these; and that in the rising and setting of the planets, and the seasons of eclipses of the sun and moon, many considerable disagreements were found, he represented it to his majesty of dignity and power ... the unrivalled pearl of the sea of sovereignty, the incomparably brightest star of the heaven of empire ... the victorious king, Mahommad Shah, may he ever be triumphant in battle.

The same preface tells us that Muhammad Shah was

> Pleased to reply, since you, who are learned in the mysteries of science, have a perfect knowledge of this matter; having assembled the astronomers and geometricians of the faith of Islam and the Bramins and Pandits, and the astronomers of Europe, and having prepared all the apparatus of an observatory, do you labour for the ascertaining of the point in question, that the disagreement between the calculated times of those phenomena, and the times in which they are observed to happen may be rectified.[603]

Jai Singh, who had already built the observatories at Jaipur, Mathura, Banaras, and Ujjain, was encouraged by the Emperor to build similar observatories in the other large cities. Accordingly, an observatory was erected in Delhi, the capital of the Mughal Empire. The observatories which had preceded it were located in territories controlled by powers as diverse as the Marathas, the Kachhwahas, and the Nawab of Awadh. Formally, however, all these lands were Mughal territory and the rulers ruled by virtue of patents granted by the Emperor. Behind the curiously shaped, yellow and pink hued observatories which can still be seen in different parts of the country today, stood the two communities of faith and the sovereign who ruled over them.

The ancient idea of the sacred space, demarcated by Jai Singh's observatories, found definite shape in the inalienable Mughal realm. Behind it lay memories of the Chakravarti Kshetra of antiquity, and of the Sultanat ruled by the sovereign Turushka *suratrānas* of Delhi. The idea of the central realm of Hindustan was six centuries old when the British troops dispatched by Lord Wellesley under the command of Lord Lake rode into the Red Fort at Shahjahanabad in 1803. For native and foreigner alike, this was one land and its political headquarters were located in the Lal Qila built by Shah Jahan. Actual power, along with control over the land as a whole, might not have been located within the precincts of the fort on the eve of the British arrival there. However, Shah Alam's reception of Lord Lake in full court in 1803 was seen as the passing of both actual and legitimate power over India to the English East India Company. Contemporary intellectuals who witnessed the scene or heard of the event grasped this fact clearly. But by subjecting all Hindis, Hindu and Muslim alike, to the arrogant power of the alien *firangi*, the Company reinforced and reconstructed the commonalty of Indians.

The 'Indians' as a Commonalty

If the land was one in 1800, so was its population. Both facts had been evident since the inscriptions of Asoka, amidst the countless transmutations over these two thousand years. Visitors from abroad were immediately aware of the identity of the population. The differences within the ethnic assortment, and the divergences of colour, facial features, constitution, etc. would have been less apparent to the outsiders than to the inhabitants. To any Chinese, Arab, Turkish, or Portuguese visitor, the population of the subcontinent was unmistakably marked out by their appearance from the peoples of other lands.

In the early days of the Sultanat of Delhi, when the roads were infested by the rebellious natives of the land, it appeared to the apprehensive visitors from Khurasan as if 'the crow-like Hindus' were 'covered with blackness'.[604] The Muslim poet born in Hind was provoked by such observations to say, 'They call Hind black and that is true enough'; and yet, he added with a play upon the word *sawad* meaning both black and country, 'it is the largest country in the world. And it was here that Adam had descended from heaven'.[605] Afanasy Nikitin, who saw everyone go naked, even the women (their breasts being uncovered), wrote, 'The men and women are all dark. Wherever I went I was followed by many people who wondered at a white man.'[606] Abdur Razzak of Samarkand said more disapprovingly: 'The blacks of this country go about with nearly naked bodies, wearing only pieces of cloth, called langots, extending from their navels to above their knees.' Only the Muslims clothed themselves properly.[607]

The Khurasani ruling class, who superimposed themselves upon the population, had an acute colour consciousness. It did not diminish with time: 'To be considered a *Mogol*, it is enough if a foreigner have a white face and profess Mahometanism; in contradistinction to the

Christians of Europe, who are called *Franguis*, and to the *Indous*, whose complexion is brown, and who are gentiles.'[608] The Mughal harem displayed a range of colour differences to those who informed credulous travellers: 'some blacke, exceedingly louely and comely of person notwithstanding; some browne, of Indian complexion; others very white, but pale, and not ruddy ...'.[609] An English visitor, dwelling on these colour differences, said: 'Of complexion the *gentues* are blacker than the *Moors*, the *Moors* than the Persians.'[610] A Portuguese visitor who stayed for some time in Goa was, however, observant enough to see that the people resembled Europeans in their facial features: 'They are formed and made both in Face, Limbes, and in all other things like men of Europe, colour only excepted.'[611] However, climate and the ethnic assortment did not allow such colour differences to survive over the generations. The same traveller saw that the third generation Portuguese of Goa, both men and women, seemed to be 'naturall Indians, both in colour and fashion'.[612]

The Indian beauty, about whom the stranger from overseas was naturally curious, appeared to him to be distinct in appearance. 'Brown, of Indian complexion', was how she appeared to be; but the complexion might shade off, in Malabar, to 'altogether blacke, yet verie smoothe both of haire and skinne, which commonly they anoynt with Oyle, to make it shine'.[613] Up north in Kashmir, they had, on the contrary, 'clear complexions' and 'fine forms ... as well made as Europeans'; it was noted that their faces had neither 'the Tartar flat nose nor the small pig eyes that distinguish the natives of *Kacheguer*, and which generally mark those of Great Tibet'.[614] The facial features of the Indian population were to such itinerant observers visibly different from those of the Tibetan (Chin) and Abyssinian (Habshi) population, and far closer to those of the Europeans.

Body postures unconsciously marked out the commonalty of the population and revealed to outsiders a visible ethnic identity.[615] The Turks from Ghazni, during their early incursions into India, were struck by the sight of the Hindus sitting cross-legged.[616] The shock they experienced wore off in time. They, too, learnt the same posture. Close upon seven centuries elapsed when Fryer saw in Surat Hindu yogis sitting 'cross-legg'd after their way of sitting'; he did not wonder much at the sight, for he had already seen aristocratic Muslims of the same town use chariots 'which are made to sit Cross-legg'd on, not their legs hanging down as ours: it being accounted among them no good breeding to let their Legs or Feet be seen while sitting'.[617]

On his visit to Goa, a Portuguese saw the local Goan women 'eate like the *Mahometans* and all other *Indians* vpon the ground'.[618] Food was served in a manner designed to prevent pollution and to preserve the distinctions of caste: 'vessels of leaves sewed together' being placed on 'the bare floor'.[619] 'All eat', noted an Englishman in Bombay, 'with their fingers, and scrupulously wash before and after meals.'[620] He saw all but the poorest people 'chew bitel (a pungent aromatic leaf) with the hard nut of the areca, mixed with a sort of lime made from shells, and with various spices, according to the person's means'.[621] Food was of incredible variety, yet somehow the diet was like no other in the world. It might consist of bowls of fowl, fish, and vegetables, each eaten with a ladle full of rice mixed with ghee, and followed at the end by curded milk;[622] or it might be the common man's diet of 'unleavened bread with boiled vegetables, clarified butter or oil, and spices';[623] in neither case could it be mistaken for the cuisine of any other country.

The cultural syncretism represented by the varied diet was rooted in a set of notions and values held in common despite the clash of religious beliefs. Badauni, a strict mulla who was not especially tolerant of the Hindus, nevertheless quoted the following verse with warm approval: 'When the good acts of the Shaikh and the Brahman shall be investigated, there shall be taken from thee not a grain that thou hast reaped.'[624] The idea was that good acts, whether performed by Muslims or Hindus, would fetch their just reward. No less powerful was the idea of the blessing. The Rana of Mewar was compelled by defeat to render unto Emperor Akbar an elephant previously demanded of him. This elephant, which bore the name 'Blessing of Ram' (Ram Prasad), was renamed 'Blessing of Pir' (Pir Prasad) by Emperor Akbar in grateful remembrance of the Chishti saint to whom he attributed this important victory. Whoever might be the source of the blessing associated with the elephant, the notion of the blessing it would bring was attractive to the Shah no less than to the Rana.[625]

Behind this lies a certain commonalty of values. By Akbar's order, four degrees of devotion to his Majesty was defined for his courtiers. 'The four degrees consisted in readiness to sacrifice to the Emperor Property, Life, Honour, and Religion. Whoever had sacrificed these four things possessed the four degrees; and whoever had sacrificed one of these four possessed one degree.'[626] The value of the four degrees, property, life, honour and religion, were placed in ascending order, except that many placed honour over religion. This was a persistent notion which repeatedly arose during the uprising of 1857, when these four degrees were declared to be the most important things in life.

The set of common physical postures and mental attitudes marked out the population of India in the eyes of European travellers of the sixteenth and seventeenth centuries. Beneath the enormous differences within that vast multitude, there lay an underlying commonalty of culture and ethnicity which no European could mistake. During his visit to Masulipatam and Madras in 1673, the English surgeon John Fryer saw that the people of Madras were 'of the same nation with Metchlapatan'.[627] These towns were located in Andhra and Tamil countries respectively, where the languages spoken were altogether different. John Huighen Van Linschoten, a Portuguese who reached Goa in 1583, observed earlier that the native agriculturists and fishermen of the town and island of Goa were the same people as 'the Canaras and Decanyns' of the Deccan, commonly called Balaghat, lying beyond Goa: 'their Religion is like the Decanijns and Canaras, for they are all of one Countrey and Custome, little differing: they goe naked, their middle only covered with a cloth'. Linschosten added that many of them were Christians, but they were all 'in a manner blacke, or of a dark browne colour', their women going about with 'a cloth bound about their middle beneath their nauels, and hanging downe to the middle of their thighes, and the other end thereof they cast ouer their shoulders, whereby half their brests are uncovered'.[628] The people of Goa, Karnataka, and Maharashtra did not appear to be different in their appearance.

It did not matter much whether the population belonged to Andhra or Tamil Nadu, Karnataka or Maharashtra; in the eyes of the overseas visitor they were the same people. They were all, in a manner of speaking, Indians, though they might belong to different 'nations' (the term being then used in the sense of 'nationalities'). Surgeon Fryer, speaking of the coolies he had hired in his journey through the Deccan, spoke naturally of 'my Indians'.[629]

Samuel Purchas, recounting the tradition of St Thomas's martyrdom in India, spoke of his preaching the Gospel 'to the Indian'.[630] Way back in the first century of the Christian era, the learned classes in the Roman Empire were in the habit of referring to 'India Proper' and to its inhabitants as 'Indians'.[631] The Brahmanical literati of the country occasionally used the Puranic term 'Bhārati' for the inhabitants of the land. The Jain merchant Banarsidas, speaking of his native land in the seventeenth century, defined it as the village of Biholi in the town of Rohtak in the midland (*madhya-desha*) of Bharata.[632]

This sense of oneness of the country, as against the rest of the world, was reflected in the fact that 'Hindustanis' thought of every place outside their country as 'Khurasan'[633] and regarded all foreigners as 'Khurasanis'.[634] The natives of the land, both Hindu and Muslim, had no difficulty in identifying aliens as a category apart, whatever might be the divisions among themselves. In the civil commotions of the Sultanat of Delhi in the period of its decline, 'foreigners' were distinguished from 'Indians' by the pronunciation of words, and killed on the spot.[635] The Persian texts also distinguished between 'the people of India' and the 'Afghans',[636] and a Mughal prince displayed his poetical skill in the Afghan court by distinguishing 'a Mughal of Iraq', 'a poet of Hind', and 'an Afghan poet' during a recitation in which Persian couplets were quoted without the names of the poets being revealed.[637] Indians abroad, wherever a settled community of emigrants from Hindustan existed, habitually spoke of themselves as 'Indians'. Seventeenth century Russian records pertaining to the settled Indian business community in Astrakhan testify to this. Thus, in a petition to the Russian authorities in 1685, Indian businessmen catalogued various groups of foreign traders in Russia, such as Armenians, Greeks, Germans, Bukharans, Chinese, etc. 'besides us Indians'. Comparing their own value to the Russian government with the taxable worth of the Russian traders, they pleaded: '... the Russian traders pay taxes much less than we Indians pay.'[638]

The 'Indians' of the Greeks, Romans, Portuguese, English, and Russians were the 'Hindus' of the Arabs and Turks. When Al Biruni spoke of 'the antagonism between Hindus and foreigners', he had in mind the ancient xenophobia of the natives of India, among whom he included the Buddhists (Shamaniyya) as well.[639] The Hindus were defined in his eyes by their ethnicity. Minhaj us-Siraj, a *qazi* on the Delhi Sultanat in its early period, spoke of 'Hindu Histories', 'Hindu era', 'Hindus', 'Infidel Hindus', in the same ethnic sense. However, he almost invariably used the term Muslim in place of Turk. In his history (1259), the Hindus meant the Indians, a race subjected to the hegemony of Islam by the Muslim conquerors from Central Asia.[640] Soon afterwards, however, a new term became necessary to indicate the Indians, for there had sprung up, under the rule of the incoming Turks, an Indian-born community of Muslims who could not be described as 'Hindus' (the term being from the outset used in opposition to 'Muslims'). As the Hindus were redefined as a particular community of faith which no longer embraced all Indians, the poet Amir Khusrau used the term Indian or 'Hindi' in opposition to the term foreigner or 'Khurasani'. A Hindi was an Indian,[641] irrespective of whether he was a Hindu or a Muslim, as distinct from the Khurasani, or foreigner (for all foreigners were Khurasanis to the inhabitants of Hind). An alternative name employed to describe an Indian was the term Hindustani. The conqueror Babur in his memoirs used both terms, 'Hindi'[642] and 'Hindustani'.[643] The collective ethnic identity of the Indians was emphasized in these terms, shorn of all religious affiliation. Ibn Battuta, who visited India in the mid-fourteenth century, clearly perceived the Indians as one people. He used the term Ahl-i-Hind, literally the people of India, in contra-distinction to the term Hindu used elsewhere.[644] 'It is a custom with the Indians', he wrote at one point of his travelogue, 'to serve curd after the meals, just as in our country.'[645] He was referring consciously to an Indian commonalty in connection with this culinary detail.

Indian lexicographers of the Persian language took some pains to explain such terms. A Hindu intellectual wrote a Persian dictionary in 1740, with suitable quotations from the poets.[646] The word 'Hindu' was thus explained there:

> ' Hindū'. Sometimes applied to thief; sometimes guard; sometimes slave, servant; sometimes infidel (kafir); sometimes the inhabitant of Hind. Khan Arzu[647] says the specific community (qaum-i-makhsus) [of Hindus] is meant, and it cannot therefore be applied to Muslims who are inhabitants of this country. The correct word for an inhabitant of Hind is "Hindi"; and what is found [to the contrary] in some texts is due to common use only. Plural [of Hindu] Hindūān. Being tall is one of the qualities attributed to him.

By a political and linguistic process, the Indians had coined a term for themselves: 'Hindian'. This, the plural of 'Hindi', was more commonly used than the Puranic term 'Bharati' and displaced the earlier Arabic/Persian term 'Hinduan' for the inhabitants of India. The term 'Hindustanis', an alternative designation for the Indians, also came into general use. Abroad, in Russia, Indian traders picked up the habit of calling themselves 'Indians'. An entity which had existed as early as the reign of Ashoka achieved at length, by around the fourteenth century, the stage of self denomination. This was self-perception as distinct from external perception. The latter went as far back as Megasthenes and Fa-hien. The emergence of the word Hindi displaced the meaning of the term Hindu and established a long term religious dichotomy, namely Hindu/Muslim. There were Indians, or Hindustanis, or Hindian; there were also amongst them the Hinduan and the Musalmanon. Collectively, therefore, the Hindian were the Muslims and Hindus of India. In the meanwhile, the original inhabitants of the land before the coming of Islam adopted the name given them by the Muslims, i.e. 'Hindu'. They adopted it in the sense of a religious category, and not in the earlier ethnic sense of the Muslim explorers of India. At the same time, the earlier sense that Muslims were foreigners as opposed to Indians gradually disappeared. They were all Indians or Hindis divided into two religious categories, Hindus and Muslims.

Popular Patriotic Sentiments

The Indians were now, in their own terms of reference, one people. Here was a felt community: an ethnic entity fused together by a historical process and a common mentality. This ethinic mass was more a cultural than a political unit. The historical record is too fragmentary to tell us what political sentiments the people might have entertained. The composite culture which they shared was not in any case politically oriented. However, occasionally, when external catastrophes overtook the country, some underlying political sentiments appeared to activate the mass. On such occasions, an unsuspected range of patriotic feelings would surface despite the fragmentary character of the record. On two distinct occasions, the sack of Delhi by Nadir Shah, and the visitation of Timur-i-Lang three and a half centuries earlier, these sentiments found expression in unmistakable popular rejection of the occupying power.

Timur's expedition to India was prompted by the news of political discord that travelled all the way from Delhi to Samarkand. The government of the Delhi Sultanat had fallen into anarchy under rival Tughlaq princes who had all laid claim to the throne of Muhammad bin Tughlaq and Firuz Shah. Civil war raged in Delhi, and as Firishta wrote, 'a scene was exhibited, unheard of before, of two kings in arms against each other residing in the same capial'.[648] Though the contentious royalty and nobility of the divided realm were in no position to oppose the conqueror's march, the people were roused to pitiful and futile resistance by his atrocities. Timur's grandson Mirza Jahangir, who was in charge of operations around Multan, was compelled by the rains to withdraw his cavalry into the town. 'There', Firishta relates, 'he was reduced to much distress by the inhabitants of the country, who closely invested the place, and withheld supplies, so that his cavalry, unable to act or procure forage, diminished daily.'[649] In retaliation, Timur carried out a massacre in the town of Bhatner, from which partisan warfare had been organized against his grandson in Multan. He then invested the fort. 'Both the Mohomedans and Hindoos, who remained within the fort, struck with horror, and dreading a similar fate, set fire to the place in despair, killed their wives and children, and sought nothing but revenge and death. The scene was awful; and the unfortunate inhabitants, in the end, were cut off to a man, though not before some thousands of Moguls had fallen by their hands.'[650]

Timur was so incensed by this desperate sally that he ordered the town to be reduced to ashes. He massacred the Indians through the provinces of Multan and Lahore on his way to Delhi. As he laid siege to Delhi, there were 100,000 Indians in his camp, taken prisoner since he had crossed the Indus. They cheered when the Delhi troops made an ineffective sortie against his reconnoitring party. Next morning it was reported to him that the prisoners in his camp 'had on the day before expressed great joy when they saw him attacked, which rendered it extremely probable that, on a day of battle they would join their countrymen against him'.[651] Timur made enquiries, concluded that most of the prisoners were Hindus, and ordered all above the age of fifteen to be put to the sword. About 100,000 men, Hindus as well as Muslims, who had carelessly exposed their loyalties, were massacred in cold blood.

Delhi was taken by storm in 1398. As Firishta puts it, 'the Indians were, in a short time, totally routed, without making one brave effort to save their country, their lives or their property'. The nobility, having submitted tamely to the invader, agreed to pay a contribution. However, several noblemen and some rich merchants refused to pay their share. 'Mughal' soldiers sent in to enforce payment began plundering the town. When news reached Timur that some of his soldiers had been killed, he ordered a general pillage. In no time Delhi was in flames, as 'the Hindoos, according to their custom, seeing their females disgraced, set fire to their houses, murdered their wives and children, and rushed out on their enemies'.[652] A general massacre ensued, some streets being rendered impassable by heaps of dead bodies. 'The desperate courage of the Delhiyans was at length cooled in their own blood, and throwing down their weapons, they at last submitted themselves like sheep to slaughter ...'[653] This was the first instance of Delhi having been subjected to a general massacre. Timur returned to Samarkand with an enormous booty, for though he had declared himself emperor, as it transpired, the 'Mughals' had no intention of staying on.

Nadir Shah's occupation of Delhi was the other incident recorded by contemporary chroniclers and intellectuals as Hindustan's 'mighty calamity'.[654] The *Tarikh-i-Hindi* of Rustam Ali recorded the 'many disasters and calamities' which he brought upon Hindustan. Yet another chronicler, a Hindu named Anand Ram Mukhlis, wondered 'how to relate the ruin and desolation that overwhelmed this beautiful country!'[655] In the narratives of these contemporary chroniclers, Nadir Shah and 'the Kazalbash invaders'[656] were pitted against the emperor, the chiefs and 'the people of Hindustan'.[657] One description of the encounter, written two years after the invader's departure, runs as follows:[658]

> The Indian warriors, saiyids, shaikhs, Afghans, and Rajputs, so fought with their cruel swords that, had Rustam and Afrasiyab lived to this time, their livers would have become water at the sight of this dreadful battle. The Iranis, dreading the swords of these brave men, left the field, and, firing their guns from a distance and from different quarters, made heaps of the corpses of Indians, who preferred death to flight.

Writing forty years later of the encounter between 'the Hindostanies and Iranians', Saiyid Ghulam Husain Khan referred to the flight and dispersion of 'the Hindostany army' and the detachment of the provinces of Sind and Kabul from 'the Empire of Hindostan'.[659] It was the opinion of eyewitnesses that 'Hindustan would have been saved' if help had been given to the garrison of Kabul.[660] The Persianized literati of 'the kingdom of Hind'[661] recorded how the Mughal ruling class surrendered Delhi to the invader and left the people to their devices, but were not particularly approving of the unilateral action of the people of Delhi as they rose against the invader with whom the ruling class was now collaborating. It is, however, evident from their account of the affray between the Kazalbash troopers and the citizens of Delhi that individual members of the nobility joined in on the side of the people after they had signally failed to defend their subjects.

On 8 March 1789, Nadir Shah of Iran entered Delhi along with the captive Mughal emperor, Muhammad Shah. The Khutba was read on Friday in the name of the Iranian conqueror. He paid a ceremonial visit to Muhammad Shah and accepted the presents offered by that hapless prince. The newly proclaimed sovereign returned safely to his camp at the close of the day, but a false rumour spread through town that he had been shot by a female guard of the Mughal harem. As evening fell, 'the bad characters within the town', according to Anand Ram Mukhlis, 'collected in great bodies'.[662] In Rustam Ali's phrase, however, 'the people of the city',[663] excited by the general confusion, fell upon the Kazalbash troopers of Nadir Shah. In the later historical narrative of Saiyid Ghulam Hussain Khan, the uprising is described as follows:[664]

> Hardly had this false rumour spread throughout the city, than armed bodies of Hindostanies made their appearance in the principal streets, putting to the sword as many Cuzzel-bashes as they could lay their hands upon; and as the latter, uninformed of the report, and unacquainted with the country-language, were rambling about by two or more together, without suspecting any harm, they were massacred with ease; and although night came on, and it was expected that the tumult would subside, it took new force on the contrary; and those seditious, without taking a moment of rest, were more eager than ever.

Evidently the Mughal ruling class, having made their compact with the invader, were startled by the popular action. Not one of them 'took the trouble to move about and to appease the tumult'. Ghulam Husain Khan adds, 'Nay, some of them that had taken from Nadyr-shah a number of cuzzel-bashes as safeguards to their families and houses, suffered them to be massacred in those very houses, or massacred them themselves ...'[665]

The tumult continued through the night, and hundreds of the Iranian troopers were killed. In the morning Nadir Shah, seeing the slaughter of his soldiers, ordered a general massacre and directed that not a soul should be spared wherever the body of a murdered Kazalbash might be discovered. At noon, when the conqueror ordered the massacre to stop, the roads were blocked by heaped bodies. 'Here and there some opposition was offered,' says Anand Ram Mukhlis, who himself defended his quarter, 'but in most places people were butchered unresistingly.'[666]

Nadir Shah had no intention of staying on, for news had reached him of troubles in his dominions. A huge tribute was rendered him by the princes and people of Delhi, and in return he delivered into the hands of Muhammad Shah 'the crown and seals of the realm of Hindustan'.[667] The Mughal prince got back 'his crown of Hindostan'[668] and a compact made between the Iranian government and 'that of Hindustan'[669] redefined the borders of the two empires. The new border was fixed roughly along the Indus, all the countries eastward of the river remaining attached 'to the kingdom of Hind'.[670]

News of the happenings in Delhi reverberated throughout India and aroused the patriotic sentiments of powers far from friendly towards the captive Mughal court. Baji Rao, the Peshwa of the hostile Marathas, had been engaged in operations against the Portuguese and the Bhonsle prince of Berar at the time of the battle of Karnal. News of the victory of the Iranians alarmed him. When he received the next newsletter intimating the plunder of the capital and the massacre of its inhabitants, he was overwhelmed. 'Our domestic quarrel with Raghoojee Bhonslay is now insignificant', he said, 'the war with the Portuguese is as naught; there is now but one enemy in Hindustan.' He was convinced that Nadir Shah would set up his own government, and further news, which proved to be false, caused him to apprehend that a hundred thousand Iranians were moving towards the Deccan. The report did not daunt him: 'Hindus and Mussulmans, the whole power of the Deccan must assemble and I shall spread our Mahrattas from the Nerbudda to the Chumbul.' He called upon the Mughals at Haidarabad to arm against the common foe, and made preparations for defence, when Nadir Shah wrote to him from Delhi that he had reinstated Muhammad Shah, and Baji Rao must now obey his sovereign. He added to this the taunt that he had been of no assistance to his master despite the large Maratha army.[671]

In Delhi, the Iranian soldiers heard the proclamation: 'Soldiers, the King of Kings and Lord of beneficence, the protector of the world, conquered the country of Hindustan and restored it. Tomorrow our victorious Banners move towards Irak. Be you prepared.'[672] Nadir Shah was anxious to reach Khurasan because of rebellions in Bukhara and Khwarizm. Every Indian was relieved when a notice reached the police chief of Delhi intimating 'that not one of the Persians remained in Hindustan'.[673] The event brought into momentary focus a common sentiment that moved diverse elements in the political world of India: the Mughal ruling class, the people of Delhi, the court of Poona. In the vision of the Mughal chronicler of the eighteenth century, all these elements were part of a category defined, in relation to 'the Iranians', as 'the Hindostanies'. This was an identity that was subsequently still more sharply focused by the dominance which the English, more patient and more determined than the 'Kazalbashis', imposed over 'the country of Hindustan'.

That identity did not, however, derive from either the English domination or the Iranian occupation. The patriotic sentiment that moved the various elements in 1739 was embedded in a longer-term collective emotional structure which had been in evidence as early as 1398. It would manifest itself, in strikingly different circumstances, in the Sepoy War of 1857. The subconscious emotional collectivity was centuries old and had clearly manifested itself during the invasion of Timur. The appearance of the same sentiment across a gulf of 341 years could be no accident. Some of the common features of the popular uprisings of 1398 and 1739 underscore the long-term commonalty of emotional response. The persistent signs of a collective psyche displayed in these popular actions expose a distinct community of sentiment. What the recurrent emotional responses amounted to was a rejection of the oppressive alien occupation of the acknowledged capital of the land. The sense of identity arose from an attachment to the country and a love of the inchoate community called the Hindis or the Hindustanis. In the English language, the nearest equivalent for describing this feeling is that of patriotic sentiment. This was ethnic patriotism of the kind that existed in many cultures before nationalism as defined by political science rebuilt the foundations of the modern state.

Notes and References

1. Mahdi Husain (trans.), *The Rehla of Ibn Battuta* (*India, Maldive Islands and Ceylon*) (Baroda, 1953), p. 41n.

2. Barbara Daly Metcalf, 'Imagining Community: Polemical Debates in Colonial India', in Kenneth W. Jones (ed.), *Religious Controversy in British India: Dialogues in South Asian Languages* (Albany, NY, 1992), p. 231. See also Benedict Anderson, *Imagined Communities: Reflections on the Origins and Spread of Nationalism* (London, 1983), pp. 30, 122; Sudipta Kaviraj, 'The Imaginary Institution of India', in Partha Chatterjee and Gyanendra Pandey (eds.), *Subaltern Studies* VII (Delhi, 1992), pp. 1, 14–18; Ernest Gellner, *Nations and Nationalism* (New Delhi, 1986), pp. 48–9.

3. *Inscriptions of Asoka*, trans. D.C. Sarkar (Delhi, 1957), pp. 33, 35.

4. J.W. McCrindle, *Ancient India as Described by Megasthenes and Arrian*, pp. 29, 43, 115, 160.

5. Or, alternatively, that such categories have existed but for a short time; 'The very assumption that there even was a religion called "Hinduism" ... was very much a product of the colonial period, an imputation of a rarefied unity to Indic religious orientations and practices that had not previously existed.' Metcalf, 'Imagining Community', p. 231.

6. The classic example of such a desperate attempt at wishing away stark realities is the pretence of V.P. Singh, the then Prime Minister of India, on the eve of the first attack on the Babri Masjid, that there was no mosque there: *'aare bhai, wahan masjid kahan hai?'* (Look here, my friend, where do you see a mosque over there?). L.K. Advani, subsequently Home Minister, stated in court: 'For the last 51 years, from 1950 to 2001, what stands there is a temple ... first a *de facto* temple and today a temple both *de facto* and *de jure*. Prior to 1992, by virtue of worship, it was a temple and the super-structure was a mosque.' This is to turn day into night.

7. 'To Alberuni in the tenth century the Hindus were a single people, one and indivisible. He does not argue the point; he simply assumes it as the basis of his discussions.' Muhammad Habib, *Politics and Society during the Medieval Period* (ed. K.A. Nizami), vol. 1 (New Delhi, 1974), p. 32. Habib, like Al Biruni, uses the word Hindu here in a dual sense: an Indian, and alternatively an adherent of the Brahmanical faith.

8. 'Whoever they may be, and wherever they may be in India, the Indian Muslims take themselves for granted. This is true of all periods of Indian Muslim history, and it is true even now, when a division of the country has taken place on a basis that does not appear to be justified by history.' M. Mujeeb, *The Indian Muslims* (London, 1967), p. 9.

9. Charlotte Vaudeville, *A Weaver Named Kabir—Selected Verses, with a Detailed Biographical and Historical Introduction* (Delhi, 1993), p. 38.

10. Samuel Beal, *Si-Yu-Ki. Buddhist Records of the Western World* (Delhi, 1981), pt. II, pp. 197–8. Bhaskara Varman of Kamarupa told Hiuen Tsang: 'Throughout the kingdoms of India there are many persons who sing about the victories of the Tsin king of the Mahachina country.' Shaktisangama Tantra, a late medieval work, distinguishes China (Maha Chin) from Tibet (Chin). D.C. Sircar, *Cosmography and Geography in Early Indian Literature* (Calcutta, 1967) p. 109.

11. Beal, *Si-Yu-Ki*, pt I, p. 69.

12. Abdul Hamid Lahori's *Badshah Nama*, for instance, describes the Portuguese, whom Shah Jahan drove out of Hugli, as 'a party of Frank merchants'. H.M. Elliot and John Dowson (eds), *The History of India as Told by Its Own Historians* (Allahabad, 1964), vol. VII, extract from the *Badshah Nama*, p. 34.

13. Zia-ud-din Barani, *Tarikh-i-Firuz Shahi*, in H.M. Elliot and John Dowson (eds), *The History of India as Told by Its Own Historians*, vol. III, pp. 182–5.

14. Irfan Habib, 'Tradition and Syncretic Talent', *The Telegraph*, 13 April 1998. Third Convocation Address to Vidyasagar University, Midnapore.

15. Radhakumud Mookerji, *The Fundamental Unity of India* (London, 1914), p. 101.

16. Rock Edict XVI, text in D.C. Sircar, *Inscriptions of Asoka* (Delhi, 1957), p. 59.

17. Muhammad Tughlaq, it was said, 'brought the people of many countries under his rule in Hindustan, Gujarat, Malwa, the Mahratta (country), Tilang, Kampila, Dhur Samundar, Ma'bar, Lakhnauti, Sat-ganw Sunar-ganw, and Tirhut'. Zia-ud-Din Barani, *Tarikh-i-Firuz Shahi*, in *History of India as Told by Its Own Historians*, vol. III, p. 236.

18. Abul-Fazl Allami, *The Ain-i-Akbari*, trans. H.S. Jarrett, (rpt New Delhi, 1988), vol. III, p. 1.

19. J.W. McCrindle, *Ancient India as Described by Megasthenes and Arrian*, pp. 115, 150.

20. B.N. Mukherjee, 'Etymology of the Indian Nation', H.C. Raychaudhuri Centenary Lecture at Presidency College, printed in the *Telegraph* 19 Aug. 1992; H.C. Raychaudhuri, *Studies in Indian Antiquities* (Calcutta, 1958), pp. 63–87.

21. Megasthenes, fragment I, in McCrindle, *Ancient India*, p. 32.

22. McCrindle, *Ancient India*, p. 185.

23. Ibid., pp. 29, 43.

24. Ibid., p. 209.

25. Beal, *Si-Yu-Ki*, pt I, p. 69; Raychaudhuri, *Studies in Indian Antiquities*, p. 79. As I-Tsing later realized, the term Hsin-tu was foreign, and not known to the people of India themselves. I-Tsing, *A Record of the Buddhist Religion as Practised in India and the Malay Archipelago (AD 671–695)*, trans. J. Takahasu (New Delhi, 1982) pp. lii, 118.

26. D.C. Sircar, *Inscriptions of Asoka*, pp. 33, 35.

27. Raychaudhuri, *Studies in Indian Antiquities*, p. 64n.

28. D.C. Sircar, *Inscriptions of Asoka*, p. 35.

29. Raychaudhuri, *Studies in Indian Antiquities*, p. 64.

30. D.C. Sircar, *Inscriptions of Asoka*, pp. 40, 54, 59.

31. Ibid., p. 53n. I-Tsing later noted that India was called 'the kingdom of the Brahmans', *A Record of the Buddhist Religion*, p. 118.

32. Bana, *Kadambari*, ed. M.R. Kale (4th edn, Delhi, 1968), p. 290.

33. Raychaudhuri, *Indian Antiquities*, pp. 75–6. See also Shashi Kant, *The Hathigumpha Inscription of Kharavela and the Bhabru Edict of Asoka* (New Delhi, 2000), p. 16.

34. Raychaudhuri, *Indian Antiquities*, p. 77; Sircar, *Cosmography*, p. 37. Somadeva Suri is said to have used the term 'Bhāratiyāh' in the tenth century *Nitivākyāmritam*, but this may be a later interpolation. B.N. Mukherjee, *The Concept of India* (Calcutta, 1998), p. 37, n. 30.

35. Ibid., p. 54.

36. Beal, *Si-Yu-Ki*, pt I, p. 69.

37. *Alberuni's India*, ed. Edward C. Sachau (rpt New Delhi, 1983), p. 21.

38. D.R. Bhandarkar, 'A List of the Inscriptions of Northern India', *Appendix To Epigraphica Indica*, vols. XIX–XXIII (Delhi, rpt 1983), pp. 109–10, no. 784; *Archaeological Survey of India, Annual Report 1907–8* (rpt Delhi, 1990), p. 216.

39. Mukherjee, *The Concept of India* (Calcutta, 1998), p. 19; see also B.N. Mukherjee, 'Etymology of the Indian Nation', text of *Naksh-i-Rustam* inscription in Niharranjan Ray et al., *A Source book of Indian Civilization* (Calcutta, 2000), p. 554.

40. *Alberuni's India*, pt I, pp. 21, 198.

41. *Tuzak-i-Timuri*, in Elliot and Dowson (eds), *History of India*, vol. III, p. 396.

42. *The Tuzuk-i-Jahangiri or Memoirs of Jahangir*, trans. Alexander Rogers (3rd edn, New Delhi, 1978), vol. I, pp. 110–11.

43. *Ain-i-Akbari*, vol III, p. 7. See also M. Athar Ali, 'The Perception of India in Akbar and Abul Fazl', in Irfan Habib (ed.), *Akbar and His India* (Delhi, 1997), pp. 215–24.

44. Ibid., p. 1.

45. Muhammad Sharif Hanafi, *Majlis-us-Salatin*, in Elliot and Dowson (eds), *History of India*, vol. VII, pp. 137–9.

46. Extract from the *Periplus*, in Sircar, *Cosmography*, p. 118.

47. *Alberuni's India*, pt I, p. 207.

48. *Alberuni's India*, pt I, p. 202.

49. Megasthenes, fragment II, in McCrindle, *Ancient India*, p. 43.

50. Fo-Kwo-ki, in Beal, *Si-Yu-Ki: Buddhist Records of the Western World*, pp. XXIX, XXXIX.

51. *Alberuni's India*, pt I, p. 198.

52. Beal, *Si-Yu-Ki*, pp. 56–8.

53. McCrindle, *Ancient India*, pp. 29, 32, 39.

54. Beal, *Si-Yu-Ki*, p. 70.
55. *Mukhtasir-ut-Tawarikh*, in Elliot and Dowson (eds), *Studies in Indian History*, pt II (Calcutta, 1953), p. 3.
56. *Malfuzat-i-Timuri* in Elliot and Dowson (eds), *History of India*, vol. III, p. 395.
57. Beal, *Si-Yu-Ki: Buddhist Records of the Western World*, pp. 198–9.
58. *O pāre te kālo rang*
    Bristi pare jham jham,
    E pāre te lankā gāchh ti rāngā tuk tuk kare
    Gunabati bhāi āmār man keman kare.
    'E mās ta thāko didi kandie kokie
    O māse te loye jābo palki sājiye'.
    Hār holo bhājā bhājā mās holo dori
    Āi re āi nadir jal jhānp die pori
    Jogindranath Sarkar, *Khukumanir Chhara* (Calcutta, 1998, 1st pub. 1905), p. 67.
59. Arrian, in McCrindle, *Ancient India*, p. 190
60. *Tabakat-i-Nasiri* of Minhaj-us-Siraj, in Elliot and Dowson (eds), *History of India*, vol. II, p. 310.
61. Arrian, p. 203.
62. Megasthenes, in McCrindle, pp. 32–3.
63. Arrian, in McCrindle, p. 222.
64. Ibid., p. 203.
65. Ibid., p. 223.
66. Ibid., p. 223.
67. Sushil Kumar De, *Bangla Prabad* (Calcutta, BS 1392), no. 8365.
68. *Alberuni's India*, vol. I, p. 204.
69. Megasthenes, in McCrindle, p. 30.
70. Jogindranath Sarkar, *Khukumanir Chhara* (Calcutta, 1988), p. 25.
71. Megasthenes, in McCrindle, pp. 29–30.
72. *The Ain-i-Akbari*, vol. III, p. 1.
73. Megasthenes, in McCrindle, pp. 38–41.
74. Beal, *Si-Yu-Ki: Buddhist Records of the Western World*, p. 82.
75. Going by Greek and Muslim impressions, close to half the World's population might have been Chinese and Indian before the dramatic increase of the European population of the world during *c*.1100–1800. See comparative figures for 1750: *The Cambridge Economic History of India*, vol. 2, ed. Dharma Kumar (Cambridge, 1983), p. 522.

76. Arrian, in McCrindle, p. 200.

77. Radhakumud Mookerjee, *Indian Shipping* (Calcutta, 1957), p. 42.

78. Megasthenes, in McCrindle, p. 34.

79. *Alberuni's India*, pt I, p. 23.

80. Arrian, in McCrindle, p. 185.

81. Ibid., p. 204.

82. Ibid., p. 224.

83. Ibid., p. 225.

84. Beal, *Si-Yu-Ki*, p. 75.

85. *Ashika* of Amir Khusrau, in Elliot and Dowson (eds), *History of India*, vol. III, p. 557.

86. *Minhaj-us-Siraj*, p. 347 and passim. For full reference, see note 125.

87. *Minhaj-us-Siraj*, p. 306.

88. Ibid., pp. 306–310, 347, 350.

89. Ibid., p. 310

90. Ibid.

91. Ibid., pp. 310–13.

92. Suniti Kumar Chatterjee, *The Origin and Development of the Bengali Language* (Calcutta, 1975), vol. I, pp. 1–149.

93. *Alberuni's India*, pt I, p. 18.

94. *Nuh Sipihr* of Amir Khusrau, in Elliot and Dowson (eds), *History of India*, vol. III, p. 556; *Ashika* of Amir Khusrau, in Elliot and Dowson (eds), *History of India*, vol. III, p. 562.

95. *Nuh Sipihr*, pp. 562–3.

96. *Ain-i-Akbari*, p. 133.

97. *Ashika*, p. 556.

98. *Ashika*, p. 556.

99. *Nuh Sipihr*, p. 562.

100. *Ashika*, p. 562.

101. Sukumar Sen, *Banglar Sahitya Itihas* (New Delhi, 1965), foreword by Jawaharlal Nehru, 14 Nov. 1959.

102. In the *Padmavat*, the poet Malik Muhammad Jayasi used the term 'Jambudip', distinguishing it from 'Singhaldip' (Ceylon), though several medieval works reckoned Sri Lanka to be a part of India: e.g., Bernier's expression: 'the whole of Hindustan, as far as the island of Ceylon'. *Jayasi Granthavali: Arthat Padmavat, Akhravat aur Akhiri Kalam*, ed. Ramchandra Shukla (Banaras, vs 2700), p. 264; Francois

Bernier, *Travels in the Mogul Empire AD 1656–1668*, ed. Archibald Constable (Delhi, 1972), p. 186.

103. Hindi text of Banarsidas, *Ardhakathanaka*, in Appendix II of Mukund Lath (trans.), *Half a Tale* (Jaipur, 1981), p. 224.

104. *Ashkalul Bilad* of Ibn Haukal, trans. in Elliot and Dowson (eds), *History of India*, vol. I, pp. 32, 33. Map facing p. 32 in Elliot and Dowson (eds), *History of India*, also text accompanying the 12th chart in Elliot and Dowson (eds), *History of India*, (henceforth ED) vol. I, p. 33ff.

105. B.N. Mukherjee, 'Etymology of the Indian Nation', H.C. Raychaudhuri Centenary Lecture at Presidency College, printed in *Telegraph*, 19 Aug. 1992.

106. *Tarikh-i-Sabuktigin* of Abul Al Baihaki, ED, vol. II, p. 126.

107. *Tarikh-i-Firuz Shahi* of Zia-ud-Din Barani, ED, vol. I, p. 234.

108. *History of the Rise of the Mahomedan Power in India till the year AD 1612. Translated from the Original Persian of Mahomed Kasim Ferishta*, by John Briggs, 4 vols (London, 1829), vol. III, p. 198; vol. IV, p. 14 (henceforth Firishta).

109. *Muntakhabu-t-Tawarikh by Abdu-'L-Qadir Ibn-I-Muluk-Shah Known as Al Badaoni*, trans. W.H. Lowe (henceforth Badauni), vol. II, p. 253.

110. Badauni, vol. II, p. 419.

111. Sayyid Sultan, *Nabivamsa*, ed. Ahmad Sharif, vol. I, (Dacca, 1978), p. 327.

112. Bernier, *Travels in the Mogul Empire*, pp. 155–6. The possibility that the story is apocryphal, based on gossip Bernier heard at court, does not affect the argument here.

113. Sanskrit text of inscription (Devanagari script) in Pushpa Prasad, *Sanskrit Inscriptions of Delhi Sultanate* 1191–1526 (Delhi, 1990), pp. 8–11.

114. Verse 6, ibid., p. 8. Translation mine.

115. Verse 7, ibid., p. 8. Translation mine.

116. Verse 10, p. 9. Translation mine.

117. *Salisilat-ut-Tawarikh* of the Merchant Sulaiman, ED, vol. I, pp. 3–7.

118. *The Babur-nama in English (Memoirs of Babur), by Zahiru'd-din Muhammad Babur Padshah Ghazi*, trans, from Original Turki by Annette Susannah Beveridge, 2 vols (London, 1921), vol. I, p. 202.

119. Afanasy Nikitin, *Voyage Beyond Seas 1466–1472*, trans. Stepan Apresyan (Moscow, 1985), pp. 23–4.

120. Raychaudhuri, *Indian Antiquities*, pp. 75–6.

121. *Mirat-i-Masudi*, by Abdur Rahman Chishti, ED, vol. I, 548.

122. Mid-seventeenth century Sufi work, cited in P.M. Currie, *The Shrine and Cult of Mu'in Al-Din Chishti of Ajmer* (Delhi, 1992), p. 66.

123. Habib, *Politics and Society*, vol. I, p. 307.

124. *Babur-nama*, vol. II, pp. 479–80.

125. *Tabaqat-i-Nasiri—A General History of the Mahammadan Dynasties of Asia Including Hindustan from* AH *194* AD *810 to* AH *658 (1260) and the Eruption of the Infidel Mughals into Islam*, by Maulana Minhaj-ul-Din Abu Amar i-Usman, trans. Major H.G. Raverty, 2 vols (London, 1981), vol. I, p. 512.

126. Ibid., vol. II, pp. 869–86. The term Mughal, which in this period meant Mongol, was later applied by Indians to the dynasty of Babur, who was himself a Turk, but with a connection to Genghis Khan on the maternal side. By Akbar's time, the dynasty adopted the Indian name for itself. It then began to frown upon the uncomplimentary references to the Mongols in the Persian chronicles.

127. Firishta, vol. I, p. 336.

128. *Rehla*, p. 242.

129. Nikitin, *Voyage Beyond Seas*, pp. 16–17.

130. Document no. 29, letter from the Department of Foreign Affairs to N. Syroezhin and V. Tushkanov, 24 June 1646, in Surendra Gopal, *Indians in Russia in the 17th and 18th centuries* (Calcutta, 1988), pp. 27–8.

131. Document no. 69, evidence submitted by the Indian merchant Marwari to the Orenburg Despatch Department, ibid., pp. 178–80.

132. Al Biladuri, *Futuh-ul-Buldan*, ED, vol. I, p. 116.

133. *Alberuni's India*, vol. I, pp. 207–10.

134. Firsishta, vol. I, p. 419

135. Sarat Chandra Das, *Indian Pandits in the Land of Snow* (Calcutta, 1965), pp. 49, 55, 56.

136. *Taranatha's rGya-gar-chos-'Gyun* (The History of Buddhism in India) (1608 C.E.) contains, as the Lama himself tells us, a 'clear account of how the True Doctrine—the precious, the glorious and the source of all glories—was spread in the arya-desa'. *Taranatha's History of Buddhism in India*, trans. from Tibetan by Lama Chimpa and Alaka Chottapadhyaya, ed. Debiprasad Chattopadhyaya (Simla, 1970), p. 352.

137. Ibid., p. 5.

138. *Rehla*, p. 16. Ibn Battuta mentioned in particular the mango, the jackfruit, the *jam* and the *mahua*. Babar listed the following as 'peculiar to Hindustan' (some of them not in fact unique to the country): Mango,

plantain, *mahuwa, jaman,* jackfruit, coconut, *tar* (palmyra from which the liquor tari is produced), etc. *Babur-nama,* vol. II, pp. 503, 510.

139. *Babur-nama,* vol. II, pp. 488–501. Babar listed under this category the elephant, the rhinoceros, the blue bull (*nila gau*), the monkey, the peacock, and the parrot. He specified no less than 3 types of crocodile, too.

140. Ibn Battuta found the rhinoceros, now confined to Kaziranga forest of Assam, roaming freely in Sind, and encountered the animal later in Bahraich (in Uttar Pradesh) (*Rehla,* pp. 5, 111). The wild ass, now found only in the Rann of Cutch, was hunted by Emperor Akbar in the Nagore desert (in Rajasthan) (ED, vol. V, p. 336). Another animal, but not unique to India, the lion, now confined to the Gir forest of Gujarat, was to be found in the grass jungles on the Delhi–Lahore road as late as the seventeenth century (Bernier, pp. 375, 379).

141. *Malfuzat-i-Timuri* (Autobiography of Timur), ED, vol. III, p. 438.

142. John Fryer, *A New Account of East India and Persia Being Nine Years' Travels 1672–1681,* ed. William Crooke, 2 vols. (New Delhi, 1992), vol. II, p. 72.

143. John Huighen Van Linschoten, 'Observation of the East Indies', in J. Talboys Wheeler (ed.), *Early Travels in India, in the Sixteenth and Seventeenth Centuries* (Delhi, 1974), p. 221.

144. Ibid., p. 220.

145. Nikitin, *Voyage Beyond Seas,* p. 28. A normal 5½ feet long cobra might appear to a fearful stranger to be 14 feet long. A King Cobra, normally over 12 feet and known to measure as long as 20 feet, would be unlikely to appear in a town (there is, of course, no likelihood of a python turning up in town).

146. *Rehla,* p. 230.

147. 'They wind them about their neckes, armes, and legges, kissing them, with a thousand other deuises, onely to get money'. Linschoten, 'Observation of the East Indies', in Wheeler (ed.), *Early Travels,* p. 137.

148. *Dabistan-i-Mazahib,* cited in Horace Hayman Wilson, 'Sketch of the Religious Sects of the Hindus', *Asiatic Researches* (1832), vol. 17, p. 182.

149. Fryer, *A New Account of East India and Persia,* vol. II, p. 293.

150. *Tarikh-i-Salatin-i-Afghana* of Ahmad Yadgar, ED, vol. V, p. 24.

151. This is so despite some minor errors. A lover of grapes and musk melons, but not so keen on mangoes or coconuts, he remarked sweepingly that Hindustan had no first rate fruits. He thought, mistakenly, that all the artisans were Hindus. For the description, see *Babur-nama,* vol. II, pp. 484–520.

152. Ibid., p. 484.

153. Ibid., p. 485.

154. Ibid., pp. 486–7.

155. Ibid. p. 486. It would appear that the canals constructed by Firuz Tughlaq had fallen into disuse by this time. In any case, outside the irrigated Delhi territory and the Tanjore delta, crops had always been fed by monsoon rains in India.

156. Ibid., p. 487.

157. Ibid., p. 484.

158. Ibid., p. 519.

159. Firishta, vol. IV, p. 542.

160. Ibid., pp. 542–4.

161. Ibid., pp. 544–5.

162. *Ain-i-Akbari* by Abul Fazl-i-Allami, trans. From original Persian by Col. J.S. Jarrett, vol. II, (Calcutta, 1894), pp. 43–105.

163. *Babur-nama*, vol. II, p. 484.

164. *Babur-nama*, vol. I, pp. 74, 199.

165. *Ain-i-Akbari*, vol. II, p. 44.

166. Malik Muhammad Jayasi's *Padmavat* provides typical examples of both: Padmini's erotic dalliance with her ardent lover through the six seasons in distant Ceylon, while the anguished wife Nagmati pines away at Chittaur through the twelve months. Chapter 30, 'Shat Ritu Varnan Khand', and Chatper 30, 'Nagmati Viyog Khand', Jayasi, pp. 133, 137–46. Prithviraj Chauhan's diasastrous dalliance with Samjogita through the six seasons prior to his mortal encounter with Muhamad Ghori is described in ch. 9, *Prithviraja Rasau* of Chand Bardai, ed. Mataprasad Gupta (Jhansi vs 2020), pp. 241–50.

167. Firishta enumerates these as follows: Sawan and Bhadon (Varsha ritu), Ashwin and Kartick (Sharad ritu), Margshirsh and Poos (Hemant ritu), Magh and Phalgun (Shishir ritu) and Jaist and Ashar (Grishma ritu), vol. 4, p. 547.

168. *Babur-nama*, vol. II, p. 515.

169. Ibid., p. 520.

170. Bernier's letter to Monsieur de Merveille, en route Lahore to Kashmir, 10 March 1665, *Travels in the Mogul Empire*, p. 389.

171. Ibid., p. 240.

172. Ibid., p. 254.

173. Ibid., p. 433.

174. Ibid., p. 432.

175. Fryer, *A New Account of East India and Persia*, vol. II, pp. 85–6.

176. Firishta, vol. IV, p. 545.

177. McCrindle, *Ancient India*, p. 31.

178. *Rehla*, pp. 18–19.

179. *Ain-i-Akbari*, trans. Jarrett, vol. II, p. 10.

180. McCrindle, *Ancient India*, p. 29.

181. Ibid., p. 39.

182. Ibid., pp. 31–2.

183. The usage among the Indians not to molest non-combatants, and not to ravage an enemy's land by fire, were designed, according to Megasthenes, 'to prevent the occurrence of famine among them'. McCrindle, *Ancient India*, pp. 31–2.

184. Contrary to the prevailing practice of the Hindu kingdoms of the south, Malik Kafur, during his campaign of 1309, laid the country waste by fire and sword, a measure that 'confounded the inhabitants, who had never injured their wanton enemies'. Firishta, vol. I, pp. 371–2.

185. Firishta, vol. II, pp. 310–16. Firishta computes that during the reign of Muhammad Shah Bahmani I, 'nearly five hundred thousand unbelievers fell by the swords of the warriors of Islam, by which the population of the Carnatic was so reduced that it did not recover for several ages'. Ibid., p. 327.

186. Ibid., p. 319. This was honoured in the next round of Vijaynagar–Bahmani warfare. Ibid., p. 338.

187. Ibid., p. 375. Subsequently, the Vijaynagar army violated the compact on one occasion, and the Bahmani army did so on another. Ibid., pp. 391, 402.

188. Ibid., p. 319.

189. *Muntakhabu-t-Tawarikh* by Al Badaoni, trans. W.H. Lowe, vol. II (Delhi, 1986), p. 240n. A Mughal officer accused of 'hovering round and harrying the Banjar-s' was deprived by Emperor Akbar of his *jagir*. Ibid., p. 182.

190. Firishta, vol. I, p. 389.

191. *Muntakhabu-t-Tawarikh* by Al Badaoni, trans. George S.A. Ranking, vol. I (Patna, 1973), p. 495.

192. Ibid., pp. 445–6; Firishta, vol. II, pp. 124–5.

193. Jean Baptiste Tavernier, *Travels in India*, trans. V. Ball, 2 vols (London, 1889), vol. I, pp. 1–8.

194. *Babur-nama*, vol. II, p. 520.

195. Bernier, *Travels in the Mogul Empire*, p. 202.

196. 'And if the King's Fleet be but ordinary, considering so great a Monarch and these Advantages, it is because he minds it not; he contenting himself in the enjoyment of the continent, and styles the Christians Lions of the Sea; saying that God has allotted that Unstable Element to their Rule'. Fryer, *A New Account of East India and Persia*, vol. I, p. 302.

197. The Mughal *sikka* rupee, 'the most refined, and purest from alloy, in the world', became the universal currency. Ibid., p. 248.

198. Ibid., p. 300.

199. Tavernier, *Travels in India*, vol. I, pp. 32, 34.

200. Ibid., p. 36.

201. Ibid., pp. 37–8.

202. Bernier, *Travels in the Mogul Empire*, pp. 248–9. The essential articles and foodstuffs travelled over long distances: rice from Bengal up the Ganges to Patna and by sea to Masulipatam, sugar to Golkunda and the Carnatic, and cotton for the whole of the Mughal empire as far as Lahore and Kabul. Ibid., p. 439.

203. Fryer, *A New Account of East India and Persia*, vol. I, p. 81; *The Book of Duarte Barbosa*, ed. Mansel Longworth Dames (New Delhi, 1989), vol. I, p. Lxiii.

204. Prasad, *Sanskrit Inscriptions*, p. 29, Sanskrit verses 3, 4, 5 and 6 of the Sarban Stone Inscription.

205. Philip B. Wagoner, '"Sultan among Hindu Kings": Dress Titles and Islamization of Hindu Culture at Vijayanagara', *The Journal of the Asian History*, vol. 85, no. 4, Nov. 1996, pp. 851–80. He used the title Hinduraya-Suratrana; Brajadulal Chattopadhyaya, *Representing the Other? Sanskrit Sources and the Muslims (Eighth to Fourteenth Century)* (New Delhi, 1998), p. 54.

206. D.R. Bhandarkar, 'A List of the Inscriptions of Northern India', *Appendix to Epigraphica Indica*, vols XIX–XXIII (Delhi, rpt 1983), p. 109. Kumbha used the title 'Hindu-suratrana'; Krishna Deva Raja Raya, in a Sanskrit inscription dated the 3rd day of the moon in the month of March 1514, referred to himself as 'Hindu-raya-Suratrana-dushta-shārdulla-mardana'. *Asiatic Researches*, vol. 22, 1836, p. 37.

207. *The Prithviraja Rasau* (p. 277), *the Kirtilata* of the Maithali poet Vidyapati (ed. Baburam Saksena, Kashi 1924 p. 44), and the *Ranamalla Chhanda* (ed. Mulchand Pranesh, Bikaner, 1972, verse 11), all contain the term Hindu. The *Prithviraja Rasau* is reputed to have been composed by

Prithviraj Chauhan's bard and companion Chand Bardai, but the work in its existing form is judged to be no earlier than 1400. The *Kirtilata* is said to have been composed in 1380, and *Ranamalla Chhanda* is assigned to 1408–11.

208. The *Ranamalla Chhanda* refers to the Muslim opponents of the protagonist indiscriminately as Yavana, Shaka, Pārasikka Mlechchha, Mungala, Mungala Mahāmālikka, Turakka, Turakki, Tara, Tatara, etc. See verses 1, 5, 41, 50, 57, 59. References in Sanskrit inscriptions occur earlier: Turaka (AD 1191) Mlechchha (*c*.1200), Yavana (*c*.1200), Shaka (1276). Prasad, *Sanskrit Inscriptions*, Sanskrit texts nos. I, 4, verse 3; II, 1, l.15; II, 18, l.12.

209. Brajadulal Chattopadhyay, *Representing the Other? Sanskrit Sources and the Muslims* (New Delhi, 1998), pp. 28–30, 92–7.

210. D.C. Sircar, 'Veraval Inscriptions of Chaulukya Vaghela Arjuna, 1264 AD', in *Epigraphica Indica*, vol. XXXIV, 1961–62, no. 21, p. 149.

211. *Alberuni's India. An Account of the Religion, Philosophy, Literature, Geography, Chronology, Astronomy, Customs, Laws and Astrology of India about AD 1030*, trans. Edward C. Sachau (New Delhi, 1983), vol. 1, p. 17.

212. Ibid., p. 21.

213. Ibid., p. 22.

214. Ibid., p. 19.

215. Abdul Rahman, *Sandesh Rasak*, ed. Hazari Prasad Dwivedi and Visvanath Tripathi (Bombay, 1960), verse 3. According to Muni Jinavijaya, the work was written before the Ghori conquest, i.e. before 1192. Rahul Sankrityana assigns it to the eleventh century, and Hazari Prasad Dwivedi to 1200 or thereabouts.

216. *Tarikh-i-Firuz Shahi* of Zia-ud-Din Barani, ED, vol. III, p. 225.

217. Ibid., p. 227.

218. Ibid., p. 100.

219. *Tarikh-i-Firuz Shahi*, quoted by M. Mujeeb, The Indian Muslims (London, 1969), p. 32.

220. *Ashika* of Amir Khusrau, ED, vol. III, p. 544. Mughal = Mongols.

221. *Tarikh-i-Firuz Shahi*, ED, vol. III, p. 213.

222. Firishta, vol. III, p. 346.

223. A couplet by the Punjabi Muslim poet Siri, included in Badauni's large collection of Persian poetry during the reign of Akbar. Badauni, vol. III, p. 346.

224. *Muntakhab-ul-Lubab* of Kafi Khan, ED, vol. VII, p. 293.

225. *Prithviraja Rasau*, I.28.

226. *Hindu Turake milala vāsa*
     Ekaka dhamme aoka upahāsa
     Katahu bānga katahu veda
     Katahu misimila katahu chheda
     [*Kirtilata*, p. 44 (translation mine)].

227. *Padmavat*, 42.13, *Jayasi Granthavali*, p. 202.

228. *Muruj-ul-Zahab* of Al Masudi, ED, vol. I, p. 20.

229. *Taj-ul-Maasir* of Hasan Nizami, ED, vol. II, p. 208.

230. Firishta, vol. II, p. 370.

231. The *Ashika* of Amir Khusrau, ED, vol. III, p. 546.

232. Firishta, vol. II, p. 474.

233. Nikitin, *Voyage Beyond Seas*, p. 28.

234. Ibid., pp. 28–34.

235. Ibid., p. 18.

236. 'Islam and the Muslims', in Hasan Nizami's narrative, mark out and
     define the 'Infidels and plural-worshippers', i.e. the Hindus, by extir-
     pating 'the enemies of religion and the state'. Qutbuddin Aibek, 'the
     pillar of Islam' and chastiser of the Hindus, is said to have 'deluged the
     land of Hind with the blood of their hearts'. Taj-ul-Maasir, ED, vol. II,
     p. 209. Iltutmish, who declared himself 'the master of the kings of the
     Turks and the Persians', was at the same time, 'the keeper of Islam and
     Muslims' and 'the subjugator of the evil-doers and polytheists'. Adhai
     Din Ka Jhopda inscription (text), in A.K. Bhattacharya,
     *Cultural, Historical and Political Aspects of Perso-Arabic Epigraphy in
     India* (Calcutta, 1999), p. 145.

237. Badauni, vol. I, p. 8.

238. For instance, *'Sunnat dile hoy Musalman, nari loker ki hoy bidhan'* (Lalan
     Fakir of Bengal), Circumcision makes a Musalman, but how about the
     woman?

239. Fryer, *A New Account of East India and Persia*, vol. I, pp. 234–41.

240. Dampakht (Persian), steamed food. Fryer omits to mention the absolute
     prohibition against pork. He does mention a point setting them apart
     from the Hindus: 'Their great scruple is about Eating together among
     all sorts of these Eastern Nations'. Ibid., p. 232.

241. *Tabaqat-i-Akbari* of Nizamuddin Ahmad, ED, vol. V, p. 392.

242. Khaliq Ahmad Nizami, *Some Aspects of Religion and Politics in India
     during the Thirteenth Century* (Aligarh, 1961), p. 160.

243. Richard Eaton dates the appearance of the East Bengali Muslim majority to the sixteenth century. Stephen Dale finds that the Mappila Muslim community formed a majority in and around Calicut in the fifteenth and sixteenth centuries. Richard M. Eaton, *The Rise of Islam and the Bengal Frontier 1204–1760* (Delhi, 1994), pp. 129–34; Stephen Dale, *The Mappilas of Malabar 1498–1922. Islamic Society on the South Asian Frontier* (Oxford, 1986), pp. 24–32.

244. Barbara Daly Metcalf argues, 'Common knowledge assumes that identities such as "Indian Muslims" are primary and of long historical standing, but in fact they are products of recent history.' *Perfecting Women: Maulana Ashraf Ali Thanawi's Bihishti Zewar* (Delhi, 1992), p. 9. M. Mujeeb said earlier that the Indian Muslims have taken themselves for granted in all periods of Indian Muslim history. *The Indian Muslims* (London, 1967), p. 9. I feel Mujeeb is closer to reality than Metcalf.

245. *Nabivamsa* I, p. 6.

246. *Tarikh-i-Firishta*, ED, vol. v, p. 546, also pp. 533–4; Badauni, vol. ii, p. 347.

247. *Tarikh-i-Firishta*, ED, vol. v, p. 545.

248. Ibid., pp. 4–41.

249. Ibid., pp. 495–7.

250. Ibid., pp. 533–69. Firishta is puzzled by the fact that the infidels of China, like the Hindus, are unaware of the Flood, and the subsequent peopling of the earth by the sons of Noah. He wonders at the assumption of the Hindus that the Brahman and Khatri castes have existed from time immemorial, and mankind from the very beginning of creation. For a treatment of popular Islamic creation myths in Bengal, see Asim Roy, *The Islamic Syncretistic Tradition in Bengal* (New Delhi, 1983), pp. 87–110.

251. There was an earlier encounter in Sind between Muhammad bin Qasim and his Hindu opponents, but the memory of it was lost as the traces of Arab rule disappeared and Sind reverted to the Hindu rulers (Firishta, vol. iv, p. 411; ED, vol. i, pp. 483–97). The memory of the expeditions of Al Biruni's master, Mahmud of Ghazni, was, on the contrary, etched into the mind of the natives on account of the destruction of the idols of Somnath, Nagarkot, and elsewhere. As soon as Ghazni fell upon hard days, new idols were re-erected in the desecrated shrines. It was rumoured that the great idol of Nagarkot had revenged himself upon Ghazni and had reappeared miraculously: an idol of the same size and shape having been surreptitiously placed there at night. 'The story raised the fame of the shrine to such a degree, that thousands came daily to worship from all parts of Hindoostan, as also to consult the oracle

upon all important occasions; and at this particular time, the offerings
of gold, and silver, and jewels, brought and sent by the different princes
from far and near, is supposed to have nearly equalled the wealth
Mahmood carried away.' Firishta, vol. I, p. 119. As regards the Somnath
idol, the Hindus believed that the Chauhan prince Kanhardev defeated
the ruler of Ghazni, recovered the idol, and reinstalled it. *Ranamalla
Chhanda*, verses 62–3.

252. *Alberuni's India*, pp. 17–20.

253. Ibid., p. 111.

254. Ibid., pp. 19–20.

255. Ibid., p. 100.

256. *Kirtilata*, pp. 42–4.

257. Ibid.

258. Badauni, vol. II, p. 268.

259. Fryer, *A New Account of East India and Persia*, vol. I, p. 95.

260. *Nabivamsa* I, pp. 495–6.

261. *Rehla*, pp. 181–2.

262. *Wakiat-i-Mushtaki*, ED, vol. IV, pp. 541, 548–9.

263. Firishta, vol. III, pp. 241–2.

264. *Tabaqat-i-Akbari* of Nizamuddin Ahmad, ED, vol. V, p. 468; Badauni,
vol. II, p. 227.

265. Ibid., pp. 312–13.

266. Badauni cites a saying of the Prophet that God curses the slaughterer
of the cow, the tree feller, and the slave dealer, yet he noted the belief of
the common people (among Indian Muslims) that unless they eat beef
their faith cannot be true. M. Athar Ali, *Elements of Social Justice in
Medieval Islamic Thought* (Indian History Congress Symposia Paper
no. 14, Delhi, 1997), pp. 12–13.

267. *Rehla*, p. 47.

268. *Matla-us-Sadain* of Abdur Razzak, ED, vol. IV, p. 103.

269. N. Venkataramayya and M. Somasekhara Sarma, 'Vilasa Grant of
Prolaya Nayaka', in *Epigraphica Indica*, vol. XXXII, 1957–8, pp. 238–68.
Sanskrit text, pp. 261–2; English paraphrase (not a literal translation),
pp. 241–2.

270. Vilasa Grant, Ll. 4–13.

271. Ll. 13–28.

272. Ll. 32–6.

273. Ll. 37–8.

274. L1. 50–2.

275. For a contrary argument, see Brajadulal Chattopadhyay, *Representing the Other?*

276. Ganga Devi, *Madhura-Viyayam-Nama-Vira-Kampa-Raya-Charitam*, ed. by Harihara Sastri and V. Srinivasa Sastri (Trivandrum, 1916), pp. 70–2.

277. *Rehla*, pp. 227–8.

278. Firishta, vol. II, pp. 310, 391.

279. *Rehla*, pp. 62–3.

280. Firishta, vol. IV, pp. 68–9.

281. Firishta, vol. IV, p. 256; ED, vol. IV, 531; Firishta, vol. II, p. 120.

282. *Tarikh-i-Sher Shahi* of Abbas Khan Sarwani, ED, vol. IV, p. 397.

283. Ibid., p. 402.

284. Ibid., p. 403; Firishta, vol. II, p. 120.

285. Firishta, vol. II, p. 497. The reason why the killing of Brahmans was considered inauspicious is that the founder of the dynasty was known to have been the trusted slave of a Brahman.

286. Firishta, vol. III, p. 121.

287. Firishta, vol. II, p. 60.

288. Fryer, vol. I, p. 309.

289. Firishta observes with regard to the Vijayanagar soldiers that 'they seemed desirous to discharge the vengeance and resentment of many ages'. Firishta, vol. II, p. 391.

290. Sanskrit text of Etawa Fort Inscription in Prasad, *Sanskrit Inscriptions*, pp. 92–3.

291. *Muntakhab-ul-Lubab* of Kafi Khan, ED, vol. VII, pp. 404–5.

292. Firishta, vol. II, p. 431.

293. Bernier, *Travels in the Mogul Empire*, p. 306.

294. *A Pepys of Mogul India 1653–1708: Being an Abridged Edition of 'Storia Do Mogor' of Niccolao Manucci*, trans William Irvine, ed. Margaret L. Irvine (London, 1913), p. 113; Tavernier, *Travels in India*, vol. II, pp. 224–43.

295. Muhammad bin Qasim converted no temple into a mosque, but built an independent mosque at leisure, presumably because he was in no hurry to have the Khutba read at the 'Central' place. *Futuh-ul-Buldan* of Al Biladuri, ED, vol. I, p. 122.

296. The list includes the Brihadishvara temple at Thanjavur, the Kandariya Mahadeo temple at Khajuraho, and the Lingaraj temple at Bhuvaneswar.

The Somnath temple itself was no more than a hundred years old. The Sun temple of Konarak would be built two centuries later. Krishna Deva, *Temples of North India* (New Delhi, 1969), pp. 48, 78–9; A.L. Basham, *The Wonder that was India* (New York, 1954), p. 357.

297. *Futuh-ul-Buldan* of Al Biladuri, ED, vol. I, p. 122.

298. *The Dabistan or School of Manners. The Religious Beliefs, Observances, Philosophic Opinions and Social Customs of the East*, trans. from Persian by David Shea and Anthony Troyer (Washington, 1901); H.H. Wilson, 'A Sketch of the Religious Sects of the Hindus', *Asiatic Researches*, vol. 16 (1828) and 17C (1832).

299. *Alberuni's India*, pp. 101–2; *Ardhakathanaka*, p. 225

300. Firishta, vol. I, pp. LXiii– LXiv, 373; ED I, p. 151. That the most ancient clan of Banias, the Agarwals, had sprung up by the mid-twelfth century at the latest is evident from the internal evidence of the Sarban stone inscription of 1328. Prasad, *Sanskrit Inscriptions*, pp. 22–30.

301. The differentiation of the vernacular languages in the Vijayanagar kingdom was sufficiently clear for the Portuguese to identify, around 1518, the Tulu, Marathi, Telugu, Kanara and Tamil languages, and also Malayalam beyond Vijayanagara. *The Book of Duarte Barbosa*, vol. I, pp. 182–5.

302. Balban is said to have subdued the Gaudas, Andhras, Keralas, Karnatas, Maharashtras, Gujjaratas, and Latas in an inscription of 1276. Prasad, *Sanskrit Inscriptions*, p. 4. It is also interesting to note the ethnic and provincial categories used by Firishta to classify the numerous mistresses maintained by a Bahmani Sultan: Arabian, Turk, Russian, European, Afghan, Rajput, Bengali, Gujarati, Telengani and Marathi. Firishta, vol. II, p. 370.

303. Barbosa divided the population of Gujarat into 'heathens' and 'Moors', and subdivided the former into 'Resbutos' (Rajputs), 'Baneanes' (Banias), 'Bramenes' (Brahmans), and 'Pateles' (Kanbi-Patidars), and the latter into 'Turks, Mamalukes, Arabs, Persians, Coraçones [Khorasanis], and Targimoes [Turkomans]; others came from the great kingdom of Dely, and others of the land itself'. *The Book of Duarte Barbosa*, vol. I, pp. 108–21.

304. Wheeler (ed.), *Early Travels*, p. 131.

305. Wilson, 'Religions Sects of the Hindus', *Asiatic Researches*, vol. 17, pp. 310–12.

306. *Dabistan*, p. 199.

307. Ibid., p. 245.

308. Ibid., p. 237.

309. Ibid., pp. 249–52.

310. Ibid., pp. 260–7.

311. Ibid., p. 275.

312. Ibid., p. 284.

313. The Sannyasis fought with the Jogis at Kurukshetra in 1564, and with the Vairagis at Hardwar in 1650. On both occasions the Sannyasis overwhelmed their opponents, and on the latter occasion the defeated Vairagis concealed themselves as Jogis to escape their wrath. Al Badaoni, vol. II, p. 95; *Dabistan*, p. 245.

314. *Dabistan*, p. 173 ff.; Wilson, 'Religious Sects of the Hindus', *Asiatic Researches*, vol. 16, pp. 3–4, 23.

315. 'At night they go to places which they call smasana, and where the dead bodies are burnt; there they intoxicate themselves, eat the flesh of the corpses burnt, and copulate before the eyes of others with women, which they call sakti puja: and if the devoted woman be that of another, the good work is so much more valuable, and it is certain that they offer their wives to each other, the disciples bring their wives and daughters to their preceptor; they unite with their mothers, sisters, paternal and maternal aunts, which is against the custom of the Hindus, who do not take daughters of near relations. ... This sect hold women in great esteem, and call them Saktis (powers); and to ill treat a sakti, that is, a woman, is held a crime.' *Dabistan*, pp. 251–2.

316. 'How far the worship of the Linga is authorized by the Vedas, is doubtful, but it is the main purport of several of the *Puranas*. There can be no doubt of its universality at the period of the Mohammadan invasion of India.' Wilson, 'Religious Sects of the Hindus', *Asiatic Researches*, vol. 17, p. 194.

317. Ibid., pp. 194–5.

318. Ibid., vol. 16, pp. 16–17.

319. Ibid., p. 14.

320. *Rehla*, pp. 164–6.

321. Wilson, 'Religious Sects of the Hindus', *Asiatic Researches*, pp. 14, 16.

322. Friedhelm Hardy, *Viraha-Bhakti: The Early History of Krishna Devotion in South India* (Delhi, 1983), p. 40.

323. Wilson, 'Religious Sects of the Hindus', *Asiatic Researches*, vol. 16, pp. 49–50.

324. Ibid., vol. 17, pp. 183–4.

325. Ibid., vol. 16, pp. 36–7.

326. Ibid., pp. 36–7.

327. Ibid., p. 44.

328. Ibid., p. 43.

329. J.T.F. Jordens, 'Medieval Hindu Devotionalism', in A.L. Basham (ed.), *A Cultural History of India* (Oxford, 1975), p. 277.

330. Muhammed Enamul Haq, *Muslim Bangla Sahitya* (Dacca, 1965), pp. 50–3, cited in Roy, *Islamic Syncretistic Tradition*, p. 190.

331. Hardy, *Viraha-Bhakti*, p. 378.

332. The same legend is recounted of Mira Bai, another real poetess of a later date.

333. Gaudiya Vaishnavas belong to the sect of Shri Chaitanya of Bengal. For comparisons of the Sufi notion of Ishq with Kabir's Viraha and Chaitanya's Prem, see Vaudeville, *A Weaver Named Kabir*, p. 105; and Roy, *Islamic Syncretistic Tradition*, p. 190ff.

334. Habib, *Politics and Society*, p. 312 (trans. Mohammad Habib).

335. Louis Dumont, *Homo Hierarchicus: The Caste System and Its Implications* (London, 1966), passim. Dumont regarded these notions as the timeless foundation of Indian society. Actually these notions evolved through history. The full articulation of the system based on these notions probably did not occur before Al Biruni.

336. I-Tsing, *A Record of the Buddhist Religion*, p. 19, see note 25.

337. *Ain-i-Akbari*, vol. III, p. 319.

338. Ibid., p. 320.

339. Ibid., pp. 321–2.

340. *Alberuni's India*, pp. 100–2. Hiuen Tsang earlier spoke of the four castes (Brahman, Kshatriya, Vaishya, and Sudra), but not so clearly of the outcastes specified by Al Biruni. However, the notions of pollution had already been articulated by the time of the Chinese pilgrim's visit. Beal, *Si-Yu-Ki*, pp. 77, 82.

341. *The Suma Oriental of Tome Pires: An Account of the East, from the Red Sea to Japan, written in Malacca and India in 1512–1515 and the Book of Francisco Rodriguez* (New Delhi, 1990), vol. I, p. 71.

342. Stephen Frederic Dale, *The Mappilas of Malabar 1498–1922. Islamic Society on the South Asian Frontier* (Oxford, 1980), pp. 11–32.

343. Susan Bayly, *Saints, Goddesses and Kings: Muslims and Christians in South Indian Society 1700–1900* (Cambridge, 1992), pp. 79–80.

344. Dale, *The Mappilas of Malabar*, p. 26; Susan Bayly, *Saints, Goddesses and Kings*, p. 80; Richard M. Eaton, *The Rise of Islam and the Bengal Frontier, 1204–1760* (Delhi, 1994), p. 130.

345. A Tamil Copperplate, given to Arab settlers by the ruler of Madurai, is dated AD 875. Another mid-ninth century copperplate given to the Syrian Christians mentions Muslim and Jewish witnesses at Quilon. Dale, *The Mappilas of Malabar*, p. 24; Annemarie Schimmel, *Islam in the Indian Subcontinent* (London, 1980), p. 3.

346. 'The Rais of Ma'bar fled with their treasures and valuables; but above a hundred elephants, which had been left in two cities, fell into the hands of Khusru Khan. On his arriving in Ma'bar the rains came on, and he was compelled to remain. There was in Ma'bar a merchant, named Taki Khan, a Sunni by profession, who had acquired great wealth, which he had purified by paying the alms prescribed by his religion. Relying on the fact of the invading army being Musulman, he did not flee. Khusru Khan, who had nothing in his heart but rapacity and villainy, seized this Musulman, took his money from him by force, and put him to death, declaring the money to belong to the Treasury.' Zia-ud-Din Barani, *Tarikh-i-Firuz Shahi*, ED, vol. III, p. 219.

347. This remarkable development is chronicled in a contemporary Arabic tract, *Tuhfat-ul-Mujahidin fi ba'zi ahwal-al-Purtukaliyyin*, written by Shaikh Zainuddin al-Mabari. What follows is based on the translation, *Tuhfat-Al-Mujahidin. An Historical Work in the Arabic Language*, translated into English by S. Muhammad Husayn Nainar (Aligarh, 1942).

348. Ibid., p. 12.

349. Ibid., p. 44.

350. Ibid., p. 48.

351. Ibid., p. 52.

352. Ibid., p. 51.

353. Ibid., pp. 54–6, 60.

354. Ibid., p. 22.

355. Ibid., p. 22.

356. Ibid., p. 66. These events refer to AD 1525.

357. Ibid., p. 22

358. Ibid., pp. 35–6.

359. Ibid., p. 36n.

360. *Suma Oriental* 1512–15, vol. I, p. 78; *The Book of Duarte Barbosa 1518*, vol. II, pp. 2–5; Firishta, vol. IV, pp. 531–2.

361. *Rehla*, pp. 187–8.

362. Doubts were entertained in Akbar's time as to whether there was a real person named Salar Masud, the legendary nephew of Sultan Mahmud, who is said to have been martyred and buried in Bahraich.

'What sort of a man', Badauni heard a courtier ask of a Shaikh, 'was Salar Masud, whom the common people of India worship?' The Shaikh replied, 'He was an Afghan who met his death by martyrdom.' *Muntakhabu-t-Tawarikh*, trans. Wolseley Haig, vol. III (Delhi, 1986), pp. 46–7. A letter from Amir Khusrau to a friend in Delhi (c.AD 1287–90) specifically mentions that 'the fragrant tomb of Sipahsalar Shahid [in the town of Bahraich] scents the entire Hindustan with the perfume of odorous wood'. This is positive proof that the tomb existed in the thirteenth century, though the antecedents of the warrior–saint said to have been buried there are not clear from the letter. Iqtidar Husain Siddiqui, 'A Note on the Dargah of Salar Masud in Bahraich in the Light of Standard Historical Sources', in Christian W. Troll (ed.), *Muslims Shrines in India. Their Character, History and Significance* (Delhi, 1989), p. 45. Ibn Battuta provides another early reference to the tomb during the reign of Muhammad Tughlaq: 'The Sultan crossed it [the Saryu] with the object of paying his homage at the tomb of the virtuous hero, Shaikh Salar 'ud, who had conquered these parts. Many marvellous stories are told about him and some notable battles are attributed to him.' *Rehla*, p. 110.

363. Firishta, vol. I, p. 431.

364. *Mirat-i-Masudi*, ED, vol. II, p. 527.

365. Ibid., p. 530.

366. Ibid., p. 548.

367. *Tarikh-i-Daudi of Abdullah*, ED, vol. IV, p. 448; *Zubdatu-t-Tawarikh* of Shaikh Nurul Haq, ED, vol. VI, p. 189; Tahir Mahmood, 'The Dargah of Sayyid Salar Mas'ud Ghazi in Bahraich: Legend, Tradition and Reality', in Troll (ed.), *Muslim Shrines*, pp. 24–5, 29, 35, 37.

368. *Rehla*, p. 32.

369. Ibn Battuta later heard that Shah Jalal had died in Sylhet at the age of one hundred and fifty years. Ibid., pp. 238–9.

370. Ibid., p. 239. This contemporary account is at variance with later legends which portray Shah Jalal as a warrior who conquered Sylhet at the head of an army. Ibid., p. 238n.

371. Ibid., p. 239.

372. Firishta, vol. I, pp. 376–7; Badauni, vol. III, pp. 1, 119.

373. Badauni, vol. III, p. 230.

374. Badauni, vol. III, p. 175; ED, vol. V, p. 391.

375. Khaliq Ahmad Nizami, *Some Aspects of Religion and Politics in India During the Thirteenth Century* (Aligarh, 1961), pp. 315–16.

376. *Tarikh-i-Firuz Shahi*, ED, vol. IV, p. 184.

377. Ibid., p. 185.

378. Ibid., p. 188.

379. *Nuh Sipihr* of Amir Khusrau, ED, vol. III, p. 510.

380. *Padmavat*, ch. 47 in *Jayasi Granthavali*, p. 233.

381. Ibid., Ch. 57, p. 269. Translation mine.

382. As Jayasi explained it, the Rana was 'the mind', Padmini 'the intellect', and Sultan Alauddin 'an illusion'. Ibid., p. 270.

383. Badauni, vol. III, p. 43.

384. Ibid., p. 50.

385. While visiting the tomb of Aminuddin Ala amidst the ruins of Bijapur in 1811, Capt. G. Sydenham observed, 'The striking contrast between the honors [sic] paid to the memory of these devotees, and the neglect shown to that of kings, is observable throughout India'. 'An Account of Bijapur in 1811', *Asiatic Researches*, vol. 13, 1818, p. 448.

386. Mujeeb, *The Indian Muslims*, p. 301. In the earlier half of the sixteenth century.

387. Badauni, vol. III, p. 7. Sheikh Pirak of Lucknow also lived in a cave in the forest, breaking his fast no oftener than once a week after the Friday prayers, when his old attendant would bring him a fragment of dry bread and some fruit of a plantain tree he had planted with his own hand. Badauni records the following: 'When Husain Khan was governor of Lakhnau I went with a friend of mine named Abdu-r-Rahman, who was Husain Khan's deputy, to endeavour to obtain an interview with the Shaikh. We found him nothing but skin, as it were, stretched over the bones, and great snakes darted their heads out of their holes both within and without the cave. One of those present was terrified and would have struck at them with his staff, but the Shaikh forbade him by a sign, and said, "What have they taken from you?"'. Ibid., p. 105.

388. Ibid., p. 57.

389. *The Travels of Abbé Carré in India and the Near East*, trans. Lady Fawcett (London, 1947), vol. II, p. 323.

390. Richard Maxwell Eaton, *Sufis of Bijapur 1300–1700: Social Roles of Sufis in Medieval India* (Princeton, 1978), pp. 157–64. The songs were known as Chakki Nama (Song of the Corn Grinder) and Charkha Nama (Song of the Spinning Wheel).

391. Shaikh Arif-i-Husaini, whom Badauni visited in Delhi, 'exhibited great supernatural power, in Gujarat, Hindustan, Kashmir, and Tibet, and wherever he went attempts were made on his life, and he travelled from country to country'. Badauni, vol. III, p. 99.

392. Nikitin, *Voyage Beyond Seas*, pp. 24–6.

393. Eaton, *Sufis of Bijapur*; 'Gentils' meant Hindus.

394. Running amok.

395. Haj.

396. Fryer, *A New Account of East India and Persia*, vol. I, pp. 229–30.

397. Firishta, vol. II, pp. 434–5; Badauni, vol. III, pp. 98–9.

398. Schimmel, *Islam in the Indian Subcontinent*, p. 140.

399. *Asiatic Researches*, vol. 13, 1818, pp. 418–19.

400. He refers to them as Haidari fakirs: 'They performed a dance (sima), and having kindled a fire they got into it and were not hurt.' *Rehla*, p. 145.

401. Ibid., pp. 207–8.

402. *Dabistan*, p. 279.

403. Ibid., pp. 278–9.

404. Bernier, *Travels in the Mogul Empire*, p. 320.

405. Badauni, vol. III, p. 10.

406. Ibid., p. 11.

407. Ibid., p. 15.

408. Ibid., pp. 15–16.

409. Nizami, *Religion and Politics*, p. 239.

410. Ibid., p. 238.

411. Schimmel, *Islam in the Indian Subcontinent*, p. 83.

412. Firishta, vol. I, p. 178.

413. Nizami, *Religion and Politics*, preface by M. Habib, p. xii.

414. Eaton, *Sufis of Bijapur*, pp. 90–4.

415. The establishment of Urdu-e-Mualla was followed in the reign of Sikandar Lodi, by another development: Hindus began to learn Persian systematically. Firishta, vol. I, p. 587.

416. *Rehla*, p. 166.

417. Ibid., p. 188. In Malabar.

418. Ibid., p. 239.

419. Ibid., p. 177.

420. Ibid., p. 179.

421. Ibid., p. 20.

422. Nikitin, *Voyage Beyond Seas*, p. 23.

423. Firishta, vol. II, p. 434.

424. *Matla-us-Sadain* of Abdur Razzaq, ED, vol. IV, p. 124.

425. Fryer, *A New Account of East India and Persia*, vol. I, p. 258.

426. Ibid., pp. 95, 236.

427. 'At the end of their *Quarentine*, which is Forty days, after the old law, they enter the *Hummums* to Purify ...' Ibid., pp. 237–8.

428. Shams-i-Siraj, *Tarikh-i-Firuz Shahi*, ED, vol. III, p. 366.

429. Ibid., p. 365.

430. Abdullah, *Tarikh-i-Daudi*, ED, vol. IV, p. 448; Shaikh Nurul Haq, *Zubdat-ut-Tawarikh*, ED, vol. VI, p. 187.

431. Badauni, vol. II, pp. 140–1.

432. Shah Waliullah, *Tafhimat-i-Ilahiyya*, quoted in J.M.S. Baljon, 'Shah Waliullah and the Dargah', in Troll (ed.), *Muslim Shrines*, p. 193

433. Marc Gaborieau, 'A Nineteenth Century Indian "Wahhabi" Tract against the Cult of Muslim Saints: *Al-Balagh Al-Mubin*', in ibid., p. 225.

434. Schimmel, *Islam in the Indian Subcontinent*, p. 157.

435. Ibid., p. 159.

436. Trans. D.C. Sircar, *The Inscriptions of Asoka* (Delhi, 1957), p. 51.

437. Quoted in *Asaru-l-Bilad* of Zakariya Al Kazwini, ED, vol. I, p. 97.

438. Similar to ruby.

439. *Rehla*, p. 192.

440. 'Mr. Samuel Purchas's Description of India 250 Years Ago' (henceforth Purchas), rpt. in J. Talboys Wheeler (ed.), *Early Travels in India* (Delhi, 1974), p. 155.

441. *Suma Oriental*, vol. I, p. 73.

442. Fryer, *A New Account of East India and Persia*, vol. I, p. 293; Niccolao Manucci, *Storia Do Mogor Or Mogul India 1653–1708*, trans., William Irvine, 4 vols. (London, 1907–8), vol. I, p. 63.

443. Firishta, vol. IV, pp. 531–2.

444. *Nazahutu-l-Mushtak* of Al Idrisi, ED, vol. I, p. 88.

445. *Jami'u-l-Hikayat* of Muhammad Ufi, ED, vol. II, pp. 162–4.

446. *Rehla*, pp. 184–9; *Matla'u-s-Sa'dain* of Abdur Razzaq, ED, vol. IV, p. 98.

447. *The Book of Duarte Barbosa*, vol. I, p. 202.

448. Al Biladuri, *Futuhu-l-Buldan*, ED, vol. I, p. 122.

449. *Rehla*, p. 192.

450. *Chach Nama*, ED, vol. I, pp. 185–6.

451. Sir Henry Elliot, App., 'Note Historical', ED, vol. I, pp. 481–2.

452. *Tarikh-i-Firuz Shahi* of Zia-ud-Din Barani, cited in Khaliq Ahmed Nizami, *Some Aspects of Religion and Politics in India during the Thirteenth Century* (Aligarh, 1961), p. 160.

453. *Tarikh-i-Firuz Shahi* of Zia-ud-Din Barani, ED, vol. III, p. 170.

454. Firishta, vol. I, p. 335.

455. *Zubdatu-t-Tawarikh* of Shaikh Nuru-l-Haq, ED, vol. VI, p. 187.

456. Seid-Gholam Hossein-Khan, *The Seir Mutaqherin or Review of Modern Times Being an History of India Containing, in General the Reigns of the Seven Last Emperors of Hindostan*, 4 vols (rpt.New Delhi, 1986), vol. III, p. 64.

457. Habib, *Politics and Society*, vol. I, pp. 18–19.

458. *The Tuzuk-i-Jahangiri or Memoirs of Jahangir*, trans. Alexander Rogers (New Delhi, 1978), pt I, p. 169; Habib, *Politics and Society*, vol. I, p. 23n.

459. Firishta, vol. III, pp. 24–5.

460. Badauni, vol. II, pp. 263–4.

461. 'Observations of the East Indies by John Huighen Van Linschoten', in J. Talboys Wheeler (ed.), *Early Travels in India (16th and 17th centuries)*, pp. 168, 190, 213–14.

462. *Tuzuk-i-Jahangiri*, pt I, p. 37.

463. Bernier, *Travels in the Mogul Empire*, pp. 345–9; *Majma-ul-Bahrain or Mingling of Two Oceans*, trans. M. Mahfuz-ul-Huq (Calcutta, 1982), p. 38.

464. Richard Eaton, *The Rise of Islam and the Bengal Frontier 1204–1760* (Delhi, 1994), pp. 78–81.

465. Roy, *Islamic Syncretistic Tradition*, pp. 184–6; Ali Raja alias Kanu Fakir, *Jnana Sagar*, ed. Abdul Karim (Calcutta, BS 1324).

466. The authentic Bengali works on the Bauls and on Lalan Fakir are: Upendranath Bhattacharya, *Banglar Baul O Baul Gan* (Calcutta, VS 1364); Abdul Ahsan Chaudhuri, *Lalan Shah* (Dacca, 1988); Saktinath Jha, *Fakir Lalan Sain. Desh, Kal, Shilpa* (Calcutta, 1995). On the Gorakhnath Yogis and Yoga, see the Western classic: Mircea Eliade, *Yoga, Immortality and Freedom*, trans. W.R. Trask (New York, 1958); for the popular vernacular dimension, Panchanan Mandal (ed.), *Gorkha Vijaya* (Visva Bharati, BS 1356).

467. Roy, *Islamic Syncretistic Tradition*, pp. 243–4.

468. *Alberuni's India*, vol. I, p. 113.

469. Wilson, 'Sketch', *Asiatic Researches*, vol. 17, pp. 233–4; Vaudeville, *A Weaver Named Kabir*, p. 315.

470. Wilson, 'Sketch', ibid., pp. 296–8.

471. Adapted from Vaudeville's translation in *A Weaver Named Kabir*, p. 315.

472. *Dabistan-i-Mazahib*, pp. 264–5.

473. Vaudeville, *A Weaver Named Kabir*, p. 43.

474. Ibid., p. 154.

475. Trans. Vaudeville, *A Weaver Named Kabir*, p. 249.

476. *Ain-i-Akbari*, vol. II, p. 141.

477. *Dabistan*, pp. 265–6.

478. Wilson, 'Sketch', *Asiatic Researches*, vol. 16, pp. 56–7.

479. Wheeler (ed.), *Early Travels*, pp. 20–21.

480. Schimmel, *Islam in the Indian Subcontinent*, pp. 143–4.

481. Wilson, 'Sketch', *Asiatic Researches*, vol. 17, pp. 304–5.

482. Dargah Quli Khan, *Muraqqa-'e-Dehli: The Mughal Capital in Muhammad Shah's Time*, trans, Chander Sekhar and Shama Mitra Chenoy (Delhi, 1989), p. 31.

483. Wilson, 'Sketch', *Asiatic Researches*, vol. 17, pp. 305–8.

484. East: Puri; West: Mecca. A *pad* of Kabir, trans. Vaudeville, *A Weaver Named Kabir*, p. 218.

485. Syed Liyaqat Hussain Moini, 'Rituals and Customary Practices at the Dargah of Ajmer', in Troll, *Muslim Shrines*, p. 63.

486. Wilson, 'Sketch', *Asiatic Researches*, vol. 16, p. 117.

487. Ghulam Husain Salim, *Riyazu-s-Salatin*, trans. Abdus Salam (Delhi, 1975), pp. 18–19, cited in Muhammad Umar, *Islam in Northern India during the Eighteenth Century* (New Delhi, 1993), p. 409, n. 237.

488. Wheeler (ed.), *Early Travels*, p. 74.

489. McCrindle, *Ancient India*, p. 100.

490. Basham, *Wonder*, p. 293.

491. Wilson, 'Sketch', *Asiatic Researches*, vol. 17, pp. 233–5.

492. *Padmavat*, trans. Shirreeff, p. 312.

493. *Inscriptions of Asoka*, p. 43; Badauni, vol. II, p. 331.

494. '... there is more Flesh killed for the sake of the *English* alone here in one Month, than in *Surat* for a year for all the Moors in that Populous City'. Fryer, *A New Account of East India and Persia*, vol. II, p. 177.

495. Bernier, *Travels in the Mogul Empire*, p. 381.

496. *Padmavat*, trans. Shirreeff, p. 313.

497. Basham, *Wonder*, p. 294.

498. *Padmavat*, trans, Shirreeff, p. 238.

499. Trans. Vaudeville, *A Weaver Named Kabir*, p. 319.

500. Firishta, vol. II, p. 327.

501.   Firishta, vol. III, p. 269.

502.   *Ardha Kathanaka*, p. 232.

503.   Ibid., p. 261. Translation mine.

504.   Basham, *Wonder*, p. 260.

505.   Trans. Vaudeville, *A Weaver Named Kabir*, pp. 326–7.

506.   *Saptasataka* of Hala, trans. Basham, *Wonder*, p. 46.

507.   The *Meghadutam* of Kalidas begins with the lover's 'extreme pangs of separation from the spouse' (*Kāntā-virahā-guruna*) in the rainy season, but at the end the cloud brings the message that the time of reunion is approaching.

508.   Hardy, *Viraha-Bhakti*, p. 420.

509.   *Shri Gita Govindam*, ed. Amarendranath Ray (Calcutta, BS 1391), p. 145.

510.   'Love (Prema) is the Sheltering of each other' ('*Prema paraspara-āshrayam*') *Raghuvamsa* of Kalidas, 3.24.

511.   '*Dharma-artha-kama-mokshash-cha purushartha udahrita*'—*Agni Purana*.

512.   The above examples are drawn from Haricharan Bandyopadhyay *Bangiya Shabda Kosha* (Calcutta, BS 1349), s.v. Prema, s.v. Purushartha.

513.   Jayadeva occasionally used the term Prema in addition to kama, *Gita Govinda*, p. 26.

514.   'My body which you once played with in sport now burns in the flame of viraha'. Abdur Rahman, *Sandesh Rasak*, verse 77. The Indian-born Muslim poet naturally adopted the Indian standard of beauty. He compared his heroine's thigh to the trunk of the plantain tree and wondered that her waist did not collapse under the weight of her big breasts. Verses 33 and 47. The influence of the seasons of India too was inescapable. The six seasons are described in connection with the Nayika's Viraha here. Similarly in *Prithviraja Rasau* (IX.1–13) Samjukta prevents Prithviraj from going off to war by promising the appropriate erotic sport for each season.

515.   Dinesh Chandra Sen, *Vanga Sahitya Parichaya or Selections from the Bengali Literature From the Earlist Times to the Middle of the Nineteenth Century*, pt II, (University of Calcutta, 1914), p. 996. Translation mine.

516.   *Atmendriya priti ichechha tare boli Kam*
       Krishnendriya priti ichchha dhare Prem nam.

       [Krishnadas Kabiraj, *Chaitanya Charitamrita*,
                    ed. Sukumar Sen, (New Delhi, 1983), p. 17]

517.   The adoration of Radha is a late innovation in the Hindu creed, and is regarded by H.H. Wilson as 'one of very recent origin'. The ninth

century *Bhagavata Purana* makes no particular mention of her among the milkmaids of Vrindaban who engaged in erotic-spiritual sport (*lila*) with Krishna. For the birth of Radha as his true consort we must look to the *Brahma Vaivarta Purana*, 'a circumstance which is of itself sufficient to indicate the comparatively modern date of the Purana'. 'Sketch', *Asiatic Researches*, vol. 16, pp. 125–6.

518. Two Bengali documents dated BS 1125 (1708) and BS 1138 (1721), both entitled Jayapatra, in Shiv Ratan Mitra (comp.), *Types of Early Bengali Prose* (University of Calcutta, 1922), pp. 131–4.

519. Schimmel, *Islam in the Indian Subcontinent*, pp. 139–40.

520. *Letters from Maneri: Sufi Saint of Medieval India*, trans. from Persian by Paul Jackson (New Delhi, 1990), p. 198 and passim.

521. Letter no. 93, ibid., p. 383. The tavern is a West Asian symbol. Un-Indian in origin.

522. Letter no. 49, ibid., p. 198.

523. *Sandesh Rasak*, verse 93. Translation mine.

524. 'No one knows the woe of severance (viraha dukha): only love's exile knows, she that is separated (virahin) from her beloved. My lover departed to a foreign land: for that reason I am in the guise of a Yogini. Whose is my life, my youth and my body? If my beloved has departed, everything has become dust. I have rent my silken attire and made rags of it. I will take that road whereby I will meet my beloved.' Trans. Shirreeff, *Padmavati*, p. 344; Hindi original, *Jayasi Granthavali*, p. 246.

525. Trans. Shirreff, p. 370: *Jayasi*, p. 268.

526. Wilson, 'Sketch', *Asiatic Researches*, vol. 16, p. 118.

527. Badauni, vol. III, p. 21.

528. Mujeeb, *The Indian Muslims*, pp. 293–4.

529. Trans. Vaudeville, *A Weaver Named Kabir*, p. 275.

530. Wilson, 'Sketch', *Asiatic Researches*, vol. 16, pp. 99–100.

531. Trans, Mujeeb, *The Indian Muslims*, p. 329.

532. Badauni, vol. II, pp. 113–21.

533. Trans. Lowe.

534. Trans. Basham, *Wonder*, p. 428.

535. Mujeeb, *The Indian Muslims*, p. 262n.

536. 'No nation can exist without a regular married life, for it prevents the uproar of passions abhorred by the cultivated mind, and it removes all those causes which excite the animal to a fury always leading to harm.' *Alberuni's India*, pt II, p. 154.

537. After mentioning several Hindu 'obscenities', Al Biruni added thoughtfully: 'However, I must not reproach the Hindus only with their heathen practices, for the heathen Arabs too committed crimes and obscentities. They cohabited with menstruating and pregnant women; several men agreed to cohabit with the same woman in the same period of menstruation; they adopted the children of others, of their guests, of the lover of their daughter, not to mention that in some kinds of their worship they whistled on their fingers and clapped with their hands, and that they ate unclean and dead animals. Islam has abolished all those things among the Arabs, as it has abolished them in those parts of India, the people of which have become Muhammadans. Thanks be to God.' Ibid., pt I, pp. 185–6. Here is an unmistakable hint of how Islam brought stricter sexual laws to Arabia and later to India.

538. 'Most of the princes of India, when they hold a court, allow their women to be seen by the men who attend it, whether they be natives or foreigners. No veil conceals them from the eyes of the visitor.' ED, vol. I, p. 11.

539. Fryer, *A New Account of East India and Persia*, vol. I, pp. 88–9. Fryer was referring here to the royal or aristocratic harem, filled with numerous concubines and maidservants, besides the four wives allowed by the Shariat at any one time.

540. 'The *Portugals, Mesticos*, and *Indian Christian* women in *India* are little scene abroad, but for the most part sit still within the house, and goe but seldome forth, unlesse it bee to Church, or to visit their friends, which is likewise but verie little, and when they goe abroad they are well provided not to be seene, for they are carried in *Pallamkin* covered with a Mat or other cloth, so that they cannot be scene'. Linschoten, '*Observation of the East Indies*', in Wheeler (ed.), *Early Travels*, p. 179.

541. The code of Manu laid down no such limitation.

542. *Alberuni's India*, pt II, pp. 154–6.

543. Bernier, *Travels in the Mogul Empire*, p. 259.

544. Badauni, vol. II, p. 315.

545. *Ain-i-Akbari*, trans. Jarrett, vol. II, p. 42.

546. Muhammad Umar, *Islam in Northern India during the Eighteenth Century* (New Delhi, 1993), p. 429.

547. Wilson, 'Sketch', *Asiatic Researches*, vol. 16, pp. 131–2.

548. *Rehla*, p. 21.

549. Firishta, vol. II, p. 352.

550. Fryer, *A New Account of East India and Persia*, vol. I, p. 148.

551. Tome Pires two centuries earlier was more explicit: 'In Malabar it is the custom for the woman to have her eyes on the bed during the act of coition and for the man to have his on the ceiling, and this is the general practice among the great and the small, and they consider anything else to be strange and foreign to their condition, and some Portuguese used to the country do not find this ugly'. *Suma Oriental*, vol. I, p. 67.

552. Ibid., p. 71; *The Book of Duarte Barbosa*, vol. II, p. 42. See also Abdur Razzaq's comment on the matrilineal system of Malabar in the fifteenth century. Matla'u-S-Sadain, ED IV, p. 101.

553. In place of Rabiya, one might also cite an Indian and near contemporary instance: Andal of Sri Rangam. Rabiya and Andal bear a generic resemblance to each other in their utter surrender to God. Neither girl would have been at ease in the company of the formidable Maitreyi. On the other hand, both would have instantly understood Mira though she came seven centuries later.

554. Al Idrisi, ED, vol. I, p. 92.

555. Al Masudi, ED, vol. I, p. 21.

556. *Rehla*, p. 247.

557. Taranatha, *History of Buddhism*, p. 5.

558. *Alberuni's India*, pt II, pp. 162–3.

559. Radhakumud Mookerji, *The Fundamental Unity of India (From Hindu Sources)* (London, 1914), pp. 27–9.

560. Ibid., p. 27.

561. Wilson, 'Sketch', *Asiatic Researches*, vol. 17, pp. 178–9.

562. ED, vol. I, p. 97; ED, vol. II, pp. 468–9; Firishta, vol. I, p. 73.

563. *Alberuni's India*, pt II, p. 146; pt I, p. 22; Purchas, in Wheeler (ed.), *Early Travels*, pp. 6–7. There were lesser centres of pilgrimage, too, such as the fair and temples at Parvat in the Deccan described by the Russian traveller: 'People from all over the land of India came together at the butkhanah [idol house] to see but's [the deith's] miracles'. Nikitin, *Voyages Beyond Seas*, p. 30.

564. Bernier, *Travels in the Mogul Empire*, p. 304; Tavernier, *Travels in India*, vol. II, pp. 226, 244–5. A similar multitude assembled every five years at the Kumbh Mela at Allahabad at the junction of the Ganges and the Jumna, yielding a good revenue to the Mughals. William Irvine (trans.) and Margaret L. Irvine (abridger), *A Pepys of Mogul India 1653–1708. Being an Abridged Edition of the Storia Do Mogor of Niccolao Manucci* (London, 1913), p. 113.

565. Tavernier, *Travels in India*, vol. II, pp. 244–5.

566. Wilson, 'Sketch', *Asiatic Researches*, vol. 17, p. 295.

567. Purchas, in Wheeler (ed.), *Early Travels*, p. 155.

568. *Tarikh-i-Alai*, ED, vol. III, p. 85.

569. *Mirat-i-Masudi*, ED, vol. II, pp. 538, 541-2, 544.

570. Eaton, *Sufis of Bijapur*, p. 229.

571. Firishta, vol. II, p. 398.

572. Amir Khurd, *Siyar-al-Awliya* (1388), cited in Currie, *Shrine and Cult of Muin Al-Din*, p. 45.

573. *Majalisu-s-Salatin* of Muhammad Sharif Hanafi, ED, vol. VII, p. 139; *Rehla*, pp. 218-19, 223, 247-8; Saiyid Sultan, *Nabi Vamsa*, p. 85.

574. Schimmell, *Islam in the Indian Subcontinent*, pp. 157-58.

575. *Muraqqa-e-Dehli*, passim.

576. *Alberuni's India*, pt II, p. 169. On the approach of death, the sick and the old were immersed in the Ganges 'that the soul may be washed, on taking its flight, from all impurities which it may have contracted during its abode in the body'. Bernier, *Travels in the Mogul Empire*, pp. 315-16.

577. Purchas, in Wheeler (ed.), *Early Travels*, pp. 5-6.

578. Roy, *Islamic Syncretistic Tradition*, pp. 242-3.

579. Tavernier, *Travels in India*, vol. II, p. 230.

580. *Rehla*, p. 4.

581. Bernier, *Travels in the Mogul Empire*, pp. 355-6.

582. Purchas, in Wheeler (ed.), *Early Travels*, p. 71.

583. Tavernier, *Travels in India*, vol. II, p. 230

584. Firishta, vol. I, author's preface, p. Xlviii.

585. Ibid., p. Xlvii.

586. *Ashika* of Amir Khusrau, ED, vol. III, pp. 545-6.

587. Badauni, vol. I, p. 479.

588. ED, vol. V, p. 74 n. 4.

589. Firishta, vol. I, p. 541.

590. *Babur-nama*, vol. II, pp. 481-4.

591. Ibid., vol. I, p. 584.

592. *Tarikh-i-Salatin-i Afaghana* of Ahmed Yadgar, ED, vol. V, p. 57.

593. Firishta, vol. IV, pp. 547-8.

594. From Thomas Roe's embassy during the reign of Akbar's son Jahangir, the English obtained a view of 'this countrey, and the disposition of

their King', as if these were given entities, naturally linked to each other. Purchas, p. 72.

595. *Tarikh-i-Salatin-i Afaghana*, ED, vol. v, p. 59.

596. Purchas, in Wheeler (ed.) *Early Travels*, pp. 18–19.

597. *Badshah-Nama* of Abdu-l Hamid Lahori, ED, vol. VII, p. 32.

598. Tavernier, *Travels in India*, vol. I, p. 324.

599. Briggs's preface, Firishta, vol. I, p. xi. The elimination of Bijapur and Golkunda meant that there was no sovereign prince in India except Aurangzeb.

600. Translated by me from Bengali verse quoted in Abdul Karim, *Puthi Parichiti*, ed. Ahmad Sharif (Dacca University, 1958), p. 495. The cosmology of the poet reflects the Puranic universe.

601. *Muntakhabu-l Lubab* of Khafi Khan, ED, vol. VII, p. 405.

602. Govind Sakharam Sardesai, *New History of the Marathas*, 3 vols (2nd edn, New Delhi, 1986), vol. III, pp. 236, 237, 301.

603. William Hunter, 'Some Account of the Astronomical Labours of Jayasinha, Rajah of Ambhere, or Jayanagar', *Asiatic Researches*, vol. 5, 1808, pp. 181–3.

604. *Taju-l Ma-Asir* of Hasan Nizami, ED, vol. II, p. 208.

605. *Ashika* of Amir Khusrau, ED, vol. III, p. 557.

606. Nikitin, *Voyages Beyond Seas*, pp. 16–17.

607. *Matla'u-S Sadain* of Abdur Razzaq, ED, vol. IV, pp. 100–1.

608. Bernier, *Travels in the Mogul Empire*, p. 3.

609. Purchas, in Wheeler (ed.) *Early Travels*, p. 73.

610. Fryer, *A New Account of East India and Persia*, vol. I, p. 91.

611. Linschoten, 'Observation of the East Indies', in Wheeler (ed.), *Early Travels*, p. 200.

612. Ibid., p. 169.

613. Ibid., p. 209.

614. Bernier, *Travels in the Mogul Empire*, p. 404.

615. Consider, for instance, Fryer's observations regarding some of the body postures: 'For their Easements both Men and Women keep a set hour, and go with every one a purifying Pot in their hand (for to take up water to wash after their occasions) to some Public Tank or Pond; the Men apart from the Women; neither of them concerned for Passengers, keeping their back-sides towards them till they have done their Business'. Fryer underlined the mutual contempt between Indian and other cultures in this respect: 'Among them all it is common to make

water sitting, as when they evacuate the other way; and it is a shame for any one to be seen to do otherwise, they sarcastically saying, such a one pisses like a Dog (which is held unclean) standing'. Fryer, *A New Account of East India and Persia*, vol. I, p. 94.

616. 'In their meetings they sit cross-legged'. *Alberuni's India*, vol. I, p. 182.

617. Fryer, *A New Account of East India and Persia*, vol. I, pp. 235, 259.

618. Linschoten, in Wheeler (ed.), *Early Travels*, p. 201.

619. Mountstuart Elphinstone, *The History of India, The Hindu and Mahometan Periods* (rpt Allahabad, 1966), p. 174.

620. Ibid.

621. Ibid., p. 173.

622. *Rehla*, pp. 180–1.

623. Elphinstone, *History of India*, p. 173.

624. Badauni, vol. III, p. 394.

625. Badauni, vol. II, p. 243.

626. Ibid., vol. II, p. 299.

627. Fryer, *A New Account of East India and Persia*, vol. I, p. 111.

628. Linschoten, 'Observation of the East Indies', in Wheeler (ed.) *Early Travels*, p. 203.

629. Fryer, *A New Account of East India and Persia*, vol. I, p. 321. Elsewhere, speaking of the natives of the Kanara Coast, he observed that some had received the Christian faith, but those who remained Hindu were 'the most impiously Religious of any of the *Indians*'. Fryer, *A New Account of East India and Persia*, vol. I, p. 150.

630. Purchas, in Wheeler (ed.) *Early Travels*, p. 155.

631. Arrian, in McCrindle, p. 185.

632. *Ardha Kathanaka*, p. 224.

633. *Babur-nama*, vol. I, p. 202.

634. *Rehla*, p. 60.

635. 'A search was instituted, and such as were found were put to death. Many persons, taken up on suspicion, declared they were Indians, and not foreigners, of which the household troops consisted. The King [a late Tughlaq prince] directed, that all such as could not pronounce certain words, viz, Kuhŕy Kuhŕy, or Gooŕa Gooŕy, should be put to death; and it is said many foreigners having no connection with the household troops suffered on this occasion.' Firishta, vol. I, p. 474.

636. Introduction to Firishta's History, ED, vol. VI, p. 568.

637. *Tarikh-i-Daudi*, ED, vol. IV, p. 498.

638. The same petition says earlier: 'At present in the year 193, the Russian traders want to destroy us. ... They complain that we Indians falsely call ourselves residents of Astrakhan and our wives and children live on the Indian soil and we sell our goods in all the shops of Moscow and in the Gostinny Dvor of all cities. ... We Indians do not trade in any city except in Moscow and Astrakhan and no oppression results to anybody in course of our journey. ... We Indians are truly residents of Astrakhan and not on Indian soil. ... It has been written in the New Trade Regulations that we would travel from Astrakhan to Moscow and trade there. The articles 77 and 78 say as follows—Foreigners from abroad, Persians and Indians and residents of Astrakhan will go to Moscow and other cities with their goods. ... That we Indians should not go from Astrakhan to Moscow and that we are to trade only in Astrakhan is nowhere written in that Trade Regulations.' Surendra Gopal, *Indians in Russia*, doc. No. 224. ii, dated 12 Dec. 1685, pp. 116–25.

639. *Alberuni's India*, vol. i, p. 21. Among the foreigners distrusted by the Hindus, the latest, in his view, were 'The Muslims'; here he switched from an ethnic to a religious category.

640. *Tabakat-i-Nasiri*, ED, vol. ii, pp. 324–5, 328, 347, 350.

641. M. Athar Ali, 'The Perception of India in Akbar and Abu'l Fazl', in Irfan Habib (ed.), *Akbar and His India* (Delhi, 1997), p. 217.

642. 'Hindis call these mountains Sawalak-parbat', *Babur-nama*, vol. i, p. 485.

643. *Babur-nama*, vol. i, p. 202.

644. *Rehla*, p. 41n.

645. *Rehla*, p. 226. Elsewhere he mentioned the fact that 'the Indians' chose an auspicious day for setting out on a journey. *Rehla*, pp. 151–2.

646. *Bahar-i-Ajam* of Tek Chand Bahar. Professor Irfan Habib kindly translated the relevant part of the lexicon into English for me.

647. A contemporary poet.

648. Firishta, vol. i, p. 481.

649. Ibid., p. 487.

650. Ibid., p. 489. This is an early example of the term Mughal being used in the sense of the all invaders from beyond the Oxus, though the invader on this occasion was a Turk and not a Mongol. The label stuck to Timur's dynasty in India, for Babar was identified as a Mughal, and Akbar himself adopted the designation.

651. Ibid., p. 491.

652. Ibid., p. 493.

653. Ibid., p. 494.

654. *Seir* I, p. 300.

655. ED, vol. VIII, pp.65, 80.

656. *Tazkira* of Anand Ram Mukhlis, ED, vol. VIII, 78.

657. *Tazkira-i-Chaghatai* of Muhammad Hadi Kamwar Khan, ED, vol. VIII, p. 23.

658. *Tarikh-i-Hind* of Rustam Ali, ED, vol. VIII, pp. 61–2.

659. *Seir* I, pp. 314, 316, 317.

660. *Tazkira* of Anand Ram Mukhlis, ED, vol. VIII, p. 78.

661. Ibid., p. 92.

662. ED, vol. VIII, p. 88.

663. Ibid., p. 64.

664. *Seir* I, p. 315.

665. Ibid., p. 315

666. ED, vol. VIII, p. 88.

667. Text of compact made by Muhammad Shah with Nadir Shah, ED, vol. VIII, p. 92.

668. *Seir* I, p. 317.

669. Nadir Shah's letter to Zakariya Khan, ED, vol. VIII, p. 96.

670. Compact made by Muhammad Shah with Nadir Shah, ED, vol. VIII, p. 92.

671. James Grant Duff, *History of the Mahrattas* (New Delhi, 1971), vol. I, pp. 305–7.

672. *Tazkira* of Anand Ram Mukhlis, ED, vol. VIII, p. 93.

673. *Tazkira-i-Chaghatai* of Muhammad Hadi Kamwar Khan, ED, vol. VIII, p. 16.

3

English Colonization and Indian Commonalty: The Language and Mentality of Early Indian Resistance

The Seven Years' War, which precipitated the Plassey Revolution and the English East India Company's expansion within the Mughal domain, was an occurrence of the old regime in Europe; a war between contending dynastic supremacies. The nation in arms, a formation which the French Revolution would bring forth three decades later, was a still unknown entity. In India, too, nationalism as a conception did not exist, least of all in the shape of the ideological creed which the English-educated Indian middle class would subsequently articulate. As there was no question of the Company's conquests being opposed by a movement of national resistance, the mentality that lay behind what opposition there was remains elusive to the modern mind.

In most instances, resistance to the establishment of the Company's mastery was local in character, shaped by the prevalent localized ideas and circumstances. On a wider basis, elements of patriotism were to be found at the time in the Sikh commonwealth, and in the Maratha confederacy. However, neither power had the universal appeal that would transcend the religious and regional particularism of their respective bases. Insofar as a common sentiment of political obligation bound rulers and subjects together in the land as a whole, it was the notion of the inalienable sovereignty of the Mughal Emperor.

The imperial nobility (*umara*), consisting of the ranking commanders of Mughal horse (*mansabdars*), were a class whose position marked them out as the obvious defenders of the sovereign realm of the Emperor (*mulk-i-padshah*). In association with the subordinate landholders (zamindars), who ruled in their respective areas, the Mughal ruling class ruled over the country as a whole. Their eventual resistance to the Company's encroachments raises the question of the underlying ideology. What were the mental conceptions that prevailed in the Mughal political world of the late eighteenth century? How did the Mughal officer class in the outlying *subas*, increasingly detached from Delhi, look upon the issue of political obligation in a changing world? All historians agree that the politics of Mughal resistance to the Company cannot be characterized as 'national'. They have not, however, given systematic consideration to the political sentiment conveyed through the contemporary term 'imperial' (*badshahi*). How did the Mughal ruling class view the imperial bond as crisis threatened their rule? What were the reactions of the chiefs and zamindars who shared in that rule?

The evidence suggests that rulers and subjects alike continued to regard Mughal realm as one indivisible whole. The Later Mughals might no longer rule, but they still reigned. Their *'farman'* was the universally recognized foundation of every ruler's title to rule. By order of God, the Creator of the universe, the realm belonged to the Emperor; and in every part of that indivisible realm, the local prince exercised authority as the Emperor's lawful representative. The idea was implicit in public orders proclaimed by beat of tom-tom: 'The Creation is God's (*khalq-i-khuda*), the Realm is the Emperor's (*mulk-i-padshah*), the executive authority is so-and-so's [as specified by the drummer according to whoever was issuing the order on the spot] (*hukm-i-   )*'. The rajas and zamindars, including the country powers that had emerged from their ranks, subscribed to the idea: it was their name that figured in the dash. After 1803, when the Company became the de facto master of the Mughal realm by virtue of possession of the person of the Emperor, the town criers continued to proclaim public orders in the same set form: *'Khalq-i-khuda, mulk-i-padshah, hukm-i-Sarkar Company Bahadur.'*[1]

The sense of continuity arose from the colonial hegemony being effected not so much by head on collision as by gradual penetration of the Mughal system. After all, the Company itself was a zamindar and then a holder of Mughal office before it became sovereign. It rose to power from the subordinate layer of Mughal rule assigned to landholders and country powers. By Mughal decree, the Company became zamindar of 24 Parganas in 1757, and diwan of Bengal in 1765; it stood forth as the Diwan in 1772 after seven years of cautious diarchy; having pensioned off the Mughal *nazim* of Bengal, it also appropriated the Nizamat in 1793; by then it had turned the Mughal *nazim* of Awadh into its subsidiary ally and had forced him to cede extensive territories in Hindustan; finally, it secured possession of the Red Fort of Delhi in 1803, establishing thereby its paramount position as regent of the Mughal Emperor. The Mughal system was taken over rather than blown apart.

Nevertheless, the ruptures were extensive. By the beginning of the nineteenth century, the Company had established the huge Presidency of Bengal, extending right up to Banaras. Its plundered economy was more tightly in its grasp than ever. With its hold assured over the person of the emperor, the East India Company was also visibly the supreme power in Hindustan. The Mughal ruling class had been ousted from positions of power in the *subas* of Bengal and Bihar. The Mughal governors still held court in Awadh and Hyderabad, but the substance of power had passed to the British Resident. The official Mughal bankers, the house of Jagat Seth, had once conducted money operations through the length and breadth of the empire. They were now reduced to insignificance in the world of finance. The Armenian, Mughal, and other merchants with seagoing as well as upstream operations were eliminated from the higher branches of trade. Several great zamindars stood divested of rulership over the extensive principalities they had enjoyed under Mughal rule. The peasantry of Bengal, Bihar, and Banaras were subjected to an enhanced tax collected with systematic rigour. The weavers, silk winders, and salt workers suffered untold severities. The people of the greater part of the lower and middle Gangetic valley were brought under the alien and unpredictable jurisdiction of British courts and regulations that they distrusted and which were systematically oppressive to the poor. The land on both sides of the Ganges right up to Banaras had been bled white by the pagoda hunters from across the sea. So great was the drain that territories which had once drawn huge amounts of silver from Europe and the Persian Gulf were no longer unfamiliar with acute and spasmodic scarcities of specie. Millions had perished in the famine which drought, combined with the Company's exactions in Bengal and Bihar, had precipitated in 1770. An ill wind from the West had blown a whole world away.

What resistance had the English East India Company encountered in appropriating and forming the Presidency of Bengal? None that mattered in military terms, save the wars fought by Sirajuddaulah (1756–7), Mir Qasim (1763), and the league of the three Mughal Princes, consisting of Shah Alam, Shujauddaulah of Awadh, and Mir Qasim

(1764). All subsequent resistance was sporadic and local, requiring no more than minor actions by detachments of the Company's forces. The wave of inchoate rural violence that swept the country in the wake of the famine of 1770 never coalesced into a widespread popular rebellion. The Sannyasi and Fakir raids, the tribal turbulence of the Jungle Mahals and the peasant uprising against the oppression of the tax farmer Devi Singh in Rangpur caused severe difficulties for Warren Hastings. To his relief, these were isolated incidents confined to the borders of the Company's realm. Immediate danger to his person occurred only once, but that was a momentary affair. He had a narrow escape when the troops of Raja Chait Singh suddenly rose up in Banaras. Subsequently, none of the great zamindars, whose estates were sold up by the Sunset Regulation of Cornwallis, were able to mount a determined armed resistance. True, a traders' hartal in Bihar and Bengal forced the Company to withdraw an unpopular police tax in 1796, but that was passive resistance, not armed rebellion. Other than that early instance of passive resistance, the traders and artisans more or less submitted to the colonial regulations. It thus fell to the Mughal officer class to offer what armed resistance they could to the Company.

Part of the difficulty in organizing resistance to colonial penetration lay in the spatial limits of class power in the eighteenth century. The rajas and large zamindars were powerful in their respective domains, but they were not capable of acting as a single class against the English East India Company. Peasants had no institutional mechanism for solidarity beyond their narrow local horizons. Traders and artisans had not coalesced into one class along the long and winding route of the Ganges. The Mughal *umara* (noblemen) were the one body of men capable of concerted action. What the Company had to reckon with was not concerted popular resistance, but armed encounters with the Mughal ruling class. The Mughal officers (*mansabdars*), though ruling over a shrinking territory, still commanded the revenues of the largest stretch of intensively cultivated land in the country. The fertile plains of Bengal and north India and choice parts of the Deccan, were still theirs. They, and they alone, had the wider imperial outlook.

History records that their opposition to the East India Company did not attain the scale and intensity of the military operations directed against the British by the Maratha confederate chiefs, the upstart dynasty of Haidar Ali and Tipu Sultan, and the Dal Khalsa of the Sikhs. The princes and nobles of the Mughal realm—the Nawabs of Bengal, the

Nawab Wazir of Awadh, the Nizam of Hyderabad, the Nawab of the Carnatic (Arcot), and Emperor Shah Alam himself—were undermined insidiously by the colonial penetration of the political structures over which they presided. This was a process that strongly contrasted with the Company's head-on collisions with the Marathas, Mysore, and the Sikhs.

The war between Mir Qasim and the Company is the one exception to the pusillanimous surrender of the Mughal ruling class to the British. Culminating as it did in the league of the three Mughal princes, the episode is of particular significance to the course of Indian resistance to colonial domination. The Mysore sultans, the Maratha chiefs, and the Dal Khalsa might have fought more continuously and tenaciously, but the glimmerings of patriotism in their struggle excluded the concept of the land as a whole. The struggle of the Mughal ruling class against the Company, though brief and unsuccessful, was informed by a broader political vision. This because it derived from the explicitly articulated indivisibility of the sovereign Mughal realm of Hindustan. It was a concept that survived a hundred years later to be adopted by the rebel leaders of 1857.

The ideology of the Mughal confrontation with the British has not claimed the attention it deserves from the historians. This is a curious omission, considering its importance in the history of the development of Indian opposition to English conquest. One might at any rate have expected the biographer of Mir Qasim, to have rectified the omission. However, the only major biographer in English, Nanda Lal Chatterjee, wrote at a time when India was still the brightest jewel in the British crown.[2] Concerned only to justify the actions of the English he paid no attention to the substance of what the Nawab wrote to the officers of the Company, nor to the mind reflected in those missives. The Nawab's entire correspondence with the English prior to the outbreak of hostilities was collected and published by his early ally and subsequent opponent Henry Vansittart.[3] Despite the existence of this rich source, historians have not used it to study the language of the Mughal confrontation with the English nor has there been a systematic investigation of the mentality that articulated itself through the letters.

There are, however, glimpses of Mughal psychology in the works of a number of historians who, after 1947, devoted themselves to studying the interaction between Mughal statesmen and the English East India Company. Brijen Gupta was the first historian to systematically investigate the grounds on which Nawab Sirajuddaulah went to war with the English. Atul Chandra Roy picked an unusual subject for his research—Mir Jafar's career as general and then governor—and sought the real historical person behind the stage 'traitor' of popular plays. Abdul Majed Khan produced an authentic portrait of Muhammad Reza Khan as a Mughal statesman seeking to preserve Mughal institutions during the diarchy in Bengal.[4]

These contributions point the way to a still unaccomplished exercise: probing the mentality of those involved in the initial opposition to colonial penetration. What is involved here is the nature of the British colonial penetration up the Ganges, the curious absence of concerted opposition from the devastated valley, and the one desperate war that the Mughal ruling class waged against the insidious enemy. In particular, there is the enigmatic figure of Nawab Mir Qasim. It is no easy matter to explore these themes. How does one probe the language and mentality of a vanquished and vanished party who left no full record of their own? Despite the problem, an attempt must be made to comprehend the experience of subjugation, the turmoil of wounded feelings and cherished notions, and the psychology of the early armed encounters between the Mughals and the English. The exercise will be worthwhile if it helps us probe from the point of view of the side that lost out. The dim psychic process that might have been at work before nationalism could articulate itself in the popular consciousness may be elusive, but here is an area that could be profitably explored to find the antecedents. For the notions that inspired the early opponents of the Company would place the whole story of the subsequent development of the struggle against the British in fresh perspective. What one must grasp at the outset is that these opponents spoke a political language. This was not the language of insurgents against a dominant colonial power. It was, on the contrary, a masterful pronouncement of war against rebels and aliens. This was necessarily so, as at the initial stage, the Mughals were the rulers, and the English by implication, the rebels. Interestingly, the language of resistance to colonial penetration did not subsequently abandon the early terminology of war. The Mughal terminology of the extirpation of rebels remained an important ingredient in that language even a century after Plassey. War for the expulsion of aliens, war for the extirpation of rebels, constituted the theme of opposition to the British from Nawab Sirajuddaulah's attack on Calcutta (1756) through the Battle of Buxar (1764), to the Indian Mutiny of 1857.

Bengal and the Mughal Ruling Class

The Bengal *suba* afforded the largest and most easily collected revenue surplus during the fierce struggles that erupted all over the Mughal empire after the death of Emperor Aurangzeb in 1707. The Battle of Plassey enabled the English East India Company to seize the surplus in 1757. That was the importance of the battle in history: not a straight drive to the supremacy of India, but a stroke of financial good fortune that would enable the Company to prevail over the rival contenders in the long struggle to the denouement of 1803. That year, the Company, under the energetic stewardship of Lord Wellesley, won the supremacy of India. The events that took place in Bengal during 1756–65 were therefore critical. To understand these events, two developments need to be noted at the outset: the detachment of the Mughal ruling class at Murshidabad from Delhi and the consequent changes in the structure of power in the *suba*. So long as the Mughal officers continued to be controlled from Delhi, which lay far beyond the reach of the English naval power, there was no question of the Company being king maker. When the *mansabdars* posted in Bengal formed an autonomous centre at Murshidabad they became vulnerable to the English at Calcutta. Even so, the growing English naval power would not have become a factor in the politics of Murshidabad but for a series of realignments that fostered the conspiracy of some influential groups against Nawab Sirajuddaulah, the young and inexperienced man who became Governor (*Nazim*) of Bengal in 1756.

Through the better part of the reign of Emperor Aurangzeb, *nazims* and *diwans* had come and gone in Bengal. They could not look with assurance beyond a stint of three years. Nor did they wish to do so, for Dacca (then capital of the *suba*) was not a popular posting with the *mansabdars*. Despite its designation as a 'paradise' (*Suba Jannat ul Bilad Bangla*) by the Emperor, it remained, in the eyes of the Mughal *umara* from Hindustan, a hellish green swamp where disease was rife. The mechanism for controlling the *suba* was well understood by the old Emperor: the Governor (*Nazim*) and the revenue minister (*diwan*) were answerable to him separately and directly, and he did not allow the one to interfere in the affairs of the other. No sooner did the Emperor breathe his last than the separation of powers ceased in Bengal. Murshid Quli Khan, the last *diwan* of Aurangzeb in Bengal, became the *nazim* of the *suba*, and combining the offices of the *nizamat* and the *diwani* in his person, he shifted the capital from Dacca to Murshidabad. Here he built the great Katra Masjid, an enormous rectangular mosque, which gave concrete expression to the fact that he and his line had come there to stay.[5]

Before Murshid Quli Khan found his final resting place in the humble grave within the mosque, he had succeeded in lending substance to his old master's designation of Bengal as '*Suba Jannat ul Bilad*'. It had emerged as a haven of peace and stability for the beleaguered Mughal ruling class harassed by the Sikhs, Marathas, Rajputs, and Jats. The difficulty of collecting the revenues of their assignments (*jagir*) in Hindustan and the Deccan because of the anarchy prevailing in those parts made Bengal a posting sought after by the mansabdars. Many officers from Hindustan solicited Murshid Quli Khan for postings in the *nizamat*. The appointments, transfers, and dismissals were no longer made from Delhi. These were being determined at Murshidabad. The connection with Hindustan, however, continued to be strong. The Nawabs of Bengal welcomed officers and men of learning from the north. Murshidabad emerged as a stable intellectual and political centre within the convulsed Mughal empire, its special feature being Shia prominence.

Murshid Quli Khan fixed certain limits to the position that the *mansabdar*s were to enjoy in his system. He gave no thought to the danger that this would reduce the military effectiveness of the class to which he belonged. In a deliberate move to centralize the finances of Bengal, he shifted the greater part of the *jagir*s assigned to the noblemen of the *nizamat* to the frontier province of Orissa. The lands vacated in Bengal were attached to the treasury at headquarters—the Khalisa—managed for the most part by the far from warlike local Hindu revenue officials of the *diwani*. The strength of the mounted warrior aristocracy was drastically reduced by the Nawab's decision to reduce his troops to only two thousand horse at headquarters. The token force was deemed sufficient to keep the peace and to collect the revenue. The Nawab's calculation proved for the moment to be correct. There was a considerable curtailment of expenditure, which resulted in a larger revenue surplus. However, the Maratha incursions of the 1740s exposed the reduced capacity of the immigrant Mughal noblemen who had settled down in the province. It was then discovered that the Mughal horse and their commanders were dangerously thin on the ground.

The Bengal *suba* was divided into 34 *sarkar*s. Proper Mughal practice required that a district commandant (*faujdar*) should be posted to each *sarkar* with a requisite number of horse. Actually there were no more than 13 *faujdar*s, posted to the frontier districts and the Mughal port of Hugli. In addition, three *naib nazim*s of higher rank were posted, with their respective forces, at Dacca, Patna, and Cuttack. Apart from the three *niabat*s and the thirteen *faujdari*s, the plains of Bengal were consolidated by Murshid Quli Khan into fifteen hereditary principalities, each of which constituted the revenue jurisdiction (*ihtamam*) of a trusted zamindar directly answerable to the *khalisa* at Murshidabad. Accordingly, the official Mughal collectors of revenue (*amils*) were withdrawn from the *pargana*s. This made the collection of revenues inexpensive, but the balance of power tilted against the imperial officer class.

Now that the Mughal *umara* in Bengal were no longer part of an integral officer corps controlled from Delhi, they had to share power with the local notables. More and more of the latter were admitted to the ranking commanders of Mughal horse. A number of favoured local Hindu families rose rapidly through the war office (*nizamat*) and the revenue department (*diwani*). These were the two branches in which the Mughal government was organized in every *suba*. The revenue office was dominated by Hindus. The *rai raiyan*, who presided over the Khalisa, and the collectors (*amils*) through whom he collected the revenues from the zamindars, were Hindus. So were the head *qanungo* and the *qanungo*s in the districts, an independent establishment of record keepers serving as a check upon fraud and embezzlement in the revenue department. The rise of certain Bengali families of good caste to high positions in the war office was a more recent development. Janaki Ram, a loyal Bengali Kayastha on whom Nawab Alivardi Khan relied implicitly, rose to the position of *chargé d'affaires* at Patna, deputizing for the ceremonial but absentee *naib nazim* of Bihar. His incompetent son, Rai Durlabh, held a succession of high positions in the *nizamat* at Murshidabad. Rajvallabh, an obscure man of the Baidya caste from East Bengal, got hold of the affairs of the *niabat* and admiralty (*nawara*) of Dacca as deputy to the *naib nazim* and *peshkar* to the *nawara* in the last years of Alivardi Khan. Nanda Kumar, an ambitious Bengali Brahman from the district around Murshidabad, was acting faujdar of Hugli for some time in the short tenure of Nawab Sirajuddaulah.

During the successive tenures of Murshid Quli Khan and his son-in-law Shujauddin Khan, the complexion of the court of Murshidabad was altered by the rise of the banking house of Jagat Seth. As Murshid Quli Khan drastically reduced the revenue establishment to cut down on costs, the house of Jagat Seth moved into the central position in the financial mechanism of the Bengal *suba*. The bank which acted as guarantor (*malzamin*) to the zamindars, received the instalments of revenue directly from the landed magnates, and transmitted the annual tribute to Delhi by means of *hundis* upon its branch at the capital of the empire. The appropriation of these functions by the bank rested on the formal recognition that Jagat Seth was treasurer and banker to the state. Furthermore, he managed the mint at Murshidabad. So absolute was his control over the money market that repeated attempts by the English East India Company to breach the monopoly made no headway.

The *nizamat* of Shujauddin Khan saw the emergence of a triumvirate at the court directing the affairs of state. The trio—Jagat Seth, Haji Ahmad (the senior nobleman at Murshidabad, and elder brother of Alivardi Khan who was then posted as *naib nazim* of Bihar), and Alam Chand (the *rai raiyan*)—conspired with Alivardi Khan at Patna. In consequence of their machinations, Shujauddin's son and successor, Sarfaraz Khan, was overthrown in 1740. The commanders of the Mughal horse and several landed magnates whose troops accompanied Sarfaraz Khan in battle switched over to Alivardi Khan's side—an event that revealed Jagat Seth's excellent connections with the imperial officers and the large landholders. The large landed agglomeration encouraged by Murshid Quli Khan as a means of cutting down the cost of revenue collection and simplifying the administration of the country had fostered a class of great local magnates commanding troops of their own and ruling over extensive domains. The nexus between the commanders of Mughal horse, the house of Jagat Seth, and the large landholders produced a revolution of state that corresponded in some ways to the *coup d'état* at Plassey seventeen years later. The only new feature in 1757 was the involvement of the East India Company in the conspiracy at Murshidabad.

It did not initially dawn upon the European adventurers in India that conditions were ripe for piecemeal nibbling at the outlying *suba*s of the Mughal empire. Neither in Hyderabad, nor in Bengal, were the autonomous Mughal ruling élite devoid of creative political energy. Nizam-ul-Mulk Asaf Jah of Hyderabad and Murshid Quli Khan of Murshidabad were both innovative statesmen of whom the Mughal ruling class would have been proud even at the height of their power. The autonomous administrations that they set up in their respective provinces were viable political systems. Furthermore, as far as the European East India Companies could see, the outlying *suba*s were still visibly linked to Delhi. The Nizam-ul-Mulk, who served on more than one occasion as the Wazir of the Emperor, was closely involved in the alignments at the Mughal court in Shahjahanabad. Shujauddin Khan of Bengal was strongly attached to Khan Dauran, the commander-in-chief of the Mughal empire. The latter had a *jagir* in Bengal which the officers at Murshidabad assigned adroitly to the eastern frontier in the hope of receiving military help in case of attacks from outside. The *suba* of Bengal regularly transmitted substantial revenues to Delhi. So far as the Europeans knew, it was still effectively a part of the Mughal empire. They were not unaware of the turmoil that the Maratha occupation of Berar, Gujarat, and Malwa had caused within the realm, but to the foreign merchant, the empire was still a colossus that bestrode the subcontinent.

To understand the timing of the growth of European designs, it has to be borne in mind that until 1739, when Nadir Shah delivered his hammer blow at Delhi, the Mughal empire stretched right up to Kabul, had effective possession of the Punjab despite Sikh insurgency, and was still a real entity in Hindustan, Bengal, and the Deccan. The Mughal noblemen of Delhi, Lahore, Faizabad, Murshidabad, and Hyderabad were still attached to one another by a thousand ties. Then, Nadir Shah detached the *suba* of Kabul from the Mughal Empire. After him, Ahmed Shah Abdali tore away the Punjab in the 1750s. At the same time, as early as the 1740s, the Mughal ruling circles in Awadh, Bengal, and the Deccan, harassed by Maratha horse, become more visibly isolated from the Red Fort at Shahjahanabad.

The process was sufficiently dramatic in Bengal to foster European designs, though initially their thoughts were no more than vague speculation. Thus far, succession to the *masnad* at Murshidabad had been governed by two factors: family ties with Murshid Quli Khan, and appointment by the Emperor. The occupation of Delhi by Nadir Shah produced a sudden paralysis of control mechanisms. There was an eruption of factional disputes in the court at Murshidabad, resulting in the killing of the legitimately appointed Governor of Bengal and the usurpation by the Deputy Governor of Bihar. Emperor Muhammad Shah regarded Alivardi Khan's coup with distaste, but situated as he then was, he had no alternative but to confer the *farman* when the usurper sent him a large present with the annual revenue. The turn of events soon stopped the flow of revenue to Delhi. The Marathas attacked Bengal and laid the entire tract waste up to the river Hugli. Fighting with their backs to the wall, no longer sending tribute to Delhi, the Mughal noblemen had to defend the *suba* without any assistance from the Emperor. The blow to the tie of imperial legitimacy, and the visible isolation of the *suba* from Shahjahanabad, stoked, for the first time, speculative thoughts among the European adventurers in India.

Colonel Mill, an English soldier of fortune who was employed in the service of the German (Holy Roman) emperor, wrote to his master at the time: 'A rebel subject, named Alivardi Khan, has torn away the three provinces of Bengal, Bihar, and Orissa from the Mughal Empire. He has treasure to the value of thirty million sterling. Three ships with fifteen hundred or two thousand regulars would suffice for the undertaking.'[6] Here was an early instance of European speculation about military intervention in Bengal. The officials of the English East India Company, too, indulged in such speculations as the Anglo-French rivalry erupted in the Carnatic, and the Mughal–Maratha confrontation drew to a close in Bengal. Squeezed by the levy of extraordinary contributions which Governor Alivardi Khan needed to pay off the Marathas, Robert Orme wrote in anger to Colonel Clive as early as 1752: '... it would be a good deed to swing the old dog. I don't speak at random when I say the Company must think seriously of it or it will not be worth their while to trade in Bengal.'[7]

These were but idle speculations at the time, though eventually five battleships accomplished the burning of Hugli, and three thousand troops achieved the victory of Plassey. Colonel Mill and Robert Orme were grossly mistaken in their estimate of the military capacity of the man on whom the Emperor had conferred the title of Mahabat Jang (Great Warrior) along with the patent of the office of *nazim*. As Persian chroniclers of the Bengal *suba* recognized, the Mughal ruling class was fortunate in having Alivardi Khan as their leader. Had he not been at the helm of affairs, the Marathas might well have conquered Bengal as they had earlier conquered Gujarat, Berar, and Malwa. He successfully maintained the unity of the new social alliance of warrior, banker, and landholder that underpinned the regime at Murshidabad. Foiling conspiracies among the Mughal commanders and noblemen by conciliation and strength, he held the *umara* together in their moment of danger and rallied them in strenuous campaigns that no longer came naturally to the army of the later Mughals. He mobilized the zamindars west of the Ganges in the operations against the Marathas and raised money from the zamindars east of the river. The greater noblemen and the house of Jagat Seth made voluntary contributions. The Marathas made no systematic effort to detach the zamindars of the affected area from the Mughals. The political and military front put forth by the

Nawab held against the cracking pressure brought to bear upon it by the annual raids of the Marathas. For over a decade of bleeding operations, the *mansabdars, seths,* and zamindars maintained a united front against the enemy under their justly named ruler Mahabat Jang.

Despite the strong leadership of Alivardi Khan, ominous deficiencies in the fighting qualities of the Mughal horsemen and their commanders were exposed by the Maratha incursions. Noblemen in even minor posts had acquired immense fortunes and were so given to luxury that they could not keep up with the swift movements of the light Maratha horse. The Nawab had to remove both his top generals, Mir Jafar and Rai Durlabh, from key positions on account of their slowness and cowardice. What was even more alarming, gigantic frauds and embezzlements were uncovered in the military accounts and musters by two energetic inspectors. Most of the commanders who were supposed to maintain one thousand horse were unable to muster even a hundred. In his commentary on the *Siyar-ul-Mutakhkhirin,* Haji Mustafa, a French convert to Islam, drew attention to the insight this offered into the military events of 1757:

> Such are, without exception, all the armies and all the troops of India; and were we to rate by this rule, those armies of fifty and a hundred thousand men that fought, or were slaughtered at the decisive battles of Palasy and Bacsar (and by some such rule must they be rated by all means), we would have incredible deductions to make. Such a rule, however, would not answer for Mir-Cassem-Qhan's troops, where there was not a single false muster; nor would it answer for Haidar-aaly's armies.[8]

All that lay in the future, and we shall have occasion to note the contrast presented by Mir Qasim's tight military organization geared up and tautened by terror, to the loose and cooperative front, willed on to continual fighting by Alivardi Khan's tactful combination of conciliation and coercion. What is worthy of immediate attention is that the united class front of the Murshidabad regime did not survive the peace purchased from the Marathas by the cession of Orissa. The Nawab undermined it by rejecting the consensus of his courtiers that Nawazish Muhammad Khan, the generous and popular husband of his elder daughter Ghasiti Begam, should succeed him. Instead, he named his unpopular grandson, Sirajuddaulah, who had alienated the commanders and grandees by his dissolute and violent conduct, as his successor to the *nizamat.* To ensure the prodigal grandson's smooth succession, he egged on the rivalries between the two main opponents of the young prince:

Mir Jafar and Husain Quli Khan. The growth of squabbles among the Mughal noblemen in the last years of his life, the assassination of Husain Quli Khan in broad daylight by his grandson's order, the precautionary dismissal of a large number of troopers from Mir Jafar's risala by the old Nawab, the growing alarm of Jagat Seth at the violent disposition revealed by the young prince, and the reported unsuccessful attempt by the latter to carry off the widowed daughter of Rani Bhavani of Rajshahi were all events signifying the end of the political and social consensus that had preserved the Mughal realm in Bengal amidst heavy odds during the Maratha incursions.

The Governor of Bengal had achieved the apparently impossible: like the contemporary Governor of the Punjab, Zakariya Khan, who had held the Sikhs at bay, he too had beaten the Marathas back. However, the maintenance of the Mughal realm in either *suba* proved beyond the capacity of the Mughal *umara* after the two great governors passed away. The Punjab was destined to be annexed by the Afghans, as was Bengal to pass into the control of the British, in the same decade: the 1750s. The Mahabatjangi *umara*, the core of Mughal noblemen and commanders who had been led into battle against the Marathas by Nawab Alivardi Khan, were no better equipped to face the East India Company without their leader, Mahabat Jang, than were the Mughal noblemen in the Punjab able to face the onslaught of Ahmad Shah Abdali.

The death of Alivardi Khan in 1756 precipitated a series of armed encounters between the parties that had cropped up among the grandees and commanders since the conclusion of the peace with the Marathas four years earlier. The designated successor Sirajuddaulah, was opposed by two parties, each with its niche in the structure of Mughal power in the *suba*: Ghasiti Begam's party at Moti Jheel, which controlled, through her Diwan Rajvallabh, the *niabat* and *nawara* of Dacca (but the party had been much weakened by the assassination of her paramour Husain Quli Khan and the demise of her husband, Nawazish Muhammad Khan); and the more distant party of Shaukat Jang, another grandson of Alivardi Khan on whom the old Nawab had conferred the *faujdari* of Purnea. The man who held the office of *bakshi* (paymaster), Mir Jafar, and the other commanders, were opposed to the Moti Jheel party, and were therefore passive spectators as the young Nawab had his aunt arrested. Returning in triumph from Moti Jheel, he promoted two upstarts, Mohan Lal and Mir Madan, at the expense of the old Mahabatjangi *umara*. The young and inexperienced Nawab rushed impetuously into murky waters, full of hidden malice. He paid no heed to the sullen resentment within the ruling circle of noblemen, commanders, officers, bankers, and landholders, who prudently recalled the fate of Husain Quli Khan and maintained a cloak of silence and secrecy over their intentions. Fear of the violent young man on the *masnad* induced them to hide their resentment, and to accompany him on his triumphant march to Calcutta, but soon afterwards they made a secret approach to the party at Purnea. When that conspiracy failed, they turned to the British, not with the intention of handing power over to them, but with the plan to use them as mercenaries to bring off yet another coup within the circle of Mughal power. Virtually no one among the courtiers and commanders of Alivardi Khan could be counted upon to support Sirajuddaulah as the crisis approached.[9] The social basis of the autonomous Mughal regime in Bengal was fast crumbling. The dissolution of the consensus at the Murshidabad court paved the way for the penetration of the English East India Company into the Mughal political order in Bengal. The British fell in with the design of the Mughal courtiers, not with the Machiavellian scheme of engineering a secretly conceived British empire, but from raw greed, sensing an opportunity to shake the pagoda tree.

The Mughal Ruling Class and the East India Company

The British, whom luck had placed at the right place to turn overnight into 'Nabobs', were a bunch of bullies, cheats, and swindlers whose greed knew no limit and who yielded to none in their boldness and cunning. The Directors of the East India Company had issued strict instructions from London that the men on the spot were not to involve the Company in any dispute for succession after Alivardi Khan's death. The Court of Directors were apprehensive of a costly misadventure involving financial loss and their instruction to Fort William on 25 August 1752, in the event of the old Nawab's demise, was 'standing upon defensive to observe to the utmost of your power the strictest neutrality between the competitors'.[10] However, the self aggrandizement of the Company's servants produced a revolution of state which neither the Company nor even they themselves had either planned or foreseen. The materials of the Mughal–British passage of arms had existed for a long time. What precipitated it was the growth of factions in the court at Murshidabad. This development allowed full play to the individual greed on the part of Englishmen. The armed encounter began with

Sirajuddaulah's attack on Calcutta and his renaming the town Alinagar in 1756. It continued intermittently until an uneasy resolution was reached in 1765 with the fragile construction of the Anglo-Mughal Diarchy of Bengal.

The alternative names, Calcutta and Alinagar, reflected contending English and Mughal conceptions of the legitimate status of the town. It is important to examine where exactly the rival conception clashed, for this lies at the heart of the confrontation between the Mughal ruling class and the English East India Company. The name Alinagar represented a range of Mughal political and economic notions that clashed at every point with the manner in which Calcutta had grown under the Company. For the moment, however, the English East India Company, too, found it advantageous to argue its case in terms of the rights conferred upon it by the Mughal farman of 1717.

The town of Calcutta sprang up at the far end of the Mughal empire, on the low-lying delta at the edge of the Sundarbans. It was not possible to maintain regular Mughal administration there, with the full complement of a district commandant's establishment. Further north, on the opposite side of the Ganges, lay the older Mughal port of Hugli. There the Emperor himself appointed and maintained a commandant with proper garrison to control the seagoing traffic of the *suba*. The task of the *Faujdar* of Hugli was to keep the Mughal, Armenian, and other shipping merchants of the town, as well as the Dutch, British, and French settlements, under proper subordination to the Mughal law. Being a ranking commander of Mughal horse, he had his own force to command, but if necessary, he could call on his superior officer, the *nazim*, to help him. The *nazim*, being a *haft hazari mansabdar* (commander of 7000 horse), was a nobleman of higher rank. Both officers were concerned to keep a close watch on the foreign settlements. The Dutch and French colonies, namely Chinsura and Chandernagore, were less than a day's march form Hugli, and were vulnerable to the *faujdar's* forces. Not so the English colony, which lay further to the south. Beyond the watchful supervision of the *Faujdar* of Hugli and the *Nazim* of Bengal, Calcutta grew steadily to emerge as an even larger centre of seagoing traffic than the official Mughal port of Hugli.[11]

One look at its origin would explain how the town came to acquire its unwarranted autonomy within the Mughal territory. Its very birth was the consequence of English rebellion against the Mughal government in the latter part of Aurangzeb's reign. This was the first of the occasions on which they defied the sovereign authority of the Mughal government. The consequence was quite different from the outcome of their second encroachment, which overturned the *nizamat* of Sirajuddaulah. They thoughtlessly provoked the wrath of an Emperor whose sway extended from Kabul to Chittagong. The *faujdar* promptly drove them from Hugli. The fleeing merchants took shelter in a place on the edge of the Sunderbans which eventually grew into Fort William. When the British obtained the Emperor's pardon, they resolved to stay on there rather than return to Hugli and the *faujdar's* watchful supervision.

The death of Aurangzeb was followed by a gradual transformation of the Mughal empire. Textbooks of Bengal history nowadays characterize the new phase as the period of the Nawabs, distinguishing it from the age of the Great Mughals. Contemporaries did not draw this distinction. In popular conception, the country still belonged to the Emperor, just as the creation belonged to God (*khalq-i-Khuda, mulk-i-padshah*). The law of the land was still the Mughal law. The *khutba* was read in the Katra Masjid every Friday in the name of the reigning Emperor, and the new year's *sikka* rupee was turned out from the mint at Murshidabad with the regnal year of the current sovereign stamped on the obverse. The Nawabs of Murshidabad continued to be *haft hazari mansabdars* of the Mughal Empire.[12] No appointment to the office of *nazim* was valid without a *farman* from the Mughal Emperor. Not to possess one would expose the incumbent to immediate danger. Sirajuddaulah, who knew this, was hoping to obtain the patent from Delhi, but he had not got it yet, and his rival Shaukat Jang was trying to secure the appointment to the *nizamat* for himself. The new Nawab, in all *parwanas* to his subjects, styled himself as the servant of the Mughal Emperor. There was an anxious note to the insistence with which he did so. In confronting the East India Company, the issues he singled out were the violations of the Mughal law which the English had committed. The Nawab went to war with the English because they were rebels against his Mughal sovereign.[13] Time and again he invoked the sovereign authority of the Emperor as if he was his imperial Majesty's undisputed servant. The weakness in his position was that he was not yet formally recognized as such by a *farman* from Delhi.

Nervously awaiting confirmation as the lawful representative of the Mughal Emperor, the Nawab was careful to spell out the grounds on which the English were deemed to have defied the sovereign authority of the land. He picked out those long-standing issues on which the

Company had incurred the displeasure of one Governor of Bengal after another. There were three problems bothering the Mughal administration in Bengal ever since the English had obtained their controversial charter from Emperor Farrukhsiyar in 1717 by which the Company was permitted to trade free of duty. One was the sheltering of fleeing Mughal subjects by the English at Calcutta. Another was the building of a fort around the town, a privilege not permitted to the merchants of the Mughal empire. The third issue was the privilege of duty-free trade enjoyed by the English East India Company, and more specifically, the abuse of the privilege by the Company's servants who had extended their own private trade under its cover. This was the most persistent issue throughout the armed encounters between the Mughals and the English from 1756 to 1764, an issue that continued to breed tensions even after the Anglo-Mughal Diarchy was set up in 1765.

The broad changes in the character of the Mughal empire after 1707 had helped the English to find a surer footing despite the failure of their initial rebellion. It would not have been possible for them to obtain the sort of charter from Emperor Aurangzeb that they cajoled out of his weak and ineffective grandson Farrukhsiyar in 1717. With Governor Murshid Quli Khan controlling all appointments in Bengal, including that of the *Faujdar* of Hugli, the imperial court of Delhi had no interest in maintaining proper control of the European colonies below Hugli. Because of the disorganized finances of the empire, the need for ready money was pressing. Therefore, when an embassy of the English company waited upon Emperor Farrukhsiyar with a large present of money, the court departed from proper imperial practice and gave the English an unprecedented *farman* without asking the opinion of the Governor of Bengal. Under the charter, the Company was entitled to a zamindari around Calcutta, and could carry on trade without paying any duties. Under cover of its landed right, the Company built up an extraterritorial jurisdiction in Calcutta, where the Mughal writ did not run. The Company servants promptly exceeded the Company's right of free trade by trading duty free on their own account, and by selling duty-free trade permits (*dastaks*) to their native associates.[14]

Murshid Quli Khan was furious, but his hands where tied by his master's dispensation. Shujauddin Khan, the next Governor of Bengal, wrote anxiously to the commander-in-chief of the Mughal empire in 1733:

I am scarce able to recount to you the abominable practices of this people. When they first came to this country they petitioned the then government in a humble manner for liberty to purchase a spot of ground to build a factory house upon, which was no sooner granted but they ran up a strong fort, surrounded it with a ditch which has communication with the river and mounted a great number of guns upon walls. They have enticed several merchants and others to go and take protection under them and they collect a revenue which amount to Rs. 100,000.[15]

Shujauddin Khan anticipated here practically all the grounds on which Sirajuddaulah went to war with the English. At every point, the manner of Calcutta's growth clashed with the Mughal notions of a proper political and economic order.

The maritime power of Calcutta grew rapidly: between 1730 and 1750 the ships visiting the English settlement were twice the number of those that went further up to the Mughal port of Hugli.[16] While Murshidabad still remained the centre of the money market under the control of the Jagat Seths, the centre of foreign trade visibly shifted to Calcutta. Despite this, the trade of the English did not fare too well. Severe difficulties were experienced during the *nizamat* of Alivardi Khan, especially on account of the Maratha raids. The conclusion of the peace with the Marathas did not restore the Company's trade to its old level. In 1754, the Company broke off with the independent merchants who had so long supplied the Company's export items (called the 'Investment') against advances (*dadni*). In place of the so called *dadni* merchants, the Company servants appointed their own native assistants (*gumashtahs*) at various up-country factories (*aurangs*) to collect the items of the Investment under their direct supervision. While the break with the independent merchants of Calcutta resulted in an immediate catastrophic drop in the Company's Investment, the covenanted servants, immune under the Company's *dastaks* to paying duty, increased their private trade rapidly by manipulating the new system of obtaining supplies directly from the *aurangs* through the *gumashtahs*. The young prince is said to have calculated a loss of customs duties worth one crore and a half on account of the use and misuse of *dastaks*.[17]

There had been other disquieting developments. In the 1740s, when news of the Carnatic War arrived at the court of Siraj's grandfather, alarm grew in Murshidabad at the energy with which the English and French were fortifying their respective settlements in preparation for war with each other. It was also impressed upon the court that fleeing Mughal subjects might take shelter from Mughal law in the fortified

English colony of Calcutta. The English had long set up a Mayor's Court there, which not only exercised jurisdiction upon the European inhabitants of the town, but even tried disputes between them and Mughal subjects.[18] In addition, J.Z. Holwell, upon being appointed perpetual zamindar of Calcutta by the Company in 1750, set up an oppressive 'cutcherry'. It extended a greedy jurisdiction over all the native inhabitants of the town, extorting greatly enhanced sums as revenues, fines, and fees without paying a pie to the government.[19] It was more obvious than ever that the imperial jurisdiction did not extend here. In a notorious case in the last year of Alivardi Khan's administration, the court sent horsemen and peons to demand the effects of the Cotma family of Kasimbazar, a leading house of silk merchants who had taken shelter with the English. The latter chased the messengers out of Calcutta. Hukum Beg, the court notable in charge of merchant affairs, had half a mind to inform the Nawab of the insolence of the English when the British chief at Kasimbazar, fearful of the old man's wrath, advised his Calcutta superiors that the Cotmas had better be escorted back.[20]

While the old Nawab was on his deathbed, the issue of the fleeing subjects, which had been confined so far to the native merchants, became a grave political matter as it linked up unexpectedly with the succession to the *nizamat*, and the alignments at the court. Krishnadas, a functionary suspected of embezzlement at the *niabat* of Dacca, fled from the young prince's inquisition, and took shelter in Calcutta, taking with him the Dacca treasure. Krishnadas was Rajvallabh's son, and he belonged to Ghasiti Begam's party at the court. Drake, the English chief of Calcutta, befriended him as he judged that on the old Nawab's death Ghasiti Begam would manage to capture power in Murshidabad.[21] As it happened, she was promptly arrested after her father's demise, and her newphew, having occupied the *masnad*, demanded that Krishnadas be handed over. Drake had the temerity to turn the new Nawab's agent out of Calcutta. This was clear defiance of constituted authority by the English. The manner in which these merchants were dabbling in the high affairs of state was obviously inconsistent with the Mughal political order. Equally obviously, they had been emboldened to do so by virtue of their fortified settlement, and their autonomous jurisdiction, which they had unlawfully erected in Mughal territory. Calcutta, on account of the rapid growth of its shipping and traffic, had already overshadowed Hugli as a centre of foreign trade. If Drake were to be allowed to pursue his course, it might emerge as a rival to

Murshidabad and become an alternative political centre. That, of course, no Mughal *nazim* worth his salt would allow.

Matters soon came to a head. Having issued an order to Drake that the new fortifications erected at Calcutta during his grandfather's illness be demolished at once, Sirajuddaulah marched out of Murshidabad to attack Shaukat Jang of Purnea, a cousin with claims to the *nizamat*, and to all appearances a more formidable enemy. However, Drake's insolent refusal to comply with his orders, together with misleading gestures of submission from Shaukat Jang, caused the young Nawab to veer around from Rajmahal, where he had arrived on the march to Purnea. Drake had the hardihood to maintain that the fortifications were necessary in view of the likelihood of war in the *suba* between the English and French.[22] This was an open declaration that the English were preparing for hostilities with the French within the Mughal domain, challenging the monopoly that the Mughal government claimed over the legitimate use of force in that territory. There could be no clearer challenge to Mughal sovereignty than this assertion that 'we were on the eve of a French war, which would probably be brought into his country'.[23] No sooner did the young Nawab hear the answer than he jumped up in a torrent of rage and, pulling out his sword, declared: '[W]ho shall dare to think of commencing hostilities in my country, or presume to imagine that I have not power to protect them?'[24]

Coming swiftly down the river, he stormed the factory at Kasimbazar, and had its chief seized. In a dramatic scene the proper submission of the foreign merchants to the rightful Mughal authority was symbolically enacted. William Watts, the English chief at Kasimbazar, was brought bound to the Nawab and made 'to hug his excellency's feet with folded hands (*Hat bandky Sahebka kuddum pukkerna*)'.[25] Watts wept all the while and said repeatedly 'that he was his slave—"toumar Zholam, toumar Zholam" [*tomar ghulam, tomar ghulam*]'.[26]

The symbolic reduction of merchant pretensions and the ceremonial enactment of proper submission to the person of the Mughal Governor was accompanied by the handing over of a written undertaking (*muchilka*) by Watts to the following effect: '1st, No protection to be given in Calcutta to any of the Nawab's subjects, 2nd, the drawbridge at Perrings and the new fortifications are to be demolished, and 3rd, no dusticks to be given to any of the black merchants.'[27] As the Governor of Bengal marched down to Calcutta, he set out what he considered British violations of his sovereign master's authority in a letter to Khoja

Wajid, the Armenian merchant prince of Hugli and his trusted adviser in merchant affairs.[28]

> I have three substantial motives for extirpating the English out of my country; one that they have built strong fortifications and dug a large ditch in the King's [i.e. the Mughal Emperor's] dominions contrary to the established laws of the country; the second is that they abused the privilege of their dusticks by giving them to such as were by no means entitled to them, from which practices the King [the Emperor] has suffered greatly in the revenue of his customs; the third motive is that they give protection to such of the King's subjects as have by their behaviour in the employs they were entrusted with made themselves liable to be called to an account and instead of giving them [up] on demand they allow such persons to shelter themselves within their bounds from the hands of justice. For these reasons it is become requisite to drive them out. If they will promise to remove the foregoing complaints of their conduct and will agree to trade upon the same terms as other merchants did in the times of Nabob Jaffeir Cawn [Murshid Quli Khan] I will then pardon their fault and permit them residence here, otherwise I will shortly expel that nation.

In an earlier letter from Rajmahal, too, the Nawab had emphasized the same points: he, as the *subadar* of Bengal on behalf of the Mughal Padshah at Shahjahanabad, could not overlook the breaches of law involved in the construction of private fortifications in Mughal territory, the sheltering of Mughal subjects and officials liable to render accounts to the appointed Mughal authority, and the purchase and sale of goods without payment of duties at the rates established of old throughout the Mughal empire.[29]

Nothing is more revealing of his underlying assumptions regarding the proper role of the merchants in the Mughal realm than the official favour (*parwana*) which he issued to the chief of the English factory at Madras after expelling the English from Calcutta:[30]

> Director Pigot, of high and great rank, May you be possessor of the Patcha's [Padshah's] favour.
>
> It was not my intention to remove the mercantile business of the Company belonging to you from the Subah of Bengal, but Roger Drake your gomasta was a very wicked and unruly man and began to give protection to persons who had accounts with the Patcha [Emperor] in his koatey [factory]. Notwithstanding all my admonitions, yet he did not desist from his shameless actions. Why should these people who come to transact the mercantile affairs of the Company be doers of such actions? However that shameless man has met with the desert of his actions and was expelled this Subah.

The man he addressed was nothing more to him than the manager of the English traders at the *kothi* (factory) at Madras. The message, too, was not without condescension: as an officer of the Mughal government charged with upholding the Emperor's authority, which extended everywhere and over every inhabitant of Mughal territory, he had punished a mere merchant who had presumed to dabble in affairs of state. Oblivious of his place, Drake had dared to shelter a functionary of the Mughal government charged with embezzling the imperial revenues at Dacca. So bold a violation of Mughal sovereignty could not be ignored. But there was a hint that the English would be allowed to return if they accepted the proper terms on which all merchants might carry on business in the Mughal empire. The terms the Nawab had in mind were those that had obtained in the time of his predecessor Murshid Quli Khan. This meant, as Holwell gathered during his captivity, the rates of duty before the grant of the imperial charter of 1717, which, in the Nawab's view, had improperly done away with the customary duties payable by the English.[31]

It is said that the young Nawab's thoughts had been influenced by the anxieties of his grandfather, who had pointed out to him on his deathbed how the English and French parties of the Carnatic had 'seized and divided the country of the king [the Mughal sovereign] and the goods of his people between them'. While a prisoner at Murshidabad, Holwell heard that Alivardi Khan had long thought it desirable 'to destroy the forts and garrisons of the Europeans, and to reduce their trade on the footing of the Armenians'.[32] The Armenians were, indeed, the key to the new Nawab's thinking: they were as merchants should be; the English, those unruly subjects, must learn to be like them. The language he adopted was that of a Mughal viceroy who would expel the alien nation of traders from his country if they did not desist from violating the laws of his Mughal sovereign. Either the disobedient merchants must be reduced to Mughal authority; or, failing that, the unruly aliens would have to be expelled from the country. Such were the sentiments that lay behind his thinking at the time.

Calcutta or Alinagar

It was not the Nawab's intention to be too severe with the 'unruly' men who had after all annually imported so much treasure to conduct their mercantile transactions in his *suba*. However, Calcutta was taken by storm. Drake and other senior servants of the Company fled on board the ships leaving behind over a hundred Englishmen to offer futile resistance under the command of his junior, J.Z. Holwell. In the confusion during the overrunning of the fort, the remnants of the party were herded by the Nawab's men into a cell locally known as the Black Hole, which was in fact the military prison of the fort, a room 18 feet long by 14 feet 10 inches wide. During the hot summer night, some of the Englishmen who had fought died of their wounds, and many more died of suffocation, fright, and thirst. No more than 23 persons emerged from the cell in the morning. The nights' imprisonment made an indelible impression on Holwell, who, after the Nawab set him free with gracious words, penned a narrative of frightful atrocities, in which he himself figured as a heroic man.

Holwell was a raconteur who was carried away by his own tale, the details of which are somewhat doubtful. He claimed that 146 English prisoners were packed into the cell, which, as nationalist writers demonstrated later on, was physically impossible. It is not known how many prisoners were actually locked up in the small prison of Fort William on that hot summer night. The Nawab had no knowledge of their fate, nor did the guards actually intend their suffocation. The deaths that occurred, and doubtless deaths did occur though the number and exact details are not certain, were due to the confused circumstances of the storming of the fort and the indifference of the guards in charge of the hapless prisoners.[33] There were no executions, no torture, and by contemporary Mughal standards, the treatment of prisoners, who in the eye of the Mughal law were rebels, was lenient when we recall the treatment meted out to the rebel Sikh leader Banda and his fellow prisoners. Even the English did not make much of the incident in the eighteenth century. For over fifty years, little notice was taken of 'the Black Hole Tragedy', until Macaulay and other compilers of the new imperialist hagiography popularized the legend during the age of Victoria.

What the lower Ganges witnessed at the moment was not a confrontation of barbarity with civilization, nor of nationalism with imperialism. It was, on the contrary, an armed encounter between an agrarian bureaucratic regime seated away from the Indian Ocean (the Mughal ruling class) and a seaborne armed corporation from Europe (the English East India Company). After Job Charnock's act of defiance against Emperor Aurangzeb, which led to the settlement of the English at Calcutta, this was the second rebellion of the English against the

Mughals, though the policy of the Governor of Bengal indicated that in his estimation this, too, was an act of defiance rather than a full blown rebellion. The occupation of the defiant English settlement on 20 June enabled the new *nazim* to give effect to his conceptions regarding the proper place of the town in a well-ordered political set-up. The next day 'orders were given out by beat of tomtom, that the town should no longer be called Calcutta, but Alinogore'.[34]

As a scion of the ruling Shia family of Murshidabad, Sirajuddaulah named the town after Ali, the Imam of the Shia reckoning. He was evidently determined to rebuild the town from altogether different foundations. The name did not last long. On 9 February 1757, Clive, having reoccupied the town, successfully concluded the Treaty of Alinagar with the Nawab, and that was the last official mention of the name. Before the summer was over, the Nawab was dead, and no more was heard of Alinagar after Plassey. In the contending Mughal and English conceptions about the legitimate status of the town, it was the English conception that prevailed. Had the town continued to be the Alinagar of Mughal conception, it would not have developed as the greatest colonial port-city east of Suez. On the contrary, it would have been a satellite to the Mughal provincial capital of Murshidabad, part of a vast agrarian regime extending further up the Gangetic valley. The contest over the name of the town proved, in that perspective, to be ultimately a contest over the future of the country. The name Alinagar summed up in one word the Murshidabad darbar's vision of the correct place of the English settlement in the Mughal realm. The English on their part, could not accept the changed mode of control signified by the altered name. Large issues depended on whether the English settlement was to become Alinagar, or to revert to being Calcutta. If the former, then the English would not trade as before; if the latter, then the Mughals would not rule as earlier. In 1756–7, it was not the town of Job Charnock alone that stood at the crossroads, but also the country of Emperor Aurangzeb.

Soon after being driven from Calcutta to the riverside halt at Falta, the English activated diplomatic contacts with the darbar through various bankers and merchants. They were anxious to learn the terms on which the Nawab might allow them to return to town. Jagat Seth, the principal banker of the Mughal empire, Khoja Wajid, the Armenian shipping magnate of Hugli, Amirchand, the biggest native merchant of Calcutta, and Khoja Petross, a smaller Armenian trader of what was now Alinagar, provided contacts with the court. It was soon evident that the Nawab was not averse to having such useful merchants back. However, the terms on which he would permit them to settle were quite different from those obtaining earlier. The English harped on their *farman* and on the rights they had obtained under it since 1717.[35] They had lost the original during the flight from Calcutta, but with Khoja Petross's assistance they secured a certified copy from the Mughal *qazi* at Hugli.[36] Evidently the English were now reduced to arguing their case in Mughal terms, but the Nawab would not hear of the *farman*. The terms for resettlement elicited from the darbar disheartened the party hanging on at Falta, and were rejected out of hand when Clive and Watson arrived with their forces.

The Nawab had the Mughal mentality as regards the proper place of merchants in the realm. Merchants, as the letter he now sent to Pigot at Madras conveyed so vividly by its nuances,[37] were subjects and they should conduct themselves as such. Drake, the manager (*gumashtah*) of the English company, had no call to interfere in the affairs of state. Such 'shameless actions' were inconsistent with the proper order of the Mughal empire. He found it outrageous that 'these people who come to transact the mercantile affairs' should conduct their business from a fortified settlement mounted with guns. The fact that they had done so, and had the temerity to set up their own jurisdiction there, was contrary to the laws of the empire. Protection of the merchants was to be provided, as in the instance of the Armenian merchants, by the Governor of Bengal, in accordance with the Mughal law. It was not for a band of tradesmen to garrison a fort or arrange their own defence. There could be no greater presumption than for them to imagine that the Mughal *nazim* of Bengal had 'not power to protect them'. Their proper role was to buy and sell, to pay duties upon it, and to obey the officers and noblemen of the Emperor's realm. In the Mughal notion of a properly constituted order, the distinction between ruler and merchant was self-evident. The Nawab, whose notions were those of his class, might well have recalled a verse communicated by Emperor Aurangzeb to a former viceroy of Bengal by way of warning:[38]

> Those who purchase—sell;
> We neither purchase nor sell.

It was important, as the Emperor's precautionary couplet which was still current in the *suba*, implied, to maintain a proper division of functions between rulers and merchants. It was not for the rulers to engage in buying and selling. By the same logic, it was not for the merchants to conduct war and peace. True, the said Viceroy of Bengal, who was in fact Aurangzeb's own grandson, had made a monopoly of several items of export, to the Emperors' displeasure; it was also true that the present Nawab's own mother, Amina Begam, had been busy exporting commodities through the Mughal port of Hugli while her father Alivardi Khan was still alive. However, if such a confusion of roles were left unchecked things would go out of hand. The young Nawab, upon entering Fort William, could not get over his surprise at the prodigious heap of cannon, cannon balls, and other munitions. He was so struck by the beauty of the Government House, that he considered it to be worthy of 'the dwelling of Princes rather than merchants'.[39] He just could not grasp the fact that the building was the Government House: how could a body of merchants have one? And therefore, had it destroyed out of hatred of Drake, whose private property he thought it was.[40]

By building additional fortification for 'protection' in an anticipated war with the French, Drake in the Nawab's view had done nothing less than question his overriding power, as the Emperor's viceroy, to protect all His Majesty's subjects. Also, by shamelessly invoking the pretext of a French war in an open letter to him, that 'wicked and unruly man' posed a public challenge to his sovereign master's legitimate monopoly of the use of force. He, therefore, had left him with no choice. The Nawab was aware that the former Governors of Bengal had found it convenient to turn a blind eye to the private wars habitually waged by the zamindars of the *suba* against one another. But he could hardly afford to ignore the fact that the English and the French had actually overturned the Mughal order in the Deccan by fighting each other. And now the *gumashtah* of the English at Calcutta, forgetful of his place as a merchant, had arrogated to himself the role of a warrior in the Nawab's own *suba*. There was no choice left but to introduce the correct forms of Mughal administration in the town of Alinagar.

Before the Nawab departed for Murshidabad, he set up a regular system of Mughal administration in the settlement. His first step was to appoint a favourite, an incompetent upstart named Manikchand, as the *Faujdar* of Alinagar.[41] A mosque was erected in the town, but in accordance with the Mughal practice of balancing the communities in the administration, the new *faujdar* was a Hindu. 'There now', reported the Dutch at Chinsura to their Batavia headquarters,

is that beautiful place, whose blooming and flourishing condition caused
every one to admire it, and from which the English Company drew a
great and princely income. The fort and all the other costly buildings
have been pulled down, the shops erected before this disaster have been
plundered, and the timber wharf destroyed, the place re-named Alinagar,
and put under the government of a Faujdar.[42]

The most notable feature of these Mughal reforms was the introduction of a *faujdari* administration. It had long been the Mughal practice
to maintain *faujdars* at strategic centres such as Rajmahal, Ghoraghat,
and the port of Hugli. The colony of the English at the edge of the
Suderbans had hitherto escaped this means of control and had even
been suffered to spawn a Mayor's Court and a perpetual zamindar's
cutchery. Now the extraterritorial jurisdiction was done away with,
the fort placed under Mughal garrison with a *faujdar* in command, and
the settlement fully brought under Mughal law and nawabi
administration. The order announcing the renaming of the town would
in these circumstances have begun with the formula '*Khalq-i-khuda,
mulk-i-padshah, hukm-i-Nawab Sirajuddaulah Bahadur ...*' to the
accompaniment of the beat of tomtom. This would din it into the heads
of the inhabitants that the town was now fully under Mughal rule.

Notwithstanding the changes, the Nawab was eager that the English
merchants should return to town. An order was issued before he left
that they might return to their homes. However, soon after he left, a
drunken European sergeant killed 'a Moorman', whereupon the Mughal
faujdar left in charge of the town ordered all Europeans to quit the
settlement.[43] It was resolved that the English should learn the proper
manner of merchants, the Armenians being held out as the model,
before the issue of resettling them might be put on the darbar's agenda.
No steps were taken, however, to drive them from Falta, where they
were hanging on in their ships. On the contrary, the *faujdar*, persuaded
by the influential native merchant Amirchand, agreed to let the English
at Falta have all the necessary provisions. This was a clear sign that the
government was aware of the benefits of the European trade. However,
the Nawab was anxious to put the trade on a proper basis. On the way
back he ordered his men to pull down the flags and fortifications of the
French at Chandernagar and the Dutch at Chinsura. The orders were
not carried out. The French and Dutch settlements avoided the fate of
the English settlement by paying large sums as presents.[44] All the same,
the Nawab let it be known to both the Dutch and the French that 'he
wanted all the nations to be without forts or flags like the Armenians'.[45]

The interruption of trade in course of the political trouble between the Mughal *nazim* and the English East India Company had affected bankers and merchants everywhere. Eager for the resumption of normal trade, they became active in court seeking to settle the differences. Not that these merchants wanted the English to get their own terms. On the contrary, the Mughal bankers and merchants wanted the Mughal order, within which they had a privileged financial position, to be enforced. What they envisaged was that the English might be brought back with due regard to trade, which would actually strengthen the Mughal order. Khoja Wajid, the Armenian merchant prince, put out feelers to the Nawab on behalf of all men of business.

The Nawab's immediate reaction was that the English should conduct themselves in the same manner as Wajid's own community. The Armenians, too, were foreigners, but they had always behaved as merchants should. As far as the official Mughal point of view was concerned, they were the ideal merchant community. The terms offered by the Nawab through Khoja Wajid before he invaded Calcutta, were the same terms on which the Armenians had traded in Bengal since the last century. The then Mughal government had given them land for settlement at a place called Saidpur in the flourishing town of Kasimbazar. There they had carried on their vocation as peaceful merchants without ever fortifying the settlements, deeming it sufficient to have the protection of the Mughal administration. They traded as Mughal subjects, paying the same rate of duty as the Muslim merchants of the Mughal empire. This was the privileged rate, lower than that payable by the Hindus. This same privileged rate has been obtained by the Europeans trading in the Mughal empire. Not content with that, the English had bypassed the provincial government to obtain by underhand means a charter of duty-free trade from the Delhi durbar. The new Governor of Bengal saw no reason why they should not return to Alinagar on his terms, which were, as Luke Scrafton noted down soon after the events, 'to live under government, without laws or fortifications of our own; and to carry on our trade like the Armenians and his own subjects'.[46]

These were the very terms which Drake had received from Sirajuddaulah while Calcutta had been under siege, and from the Mughal point of view, they were deemed perfectly reasonable. Not so, however, from the English point of view, which had been long conditioned to privilege as under the Charter of 1717. Had Drake then agreed to the Nawab's terms, Calcutta would have lost its privileged corporate status, a concept quite alien to the Mughals. As his minute on the siege of Calcutta, justifying the grounds on which he had rejected the nawab's terms, put it to the Court of Directors, '... any terms we would propose to the Nawab would not be listened to except that we consented to deliver up our cannon, pull down our bastions and all our fortifications, and submit to inhabit in these dominions as Armenians, which articles had we dared to comply with, would, with this rash Nobob, have submitted us to an easy prey at the expense of being plundered and no security left for future times.'[47] Drake was of course concerned to justify his conduct to his critical superiors. It is nonetheless true that the English were not prepared to carry on trade except as a privileged and armed commune. Nor, for that matter, were the Dutch and French. Here lay the root of the contradiction; a conflict that would have to be resolved one way or the other.

It was part of the Nawab's policy to reduce the French, the Dutch, and especially the English to the same level as the other merchants of the Mughal empire. In his view, these three nations had been allowed for too long and wholly improperly to carry on trade from fortified settlements under their own laws. If the political lessons of the Carnatic War were to be taken to heart, nothing was more urgent than to reduce them to the status of Mughal subjects, a status which the Armenians had been good enough to accept. Not to speak of the Armenians, even some European nations had not been allowed the privilege of trading under arms. As the young Nawab saw, the Danes and Prussians had been allowed the liberty of trade, yet they were prohibited to run up fortifications or to put in garrisons. From what Holwell gathered during his captivity in Murshidabad, it was the resolve of the government to divest all the Europeans of their forts and garrisons: 'we were the objects of his policy and not of his resentment only'.[48]

Accordingly, when the English at Falta got in touch with the Nawab through Khoja Wajid, they found that Sirajuddaulah was determined not to allow them any privilege that would mark them out from other Mughal subjects. Khoja Wajid let out that 'if the Nawab did so far comply with his request to admit the English into Calcutta, it would not be upon better terms than the Portuguese and Prussians trade on, which is to pay duties and hire houses and ware houses for themselves and goods'.[49] Wajid further informed the English that they must not expect to be put in possession of Fort William again. He also hinted that 'the only method to re-establish Calcutta upon creditable terms would be to proceed to Madras and there concert measures with the

Governor and Council, and to return with strength sufficient to enforce any petitions we had to make'.[50]

Unwilling to trade on the same terms as the Armenians, the Prussians, the Danes, and the Portuguese, the refugees at Falta had no choice but to take Wajid at his word. They haplessly awaited the arrival of reinforcements from Madras. As trade was at a standstill, Jagat Seth and Amir Chand were busy trying to patch up matters. At length the nawab relented. Khoja Wajid was summoned from Hugli. Sirajuddaulah, it appeared, was ready to soften his stand to some extent: 'There is two things they say that the Nawab will not give up, that is the mosque and the name he gave Calcutta; that a Fouzdar's [residence in Calcutta], and some other articles he made a point of, is dropped or at least will not be insisted on.'[51] The Nawab's insistence on the mosque was perhaps more political than religious. As it was a public mosque it was the Jami Masjid of Alinagar where the Khutba was read in the name of the reigning Mughal Emperor every Friday. This was symbolic of Mughal sovereignty.

The gulf between the Mughal and English notions was wide and the clash of positions fundamental. Still, a compromise might have been arranged in normal circumstances. The English, driven to the pestilential island of Falta and reduced to dire straits, were desperately seeking for terms, and the Nawab, in view of the large influx of silver he might expect from the Company's trade, was not averse to resettling the English on terms consistent with the ceremonial sovereignty of his imperial master. However, circumstances were not normal. War was known to be imminent between the English and French. It happened that the Madras Presidency had at its disposal a well equipped fleet and army for operations against the French. The President and the Council of Madras, after debating the matter, decided that they would temporarily divert this opportune resource to an expedition to Bengal. It would be commanded by Admiral Watson and Colonel Clive, with a view to 'securing their colonies and trade from future insult and exactions'.[52] The English idea of how this was to be achieved was irreconcilable with the Mughal notion of the proper constitution of the realm.

Still, the English had no design at this stage for the political conquest of Bengal. The Madras authorities instructed Watson and Clive to conclude peace with the Nawab if he offered to return Calcutta, pay compensation for its plunder, and allow duty-free trade as before. Financial prospects, more than political schemes, guided the expedition from the start: compensation, recovery of losses, and reprisals upon the Moors with a view to winning 'prizes'⁵³ for the navy (i.e. Admiral Watson) and the army (i.e. Colonel Clive). The *Faujdar* of Alinagar fled from town on the approach of the English forces, which proceeded to burn and plunder the Mughal town of Hugli. An inconclusive engagement outside Alinagar frightened the Nawab into making an offer of peace. The English were promised all the privileges under their *farman*, together with compensation for losses, permission to coin *siccas* 'in your mint at Calcutta or Alinagar, and the right to fortify the town'.⁵⁴ Clive, delighted at the offer of all the conditions laid down by Madras at the start of the expedition, was much relieved. The Treaty of Alinagar was concluded on that basis. Although the treaty officially confirmed the name of Alinagar, the town that emerged from it was no longer under a Mughal *faujdar*. The Nawab resiled from his earlier position that the conditions in force before the notorious farman of 1717 must be restored. In substance, if not in name, the town was now reinstated as the English colony of Calcutta it had been since 1717. Even so, the treaty was well within the parameters of the Mughal order, which the English for the moment had no notion of replacing with a colonial order. The Madras authorities, highly pleased by the terms of the peace, pressed Clive to return immediately for operations in the Carnatic. Clive had every intention of doing so, and he wrote confidently to his father, 'I expect to return very shortly to the Coast as all is over here.'⁵⁵

The matter might have rested there but for the fact that a conspiracy which had sprung up earlier in Murshidabad became active again in consequence of a dual crisis which shook the Nawab's power to its foundations: the outbreak of hostilities between the English and the French, and the rumoured march of Ahmad Shah Abdali upon Bengal. Siraj had been provoked into commencing hostilities by Drake's insolent declaration that the English might shortly be at war with the French. This was a violation of imperial territory which no viceroy could ignore. No sooner, however, had he concluded peace with the English than news arrived from Europe that England and France were finally at war. The English might have remained quiet on the Ganges but for the rumour that the Afghans had left Delhi for Bengal. Fear of an Afghan invasion, which in the event did not materialize, immobolized the Nawab. Taking advantage of the paralysis of the Mughal government, the English drove the French from Chandernagore. The Nawab held his hand because he counted on English military assistance in the event of an Afghan march upon Bengal. He, however, refused to hand over

Jean Law, the French chief at Kasimbazar, to Clive: '... it is not the custom of Hindustan to bind or deliver up to their enemies the weak, or those who have begged their protection.'[56] The courtiers at Murshidabad, whose deep designs might be foiled by any junction between the Nawab and the French, persuaded him to turn Jean Law out of the capital. The same fear induced Clive to explore the possibility of arranging countermeasures with the Nawab's opponents at the durbar.[57]

The conspirators at Murshidabad were playing a fresh hand at an old game. Their original plan was to mount a coup from within the Mughal set-up, without English help. Shaukat Jang had become, by virtue of a *farman* obtained at great expense from Delhi, the legitimate Governor of Bengal in the autumn of 1756. A conspiracy by Mir Jafar and other noblemen of Murshidabad to set up Shaukat Jang in place of Sirajuddaulah miscarried when Shaukat Jang's rashness resulted in his death in battle.[58] The subsequent imperial confirmation of Sirajuddaulah[59] as viceroy did not put a stop to the spasmodic conspiracies against him: rumours in the capital focused upon a son of Shaukat Jang, surviving sons of the former nawab Sarfaraz Khan, the Mughal deputy governor of Cuttack who was said to be backed by the Marathas, and Mir Khuda Yar Latif Khan, a commander of 2000 horse who had been disappointed in his hopes of being appointed *Faujdar* of Hugli.[60] Finally the conspirators turned to the English, convinced by the latter's taking of Chandernagore that it would be useful to employ fighters as mercenaries against the nawab. In doing so the Mahabatjangi *umara* ignored their master's warning that in the event of his death 'the hat-men would possess themselves of all the shores of Hindia'.[61]

In a secret treaty the English promised to help Mir Jafar become Nawab in return for Rs 2.5 crores, a sum approaching the entire annual revenue of Bengal. The treaty, however, made no provision to enhance the Company's position in the land and trade of Bengal beyond the fullest extent of the imperial charter of 1717 and the Alinagar Treaty of 1757. Between them, Emperor Farrukhsiyar and Nawab Sirajuddaulah had already granted the privileges aimed at by the Company: duty free trade, privilege to mint coins in Calcutta, and a small zamindari around the town. The Mahabatjangi *umara* had no intention to yield anything beyond this. Nor did the English themselves envisage it. As the terms of the secret treaty revealed, what they wanted above all was money. Had the relations between Nawab Mir Jafar and the English been regulated on the basis of the treaty alone, the English would have retired from Murshidabad after the payment of the promised sums. The conspirators intended to seize power for themselves, not to hand it over to the English.

Powerful elements, well entrenched within the political and social structure created by Murshid Quli Khan forty years ago, combined against the Nawab. The ranking commanders of Mughal horse, the banking house of Jagat Seth, merchants with an entrée to the durbar, and some leading zamindars, were all involved in the intrigue. The internal constellation of power within the *suba*, which had fallen into line behind Alivardi Khan in his campaign to hold the Marathas at bay, lined up against Sirajuddaulah in his bid to keep the English out. Plassey in consequence was no real test of the forces engaged on the two sides: the Mughal warrior–aristocracy staged a mock battle to unseat their formal head. The unfolding of material realities in the years to come would make the Mughals and the English each other's natural enemies and a real reckoning of strength would have to come. In the meanwhile, the huge sums that the English extracted from the new Nawab Mir Jafar enabled them to station troops which they had earlier intended to withdraw. A symbolic event indicated the altered balance of power. In the official Mughal records, Calcutta regained its name, and ceased to be described as Alinagar.[62]

The Crisis of the Mughal Nobility

Mir Jafar, the new Nawab, distributed large presents among the English chiefs of Calcutta, hoping thereby to escape the staggering obligations under his treaty with the English. The illusion was speedily dispelled. The Marathas who had laid Bengal waste were remembered as cruel and greedy. The English were more systematic, and their avarice was deadlier because it was relentless. Where the sky is the limit to man's conceptions of acquisition, he is surprised at his own restraint. 'I stand astonished at my own moderation', Clive subsequently declared before Parliament.[63] Contemporary English witnesses record that the people of Murshidabad stood by sullenly and watched as the flotilla of boats carried away the first great consignment of treasure to Calcutta. Calcutta, now no longer Alinagar, loomed ever larger as a peril to the Mughal order. The people most immediately affected were the Mughal officer class. It was they who lived off the income and savings of the government at Murshidabad. They turned against the English. Driven to his wit's end by the English demand for ever more money, the new Nawab looked to the Dutch for deliverance. However, this hope too was speedily laid to rest as a Dutch expedition to Bengal ran aground.

Old and weak willed, Mir Muhammad Jafar Khan was totally ill-equipped to lead the Mughal ruling class. Their natural resentment of the plunder of Murshidabad put the *Nizamat* and the Company on collision course. Mir Jafar's cruel and energetic son, Miran, wanted the *nizamat* to break free from the crippling military dependence on the English. His attempt to avoid the use of English troops was calculated to this end. The object however proved beyond the incompetent young man's grasp. The Mughal forces had disintegrated at Plassey. The blunted edge of the *nizamat's* military power encouraged the zamindar of Birbhum, the *Faujdars* of Midnapore and Purnea, and the *Naib Nazim* of Bihar to defy the *nazim's* authority and to withhold the payment of the land revenue. Miran had neither the courage to lead the troops in battle, nor the ability to reorganize the Mughal army. Inevitably, the Nawab had to take English help to suppress the challenges to the *nizamat*. When lightning struck his son dead, he was left helpless.

Under the crushing financial burdens imposed on the *nizamat* by the Company, the framework of Mughal governance gave way. The troops were in mutiny for arrears of pay. Their commanders were fiercely resentful of the tribute to the English which was depriving them of those payments and grants from the treasury that financially sustained the Mughal nobility. As head of the *diwani*, Rai Durlabh somehow kept the tribute flowing to Calcutta. Mir Jafar saw him as the Trojan horse of the English in Murshidabad. In fear of life the *nizamat diwan* fled to Calcutta. The confidence of the Jagat Seths in the solvency of the *nizamat* was so severely shaken that they refused a loan for the expedition against Raja Ramnarayan, the *Naib Nazim* of Bihar. Leaving Murshidabad, they went off on the pilgrimage to Parasnath. When the nawab's troops were ordered to block their passage, they forced their way through. To meet the financial obligations to the English, the *nizamat* was then obliged to make over to the Company the revenues due from the *Faujdar* of Hugli and the zamindars of Nadia and Burdwan. In the process it began to lose its control over important holders of office and land. Even these concessions (*tankhas*) did not suffice to make up the deficit in the payments. The English, however, would not ease the unremitting pressure for more money as the plunder of Bengal was financing their war with the French in the peninsula. The zamindars, taking advantage of the government's weakness, held back on the instalments of revenue. They would not pay up until troops were sent down to chastise them. That in turn increased the cost of collection.

In short the alliance of interests that had enabled Alivardi Khan to overcome the Maratha raids broke down on account of a circular process: exactions by the English, accumulating arrears in the pay of Mughal troopers, the military paralysis of the government, rebellions in the country, further use of English troops, and more exactions by the Company. The squabbles and rivalries within the Mughal ruling class of Bengal intensified as the pressure mounted on their dwindling incomes. At the same time, their political sentiments turned against the weak and dependent Nawab who had signed away their rights and privileges in the government. Those very noblemen who had helped Mir Jafar bring down Sirajuddaulah recalled the latter's forceful rule with regret. The change of mood led to a contretemps of court. As it happened, the troops of one Mughal commander, Mirza Shamsuddin, were involved in a brush with colonel Clive's men. The Nawab pulled him up in full durbar: 'Sir, your people have had a fray with the Colonel's people. Is your honour to know, who is that Colonel Clive, and in what station Heaven has seated him?' Standing upright, the Mirza replied, 'My Lord Nawab, Me, to quarrel with the Colonel! Me! Who never get up every morning without making three profound bows to his very jack-ass? How then would I be daring enough after that, to fall out with the rider himself?'[64]

Driven by their miseries, a number of officers formed a compact to rid themselves of 'Clive's jack-ass'. The conspiracy was discovered: they were assassinated by Miran before his crimes (as contemporaries saw it) brought down the wrath of heaven on his own head. Some noblemen who escaped joined the Mughal prince Shahzada Ali Gauhar on his expedition to restore Mughal power to Bengal. A conjunction of forces threatened Mir Jafar and the English. The Shahzada, who shortly afterwards became Emperor Shah Alam, was supplied with troops by the Governor of Allahabad. The *wazir* of the Mughal empire, who held the office of Governor of Awadh, also made threatening noises that he might come to the aid of the prince in his project to recover the Mughal dominions in the east. Simultaneously, the Pathan zamindars of Birbhum, the *Faujdar* of Purnea, several Bihar zamindars, and the Maratha chiefs of Orissa took up arms against Mir Jafar, with a view to effecting a junction with the Shahzada. This was the first real challenge by the Mughal ruling class and the subordinate country powers of the rising English power in Bengal. The challenge emanated not just from an isolated segment of the *mansabdars* of Bengal, but in a sense from the body of the Mughal nobility, the only all-India class in the troubled politics of the eighteenth century. Associated with this class were the country powers, occupants of appropriate levels of the power structure of the Mughal empire. The Mughal structure, in which the country chiefs were recognized in their respective areas while over them the nobility exercised sovereign power in the land as a whole, was at length responding to the crisis.

The Mughal crisis in upper India had become deeper with the death of Emperor Muhammad Shah. He had somehow piloted the realm through the sack of the capital by Nadir Shah, losing no territory other than Kabul to the invader from Iran. However, soon after his death (1748), Ahmad Shah Abdali seized the vital frontier provinces of Lahore and Multan (1752). The rival families of the Nizam of Hyderabad and the Wazir of Awadh then engaged in a violent contest for the possession of Delhi and the person of the emperor. Ghaziuddin, a grandson of the Nizam, won out in this struggle. He blinded one emperor and murdered another. The crown prince, Shahzada Ali Gauhar, fled from the capital to save his life. A band of impoverished Mughal officers and noblemen joined the prince in his wanderings. The powerful Mughal satraps of Allahabad and Awadh turned up with unexpected promises of support for the Shahzada's ventures in the east. Muhammad Quli Khan, the Mughal Governor of Allahabad, egged on by his scheming kinsman, Shujauddaulah of Awadh, sent an expedition to the *suba* of Bengal and Bihar with the Shahzada's wandering regiment at the head of his troops. A number of disillusioned Mughal officers from Murshidabad and several embattled zamindars of Bihar joined the imperial expedition. The rebellious *Faujdar* of Purnea, with another band of Mughal officer up in arms against Clive's nominee for Murshidabad, moved out to effect a junction with the Shahzada's forces. The Maratha chiefs moved up from Orissa at the same time with professions of allegiance to the Mughal crown prince. Virtually every officer and nobleman of Murshidabad prayed for the success of the Shahzada's expedition to restore Mughal rule in Bengal.

The sudden appearance of so formidable a combination reflected an intangible bond of community among the Mughal ruling class. The continuing force of Mughal legitimacy was a factor to reckon with in all parts of the fragmented realm. Left to themselves, the Mughal officers in Bengal and Bihar would no doubt have submitted to the Shahzada. Ramnarayan, deputy governor of Bihar, was the first in the firing line of the army advancing from Allahabad. He chose to play a waiting game, prepared to join whoever, Mughal or English, were to prove mightier in the contest. Mir Jafar, Governor of Bengal, was inclined to submit to the crown prince. This did not suit the English at all. A strong Mughal presence in Bengal would check their rising power. They therefore forced Mir Jafar to send an expedition to resist the advance of the Shahzada and the Governor of Allahabad.

The imperial army with the Shahzada at their head besieged Patna for several months. At this stage, Shujauddaulah, who had deviously persuaded Muhammad Quli Khan to leave his headquarters, suddenly seized Allahabad. This forced the betrayed Governor of Allahabad to abandon the prince. As the overthrown governor beat a precipitate retreat, some officers from Murshidabad took up the imperial cause. They were joined by Kamgar Khan, a warlike zamindar of Bihar from Narhat Simai. The imperial army defeated Ramnarayan's forces and a small detachment of the English, but failed to seize the favourable moment to occupy Patna. As the siege dragged on, two Maratha officers from Orissa, along with the Raja of Bishnupur, joined the prince. In the meanwhile Shahzada Ali Gauhar received news from Delhi that his father had been assassinated. He crowned himself Emperor Shah Alam. Kamgar Khan, who proved himself a loyal adherent of the new Emperor, made a bold move upon Murshidabad in the company of the light Maratha horse. Energetic action on the part of the Nawab's son-in-law, Mir Qasim, foiled the move. Shah Alam was reduced to fruitless plundering in the plains of Bihar. Had Shujauddaulah of Awadh backed the imperial expedition instead of backstabbing his cousin, the English position in Bengal would have been critical. As it was, the Mughal project for the recovery of Bengal came to nought. Jean Law, the expelled French chief of Kasimbazar, was in the camp of the Emperor when this happened. Frustrated by the short-sighted conduct of the Mughal ruling class when faced with the English challenge, he told Ghulam Husain Khan:

> I have seen all the country from Bengal to Shahjahanabad and have been able to observe nothing but the ruin of the poor and the oppression of the lesser ones, by their rulers and superiors. And although I have proposed to some of these ignorant inconsiderate Princes, namely to Wazir Imad-ul-Mulk [Ghaziuddin, the murderer of Shah Alam's father] and Shujauddaulah [the governor of Awadh] to endeavour to bring order, tranquility and union in the Empire, after which Bengal might be easily recovered from the English, I have found attention nowhere.[65]

Meanwhile, Mir Jafar's government had collapsed in Murshidabad under the weight of the English exactions. Yet another coup was in the offing, assisted by the English. The Mughal commanders, even those who had been consistently loyal, besieged the Nawab in his own palace, and their troopers prevented ingress and egress until their pay, in arrears for months and years, was forthcoming from the treasury. The Nawab was in no position to meet their demands, for his coffers were empty. He turned to his ambitious son-in-law, Mir Qasim. The latter had carefully husbanded his resources as *Faujdar* of Rangpur. An altogether abler man than his drug-addicted father-in-law, he paid part of the arrears and quelled the mutiny. The commanders and troops turned to him hopefully, for they were convinced that no money would be forthcoming from the treasury while Mir Jafar's minions, Chunilal and Munilal, had the keys in their grasp. Ali Ibrahim Khan, a senior and respected officer, put together a following for Mir Qasim at the court. The *seths*, Jagat Seth Mahtab Rai and Raja Sarupchand, secretly helped the party, little suspecting what the change of regime held in store for them.[66]

The collapse of the machinery for revenue realization was a matter of grave concern to the English. They had no adequate and assured source of income from the land, only a certain sum from the zamindari of Calcutta. Much larger sums were needed to finance the war against the French in the peninsula, so they were counting on every penny due from the Nawab under the treaty of 1757. As the authorities in Madras, who had fitted out the successful expedition to Bengal, pressed for funds, Fort William was reduced to explaining its own distressed financial condition and apologizing for the delay in the dispatch of the sorely needed treasure.[67] This brought home the urgent need for a strong hand to reorganize the finances at Murshidabad. A more skilful Nawab would ensure payment of the sums promised to the English. Henry Vansittart, who had risen to be governor of the English in Calcutta, concluded that Mir Qasim would be the man for the job. As Mir Jafar was deemed to have betrayed the Company during the Dutch expedition to Bengal, his son-in-law appeared to be more suitable.

Mir Qasim had broached the matter to Vansittart when in Calcutta some time earlier in connection with official matters. He was however ready, if nothing came of his approach to the English, to move with his men and money towards Birbhum, enter into a league with Shah Alam and Kamgar Khan, and declare war against his father-in-law. While the English hesitated, Ali Ibrahim Khan urged Mir Qasim, '... send for your troops and money hither; and taking your departure from this

very spot, march towards Beerbhoom, and canton yourself there, act as
one revolted, and live by plunder and rapine. As most of the troops are
attached to you, and the Emperor and Cam-car-qhan will favorise your
views undoubtedly, it is probable that even in this manner your scheme
may succeed.'[68] Mir Qasim's party at the court had a Mughal card up
their sleeve while playing the English card. Had Mir Qasim decided to
throw in his lot with Shah Alam and the rebellious zamindars of
Birbhum and Narhat Simai, he might well have come to power through
an insurrection rather than a coup. This, however, did not come to
pass, for Vansittart forced Mir Jafar to abdicate. In conformity with a
bargain made between Mir Qasim and Vansittart, the English obtained
permanent possession of the districts of Chittagong, Midnapore, and
Burdwan. The new Nawab, moreover, got the tribute once again flowing
in to Calcutta. Beneath this visible accretion to English power, a
challenge was brewing that would bring the Mughal ruling class out
against the aliens in one last desperate bid for recovery of Bengal. It was
a battle for their very survival.

Mir Qasim and the Mughal Rally

Within a few months of coming to power Mir Qasim surprised everyone
by mobilizing sufficient finances to pay off not only the unpaid sums
due to the English East India Company but also the accumulated arrears
of the Murshidabad troops. It was a remarkable financial and administrative feat, and was recognized as such.

This initial success, by easing Calcutta's pressure upon Murshidabad,
opened the way to a wide-ranging financial, political, and military effort
to rebuild the Mughal government in Bengal from its foundations. The
social alliance of warrior, banker, and landlord, which had underwritten
the Murshidabad regime and had enabled Alivardi Khan to beat back
the Marathas, had collapsed in the turmoil following Plassey. The
Nawab's authority, which was the magnetic centre of the alliance, had
been set at nought. Mir Qasim's task was to restore authority. The
means by which he achieved this was terror, for conditions no longer
favoured the blend of conciliation and coercion with which Alivardi
Khan had rallied the Mughal officers, the *seths*, and the zaminders against
the Maratha invaders of the Mughal realm. The terror which Mir Qasim
let loose was balanced by strict justice. The fear he aroused among his
officers and the subordinate zamindars of the realm restored cohesion

and enabled the Mughal ruling class to wage its last all-out war against the English.

The officer and historian, Ghulam Husain Khan, feared and disliked the Nawab, but was impelled by respect for truth to observe that 'he had admirable qualifications that balanced his bad ones'. The treasons and duplicities which he had seen through the preceding administrations had soured his temper. He had concluded that the faithless Mughal troopers and the commanders and grandees of the realm required an iron hand to control them. He was therefore 'ever prone to confiscation of properties, confinement of persons and effusion of blood'. All the same, Ghulam Husain Khan could not help admiring his qualities:

> In unravelling the intricacies of affairs of Government, and especially the knotty mysteries of finance; in examining and determining private difference; in establishing regular payments for his troops, and for his household; in honouring and rewarding men of merit, and men of learning; in conducting his expenditure, exactly between the extremities of parsimony and prodigality; and in knowing intuitively where he must spend freely, and where with moderation—in all these qualifications—he was an incomparable man indeed, and the most extraordinary Prince of his age.[69]

Soon after coming to power, Mir Qasim resolved to move his headquarters further up the Ganges, away from the reach and influence of the English. Leaving his uncle Abu Turab as *naib nazim* in Murshidabad, he marched out of town with all his horses and treasure, bidding farewell to the *suba* of Bengal.[70] Arriving in Patna where the courtiers had gone out of hand after the defeat at Plassey, he soon removed the fickle Raja Ramnarayan and possessed himself of the treasure. He did not stay there long. The chief of the English factory in Patna, a man named Ellis, belonged to the faction of the Company opposed to his accession. The hostile presence of Ellis induced him to move back to Bihar's border with Bengal. He set up headquarters in Monghyr.

Here, amidst new fortifications which commanded the Gangetic route between Patna and Murshidabad, he built a centre of power untramelled by the English presence. To keep himself informed of the activities of his officers, he employed three head spies. Each had hundreds of spies under him, their business being to watch the Mughal noblemen, officers, landholders, and notable townsmen. The spies were themselves under scrutiny. The three head spies were executed for entering into correspondence with the disaffected zamindars. The Nawab also executed a Mughal commander, and then a Hindu revenue officer. These executions spread fear among the high and mighty. There was not a man at court, however considerable, who could sleep in peace.[71] The Mughal nobleman and jagirdar, Ghulam Husain Khan, was detained at one of these trials. He nearly fainted with fear that he would be the next to be accused.[72] 'So suspicious a government', he wrote, 'soon interrupted all social intercourse; and people, accustomed to a certain set of actions, acquaintances, and visits, now found themselves under the necessity of abandoning them at once and of living at home altogether.'[73]

With the object of accomplishing the ruin of Ramnarayan, the Nawab set Rajvallabh of Dacca upon him to discover the suspected embezzlements at Patna; and when the astute Rajvallabh accomplished the task, he himself was charged with misappropriations, his treasure in Dacca was confiscated, and the auditor was thrown into prison along with the man he had ruined. Mir Qasim was well aware that a party had been formed among Englishmen against him in Calcutta. He decided not to leave behind any magnate who might be influential enough in Murshidabad or Patna to enter into a conspiracy with his enemies. The Jagat Seth cousins were brought under guard to Monghyr and were confined in the fort. The *Riyaz-us-Salateen* gives a list of officers and landholders who were suspected of conspiracy and were placed under detention. The list of those detained in Monghyr included Umid Rai, the *Rai Raiyan* or chief officer of the *Diwani*, his son Kaliprasad, Ramnarayan, the former *Naib Nazim* of Bihar, his successor Rajvallabh, Jagat Seth Mahtab Rai, his cousin Raja Sarupchand, the zamindars of Dinajpur, Nadia, Kharakpur, Birbhum, and Rajshahi, Dulal Rai, Diwan of Bhojpur, Fateh Singh, the Raja of Tikari, Ramkishore, Muhammad Masum, Munshi Jagat Rai, and others.[74] Through these measures, the Nawab sought to neutralize the elements among the officers and landholders whom he judged to be capable of conspiring with his enemies. His terror tactics were designed to crush the centres of disaffection among the subordinate zamindars and to coerce the officers, commanders, and noblemen of the Mughal ruling class into a united effort to reassert Mughal rule in Bengal and Bihar.

Rallied by the coercion and terror of the new *Nazim*, the Mughal officers fought with unity and determination in the ensuing war with the English. Mir Qasim thus restored some degree of consensus among the nobility through his cold, calculated, and cruel methods. However, such methods could hardly be expected to suppress altogether the jealousies, rivalries, and covert feuds among his officers. Ali Ibrahim Khan, the man who had arranged the conspiracy in Murshidabad that brought Mir Qasim to power, was an able minister and completely loyal to him. So was Muhammad Taqi Khan, an outstanding general whom he appointed *Faujdar* of Birbhum to keep an eye on the turbulent Pathan zamindar of the district. These and other Mughal officers were confounded by the rise of an Armenian in the Nawab's favour. This man, Gurghin Khan, was an able general who reorganized the artillery and other branches of the antiquated Mughal army. Ghulam Husain Khan, a typical representative of the class of Mughal noblemen and warriors, had not a word to say in favour of this innovative Armenian. Without producing any hard evidence, he accused Gurghin Khan of conspiracy and treachery, and held him responsible, in some undefined manner, for Mir Qasim's downfall.

At Mir Qasim's accession to the seat of power, the army in Bengal stood on paper at upwards of ninety thousand men.[75] The real number, after deducting the false musters expected of a Mughal army, would have been less than half of this. Even among them, the majority had put up no fight at Plassey. After the defeat of 1757, the Mughal army of Bengal was little more than a rabble. In good old Mughal fashion, this was an army of horsemen, but without the commanders who had served under Alivardi Khan. The troops, recruited in great numbers by Mir Jafar and his son Miran, were led by incompetent generals, and were totally unreliable.[76] Their cowardice and incompetence was brought home to Mir Qasim in his very first campaign. English intervention alone saved the day against the refractory Raja of Birbhum. Mir Qasim concluded that a new basis would have to be found for restoring Mughal military power. He paid off the arrears of the disaffected troops and then dismissed most of them, retaining only those whom he liked best. In addition, he raised a number of troops, but upon a different establishment.[77]

When Vansittart visited Monghyr to stave off a breach between the new Nawab and the English, he saw on parade sixteen thousand horse, out of which the newly raised cavalry numbered about two thousand. He also saw three battalions of sepoys on foot organized by Gurghin Khan upon the English model.[78] Haji Mustafa, the French born commentator on Ghulam Husain Khan's history, confirms these figures, and adds that besides sixteen thousand horse, Mir Qasim had at his disposal twenty-five thousand infantry,[79] which presumably included the European model sepoy battalions Vansittart saw on parade. This was not 'an army as numerous as the multitude at the Day of Judgement' spoken of by Ghulam Husain Khan, but the sight might have appeared to him as such since every trooper and every footman mentioned in the army roll actually happened to be there—an event unheard of in Mughal history since the days of Emperor Akbar. Mir Qasim was too exacting and terrifying a master for any commander to dare attempt a false muster, or to withhold any soldier's due.[80]

In enforcing this strict muster, Mir Qasim hardly went beyond what a good Mughal statesman would have done. Where he innovated was in the branch of firearms. He sought to link the numerous body of Mughal horse to the use of firepower. Guns, he was quick to gather, had shifted the balance of power drastically from the Mughal ruling class to the *firangis* from overseas. This realization lay behind his project to build up a firearms industry in Monghyr. There the reconstituted government started collecting and manufacturing as many guns and flint muskets as possible in order to equip the new model infantry and artillery. The firearms manufactured in Monghyr were said to be better than the best Tower-proofs sent to India for the Company's troops. Such, at any rate, was the opinion of English officers at the time, based on a comparison made to the order of the Council of Calcutta. The flints of the guns were Rajmahal agates and their metal was more mellow.[81]

The man whom Mir Qasim placed in charge of this newly developing branch of the armed forces was the Armenian organizer Gurghin Khan. He started training the Nawab's infantry and artillery in the English manner, but there was no time to complete the job. Half trained as they were, a detachment of them prevailed against the troops of Major Carstairs, as numerous as those of Clive at Plassey. The Frenchman, Haji Mustafa, was convinced that had the new troops been trained for two more years, they would have brought about the defeat of the English. Gurghin Khan enforced discipline on the Mughal troops—Persians, Tartars, Afghans, and Hindustanis—with a strictness unheard of. This, however, earned him the hatred of the soldiery, a feeling accentuated by the natural Mughal animosity against the Armenian upstart.[82]

Mir Qasim's army was all the same a recognizably Mughal army. Mughal horse was still its backbone. The Nawab, with his deep pride in the Mughal tradition, was not one to ignore this branch of the forces. Mughal cavaliers constituted the principal branch of the army in the confrontation with the English. He, however, saw to it that a part of the cavalry was disciplined in the English manner. The newly trained cavalry numbered five thousand, according to the figure given by Ghulam Husain Khan (a higher estimate than that of Vansittart). These troopers were placed under the graded command of *havildars*, *jamadars*, *subadars*, and *comidans*. There was one guard for every ten troopers, a hefty man with a drawn sabre, whose business was not to fight himself but to kill on the spot anyone who turned his back on the battle.

Building the new army required money. Mir Qasim sought right from the start to find a viable financial basis for the government. Finance was central to the Mughal state which he was seeking to reconstitute. He collected large sums at the beginning of his *nizamat* by setting auditors on all officers who were suspected of ill-gotten gains. Embezzlements were traced right back to the *nizamat* of Alivardi Khan. This was unprecedented. The Nawab also cut back on non-essential expenditure. These preliminary measures brought in enough sums to pay off the arrears of the troops and the sums due to the English. He then set about building a new financial and revenue system which was by far the most exacting and rigorous that Bengal had ever experienced before colonial rule. Alivardi Khan had allowed a lot of slackness in the financial system: this had enabled him to raise special contributions from noblemen, landholders, and bankers. Mir Qasim could not afford such latitude; instead he sought to build the exactions into the system itself in a desperate race against time. The severe pressure undermined the position of the zamindars and strained the fabric of rural society. The succeeding *diwani* administration of the English East India Company accentuated these adverse trends, bringing about the devasting famine of 1770.

As Ghulam Husain Khan put it laconically, Mir Qasim was an enemy of the zamindars. He ordered a *hast-o-bud*, a detailed investigation into the past collections from the big zamindars of Bengal. After the cession of the zamindari of Burdwan to the English, the ones that remained under the jurisdiction of the Nawab were Rajshahi, Dinajpur, Nadia, and Birbhum, all of which were severely squeezed. In the settlement made in 1763, the Nawab fixed an additional sum of Rs 1.24 crore, and this on a shrunken territory, after 24 Parganas, Burdwan, Midnapore, and Chittagong had been ceded to the Company's revenue jurisdiction. On the remaining territory, the Nawab sought to collect Rs 2.66 crores as compared to the previous amount of Rs 1.42 crores collected from the larger area in the days of Murshid Quli Khan. The incidence of the land tax thus virtually doubled under this draconian settlement.

The Nawab did not spare his own officers, *faujdars*, and *jagirdars* while fleecing the subordinate class of zamindars. The Mughal realm was built out of two distinct elements: the ruling class of officers, commanders, and noblemen, and the class of subordinate landholders. It was part of Mughal policy to bind the latter class in order to ensure proper subordination of the rural population. This, because it was the zamindar who would lead the odd rural uprising, despite his designated role as the prop of rural Mughal administration. To keep the zamindars in control, which was the declared aim of Mir Qasim's financial and political policy, the new Governor of Bengal had to unite his officers to assert their rule. Typically, Mir Qasim sought to achieve the latter objective by coercion and by arousing fear of his masterful scrutiny. While the *kifayat hast-o-bud*, or profits from the reassessment of the zamindaris of Birbhum and Dinajpur, yielded an additional revenue of Rs 14 lakhs, the *kifayat faujdari*, or profits from the reassessment of frontier jurisdictions of the *faujdars*, amounted to Rs 32 lakhs. The Raja of Dinajpur was set aside by a revenue farmer who undertook to pay double the existing amount. Abid Ali Khan, the *Faujdar* of Rangpur, took a farm of the district on the basis of a similar enhancement. The entire landholding class, along with the officers, supported by assignments of the land revenue came under the severest pressure in living memory.[83]

Mir Qasim's land policy had an additional feature. This was his fixed resolve to disarm all zamindars whose forces spelt danger to the *nizamat*. Taking advantage of the turmoil following the battle of Plassey, zamindars and rajas all over Bihar and Bengal had fortified themselves and assembled their troops. Mir Qasim put in motion three expeditions to chastize the landholders. The first was directed against the overmighty Pathan Raja of Birbhum, whose capital Rajnagar was in striking distance of Murshidabad. Related to the warlike Kamgar Khan of Narhat Sinai, this magnate had gone over to Emperor Shah Alam, who was at this juncture the common opponent of both the Company and the Nawab. A joint expedition by the forces of the *Nizamat* and the Company compelled Asad Zaman Khan of Birbhum to offer his submission. Mir Qasim then turned his attention to the refractory zamindars of Bihar.

Taking advantage of the presence of Shah Alam, the zamindars of Shahabad, who were collectively referred to as the Bhojpuriah, had set the authority of the *niabat* of Patna at nought. Mir Qasim came to an amicable understanding with the Emperor and persuaded him to leave Bihar. He then issued a summons to the principal zamindars of Bihar to attend the durbar at Patna. Some zamindars obeyed the summons, but Kamgar Khan did not comply and was driven from his estate. Several Bhojpuriah landholders were also driven by the Nawab's forces to the neighbouring country of Banaras. This expedition was followed up by a third campaign which restored the durbar's authority in the territory of the Raja of Betia.[84]

Mir Qasim dispossessed several rebellious zamindars and put district collectors (*amils*) and revenue farmers in charge. His coercive policy effectively brought to submission a class he regarded as dangerous to the state. This ensured their material cooperation with the *Nizamat* in the coming war against the English. Even Kamgar Khan joined the Nawab with his forces when the latter emerged as the focal point of the opposition to the alien English power. As Vansittart saw, not a single zamindar in the country ever lifted his hand against the Nawab since the beginning of his dispute with the Company.[85]

The Collision with English Private Interests

Though the Nawab prepared well for the contingency of a war against the English, it was not his intention to wage it unless it was forced upon him. It was one party among the English, opposed to both Vansittart and the Nawab, who precipitated and, indeed initiated the hostilities. They did so in pursuit of their private commercial interests. Mir Qasim tried to the very last moment to avoid an outright war. That he was not contemplating an attack on the English position is demonstrated by one revealing fact: just prior to the commencement of the Mughal–English war of 1763, he sent his new model army to Nepal, an expedition from which it returned badly mauled. He needed breathing space to recover from this disastrous retreat. However, the embattled English private trading interests gave him no respite. He bore with supreme patience the provocations by the hostile party of Amyatt and Ellis right up to the surprise attack of Ellis on the citadel of Patna. That he was anxious to avoid war can be judged, as Vansittart pointed out, both from his letters and his actions: '... his letters, though filled with the most bitter remonstrances of the violence committed against him, shewed always a fear of coming to extremities, and a desire to treat ... while ours, which he was answering, contained the most absolute commands, enforced with a denunciation of war, if he refused to submit to them.'[86]

Fortunately for historians, Vansittart published this entire correspondence to defend himself against his English opponents,[87] and in addition provided his own commentary on the conflict.[88] In the Nawab's letters, we have a rare corpus of evidence regarding Indian reactions to the English colonial penetration. Mir Qasim's letters, along with the letters of some of his officers, reveal, as nothing else could, the Mughal attitudes in the confrontation leading to Buxar. English historians virtually ignored this body of evidence and even Mir Qasim's Indian biographer paid no attention to the Nawab's point of view in the developing conflict.[89] An important dimension is thus missing from the existing accounts of the war that displaced Mughal power and established English colonial government in the lower Gangetic valley.

Mir Qasim ascended the *masnad* with the expectation that the territorial division of Bengal's revenues, and the assignment of Burdwan, Midnapore, and Chittagong, in satisfaction of the Company's financial claims, would produce a lasting accord with the English. Not once did he interfere in the affairs of these three districts. In return he expected that the Company would not interfere in the *Nizamat's* affairs in the rest of Bengal and in Bihar. The aggressive conduct and hectoring demands of Carnac, Coote, and Ellis, who succeeded one another in Patna, quickly dispelled the illusion. In truth, the Nawab's desire to be master in his own house was quite incompatible with burgeoning English private trading interests, especially those less favoured Englishmen who were jealous of Vansittart's protected private trade.

Before Plassey, English private fortunes were made or lost principally at sea. After Plassey, however, the inland trade of Bengal emerged as the most attractive field for making a quick fortune. The Company servants and army officers transformed the character of this trade by an illegitimate and unfettered extension of the Company's freedom from customs duties to their own private trade in Bengal and Bihar. In illegally enlarging this privilege, they contravened the orders of their masters in London.[90] Alarmed by the growth of private interests at the cost of the Company's concerns, the Court of Directors positively directed Fort William on 30 December 1762, if the latter valued their service, to immediately acquaint the Nawab in the Company's name that the Directors disapproved of every measure that had been taken to the prejudice of the authority and government, 'particularly with respect in the wronging in his revenues by a shameful abuse of dusticks'. However, Fort William's involvement was far too deep for them to carry out this instruction. For that matter, many a director, in his individual capacity as partner of one or other group of Company servants involved in private trade in Bengal, had a finger in the pie too.

The distinction between the Company's interests and the private interests of its servants on the spot is theoretically important in order to locate the dynamics of the growth of English imperialism in Bengal. It was the private aggrandizement of the Company servants that constituted the cutting edge of the colonial expansion up the Gangetic valley. The East Indian fortunes which the 'Nabobs' shipped down the Ganges were integral to English imperialism; their scope so great as to fudge, in practice, the distinction between the Company's interests and the private interests of the Company servants. That is why, despite repeated remonstrances from London, the latter were not brought under effective control until Cornwallis undertook the task.

While it cannot be said that English colonial expansion had any corporate or national impulse at this stage, all the same the private interests of the Company servants, by breaking apart the Mughal order in Bengal, steadily expanded the Company's corporate, and England's national, domain. In that long term perspective, the contradiction between the Company's interests and the private interests of its servants is misleading. The commercial and political realities of the age were more complex. Private interests, ranging from the lowest Company servants in Bengal to the highest director in London, set aside the restraining hand of the Company, so that colonial aggression, propelled by the private trading interests, was virtually unimpeded by the theoretically contradictory interest of the East India Company.

Factions within the Company, formed on the basis of contentious private trading interests, precipitated the English confrontation with the Mughals. Amyatt, who had expected to be governor at Fort William, was much put out by Vansittart's elevation. He formed a party in Council to oppose the man whom Vansittart in turn had promoted to the *masnad* at Murshidabad. Not that Amyatt was insensible to the superior ability of his rival's protegé. However, Ghulam Husain Khan explains, 'nothing of Aaly's will ever please Moaviah'. Amyatt and his party were, therefore, against the new Nawab. There was more to it than the personal rivalry between Vansittart and Amyatt. As governor of Fort William and a man suspected to be thriving on the secret favour of the Nawab, Vansittart was thought to be doing far too well for himself. He soon engrossed a share of the salt trade which equalled that of all the other Company servants put together. Jealous opponents spoke of his 'trying to encircle the general trade of Bengal'.[91] They rallied in the Council under Amyatt's leadership. The partnership of Johnstone, Hay, and Bolts was a concern almost equal in size to Vansittart's, and a bitter rival in the field of salt. These men, along with Ellis at Patna (he, too, had a large private trade), joined Amyatt in the opposition to Vansittart. They hit out at the Nawab, because they thought his favour to be the key to Vansittart's prosperity.[92] The occurrence of vacancies in the Council reduced the number of Vansittart's supporters. As vacancies filled, the party determined to overthrow the Nawab became the majority.

There was yet another private reason for the animus of the majority against the Nawab; they suspected Vansittart of having obtained presents secretly as the price of Mir Qasim's elevation, and considered themselves cheated of their due share. Vansittart denied this, but like every single man among his opponents, and indeed every Englishman in Bengal, he was a liar. Greed was the common characteristic of the rivals: they had all come to shake the pagoda tree. However, while Vansittart and his supporter Warren Hastings lied fluently, the majority opposing them lied and bullied simultaneously. At the time of his coming to power, Mir Qasim secretly promised, in writing, to pay Vansittart Rs 20 lakhs. Vansittart, an honourable man by the standards then prevailing among Englishmen in Bengal, resolved not to take the money until the Company's claims and the troops' arrears were paid off by the Nawab. News of this deal, not a part of the formal agreement between Mir Qasim and the Company, leaked out. Once the Mughal government paid off all the dues, the majority passed a resolution in Council asking Mir Qasim to hand over the promised twenty lakhs to the Company. Their move was intended to embarrass Vansittart. The latter claimed he had refused the offer altogether.

Mir Qasim was well acquainted with the affairs of the Council. He was scornful of the majority. Their demand, which was clearly not provided for in the treaty, was rejected by him with the contempt it deserved: 'That you, gentlemen, should unreasonably demand twenty lakhs of me, surprised me greatly. This is a behaviour unbecoming men of dignity, in whom it is doubtless improper, after having refused a thing, to repent of it, and demand it in the name of their masters. ... I owe nobody a single rupee, nor will I pay your demand.'[93]

This dignified rebuke earned him the hostility of several powerful men. He saw that it would be prudent to buy the support of Vansittart's party in Council. When the latter was in Monghyr to negotiate a deal over the private trade of the Company servants, he paid the Englishman a tidy sum of 7 lakhs. Further payments to others who had promoted him brought the amount up to the full 20 lakhs previously agreed upon.[94] His father-in-law, Mir Jafar, had bought the whole council in 1757. His mistake was that he bought less than half and antagonized the rest.

Major Carnac and Colonel Coote had been posted at Patna to counter the danger of Shah Alam's presence in Bihar. Encouraged by the opposition in Council, they intrigued with various officers and landholders to undermine the Nawab's authority. One early act on their part was to encourage Raja Ramnarayan, at the time deputy governor (*naib nazim*) of Bihar, to defy Mir Qasim. They acted as if they and not the Nawab were master. Carnac's insolence obliged the nawab to ask whether the major looked upon him as the *subadar* of the provinces. The latter told the Nawab bluntly that Mr Vansittart was two hundred leagues from hence. He would do what he thought advisable. Colonel Coote too presumed that he could dictate terms, and was no less insolent. He told the Nawab that the latter must comply with everything he recommended. While parleying with him the Nawab gathered:

> I must appoint Nundcoomar to the fougedarry of Hooghly, give the government of Purnea to the son of Allee Cooley Cawn, restore Muzuffer Allee (who plundered Nasir-ool-moolk's jewels to the amount of eight lacks of rupees) to the Zemindaree of Carrackpore, restore Camgar Khan to the Zamindaree of Mey, and regulate the Zamindarrees of Radshay and Dinagepoor, according to his pleasure.[95]

One night the drunken colonel was informed by the intriguing deputy governor that the Nawab intended to attack him in his camp. In the early hours of the morning the Colonel invaded the *subadar's* quarters with a cocked pistol in each hand and came swearing into the latter's tent. 'It so happened', Mir Qasim subsequently wrote to Vansittart, 'that I was asleep in the Zenana, and none of my guards were present. How shall I express the unbecoming manner in which the Colonel went about from tent to tent, with thirtyfive horsemen and two hundred sepoys, calling out, "Where is the Nobob?"'

There was method in this madness: the colonel prevented Shah Alam, as long as possible, from conferring the *nizamat* on Mir Qasim. It appeared as if Carnac, Coote, and Ellis were plotting behind Governor Vansittart's back for the overthrow of Mir Qasim and the cancellation of the arrangement between the nawab and the governor. They were not above intriguing with the external powers in Hindustan in order to carry out their secret design. As letters, which came into Vansittart's hands, showed later, Carnac and Coote conducted a concealed correspondence with the imperial court and the Nawab Wazir of Awadh. The purpose behind this was to set them against Mir Qasim and to impede his confirmation as the *subadar* or *nazim* of the *subas* of Bengal and Bihar. Mir Qasim foiled these moves by reaching an agreement with Shah Alam, a step which eventually culminated in the alliance between Emperor Shah Alam, his *wazir*, Shujauddaulah, who was *subadar* of Awadh, and Mir Qasim, the lawfully appointed *subadar* of Bengal and Bihar. In the meanwhile, Mir Qasim had to reckon with the malignance of Ellis, the English chief of Patna who was destined to start the hostilities in the war of 1763–4.

Ellis, who had large private trading interests in Bihar, made it his business to seize any officer of the Nawab who dared put the slightest obstruction to the *gumashtahs* managing the illicit private trade of Englishmen in the country. Setting the *subadar's* authority at naught, he ordered the seizure of a Mughal official of Arrah bold enough to stop some opium belonging to his friend Hay. He put into iron shackles the *amil* of Monghyr who had committed a minor and unintended violation of the Company's saltpetre farm. He then laid siege to a fort in the vicinity of Monghyr on the false pretext that some English deserters were hiding in it. Mir Qasim proved more than a match for these insolent opponents. Outmanoeuvring Carnac, Coote, and Ellis at every step, he managed to establish his authority in Bihar within a year.

At this stage, the illegal use of free passes (*dastaks*) by the Company servants and their Indian *gumashtahs* set the Mughal *Nizamat* of Bengal and the English East India Company on collision course. An additional issue in the conflict was the frustration of the English regarding the rates of exchange and their resolve to gain control over the money market at the expense of the *subadar* and the *sarrafs*.

The Calcutta mint had started issuing *sikka* rupees in the name of the Mughal government since 1757. The *sarrafs*, who were able to detect the Calcutta issue on account of the inferior manufacture, charged a discount (*batta*) upon it. The Company therefore wanted the *subadar* to strike in his mints only one species of rupees, to be current throughout the two *subas* without any discount. As this was known to be beyond the Nawab's ability to effect in view of the growing scarcity of coin caused by the drain of silver to England, the Company wanted at least to impress upon him the impediment which its business suffered from the contrariness of the *sarrafs* regarding the exchange and circulation of the Calcutta *sikkas*.

Amyatt and Hay, when they went on their final fateful journey to visit Mir Qasim with the 'copy of the Demands' by the Company, had instructions to 'get him to issue peremptory orders to the shroffs and others, for effectuating the currency of the rupees coined in our mint, that our business may no longer suffer such interruptions and losses from this source'. The English also demanded permission to coin three lakhs of rupees annually at the mints of Patna and Dacca for the trade of their factories. It was calculated that the additional coins, together with the elimination of the discount, would substantially increase the money invested in the trade of the English, both corporate and private. This would remove the constraints on the supply of capital because of which they were still dependent on the *sarrafs*, despite the political influence they had won. The Nawab, for his part, refused to let the English coin any money at the Murshidabad, Dacca, or Patna mints as it would occasion a loss to the Mughal government. He would permit them to mint their coin in Calcutta alone.[96] The dispute regarding the coinage of the realm arose from a deeper problem which the two contending parties had not yet grasped: the shortage of bullion supply and the circulation of debased coinage caused by the drain of specie following Plassey.

However, the fundamental issue that put Amyatt's party on the warpath and brought Mir Qasim's defensive Mughal patriotism into play was the English misuse of free passes. We have seen how the same issue had galvanized the former Mughal Governor Sirajuddaulah into an imperious attempt to bring the rebels against the realm to book, and how his defeat in this project had torn apart the Mughal realm in Bengal. As the new Mughal governor was on the defensive, the patriotic element in the Mughal outlook was now somewhat better defined, both in the consciousness of Mir Qasim and in the outlook of the class he led into battle. The *Nazim*, who had all the pride of his class in the Mughal

tradition, had schooled himself long and hard to master the administrative and constitutional precedents in the *suba*, not least the exact
limits of the rights and privileges which the English claimed under
Mughal charter. He consciously defined his role as the champion of the
Mughal administration in Bengal. What is more, unlike Sirajuddaulah,
he was able to rally the Mughal *umara* behind the cause. Thus, the
Mughal cause was charged with a new patriotic fervour.

Mir Qasim's mental identification with the Mughal administrative
tradition in Bengal, his pride in having mastered its precedents and
charters, and his championship of the Mughal officers as a class (rather
than his own personal power) all come out strongly in his ironical
response to the English claim that they had Mughal charters for the
license they were claiming and exercising: 'I am not ignorant of the
nature of your Firmaunds and Husbulhookums. I have been twenty or
thirty years in Bengal, and am perfectly acquainted with every article
in them.' Referring then to the assaults of the English chiefs upon the
Mughal officers in the *suba*, he went on to say: 'The justice of the Chief
of your factories is this; they abuse and beat my Officers, and carry
them away bound.' What comes out here is the collective sense of shock
experienced by the Mughal ruling class: the bitter realization that they
were now objects of physical coercion.[97]

The Mughal officers and noblemen were startled by the unexpected
consequences of the battle of Plassey. Mir Qasim, along with other
noblemen who had rallied behind Mir Jafar, had intended it as a coup:
not a revolution that would threaten the Mughal system and their
commanding position in it. As the realization dawned that their fate
was tied to a collapsing system which they must defend if they were to
survive, it became urgent to identify the element threatening the system.
They appraised it as the untrammelled private trade of the English.
There was more than class feeling behind this appraisal. It goes without
saying that they had the superior position in the order under attack,
but their concern went beyond their own situation. The Mughal officers'
crusade against private English trade embraced the interests of the people
at large. The *nazim's* pronouncements, in particular, showed a concern
for the poor. The vanishing supremacy of the Mughal ruling class
brought into play an old world patriotism within a collapsing social
order. Far removed from modern nationalism, it nonetheless expressed
an organic concern for the community as a whole. The earliest
remonstrance of Mir Qasim on the issue of free passes for private trade

showed a threefold concern: the challenge to the authority of the *nazim*, the disempowerment of the Mughal officers, and the novel attempt of the English to engross the necessities of life on which the people subsisted:

> ... from my accession to the government, I have perceived, that many English gentlemen were ill affected to me, and that the country was not in my hands. The cause of the dissatisfaction of these gentlemen. I know not; you may. The cause of the country's not being in my own hands is this; that from the factory of Calcutta to Cossimbazar, Patna and Dacca, all the English chiefs, with their gomastahs, officers and agents, in every district of the government, act as collectors, renters, zamindars and talookdars, and setting up the Company's colours, allow no power to my officers. And besides this, the gomastahs and every other servants in every district, in every gunge, perganah and village, carry on a trade in oil, fish, straw, bamboos, rice, paddy, betel-nut and other things; and every man with a Company's dustuck in his hand regards himself as not less than the Company.[98]

Mir Qasim's first remonstrance was concerned primarily with the threat to his authority and the challenge to the Mughal ruling class. However, as the conflict mounted, the Nawab's ideological counter-offensive shifted to the cause of the people of the country. The English gentlemen and their *gumashtahs*, he told Vansittart, had set up a trade in salt, tobacco, dried fish, timbers, and other necessaries, which they purchased 'from the country people with force and extortion, ... so that the poor, the inhabitants, merchants, and manufacturers of my country are oppressed'.[99] The expressions 'my country' and 'the poor' constituted a new language indicating the sense of disempowerment suffered by the ruling class and the newly felt need to invoke a popular basis for Mughal rule. In his final remonstrance to the Company in London, his championship of the people achieved clear definition:

> On any taxable goods imported I have never troubled them [Company servants] for one rupee; and such of the most valuable commodities of the country, as they have brought and carried to other ports, have passed in like manner, without any demand from me for duties upon them. Yet not content with this extensive trade in all articles free from duties, they carry on a trade in many things not customary, such as dried fish, straw, bamboos, betel-nut, salt, tobacco, timbers and such other trifling articles which used to afford the means of subsistence to the poor and indigent in the country, nor are they fit for exportation, nor can produce any profit to the Company; and for their own trade and advantage they raise disputes.[100]

The Nawab's concern for the poor invested his determination to resist the aggression of the English with a significance beyond class sentiment or self esteem. His sense of the crumbling Mughal order and his outrage at the exploitation of his subjects found private expression in a letter he wrote to Vansittart in May 1762. This was his most detailed pronouncement on the subject. It revealed the Mughal *Nazim's* own perception of the crisis of his times. The unusual letter shows the mind of an eighteenth century Mughal nobleman preparing to defend 'his country'. It thus deserves to be quoted at some length:

> And this is the way you gentlemen behave; they make a disturbance all over my country, plunder the people, injure and disgrace my servants, with a resolution to expose my government to contempt; and from the borders of Hindustan to Calcutta, make it their business to expose me to scorn. In every perganah and every village, they have established ten or twenty new factories, and setting up the colours, and shewing the dustucks of the Company, they use their utmost endeavours to oppress the reiats, merchants and other people of the country. The dusticks for searching the boats, which you formerly favoured me with, and which I sent to every chokey, the Englishmen by no means regard, but bring shame and disgrace upon my people, holding themselves in readiness to beat and abuse them. Having established these new factories, they carry on such business as the Company never heard of; and every Bengal gomastah makes a disturbance at every factory, and thinks himself not inferior to the Company. In every perganah, every village, and every factory, they buy and sell salt, betel-nut, ghee, rice, straw, bamboos, fish, gunnies, ginger, sugar, tobacco, opium and many other things, more than I can write and which I think it needless to mention. They forcibly take away the goods and commodities of the reiats, merchants, &c. for fourth part of their value; and by ways of violence and oppressions, they oblige the reiats &c. to give five rupees for goods which are but worth one rupee; and for the sake of five rupees, they find and disgrace an Assamese, who pays me one hundred rupees malguzarree; and they allow not any authority to my servants. Near four or five hundred new factories have been established in my dominions; and it is impossible to express what disturbances are made at every factory, and how the inhabitants are oppressed. The officers of every district have desisted from the exercise of their functions; so that by means of these oppressions, and my being deprived of my duties, I suffer a yearly loss of near twenty five lakhs of rupees. In that case, how can I keep clear of debts? How can I provide for the payment of my army and my household? ... And every one of these gomastahs has such a power, that he imprisons the collector and deprives him of all authority whenever he pleases.[101]

The recurrent expressions 'my country', 'my people' used by Mir Qasim, had more of a patriotic and less of an imperial flavour than the earlier pronouncements of Sirajuddaulah. The changing mode of expression exhibited how the ground was shifting from under the Mughal ruling class, besieged by the intrusive English gentlemen and their Bengal *gumashtahs*. Apparently more powerful than the Mughal *nazim's* 'officers' and servants', the gentlemen and their *gumashtahs* obliged the Mughal ruling class to call upon 'the people of the country'. The late Mughal political ideology was based on a sense of legitimate dominion over the country which acquired, under a sense of siege, an added patriotic component. The *Subadar's* use of the term 'my country' reflected a sense of identity as well as the pride of possession. Referring to the fact that the Company now peremptorily held saltpetre land at Rs 1¾ maund, whereas formerly it paid him Rs 3 or 3½ per mound, Mir Qasim wrote, 'So my country is to go to ruin and I am not to say a word.'[102] The Nawab's voice here is more consciously patriotic than Sirajuddaulah's earlier declaration that he would expel the English from his country, but it is not to be confused with a sense of subordination of the self to the country. The tone of lordship is evident in his use of the term 'my people':

> To be sure whatever your Gomastahs write is all just and proper, and my people tell nothing but lies and bare-faced falsities. I must have all losses in your trade made good to you; but who will indemnify me for the loss of revenues justly due to my Government? I must cut off my officers' heads, but your Gomastahs, who are guilty of oppression, you highly extol.[103]

As the Nawab set 'my Government', 'my officers', 'my people', and 'my country' against 'you gentlemen', 'your gomastahs', and 'your people',[104] Mughal imperialism was transformed into a conscious resistance to the aggression of alien 'usurpers'. The simmering resentment among the Mughal officers against the English and their *gumashtahs* burst forth as soon as the *Nazim* confronted the Company. The zamindars, too, the subordinate chiefs under the Mughal ruling class, were associated with this resistance, for they were equally hurt by the private trade of the English. The *mansabdars* and zamindars saw this trade spread across the country. The authority of the Mughal officers and the country chiefs was threatened by the tightening hold of the English and their *gumashtahs* over the ordinary producers and traders around the factories springing up all over the countryside. The severe oppression of the peasants, artisans, and small traders was undermining every constituted authority from the *Nazim* and his officers down to the local zamindars. It was, in Mir Qasim's vision, a crisis that enveloped the Mughal government, the Mughal officers, and the Mughal subjects, including the zamindars. That the local zamindars shared his alarm is clear from a letter which he received from Saiyid Rajab Ali, zamindar of Barabazu *pargana*, in mid-1762.

> From the beginning the Company's factory has been in Beelcoochy, and a cloth business has been carried on there; and I do not neglect doing, to the utmost of my power, whatever the gomastahs of the factory desire, nor was any oppression practised. Whoever traded in copper, toothenague, or cotton, which was sent to the factory by the Company, traded freely and at the market price. Now from Calcutta, Dacca, Chellmary, and Rangamatty, numbers of Englishmen and merchants, and people of Monsieur Chevalier &c. bring into the perganah, copper, toothenague, cotton, tinkal, salt, betel-nut, tobacco, rice, muggadooties, seringa-boats, lack, stick-lack, dammer, dried fish, &c. and all these people assuming the name of the Company, force the reiats, who never dealt in such commodities, to purchase them at an exorbitant price. Besides this, they violently exact large sums for presents, and for their peons' expenses, and take, at a low rate, whatever oil &c. they buy. By means of these oppressions, the merchants, peons, reiats, &c of the perganah, have taken to flight, and the hauts, gauts, gunges, and golahs, are entirely ruined. Moreover, they prevent the reiats from carrying on their business; they rob and plunder them wherever they meet them on the road; and giving colours and certificates to the merchants of the perganah, who formerly paid duties, they will not suffer any to be taken from them. Thro' these oppressions, the revenues of the government have been absolutely ruined, and the Company's business obstructed ... I hope, that regarding my distressed condition, you will send a seepoy, with a dustick, to take my country under his protection; and will order the gomastahs of the Beelcoochy factory, to put a stop to the power of such as trade by force and oppressions; to make every one refund what profits he has exacted by violence; to put oppression and injustice to flight, and to have the Company's business carried on as formerly.[105]

The coercive trade of the Company, the gentlemen, and the *gumashtahs* was not simply an economic issue, nor just a new source of oppression of the poor; it was also a political issue and one that undermined the power and authority of the Mughal officers and the zamindars, and indeed threatened their very survival. The oppressed *raiyats* were Mughal subjects; when the Mughal officers sought to give them protection they were immediately subjected to the wholly unfamiliar experience of being physically coerced by the Company's forces. The question, in other words, was one of the legitimate monopoly of force, and who was to exercise this power. The Mughal governor of Bengal was as much concerned about the authority of his officers as about the oppression of his subjects. It was unheard of that Mughal officers, who had legitimately claimed a monopoly of the means of physical coercion over *raiyats* as well as zamindars, should themselves become the object of such coercion. The *Nazim* and his officers were amazed when they saw this happen. The two issues, economic and political, became intertwined in the Nawab's complaints to Vansittart, whom he still regarded as his ally: 'Now', he wrote on 22 February 1763, 'the gentlemen of all the factories do not regard your direction, but require the orders of the Council, and they ruin the affairs of the Province of Bengal, the zamindaries, the Merchandize, the Ryots &c. for what reason I cannot conceive.' Four days later, the *subadar* touched on the other issue, the authority of his officers, and asked pointedly whether 'your gomastahs are to carry on these branches of trade, which were never practised in the country ... and the officers of my Government are to have no concern in the affairs of the administration, nor allowed to say a word?'[106]

At the moment when the Nawab wrote this, an instance of a Mughal officer being subjected to physical violence, the first of its kind, had already occurred and the issue was no longer just the threat to the power that the officers claimed for protection of their subjects against oppression. A minor official of the Nawab sent to inspect the English factory at Dacca was seized by the chief of the factory and was held in confinement for three days. [107] This sent shock waves through the Mughal ruling class. The Nawab was provoked to write to Vansittart: ... contrary to your agreement with me, you detached forces to carry on the business of the Company and the English gentleman by compulsion and to beat and chastise my officers if they dared to speak a word.'[108] Encouraged by the majority in the Council to defy Vansittart's compact with Mir Qasim, the Company servants had resorted to a campaign of physical violence against the Mughal officers. In less than a month they went so far as to arrest the Mughal *Faujdar* of Rangamati on the Assam frontier. This high ranking officer, whose name was Saiyid Jalal Bukhari, was seized by English troops. In a state of shock the Nawab wrote to Vansittart:

Such tumults as the English have set on foot, were never known in any
Government till the time of Meer Mahomed Jaffier Cawn: That they
should send Seapoys, and seize the Officers of the Government and carry
them away, at the same time the Nazim was looking on without taking
notice of it. All my remissness has been owing to the friendship between
you and me. If the English Gomostahs will carry on their trade according
to the custom practised by other merchants, well and good; if not, I have
no recourse but to make use of the same expressions, favouring of
disagreement, that ye do.[109]

From the distant quarters of the *suba*, from as far afield as Rangpur,
Dinajpur, Rangamati, Goalpara, Sylhet, and Bakarganj, officers and
zamindars had begun to bombard the court with complaints similar to
the petition of the Barabazu zamindar quoted above. The Bengali
gumashtahs and their English masters, were reported to have committed
unheard of misdemeanours. They treated Mughal officers with contempt, set themselves up as judges and magistrates, extorted fines, forced
the merchants to buy goods from them at more than the market price
and sell what they required at much below it.[110] What the officers and
landholders of the Bengal *suba* objected to was not the seaborne trade
of the Company, which consisted of duty-free and high-value articles of
import and export. They objected rather to the novel additions to the
trade of the English, above all to the inland private trade of the Company
servants and the 'free merchants' in the necessaries of life. To be more
specific, they clamoured against the coercive and monopolistic character
of this new trade, because the use of force by the *gumashtahs* was
disorganizing life in the interior, oversetting constituted authority,
disrupting the cycle of economic activity, blocking the free flow of
trade and causing distress to the poor.

The officers and zamindars were well aware of the distinction
between the legitimate trade of the Company under the Mughal *farman*
and the bastard trade of the Company servants and the free merchants
under illicit English *dastaks*. Their alarm and anger was directed at the
replacement of market mechanisms by coercive monopolies (that is,
forced selling of goods at high prices) and monopsonies (that is, forced
buying of goods at low prices) in the interior. The remote corners of
the *suba*, which had not till then been affected by the Company's
import–export trade, were being disturbed by the extension of private
inland trade since 1757. From the very beginning of the dispute, Mir
Qasim insisted 'that the gomastahs shall not force their goods on his
subjects against their will, or at their own prices, nor compel the

workmen to provide goods for them at unreasonable prices; but that every man be left at his own option to buy or sell, as he finds his advantage in either'.[111] The Mughal government appeared here as the champion of free trade; it was the English company which stood for monopoly. In this struggle, as the Nawab saw it, the issue was the fate of the poor, and the welfare of the country.

The greedy and cunning cabal led by Amyatt sought to confuse matters by representations to London that the Nawab and his officers were bent on stopping the Investment of the Company. The Company authorities were not deceived. The facts of the matter were self-evident. What precipitated the war was the private aggression of the Company servants towards the lawful government and its subjects, and what motivated their aggression was their monopolistic and coercive participation in the inland trade in an entirely private capacity. As they encountered opposition to this trade from the Mughal officers, they resorted to open threats of war. Cartier, the Chief of the Dacca factory, threatened the *amil* of Dacca, Muhammad Ali Beg, with dire consequences for interrupting private trade under free pass: 'you know that a disturbance will arise between us; and by the grace of God you have seen, and will see, what our strength and power has shewn itself, and will shew itself'.[112] The partnership of Johnstone, Hay and Bolts, interrupted in their business by Mir Sher Ali Khan, the *Faujdar* of Purnea, expressed surprise at his having dared to 'violate' the charter of Farrukhsiyar: '... you shall repent having thus interrupted our business, in despite of the royal firmaun.'[113] Vansittart condemned these communications for their improper tone, but his own private trade was at least as large if not larger than that of Messrs Johnstone, Hay and Bolts. Indeed, it was their mutual rivalry that precipitated Ellis's surprise attack on Patna. That began the war.

The truth was soon out, but not soon enough to prevent the war which the English thrust upon Mir Qasim. Even as the East India Company heard of what was happening in Bengal, Amyatt's party managed to depose Mir Qasim by their violent manoeuvres. The Court of Directors, without having at that stage heard of the outbreak of war, condemned 'the licentious trade of our said servants'. They called for 'the strictest friendship and harmony' with the Mughal government, and dismissed Amyatt (already killed), Johnstone, Hay (already killed), Carnac, Ellis (already killed), and others.[114] By then, Mir Qasim had been overthrown. The Company servants, free at that distance of any effective supervision by London, had effected their private purpose: to remove the barriers posed to their trade by the last determined Mughal government in Bengal. The size of their private trade is indicated by their claim for restitution. A claim, on account of 'plunder' by Mir Qasim's officers during the war, for Rs 5,300,000, was eventually passed.[115] The amount of private trade would appear from this to be not less than a third of the annual revenue of Bengal before the latter was enhanced by Mir Qasim. Private trade had obtained, by 1763, the critical mass for a second explosion in Bengal. The Court of Directors had no difficulty in identifying this as the cause of the war when they heard the news. They saw the inland trade of their servants as a breach of their orders, a violation of the imperial charter granted to the Company by the Great Mughal, and, in a great measure, the cause of the wars with Sirajuddaulah and Mir Qasim. 'The amazing sums demanded for restitution in respect of losses sustained in this trade have opened our eyes to the vast extent to which it has been carried,' wrote the Directors. This illegal traffic, they declared, was 'the foundation of all the bloodshed, massacres and confusion which have happened of the late years'.[116]

Events occurred too fast for London to intervene. As the Mughal officers and the Company servants drifted into an undeclared war, Vansittart and Warren Hastings made one last attempt to patch up matters. The Nawab had told them that it would be much more to his interest 'to lay the trade open, and collect no customs from any person whatever upon any kind of merchandize, which would draw a number of merchants into his country and encrease his revenues, by encouraging the cultivation and manufacture of a large quantity of goods for sale'. This alarmed them, 'as it would immediately render the dustuck useless, and prejudice our Honourable Masters' business, by enhancing the number of purchasers'.[117] In order to avoid the undermining of the Company's free pass, Vansittart pleaded in Council that Englishmen should participate in the inland trade on a legitimate basis by paying duty at 9 per cent on their private transactions. The majority in the Council tumultuously rejected the proposal. They would pay no duty but grandly consented to pay the Nawab 2½ per cent on salt. The Nawab wrote back with biting irony, 'why should you take upon you so great a hardship?'[118] He then proceeded to deliver the *coup de grâce*: neither European nor Indian merchants need pay duty for the next two years.

This was a body blow to the private trade of the Company servants. The confrontation with them drove the beleaguered Mughal government to a radically new measure that had no parallel. The step was all the more novel because Mir Qasim abolished not just the customs duties on his Indian subjects to free them from the tightening English grip, but in addition all minting charges in view of the English offensive in the money market. The terse communication ran: 'Since all this wrangling on the part of the gentlemen has arisen on account of duties, I have, for that reason, put a stop to the collecting of duties in all districts of the provinces, subject to me, as well as to the coining of money in all my mints.'[119]

The exact mode of the latter measure is nowhere explained in the documents, and Mir Qasim's biographers[120] do not comment upon it. Obviously coinage could not be stopped; it would have to continue. What the Nawab presumably meant was that there would be no restrictions on minting and that all coins, and not just the current coins of the regnal year (called *sikka* rupees), would be accepted at the public treasury. The official rule had been that the revenues must be paid in current and not old coins. Mir Qasim would no longer insist on this. The public revenues might be paid in both the current (*sikka*) and old (*sanwat*) coins of the Mughal realm.[121] Nor would he interfere in the rates of exchange between the various coins circulating in his realm. Despite English insistence that he bring the private banking exchange operations under control, he would leave the regulation of the rates between the current and old coins of the realm and between these and external coins (Arcot), entirely to the private and free operations of the bankers. Previously, only those state bankers who had taken a farm of the Nawab's mints had the right of free coinage, in consideration of the money they had paid into the treasury. Now that the English also claimed the right of free coinage in all his mints, he apprehended that his income would dwindle. Beyond that, the English would get a grip on the money market, and thereby extend their control over the economy. To forestall this, he made minting free for all, enabling Indian bankers and merchants to escape the English monopoly.

By abolishing customs and by withdrawing minting monopolies, Mir Qasim, at the sacrifice of his own income, removed all ostensible cause of complaint by the English. Perfectly aware of the blow he had delivered, he declared innocently to Vansittart that he had done this 'to avoid all disputes between your government and mine'. It was a bold new move, imaginative in its sweep, designed to deprive the enemy of all rational argument. It was not his original intention to create a free economy in Bengal: the enhanced revenue assessment upon the land had pointed in a contrary direction. However, the tide of events advanced his plans, and his wish to save the country came to the fore. The Mughal *subadar* of Bengal stood forth as the champion of 'the merchants, the poor, and all my officers, and mutaseddees of the public and private receipts of custom', who had been distressed by 'the oppression of the English agents and gomastahs' and had been 'deprived of their daily bread'.[122]

When the Nawab abolished his dues, he pretended that he had removed all grounds of conflict with the English. He reckoned without the proverbial wolf. It will be recalled that the wolf, deprived of all arguments, had told the lamb, 'You are good at finding excuses, but I shall eat you all the same.' Mir Qasim, of course, was not exactly a lamb. In the Council, Johnstone declared the Nawab guilty of a fixed resolve 'to ruin our trade, superiority and influences through the country, by reducing us on a footing with all other European or foreign traders, and even with the very Bengal inhabitants'.[123] The wolf bared its fangs. Amyatt and Hay went on embassy to Monghyr not for the freedom of English trade, but to insist that Indian traders remain bonded. They must pay duties, and the *sarrafs* must effect the circulation of rupees coined at the English mint. The Nawab would have to issue peremptory orders for this, and allow the English to coin three lakhs of rupees annually at each of the Mughal mints of Dacca and Patna.[124] Rejecting these senseless demands, the Nawab replied '... the shroffs and merchants are no one's servants, but for the sake of a small profit, deal with one another. Let every man of his own fancy buy and sell whatever he pleases, I shall interrupt no one.'[125] Aggrandizement has seldom been so thinly guised in history. Confronted with the astonishing actions and arguments of his opponents, the Nawab might well exclaim, as indeed he did, 'O gracious GOD! this is a matter of astonishment which my understanding cannot reach'.[126]

Even at this stage, he had no plans for a war of offence; he waited for the English to make their move. 'My reputation and honour', he wrote, 'are dearer to me than life.' If the English were inclined to let friendship subsist between the two parties, let them set aside these disturbances and altercations, which would surely produce a rupture: 'and if you are inclined to break with me, let know it immediately, that I may have nothing further to do with these things, for I can bear them no longer'.[127] The English were afraid at the time that the Nawab's general in Birbhum, Muhammad Taqi Khan, would commence the hostilities by attacking the English district of Burdwan. Had the Nawab ordered this, the Company might have been paralysed, for it derived its chief supply of money from that district. Instead, the English made the first move. Ellis, who had long plotted a showdown with the connivance of the party of Amyatt in Council, commenced the hostilities by a surprise attack on Patna. 'Like a night robber', wrote the Nawab, 'he assaulted the Kella of Patna, robbed and plundered the Bazar, and all the merchants and habitants of the city, ravaging, flaying from the morning till the third pahr [afternoon].'[128] Mir Qasim's soldiers quickly retook the fort. The *naib* at Patna, Mir Mahdi Khan, apprehended the roguish English chief who had long made life impossible in town. 'You gentlemen', said the Nawab, 'were wonderful friends, having made a treaty to which you pledged the name of Jesus Christ. You took from me a country to pay the expenses of your army, with the condition that your troops should always attend me. In effect you keep up a force for my destruction, since from their hands such events have proceeded.'[129] If Mughal justice required the execution of one man, Ellis was that very person. He, along with his connivers, Amyatt and Hay, were put to death during the bloody events that now followed. What the English dubbed the 'Patna massacre' was, from Mir Qasim's point of view, the just execution of traitors and rebels.[130]

At the heart of the dispute lay the issue of customs and the relentless drive of the English gentlemen and their *gumashtahs* to monopolize the inland trade of Bengal. However, as the dispute progressed to the outbreak of hostilities, a political dimension was revealed. This was the defence of the Mughal realm in Bengal and the *subadar's* attempt to construct a reformed Mughal order capable of withstanding the pressure of the pagoda hunters. Such a regime was inconsistent with the private interests of the Englishmen in Bengal. This was no longer simply a question of duties, which Mir Qasim had unilaterally settled in so unprecedented a form (it may be noted in passing that France, the most advanced country on the continent of Europe, abolished internal customs duties no earlier than 1791, whereas the Nawab abolished them in 1763). Amyatt and Hay had been deputed to Monghyr not to discuss this question alone, but 'other articles of business' as well. This meant in effect who should be in charge, the *Subadar* and his officers, or the Company servants and their *gumashtahs*.[131] The Nawab grasped this well, as is evident in his communication expressing displeasure at the embassy of Amyatt and Hay:

By what you write of other articles of business, besides the customs, I understand, that for this remaining country, which is left for my share, you have appointed me aumil, or regard me as wadadar, or zamindar, or gomastah, or mutaseddee; that you have given in charge to the said gentlemen other articles of business, exclusive of customs. Write me fully and explicitly of this that I may be acquainted and act accordingly.

The bitter and heavy sarcasm was characteristic of a man driven from pillar to post; a self-respecting man to whom his reputation and honour were more important than life; a natural ruler of men who had the interests of his subjects at heart, and who refused to be an *amil* (collector), or a *wadadar* (deputy sent to attach a property), or *gumashtah* (manager), or *mutasaddi* (officer) to an alien merchant company. As Governor of Bengal duly appointed by the Emperor, he saw it as his duty to defend the Mughal realm against the interlopers. His mission was to protect Mughal subjects whom the usurpers had grown powerful enough to exploit and oppress. These were patriotic sentiments, and not just imperial sentiments. Such sentiments were characteristic of the vanishing Mughal world of the mid-eighteenth century. The events that followed were reminiscent, in some ways, of the anti-foreign uprising in Delhi during the occupation of Nadir Shah, but on this occasion the people were led by the Mughal officer class.

The Mughal–English War of 1763–4

The war which the Mughals fought with the English in 1763–4 had no precedent in their history. They fought and lost and the English emerged as the ruling class. It was the first, and the last, occasion when they fought the English as a class—not a united class, perhaps, but still an all-India class despite the persistence of internal rivalries.[132] The provincial Mughal *umara* of the *subas* of Bengal, Bihar, and Awadh, and the imperial noblemen of the roving court of Emperor Shah Alam, claimed legitimate authority over the entire stretch of the Ganges and made a last desperate attempt to restore Mughal rule over the extensive valley. What this involved was not just the contention of an old ruling class against a thrusting new one. This was a conscious bid to break the stranglehold of an alien and exploitative trading system, which was threatening to upset the entire Mughal order. The war had a popular dimension, arising out of the oppression of the entire population. It was a patriotic Mughal war; one in which defeat would imply the passing of real power to the

English over the whole stretch of the Ganges (unless, somehow, the Marathas could beat them to it). The Mughal *subas* of Bengal, Bihar, and Awadh, territories constituting the valley of the Ganges from the source to the mouth of the river, were poised on the brink. At no time had the interests of the people and the Mughal ruling class fused so organically as in this war.

A glance at the 'Copy of the Demands presented by Messrs' Amyatt and Hay to the Nabob', especially the third and fourth clauses, would reveal how alien oppression had brought about this identity of interests. It was fusion brought about by inconceivable English demands. The third demand hit out directly at the people of Bengal and Bihar:

> 3rd, That the Sunnuds granted by your Excellency for the exemption of all duties for the space of two years, be immediately annulled, and all duties collected as before, as it in a great measure deprives the English of the advantages, which the tenor of the Royal Firmaund has ever entitled them to above other merchants, and is entirely repugnant to their interest, and prejudicial to the good harmony which ought to subsist between your Excellency and the English.[133]

No assertion of self interest could be more barefaced than this, no demand couched in terms so entirely injurious to an entire population. Since the Mughal officer class had resisted this, the fourth demand followed automatically from the third: in the disputes that had arisen between the Mughal officers and the English in the subordinate factories all over the country, the chief of the English Factory and not the Nawab's officer would arbitrate, 'giving a copy of his determination to the Officer of the Government who made the complaint'.[134] This demand, that government officers should be governed by private and alien parties, had been preceded by the proposal that government should not govern. Even before the embassy of Amyatt and Hay, the English had the effrontery to tell the Nawab: 'With respect to our Gomastahs, we cannot admit that they should be under any actual control of the Officers of your Government'.[135] The Nawab, shocked out of his wits, replied: 'You are resolved that the determination of all the disputes with my Officers shall rest in the power of the Chiefs of your factories. The justice of the Chiefs of your factories is this: they abuse and beat my Officers, and carry them away bound.'[136]

This was not figurative speech. Such things were literally happening. At length the Mughal officers stood up to the bullies. They were the warriors who came forward to lead the people in an all-out war. Not that the popular element counted for much in terms of fighting. That was done by the Mughal officers and their troopers. This was no war in which mobs could play an effective role. Occasionally, however, fakirs and sannyasis and the retainers of zamindars appeared on the battle scenes. Besides, popular discontent with the coercive monopolies of the Company and private English traders invested the military operations of Mir Qasim's officers with the character of a crusade. This was evident above all in the prelude to the formal outbreak of hostilities, in those preliminary months in the spring of 1763 when the two sides drifted into an undeclared war in various places in the interior where private English factories had mushroomed after Plassey. The people and their country chiefs had altercations with the factories; they were encouraged by the Mughal officers who intervened on their behalf. The zamindars and people, in turn, lent the officers support in laying siege to the factories.

The rumours that spread in the market towns at this time reflected obscure popular wishes, lacking the power of coherent speech. If the wish is the father to the thought, then the mentality reflected in these rumours was charged with an antagonism that boded the factories no good. The popular mood in the countryside seemed to be anticipating the violent extermination of the alien monopoly trades. On the eve of the war, Chambers, the deputy chief of the Kasimbazar factory, heard rumours of measures being afoot to hit at the foundation of the Company's trade. 'There is an order', he heard from his *vakil* and from a large silk dealer and several other merchants, 'passed for destroying all the mulberry trees in the country, and they have actually commenced putting it in execution; so that we can expect no silk or silk piece-goods for the ensuing year, if it is not put an immediate stop to. I hear there is the same order concerning all the cotton plants, which will be detrimental to the white cloth trade.' Amyatt and his friends in the Council were only too willing to seize on this rumour for action against the Nawab, but Vansittart was plainly sceptical. When asked to confirm his earlier report, John Chambers become evasive. It was beyond dispute, he said, that tom-toms had been beaten in several places by the *zilladars*, who pretended to have received orders from the Nawab to destroy the mulberry trees on both sides of the Ganges. He could not, however, say for certain that they had yet put it into execution. Pressed further, Chambers asked the *Naib Nazim* at Murshidabad about the purported order. Saiyid Muhammad Khan said he had received no such order from the Nawab, nor had he given any. Chambers asked him to find out the persons who had spread the report and to punish them. This was a tall order. 'The report', Chambers maintained, 'was not only here, but on the other side of the great river. It will be impossible for me to trace it to the foundation; I have used already every method in my power, but in vain.' There the matter rested.[137] This was a rumour: country people apparently anticipated the uprooting of plants, oblivious of the misery this would cause, because the wish to see harm done to the English was stronger. They wanted to get rid of the violent monopolies which the aliens had imposed on their crops and manufactures.

The link between popular anticipation and Mughal officialdom (*zilladars*—tom-toms—rumours) was a notable feature of the 'news' circulating on both sides of the Ganges at Kasimbazar. The Mughal officer class was the spearhead of the popular antagonism to the *firangi*. The dismissals, appointments, and reappointments since Mir Qasim's coming to power had resulted, on the eve of the war, in the promotion of a set of strongly anti-English imperial officers to key postings. They were all imbued with a determination to obstruct English trade and were collectively pressing the *Subadar* on. Having encompassed the ruin of Ramnarayan and Rajvallabh (both suspected of pro-English tendencies) by setting them against each other, Mir Qasim had appointed the faithful Nobit Roy as *Naib Nazim* at Patna. However, Nobit Roy was no warrior and as the confrontation with Ellis shaped into a series of armed clashes, Mir Qasim had to find a more formidable man to confront the bully. Recalling Nobit Roy at Monghyr to serve him as minister in attendance, the Nawab posted the warlike Mir Mahdi Khan, a ranking Mughal commander, as the deputy governor at Patna.

Jasarat Khan, the *Naib Nazim* at Dacca, was no crusader for customs, but the nawab took care of the matter by appointing Muhammad Ali Beg as under-officer (*amil*) there. This man at once proceeded to discipline the aggressive and disorderly set of English factors who had spread over the *niabat* of Dacca. Mir Sher Ali Khan, the *Faujdar* at Purnea, was another man the English had to reckon with as an early opponent of their misdeeds. They pressed repeatedly for the removal of these two thorns in their flesh. The Nawab promised, at one time or other, to remove Muhammad Ali Beg and Mir Sher Ali Khan. In the event, he maintained both at their crucial frontier posts.

Mughal officers at other disturbed frontiers were thereby encouraged to put a check upon the disorderly activities of the English. On the frontier at Assam, Saiyid Jalal Bukhari, the man posted as *Faujdar* of

Rangamati, insisted on controlling all items of export and import, refusing to make special concessions to English goods. Infuriated by the check upon free private trading to Assam, the English authorities in Fort William ordered the seizure of this imperial officer in startling defiance of Mughal sovereignty. At the nearby frontier post of Rangpur, the *Faujdar*, Abid Ali Khan, also began to insist on duties. He subsequently became one of the principal fighters against the English. Muhammad Taqi Khan, the *Faujdar* of Birbhum, had no English factories in his jurisdiction to contend with, but the troops he had raised were a cause for alarm at the nearby English revenue post of Burdwan. Collectively, these officers represented the hostility of the mounted imperial warrior class to the alien usurpers. Exposure to the unfamiliar experience of physical humiliations infused in them a patriotic spirit and a strong determination to resist the bullying by the English gentlemen and their lowly *gumashtahs*. Aside from the *niabat* of Patna, where the head on clashes between Mir Qasim and Ellis were staged, the principal theatres of armed confrontation were the *niabat* of Dacca in the east, and the *faujdaris* of Purnea, Rangpur, and Rangamati in the north. When war broke out, the theatre shifted up the Ganges all the way to Buxar, where the decision was reached on the basis of which the mounted Mughal warrior class would be compelled to concede military supremacy over the valley of the Ganges to an emerging white ruling class.

The documents which make it possible to study the initial armed encounters from the point of view of the Mughal officers can be counted on one hand. Apart from the correspondence of Mir Qasim which Vansittart (a Persian scholar) took care to translate and publish for his own reasons, there are only a few other letters, which are, however, important as they reveal the attitudes of his officers. Communications by Muhammad Ali Beg of Dacca and Mir Mahdi Khan of Patna were among the few that fell into English hands during the armed clashes leading to the war. Available in translation (by Vansittart), these letters, from two key members of the Mughal administration in Bengal and Bihar, afford some scraps of material to the historian for a study of the Mughal officers' mentality on the eve of the Mughal–English war of 1763–4. It is evident that they had a notion of laws established for the good administration of the country, and a notion of what is not done. Hence their outrage at the doings of the English. Mixed with this was a growing alarm at the chaos spread by these lawless bullies from abroad, a concern for the country and the inhabitants, and the birth of a determination, hardened by the experience of physical humiliation, to defend the land and the realm which was theirs. These officers were straining at the leash, pushing the Nawab to defend the subjects of the Mughal government and to expel the usurpers from the territory of their mutual sovereign by the force of arms. Such sentiments were inseparably imperial and patriotic.

Upon his appointment as the collector for the extensive *niabat* of Dacca, Muhammad Ali Beg, along with his official but inactive superior Jasarat Khan, received notice from Mir Qasim of the agreement with Vansittart that Englishmen were to pay 9 per cent duty on their private trade. Not having anticipated the rejection of the agreement by the majority at Fort William, the Nawab issued a directive to Muhammad Ali Beg to enforce the trade agreement, and to expel those Englishmen who would not conform. Even before he received this *parwana*, Muhammad Ali Beg had taken certain steps on his own. In the autumn of 1762 he had written respectfully but firmly to Vansittart that the latter should order the English chiefs of Dacca and Luckypoor not to oppress the merchants, artisans, and cultivators in his jurisdiction. Here he gave a succinct account of the state of affairs around the Dacca and Luckypoor factories and the new factories set up by Mr Chevalier:[138]

> In the first place, a number of merchants have made interest with the people of the factory, hoist English colours on their boats, and carry away their goods under the pretence of their being English property, by which means the Shahbundur and other customs are greatly detrimented. Secondly, the gomastahs of Luckypoor and Dacca factories oblige the merchants &c, to take tobacco, cotton, iron and sundry other things, at a price exceeding that of the bazar, and then extort the money from them by force; besides which, they take diet money for the peons, and make them pay fine for breaking their agreement. By these proceedings, the aurungs and other places are ruined. Thirdly, the gomastahs of Luckypoor factory have taken the talookdars' taloocs from the tahsildar by force for their own use and will not pay the rent. At the instigation of some people they, on a matter of complaint, send Europeans and sepoys with a dustuck into the country, and create disturbances. They station chokeys at different places, and whatever they find in poor people's houses they cause to be stolen and take the money. By these disturbances the country is ruined, and the reits cannot stay in their house, nor pay the malguzarree. In many places Mr Chevalier has by force established new markets, and new factories, and has made false sepoys on his part, and they seize whom they want, and fine them. By his forcible proceedings many hauts and

perganahs are ruined, and the malguzarree of the government suffers greatly.

Muhammad Ali Beg's remonstrance to Vansittart was a sign of the consensus of opinion then emerging within the imperial officer corps against the coercive private trade of the Company servants and the free merchants. He proceeded from word to action. The gentlemen at Luckypoor were much alarmed at being informed by his deputies that 'they had orders from the Nabob to stop and demand duties from every English boat that passed and on no account to let them go free, as the English dustuck was of no consequence in the country'. The unlucky gentlemen of Luckypoor lamented in their report to the Governor and the Council: 'This has occasioned an entire stoppage to our trade, greatly to the detriment of our private fortunes, as we have now large quantities of goods, detained at the different chokeys, which we cannot get released; unless we submit to the extravagant custom they require.'[139] Amyatt's party pressed the Nawab hard to dismiss the redoubtable collector of Dacca. As the Nawab lent them no ear, Cartier sought to intimidate Muhammad Ali Beg by talking of dire consequences. On the basis of the provisional agreement with Vansittart on customs (9 per cent duty on English private trade), Mir Qasim then issued a directive addressing Muhammad Ali Beg as 'You of noble rank'. The Englishmen, he directed, 'in no wise are to use violence or extortion'. He assured the collector of Dacca, 'If they act contrary thereto, I will not suffer such behaviour in the country, but will turn them out.' He added: 'And you, our well beloved, are to act agreeable to this written security. If any of the factors shall bring to pass anything, contrary to this written security, you shall remove him.'[140] The Mughal collector took his master at his word, thereby tempting the fate that awaited both master and servant.

The Englishmen in Bengal, busy making their private fortunes, had no imperial ambitions, but the design of the ruler and his officers to prevent the oppression of Mughal subjects was quite inconsistent with their burgeoning interests. When Muhammad Ali Beg tried to stem the erosion of Mughal authority, they struck. The chief of the Luckypoor factory had the effrontery to arrest a messenger sent by the nawab. He kept him in confinement for three days. On 14 February 1763, Vansittart complained to the Nawab of 'the oppressions and insolences of Muhammed Aly Beg,' and as evidence enclosed a letter written by him to Mir Abdullah, the collector of Sandip *pargana*: 'consider it is his design "not to suffer a single Englishman in the country, and to punish whoever shall take the name of an Englishman"; accordingly the Company's business and that of private Gentlemen has been everywhere stopt'.[141] Two days later Middleton reported from Luckypoor that Muhammad Ali Beg's officers had seized the houses of two Muslim servants of the factory. Both men escaped by the back door. A mother and a sister left behind consumed poison but were revived by treatment. Englishmen at Dacca dubbed Muhammad Ali Beg as 'powerful inveterate enemy' of all trade, 'both Company's and private, but more particularly the latter'.[142] The latter was of course what mattered most to them. At this stage, they turned violent. A clash occurred at Jafarganj. This was the first of the armed confrontations between Mir Qasim's officers and the Company servants. A party of sepoys went down to snatch some boats detained by Muhammad Ali Beg's officers. In the ensuing fray, the brother of the officer in charge of the police station (chaukidar) at Jafarganj was killed. This was the beginning of the undeclared war which was to lead in less than a year to Ellis's fateful assault on the citadel of Patna. The zamindars were already stirring against the English. In a dispute between the uncle and nephew about the zamindari of Baboopoor, unwelcome interference by the Company servants had resulted in three or four of their sepoys being killed.[143] As Muhammad Ali Beg laid an embargo upon the factory of Luckypoor, the retainers of Baboopoor and other zamindars lent him their militia.

Armed clashes broke out simultaneously in Luckypoor, Rajmahal, and Rangamati as Mughal officers sought to curb the lawless activities of the Company servants and their Indian staff.[144] The Nawab formally noted Vansittart's complaint that 'Mahomed Aly Beg's intention is, that not a single Englishman shall be suffered in the country'. Interestingly, he did not rebut the charge.[145] Mir Jafar had granted a *taluk* to the Company at Luckypoor. Muhammad Ali Beg seemed bent on arresting the Indian staff managing it and the factory.[146] Syed Buddul Cawn, his officer at Luckypoor, was in charge of the operations. The collector wrote to his subordinate, working out the plan for a siege:[147]

Your agreeable letter is arrived. I fully understand the particulars contained therein, and from the Hircarah likewise I learn the account of the villainies of the English in Luckypoor. I have wrote pressingly to Aga Mahomed Nazim, and Samadam, and Aumur Sing, and Jangaut Sing, to repair all of them with their people unto you; I have also sent Perwanas with the utmost dispatch unto the Zamindars of Bulwat, Baboopoor, &c. and I have taken engagement from every zemindar's Vackeel, about Luckypoor, that their masters the Zemindars will attend upon you, and act as you shall direct them. It behoves you with the utmost dispatch, to repair thither immediately, and blockade the passages for going in, and coming out on all sides of Luckypoor, and place strong sentinels, that no person whatever may pass or repass, to and from Lackypoor; and that a soul does not escape of those who claim the English protection, and make use of their name; take two or three and crucify them, and seize their houses and effects; lay hold of their wives and children, and send them straightaway to me.

Be sure not to fail in this respect; his Excellency having honoured me with his orders to this purpose, as you must be informed from the copy of the Governor's [Vansittart's] engagement, and of his Excellency's [Mir Qasim's] Perwana in consequence, which I heretofore sent you. And do not entertain the least diffidence; regard this my short letter, in the light of a thousand letters, and act accordingly. Moreover, let guards be placed to keep a good look-out about Luckypoor, and the parts adjacent; until the Nabob's orders arrive, when they will proceed to act, as I shall write to you: at present surround it on all sides, and keep a constant watch.

You will take extraordinary good care of the Europeans at Luckypoor, that they get no intelligence from any of their dependents, either by land or water, and for security you will send 200 men, with a commander whom you can rely upon, and direct above all things to be ready for action, both night and day.

This was a plan for economic blockade of the Luckypoor factory, preparatory to military assault by the Nawab's forces expected to arrive shortly. In accordance with his instructions, Syed Buddul Cawn placed a former servant of the Luckypoor factory under house arrest. In retaliation, Middleton had him seized and sent him down to Calcutta. In self-defence he produced the letter of instructions from Muhammad Ali Beg. On the basis of the letter the English asked the Nawab to punish his lieutenant in Dacca. The Nawab replied that he had dismissed his servant. In point of fact, Muhammad Ali Beg remained in Dacca, mobilizing the people of the country and the zamindars for a siege of the hated bastion of English oppression. The English then took the extraordinary step of having him arrested.[148] Interestingly, a popular siege did occur at the outbreak of war even without his directing presence. The Baboopoor zamindars in particular persisted with these operations even after the English forces recovered the factories in the *niabat* of Dacca. Officers, zamindars, and people around the factories coalesced in a combined front which aimed at starving the English out and ruining their trade.[149] The cementing factor was a common perception of the English as an alien race bent upon 'villainies' in 'this country'.

The Mughal officers emerged at the head of the oppressed people in many other areas in the spring of 1763, on the eve of Mir Qasim's fateful decision to abolish customs altogether. Having been so long under the yoke of the *gumashtahs*, no sooner had they a prospect of being freed from it than they swung from sullen subservience to avowed hostility.[150] English gentlemen privately exporting salt to Assam found their boats stopped at every *ghat* and were obliged to pay duties at every *chauki* by the orders of the *faujdar* of Rangamati. Saiyid Jalal Bukhari's orders were said to be so strict that the gentlemen there could 'scarce get anything to eat'. If an Englishman sent a peon with a letter for a *dastak* or any other business, the irascible commandant kept the man in prison for a week or a fortnight, and then he sent him back 'half dead without an answer'. There was a public announcement at the border that nobody should have any dealings with the English. Bukhari's men put out that the English had at present little power in the country. The saddened gentlemen at the frontier took this to imply that 'every one should take from them as much money as he pleases'. Rangpur, which constituted a contiguous part of the north-eastern border, had a no less formidable *faujdar* in Abid Ali Khan. He imposed duties on cloth and silk. The business of the English gentlemen and their *gumashtahs* was at a standstill as the concerned *paikars* and *dalals* had been arrested by the *amil* acting under the *faujdar's* orders. In the neighbouring zamindari of Dinajpur, beyond Abid Ali Khan's jurisdiction, the manager Ramnath Bhaduri, at his own initiative, set ten matchlockmen on each of the six *gumashtahs* carrying on the business of the English. Contributions were raised by him from them, and the money was used to pay off a marauding band of fakirs. All over the north-eastern parts the gentlemen were made to feel the altered equations of power. In drastic retaliation, they had Saiyid Jalal Bukhari arrested.

The undeclared war between the Mughal officers and the English gentlemen reached its climax in Bihar. The bitterness here was the effect of Ellis's bullying. Qutb Alam, the *faujdar* of Rajmahal at the junction of Bengal and Bihar, caused tension to rise in both *subas* as he stopped four boats from Dacca laden with betel-nut. He demanded duties despite a *dastak* from the chief of the Dacca factory, causing an uproar among the English by his daring act. Further up the Ganges, saltpetre and opium provided the issues in the contest, exacerbated by the violence of Ellis. The saltpetre business of the Company itself was impeded by an assortment of resentful Mughal *amils* posted at various places in the *niabat* of Patna. Opium, which was becoming an important item of English exports from Bihar, was subjected to levies by Rai Mohan Lal, one of the *amils*. Yet another *amil*, posted in the district of Saran, stopped bullocks loaded with saltpetre, and pulled the goods off their backs. At Seisaun (Sasaram), the local *daroga* stopped a boat laden with the Company's saltpetre and had it landed.

Matters came to a head at the fort of Tajpur in Monghyr. The Nawab's officer posted there, a *naib* named Mir Akbar Ali, had seized some saltpetre belonging to the Company. This gave Ellis the excuse he had been waiting for. At the Patna chief's order, Lieutenant Downie invested the fort, seized the *naib* and sent him prisoner to Patna. The lieutenant took charge of the saltpetre and had it dispatched under guard to Mow. News reached the Nawab that Ellis had sent three companies with two guns to surround the Fort of Tajpur. Apparently the Patna chief had also sent other companies towards Darbhanga, Teegra, Sarkar Saran, Tikari, and other districts. The Nawab knew not in what light to consider 'all these disturbances, plunderings, and ravages'. Even before the arrival of the news that the *naib* had been seized at Tajpur by an English party, the Nawab had sent Muhammad Amin Khan, one of his *jamadars*, towards the fort. At the head of 500 horse, the Nawab's *jamadar* attacked the English guard, killed four and wounded three. The rest, including the English *gumashtah* at Tajpur, were carried prisoner to the Nawab. The Nawab dismissed the *gumashtah* with a warning.

Like an enraged bull, Ellis pounced upon Patna. The newly posted *Naib Nazim* had repeatedly expressed his alarm and anger at this man's inexcusable conduct. Some time before Ellis's attack, Mir Mahdi Khan wrote to his master, expressing his apprehension that the Mughal administration was collapsing in the *niabat* of Patna. He dwelt particularly on the effect the dispute would have on the turbulent zamindars and raiyats of Bihar:

> I have frequently and repeatedly advised your Excellency, that Mr Ellis and the troops which are with him, creating troubles and disputes with the people of the Sircar, seek for a rupture. And the tenants and inhabitants of the city, and the Sepoys of this place, feeling this state of things, are fallen into apprehensions and alarm, and are providing for their own security. The people judging from hence that there is no longer a friendship and good understanding between us, raise many reports of different kinds; and the zemindars, taking the occasion of their not being called upon, withhold their rents, so that the revenues are entirely obstructed. I cannot

describe to you how much the affairs of the Nizamut are fallen into confusion. In whatever light you regard these affairs, you will graciously be pleased to issue your orders for quieting these disorders and troubles, otherwise the whole business of the Government is destroyed, and these mutual animosities, which tend to ruin the interest of both parties, raise suspicion in the mind of the people.[151]

This was the reaction of a Mughal nobleman, and a typical one: a sense of the Mughal order being violated, fear of the loss of control, alarm at the restiveness of the zamindars, and above all a determination to defend the government ('sarkar') against the encroachments of the aliens. As Ellis's conduct became more and more insufferable, he wrote once again to his master: 'If that Chief is determined on a quarrel, I will put up with no more insults, but will fight with him.'[152] Ellis, however, a rogue and a bit of a fool, did not take account of the possibility of counter-attack, and the risk to himself and other Englishmen such as Amyatt, and Hay, exposed in the Nawab's territory. He struck, and thereby sealed his fate, and that of his opponent the Nawab. Referring to the series of clashes that led to the war, Vansittart later commented on the 'national' focus of Mir Qasim's antagonism to the English. 'In a word, as the influence of those who were the Nobob's avowed enemies among us, had encouraged the contention which at length became universal against him; his resentment no longer limited itself to particulars, but became national; and the English in general as well as their adherents, were the natural object of it.'[153] Vansittart used the term 'nation' in the eighteenth century sense, of a people.[154] Mir Qasim, in other words, resented not this Englishman or that particular one: he wanted to get rid of that entire people. These were very much the sentiments of a Mughal statesman of the eighteenth century, at once imperial and patriotic.

The people, including the zamindars, were with him. It was not the officers alone who attacked the factories at the beginning of the war. There was a popular element in the sudden outburst of violence against the English all over Bengal. The attack on the English at Dacca, for instance, was made by 'a rabble of faquiers'. They invaded the factory, forced the English to retreat in total disarray, and captured a considerable portion of the Company's treasure and merchandise. When Captain Grant with a small detachment retook the place, the fakirs taken prisoner were gang-pressed as coolies to repair the sacked factory.[155] The zamindars participated in the siege of the English factories in the countryside. As trouble erupted all over the *suba*, Dayaram Ray, the *diwan* of Rani

Bhavani of Rajshahi, intercepted a hundred maunds of silk on its way from Rampur Boalia to the English factory at Kasimbazar. An officer of the *Nizamat* took charge of the goods.[156] The zamindar of Baboopoor, in whose internal affairs the gentlemen of Luckypoor had made an unwelcome intervention, took up arms against the Luckypoor factory.[157]

The social alliance which Mir Qasim forged against the English by coercion and terror held firm until the war began to go against him. It was not his coercive methods alone that produced this solidarity. Vansittart was inclined to attribute it to the loyalty of his subjects, or at any rate to 'their contempt for Mir Jafar, or their resentment of our oppressions'. He found it remarkable that when the war broke out, despite the Nawab's want of courage to face his enemies in person, his soldiers fought for him with great bravery and fidelity. Nor did any of his officers, in the most distant part of his dominions, revolt from his authority to join the English, till Patna was lost and he prepared to fly the province.[158] The Mughal officers, united by a common political sentiment, appreciated the mortal danger to their class, and fought for their very survival. When their fellow officers in Awadh and the courtiers of the Emperor joined them in their war of survival, it acquired the dimension of a patriotic Mughal war. It was an all-out campaign that would decide the fate of the valley of the Ganges as far up as Faizabad and Lucknow. There would be no walkover for the English this time, as a Mughal plot had ensured on the former occasion at Plassey.

Yet, despite the organizational and technical improvements of their military capability under Mir Qasim's innovative statesmanship, the Mughal officers fought the war far too soon, before they could perfect the art of coordinating their cavalry with the new firepower. It was superior firepower that gave the English victory. This was a power more formidable than the light Maratha horse that the Mughal troopers had coped with twenty years earlier. The English imported into Bengal novel European methods of warfare tried out in the Carnatic. The key to these methods was concentrated fire by trained and disciplined bodies of infantry who advanced in tight formation with muskets fixed with bayonets. This had worked with deadly effect on Mir Madan's cavalry at Plassey, despite the absence of horse in the English ranks which had worried Clive so much on the eve of the battle. With the greater funds available after Plassey, the English expanded and improved their forces considerably. Impressed by their success, Mir Qasim raised select bodies of infantry equipped with muskets as good as those of the English and disciplined after the European manner by his Armenian general Gurghin

Khan. As Mir Qasim's brief campaign in Bundelkhand proved after his defeat and exile from Bengal, the troops of Hindustan were no match for his deadly body of musketeers and his new model cavalry. All the same, these very forces were repeatedly defeated in Bengal by the expanded and improved English troops. As there was no political collapse under the strong leadership of Mir Qasim, the explanation for his defeat must be sought in the military sphere.

The English guns were no better than those of the Nawab. Their trained and disciplined body of musketeers, who had proved themselves capable of beating back any frontal attack by Mughal horse, were now opposed by the corps of musketeers raised by the Muhammad Taqi Khan and Gurghin Khan. The Nawab, though he did not take part in the action himself, was not deficient in strategy. His choice of Udhua-nala as the site at which to concentrate all his forces in a last-ditch defence showed his grasp of the essentials of the art of warfare. It was a strongly defended position guarded naturally by river, mountain, and morass, and still further strengthened by artificial ditches and earthworks. The English could not have overwhelmed his superior forces by a frontal attack on this impregnable position. A surprise night attack did the trick: the Nawab's camp was broken up. Even earlier than that, in the initial confrontation that led to the death of Muhammad Taqi Khan, an English ambuscade on the path of his charge felled the brave general from his horse, breaking up his army at the critical point when the English were retreating from the battlefield under the frontal assault of the Mughals. These instances show that the English were superior in terms of tactics, if not strategy. They had greater reserves of resource in the new art of warfare on foot. The Nawab's army lacked this staying power. Not having the requisite discipline, the Mughals betrayed the old tendency to break up at moments of adversity. The commanders of the Mughal horse fought with courage and determination in the first stages of the war. However, no sooner did the Mughal army retreat past Rajmahal to Bihar than instances began to occur of rank cowardice, desertion, and even treachery. The underlying defects of Mughal military organization were thereby exposed.

These defects may be classified under two headings. There were the older weaknesses inherent in the organization of Mughal horse, and then there were the newer problems arising out of the incomplete transition from the method of fighting on horseback to that of fighting on foot. Such problems were apparent right at the start: that crucial stage when the Mughals might well have won. After the first defeats their morale broke: they no longer had the will to win. The Mughal noblemen were essentially a class of mounted warriors. It was in the course of fighting that the worth of the class was put to the test. The conduct of particular *mansabdars* and officers shows that the class failed as a whole to pass the test. It is further evident that the problem lay in the organization of their cavalry and its coordination with the fighting force of musketeers.

As regards the organization of Mughal horse, the *mansabdars* led their own troopers. There was no chain of command to convert their separate forces into a single well-knit cavalry. Individual commanders would follow their own policy in any campaign. They might stay out of battle with perfect impunity, or even join the enemy. Only the presence of rulers of towering stature in the camp would ensure coordination. Nawab Alivardi Khan had joined the strenuous marches against the Marathas, and had kept the Mughal forces together, but concerted action was all too often disrupted by the mutual rivalries and bickerings of the ranking commanders. Mir Qasim stayed behind in the headquarters at Monghyr during the first encounters with the English, and took no part in the subsequent campaign. This resulted in his officers fighting independently along with their troopers. They fought one by one and not in unison. While some fought with great determination, others fled on the first intimation of defeat. The problem was that Mughal troopers had been raised individually by the *mansabdars* and were habituated to fighting as detached bodies. The absence of a general staff and a chain of command meant dispersal of the body immediately upon the death of the commander.

It was just such an accident that prevented the Mughals from winning the first battles. This was the death of Muhammad Taqi Khan. The *Naib Nazim* of Murshidabad, an old uncle of the Nawab, was jealous of the young *Faujdar* of Birbhum. He withheld vital supplies from Muhammad Taqi Khan as the English approached Katwa. Shah Haibatullah, the *Faujdar* of Nadia, and another commander named Alam Khan, were encouraged by the jealous old man not to cooperate with the young and able *faujdar*. Sent by Mir Qasim to assist Muhammad Taqi Khan, they insisted on setting up a separate camp on the opposite side of the Ganges. They fought a separate action in which they were soundly defeated. In the subsequent action at Katwa, where Muhammad Taqi Khan might have carried the day but for his sudden death, Shah Haibatullah and the other commanders were silent spectators.

With the death of this brave commander, the other problem, that of coordinating the Mughal horse with the firing arm recently added to the army, came to the fore. Muhammad Taqi Khan was the most forward looking of the Mughal generals. He had raised a much admired body of musketeers who fought in concert with the Mughal troopers under his unified command. The other Mughal generals were appreciative of the havoc wrought by the musketeers, but were apprehensive of the social impact which the new style of warfare would have on the position of their own class. They were bitterly opposed to the rise of Khwaja Gregore, the Armenian organizer of the musketeers, who became known as Gurghin Khan.

Mughal horse represented the military sanction behind the rule of the nobility: a force recruited and commanded entirely by themselves. The successful resistance to the roving bands of Maratha horse by Alivardi Khan in the 1740s had been based on his masterly use of Mughal horse. In the 1750s, however, and especially after the battle of Plassey, the realization dawned that this critical instrument of their class rule was being overtaken by new military instruments. Mir Qasim sought to take account of these new developments by resorting to Armenian (Gurghin Khan and Marcar) and European (Somroo) mercenaries to form a corps of musketeers. This threatened the very basis of aristocratic Mughal dominance. The musketeers were recruited from the lower strata of society. Being recruited centrally, they represented a perceptible strengthening of the ruler against his courtiers. Hence the violent dislike of the new Armenian favourite of the Nawab by the Mughal noblemen, who expressed their contempt of Khwaja Gregore's origin by referring to him as 'a seller of cloth by the yard'. The tension between the Mughal officers and the Armenian general reflected the fact that the musketeers were an alien arm artificially grafted on to the decrepit body of Mughal horse. Hence they were not absorbed, digested, and internalized by the Mughal forces.

The Mughals reassembled at Suti to face the enemy once again. Shah Haibatullah, who had retreated up the Ganges, was joined here by Asadullah Khan, the *Faujdar* of Narhat Simai, and Mir Sher Ali Khan, the forceful *Faujdar* whom the English had so long sought in vain to remove from Purnia on account of his opposition to their private trade. The bands of cavalry they led were reinforced by a corps of musketeers under Marcar and Somroo and a corps of rocket-men under Mir Nasir. The commanders had strict instructions from the *Subadar* of Bengal to fight in concert and to avoid the jealousies and dissensions characteristic of the Mughal ranks. This time the Mughal forces went into battle together, but coordination between the various bands of Mughal horse under their respective commanders and between the horse and the firearms proved beyond their capacity to sustain. The English established an edge over the troops commanded by Marcar and Somroo right at the outset. This was a sign of the immaturity of the new firing arm of the forces of Nawab Mir Qasim. Marcar and Somroo quit the field disgracefully, followed by a large body of horse belonging to Asadullah Khan who was intimidated by the firepower of the English. These retreats exposed a small body of eighty horse commanded by Mir Badruddin and the rocket men commanded by Mir Nasir, just when they had attacked the English troops so vigorously as to force them to retreat in total disorder to the river behind them. The English had been fairly done for at Suti when the failure of Asadullah Khan to make a well coordinated cavalry charge enabled them to regroup, disengage their artillery, and make the counter-attack that gave them victory. The Mughal army lost the battle because it lacked a high command to coordinate the cavalry and the corps of musketeers and rocket-men.

The same problem recurred at the next action at Udhua-nala, an apparently impregnable position from which the enemy could scarcely have dislodged the Nawab's more numerous forces but for one thing. This was the lack of a commander-in-chief capable of enforcing the requisite discipline to keep the troops alert and battle ready. The antagonism between the Mughal *mansabdars* and Gurghin Khan resulted in no generalissimo being in overall charge of the sprawling Mughal camp. Kamgar Khan had recently joined the Mughal camp under the patronage of the Nawab's trusted adviser Ali Ibrahim Khan. He advocated that 'some commander-in-chief should be sent thither to bring that multitude under some order, and to make it fight in concert'.[159] Gurghin Khan opposed this. Kamgar Khan asked him insolently what he could possibly know of war and whether he had ever seen a battle. The infuriated Armenian general insinuated that the Pathan chief would turn against the Nawab as soon as an opportunity presented itself. In a swift counter-move Ali Ibrahim Khan proposed that Gurghin Khan should be the commander of the Mughal forces. However, the Armenian, unsure of his hold over the Nawab, would not go forth. The leaderless Mughal camp was a scene of utter confusion. There were no less than five separate bands of cavalry: those of Asadullah Khan, the *Faujdar* of

Narhat-Sinai; Mir Himmat Ali, the paymaster; Shah Haibatullah, the *Faujdar* of Nadia; Alam Khan, Muhammad Naqi Khan, and Jafar Khan. In addition the two Armenians, Marcar and Aratoon, and Somroo, the European mercenary, commanded their own corps of artillery. These officers, records Saiyid Ghulam Husain Khan, so greatly relied on the natural strength of the post, and to the impracticability of the enemy's forcing a passage, that they became negligent in their duty. Most of the officers who had any money made it a practice at the beginning of the night 'to gorge themselves with wine, and to pass the remainder of it in looking at the performances of dance-women, and in taking them to their beds'.[160]

The English, chancing upon a secret ford through marsh and lake to the Mughal camp, made a surprise attack at night. Such was the fear and dismay everywhere that whoever woke up 'thought of nothing but of making his escape and flying with all his might'.[161] In their headlong flight, many drowned in the river. Those who could not escape were killed, maimed, or disarmed. Somroo and Marcar, adroit as ever, made their escape. So did the nimble Asadullah Khan. The bedraggled Mughal army of Bengal now fell back upon Bihar. During the retreat, Mughal resentment of Gurghin Khan crystallized into a plot. Some Mughal troopers assassinated the overbearing Armenian general. Monghyr was treacherously surrendered by its Arab commandant. A coup in Purnea by the son of a former *faujdar* resulted in that district going over to the now restored Mir Jafar. At Patna, the Mughal troopers fled at the first sight of the red-coated Telinga musketeers. Mir Raushan Ali Khan, the new paymaster, could not find his horse and turban, and escaped with his slippers in hand. As the *Nazim* of Bengal retreated from Bihar to the dominions of the imperial Wazir and Governor of Awadh, it might well have been said of the mounted warrior class which had once ruled an empire from Kabul to Chittagong: 'Thou art weighed in the balance and found wanting.' Crowds of peasants, intent on plunder, harried the retreating Mughal warriors.

The Mughal ruling class was destined to put up one more fight, further upstream in the heart of Hindustan. Mir Qasim had been careful, since the eruption of the conflict with the English, to keep a line open to Emperor Shah Alam and his wazir Shujauddaulah of Awadh. Najaf Khan, the only general to acquit himself with honour in the disgraceful flight from Udhua-nala, strongly opposed an alliance with the *Subadar* of Awadh whose treacherous disposition he knew well. He proposed that the Nawab should join the Marathas and move with his army into

Bundelkhand rather than Awadh. However, the unnatural alliance did
not commend itself to the *Subadar* of Bengal, who thought of the
difference of his temperament and that of the Marathas, and of the
latter's rooted inclination for plunder and blackmail. With the natural
sentiments of the Mughal nobleman in his heart, Mir Qasim thought
that his troubles would cease if he could get into the Wazir's territory
and join the Badshah's court.[162] Even before the war broke out, he had
sent Mirza Shamsuddin with a commission to Shujauddaulah and Shah
Alam in order to request their assistance against the English and to
prepare them for every contingency.[163] The Wazir now responded
positively to the fleeing governor's call. A Mughal alliance, consisting
of the court of Shah Alam, the government of Awadh, and the exiled
Governor of Bengal, sprang up against the English.

The three potentates marched towards the eastern dominions of
the Mughal empire with a view to expelling the English usurpers. The
agreement was that Mir Qasim would pay the Wazir's army a subsidy
of eleven lakhs per month as long as the expedition lasted. On their
way, the Badshah, the Wazir, and the exiled *Nazim* halted at Banaras to
pay a ceremonious visit to a holy man. Shah Muhammad Ali Haji
proved to be something of prophet. He sought to dissuade the allied
Mughal princes from marching against the English, as they were inferior
to those strangers in the art of war and lacked unity and concert. The
prediction was speedily realized as Shujauddaulah turned against Mir
Qasim and seized his effects, violating all the rules of hospitality. The
Wazir literally reduced the Nawab to a fakir. However, despite this rank
treachery, the league of the Mughal princes did reflect an imperial bond,
forged by a general alarm at the English advance up the Ganges. The
Wazir's declaration of war clearly expressed these sentiments:[164]

> Since you have turned out and established Nawabs at pleasure without
> the consent of the Imperial Court; since you have imprisoned dependants
> of the court and exposed the Government of the King of Kings to contempt
> and dishonour; since you have ruined the trade of the Merchants of the
> Country, granted protection to the King's servants, injured the revenues
> of the Imperial Court, and crushed the inhabitants by your acts of violence
> and oppression, and since you are continually sending fresh people from
> Calcutta and invading different parts of the Royal dominions, and have
> even plundered several villages and pergunahs belonging to the province
> of Allahabad, to what can all these your proceedings be attributed but to
> an absolute disregard of the court and wicked design of seizing the country
> for yourselves. If you are naughty and disobedient (which God forbid),

the heads of disturbers will be devoured by the swords of justice, and you will feel that weight of His Majesty's displeasure which is the type of the wrath of God.

The Wazir threw a bridge of boats across the Ganges and crossed over with an army so numerous that 'it covered the country and the plains, like an inundation, and moved like the billows of a sea'.[165] The English, intimidated by the number and fighting reputation of the troops of Hindustan, retreated behind the walls of Patna. However, Somroo, the mercenary who commanded Mir Qasim's five regiments of Telinga musketeers and field pieces, did not lend support to the advancing Mughal horse. Shujauddaulah's troopers were eventually worsted by the incessant artillery fire of the English. The Dasnami Naga sannyasis, who had come to fight as mercenary troops, were mowed down, as were the Rohilla troopers of Inayat Khan, and the Wazir's own Mughal troopers. Beaten back from Patna, the league of Mughal princes retired to Buxar. Here the action was fought which decided the fate of the Gangetic valley. In this final battle between the Mughals and the English, Shujauddaulah's troops plundered one another instead of concentrating on the enemy. Unaccustomed as they were to any order and discipline, the Mughal horse faced a line of English infantry 'that looked very much like a wall vomiting fire and flames'.[166] Without an instituted high command to rally them, they retreated in total disorder before the advancing musketry. After this signal and decisive defeat the Wazir made one last attempt at recovery by enlisting the help of the Maratha's horse and their seasoned commander Malhar Rao Holkar. However, the Maratha horse proved no more capable of overcoming the unaccustomed English fire. The Wazir then conceded defeat. The subsidiary alliance which he entered into with the English extended the Company's power right up to the upper reaches of the Ganges.

While the campaign was in progress, some perceptive Mughal commanders argued that the strength of the English and the secret of their success lay in their ability 'to range themselves in battle array, according to their own rules, with their field pieces properly stationed, and their talingas upon the wings'. These commanders saw the only chance of Mughal success in preventing the array of the English in set-piece battles. In that type of action, 'so few as a few thousand of them would always prove an overmatch for an army of fifty thousand Hindustanies'.[167] Najaf Khan, Kamgar Khan, and some of the more intelligent generals of the Wazir advocated a different type of warfare.

The Mughal horse, they urged, should range the country, avoid head-on collisions with the wall of fire, cut off the supplies and communications of English, harry them in the rear, and make their trade impossible.[168] This was indeed the kind of war which the people of Bengal had expected at the beginning of Mir Qasim's war with the English. They thought they would support the bands of Mughal horse skirmishing with the English and thereby put a stop to the latter's monopolistic traffic. Such a mode of warfare, by making the operations too expensive over an extended period, might have hit at the very rationale and existence of a trading company out to earn a profit. However, Mir Qasim, Shujauddaulah, and the imperial officer class did not place their faith in a mode of war which was so alien to the Mughal ethic. They opted for a mode of warfare in which the people would scarcely have any part to play. Their preference was for set-piece battles, relying on their horse and élite band of commanders.

Whether a mode of warfare relying on popular support and one which avoided action might have succeeded against the Company is an unresolved question. What is evident is that the Mughal imperial class had thrown its entire resources into the campaign. Unlike the untested outcome at Plassey, their successive defeats in the hard-fought battles beginning with Katwa and ending with Buxar proved decisive. In his private conversation with Mir Qasim during the visit to Monghyr to negotiate an agreement on private trade, Vansittart had anticipated the political consequences of such defeat. Saiyid Ghulam Husain Khan puts these words into his mouth:[169]

> I have seen your troops and acknowledge that you have accoutred and disciplined them very well; but these are only good against Indians, and people of this climate. Beware of ever opposing them to Europeans, or coming to a rupture with the English upon a confidence reposed in your people; for rest assured that you shall find yourself disappointed, and that these men will never stand the brunt of European soldiers. Beware therefore of trusting your honour to such hands. They will disappoint you assuredly, and with the loss of your honour, you shall take away the honour of every Hindian nation, and of every Hindostany Prince; for if you come to be defeated, with these your choicest troops, the people in Europe will from thence conceive the most contemptible idea of the rest of the Hindians; and they will come to despise everything that is in Hindostan. Reckon then that in your fate is involved the fate of all Hindustan.

'Every Hindian nation', 'the rest of the Hindians', 'the fate of all Hindustan': these words are evocative of a contemporary perception of 'the Hindian' making a last desperate stand against the English East India Company. The English governor and the Mughal chronicler were right in reckoning that the fate of all Hindustan was involved in the outcome of the Mughal–English war of 1763–4. Defeat sealed the fate of the Mughal imperial class, and not just in Bengal and Bihar, but in Hindustan as well. After Buxar, the Company would meet no opposition from the Mughals to the extension of its power. Reckonings with the Marathas, Haidar Ali and his son, and the Sikhs still lay ahead, and they would prove to be made of sterner stuff than the effete Mughals of Bengal, Awadh, Delhi, and Hyderabad. Longer and deeper acquaintance with the European organization of war and the more effective adoption of firearms enabled the successor states to fight with the English on more equal terms than the Mughals did in 1763–4. However, victory in the Gangetic valley gave the Company immensely greater resources than before in meeting these formidable adversaries. The grant of *diwani* by Emperor Shah Alam in consequence of his defeat at Buxar entitled the Company to the revenues of Bengal. The *suba* of Awadh, now tied to the rising English power, became its buffer in Hindustan against the Marathas upon their return to Delhi with Shah Alam in train. The absence of Mughal leadership would henceforth preclude the fight of 'the Hindian' against the English as one political entity.

The structure of personal and group loyalties that had enabled the Mughal ruling class to mobilize for war against the East India Company collapsed soon after their defeat. The English generals had for some time felt the need for the addition of a cavalry arm to the Company's army to meet their mounted Mughal adversaries. Major Munro, the victor of Buxar, sent a feeler to Zain-ul-Abedin, a Mughal Commander of Awadh, desiring him to come over with as many 'able-bodied and well-mounted horsemen, Moguls, Toorannies &c.', as he could. Zain-ul-Abedin reflected anxiously on how dishonourable it is to all men, particularly persons of high family, 'to desert the service they are engaged in, and go over to their Master's enemies'. In the face of this he saw how his master, Shujauddaulah, had murdered Muhammad Quli Khan, 'who was the glory of the Moguls', and had gone on to treat Mir Qasim 'in such a manner as to incur universal censure and reflect disgrace upon the Mogul name'. However, he and his class had more substantial grievances against the Wazir of the empire: '... with respect to us Moguls, who are strangers in this country, and who have nothing to depend upon but our monthly pay, are, together with our families, brought to distress whenever that is stopt. He thinks of nothing but how to oppress and ruin us, and therefore takes no notice of men of family, but places all his confidence in low and worthless people'.

The new methods of warfare, and the promotion of men of low social birth by the Mughal governors of the mid-eighteenth century, had combined to undermine the position of the mounted Mughal warriors. Zain-ul-Abedin and his compatriots therefore let Munro know that 'if the English, who are celebrated for their justice and good faith, are desirous of our alliance, and are willing to agree to our just demands, ... doubtless a great number of Moguls and Toorannies &c., will without delay join you in due time'.[170]

The restored Nawab, Mir Jafar, conveyed to Major Munro the terms on which the Mughal commanders were willing to join the service of the Company: 'you should in every respect regard the honour and reputation of us, who are strangers in this country, as your own, and make us your confederates in every business'. In particular, the leaders of the troopers, including *jamadars*, *havildars*, and other distinguished men, should receive substantially higher pay, over the 60 rupees per month received by the ordinary troopers. 'Whatever Moguls, whether Iranies or Tooranies, come to offer their service, should be received on the aforesaid terms ... .' Moreover, a month's pay should be advanced to them; and if anyone 'should be desirous of returning to his own country, let his arrears be immediately paid, and let him be discharged in peace'.[171]

The terms set by the Mughal commanders for joining the English hinted at the crisis that had overtaken the Mughal warrior class to its lowest level. Below the ranking commanders of Mughal horse (*mansabdars*), there were the leaders of the horsemen (*jamadars*, *havildars*, *dafadars*, and distinguished individuals), and below the latter, the ordinary troopers, no less proud of a supposed Irani or Turani (collectively known as Mughal) background, and all giving themselves airs as 'strangers to this country' who might wish at any moment to return to their 'own country'. The service they had given on horseback had sustained the Mughal imperial structure for two centuries. They were now willing to switch that service to the English colonial power. However, the terms they set to the service showed a gross overestimation of their market value, and their illusions were quickly dispelled. As long as the operations were under way, Munro was anxious for some Mughal horse to come over. However, once the mopping up operations were over, there was no urgent need, nor were such troops worth much. The reply which the English eventually sent to the hopeful Mughal commanders was the following: 'If you are desirous of entering into the service of the English Company, you shall be entertained with a thousand good Moguls furnished with good horses, but a greater number cannot be admitted into the service.'[172]

As far as the Mughal warriors were concerned, this reply put paid to the prospects of joining the English bandwagon and profiting from another empire. The class was dependent on resumable revenue assignments (*jagir*) or cash salaries from the paymaster. Seated high above the hereditary landholders and their local militia, the imperial warrior class were not prudent enough to acquire the prescriptive rights to the soil which would later enable the zamindars and *taluqdars* to survive under colonial rule. In Bengal the former Mughal ruling class practically ceased to exist by the end of the eighteenth century. In Awadh and Hyderabad, they were relegated to the margin under the new English dispensation.

Mughal Collapse, Rural Violence, and the Indian Confederacy

The league of the Mughal princes had fought the Company on a 'Hindian' basis. The successor states that fought with the English after the Mughal defeat at Buxar did so severally and on a regional basis. Popular resistance was of marginal importance in this struggle: it was local and sporadic, and without concert. But for one brief moment, the fate of the Company hung in the balance with the appearance of a combination of Indian powers, accompanied by wild popular expectations and turbulence. The Indian confederacy of 1780 was the last occasion when a 'Hindian' perspective informed resistance to the subjugation of Indian society. Concerted military and popular resistance collapsed after its dissolution. However, even as the Indian powers fell one by one, the memory of a universal realm persisted. The Marathas themselves invoked the doctrine of Mughal sovereignty to contest the growing English power in the Gangetic valley. An ideology of Mughal restoration permeated the political culture of late eighteenth century India even though imperial rule had ceased to exist. The Company gained visible supremacy over India only when it replaced the Marathas in the Red Fort which housed the Mughal sovereign of India.

The curious fact that the sovereign of Delhi continued to be acknowledged as the lord of the universe (*Dilliswaro Wa Jagadishwaro Wa*) long after the passing of his universal dominion may be explained by the persistent idea of Mughal legitimacy, and the practical advantages to be derived by manipulating this source of legitimization in an age of violent political contentions. Referring to the British capture of the Red Fort in 1803, Rammohan Roy was to dwell as late as 1831 on the stability that the British government attained by securing the person of a monarch who had no territorial possession at the time but was still regarded as the only source of legitimacy.[173] In 1765, Shah Alam was 'an independent sovereign and the universally acknowledged monarch of the whole of Hindustan'.[174] The contending powers, whether the Nawab Wazir of Awadh, the Nizam of Hyderabad, the Peshwa of the Marathas, the Nawab of the Carnatic, the Naik of Mysore or latterly the East Indian Company in Bengal, were all equally anxious to attach their names at the end of the well recognized formula: '*khalq-i-khuda, mulk-i-padshah, hukum-i-...*'

The 'imperialists' and the 'usurpers' both needed support to be derived from the idea of the inalienable sovereignty of the Mughal Emperor: the autonomous Mughal governors and their officers to uphold their dignity and social pretensions, and the Marathas, English, and other declared rebels and usurpers to secure legitimacy in an age when power was too uncertain to survive without the security of a title. The Marathas, who had appeared much earlier than the English as appropriators of the Mughal realm, took good care to obtain a charter in 1752 which granted them a quarter (*chauth*) of the revenues of the Mughal empire throughout Hindustan. The imperial charter admonished them to 'wholeheartedly execute our orders and punish our enemies'.[175] Haidar Ali of Mysore was not equally successful in this respect: he was referred to in Mughal parlance as 'a rebel and a usurper'.[176] However, even in the mosques of 'Haidar Naik', as the Mughal ruling class persisted in characterizing him, and in fact from every pulpit of India, the *khutba* was read invariably in the name of the reigning sovereign, Emperor Shah Alam.[177] The English had a stroke of luck in this respect: as victors at Buxar, they obtained temporary possession of the person of Shah Alam, whose capital was then under the occupation of the Rohilla family destined to blind him. Here was an opportunity for the English to fit into the framework of Mughal legitimacy: they obtained a confirmation of their new possessions which they were admonished to govern 'agreeably to the rules of Mahomed and the law of the Empire'.[178]

The English forces had not marched to Buxar with the idea of conquering Hindustan. There was some confusion in Calcutta initially as to how exactly to account for the defeat of Shujauddaulah and the possession of the person of Shah Alam. It was proposed at first to put Shah Alam in possession of the province of Allahabad as well as the hereditary domain of Shujauddaulah in Awadh.[179] However, Clive, the new Governor of Bengal, decided to restore Awadh to Shujauddaulah, who became a thankful subsidiary ally of the East India Company. The Emperor, who was put in temporary possession of Cora and Allahabad under the care of English troops, bestowed on the Company 'the most important Grants yet obtained by any European state from the Mughal Court'.

On 12 August 1765, the Company became *diwan* of Bengal, Bihar, and Orissa, an office it held from the Emperor as a gift (*altamgha*) in perpetuity, in return for standing security for imperial revenue worth Rs 26 lakhs. This sum was to be regularly remitted by Najmuddaulah, who had succeeded his father Mir Jafar as the *Nazim*.[180] On the same day Clive obtained from the Emperor a confirmation of the Northern Circars, till then formally dependent on the Mughal Viceroy of the Deccan, as a gift (*inam*) for the Company at Madras.[181] This gift was subsequently reconfirmed by the Nizam, who renounced his claims on the territory. The series of gifts made by Shah Alam to Clive on 12 August 1765 was completed by a Mughal *sanad* which confirmed the Company's Jaghire around Madras (granted some years ago by the Nawab of the Carnatic) as an *inam* in perpetuity. The Presidency of Madras was further strengthened by the imperial order that the Nawab of Arcot, till then the Nizam's deputy in law, should hold the Carnatic indepen-dently of the *subadar* of the Deccan, whereby he became an exclusive dependent of the Company.[182] In the Presidency of Bombay, the Company was already since 1759, the *Qiladar* of the Surat Castle and the Admiral of the Mughal Fleet. Its induction in the Mughal framework was formally accomplished, and its challenge to the Marathas, the rival appropriators of the Mughal realm, was sharper than ever. In the struggle for supremacy that ensued between the English and the Marathas, the *diwani* gave the Company a distinct financial edge. It enabled Fort William to shore up the weak presidencies of Bombay and Madras against their formidable adversaries in Poona and Mysore.[183]

The Englishmen had come to Bengal not to build an empire but to shake the pagoda tree. 'Do you imagine it rains rupees?'[184] asked the restored Nawab Mir Jafar petulantly before he died. Fort William was in no frame of mind as yet to take over the Mughal administration. The Mughal nobleman Muhammad Reza Khan became the deputy to the Company in the *diwani* and at the same time the Nawab's deputy in the *nizamat*, assuming formal charge of the Anglo-Mughal regime under the overriding supremacy of the Company. Dual government facilitated a more general plunder of the country by the English. The Company servants were not bothered with how to rule the country. What preoccupied them was money, and the question 'whether it should go into a blackman's pocket or mine'.[185]

The issue of duties on private trade was settled to the satisfaction of the Company servants: they decided to pay no more duties on their private trade in inland commodities, except for 2.5 per cent on salt. With this a reign of oppression was let loose which beggars description. Reza Khan was bombarded with complaints from the zamindars that 'the factories of the English gentlemen in the pergunahs are many' and 'their Gumastahs are in all places in every village almost throughout the province of Bengal'. Grain, linen, and all sorts of necessaries of life were monopolized in the process. The *Naib Nazim* emerged from being a trusted ally of the English to an ineffective champion of the disappearing Mughal order. Moved by the woes of his hapless subjects and his beleaguered Mughal compatriots, he observed: '... there is now scarce anything of worth left in the country.'[186]

While the Company servants and free merchants traded in the essentials of life by coercive and monopolistic methods, the Company collected the revenues with a new commercial spirit to meet its increased financial and military needs. Since 1757 it had ceased to import treasure in India for its business. *Diwani* implied the transformation of the revenue of Bengal into a means of the Company's Investment— henceforth a larger revenue was essentially a larger mercantile capital.[187] Mir Qasim had imposed an extraordinary assessment before this, but that was in wartime, and he did not collect even half of the enhanced revenues. The Company, persuaded by Reza Khan to set a somewhat lower figure as its aim, realized practically every pie. Richard Barwell warned on 1 January 1767, ' The enhancing the revenue of the country which appears the great aim of Lord Clive will be found, I believe, in a year the cause of its being diminished.'[188]

The same apprehension moved Reza Khan for the restoration of the older Mughal ways of governance. On the eve of the famine of 1770, he declared to Englishmen that 'the true spirit of trade' was 'the mutual satisfaction of buyer and seller'. They should, therefore, stop 'the illegal and oppressive' trade of the *gumashtahs*. Freedom of trade should be restored as in the time of Alivardi Khan. 'Men of credit and large capital', who had been forcibly retired, would then come forth once more. This would counteract 'the sudden failure of the usual supplies of specie', a phenomenon that was now familiar on account of Jagat Seth and other big merchants being reduced to distress. The business of the bankers and merchants had come 'almost to a total stand'. The revenues for want of circulating specie, were 'extorted rather than collected'. Deploring the coercive system of monopoly which the English had imposed on the trade of Bengal, Reza Khan argued that its withdrawal would enable merchants to renew commerce and import specie. The taxes would then be collected from the peasants with greater ease 'and without recourse to rigorous methods'.[189]

Reza Khan's plea for the restoration of Mughal practice exposed him to suspicions of conspiring against the Company. As early as 1767 he was embarrassed by the interception of a letter in Allahabad which he was alleged to have written to the Jat chief Jawahir Singh.[190] 'Seeing that the ordering and regulating the affairs of the [Mughal] Empire and the extermination of the traitors of this realm [the English] are points which it becomes and behoves all the Grandees of the Throne and every noble of consequence in Hindustan to pursue as his particular cause,' Reza Khan purportedly urged the Jat chief to oppose the Nazarenes and to take his due part in 'the designs laid for the expulsion of the evil-minded tribe'. The letter was dismissed at the time as a forgery. Its phraseology was, however, carefully modelled upon the language used in contemporary Mughal correspondence and conversation. The 'cause', that is, the 'ordering and regulating' of the Mughal empire, was not a figment of the imagination. The forger could hardly hope to be successful unless he convincingly imitated the language and mentality of the circle to which Reza Khan belonged.

From the last Mughal administrator's point of view, there was indeed every reason why the sedition of the Nazarenes should be described as an 'enormous evil'. Within five years of the grant of *diwani* to the English, the extraction of the revenues by the Company and the profiteering of its servants in rice and other essential commodities so deranged the trade and agriculture of Bengal that the drought in 1769 turned speedily into the famine of 1770. When the scarcity first manifested itself, Reza Khan of Murshidabad and Shitab Rai of Patna proposed certain remissions of revenue—a third of grain and a quarter of the cash crops—to supply the peasants with stock and subsistence and to enable them to undertake production for the next year. In the event, as the English resident at the durbar at Murshidabad communicated on 7 February 1769, 'The revenues were never so closely collected before.' Reza Khan further complained that the English *gumashtahs* were monopolizing rice and asked for a ban on the English trade in this commodity. His pleas fell on deaf ears. In Murshidabad itself, as people lay dead in heaps, influential Englishmen, having coercively bought rice at three maunds a rupee, sold it to local traders at fifteen seers.[191]

The Company had been prudent enough to disarm all the powers capable of opposing them soon after obtaining the *diwani*. The Nawab's 'useless military rabble' and 'the troops kept up by the Rajas and phouzdars in their several districts for the purpose of enforcing the collections' were dismissed and eight new battalions of sepoys were raised in 1766 to enforce the Company's authority on the country.[192] The Raja of Burdwan, among others, was obliged to dismiss all his *nagdi* troops, that is, the horsemen and musketeers he paid in cash, as distinct from the traditional rural militia who fought on foot without firearms.[193] Having drawn the teeth of the Mughal ruling class and the rural magnates, the Company proceeded, in a country laid waste by famine, to assume formal charge of the government in 1772. Subsequently the abolition of the *nizamat* (1791) wiped out the Mughal nobleman and officers in Bengal. At the same time, the Sunset Regulation of the Permanent Settlement (1793) laid low the great zamindars earlier brought into prominence by Murshid Quli Khan. With the bankers and merchants of Bengal in irreversible decline and their lucrative connection with the revenue management of the country terminated by the shift of the Khalsa from Murshidabad to Calcutta, the class combination of *mansabdars*, zamindars, and *seths* which had underpinned the late Mughal regime in Bengal was overthrown.

Having dismantled the social structure of the Murshidabad regime and disarmed the classes possessed of the organized means of violence, the Company had to face the more inchoate violence of the lower classes let loose by the disorganization of the rural economy following the famine of 1770. Peasant violence was by its nature confined to the specific rural locality. The Mughal officers had possessed the means to oppose the Company on a wider basis. The zamindars did not possess the means, far less the ordinary villagers. It was not simply the lack of organization: there was no commitment to the sort of 'cause' that involved 'the situation in this country'. The rural classes did not share the Mughal notion that 'the superiority of the Nazarenes' might be opposed by 'the designs laid for the expulsion of the evil-minded tribe'.[194] The absence of an articulate ideology prevented the peasants from conceiving a definite alternative to the new English dominion. There were riotous assemblies of peasants almost every year at the time when the zamindars, backed by the English, commenced operations for collecting the revenues. These demonstrations were carefully stage managed. The village heads (*mandals*) would gather a few hundred ryots and made them take an oath to pay no tax until a reduction was obtained. The local officers or tax farmers appointed by the zamindar would be chased away and the footmen sent from the *cutcherry* would be beaten up. Usually the *mandals* would manage to obtain some remissions and then their followers would calm down. Such commotions had been frequent in more than one district since 1781 and were sometimes encouraged by officers dismissed by the zamindars.[195]

The disturbances in the areas devastated by the famine fused into a peasant uprising in Rangpur; there an oppressive revenue farmer, Devi Singh, tortured, humiliated, and sometimes set aside the zamindars of the land which he had taken on farm. Consequently, the Company had to reckon without the support of the local magnates when his oppressive methods of collecting the taxes provoked the headmen (*busneahs*) to assemble crowds numbering a thousand and sometimes even ten thousand in various parts of the district. Armed with lances and bows the ryots attacked the *mofussil* officers of the farmer in 1783, beheaded some of the more hated stewards, and plundered whatever cash and records on which they could lay their hands. The rebels looked to the English Collector, Goodlad, for relief. When Goodlad opted for force rather than justice, armed clashes broke out between the Company troops and the moving bodies of insurgents. The latter had a rudimentary local organization, with a 'nawab', a '*dewan*', and a '*bakshi*' at their head and 'sardars' at local centres, drawn from the ranks of the *busneahs*, who were ryots holding leases for broad acres. The 'nawab', a Brahman named Dirjinarain, was a landholder who had paid revenues worth Rs 3500. Baneswar Pramanik, a low caste Hindu, was elected his '*dewan*', and Nuruluddin Bosneah, a Muslim headman, was his '*bakshi*'. The rebel government issued a proclamation forbidding payment of taxes and levied a sedition tax (*ding kharcha*) to defray its expenses. The ineffective replication of the forms of Mughal government in Bengal was not accompanied by any attempt to expel the English. The insurgents did not proclaim an end to Company rule: negotiations went on to obtain redress of grievances. 'We are our own leaders', the crowd told a party of footmen sent by the zamindars of Kazirhat, 'and we are going to obtain justice.' Their conventional weapons were no match for the firearms of the sepoys led by Lt. Macdonald. A few skirmishes in which the sepoys opened fire dispersed the armed assemblies. The leaders of the insurrection (*ding*) were apprehended, but the insurgents obtained the dismissal of Devi Singh.[196] A folk song recorded the joy with which the ryots received the good news:

> God gave the realm to the English
> And the Company meted out justice.[197]

In the wake of the famine, roving bands of fakirs and sannyasis began plundering the English factories and government treasuries almost every year. The fakirs belonged to the Madari sect of Makhanpur near Kanpur and the sannyasis were Dasnami Nagas from Banaras and other centres in the *subas* of Awadh and Allahabad. These bands used to come on pilgrimage annually from upper India to Bengal under the Mughal regime. What precipitated the confrontation was Fort William's instruction to the newly sent out English supervisors in 1769–70 to control or even stop the annual pilgrimages of the fakirs and sannyasis to the shrines and bathing ghats along the Ganga–Brahmaputra rivers. The contributions which these bands levied on ryots and zamindars were regarded by the Company as impediments to the smooth collection of the revenues. Captain Thomas who was dispatched by the Supervisor in 1772 to intercept the sannyasis was killed in an ambush. The sannyasis then plundered the zamindars of Dinajpur, put the zamindars and inhabitants of Mymensingh to flight, and kidnapped the *naib* of Zafarshahi, extorting from him a ransom of Rs 1600. Captain Edwards, who was ordered to advance with a detachment to pursue the Naga sannyasis, was killed with most of his sepoys in yet another encounter. At the beginning of 1773, as Warren Hastings reported from Calcutta, the province wore a somewhat warlike appearance. In the winter that followed, the fakirs, led by Majnu Shah, joined up with a body of sannyasis and moved towards the Brahmaputra. Four companies of sepoys encountered the fakirs and sannyasis on 23 December 1773 and repulsed the combined bands with heavy slaughter. Efforts by the sepoys to capture Majnu Shah were foiled by his swift movements and lightning raids. He would fall back upon Makhanpur whenever hard-pressed, and would renew his expedition whichever winter suited him. 'The velocity of their marches', reported the Magistrate of Dinajpur, 'must greatly surpass that of regular infantry.' Though Majnu Shah identified the English as the enemy and operated on a wider terrain than other rural insurgents, he never fought more than flanking actions.[198] His expeditions to Bengal were recalled by the folk poet Panchanan Das in an oral composition of 1813 as 'the cause of Bengal's ruin' (*Bangala-nasher hetu*). The martial procession of Majnu Shah riding with his flag intimidated the pacific villagers: 'The Bengali folk are put easily to flight', said the poet, and he went on to recount how the fakirs 'chased' them:

> Good wives of common folk,
> Chased into the jungle,
> Stripped, pressed for embrace,
> Plead with the fakirs, beg quarter.
> 'God see to it,' they curse Majnu
> 'Let this son of a slave die soon.'[199]

Folk memory did not recall the sannyasi and fakir expeditions as an early war of independence. Panchanan Das's view of the matter is a whole world removed from the middle class vision of Bankim Chandra Chatterjee's later novel *Ananda Math*, in which the sannyasis singing 'Bande Mataram' sought to liberate the country by the force of arms. In the eyes of the village poet, the armed mendicant is nothing but a curse upon the land, 'a base fellow who came from some foreign quarter' to oppress the village folk of Bengal.[200]

It will be recalled that the fakirs had earlier participated in more effective action against the British: as auxiliaries of Mir Qasim's troops, they drove the English from their factory in Dacca. The sannyasis, too, had fought against the English as mercenary troops of the Mughal Wazir Shujauddaulah at Buxar. That was a frontal battle, no flanking action. However, with Mughal power broken in the Gangetic valley after the battle, there was no rallying point. The focus of armed opposition to the East India Company shifted thereafter to the peninsula, where powers vying with the English and among themselves began adjusting to the European methods of warfare based on firepower.

The realization had by this time dawned on the Company's officers that 'the political system of the country'[201] hinged on an Emperor in exile with rival powers vying for his favour and sanction. Alive to 'the general balance of power',[202] which had replaced centralized Mughal control, they were resolved, as long as the Emperor remained in their care at Allahabad, 'to take every effectual means for discouraging applications to him from any quarter for Sunnuds for their provinces, as ... they might in improper hands embarrass our affairs'.[203] However, with regard to Shah Alam's repeated entreaties for help in recovering Delhi, where his family lived in the dubious care of the lusty Rohillas, the Directors of the Company instructed their officers on the spot 'Never to engage in a march to Delhi, nor enter into any Offensive War.'[204]

As *diwan* of Bengal, *inamdar* of the Northern Circars, *jagirdar* of Madras, and admiral of the Mughal Fleet at Surat, the Company appeared to have worked its way deep into the Mughal structure, when Shah Alam, attracted by the rapid recovery of the Marathas from defeat at Panipat (1761), disrupted Clive's carefully laid arrangements by 'intriguing with those freebooters, & stipulating for their assistance by the grant of territories in the very heart of his Empire'.[205] For a time it appeared as if the '*fitva*'[206] of the Marathas would prevail over the 'sedition' of the English within the crumbling Mughal framework. The new Peshwa Madhav Rao, as he advanced in years, displayed 'abilities which made him dreaded and respected by everyone'.[207] Even Haidar Ali of Mysore, a man who had forced the Company to sue for peace at the very gate of Madras in the Mysore War of 1767–9, was made to bite the dust by the young Peshwa. The English at Bombay were startled by 'the growing power of the Marathas', and they saw in this a prospect 'much to be lamented'.[208]

The alarm spread to Calcutta when the Peshwa's officers enticed the Emperor out of the custody of the English at Allahabad. Fort William stopped paying the stipulated tribute to the Emperor. Accompanied by Maratha horse, Shah Alam rode into the Red Fort. The Rohillas vacated the town as the Peshwa's troops approached Delhi in 1771. In the moment of triumph, the architect of Maratha recovery was struck down. Dying of tuberculosis, the Peshwa warned his officers in Hindustan that they must not allow themselves to be intoxicated by a deed which the English had desisted from attempting.

> The English if they had been so minded, did certainly possess the strength to place the Emperor on his ancestral throne: but as their power is mainly based on the sea, they declined to go a long way inland without a corresponding advantage. Now, you must remember never to allow the

English to make a lodgment at Delhi. If they once obtain a footing, they can never be dislodged. ... They have seized strategic points and have formed a ring around the Indian continent, from Calcutta to Surat.[209]

Apprehensive Poona watchers in Bombay had no doubt that 'had his life been longer he would have effectually restored the influence of the Peshwa'.[210] His untimely death in 1772 was a calamity that shook the Maratha confederacy to its foundations. Observing the dissensions in the world of Mughal and Maratha politics, the Mughal chronicler Saiyid Ghulam Husain Khan anticipated the artful manner of the English conquest. 'By which means the downfall of the people of those parts, especially of the great and powerful ones, is soon obtained by the hands of one another ... and meanwhile the English who seem quite passive are in fact ... turning those sots into so many objects of contempt and raillery, both in Hindustan and in Europe.'[211]

The Maratha troops, summoned hastily to Poona, left Delhi a prey to anarchy. A citizen of Delhi asked the Mughal poet Sauda, 'Why do you spend your days roaming aimlessly about? Why don't you buy a horse and ask for employment in some noble's army?' 'Employment?' Sauda was amazed. 'Don't you know that only the wealthy and great can offer—or rather *could* offer—employment? But how can they do so today? They can no longer realize the revenue from their estates. For years now the land has been a prey to lawless and rebellious men. Even the person supposed to be lord of twenty two provinces [Shah Alam] no longer controls even the district of Aligarh [less than 80 miles south of Delhi]'.[212] The poet's words summed up the fate of the Mughal cavalier and gentleman. However, he expressed not just the sentiments of his own class but those of the people as well when he commented on the 'topsy-turvy' (*inqilab*) of the age in which they lived:

See the perverted justice of this age!
The wolves roam free; the shepherds are in chains.[213]

The Maratha dispute over the succession after Peshwa Madhav Rao seemed to the Englishmen in the settlement of Bombay to be 'the very crisis wished for by the Company'. Driven by a desire to grab the cotton tract of Gujarat and territories which would furnish 'a revenue equal to the necessities of that settlement', they intervened in the civil commotion at Poona.[214] Without informing Governor General Warren Hastings and his Council, the President and Council of Bombay set up the Maratha pretender Raghunath Rao and 'engaged in a war, the object of which was no less than the conquest of the Mahratta Empire, without Resources either of Men or Money, and even without a Plan of Operations'.[215] An English army marching upon Poona was surrounded by the Marathas and compelled to surrender at Wadgaon. The thoughtless aggrandizement eventually provoked an Indian confederacy against the English Company. Its architect, the Poona minister Nana Fadnis, wrote to his old antagonist Haider Ali: 'Divide and grab is their main principle. ... They are bent upon subjugating the States of Poona, Nagpur, Mysore and Haidarabad one by one, by enlisting the sympathy of one to put down the others. They know best how to destroy Indian cohesion.'[216]

Indian cohesion was, on the face of it, an unlikely event, reckoned to be 'so improbable' that the English authorities were at first unwilling to credit the news. They questioned how an alliance might be formed between powers as diverse as the Mughal *Subadar* of the Deccan, the Poona darbar, the Raja of Berar, and Haidar Ali of Mysore.[217] However, the growth of English power in the peninsula had, in fact, encroached alarmingly on the territories of all the princes. The Mughal *Subadar*, Nizam Ali of Hyderabad, was perturbed by the possibility that English success in establishing Raghunath Rao in Poona would enable the Company to challenge his dominion in the Deccan.[218] Despite his distaste for Haider Ali, the Nizam, therefore, combined with the upstart '*naik*' of Mysore to oppose an English thrust into Guntur, a Mughal possession which the Madras Council wanted in order to link up the Carnatic with the Northern Circars. Haidar Ali, who was not at first averse to the idea of allying himself with Raghunath Rao and the English in a bid to weaken his Maratha neighbours to the north, turned around when the English, revealing themselves to his gaze as the most faithless and usurping of all mankind, sought to grab a place so contiguous to his territory.[219] Nana Fadnis chose this moment to win over Haidar Ali: through a letter of agreement (*tahanama*) in January 1780 the Marathas allowed the ruler of Mysore to extend his northern frontier to the Krishna in return for a tribute deferred in consideration of the heavy cost of the ensuing operations against the English.[220] Remembering the hostilities with Mysore in the time of Peshwa Madhav Rao and the subsequent campaigns of Haidar Ali to recover lost ground, the Maratha envoy at Seringapatam wrote with a sense of satisfaction at the triumph of Poona's diplomacy: 'This agreement is not a small thing. We have together embarked on the same venture.'[221]

A series of confabulations in Poona, Seringapatam, and Hyderabad, in which the peripatetic agents of the Bhonsle ruler of Nagpur also took part, produced a concerted plan of operations between the confederates, 'for the expulsion of the English nation from India'. The plan entailed the following operations: 'Nizam Ali invading the northern Circars; the Marathas of Berar, Malwa, and the more northern parts of Hindoostan, attacking the territories of Bengal and Bihar; those of Poona and the south operating on the side of Bombay; while Hyder, accompanied by 2000 chosen Mahrattas, rather as a guard of observation than an aid, should direct his whole force towards Madras.'[222] This was the moment of peril for the English East India Company. It was saved by the fickleness of the Mughal governor of the Deccan, and the indifference of the Maratha confederate of Berar. The Nizam was 'on the eve of revenging' what he called 'the violence of the Governor and the Council of Madras' when Warren Hastings's insistence that Guntur be restored to the Mughals induced him to put a stop to his preparations.[223] The Bhonsle of Berar, for his part, was bribed by Hastings to spin out his march upon Bengal, and to allow English troops from Bengal passage through his territory to go to the relief of Madras. Fort William cited these developments as its reason for being 'unwilling to admit that the Power which the Company possess in Indostan is so extensive and obnoxious to the whole [Maratha] Empire as to make it the Interest of all its Provinces to unite with one another in overthrowing it'.[224]

In the event, Mysore alone joined Poona and its confederates in Malwa in the operations against the English. Haidar Ali, in the words of his son Tipu Sultan, responded to the appeal for his assistance by 'the Poona infidels', as the English were far worse. They had extended their domain by 'intrigue and chicane', and had even obliged the Saiyids and ulama of Bengal to eat the flesh of swine. Haidar Ali accordingly marched with Tipu upon Madras, 'prudently considering, that although it is declared "Heretics are impure", yet that it was more advisable to afford than refuse his assistance to the infidels belonging to the country (because the supremacy of the English was the source of evil to all God's creatures)'.[225] Tipu, who thus explained his father's action, was himself acutely conscious of the duty of 'my assisting and joining my brethren Musselmans in the general cause of religion, and defending the regions of Hindostan from the machinations of this enemy [the French and English Christians]'.[226]

In explaining the ideological basis of the confederacy of the Indian princes against the East Indian Company, Tipu was evidently constrained by the absence of a suitable political discourse. He had no claim to a legitimist position, and there was no discourse yet to construe opposition to the foreigners as a national war for the defence of the country. Sixteen years earlier the league of the Mughal princes had deployed imperial rhetoric against the Company. This was legitimist language, not nationalist discourse, but it embraced the whole of the country and had made it possible for the Emperor's *Wazir* to denounce the English as 'naughty and disobedient' rebels who had usurped 'different parts of the Royal dominions'. But with the disintegration of the Mughal domain since Buxar, the autonomous Indian powers were obliged to cast the struggle against the English in other terms. It was certainly not for Haidar Naik and his son, themselves usurpers in the eyes of the Mughal rulers, to represent the war in those legitimist terms.[227] Tipu was, therefore, obliged to shift the ground of the struggle to a defence of Islam and of Hindustan.

'God', he wrote to the Ottoman ruler of Turkey, 'is the protector and defender of the land of Hindustan; next to him, this supplicant at the Almighty Throne, does not and will not neglect the defence of the people.' The problem with this formulation, as Tipu was aware, was that the defence of Islam and the defence of Hindustan might not be the same task. 'All Hindostan', he perceived, 'is over-run with infidels [Christians] and polytheists [Hindus], excepting the Khoodadaud Sirkar, which like the Ark of Noah are safe under the protection and bounteous aid of God.' It was his hope, 'that as at the appearance of a second Adam, the religion of Islam will obtain exclusive prevalence over the whole country of Hindostan, and that the sinful heretics will with the utmost ease become the prey of the swords of the combatants in the cause of religion'. However, the political situation in the country obliged him at the same time to bear in mind the distinction between the infidels of the country and those from abroad. A jihad, he saw, must, in the first instance, be directed at the latter: 'Be it known to those who stand at the foot of the imperial throne, that the treachery, deceit, and supremacy of the Christians in the regions of Hindostan, are beyond the power of expression.'[228] Yet an ambiguity persisted in his attitude to the 'infidels belonging to the country'.

The Marathas, too, spoke of 'Swadharma'[229] and 'Dharmarajya'[230] occasionally, but they did not place their struggle against the English so squarely upon a religious ground. In the correspondence between the Marathas and the other Hindu princes, the term 'kafir' (infidel) was used to designate the English pejoratively. This was an Islamic term. When so used by a Hindu pen, it acquired a political rather than a religious connotation,[231] alternating with the term '*firangi*'.[232] For Maratha allies in Bharatpur, the cause of religion was an additional consideration; 'for in this country, which is a most sanctified place of worship, and the residence of our God, how can we support the slaughter of cows ... .' The Bharatpur courtiers, however, realized that for the Marathas, the principal consideration was 'the dominion of the Mahrattas', which the English were perceived as being bent upon removing 'from this country'.[233] As the authorities in London also saw, 'the Mahratta confederacy, though the power of the Peishwa is but imperfectly maintained, is yet so far a body politic as to make the acts of each member a matter of common concern to all'.[234] The problem was that these bonds would not stretch beyond the Maratha confederacy, nor was the flag of the Marathas,[235] a likely rallying point for other members of the Indian body politic. The Maratha confederacy was a predatory organization with a claim upon a quarter of the revenues of the Mughal realm. As such, it was feared by the Company and the country powers alike:

> The Mahrattas claim the choute of all India; and all the claims of this description centre in the Peishwa's authority. Besides this general claim, there are others of various descriptions and denominations upon every power, of all which there are records at Poonah; and it is a mistake to suppose that the Peishwa, however weak in terms of troops and resources, will not find persons in the Mahratta empire ready and willing to enforce these claims in his name.[236]

This was hardly a promising basis for leadership of India against the English Company. The Marathas had no political vocabulary to express their sentiments in terms wider than saving the 'Maratha state' (*rajya*) and the 'Peshwa's possession' (*daulat*) from its enemies.[237] 'It was mutual cooperation and good will', the Holkar declared at one point, 'which enabled our ancestors to build the Maratha State.' What moved him was that the 'Maratha state had been grasped by foreigners', and 'how necessary it was for all of us [i.e. Holkar, Sindia and Bhonsle] to join in averting foreign domination'.[238] 'The English', he warned, 'are waiting at the gate for a chance to seize the Maratha State.'[239] Sindia dwelt for his part on how 'all our hope centres in this small tender plant, the young peshwa, upon whose strength the fate of the Maratha State delicately hangs'.[240] These were not sentiments that would appeal to the Nizam, or to Haidar Ali and son. The Mughal declaration of war upon the Company had been couched in terms of imperial restoration deriving from a legitimate sovereignty over India as a whole. Unlike the league of the Mughal princes (1764), the Indian confederacy (1780) had no coherent ideology, nor a common vocabulary. The political framework of India built around the acknowledged authority of Shah Alam had in the intervening period broken down. As a Mughal poet of Delhi declared:

> Sikhs, Marathas, pickpockets, beggars, kings—all prey on us
> Happy is he who has no wealth; this is the one true wealth today.[241]

Despite the dismantlement of the Mughal structure, Mughal sentiments were by no means reconciled to the ascendancy of the English. In order to collect money for the war in the Deccan, Warren Hastings bullied and imprisoned Raja Chait Singh of Banaras in 1781. No sooner was it reported that the Raja's retainers had risen in arms than Mughal noblemen in Murshidabad, Banaras, and Faizabad contemplated pouncing upon the fleeing Governor-General. 'Kill that man', a young Mughal from Murshidabad urged Mirza Saadat Ali at Banaras.

> Kill that man: he is only with another Frenghee in the field yonder, flying for his life; say but one word, and four of us shall go and dispatch them both, and bring you his head; and after that, march down from hence to the very gates of Calcutta. There is not one man in arms from hence to Moorshoodabad, or if there be any, on seeing the head they will all desert to you; all the Zemindars will join you with a whistle; this day two months I will salute you Lord of Bengal ... .[242]

Mirza Saadat Ali, brother of the ruling Nawab of Awadh, asked the man to take a dip in the Ganges to cool his fever. English suspicions were aroused, and the Begams of Awadh, whom Warren Hastings had caused to be dispoiled, were accused of having instigated the zamindars in the disturbances that spread through Banaras, Bhojpur, and Awadh.

Divested of the means for waging war, the dispossessed Mughals merged with the crowd in the popular uprisings against the Company. 'What! are we not men as well as Cheyt-Sing's people?' the cry was heard among the best Mughal company in Murshidabad. Any man, it was argued in this circle, could kill the fleeing Governor-General with ease—'and this would have at once produced a revolution'. When it was pointed out that the English had an army of sepoys at Berhampore, the dispossessed Mughal shot back, '... are they not Hindostanies? And at all events we are much multitudes here—with each a brick-bat in our hands we could knock them down to a man.'[243]

The under-tide of popular anger carried the confederacy of the Indian princes forward in their confrontation with the Company. English reverses at one end of India caused rumours and signals to fly to the other. A full fifteen days before the Presidency of Bengal got an official account of the disaster that had befallen English arms at Wadgaon, a Muslim Frenchman living in Murshidabad and going about in Hindustani attire found the town in ferment. The 'signs of this national sullenness'[244] appeared to him even more unmistakably when news of the flight of Warren Hastings from the wrath of Chait Singh's retainers reached Murshidabad. M. Raymond, alias Haji Mustafa, seeing that the English had 'alienated all hearts', wrote to an English acquaintance, 'All hearts! *Can that be true?* ... and yet behold! Hardly is this man supposed killed, than *all, all* Sir (it is the very word), *all* think of rising on the English.'[245] In Banaras itself, as a toothless old broker recalled with pleasure, the sabre had worked well ('*Talwar Khoob Chelaw*'). Raymond pointed out to the man that the English forces had no supply of shot when Chait Singh's men broke out without warning. 'And suppose they should have had,' the old man turned in fury, 'Ten Thousands would have been pouring upon them, instead of Ten Hundreds; and the whole city would have risen upon the Frenghees and their adherents.'[246]

At this very time the people of the Carnatic hailed Haidar Ali as a deliverer notwithstanding the devastation caused by his expedition. They informed him of every movement made by the English columns, and helped him storm the fort of Arcot. All English letters from the Coromandel coast seemed to concur 'that from Ganjam to Cape Comorin, there was not a native, but proved disaffected to the English ...'[247] The oppressive rule of the Nawab of Arcot had alienated every subject, and rumours were rife throughout the peninsula that the English, upon their ascendancy in Bengal, had 'forcibly taken prisoners, wives and daughters, violated their chastity, and carried them off to their own islands and country ...'.[248]

As if in concert, rumours of English defeat in the peninsula caused wild excitement in the Gangetic valley. As the confederacy won important military points in the contest with the Company, the news spread that General Goddard had been forced by the Marathas to retreat to Bombay (true); and that General Eyre Coote of Wandiwash fame had been obliged by Haidar Ali to shut himself up in the fort of Madras (not quite true).[249] Popular support of the military operations of the confederacy exposed the English forces to peril in theatres of war uncomfortably close to their bases at Bombay and Madras. The Maratha tactic 'of retiring before us and ravaging the country' starved the Bombay troops marching upon Poona into surrender at Wadgaon, where the hostility of the population confronted them with the 'total impossibility of a supply'.[250]

The better prepared forces of General Goddard won no better success in a more organized march upon Poona. Maratha horse chased him down the Ghats all the way to Bombay. The Maratha mode of war—of 'repeated skirmishes' by light cavalry with the aim of cutting off the enemy's supplies[251]—deprived him of the edge which Munro had earlier enjoyed at Buxar. Heavy Mughal cavalry charging *en masse* in frontal assaults had been destroyed by concerted English firing in 1764. The Marathas, whose mode of fighting avoided engaging at close quarters, harassed Goddard's fleeing column by 'irregular and unexpected assaults'. The light Maratha horse pursued the English from the hills of the Deccan to the Konkan coast through 'a country full of bushes, thickets and narrow defiles'.[252] In the Carnatic, too, the military balance changed perceptibly: no longer might 'such an undisciplined, disobedient rabble as can be collected in India', crumble before 'such a rain of fire as might be poured by the English.'[253] Instead, Madras troops fled before Mysore horse which Haidar Ali combined skilfully with fire-power. Munro, the man who routed the Wazir's forces at Buxar, fled headlong to Madras, spiking his guns to deny their use to Haidar Ali's advancing troops.[254] Eyre Coote, Munro's successor, swore that he had never *retreated* in his life, but was obliged to add that he would permit the army to *fall back*.[255] The withdrawal was unavoidable because the numerous Mysorean cavalry combined skilfully with a body of musketeers disciplined by Haidar Ali in the European manner. The Mughal chronicler noted admiringly: 'His army accoutred and furnished with every necessity, exactly as in Europe, is kept under the strictest order and discipline.'[256] Haidar's tactics—avoiding close quarters, disciplined use of firepower, and harassing the enemy by rapid movements of horse—proved more than a match for the dispirited and unpaid troops of Madras.[257]

The military balance between the Company and the confederacy proved therefore to be more even than that between the Mughals and the English. The light Maratha horse and the disciplined troops of Mysore fought the redcoats to a standstill. However, the confederacy could not press the advantage home because it lacked political and ideological cohesion. No sooner had the Marathas achieved their object of saving the state from the attack by Bombay than they concluded a separate peace with the English (1782). Tipu Sultan, who had succeeded Haidar Ali, was left to fight on alone. In the end Tipu, too, made his terms with the English (1784), neither side gaining an advantage. Incomparably more successful than the league of the Mughal princes in the fields of battle, the Indian confederacy collapsed no sooner than it was constructed because it had no ideological foundation. Had the embattled Indian princes had the perspicacity to combine under the universally acknowledged sovereignty of Shah Alam, a legitimist banner that was perhaps not altogether beyond their grasp, the tables might have been turned on the Company politically. At the crucial moment when the confederacy was born, the Marathas had, however, no presence in the Red Fort at Shahjahanabad. The Mughal state of Delhi, which had passed into the hands of the new regent Najaf Khan upon the Maratha withdrawal to Poona following Peshwa Madhav Rao's calamitous demise, was too preoccupied with local enemies to the north (Sikhs, Rohillas, et al.) to show a disposition to back the confederacy against the Company.

Scarcely had peace been restored in the peninsula, much to the relief of the English, than Maratha horse reappeared in Delhi, this time under the independent initiative of Mahadji Sindia. The new chief secured on behalf of his formal masters at Poona (the Peshwa) and Satara (the Raja) the appointment of regent (*wakil-i-mutlaq*) to Emperor Shah Alam (1784). C.W. Malet, the English Resident at Poona, wrote apprehensively in his diary:[258]

> The characters of Prime Minister to the Raja of the Deccan and the King of Hindustan, now rest with members of the Maratha Empire; and under this strange heterogeneous junction of power is united the absolute and executive management of the two empires. With the force of the one, and the claims of the other, everything is to be apprehended by the Company and their allies, and by this extraordinary concentration of powers and title, not only the Company's own possessions are open to vexatious demands, nay absolute resumption at a convenient season, but the safety of the dominions of their allies, Asoph-ud-Dowla [Awadh] and Wala Jah [Arcot], must in future rest on the will and power of the Marathas, which, if we may judge from the rapacious turn of their politics, will not be slow

in their operations, particularly under the influence of such a cheif [sic] as Sindia, who will be the grand benefiter by any acquisition of territory or revenue in the new character of Vakil-i-Mutluk.

In the event, the power of Mahadji Sindia proved unequal to the task of protecting his imperial master. An unexpected raid upon Delhi by the Rohilla chief Ghulam Qadir resulted in an event that shook all of India on 10 August 1788. The Mughal poet Mir lamented a world turned upside down, an unthinkable *inqilab*:[259]

> I lived to see the needle drawn across the eyes of kings
> The dust beneath whose feet was like collyrium ground with pearls.

The blinding of Shah Alam by the Rohillas, who were expelled with great difficulty by Mahadji Sindia, seemed to preclude any possibility of glory ever returning to the Red Fort. 'How can I describe the desolation of Delhi?' Sauda, Mir's great contemporary, wrote in his book. 'There is no house from where the jackal's cry cannot be heard.'[260]

Meanwhile, events in the peninsula seemed to be moving towards a decision with fateful implications for Delhi. No irony of politics could be keener than the diplomatic revolution by which a coalition between the Nizam, the Marathas, and the English against Mysore replaced the Indian confederacy against the Company. With incredible folly, Nizam Ali and Nana Fadnis cooperated with Lord Cornwallis in reducing Tipu's realm by half in 1792. Tipu, who had assumed the dignity of independent ruler to everyone's alarm and had emerged as the sworn enemy of the English, warned the Marathas after his defeat, 'You must realize I am not at all your enemy. Your real enemy is the Englishman of whom you must beware.'[261] It was too late. Through Pitt's India Act, the British government had imposed unified control over the English East India Company. This, and the introduction of the rule of regulations by Lord Cornawallis, forged the English colonial state in India into a powerful instrument which the imperious Lord Wellesley found ready to use for the realization of his vision of an Indian empire ruled from Calcutta.

Wellesley tied the Nizam into a subsidiary alliance, and drew the Mughal realm in the Deccan into the Company's sphere. He then proceeded to destroy Tipu. The fall of Seringapatam (1799) brought the forces of the young Wellington within striking distance of Poona at a moment when the Maratha confederacy was convulsed by yet another civil war. The new Governor-General's massive intervention destroyed the confederacy. The second Maratha war, in which Daulat Rao Sindia's forces were routed before Delhi, substituted for the balance of power the hegemony of the East India Company (1803). The symbol of this new hegemony was the English possession of the Red Fort and its blind sovereign. The 'men with turbans' had yielded there to those 'who wear hats'.[262]

Wellesley considered 'placing the person, family and nominal authority of his Majesty Shah Alam under the protection of the British Government' to be 'a principal object, though not a cause of the war, and an indispensable condition of the peace'.[263] He was concerned by the declarations of French officers in India, some of them employed in the service of Sindia, that 'Shah Alam ought to be the undisputed sovereign of the Mughal Empire'. A French 'Memoir on the Real Importance of India and the most efficacious means to re-establish the French Nation in its Ancient Splendour'[264] dwelt on the fact that 'his [Shah Alam's] sovereignty is universally acknowledged although his power is no more', and hinted threateningly that 'the English Company derived its own constitutional power from his infinite goodness'. The document then went on to draw the following inferences from this fact:

> The English Company, by its ignominious treatment of the great Moghul, has forfeited its right as dewan and treasurer of the Empire; the Nobobs of Oude and Bengal are equally criminal, because they have acted as traitors towards their lawful sovereign: thus the Emperor of Delhi has a real and indisputable right to transmit to whomsoever he may select, the sovereignty of his dominions, as well as the arrears due to him from the English.

The importance of securing the nominal authority of the Mughal against the designs of France prompted Wellesley to offer what he called an honourable and tranquil asylum to Shah Alam. Once the Red Fort was under English occupation, however, the Governor-General declared that 'no obligation was imposed upon us to consider the rights and claims of his Majesty Shah Aulum as Emperor of Hindoostan'.[265]

'The Progress of Political Philosophy'

The overthrow of the lawful power of the Mughal sovereigns, the usurpation of their dominions by rival upstarts, the ascendancy of strangers from overseas—these confusing developments appeared in the eyes of contemporary Mughal poets and historians as topsy-turvy (*inqilab*). The word revolution or *inqilab* was thus explained in the Persian dictionary of Tek Chand Bahar (1740): '*Inqilab*. To be turned topsy-turvy (*wazgūn shudan*). Used with the words *giriftan, uftādan,* i.e. [for fortune] to be changed totally ....'[266] Contemporaries understood by it an inversion of the time-honoured scheme of things, an overturn (*inqilab*) in which the high and noble fell and the lowly rose to the top. 'How can one describe the ups and downs of the world,' lamented a late Mughal poet to whom the world appeared to be upside down as those who had ridden elephants in the good old days went around barefooted while those who had once craved for parched grains now owned palaces and elephants. As the once prosperous Mughal towns of Delhi, Agra, Patna and Murshidabad withered away, the catastrophe evoked a brand of poetry known as the 'Town in Lament' (*Shahr-i-Ashob*), with *inqilab* at the centre of its theme. A poet of Patna complained that Mughal troopers were so afflicted by poverty that they could not afford a toy clay horse; another poet of the same town pointed to the contrast presented by 'the cavalry of Lalas and Babus' going tumultuously through town.[267] Overwhelmed by 'the impression of changing fortune', these poets saw the age as one in which everything had been 'turned upside down'. 'We are living in a special kind of age', wrote Sauda. 'Ours is a dark age', said Mir.[268]

> This age is not like that which went before it.
> The times have changed, the earth and sky have changed.[269]

Late Mughal historians subjected this *inqilab* to a closer analysis. Among them, the most prominent was Saiyid Ghulam Husain Khan, whose analysis of the economic effects of early English rule and the reversal of the flows of trade, specie, and consumption under the Company marked him out as the first Indian proponent of the doctrine of the drain of wealth to Britain. Unlike Dadabhai Naoroji, M.G. Ranade, or R.C. Dutt, this Mughal nobleman was incapable, by birth and social affiliation, of envisioning a new world. However, although he yearned for the older order disappearing around him, his roots gave him an insight into the evils of the English system that could not but add a radical dimension to his political philosophy. In those days Englishmen themselves were not circumspect about the effects of their rule: an English 'plan for the conservation and augmentation of current specie of Bengal' (1785) estimated that prior to Plassey, European and Indian merchants annually imported bullion worth Rs 2 crores.

Subsequently, the flow was reversed and there was an annual specie drain of Rs 1 crore, 'to the impoverishment of this country, to the great Detriment of the Revenue, and to the Ruin of Commerce'.[270] The reversal of the flows, which in the eyes of Ghulam Husain Khan was part of the *inqilab*, caused an evident reduction of consumption and employment in the country, and a melancholy revolution of the classes. He saw these as 'hard times' in which 'the remaining stock of the ancient nobility' had 'not a single resource left under the canopy of the Hindostany heaven'. Their precipitous fall from the command of horse threw between forty and fifty thousand troopers out of pay in Bengal. Handicraftsmen, deprived of aristocratic purchasers of their products, were at the same time reduced to 'begging or thieving'.[271]

In an implicit plea for the restoration of the Mughal way of governance, Ghulam Husain Khan pointed out that during the time of Alivardi Khan, the revenues received at Murshidabad and the fortunes of the Mughal nobility were spent upon the country. Not so under the English. They 'had a custom of coming for a number of years, and then of going away to pay a visit to their native country, without anyone of them showing an inclination to fix himself in this land'. To this custom they joined another, 'which everyone of these emigrants holds to be of divine obligation': this was 'scraping together as much money in this country as they can and carrying it in immense sums to the kingdom of England'. Ghulam Husain Khan could distinctly recall a time when these very gentlemen imported gold and silver every year 'which procured an abundant circulation and promoted everyone's good'. Seeing this revolution of fortunes, the Mughal nobleman was not surprised that 'these two customs, blended together, should be ever undermining and ruining this country'.[272]

As noblemen, soldiers, merchants, and artisans alike fell upon hard days, Ghulam Husain Khan saw how the 'Gentlemen' and 'their Mootsuddies or officers and dependants' rose to power over the ruin of the old order. The *mutasaddis* were a breed that prevented high and low alike from approaching their masters for justice, as the complaints were as often as not against these very people. The aversion which Ghulam Husain Khan saw Englishmen evince for the company of Indians, and the disdain with which the *mutasaddis* treated visiting Indian gentlemen of ancient and illustrious families, filled him with a sense of indignation.[273] This revolution of the classes, a process accompanied by 'a variety of affronts and indignities', was acknowledged by the English judges and magistrates newly appointed by Lord Wellesley:

The greatest men formerly were the Musalman rulers, whose places we have taken, and the Hindoos zemindars—These two classes are now ruined and destroyed—the natives mostly looked up to, are our Omlah and our domestics: these are courted and respected: they must necessarily be the channel through which every suitor and every candidate looks up for redress and preferment.[274]

This was *inqilab*, in the negative contemporary sense of the term. As Wellesley saw, the Muslim gentry (*ashraf*) of the reduced Mughal towns raged over it. His arrival in India coincided with the suppression of the rebellion of the banished Nawab of Awadh, Wazir Ali. The dethroned ruler of Lucknow killed the British Resident and fled from Banaras in 1799. The inquiries following this abortive rebellion led to the apprehension of Shamsuddaulah, a relation of the Nawab of Bengal. It appeared that this young Mughal had invited Zaman Shah of Kabul to redress what he perceived as the fall of Muslim power in India. These events put Wellesley 'in possession of sufficient evidence to prove that a conspiracy has been formed for the purpose not only of restoring Vizier Ali to the throne of Oude, but also of favouring the invasion of Zemaun Shah, and of expelling the English nation from the provinces of Bengal, Bihar and Orissa'.[275] Wellesley observed that the persons concerned in 'this treason' were 'almost exclusively Mahommedans, and several of them of high rank'. He dwelt anxiously on 'the disaffection of this description of our subjects, whom we found in possession of the Government, and whom we have excluded from all share of emolument, honour and authority, without providing any adequate corrective of those passions incident the loss of dignity, wealth and status'.[276]

The Persian and Urdu poetry of the eighteenth century conveys the impression that the notion of *inqilab* was generally shared, and was not confined to the fallen aristocrats alone. The sense of topsy-turvy extended to the Hindu section of the population, and could be traced as far down as the Carnatic. A Smartha Brahman of the south, who composed *The Pleasure of All Gods* in Sanskrit some time between 1767 and 1817, referred disparagingly to the whitefaced upstarts (*sveta-mukhas*) and posed the question, 'So now how do they put up with the upstarts who have uprooted the righteous order of varna and ashrama? Tell me.'[277] The simple answer to the question, as one English Judge and Magistrate suggested, was that the overthrow of the former Muslim rulers, and the disarming of the country magnates, had left their subjects with no leader to keep them 'in a state of union'. The greatest zamindar in his district, though possibly a proud man, would not refuse to court the friendship of the lowest dependent of a European: 'There is scarcely a native in this district, who thinks of sitting down, in the presence of an English gentleman.'[278]

The mud-forts dotting the country had fallen into decay and nothing remained of them but the ditches and the bastions covered with jungle.[279] The population, disarmed for all practical purposes except the thick bamboo bludgeons and spears left in the hands of the lower classes of natives, was under the rule of 'the Regulations' promulgated by the East India Company which the majority of them could barely comprehend. The English government under Lord Wellesley appeared to be strong and secure, though the natives could 'hardly be said to be attached to it': for 'none of them understand it'. Indeed, 'No Government ever stood more independent of public opinion.'[280] Henry Strachey, the Judge and Magistrate of Midnapore, could see 'no tendency whatsoever to improvement among the natives, except their increasing knowledge of the Regulations, which in speaking of the progress of political philosophy, is scarcely worth mentioning'.[281]

Imperceptibly, however, in the coastal presidencies of the English, the rule of the law was fostering the growth of a civil society. The insensible emergence of public opinion was effecting a deeper revolution in political thought and sensibilities beneath the *inqilab* lamented by the poets and historians of the old order. As early as 1765, the first Indian visitor to England, Mirza Shaikh Ihtisamuddin, had discerned that the laws of England, made with the consent of the king's subjects, provided greater stability than Mughal rule in India which lacked a set of rules and was, therefore, vulnerable to intrigues, civil wars, and revolutions. The Englishmen's love of liberty, and their sentiment, 'We are no one's slave and servant', impressed this Mughal gentleman from Bengal, who nevertheless felt homesick: 'Love of one's own land is nobler than the throne of Solomon. The thorn of one's land of birth is sweeter than a fragrant flower.'[282] As English rule was set firmly into a 'constitutional' framework by Cornwallis, it guaranteed personal security and absolute rights to property through the courts of law, even against the Company's government, to a new breed of Indians able to operate within the colonial legal system.

In many ways this was but a caricature of the system which Mirza Shaikh Ihtisamuddin admired in England. 'Such is the justice of the courts that no one has the power to oppress the poor people,' he said of the courts of law he saw there.[283] The Company's courts in India were a different proposition altogether. The generation that would operate successfully within the system, 'Natives of wealth and respectability, as well as the Landholders of consequence', were well aware of the arbitrariness of the system of courts and regulations within which they had consolidated their position. The reformer Rammohan Roy, who belonged to that generation, was to point out how 'the present system of English judges and Native Pleaders' fostered the crime of perjury to such a degree that 'it is impossible to distinguish what is true from what is not'.[284] All the same, he was profoundly aware that the Permanent Settlement and the rule of the Regulations was the *magna carta* of the new society around him: an irrevocable guarantee that 'their lives, religion and property [would] be secured'.[285]

The collapse of the Mughals, Marathas, and other powers led to a perceptible shift in the nature and basis of opposition to the Company. After 1803, the restoration of Mughal rule was no longer a tenable creed either politically or even ideologically. Reactions to the establishment of the hegemony of the East India Company, however, differed markedly from one section of Indian society to another. The rule of the regulations and the creation of absolute property crystallized a range of attitudes to the new dispensation which ran counter to one another, fostering thereby an unlooked for 'progress of political philosophy'. The essence of the new order, as Lord Wellesley conceived it, was the rule of law. He was quick to identify those who were inclined to defy that law and its rule altogether, but he was not quick enough to anticipate those who might try and turn that law upon its framers.

'The early administration of the Company', wrote Lord Wellesley to the Court of Directors in 1800, 'succeeded to the despotic power of the native princes.' Those princes, he thought, united in their persons the whole executive, legislative, and judicial powers of the state, and exercised them according to 'the dictates of their own discretion'. Experience of 'the evils attendant on this form of Government' induced the Company to adopt a model of Government 'analogous to that which forms the basis of the British constitution'. The lines between the legislative, executive, and judicial authorities were 'distinctly drawn'. However, the situation dictated one departure from the English model: the Governor-General in Council found it necessary to exercise the entire legislative authority. Wellesley acknowledged the implication of this deviation: '... we excluded our native subjects from all participation in the legislative authority.' However, in his view an effectual guarantee against every abuse of this was 'the fundamental principle of the new constitution' that the Governor-General in the Council should print and publish every legislative Act. 'His executive authority as far as regards the internal government, will be subject to the control of laws, and the due administration of laws, will be secured by the courts appointed to administer them being rendered entirely distinct, both from the executive and legislative authority ....'[286]

The doctors of Islamic law (*ulama*) and the Muslim gentry (*ashraf*) of the towns of northern India were not intellectually conditioned to accept these definitions of despotism, law, and liberty; but in Bengal a great many Hindus of wealth and respectability (*bhadralok*) were inclined to recognize 'the security of private rights and property'[287] which Wellesley's government claimed to have conferred on the country.

Throughout the period of Maratha occupation of Delhi, the ulama had continued to regard the country as a land of peace (*dar-ul-Islam*) in view of the careful preservation of the external forms of Mughal sovereignty. No sooner, however, did Lord Wellesley do away with these pretensions than the leading Muslim theologian of the capital declared that Shah Alam, the imperial protector of the Muslims (*imam-al-Muslimin*) no longer had any authority in the town. 'From here to Calcutta', pronounced Shah Abdul Aziz (1746–1824), 'the Christians are in complete control.' Eldest among the sons of Shah Waliullah, he followed his father's puritanical line and decreed that the areas under English control were now a land of war (*dar-ul-harb*).[288] There was no longer any check on the Christan authorities, and the promulgation of their sinful commands meant 'that in administration and justice, in the domain of trade, finance and collection of revenues—everywhere the kuffar are in power'.[289]

The implication which his disciple Saiyid Ahmad Khan of Rai Bareilly and his own nephew Shah Ismail Shahid drew from this was that holy war (*jihad*) was obligatory. Ismail Shahid set out Saiyid Ahmad Khan's sayings in a tract entitled *The Straight Path* (*Sirat-i-Mustaqim*). A despot was defined therein as 'a person ... who does what he wants without any regard for the shariah and for custom'. 'It is such people,' the tract pronounced, 'whose government I call despotism and whom I call despots.' These definitions constituted, of course, the very antithesis to Wellesley's ideas. The leaders of this movement for puritanical reform forbade Muslims from serving the English as clerks, servants, or soldiers, and laid an injunction upon learning English for the promotion of better relations with the rulers.[290] Dubbed 'Wahabis' by the British, the followers of the straight path of Shah Waliullah and Saiyid Ahmad Khan were destined to become a prominent element in the Mutiny.

Among the *bhadralok* of Bengal, by contrast, the 'increasing knowledge of the Regulations' produced an advance in political philosophy of quite a different sort, and sooner than the prescient Judge and Magistrate of Midnapore had anticipated in 1802. Not seven years elapsed before Rammohun Roy called out the Collector of Bhagalpur for the personal indignity of requiring him to alight from his palanquin to perform the *salaam* expected of a native. His appeal to the Governor-General, with the admonition that 'the spirit of the British laws would not tolerate an Act of Arbitrary aggression' against the lowest individual, not to speak of 'persons of respectability', resulted in the English collector being warned 'against having any similar altercation with any of the Natives in the future'.[291]

Rammohun Roy and his generation were aware 'that the more valuable privileges of the English Law, and the rights which it bestows were confined to the ruling class, to Europeans ...'.[292] Their demand for 'an equality of privileges'[293] initiated the constitutional agitation of the new generation of Indians for the right of self-determination. Rammohun Roy had the premonition that he would not 'live to see liberty universally restored to the nations of Europe, and Asiatic nations, especially those that are English colonies, possessed of a greater degree of the same blessing than they now enjoy'. Nevertheless he wrote to an English friend, 'Enemies to liberty and friends of despotism have never been and never will be successful.'[294] This was neither Lord Wellesley's judgement that liberty had replaced despotism, nor Saiyid Ahmad Khan's belief that despotism had replaced liberty. Embodying both views, it exposed the paradox of a despotism professedly based on the rule of law. The internalization of the notions of individual liberty and national self-determination indicated the extent of the progress of political philosophy.

Nearly half a century had passed since Mirza Sheikh Ihtisamuddin had remarked on 'a new mode in England, that is, the printing of books'. The first Indian visitor to London still preferred calligraphy.[295] The Company's press in Calcutta was confined to printing Acts and Regulations in English and the vernacular languages. The growth of the bench, the bar, and the press, and the consolidation of a class of 'persons of respectability' within the framework of property and the rule of the regulations changed all this. Between 1810 and 1820, 15,000 works were printed and sold in the Bengali language,[296] a sure sign that a printing and information revolution was on the way, and that public opinion was making itself felt in the emerging civil society. A petition by the citizens of Calcutta to the Supreme Court against an ordinance of the government imposing new restraints on the vernacular press dwelt in 1823 on the fact 'that ever since the art of printing has become generally known among the Natives of Calcutta, numerous Publications have been circulated in the Bengallee Language, which by introducing free discussion among the Natives and inducing them to reflect and inquire after knowledge, have already served greatly to improve their minds and ameliorate their condition'.[297] Unlike the Muslim divines of northern India, these men of affairs in Calcutta appreciated the importance of providing their sons with an English education, a purpose for which they set up the Hindoo College in 1817. The new nationalism conceived in the minds of the young students of the college conveyed itself in the unmistakable language of their Eurasian teacher, Henry Louis Vivian Derozio:[298]

> My country! in thy days of glory past
> A beauteous halo circled round thy brow,
> And worshipped as a deity thou wast,
> Where is that glory, where that reverence now?
> The eagle pinion is chained down at last
> And grovelling in the lowly dust art thou:
> Thy minstrel hath no wreath to weave for thee,
> Save the sad story of thy misery!

Did this nationalism, which would find organizational shape in the Indian National Congress of 1885, have any connection with the resistance to the establishment of colonial domination in the late eighteenth and early nineteenth centuries? Quite the contrary. During the Pindari and Maratha wars of 1817–18, which led to the acknowledgement of the Company's paramountcy, the classes patronizing the Hindoo college offered prayers for the success of the English 'from a deep conviction that under the sway of that nation, their improvement both mental and social, would be promoted, and their lives, religion and property be secured'.[299] The social basis of this English-inspired nationalism being so different, its ideas, too, could not but be radically opposed to those of the earlier Indian resistance to colonial subjugation. In view of this discontinuity between the initial resistance to the English and the later Indian nationalism, it is important to try and trace the changing forms of discontent, identity, and patriotism in the first century of British rule in India. One problem that arises in connection with the trajectory of the ideas of early Indian resistance is the question whether the Company's opponents in the old order had any sense of Indian identity, a component, as it were, of national feeling, howsoever different it might be from the sensibilities of the nationalist movement of the nineteenth century.

In response to a query from Wellesley's government, whether there were persons '"supposed to be" disaffected to the British Government',[300] the judges and magistrates of the districts of Bengal could see no such sentiments in the population. The natives had 'no idea of loyalty, or disloyalty, except to their masters who support them'; indeed, 'they would see a revolution with apathy and indifference, and would submit to the tyranny of any future Government, with perfect resignation. The magistrates made only one tentative exception to this: the displaced Mughal nobleman. They alone were capable of conceiving the political destiny of the country as a whole, and they alone had a clear view of the alternative to English rule. The Mughal wars (1756–64) and the Mughal conspiracies against the Company (1799) were inspired by notions of preservation or restoration of the Mughal order. The confederacy of the Indian princes (1780–1782) had no such positive vision, but they did enjoy the support of the population in their opposition towards the foreigners.

What could be the emotional basis of the resistance of the 'men with turbans' to those who 'wear hats', except some sense of Indian nationality, however elusive? Sirajuddaulah's conquest of Calcutta, Shah Alam's expedition to Bengal, the all-out war of Mir Qasim, the league of the Mughal princes at Buxar, the conspiracies of Wazir Ali and Shamsuddaulah, were all actions and engagements informed by an old world Mughal patriotism in which membership of the political community was by no means confined to the Muslim noblemen alone. Various classes of the population, and both Hindus and Muslims were involved in the commonalty of action and sentiment against the foreigner. One European who went native, and who was in a position to feel the pulse of the people, was convinced that the Indian body politic was not devoid of national feeling. Living in the centre of Murshidabad, wearing the dress of a Muslim, and making a practice in the evening to walk the streets to mix with the company there or in the market place, M. Raymond, known there as Haji Mustafa, had access to a variety of information denied to the ordinary European.

While translating the *Siyar-ul-Mutakhkhirin*, Raymond felt in Saiyid Ghulam Husain Khan's narrative 'a subterranean vein of national resentment, which emits vapours now and then, and which his occasional encomiums of the English can neither conceal nor even palliate'. The translator was convinced that the author was 'but a voice that has spoken among a million others that could speak but are silent: nor have signs of this national sullenness been wanting these sixteen years'.[301] Raymond then went on to recount various incidents, both from his personal experience and from the *Siyar*, which formed 'the loose links of a chain that seemed once to bind the whole nation at large'.[302] The word nation was used in eighteenth century English and French in a looser sense than political scientists interpret it now, and in that looser sense Raymond as well as other Europeans did use the word with regard to the people of Hindustan. Raymond warned the English readers of his translation: 'The general turn of the English individuals in India seems to be a thorough contempt for the Indians (*as a national body*). It is taken to be no better than a dead stock, that may be worked upon without much consideration and at pleasure. But beware! that national body is only motionless, but neither insensible nor dead.'[303]

Ghulam Husain Khan, the man whom this French Creole born in Istanbul translated into English, would have used the term '*qaum*' in the Persian text for the equivalent 'nation' substituted in the English translation; both terms would have signified, with equal facility, a race, a community, a people, at the time; for political science had not yet made that linguistic intervention which would indelibly stamp upon the term a new concept. This is the sovereign national state exercising a legitimate monopoly of the means of violence in a defined stretch of territory, and deriving the right to do this from the will of all the subjects, or citizens, arrayed behind this unhindered authority. Nation, community, race, people, all these meanings still slid into one another at ease, and all might bear the connotation of patriotic feelings which coalesced the mass. Nation, in other words, did not have to signify nationalism, a term which did not then exist. What nation meant at the time was a community of persons united by the patriotic sentiments adhering to that people. Such sentiments might be religious, ethnic, or political. The Latin derivative 'patriotism' did not adequately cover this range of feelings, but the term was in English usage then and it did connote the keen sentiments that might be common to a religious community, an ethnic group, or a people striving to acquire or protect their own political space. It is in that sense that Saiyid Ghulam Husain Khan spoke of *qaum*, or nation, in his *Review of the Moderns*.

The Mughal historian conveys a sense of the nation at large while dwelling on the differences between Hindus and Muslims; and, of course, Hindustanis, Muslims, Hindus, are all equally, as far as he is concerned, *qaum*s. Saiyid Ghulam Husain Khan was of the view that the Muslim conquerors, despite their foreign origin, were assimilated among the people of India. They learned the language of the country; and unlike the English, they behaved to the native inhabitants of the land 'as brothers of one mother and one language'.[304] Although the Hindus appeared to the Muslims a strange people, differentiated from the rest of mankind by rites and tenets that rendered all Muslims aliens and profane, yet the two *qaum*s drew nearer in course of time. Dissimilarity and alienation gave way to friendship and union, and 'the two nations'[305] coalesced together 'into one whole.'

As soon as the initial state of warfare, slaughter, and confusion came to an end, the Muslim sovereigns of Delhi settled down to living among their subjects 'as kind and condescending parents amongst their children'. Under the Mughal emperors, 'everything in Hindostan was quietness, love and harmony',[306] until the empire was torn by cabals, and 'European foreigners' began 'casting their eyes upon the conquest of India'.[307] But even in the empire in its enfeebled state, there were outstanding rulers like Alivardi Khan of Bengal whom Ghulam Husain Khan recalled with personal fondness: 'he looked upon all his subjects to be creatures of one and the same God, and brothers of one and the same mother; and used to promote Gentoos and other dissenters, according to their merits, and just on the same footing with the Mussulmen themselves.'[308] It was quite otherwise with the English, who came as strangers and remained so: '*such is the aversion which the English openly shew for the company of the natives, and such the disdain they betray for them, that no love, and no coalition ... can take root between the conquerors and the conquered ...*'.[309]

Ghulam Husain Khan then went on to make certain deductions about the altered equation of identities in the new situation: the people of Hindustan, both Hindus and Muslims, were one *qaum*, and the English, their conquerors in Bengal, another, with a strange and alien government opposed to the Mughal government of the country. 'In one word, it may be said in general, and indeed in almost every institution and custom, that there is a wide difference betwixt the two nations and Governments; and that it is of such a nature as cannot be remedied at all.'[310] If the Hindus and Muslims at one time were two nations, so were the Indians and the English two nations now.

Ghulam Husain Khan had no doubt in his mind as to which one of the two governments 'the people of this country'[311] preferred. He saw with his own eyes how quickly a political union of the subjects of the Mughal emperor occurred in Patna at the time when Shahzada Ali Gauhar came there for the purpose of 'waging war against the English nation'. When the glad news spread that the prince was coming to Patna, 'there was not an inhabitant, or a citizen, who, on the strength of the favours and the good government they had formerly experienced under the Prince's forefathers and ancestors, did not pray for victory to him, and for prosperity in his undertaking'. The people seemed to Ghulam Husain Khan 'to have but one mouth and one heart, although not one of them had yet received any favour from him, or tasted of the crumbs that might have fallen from the table of His Goodness'.[312] Ghulam Husain Khan added impartially that the people turned against the prince when his troops plundered the country. They then prayed for the victory of the English army, but not for long. '[T]he Hindians'[313] were rapidly disillusioned with their new English rulers: 'those same people feel nothing for them now, fully sensible that these new rulers pay no regard or attention to the concerns of Hindostanies'.[314]

'... Those same people, I say, reduced now to despair, have altered their language, and totally changed in their hearts,' said the Mughal historian in 1780. These same anti-English sentiments, that formed the basis of Mughal patriotism at the time, would provide the emotional foundation of later Indian nationalism. The mind, it should be noted, operates at two levels: the brain and the heart. Looking at the successive generations of Saiyid Ghulam Husain Khan and Rammohun Roy, it is evident that the intellectual attitudes of the Indians towards the English changed considerably in these two generations. However, with regard to the aliens the same emotional otherness persisted in the psychic sphere. The Indian patriotism/nationalism of Henry Louis Vivian Derozio in the third generation derived as much from the altered intellectual attitudes as from the persistent instinctive otherness. No history impervious to this will delve deep.

The Mughal cause, however popular, was a lost cause. It appealed to a past that was beyond recall, and it was unable to evoke a new vision. Even so, it lived on. The widespread loyalty of all sections of the population to the Mughal throne was capable of producing an instant coalition of sentiments and aspirations at moments of political crisis. The founder of the English empire of India was aware of this. 'Notwithstanding his Majesty's total deprivation of real power, dominion and authority', Wellesley said in 1804, 'almost every state and every class of people in India continue to acknowledge his nominal sovereignty.' Though His Majesty was no longer the master of the Red Fort, he pointed out at the time:

> The current coin of every established power is struck in the name of Shah Aulum. Princes and persons of the highest rank and family still bear the titles, and display the insignia of rank which they or their ancestors derived from the throne of Delhi, under the acknowledged authority of Shah Aulum, and his Majesty is still considered to be the only legitimate fountain of similar honours.[315]

In 1831 Rammohan Roy, representing the case of the Mughal Emperor in London, dwelt on 'the greater stability to the power of the British Government, attained by securing the grateful friendship of a monarch, who though without territorial possession, was still regarded by the nations of Hindoostan as the only legitimate foundation of either honour or dominion'.[316]

The mystique of the person of the Mughal Emperor was a factor that could not be ignored in Indian politics. In 1857 the British lost their control over his person to a group of mutinous sepoys from Meerut; immediately English rule collapsed all over the Ganga–Jumna valley as far down as Allahabad. It would be yet another generation before a national congress could replace the person of the emperor as the focus of 'the people of this country'. In the intervening period the intellectual outlook changed profoundly, but the spontaneous sentiments that distinguished all turbaned men from the hat-wearers were exactly the same. The fact that many a turbaned man's son now wore the hat did not alter this emotional polarity.

Notes and References

1. *Freedom Struggle in Uttar Pradesh. Source Material*, ed. S.A.A. Razvi (Publications Bureau, Uttar Pradesh, 1957–), henceforth *FSUP*, vol. v, p. 331.

2. Nanda Lal Chatterjee, *Mir Qasim* (Allahabad, 1935).

3. *Original Papers Relative to the Disturbances in Bengal Containing Every Material Transaction from 1759 to 1764*, 2 vols (London, 1765) (henceforth *Original Papers*). Shorter extracts are given in Henry Vansittart, *A Narrative of the Transactions in Bengal 1760–1764* (henceforth *Narrative*) (rpt Calcutta, 1976; first published 1766).

4. Brijen K. Gupta, *Siraduddaulah and the East India Company 1756–1757: Background to the Foundation of British Power in India* (London, 1962); Atul Chandra Roy, *The Career of Mir Jafar Khan (1757–1765 AD)* (Calcutta, 1953); Abdul Majed Khan, *The Transition in Bengal 1756–1775: A Study of Saiyid Muhammad Reza Khan* (Cambridge, 1969).

5. The following account of political changes in Bengal is based on Ghulam Husain Salim, *Riyazu-s-Salatin* (henceforth *Riyaz*), tr. Abdul Salam (Calcutta, 1902–1904); the English translation of Salimullah's *Tawarikh-i-Bangala* by Francis Gladwin, entitled *A Narrative of the Transactions in Bengal* (n.d.); Saiyid Ghulam Husain Khan, *Sèir Mutaherin* (henceforth *Seir*) tr. Nota Manus, or Haji Mustafa, rpt, (Calcutta, 1902); James Grant, 'An Historical and Comparative Analysis of the Finances of Bengal'. (henceforth 'Analysis') in *The Fifth Report from the Select Committee on the Affairs of the East India Company* (henceforth *Fifth Report*), vol. 1 (London, 1812).

6. Brijen Gupta, *Sirajuddaulah*, p. 36.

7. Sushil Chaudhury, 'Sirajuddaulah, the English Company and Plassey Conspiracy—A Reappraisal', *The Indian Historical Review*, vol. XIII, no. 1–2, July 1986 and January 1987.

8. *Seir*, vol. II, p. 89 n.

9. The foregoing account of the intrigues in the last years of Alivardi Khan and the alignments in the court at the accession of Sirajuddaulah is based on Karam Ali, *Muzaffarnama* tr. Jadunath Sarkar, *Bengal Nawabs* (Calcutta, 1952); *Seir*, vol. II. I have explored the alignments in greater detail in *Palasir Sharajantra o Sekaler Samaj* (Calcutta, 1993).

10. Quoted in Brijen Gupta, *Sirajuddaulah*, p. 37.

11. *Riyaz*, pp. 399–414.

12. Ibid., p. 290.

13. Nawab to Coja Wajid, 1 June 1756; Parwana from Nawab to Gomasta of the English Coatey at Madras, undated; both printed in *Indian Records Series. Bengal in 1756–1757: A Selection of Private and Public Papers Dealing with the Affairs of the British in Bengal during the Reign of Sirajuddaulah*, ed. S.C. Hill (London, 1905) (henceforth Hill), vol. I, pp. 3 and 196.

14. 'If I am not mistaken the Company also indulged their covenanted servants with *dusticks* [warrants for duty free trade] for their private goods too ... which was certainly no small benefit to us as it gave us a considerable advantage over all the other merchants,' William Tooke's narrative, Hill, vol. I, p. 282.

15. Brijen Gupta, *Sirajuddaulah*, pp. 43–4.

16. P.J. Marshall, *East Indian Fortunes. The British in Bengal in the Eighteenth Century* (Oxford, 1976), p. 57.

17. Narendra Krishna Sinha, *The Economic History of Bengal from Plassey to the Permanent Settlement*, vol. I (Calcutta, 1965), p. 9.

18. One such case was a dispute between an Englishman and a functionary of the Raja of Burdwan residing in Calcutta. The latter challenged the jurisdiction of the Mayor's Court as he was a Mughal subject. The English paid no heed. Tooke's narrative, Hill, vol. I, pp. 280–1.

19. Ibid., pp. 266–75.

20. Rila Mukherjee, 'The Story of the Kasimbazar Silk Merchants and Commerce in the Eighteenth Century', Occasional Paper no. 103, Centre for Studies in Social Science, Calcutta, 1988, p. 54.

21. The 'more especially as for some days advices from all quarters were in favour of the Begum's party'. J.Z. Holwell to Court of Directors, 30 Nov. 1756, Hill, vol. II, p. 5; Drake to Fort William, Hill, vol. II, p. 143.

22. Cooke's written evidence to Orme, Hill, vol. III, p. 394.

23. J.Z. Holwell to Court of Directors, 30 Nov. 1756, Hill, vol. II, p. 15.

24. Ibid., Memoirs of Jean Law, Hill, vol. III, p. 165.

25. Tooke's Narrative, Hill, vol. I, p. 252.

26. British Museum manuscript by a Frenchman, entitled 'Revolutions in Bengal', Hill, vol. III, p. 222. Hill is unwilling to accept the veracity of the scene, but that is understandable, for no Englishman in the heyday of empire could have stomached the thought that an ancestor could have referred to himself as 'your slave, your slave', before a native prince.

27. Francis Sykes to Fort William Council, 4 June 1756, Hill, vol. I, p. 10.

28. Nawab to Coja Wajid, Murshidabad, 1 June 1756, Hill, vol. I, p. 4.

29. Nawab to Coja Wajid, Rajmahal, 28 May 1756, Hill, vol. I, p. 3.

30. Parwana from the Nawab to the Gomasta of the English koatey or Trading House at Madras, Hill, vol. I, p. 196.

31. J.Z. Holwell to Court of Directors, 30 Nov. 1756, Hill, vol. II, p. 15.

32. Ibid., p. 16.

33. Ten years after Indian independence, this was the judgement T.G.P. Spear reached while revising the *Oxford History of India*. Third edition, Oxford, 1958 (this rpt 1961), p. 479.

34. Took's narrative, Hill, vol. I, p. 264.

35. Watts and Collet to Council at Falta, 14 July 1756, Hill, vol. I, p. 57; Pigot to Nawab, 14 Oct. 1756, Hill, vol. I, p. 242.

36. Petross Arraton to Court of Directors, 25 June 1759, Hill, vol. III, p. 365.

37. Hill, vol. I, p. 196.

38. *Riyaz*, p. 247.

39. French letter from Chandernagore, 3 July 1756, Hill, vol. I, p. 51.

40. Ibid.

41. Lindsay to Orme, July 1756, Hill, vol. I, p. 170; *Seir*, vol. II, p. 192.

42. Dutch Council, Hugli, to Supreme Council, Batavia, 5 July 1756, Hill, vol. I, p. 54.

43. Capt. Mill's account, Hill, vol. I, p. 194.

44. Letter to Demonterein from Chandernagar, 1 Aug. 1756, Hill, vol. I, p. 181.

45. 'Revolutions in Bengal', Hill, vol. II, p. 225.

46. Luke Scrafton, *A History of Bengal Before and After the Battle of Plassey: 1739–58* (rpt Calcutta, 1975; 1st ed. 1763), p. 63.

47. Drake's narrative, 19 July 1756, Hill, vol. I, p. 154.

48. Holwell to Court of Directors, 30 Nov. 1756, Hill, vol. II, pp. 16–18.

49. Watts and Collet to Court of Directors, 17 July 1756, Hill, vol. I, p. 117.

50. Ibid., p. 118.

51. Dr Forth to Council at Falta, 11 Dec. 1756, Hill, vol. II, pp. 53–4.

52. Select Committee, Fort St George, to Select Committee, Fort William, 13 Oct. 1756, Hill, vol. I, p. 239.

53. Hill, vol. I, p. 222.

54. Ranjit Rai to Clive, 6 Feb. 1757, Hill, vol. II, p. 214.

55. Clive to father, 23 Feb. 1757, Hill, vol. II, pp. 242–3. But Sushil Chaudhury argues that the English intended conquest. See *The Prelude to Empire: Plassey Revolution of 1757* (New Delhi 2000), pp. 87–103.

56. Nawab to Clive, 26 April 1757, Hill, vol. II, p. 359.

57. Watts to Clive, 11 April 1757, Hill, vol. II, p. 323.

58. *Seir*, vol. II, pp. 192–214; Law's Memoir, Hill, vol. II, pp. 173–4;

59. Dr Forth to Council at Falta, 11 Dec. 1756, Hill, vol. II, p. 53.

60. Clive to Secret Committee, London, 1 Feb. 1757, Hill, vol. II, p. 207; from Dacca factory to Roger Drake, 14 April 1757, Hill, vol. II, p. 331; Law's Memoir, Hill, vol. III, p. 210.

61. *Seir*, vol. II, p. 163.

62. J. Long, *Selections from Unpublished Records of Government for the Years 1748 to 1767 Inclusive*, ed. Mahadevprasad Saha (Calcutta, 1973), doc. no. 274, letter to Court of Directors, 10 Jan. 1758, p. 149.

63. Percival Spear, *Master of Bengal: Clive and His India* (London, 1975), p. 189.

64. *Seir*, vol. II, p. 262.

65. Ibid., p. 319.

66. Ibid., p. 383.

67. Vansittart, *Narrative*, p. 33.

68. *Seir*, vol. II, pp. 382–3.

69. Ibid., pp. 431–2.

70. *Riyaz*, p. 385.

71. *Seir*, vol. II, p. 429.

72. Ibid., p. 442.

73. Ibid., p. 427.

74. *Riyaz*, pp. 393–5.

75. Vansittart, *Narrative*, p. 230.

76. *Seir*, vol. II, p. 395.

77. Ibid., p. 393.

78. Vansittart, *Narrative*, p. 231.

79. *Seir*, vol. II, p. 425 n.

80. Ibid., p. 434.

81. Ibid., p. 421 n.

82. Nandalal Chatterjee, *Mir Qasim* (Allahabad, 1935), pp. 268–9.

83. James Grant, 'An Historical and Comparative Analysis of the Finances of Bengal', in *The Fifth Report from the Select Committee on the Affairs of the East India Company*, vol. I, (London, 1812), passim.

84. *Seir*, vol. II, passim; Chatterjee, *Mir Qasim*, passim.

85. Vansittart, *Narrative*, p. 427.

86. Ibid., p. 49.

87. *Original Papers Relative to the Disturbances in Bengal*, 2 vols.

88. Vansittart, *Narrative*.

89. Nandalal Chatterjee wrote a pro-English and anti-Mir Qasim thesis. Mir Qasim still awaits a proper historian.

90. P.J. Marshall, *East Indian Fortunes*, passim.

91. Ibid., p. 115.

92. Vansittart was much embarrassed in the Council by the disclosure of a letter from Mir Qasim to his *amil* in Dacca. The Nawab had instructed his servant not to impede Vansittart's *gumashtah* in his private trade. Johnstone seized the letter and submitted it gleefully to the Council. *Narrative*, pp. 420–1.

93. Vansittart, *Narrative*, pp. 166–7; *Original Papers Relative to the Disturbances in Bengal*, vol. I, pp. 170–3.

94. Marshall, *East Indian Fortunes*, pp. 168–70.

95. Letter from Nabob to Vansittart, 16 June 1761, full text in *Original Papers Relative to the Disturbances in Bengal*, vol. I, extract in Vansittart, *Narrative*, pp. 82–3. These two works contain respectively the full text and extracts from Mir Qasim's letters. These letters have made it possible to reconstruct the story of his confrontation with the English from his standpoint. Long's *Selections* also contain a few letters from his officers and himself. Unless otherwise stated, what follows is based on Vansittart's *Narrative*, which is essentially a collection of documents interspersed with his comments.

96. *Original Papers*, vol. I, pp. 229–31; vol. II, H5, 'Copy of the Demands presented by Messrs. Amyatt and Hay to the Nobob.'

97. *Original Papers*, vol. II, p. 137.

98. Vansittart, *Narrative*, p. 148–9.

99. Original Papers, vol. II, p. 99.

100. Vansittart, *Narrative*, p. 431.

101. Ibid., pp. 191–2. Full text: no. L3, Nabob to Gov., received May 1762, *Original Papers*, vol. I.

102. Nabob to Gov., 5 March 1763, *Original Papers*, vol. II, p. 113.

103. Nabob to Gov., 26 Feb. 1763, ibid., pp. 97–8.

104. All these expressions occur in the Nawab's various letters to Vansittart.

105. Vansittart, *Narrative*, pp. 193–4.

106. Nabob to Gov., 26 Feb., *Original Papers*, vol. II, p. 99.

107. Ibid., p. 101.

108. Nabob to Gov., 5 March 1763, ibid., p. 111.

109. Nabob to Gov., 5 March 1763, ibid., pp. 121–2.
110. Vansittart, *Narrative*, p. 256.
111. Ibid., p. 256.
112. Cartier to Mahomed Aly, *Original Papers* I, pp. 220–2.
113. Vansittart, *Narrative*, pp. 214–15.
114. Long, *Selections*, no. 740.
115. Marshall, *East Indian Fortunes*, p. 116.
116. Long, *Selections*, no. 894.
117. Letter from Gov. and Mr Hastings to Council, 15 Dec. 1762, *Original Papers*, vol. II, p. 227.
118. Nabob to Gov., 22 March 1763, *Original Papers*, vol. II, pp. 136–7.
119. Vansittart, *Narrative*, p. 362.
120. Akshay Kumar Maitreya and Nanda Lal Chaterjee.
121. Vansittart, *Narrative*, p. 450.
122. Ibid., p. 358.
123. Ibid., p. 370.
124. Ibid., p. 447.
125. Copy of the demands presented by Messrs Amyatt and Hay to the Nabob, *Original Papers*, vol. II, pp. 214–15.
126. The Nawab was referring in this instance, to the arrest of his officers by the English, and to the paradoxical objections of the English to his arrest of Jagat Seth, Nabob to Governor, 2 May 1763, *Original Papers*, vol. II, p. 207.
127. Vansittart, *Narrative*, p. 366.
128. Nabob Cossim Aly Cawn's letter to the Governor, 28 June, 1763, *Original Papers*, vol. II, p. 274.
129. Ibid.
130. Vansittart observes in this connection: 'That we were the first aggressors, by the assault of Patna will not be disputed. I will not take upon me to pronounce how far Mr Ellis, in taking this ill-fated step, or the Board in authorizing him to do it, were to blame. ... My own opinion is, that Mr Ellis's intention was, from the beginning, to break with the Nabob; and the discretionary powers which he so earnestly solicited, and so passionately complained of being withheld, were wanted only as a sanction for executing what he had already resolved on: of this I repeatedly declared my apprehensions; and for that reason always refused to give any consent to any orders that put it in the power of Mr Ellis to begin the war, when he should think proper; and, in effect,

no sooner was he in possession of such authority, than he immediately made the use of it which I had dreaded.' *Narrative*, p. 552.

131. The English had at this point sent troops and seized the *amils* of Dacca, attached and beaten the *thanadars* of Jatirapoor, and on the Patna side seized *amils* and kept them in prison. Nabob to Governor, 11 April 1763, *Original Papers*, vol. III, p. 190.

132. The term 'class' is used here in the loose sense of ordinary conversation. Max Weber's 'status group' might be more appropriate, but not so familiar. Whether class or élite, what is not in doubt is the reality of the group of officers, commanders, and noblemen who ruled the country before being replaced by the English. The Mughals, furthermore, were an all-India class in a way which no other group that resisted the English could aspire to be. The Pathans of Rohilkhand, the Dal Khalsa of the Sikhs, the dynasty of Haidar Ali and Tipu Sultan, or even the Maratha confederate chiefs were regional rulers.

133. Document H5, *Original Papers*, vol. II, p. 214.

134. Ibid., p. 215.

135. Gov.'s letter to Nabob, ibid., p. 103.

136. Nabob to Gov., 23 March 1763, ibid., p. 137.

137. Vansittart, *Narrative*, pp. 410–14.

138. Ibid., pp. 199–200; *Original Papers*, vol. I, pp. 205–7.

139. Vansittart, *Narrative*, p. 202.

140. Ibid., p. 250.

141. Long, *Selections*, no. 696; *Original Papers*, vol. II, pp. 99–100.

142. Vansittart, *Narrative*, p. 288.

143. *Original Papers*, vol. I, p. 228.

144. Nabob to Governor, 11 March 1763, *Original Papers*, vol. II, p. 116.

145. Nabob to Governor, 26 Feb. 1763, ibid., pp. 99–100.

146. Nabob to Governor, 11 March 1763, ibid., p. 116.

147. From Mahomed Aly to Syed Buddul Cawn, ibid., pp. 167–8; Vansittart, *Narrative*, pp. 405–6.

148. *Original Papers*, vol. II, pp. 167, 169, 209.

149. The gentlemen at Luckypoor wrote: 'We must observe to you, that within these few days past, we have received advice from our gomasthas, in different parts of the country, that our business is entirely put to stop to, by the Nabob's people, and boats not suffered to pass the chokeys, the zemindars demand very considerable duties to be paid to them, declaring they have orders from Cossim Ali Cawn to do so, and unless we use force to prevent it, they will see his directions strictly

complied with. Several of our boats are now lying confined at different chokeys.' Vansittart, *Narrative*, p. 203.

150. Ibid., p. 261.

151. Letter from Meer Mahdi Cawn to the Nabob, n.d., *Original Papers*, vol. II, p. 223.

152. Meer Mahomed Mahdy Cawn Bahadre to the Nabob, n.d. ibid., p. 264.

153. Vansittart, *Narrative*, p. 527.

154. Vansittart's contemporary, the philosopher Adam Ferguson, used the term 'nation', 'tribe', 'race', 'people', interchangeably in 1767. Adam Ferguson, *An Essay on the History of Civil Society*, ed. Fania Oz-Salzberger (Cambridge, 1995), p. 78 and passim.

155. Long, *Selections*, nos. 690, 754, 839.

156. Ibid., no. 776.

157. Ibid., no. 798.

158. Vansittart, *Narrative*, p. 526.

159. *Seir*, vol. II, p. 494.

160. Ibid., p. 496.

161. Ibid., p. 498.

162. Ibid., pp. 512–13.

163. Ibid., p. 450.

164. Long, *Selections*, no. 802.

165. *Seir*, vol. II, p. 526.

166. Ibid., p. 566.

167. Ibid., p. 526.

168. Ibid., pp. 495, 512, 526–7.

169. *Seir*, vol. II, p. 444.

170. Long, *Selections*, no. 716.

171. Ibid., no. 718.

172. Ibid., no. 815.

173. Rammohun Roy to the Chairman and Deputy Chairman of the East Indian Company, 25 June 1831, Annex. A, in Dilip Kumar Biswas (ed.), *The Correspondence of Raja Rammohun Roy*, vol. I, 1809–1831 (Calcutta, 1992), p. 596.

174. Ibid.

175. Andre Wink, *Land and Sovereignty in India, Agrarian Society and Politics under the Eighteenth Century Maratha Swarajya* (Cambridge, 1986), pp. 40, 102, 133, 144 n.

176. Proclamation of the Nizam in his capacity as Mughal Viceroy of the Deccan, in C.U. Aitchison (ed.), *A Collection of Treaties, Engagements and Sunnuds Relating to India and Neighbouring Countries*, vol. v (Calcutta, 1864), p. 26.

177. Mark Wilks, *Historical Sketches of the South of India in an Attempt to Trace the History of Mysoor from the Origin of the Hindoo Government of that State to the Extinction of the Mohammedan Dynasty*, 3 vols (London, 1810–1817), vol. i, p. 173.

178. Shah Alam's *farman*, 29 Dec. 1764, in Aitchison, *A Collection of Treaties*, vol. ii (Calcutta, 1863), p. 6.

179. Ibid.

180. 'Grant of Diwani', 12 Aug. 1765, in Aitchison, *A Collection of Treaties*, vol. i (Calcutta, 1862), p. 60.

181. Aitchison, *A Collection of Treaties*, vol. v (Calcutta, 1864), p. 12.

182. Ibid., pp. 21–31.

183. Lakshmi Subramaniam, *Indigenous Capital and Imperial Expansion: Bombay, Surat and the West Coast* (Delhi, 1996), p. 320 and passim.

184. Atul Chandra Roy, *The Career of Mir Jafar Khan* (AD 1757–65) (Calcutta, 1953), p. 282.

185. Abdul Majed Khan, *The Transition in Bengal 1756–1775. A Study of Saiyid Muhammed Reza Khan* (Cambridge, 1969), pp. 160, 162.

186. Ibid., pp. 142–3.

187. As Richard Barwell wrote home to his father in 1769. '... all the revenue is anticipated for the payment of the army and for the provision of the Company's Investment.' Ibid., pp. 120, 211.

188. Ibid., p. 160.

189. Reza Khan's Propositions, Bengal Public Consultations, 28 March 1769, ibid., pp. 171, 177.

190. Ibid., pp. 148–9.

191. Nikhil Sur, *Chiattarer Manvantar o Sannyasi-Fakir Bidroha* (Calcutta, 1981), p. 20.

192. Long, *Selections*, no. 888, pp. 615–16.

193. Ibid., no. 995, p. 670.

194. Reza Khan's purported letter to Jawahar Singh, in Khan, *The Transition in Bengal*, pp. 148–9.

195. Ratnalekha Ray, *Change in Bengal Agrarian Society 1760–1850* (New Delhi, 1979), pp. 67–9.

196. J.A. Vas, *Eastern Bengal and Assam District Gazetteers, Rangpur* (Allahabad, 1911), p. 30; Narahari Kaviraj, *A Peasant Uprising in Bengal 1783: the First Formidable Peasant Uprising Against the Rule of the East India Company* (New Delhi, 1972), passim.

197. The song is quoted in full by Kaviraj, op. cit., pp. 97–102. Translation mine.

198. For a more detailed account, see A.N. Chandra, *The Sannyasi Rebellion* (Calcutta, 1977); Atish Dasgupta, *Fakir and Sannyasi Uprising in Bengal* (Calcutta, 1992); Ananda Bhattacharya, 'Sannyasi and Fakir Uprising in Bengal in the Second half of the Eighteenth Century', PhD Thesis, Jadavpur University, Calcutta, 1991.

199. Quoted by Ranjit Kumar Poddar, *Bangla Sahitya o Samskritite Sthaniya Bidroher Prabhab* (Calcutta, 1982), pp. 62–5. Translation mine. There is a contrary view of Majnu Shah, which sees him as a valiant fighter against the British, in a considerably later poem, *Majnu Shaher Hakikat*, by Jamiruddin Dafadar. A doubtful colophon dated the poem to 1872. It is quoted in M. Abdur Rahman, *Bidrohi Fakir Nayak Majnu Shah* (Calcutta, BS 1372), pp. 37–42.

200. In yet another folk poem by Dwija Gaurikanta (1813), the Sannyasis are seen as 'thousands of bastards intent on loot'. Ibid., pp. 72–3.

201. Fort William to the Secret Committee of the Company, 30 October 1762, *Fort William–India House Correspondence and other Contemporary Papers Relating Thereto (Secret and Select Committee)*, vol. xiv, 1752–81, ed. Amba Prasad (Delhi, 1985), p. 156.

202. Wellesley to Dundas, 23 Feb. 1798, *The Despatches, Minutes and Correspondence of the Marquess Wellesley*, ed. Montgomery Martin (rpt New Delhi, 1984), vol. i, p. 28.

203. Fort William to Court of Directors, 24 March 1766 and Fort William to Court of Directors, 8 Feb. 1765, *Fort William–India House Correspondence*, vol. xiv, pp. 162–3, 185.

204. India House to Fort William, 26 Nov. 1767, ibid., p. 15.

205. Fort William to Court of Directors, 24 March 1766, ibid., p. 185.

206. Wink, *Land and Sovereignty in India*, pp. 33, 102, 113.

207. Representation of W. Taylor on behalf of Bombay to G-G & Council, 9 Oct. 1775, G.W. Forrest (ed.), *Selections from Letter, Despatches and Other State Papers Preserved in the Bombay Secretariat. Maratha Series* (Bombay, 1885), vol. i, p. 250.

208. Bombay government's instructions to Thomas Mostyn on embassy to Poona, 18 Nov. 1767, ibid., p. 141.

209. Govind Sakharam Sardesai, *New History of the Marathas* (New Delhi, 1986), vol. II, p. 515.

210. Representation of W. Taylor, 9 Oct. 1775, Forrest (ed.), *Selections*, p. 250.

211. Seid-Gholam Hossein-Khan, *The Seir Mutagherin or Review of Modern Times: Being an History of India from the year 1118 to the year 1194, of the Hedgirah* (rpt New Delhi, 1986), vol. III, pp. 94–5.

212. Khurshidul Islam and Ralph Russell, *Three Mughal Poets: Mir, Sauda, Mir Hasan* (Delhi, 1991), p. 64.

213. Ibid., p. 60.

214. Representation of W. Taylor, Forrest (ed.), *Selections*, p. 257.

215. Warren Hastings, J. Clavering, and P. Francis to Court of Directors, 28 July, *Fort William–India House Correspondence*, vol. XIV, p. 409.

216. Sardesai, *New History*, vol. III, p. 97.

217. James Mill, *The History of British India*, 10 vols (5th edn, London 1858), vol. IV, p. 121. Narendra Krishna Sinha, *Haidar Ali* (Calcutta, 1959), p. 180.

218. Ibid., p. 173; Fort William to India House, 29 Nov. 1780, *Fort William–India House Correspondence*, vol. XIV, p. 550.

219. Mill, *History*, p. 120.

220. Sinha, *Haidar Ali*, p. 180.

221. Ibid., p. 180.

222. Mark Wilks, *Historical Sketches*, vol. II (London, 1817), p. 210.

223. Sinha, *Haidar Ali*, p. 178.

224. Fort William to India House, 29 Nov. 1780, *Fort William–India House Correspondence*, vol. XIV, p. 555.

225. Letter from Tipu Sultan to the Grand Seignior (Constantinople), in *The Despatches, Minutes and Correspondence of the Marquess Wellesley, K.G. during his Administration of India*, ed. Montgomery Martin (rpt Delhi, 1994), vol. V, p. 29.

226. Ibid., p. 24.

227. Haidar Ali sent an embassy to Delhi in 1779 to obtain an imperial grant of the two Carnatics (Bijapur and Hyderabad) in the hope that he might acquire these possessions in the future and obtain prior legal sanction for this. Nothing came of the mission. However, rumours, including 'certain intelligence' that Shah Alam had given the Nizam's entire dominion to Haidar Ali, induced Nizam Ali to abandon the Indian confederacy and settle his differences with the English. Wilks, *Historical Sketches*, vol. II, pp. 203, 238.

228. Tipu to Grand Seignior, *Wellesley Despatches*, vol. v, p. 25.

229. Gopalrao Patwardhan to his Karkun, 7/17 July 1763, *Survey and Calendar of Marathi Documents 1600–1818. Documents from Aitihasika Lekha Sangraha*, trans. V.T. Gune (Calcutta, 1996), p. 190.

230. Govind Hari to Gopalrao, May 1763, ibid., p. 116.

231. Holkar, for instance, was praised in 1804 by a functionary of Bharatpur for having 'formed such a plan as will put all the Caffers [English] to flight'. Nerunjun Lall to Jeswunt Rao Holkar, *Wellesley Despatches*, vol. IV, p. 188.

232. Jeewan Khaun and Elahi Bucksh Khaun to Seo Lalla, ibid., p. 187.

233. Nerujun Lall to Jeswunt Rao Holkar, ibid., p. 188.

234. Castlereagh to Wellesley, 4 March 1804, ibid., vol. v, p. 313.

235. Letter from Karkun, 12/5 Nov. 1764, *Survey and Calendar of Marathi Documents*, p. 247.

236. Major-General Arthur Wellesley's observations on note sent by Castlereagh, Nov. 1804, *Wellesley Despatches*, vol. v, p. 336.

237. Gopal Hari to Govind Shivaram, June 1763, *Survey and Calendar of Marathi Documents*, p. 187; see also Ahalyabai Holkar's letter cited in V.S. Kadam, *Maratha Confederacy: A Study of Its Origin and Development* (New Delhi, 1993), p. 58, n. 173.

238. *Holkar State Papers*, Marathi, vol. 2, no. 72, cited by Sardesai, *New History*, vol. III, p. 436.

239. Ibid., p. 373.

240. Ibid., p. 255.

241. Mir cited in Islam and Russell, *Three Mughal Poets*, p. 231.

242. *Seir Mutaqherin*, in vol. 1, preface by Haji Mustafa (M. Raymond), pp. 8–9.

243. Ibid., pp. 7–8.

244. Ibid., p. 6.

245. Letter from Raymond, the translator, to William Armstrong, 15 May 1790, *Seir*, vol. IV, App., p. 24.

246. *Seir*, vol. I, translator's preface, p. 10.

247. *Seir*, vol. IV, Raymond to Armstrong, p. 26; Mill, *History of British India*, vol. IV, pp. 127, 142.

248. Tipu to Grand Seignor, *Wellesley Despatches*, vol. v, p. 28.

249. *Seir*, vol. IV, pp. 115–16.

250. Committee meeting, Bombay, 6 Jan. 1779, Forrest (ed.), *Selections*, vol. I, p. 360.

251. *Seir*, vol. III, p. 358.

252. Mill, *History of British India*, vol. IV, p. 215.

253. *Seir*, vol. IV, p. 54.

254. Mill, *History of British India*, vol. IV, pp. 136–7.

255. Ibid., p. 151.

256. *Seir*, vol. III, pp. 123–4.

257. Mill, *History of British India*, vol. IV, p. 149; Sinha, *Haidar Ali*, pp. 87, 91.

258. Diary of C.W. Malet on a Journey from Bombay to Calcutta 1785–86, 13 Feb. 1785, in Forrest (ed.), *Selections*, vol. I, p. 509.

259. Islam and Russell, *Three Mughal Poets*, p. 28.

260. Ibid., p. 67.

261. Sardesai, *New History*, vol. III, p. 192.

262. *Wellesley Despatches*, vol. IV, p. 567 and passim.

263. Gov.-Gen. in Council to Secret Committee of the Court of Directors, 13 July 1804, ibid., p. 156.

264. French text, App. L, ibid., pp. 648–60.

265. Gov.-Gen. in Council to Secret Committee of the Directors, 2 June 1805, ibid., p. 555.

266. *Bahar-i-'Ajam* of Tek Chand Bahar (AH 1152). I am indebted to Professor Irfan Habib for translating the entry.

267. Kumkum Bandyopadhay, 'Indigenous Trade, Finance and Politics—A Study of Patna and its Hinterland, 1757 to 1813', PhD thesis, Calcutta University, 1987, pp. 440–9. See also the printed version, Kumkum Chatterjee, *Merchants, Politics and Society in Early Modern India, Bihar: 1733–1820* (Leiden, 1996), pp. 222–30. The poets of Patna quoted above are Rasikh and Jauhari.

268. Islam and Russell, *Three Mughal Poets*, p. 68; Ralph Russell, *The Pursuit of Urdu Literature, A Select History* (Delhi, 1992) p. 59.

269. Islam and Russell, *Three Mughal Poets*, p. 22.

270. Home Misc. 434, India Office Library and Records.

271. *Seir*, vol. III, pp. 46, 192.

272. Ibid., p. 194.

273. Ibid., p. 29, 161–2, 170–1, 190–1.

274. Answers from Sir Henry Strachey, Judge and Magistrate of Midnapore, 30 Jan. 1802, *The Fifth Report from the Select Committee on the Affairs of the East India Company* (London, 1812), p. 701.

275. Earl of Mornington to Select Committee of Court of Directors, 22 April 1799, *Wellesley Despatches*, vol. I, p. 535. See also Aniruddha Ray, *The Rebel of Nawab of Oudh: Revolt of Vizir Ali Khan* (1799) (Calcutta, 1990), pp. 195–6. Ray contends that this was not one master conspiracy, but several fragmentary incidents. Wellesley, however, was not off the mark in seeing the thread of Mughal discontent that ran through these simultaneous incidents in Banaras and Dacca.

276. *Wellesley Despatches*, vol. I, p. 536.

277. '*Tad–adhunā varna–āshrama–dharma–uchchhed–kārinim–etad–nicha–uddhati katham sahante? Bruhi.*' *The Sarve–Deva–Vilasa*, ed. V. Raghavan (Adyar, Madras; rpt from Adyar Library Bulletin, 1958), pp. 2, 80, 90.

278. Henry Strachey, 30 Jan. 1802, *Fifth Report*, pp. 691, 701.

279. Ibid., p. 698; Judge and Magistrate of Burdwan, 9 March 1802, *Fifth Report*, p. 721.

280. Henry Strachey, *Fifth Report*, p. 700.

281. Ibid.

282. Mirza Shaikh Ihtisamuddin, *Vilayet Nama*, trans. from Persian (*Shigurf Nama-i-Vilayat*) into Bengali by Abu Mohamed Habibullah (Dacca, 1981). pp. 2–3, 10, 18, 108.

283. Ibid., p. 112.

284. Dilip Kumar Biswas (ed.), *The Correspondence of Raja Rammohun Roy*, vol. 1 (1809–1831), (Calcutta. 1992), pp. 211, 343–4.

285. Ibid., p. 211.

286. Gov.-Gen. in Council to Court of Directors, 9 July 1800, *Wellesley Despatches*, vol. II, pp. 312–18.

287. Ibid., p. 315.

288. M. Mujeeb, *The Indian Muslims* (London, 1969), pp. 390–8.

289. Schimmel, *Islam in the Indian Subcontinent* (London, 1980), p. 182.

290. Mujeeb, *Indian Muslims*, pp. 390–8.

291. Biswas (ed.), *Correspondence of Raja Rammohun Roy*, pp. 1–19.

292. Ibid., p. 372.

293. Ibid., p. 363.

294. Rammohun Roy to J.S. Buckingham, 11 Aug. 1821, ibid., pp. 60–1.

295. *Vilayet Nama*, p. 146.

296. A.F Salahuddin Ahmed, *Social Ideas and Social Change in Bengal 1818–1835* (Calcutta, 1976), p. 90.

297. Biswas (ed.), *Correspondence of Raja Rammohun Roy*, p. 214.

298. Rajnarayan Bose, *Hindu Athaba Presidency Colleger Itibritta* (1875), ed. Ashok Kumar Ray, p. 31.

299. Biswas (ed.), *Correspondence of Raja Rammohun Roy*, p. 211.

300. *The Fifth Report*, App. 10, p. 668 ff.

301. *Seir*, vol. I, translator's preface, p. 6.

302. Ibid., p. 12.

303. Ibid., p. 6. Emphasis mine. The phrase 'national body' is the Frenchman's.

304. *Seir*, vol. III, p. 188.

305. Ibid., p. 189.

306. Ibid., p. 159.

307. Ibid., p. 161.

308. Ibid., p. 180.

309. Ibid., pp. 161–2, emphasis in text.

310. Ibid., p. 162.

311. Ibid.

312. Ibid., pp. 189–90.

313. Ibid., p. 192.

314. Ibid., p. 190.

315. Gov.-Gen. in Council to Secret Committee of the Court of Directors, 13 July 1804, *Wellesley Despatches*, vol. IV, p. 153.

316. Biswas (ed.), *Correspondence of Raja Rammohun Roy*, p. 596.

Part Two

Storm Across
The Ganges

4

The Mentality of the Mutiny: Conceptions of the Alternative Order in 1857

I
The Nature of the Mutiny

> May all the enemies of the faith be killed to-day
> The Feringhis be destroyed, root and branch!
> Celebrate the festival of the Eed Kurban by great slaughter;
> Put our enemies to the edge of the sword—spare not!
> [*Emperor Bahadur Shah Zafar*[1]]

> Kill the English, Mother Destroyer! Destroy them altogether
>   Mother Chandi! Let him not live—the enemy!
> Protect your offspring, Mother Destroyer! Protect Shankar
>   Sustain the poor one—your own devotee!
> [*Raja Shankar Shah, Gond Chief*[2]]

The spirit of the Mutiny was embodied in a collective mentality: a blend of fear and outrage gripped the minds of the sepoys of the Bengal Army and communicated itself, as if by an electrical impulse, to the villages and towns of Hindustan from where they had been recruited. Where that particular mentality, or temperament, did not grip the people—and this was so both in the Punjab and in Bengal at the opposite ends of Hindustan—the mutinies in the cantonments did not ignite rebellions in either town or country.[3] In Hindustan, on the contrary, the popular mood was finely attuned by bonds of kinship and mental sympathy to the mood of the sepoys. Here, as nowhere

else, a particular mentality coalesced diverse grievances into a comprehensive challenge to the hated English rule, and this was accompanied
by coherent notions of an alternative form of government.

What was the mentality that lay behind the formidable insurrections in the cantonments, towns, and villages of Hindustan?[4] and what
were the contours of the alternative political and social order constructed
by the mutinous crowds and sepoys in that stretch of territory?

The rebellion indicated the people's realization that the mutinies
in the cantonments had brought forth a keenly desired but wholly
unexpected reversal in the relations of power. The natives of Hindustan
had experienced the English regime as a race rule in which power and
privilege lay with the sahibs, their women, and their children.[5] The
rule of the white race, as *The Times* correspondent accompanying the
vengeful English soldiers to Lucknow saw so clearly, was based on force.
'That force is the base of our rule', wrote W.H. Russell in his private
diary of 14 February 1858. 'I have no doubt; for I see nothing but force
employed in our relations with the governed.'[6] All of a sudden and
without the slightest warning, the people's outrage at racial subordination imposed by superior physical force, and the associated fear
of emasculation and abasement arising out of the necessity of having to
submit to it, found cataclysmic release. The breaking forth of the pent-
up emotions of the coerced people of Hindustan was fuelled by the
sudden sense of the reversal of the relations of power—a sense that the
world had turned upside down, and that their turn had now come to
exercise force upon those who had hitherto coerced them. It is no
accident that on the eve of the outbreak, proclamations appeared in
Lucknow in Hindi, Urdu, and Persian, calling upon the Hindus and
Musalmans to exterminate all Europeans: 'These proclamations, there
is reason to believe, are written by people in the city—the scum of the
populace who like the Scottish robber, would like to see the world
turned upside down ....'[7]

Shortly afterwards, white men, women, and children perished in
Cawnpore; and from the English point of view, the peculiar aggravation
of the massacre, as Russell recorded in his diary, was that 'the deed was
done by a subject race—by black men who dared to shed the blood of
their masters'.[8] He added perceptively: 'Here we had not only a servile
war and a sort of jacquerie combined, but we had a war of religion, a
war of race, and a war of revenge, of hope, of some national promptings
to shake off the yoke of a stranger, and to establish the full power of the

native chiefs, and the full sway of the native religions.' Russell's insight enables him not merely to see the reversal of the power relationships hitherto obtaining between the white rulers and their black subjects, but to grasp the idiom of faith through which the sense of reversal expressed itself. The proclamations issued in Lucknow on the eve of the outbreak had denounced all who remained passive as 'born of the pigs of Europeans, born of cows, despised by the Gods, hated and spat at by all true sons of Mahabeer Jee, and of Mahomed'.[9] What is of interest here is that the combination of the black subjects against the white rulers is ideologically conceived, not in terms of a nation asserting its independence of colonial rule, but in terms of the Hindus and Muslims jointly asserting the sway of their respective religious creeds against the hated Christian 'Nasara' (Nazarenes).[10]

Was there, then, a true sense in which the Mutiny could be called, as indeed Jawaharlal Nehru (and thirty years before him V.D. Savarkar) called it, 'a war of Indian independence'? Why did he say this despite his careful qualification that 'Nationalism of a modern type was yet to come'?[11] It must be remembered, for the clarity of the argument here, that patriotism is a far older phenomenon than modern day nationalism. The resistance of the Greek city states to the Persian invasion, the crusade of Joan of Arc against the aliens from across the English Channel, and the uprising of the people of Delhi against the Iranian troopers of Nadir Shah, all exhibit patriotism in various antique forms.[12] Patriotism signifies that spontaneous desire for independence from alien rule which, in all human societies, must long precede the modern concept of national unity embodied in the sovereign national state. The patriotism of those who mutinied in 1857 expressed itself in the specific form of a combined religious crusade.

Unlike the Indian National Congress of 1885, or even the contemporary members of the British Indian Association who denounced the Mutiny so vehemently, the rebels of 1857 belonged to a society that had no political notion of national sovereignty. Devoid of that notion, they were thrown back upon 'the full power of the native chiefs, and the full sway of the native religions'. Even so, it would be unduly simplifying matters to dwell on the chiefs and religions alone; for the people's power that surged through these old methods of mobilization invested the apparent restoration of the chiefs with a content that was no longer the true substance of the old regime. Indeed, what the Congress leaders later called 'the Indian nation', the rebel leaders already spoke of distinctly as 'the Hindus and Musalmans of Hindustan'. Interestingly Rabindranath Tagore, who was mentally close to the age, used the same expression—'all the Hindus and Musalmans of Hindustan felt a rush of hot blood'—in a Mutiny story written in 1898, though by then the term 'Indian nation' had been familiarized by Congress agitation.[13]

Outwardly, it might indeed appear as if everywhere the ancient supremacies that the British had overthrown were once again coming into their own. To that extent, as Jawaharlal Nehru saw it in the later perspective of a socialist age, the rebellion was 'a feudal outburst'; one led by feudal chiefs and their followers, albeit inspired by the widespread popular sentiment against foreign rule.[14] Even so, the question that arises is how substantive was the 'restoration'? After all, the old supremacies had disappeared without a trace in large parts of the Doab, necessitating, as we shall see, all sorts of improvisations by the rebel crowds of Cawnpore, Allahabad, Bulandshahr, and elsewhere in the selection of chiefs. Even where the surviving remnants of overthrown supremacies were more clearly marked, as in Awadh, Rohilkhand, and Bundelkhand, there were keen struggles for succession to the departed British magistrates, restoration being by no means automatic. What is more important, the restored chiefships had to come to terms with the sepoy councils that were then the most organized embodiment of the people's power.

This was so because the mutiny of the sepoys lay at the very heart of the people's rebellion.[15] It was, indeed, its most democratic part. Eric Stokes, breaking through the false distinction between the mutiny and the popular rebellion, puts the matter succinctly: 'In a real sense the revolt was essentially the revolt of a peasant army breaking loose from its foreign master.'[16] It was however more than that. The sepoy was not simply a peasant in uniform: when he donned the uniform, he acquired a perspective wider than the little world of the typical villager. Peasant rebellions before 1857, and indeed subsequently (until they were linked to the Congress in the 1920s), tended to be spatially restricted insurrections based on ties of kinship and locality. The 200,000 strong native army, as the journalist Karl Marx commented during the Mutiny in the *New York Daily Tribune*, was the 'first general centre of resistance which the Indian people was ever possessed of'.[17] The sack of potatoes, as Marx described the peasantry, thereby acquired a hard, pointed spearhead. They strained towards a form of government that was indeed neither libertarian nor egalitarian, but which nonetheless accommodated a curiously republican–democratic component within its hierarchical, princely structure.[18]

The restored 'feudal' chiefships of 1857 could not thus be likened to the old regimes of the eighteenth century. Behind the reassertion of Mughal legitimacy lay the entire force and dynamism of a people who had risen in the mass. At the instinctual level of the collective mentality, it was the violent protest of a black subject people against their white oppressors. They provoked a vengeful master race who, in retaliation, unleashed the most naked race war that the world was to see in the nineteenth century. It was not, however, the rebels who put the struggle in terms of a war between the races: that was, distinctively, the language of the masters.[19] Although the mutinous crowds and sepoys gave vent to racial antipathy in word as well as deed, this was not the most typical expression of their considered thinking. At the level of conscious thought, they clothed the underlying race war in the ideological garb of a struggle between the true religions and the false one.[20] It was, in their view, a struggle of the Hindus and Muslims against the Nazarenes— not so much because the latter were supposed to be determined to impose the false doctrine of the Trinity, but because the identity of 'the Hindus and Muslims of Hindustan' was being threatened by the moral and material aggrandizement of the arrogant imperial power.[21] The joint brotherhood of the religions expressed, in so far as they were capable of expressing it, the instinctive feeling that the native subject race constituted one people[22] as against the white Christian rulers. The inchoate sense of the nation embedded in the mass psychology and expressed in terms steeped with religion was the dynamic factor that invested the restoration of the vanished supremacies of the eighteenth century with a new meaning.

Conceptually, then, the Mutiny is a peculiarly difficult phenomenon to define: a war of the races that was not a race war because the subject race conceived it as a war of religion; a religious war that cannot be called truly and purely a war of religion because what was being opposed was not the creed of the master race but their political domination; as such, then, neither a war of race, nor a war of religion, but a patriotic war of the Hindu–Muslim brotherhood, or the inchoate social nationality of Hindustan; yet not a national war either. It was all these things and therefore none of them: the product of a mentality rooted in the past, yet forced to reckon with the dynamic world of the

nineteenth century. The truth after all is that while the rebels spoke of
a war of restoration, their actual proceedings groped falteringly
towards finding an effective alternative to the technologically advanced
regime of the British. Racially abused by the superior colonial power,
they sought to meet the challenge by developing a new sense of identity: the idea of a political community couched in terms of two combined religions. In doing so, they tragically fell short of conceiving and
realizing the only effective alternative to the bureaucratically organized
imperial power, i.e. the sovereign national state. Circumstances forced
upon the mutineers, as upon their contemporaries the Taipings, the
need to envisage a brave new world with an outlook belonging to the
shattered past.

In the strain of the effort, they produced an inchoate, indeterminate cosmos: not in the true sense traditional, but hardly one capable
of coping with the challenges of the modern world. Their language was
not the language of 'revolution', for which no word existed then.[23] They
spoke, instead, of 'government', of the legitimate Mughal sovereign, of
restoring the rightful chiefs of Hindustan to their respective positions.[24]
As far as they were concerned, the English were the rebels, not they.[25]
The Mutiny constitutes the great disjuncture in the development of the
Indian nation: it is not a part of the national movement, nor is it the
dying throes of the old order. The best term for it is the one used by the
mutineers themselves: the 'war'[26] of 'the Hindoostanis' (or alternately
'the Hindus and Musalmans of Hindustan')[27] to protect their '*dharma*'
and '*deen*' and to 'save the country'.[28] In other words, the patriotic war
of a people who expressed their sense of national identity in terms of
the attributed brotherhood of the two principal religious communities
of a single land.

What we have here is a foetal national community with a mentality
opposed to the civil society that was already appearing in Calcutta,
Bombay, and Madras. Common racial abasement had produced in
Hindustan a sense of reactive oneness untouched by the modern doctrine
of national sovereignty and steeped in a mentality that could only express
the struggle in the older language of restoring the chiefs and reinstating
the religions. All the same the political vocabulary underwent an
important modification when the foetal nationality coined the significant expression 'Hindus and Musalmans of Hindustan'[29] to articulate
itself. No less significant were the constitutional changes arising from
the process of reconstituting authority. The sepoy council, that new

embodiment of the people's power, modified the working of the older institutions—the legitimate Mughal sovereign and the rightful country chiefs—in such a manner that the political order of the Mutiny could be likened neither to the integrated bureaucratic Mughal empire of the seventeenth century, nor to the squabbling federation of the eighteenth-century chiefs. The idea of popular authority embodied in the joint rule of the two religions ('the two religions govern')[30] and the act of exercise of power by the elected council of the sepoys ('the command belongs to the sipahi bahadur')[31] amounted together to an unprecedented expression of the power derived in 1857 from the people's will, and there was no question of reconstituting it entirely in the manner of the past. Incapable of generating a new world, imprisoned within a fragmented, timeworn cosmos, yet strenuously driven by circumstances to reorder the fragments into a different, unfamiliar constellation, the Mutiny was at once a 'traditional resistance movement'[32] and a movement unrecognizable to tradition.[33]

The dialectic of the Mutiny moved through a process of dual inversion that took the world back to the past and yet did not leave it as it had been then. The frightened message of a white man from Lucknow that the scum of the populace were determined to turn the world upside down, did not accurately represent the popular point of view; to the rebels' way of thinking, the white men had turned the world upside down, and they were merely turning it back.[34] However, too much shattering had occurred in the course of these multiple inversions for the older cosmos to be restored in its original outline. The alien regime, by threatening the popular religious identities embedded in the old political order, had forged them into a national religious front, and had made it explicit in a manner not known before. The idea that 'the two religions govern'—a slogan counterposed by the sepoys to the claims of the Rani of Jhansi[35]—was an implicit check upon the legitimate authority of the restored chiefs. The old chiefships had been tried and found wanting against the onslaught of the colonial power and would now have to be buttressed by the sepoy army. In popular memory the mutiny was always remembered as a chaotic struggle that, in attempting to restore the old regime, altered and distorted its shape fundamentally. Thus, Abdul Halim Sharar, born in Lucknow after the Mutiny, recreated the event in the following terms:

> At the time Birjis Qadar, with the royal consort, Hazrat Mahal, had become the effective ruler in Lucknow. The authority of Birjis Qadar

was acknowledged, coins were issued in his name, officials were appointed to the State, taxes began to be collected, and the siege [of the Residency] itself was continued only as a sort of pastime. People praised the efficiency and good intentions of the Queen, who had great regard for the soldiery and would reward them highly for their work and prowess. But to what avail? It was impossible for her to discard her purdah and become commander-in-chief of the army. Her advisers were bad and her soldiers useless. Everyone was a slave to his own desires and no one agreed with what anyone else said. The mutineers of the British army were so arrogant that they thought that everything happened by their grace and considered themselves the true rulers and the only 'king-makers'.[36]

The sepoys, the people, the community, were sovereign: hence the coinage, 'Hindus and Musalmans of Hindustan'.

II
Mentality

Race, Religion, and Realm

On the eve of the Mutiny outbreak at Meerut, a captain, worried about the feelings of his men regarding the 'cartoos', wrote to a colleague at headquarters:

> Feeling ... is as bad as can be and matters have gone so far that I can hardly devise any suitable remedy. We make a grand mistake in supposing that because we dress, arm and drill Hindustani soldiers as Europeans, they become one bit European in their feelings and ideas. I see them on parade for two hours daily, but what do I know of them for the other 22?
>
> What do they talk about in their lines, what do they plot? For all I can tell I might as well be in Siberia.
>
> I know that at the present moment an unusual agitation is pervading the ranks of the entire native army, but what it will result in, I am afraid to say. I can detect the near approach of the storm, I can hear the moaning of the hurricane, but I can't say how, when, or where it will break forth. Why, whence the danger, you say. Everywhere far and near, the army under some maddening impulse, are looking out with strained expectation for something, some unseen invisible agency has caused one common electric thrill to run thro' all.
>
> I don't think they know themselves what they will do, or that they have any plan of action except of resistance to invasion of their religion and their faith.

But good God! Here are all the elements of combustion at hand, 100,000 men, sullen, distrustful, fierce, with all their deepest and inmost sympathies, as well as worst passions, roused, and we are thinking to cajole them into good humour by patting them on the back, saying what a fool you are for making such a fuss about nothing. They no longer believe us, they have passed out of restraint and will be off at a gallop before long.

If a flare-up from any cause takes place at one station, it will spread and become universal.[37]

The 'elements of combustion', vague and as yet undefined in Captain Martineau's letter, may be better identified by tracking down rumours. A novel by an eyewitness, which begins with an imaginary speech by a real maulvi, fuses these rumours into an integrated sketch of the prevailing mentality. Its ingredients stand out in the clearer outline of hindsight:

You are aware that the firangis became our masters through subtilty [sic]. After entering the country as traders, they mixed themselves in politics, set one *subedar* against another reaping the benefits of the quarrel themselves ....

... Consider what instruments they used to conquer the country? Why, they set our own swords against our own throats. It is the *sipahi* army which conquered India for them, and by the sword of Ali! that very instrument shall be employed to destroy them.

But you will perhaps ask: 'what have they done to receive this treatment?' I answer: If *suar gadha* (swine, pig or hog; ass or donkey: very common epithets applied by the Europeans to the native of India— [footnote in original]) in the public streets and 'damn your eyes' in the public courts is a form of compliment acceptable to you, they then have deserved well at your hands. Have you never seen a fellow-countryman of yours being kicked by the whites, and sometimes the cane laid across his back? Have you ever known them to be addressed other than 'nigger' and 'kala-suar?'[38] These are every-day occurrences ....

You will say: 'this is our natural lot as a subject race, and we have no right to complain'. But ai bbaio! Our religion is now in danger. Having lost the sovereignty of the land, having bowed in subjection to the impure kafir, shall we surrender the inalienable privileges which we received from the prophet, upon whom be peace?

Again perhaps you will be desirous to know upon what facts this allegation is founded? ... Have not their padris spread through the length and breadth of the land, sowing the seeds of the baneful *nasri* (Nazarene) doctrine, and drawing away from the truth the ignorant and the simple-minded? Have they not ordered wheat-flour to be mixed by bone-dust? Have they not issued cartridges to the *sipahi* army greased with cows' and pigs' fat? And to enforce the use of the abomination, have they not forged irons and have sent 2000 to each town where there is a native corps with orders that whoever refused to cut them with his teeth shall at once be placed in arrest and sent off to jail?

O brothers of the Hindu race! the purity of your caste is threatened, and the religious distinctions so prized by you invaded by the proselytizing and annexing firangi! Rise in arms! ...

Just a hundred years ago the rule of the infidel began, and I declare to you that it must now end. Remember the words of the pir dastgir that the centenary of Plassey shall see the termination of kafir rule. That centenary approaches ... .[39]

The racial humiliation of an entire population hitherto lacking a clear sense of national identity, their patriotic rallying in defence of the most cherished part of their identity, i.e. religion, the flying of rumours preparatory to the great reversal of the relations of power obtaining between whites and blacks, and finally—a step missed out in the fictional account above—the contagious fear of the whites coming to massacre the blacks, were all steps in the psychic process through which the Mutiny, in essence a turning of the tables by the massacre of the whites, precipitated itself. In terms of the succession of emotions, the common experience of racial abasement stands right at the base of the mental process behind the Mutiny. Its importance, at the level of the formation of a mass national identity, cannot be overemphasized. It created a bitter commonalty by obliterating degrees and distinctions,[40] by subjecting the prince to the same servitude as the pauper, by levelling sepoy with servant,[41] by thrusting the iron into each self-contained and hitherto separated soul—providing thereby a mass dimension to the dawning self-realization of the people of Hindustan.[42]

So pronounced was the racial character of British domination and so twisted out of shape the degrees of consequence under its forceful dispensation, that the highest man of the land would have to grovel before the lowest of the European ladies, with a sick realization at heart that only a reversal of the relations of power, by some sudden external intervention, could set matters right. Thus, we find Prince Jawan Bakht, youngest son of the last Emperor, being treated like dirt by a Mrs Scully, an English sergeant's daughter, inside the very Red Fort from which his ancestor Shah Jahan had held sway from Kabul to Chittagong. Sergeant Fleming's wife and daughter were visiting Queen Zinat Mahal in April 1857, and the daughter was talking to the prince, when she suddenly exploded: 'Mother, do you hear what this young rascal is saying? He is telling me that in a short time he will have all the infidel English under his feet, and after that he will kill the Hindus.' Mrs Fleming turned upon the young prince: 'What is that you are saying?' He replied that he was only joking. The sergeant's wife retorted: 'If what you threaten were to be the case, your head would be taken off first.' Prince Jawan Bakht, a boy only recently married, could do nothing except make the dignified reply: 'that the Persians were coming to Delhi, and that when they did so, we, that is, myself and daughter, should go to him, and he would save us'.[43]

The young prince's predicament—his suppressed yearning for release from bondage, his humiliation at the hands of a sergeant's daughter for daring to express it, his realization that there would be no rescue unless the relations of power were to change by an unforeseen external event such as the Persians winning against the British in the war then proceeding at Herat—illustrates the lot of all natives under white rule. If princes could be treated like this in their palaces, what security could ordinary men expect for their 'religion, honour, life and property'?[44] An incident in Meerut prior to the Mutiny, recorded in a native paper after the European press decided to suppress the news, reveals the sense of oppression weighing upon the people:

An act of retributive justice has been committed by the worthy magistrate of this district. It was supposed that an escaped convict from jail was secreted in a village about four miles distant from this cantonment. In the dead of the night the magistrate, at the head of a large body of police, visited the village, aroused the inhabitants from their slumbers, and demanded the culprit. The villagers denied any knowledge of him. The magistrate with characteristic kindness and consideration, gave them half an hour to make up their minds. At the expiration of that time, as the culprit was not produced, he set fire to the village. In those flames, which illuminated the country for miles round, thirteen lives were sacrificed; namely, those of three men, four women and six children. One of the unfortunate women was in labour at the time. Some malicious natives in the neighbourhood of Meerut give out that the Sahib has been notoriously mad for several years past. Let us hope, however, that the Lieutenant Governor will not heed such insinuations, but after complimenting the magistrate on his vigour and zeal, appoint him to the first judgeship that may become vacant. No less than six hundred persons are, by this fire, rendered homeless beggars. But what of that? Must justice be obstructed?

It remains for us to add that the escaped convict of whom the magistrate was in search, has been in Oude for the past month, and that no notice of this affair will appear in any of the papers printed in England and edited

by the Sahib Logue. Those gentlemen are far too modest to make known
the manifold blessings which arise out of British rule in India.[45]

The belief was ingrained in the mind of the Englishman in India
that the natives were subhuman;[46] and in truth loyal servants as well as
rebel sepoys were all alike 'niggers' as far as the English were concerned.[47]
The impact of these attitudes was to create a single new category
('natives', 'niggers') out of an entire population, and to invest it, willy-
nilly, with an existence and mind of its own. Contrary to the belief of
William Muir, Charles Raikes, and other officials that crowd behaviour
in 1857 was an instance of mere anarchy let loose by the sudden removal
of the restraining hand of authority, there lay behind the Mutiny a
collective will to purge the land of all foreign authority and to restore
native rule at all levels of the political and social structure.

Mentally, the British had come to regard India as a possession
assimilated to, and identified with, the white master race.[48] Every white
man, woman, and child was a proprietor, by virtue of colour, with an
invisible share in dominion.[49] This was evident in the manner the 'Mem
Sahibs' and the 'Baba Logue' treated the expropriated natives of the
land;[50] a form of treatment that could not but evoke the suppressed
hatred of its helpless objects.[51] It was an integral part of the exercise of
dominion that the whites should be served by the natives. For that to
come to an end was tantamount to the world coming to an end—the
ultimate and inconceivable misfortune that could befall white women
and men. Consequently, when the inconceivable came to pass in 1857,[52]
the 'Goras', those white monsters who became the objects of nightmare
and screaming terror,[53] fought back with the most incredible savagery
the world has known—in a manner 'as relentless as Lords of the Pale in
Ireland, Danes in Britain, or Spaniards in Mexico'.[54] It was a race war
which, in its scale,[55] cruelty, and meanness, had no parallel in the
nineteenth century, and was not to be outdone until Hitler launched
his war for *lebensraum* against the *untermenschen* of Slavonic Europe.[56]

Long before the Cawnpore massacre (by which all the excesses of
the white soldiery were explained away at the time)[57] became known,
John Bull had turned the war into a blood sport; a game in which the
fun consisted in 'potting pandies' and 'finishing off niggers',[58] and the
serious object of which, literally, was to take away from 'Pandy' what
he cherished most—'1st Religion, 2nd Honour, 3rd Life, 4th Property'—
in a bid to dehumanize the victim in the act of putting an end to him.
Violence assumed, in other words, the character of transgression, of

violating the enemy's innate substance with a view to reducing him to less than nothing in his own eyes. Such a war could not have been fought unless the enemy had not been regarded as subhuman. The aim was to fix him indisputably and immutably in that category. 'The fierceness of the men', wrote an eye witness of the siege of Delhi, 'increased every day, often venting itself on the camp servants, many of whom ran away. The prisoners, during the few hours between their trial and execution, were unceasingly tormented by the soldiers. They pulled their hair, pricked them with their bayonets, and forced them to eat cow's flesh, while officers stood by approving'.[59] The soldiers were determined to take not only life but also religion, and they thought as little of taking it from the common sepoy as from the prime minister of the Nawab of Farrukhabad. That high dignitary of the rebel government was brought into camp 'tied down on a charpoy', and preparatory to hanging him 'the Highlanders made him partake heartily of swine's flesh'.[60]

Because the white soldiery regarded their opponents as 'savages', they had no compunction in outdoing the latter in savagery. The sepoys massacred men, women, and children, but they went in for straight execution and not torture, and except in rare instances, they did not rape women.[61] The British sought proof of their higher civilization in the claim (quite contrary to the facts) that women and children had nothing to fear from them;[62] and because the natives appeared to them as one undifferentiated race of inferiors, among whom careful distinctions of age and sex were difficult if not redundant, they quite believed (here they had the advantage over Dr Goebbels) in their own propaganda. The natives knew, to their bitter experience, that the British not only executed thousands of men, but also raped women;[63] that thoughtless boys, who displayed the rebel colours beating the tom-tom, had not a chance of being spared their young lives; and that the European officers and their soldiers were quite capable of slaughtering 'thousands of innocent and insignificant men, including women, blind men and mendicants'.[64] 'O brethren!', ran a rebel proclamation, 'at this present time, the execrable Christians ... are killing innocent men, plundering their property, setting fire to their houses, and shutting up their children in houses, some of which they burn down and the doors of others they build up.'[65]

The white soldiers strung up corpses by twos and threes from every branch and every signpost at Allahabad; systematically burned down the villages along the road from Allahabad to Cawnpore hanging all whose faces were turned the wrong way;[66] gave vent to their macabre sense of art by making figures of eight with corpses hanging from the branches;[67] and made a particular speciality, in Lucknow, of roasting sepoys alive on slow-burning fire.[68] Small wonder, then, that for the ordinary fleeing villagers, there was no room for doubt as to who was the enemy: 'It is melancholy that the people should think we are their enemies. Amid the fugitives from our advance today were women with children in their arms, and men carrying charpoys and bundles on their backs.'[69] The incident lit up in one flash how the white terror drew out the lineaments of one collective psyche burnt and blackened into an identifiable mass. If for no other reason, here was a nation in the making engaged in a mortal struggle for religion, honour, life, and property. True, for every rebel who fought, many others stood by silently trembling in fear; but if one onlooker's record in Marathi, the *Majha Pravas*, is any guide, there is no doubt as to where the sympathies of the bystander lay in the struggle.[70] On the British side, it was unmistakably a war to suppress an incipient nation, and to pulverize it by stamping upon its heads. Therefore, 21 *shahzadas* of the Mughal dynasty, against whom no evidence could be found except that they belonged to the royal family, were 'all condemned, hanged and carted off on the same day';[71] and it was left to Ghalib, the poet of the Mughal twilight, to write in anguish: 'If you were here ... you would see the moon-faced Begums of the Red Fort wandering around in the streets in filthy clothes, ragged pyjamas, and broken shoes.'[72]

By waging a brutal war to put an 'inferior race' in its place, the British imparted to the struggle a predominatly racial character; but it must not be forgotten that from the point of view of the rebels, the governing motive was 'religion'.[73] Even in any act of overt racial animosity such as the massacre of the whites, the rationale behind the action, as captured sepoys consistently maintained when cross-examined, was this: 'the slaughter of the British was required by our religion'.[74] This was so right from the beginning of the outbreak at Meerut, where the men of the 3rd Cavalry broke out with the cry, 'Our fight is for the cause of religion.'[75] 'Brothers, Hindoos and Musalmans', cried a *sawar* galloping towards the jail with sword unleashed, 'We are going to a religious war. Be assured we will not harm those who join us, but fight only against the Government.'[76] The *sawars* rushed on, riding without saddle, bareheaded, armed with drawn swords and pistols, pausing here and there to cry out: 'Babas, this war is in the cause of religion, whoever likes to join, come along with us'; and soon enough they were followed by the Muslim weighmen from the bazaar and butchers armed with stones, crying, 'Yah Ali! Ali!'[77]

'This day orders have been given to the whole force to turn out and plunder the English and to remember that the war is one of religion.'[78] Here, the primary racial impulse to hit back at the white men is converted into a religious crusade against the infidels enjoined by one's inner sense of duty—a process reminiscent, in some respects, of the Freudian transition from the id to the superego. Racial antagonism is the primary impulse which from time to time breaks through the surface: 'the yellow faced and narrow minded people', exults Nana Sahib, 'have been sent to hell';[79] 'these people with white skins and dark fortunes', promises a minor Muslim nobleman to Bahadur Shah, would be totally exterminated in three days if command of the operations were to be given to him;[80] and an armed Rajput retainer, pointing a matchlock at one Mr Corridon's breast, says more bluntly that it 'made his blood boil to see a Feringhee'.[81] However, the injunction laid by religion upon every mutineer's conscience was so far internalized that the enemy, rather than being perceived in stark terms of colour, was more usually referred to as 'kafir':[82] an unclean infidel on naming whom 'a man's mouth became impure [for] forty days'.[83] Thus, a trooper and some townsmen of Meerut, chasing a white man, cry out '*Māro kāfir ko*' (kill the infidel) even as they manage to sever his head. Joseph Henry Jones trembles as he hears a party of insurgents led by some policemen exclaim: '*Ali, Ali, aj marlia haie kafron ko*' (Ali, Ali, we have finished off the infidels today). Then, in a significant reversion to the underlying racial categories, a native informs him: '... the sepoys are killing the European soldiers, and no Feeringhee will be allowed to exist on earth.'[84]

Race and religion were thus fused into an explosive psychical compound. A group of disaffected policemen lounging on the charpoy on the eve of the outbreak in Lucknow put the matter simply: '*Kala Kala admee sab eyk hyn. Deen kee bat hyn. Hum log kahi ko bey dhurm ho*' (All black people are one. It is a matter of religion. Why should we incur loss of faith?).[85] The matter was debated at somewhat greater length between Vishnubhat Godase, travelling north to Hindustan, and a Marathi-speaking sepoy who was making his way back to Goa from the scene of the Mutiny. On being urged by the fleeing sepoy to go back, the Brahman reflected that he, as a mendicant, had nothing to fear from a war of religion by the assembly of blacks. 'We are not, after all, involved as fighting men, I am a poor begging Brahman (*Garib Bhikshuk Brāhman āhon*). I have nothing at all to fear from black people getting together to fight for the sake of religion (*Kāle lok ekatra hôun dharmakaritā bhāndanāt tar āpanyās bhaya nāhiñ*).' Further up he encountered a group of threatening sepoys, and managed to conciliate them by putting forth the same argument: 'O sepoy sons! I am a poor begging Brahman ... I have, however, no fear. Because a poor scripture-trained mendicant like me has nothing at all to fear from black people uniting to fight for the sake of religion' (*Kāran kāle lok jar dharmasāthi bhāndanār tar āmhā vedashāstrasampanna garib bhikshukāngsa bilkul bhaya nāhiñ*).[86] The heart of the matter, the root of what Shahzada Feroz Shah called 'the bitterest enmity between the natives and the English', was the perceived intention of 'these wicked Christian *Kafirs*' to spread Christianity by violence and 'to do away with the religion of Hindoos and Mussulmans';[87] that is why all subjects who did not wish to become Christians were urged to unite with the sepoys and not to leave 'the seed of these devils anywhere'.[88] The 'unclean infidels', in their 'pride', had committed the ultimate excess: a transgression that must be made to recoil totally upon itself by the traceless elimination of the perpetrators.[89]

One of the many minor outbreaks that set the pattern of the Mutiny has as its protagonist an unknown and forgotten Brahman, caught in the act of carrying messages from some disaffected villagers to the sepoys at Aligarh. The English had good reason to believe till then that the sepoys would be 'true to their salt'. Scarcely had the man been hanged in the presence of the troops that one of them stepped out and shouted to his comrades: 'Behold a martyr to our faith!'[90] That is how the ranks which broke out immediately into mutiny perceived the man: a martyr to faith. Note that the man was not cast here as a patriot sacrificing himself for the nation. Again, the Charkhari Raja, a loyalist, was upbraided by the mutinying troops of the Gwalior Contingent, not for being a traitor to the country, but for 'being regardless of the next world'.[91] What we seem to have here is a collective superego that pitted the rebellious people of Hindustan against the infidels as a matter of religious duty—apparently with no overt injunction from the 'higher self' to fight for the country as such.[92] The pervasive religious fervour of the Mutiny, then, seems on the surface to preclude the people's awareness of themselves as a political nation.[93] We must, however, look below the surface. Unless we do so, we shall not plumb that inarticulate unconscious in which a nation was in the making, nor shall we interpret correctly what lies behind the signs of religious symbolism.

Religion, constituting as it did the very basis of the community in 1857, was an immensely complex phenomenon with many different shades of meaning in that society: alternative senses that contained in consequence the possibility of vital encounters and resolutions within its own parameters, and which cannot be grasped if the deceptively easy formula of 'a war of religion' is seen as a self-explanatory theorem precluding deeper investigations into its multiple inner dynamics.[94] To start with, some of the simpler variations on the theme: Muslim women in Delhi taught their children to pray for the success of their faith during the Muharram of 1857, and their own fervent prayers were 'generally accompanied by execrations against the English'.[95] The Hindus, with whom it was not so straightforward a matter of creed,[96] were thought by one Christian prisoner of the palace to be less averse to the Company's government than the Muslims.[97] What he meant, perhaps, was that the grievances of the Hindus had a less doctrinal form:[98] as Sindia and his prime minister assured the English, 'Benares, Gya, and the other centres of Hindu opinion, to which all had looked, had abstained from sanctioning any religious pretext [for the revolt].'[99] Passages from the Qur'an, however, were quoted time and again to set out the grounds on which it was obligatory for the Muslims to oppose the Christians.[100]

One miscellaneous group that joined in the Mutiny—the misnamed 'Wahabis' (more correctly, the men of the Waliullahi tradition going back to Shah Wali Ullah of Delhi)—had long been active in preaching jihad. The widely circulated tract *Rissalah Jehad*, composed some thirty years earlier by Maulvi Muhammad Ismail and translated into the Hindustani language in 1850, was to be found in Delhi, Lucknow, and Cawnpore on the eve of the Mutiny, exhorting Muslims to attain heaven 'by dying in Battle with the Infidel'.[101] No sooner had the mutinies broken out in the cantonments than bands of Ghazis (or Mujahideen) appeared in Delhi from Tonk, Gwalior, Bareilly and elsewhere: fine-looking fellows, 'grizzly-bearded elderly men for the most part', with green turbans and cummerbands, and every one of them wearing a silver signet ring with a long text from the Qur'an finely engraved upon it. Men without fear, they would come on 'with their heads down below their shields, and their tulwars flashing as they whirled them over their heads, shouting "Deen! Deen!" and dancing like madmen'— only to be shot between their eyes by white soldiers stepping out with their Enfield rifles.[102] To all appearances, they were the same sort of men whom Saiyid Ahmad Khan of Rai Bareilly had led in jihad against the Sikhs in the Punjab. Such men had appeared even more recently at the imagined birthplace of Rama, 'with a fanatic môlovee at their head, ... resolved to enter the Hindoo shrine or die'.[103] However, in consequence of a dramatic realignment of forces, the mujahideen were transformed in 1857, fighting shoulder to shoulder with the Purbeah Hindu sepoys against the British batteries mounted on the Ridge outside Delhi.

The *Risala' Fath-i Islam*, one of the pamphlets that appeared during the Mutiny calling upon the Muslims to wage holy war upon the infidel, also carried an *ishtihar* (proclamation) 'meant for the Hindus and the Muslims of India, so that they should think over, and should prepare themselves for the slaughter of the English in order to protect their din and dharam'.[104] There could be no clearer manifestation of the Mujahi-deen's conscious acceptance of the altered context of holy war. *Deen*, the use of the word now dramatically extended, became a political rallying cry for both Muslims *and* Hindus amidst the sounds of battle.[105]

There were, however, still more dramatic transformations of '*deen*'. Its remarkable shift from one meaning to another, from a code of personal conduct to a matter of public duty, transformed the lives of some remarkable Muslim women who appeared in Delhi as *jehadins*— women who, if they had abided by the conventional sense of religion, should have stayed back at home and contented themselves with a daily prayer for the defeat of the infidel.

Colonel Keith Young, encamped on the Ridge, wrote to his wife in Simla on 29 July 1857: 'Did I tell you that they took a woman prisoner the other day, who they made out was leading a charge of Cavalry and who killed two of our men with her own hand? I believe the greater part of this to be fiction, and she is old and ugly, not much romance attaches to her, though she is wounded!'[106] The dour civil commissioner in the camp, H.H. Greathead, to whom the elderly *jehadin* was taken in captivity, made a more exact mention of the event: 'A Joan of Arc was made prisoner yesterday, she is said to have shot one of our men, and to have fought desperately. She is a Jehadin, a religious fanatic, and sports a green turban, and was probably thought to be inspired. She is to be sent prisoner to Umballa.'[107] History does not record who these elderly women were, how they were displaced from home, and what the circumstances were that inducted them into the war, but we have one indigenous record of the impression they made on the rebel camp in Delhi.

The police chief of rebel Delhi (the second in succession) recalled later:

Frequently two old withered Muslim women from Rampur led the rebels, going far in advance with naked swards and bitterly taunting the sepoys when they held back, calling them cowards and shouting to them to see how women went in front where they dared not follow—'We go on without flinching among the showers of grape while you flee away.' The sepoys would excuse themselves saying: We go to fetch ammunition, but the women would reply: 'You stop and fight and we will get your ammunition for you.' These women frequently did bring supplies of cartridges to the men in the batteries and walked fearlessly in perfect showers of grape, but by the will of God were never hit. At length one of them was taken prisoner and brought before Mr Greathead, the Commissioner, who after enquiring into the state of the city and the rebel army gave her five rupees and released her, at the same time issuing strict orders that no men should molest her. As she never returned to the mutineers she was considered by many to be a British spy. When the band of ghazis moved off to assault the women invariably went in advance of all.[108]

The better known career of the Rani of Jhansi illustrates the same shift from one meaning to another, with regard to the use of the word *dharma*: a transcendence her own words on one occasion capture unconsciously. The incident is related by Vishnubhat Godase. On the way to Kalpi the poor pilgrim was resting by the shade of a well when the young Rani, riding away from a disastrous encounter with the English at Charkhari, came up with four or five sawars who were then her only attendants. Here is the pilgrim's account of the encounter:

She was dressed from head to foot as a Pathan and her body was full of dust. Her face was slightly flushed and she looked a bit pale and dejected (toṅda ārakta asun mlān wa udās disat hote). Seized by extreme thirst she got down from the horse and, coming up to me, she asked: 'who are you?' Stepping quickly forward I said with folded hands, 'I am a Brahman' ... As I started lowering the earthen vessel into the well, the Bai Saheb interrupted: 'You are a learned Brahman (tumhi vidvān Brāhman), please don't draw water for me. Let me draw it up myself.' As I listened to these generous words, I felt ever so bad, but being helpless I put the ropes and earthen vessel down. The Bai Saheb, drawing the water up, quenched her thirst by drinking with cupped hands from the earthen vessel (Bāi Sahebāni pāni kātun tyā mrinmaya pātrātun oñjaline pāni

piyun trishā haran keli). Strange are the ways of providence. Thereupon
she said with an acute expression of despondence: 'I am entitled to half a
seer of rice only (mi ardhā sher tāndulāchi dhanin): I need not have
given up the common widow's dharma and taken up all these enterprises
(majlā rāṇdmuṇdesa vidhabādharma sorun hā udyog karanyāchi
kāhi jarur ṇābhati), nevertheless I have set my hand to these endeavours
to uplift the honour of the Hindu dharma (*parantu hindudharmāchā
abhimān dharun yā karmāsa pravritta jhāle*), and to this end I have
given up everything—the hope of riches, of life, of all things on earth
(wa yājakarita vittāchi, jivitāchi, sarvāchi āshā sorali).'[109]

The unconscious shift in the meaning of dharma, from 'the common husbandless woman's widow religion' (*rāṇdmuṇdesa vidhabā
dharma*) to the mounted warrior woman's 'proud Hindu religion'
(*Himdudharmāchā abhimān*), bears the traces of a remarkable trans-
figuration that lived on in the popular memory. Over half a century
after the event, William Crooke recorded a Mutiny song by the village
muse Rameshwar Diyali Mishra, who still remembered it after the lapse
of fifty-three years:

> She fought well, that brave one, the Rani of Jhansi,
> There were guns in the towers, and the magic shells were fired
> O the Rani of Jhansi, how well she fought that brave one
> Her soldiers were fed on sweetmeats but she took only coarse sugar and
> rice
> O Rani of Jhansi, how well she fought, that brave one.[110]

What was the passion in the breast of the young Rani, and those
elderly Jehadins, that drove them to these deeds? Without question it
was the passion of martyrdom for the faith, for faith alone could have
moved women so intensely in that age. Even so, the feeling itself, as
recorded in folk song, is indistinguishable from patriotism, for all intense
feelings are alike when they reach the ultimate pitch of transfiguring a
person. Crusader or patriot—what does it matter? The same word, *shahid*
(martyr), describes both in the Hindustani language of today and the
shift from one to the other is too elusive to track. That the assimilation
of the two is not a later development, but on the contrary a contemporary one, seems to be indicated by an utterance attributed to Nana
Sahib during his retreat from Cawnpore: 'An effort will have to be
made once again for the sake of the Hindu religion and the Hindu
realm' (*Hindudharmakaritā wa Hindurājyakaritā punhā ekbār jhatle
pāije*).[111] As realm and religion were even more closely tied together in

the Islamic faith, not surprisingly the implications for the country's governance were no less clearly articulated in the proclamations of jihad in 1857. Thus, Maulvi Liaqat Ali exhorted his co-religionists: 'O My Mussulman Brethren! as soon as you hear the above glad tidings prepare yourself for *Jehad*, come to Allahabad, subdue and put to sword the besieged Christians there, and then rule the Country according to Laws and Institutions of Mohammed.'[112]

The question may now arise as to how these apparently conflicting Muslim and Hindu visions of realizing the sacred realm were to be reconciled in the actual sphere of governance. It is here that the mutineers made a striking contribution to the development of political concepts. Though original, these concepts were profoundly embedded in the past. A clue to these not so well articulated conceptions is found in the words of an unknown Muslim nobleman whom a native Christian heard conversing on the verandah of the Bijnaur Collector's bungalow six weeks before the Mutiny. The company present consisted of the Muslim nobleman whom the Collector's chupprassee addressed respectfully as nawab (he apparently had a brother who was tahsildar in the district), another Muslim who was serving as *jamadar* in the Canal Department, and the native Christian, Francis Shester.

> The Nawab commenced the conversation by observing that two regiments to the eastward had taken their discharge, because the Kafirs had mixed pigs' and cows' fat with the new cartridges, that the Kafirs had determined to take away the castes of all Mahomedans and Hindoos, and that these infidels should not be allowed to remain in India, or there would be no difference between Mahomedans and Hindoos, and whatever they said, we should have to do.[113]

Note the Nawab's unstated commitment, a value attached unconsciously as it were, to 'the difference between Mahomedans and Hindoos' (which lay at the very heart of the traditional Indian social and political system),[114] the destruction of which, he knew instinctively, would result in all of them being obliged to do whatever 'they', the foreign masters, would have them do. The nawab was only voicing a thought then in the mind of every sepoy, and indeed the population at large. Just a day before the Mutiny, Henry Lawrence heard a trusted sepoy in Lucknow say: 'That is just it. You want us all to eat what you like that we may be stronger, and go everywhere.'[115] Captain Martineau, posted at Ambala, heard a belief then current that the people of Hindustan 'should be all compelled to eat the same food', which was taken to be a token that 'they would likewise be compelled to embrace one faith, or as they termed it, 'One food and one faith'.[116] As the Mutiny broke out, the instinctive and subconscious commitment to the fundamental principle of Indian society, unity in diversity, took firmer ideological shape. That ideology was set out in the celebrated proclamation of Emperor Bahadur Shah to the Hindu rajas and zamindars of Hindustan, which the English prosecutor produced in extenso at his trial:

PROCLAMATION[117]

'With the approving sanction of God, the Lord of the Nation'[118]

'Exposition of a letter written regarding the victory of the faith'

All you Rajahs are famed for your virtues, noble qualities, and liberality, and are moreover the protectors of your own faith and of the faith of others. Keeping your welfare in view, I humbly submit that God had given you your bodily existence to establish his different religions and requires you severally to learn the tenets of your own different religions, institutions, and forms, and you accordingly continue firm in them. God has moreover sent you into the world in your elevated position, and given you dominion and Government, that you may destroy those who harm your religion. It is incumbent, therefore, on such of you as have the power, to kill those who may harm your religion, and on such as have not, to engage heartily in devising means for the same end, and thus protect your faith; for it is written in your scriptures that martyrdom is preferable to adopting the religion of another. This is exactly what God has said, and what is evident to every body. The English are people who overthrow all religions. ... It is now my firm conviction that if these English continue in Hindoostan they will kill every one in the country, and will utterly overthrow our religions. ... Under these circumstances, I would ask, that course have you decided on to protect your lives and faith? Were your views and mine the same, we might destroy them entirely with a very little trouble; and if we do so, we shall protect our religions and save the country. And as these ideas have been cherished and considered merely from a concern for the protection of the religions and lives of all you Hindoos, and Mussulmans of this country, this letter is printed for your information. All you Hindoos are solemnly adjured, by your faith in the Ganges, Tulsi and Saligram; and all you Mussulmans, by your belief in God and the Kuran, as these English are the common enemy of both, that you unite in considering their slaughter extremely expedient, for by this alone will the lives and faith of both be saved. It is expedient, then, that you should coalesce and slay them.'

Bahadur Shah's proclamation brought out the central principle of the Indian social system: coexistence and compartmentalization of the religions in their respective social spheres. Under the system, the parts were dependent on the whole in the sense that no religion would be secure in its demarcated sphere if the acceptance of doctrinal diversity were to come under threat. The patriotic commitment of the proclamation lay in the commitment to the social system evolved in Hindustan over the centuries. The argument was developed with a remarkable grasp of the mind and doctrines of the Hindus as set out in the *Bhagavad Gita*, for Bahadur Shah translated almost word for word Lord Krishna's exhortation to Arjuna in the Kurukshetra war: *'svadharme nidhanaṁ shreyah, paradharmo bhayavahah'* (it is better to die for one's own faith, for adopting the faith of another is too terrible to contemplate). It is no coincidence that the same principle is enunciated by quoting the same *sloka* in the parallel proclamation of Rani Lakshmi Bai:

> The *Shastra* declares that it is best to follow one's own religion, and not to adopt another's, and God himself has so declared; but it is evident to all men that these English are perverters of all man's religion. From time immemorial have they endeavoured to contaminate the Hindoo and Mahomedan religions by the production and circulation of religious books through the medium of missionaries, and by extirpating such books as afford arguments against them.

In an age when the mentality of the people was steeped in profound religious convictions, it may be historically misleading to try and isolate the patriotic feelings that have come to stand on their own in the course of later developments. Undoubtedly such feelings were embedded in the jihads that erupted in many parts of the Islamic world, including Hindustan, but the historian must not forget that in the people's own consciousness these were wars of religion. The Mutiny, however, while including a prominent element of Mujahideen, must, as Bahadur Shah's proclamation makes clear, stand in a category by itself. It has no exact parallel anywhere else. In those countries where one people and one religion have made possible an indissoluble blend of faith and patriotism, national identity itself must in some measure be a matter of religion. The situation was far more complex in India in 1857. Here was a country consisting of two communities striving to construct their respective sacred realms by ousting the common enemy, and at the same time profoundly moved by a sense of the land as one indivisible whole. What joined the two communities together was not just mutual opposition to 'the common enemy of both' but, as Bahadur Shah's proclamation also stressed, the country itself to which they belonged, and where both had the mutually recognized right to set up the appropriate sacred realm. Note the words: 'we shall protect our religions and save the country'. The latter was the common link and in that sense stood outside of the two religions.

As to the mechanics of the accommodation between the two, the proclamation was vague, and had nothing to say except that the Muslim rulers and Hindu rajas were naturally the protectors of their own faith 'and of the faith of others' (not an inappropriate description considering the rulers of eighteenth-century India). The same vague conceptions reappeared in the popular notions of Ram Raj and Khilafat in the Indian struggle of 1920–2. The ulama of Deoband and the Ali brothers articulated a vision of the Indian destiny not altogether dissimilar: one country with two realms, two nationalities within one people (a solution that might well have been realized if the confederation envisaged by the Cabinet Mission had not been rejected by Jawaharlal Nehru in his single-minded pursuit of the secular nation).[119]

The rebels were up in arms not because they objected to the rulers' doctrines as such, though on one occasion they were provoked by Queen Victoria's assertion of 'the truth of Christianity'[120] to pour scorn on the doctrine of the Trinity.[121] However, as Begam Hazrat Mahal put it in her rejoinder: 'What has the administration of justice to do with the truth or falsehood of a religion?' The people were driven to 'mortal desperation' (in the Begam's phrase, *'Murta kya na kurta'*: a dying man will do anything), not so much because of missionary propaganda in favour of the 'false' doctrine of the Trinity, nor because of the subtle undermining effects of the spread of English education[122] (which they were perfectly confident of coping with and taking advantage of), but because they were convinced that the government was maturing in secret the terrible master plan—kill or convert.[123]

The 'alarms' of 1857 had reference 'to the Government alone—to its news, its decisions and its designs'. The terror that gripped their minds was the completion of the physical and spiritual domination of the alien masters, the enslavement of their very souls by extinguishing the native religions of Hindustan, and the loss of the identity of the people rooted in the cherished differences of their social system. The psychical 'defensive reaction' against the feared result was translated into the rhetoric and language not of national resistance to the imperial aggrandizer (a language then being born in the Presidency towns of Calcutta, Bombay, and Madras but still unknown in the heart of

Hindustan), but of the confederate alliance of the Hindus and Muslims against the *'firangi'* or *'kafir'*, expressions indicative of the unlovely twin characteristics of the enemy looming large in the minds of the people.[124]

The manner in which the people perceived and defined themselves was most strikingly evident in these descriptions of the enemy. 'They' were sometimes addressed as *'firangis'*, 'we' being by implication Hindustanis, or the inhabitants of Hindustan; more frequently, 'infidels', 'Christians' or 'Nazarenes' were set against 'the Hindus and Musalmans' in the rebel language. The commonest term by far was kafir (infidel),[125] an expression covering not merely the English, but also the native and half-blood Christians. The Englishmen were 'accursed Christians';[126] they were enemies of religion and accursed *vilaitis* (foreigners);[127] and the 'unbelieving Nazarines' must be dispatched to hell.[128] The NWP Police Commissioner's *Synopsis* of the Cawnpore evidence tells us: '... the troopers ... were indefatigable in their search of Christians.'[129] That the latter category also included non-whites comes out in the evidence of an opium *gumashtah* who was in Cawnpore on leave: 'Many merchants expected that the sepoys would spare their property and that they would consequently be able to carry on business under the new Government. The sepoys however murdered every Christian they found, and also fired at every person they saw wearing English garments.'[130] In Lucknow, Christians, half-breeds, and *keranees* (literally clerks, a term indicating the Eurasian employees of the government) were kept in a separate prison and some of them were put to death along with the 'Sahib Logue'.[131]

The warlike instincts impelling the people to deeds of violence would appear to have consisted of two allied emotions: hatred for the whites and dislike and distrust of all others whom they instinctively associated with the white domination. One aspect of that domination was perceived to be spiritual and religious, and several missionaries, computed by Reverend Alexander Duff to be 37 in all, were killed. However, missionaries were not specially singled out. They were dealt with in precisely the same way as all other Europeans, and, as Dr Duff himself pointed out at the time, all persons 'identified by the rebels with the governing class' were made to suffer—Bengali babus as well as native Christians and Eurasian clerks.[132] There would appear to have been some sort of instinctive gradation of the victims according to the severity of the punishment they deserved. Each European was singled out and slaughtered in Hamirpur, whether he be a high government

official or a private landholder and merchant. The native catechist of
the Church Missionary Society, a man named Jeremiah, was also
murdered with his wife and four children. However, Bengali babus,
while relieved of everything they possessed, were all able to beg
successfully for their lives. The half-breed judicial clerk, Mr Bunter,
and his wife, were also given their lives on promising to become Muslims,
but later the couple was cut down by the infuriated mutineers when
Mr Bunter unadvisedly came out and bowed to the European magistrate
and joint magistrate as they were being marched out to the firing squad
at the Cutcherry.[133]

Nothing revealed the alignments in the Mutiny more clearly than
the census of people who took refuge in the Agra Fort when the town
fell into the hands of the mutineers. Charles Raikes observed in the
motley six-thousand-strong assemblage 'unwilling delegates from many
parts of Europe and America', for what mattered was colour, and next
to it creed, but not distinctions of nationality:

> Nuns from the banks of the Garonne and the Loire, priests from Sicily
> and Rome, missionaries from Ohio and Basle, mixed with rope-dancers
> from Paris, and pedlars from America. Besides these we had Calcutta
> Baboos and Parsee merchants. Although all the Christians alike were
> driven by the mutinous legions into the Fort, the circumstances of the
> multitude were as various as their races.[134]

The Parsees and Bengalis were, of course, neither whites nor
Christians, but the mutineers could hardly have overlooked the fact
that there were Parsee merchants on the Ridge outside Delhi supplying
wines, spirits, and beer to the English camp,[135] and cowering Bengalis
in Cawnpore, suspected of sending messages to the English force
marching up from Allahabad. Orders were issued by Nana Sahib that
'the baboos of the city, and every individual who could read or write
English, should have their right hands and noses cut off', but the timely
arrival of the British troops saved them.[136]

Such were the spontaneous impulses of a population smelling out
and identifying the enemy. In seeking to put these feelings into
ideological terms, however, they adopted the only universal definitions
familiar to them: those derived from the phraseology of religion with
its opposed categories of *kafir* and *mujahid*.[137] So deep was the impression
of these categories on the popular mind that those natives who where
prepared to help the English were denounced as Christians and pariahs,[138]
and the Christians themselves were recognized to have a right to

protection on abandoning their infidel Nasri doctrines and embracing the true faith. From the standpoint of the rationalist Indian of 1885–1947, these redefinitions might have appeared embedded in an outmoded false consciousness, but to the rebels of 1857 and their ways of articulate thinking, the categories were real enough.

Thus the diary of the Nannhe Nawab, at first a reluctant and then an enthusiastic rebel leader of Cawnpore, opens with two common troopers taunting him in the following manner:

> As I had not joined with the men of the Jhunda [Muslim flag], two troopers were sent by the Nana to fetch me, saying that they have waited long for me, how it was that I did not join the Jhunda, it appears that I was not a Mahomedan but a Christian (an expression of contempt), I had better soon attend the Nana's Court, or they have orders to take my head to the Nana.[139]

A variant of the same logic is illustrated in the following petition of the vacillating Jat Raja of Ballabhgarh to Emperor Bahadur Shah:

> Further I heard from some persons who had requests to make to me, that it has been represented to your Majesty, that the Chief of Ballabhgarh has secreted two Englishmen, with their wives and children. God is witness that this is entirely a false and unfounded calumny. How could your slave dare to commit an act of the kind, without your Majesty's wishes and orders! A native, however, who was formerly a Christian, had been twelve years in my service; but I put even him away, fearing Your Majesty's displeasure. This man has now discarded Christianity and embraced the Mahomedan religion, and he is accordingly deserving of mercy and forgiveness.[140]

It should appear from the tone of the letter that Europeans were not supposed to be allowed the same dispensation. However, we have on record from the rebel police chief of Delhi the following instance of the logic of the doctrine being pushed to its furthest extent by General Bakht Khan, who is said to have been a 'Wahabi':

> A European sergeant whom they called Abdullah was with the Bareilly brigade, as well as two or three Christians, half castes of the poorest class. Mr John Powell, son of Mr Powell of Saharanpur, whom they had seized and brought from Moradabad, was also with them but under surveillance. The 29th Native Infantry were favourably disposed to these persons and would let no one molest them, saying they had made them Moslems. The regiment indeed took considerable care of them, provided their wants and would not permit sepoys of other corps or the town people to approach them.[141]

A slightly different version, by another rebel police chief of Delhi (a predecessor), makes it clear that Abdullah played an active role in the defence of Delhi against the British. According to this version, he was a discharged European soldier of the 17th foot at Meerut: he converted to Islam and, as Abdullah Beg, become leader and adviser to the mutineers in Delhi.[142] The incident, too well authenticated to be doubted, forms a curious instance of the impulse of race animosity being overlaid by the ideology of religious solidarity. In the process the particular definition of the rebellious native race or nation itself was superseded by the universal category of the brotherhood of faith.

No wonder then that the language of religion preponderates in the scores of Mutiny proclamations and letters recovered by the patient researches of the archivist and historian: and unless we suppose that the feelings of patriotism are concealed and embedded within those religious sentiments, we look in vain for any patriotic rhetoric in the numerous specimens of Mutiny language now available in print. Consider, for instance, a proclamation discovered as far afield as Hyderabad, in which patriotic solidarity, if at all to be looked for, must be taken to be a function of religious excommunication:

> A Muslim who resolves to kill a Kafir, i.e. a Christian, and delays will be cut off from the society and called a descendant of the pariah caste, of a pig, and of a dog. He will be a descendant of Yazeed and Shumar. It is an oath on God to a Muslim whether he is rich or poor, or the Dewan, or spiritual head, or Moulvi, Kazi, Mufti, Suba or Kootwal, to participate in the task and get the blessings of God. If he succeeds he will be called a victor (Ghazi). If he dies he will be counted among those who died in the holy wars and will get a place in Bliss.[143]

The only hint (a negative one) that this is not an Islamic jihad in the hitherto known style is the implicit exclusion of the Hindus from the definition of Kafir. The infidel, it is taken care to define, is a Christian. Negative though it is, the hint is nonetheless vital for behind it lies an underlying commitment to the caste-bound social system of the country with which the Indian Muslim had adjusted for several centuries. It is made clear that if he does not spring to its defence, he will be declared a pariah.

If the infidel is by definition a Christian, the extension of the same logic points to the Hindus and Muslims as the faithful: therein lies embedded the inchoate, inarticulate notion of the nation, concealed and overlaid by the Weltanschauung of religion.[144] While sensing out the unformed outlines of that foetus may be an interesting historical exercise, it may lead the investigator astray if he looks upon the enveloping corpus of *deen* and *dharma* as a mere veneer concealing the real thing. The notions that sustained the rebels till the last hour of doom derived from faith. An individual who assisted at their systematic hanging in Cawnpore was constrained to observe: 'As a rule, those who had to die died with extraordinary, I was going to say courage, but composure is the word; the Mahomedans, with a hauteur and an angry kind of scorn; and the Hindoos with an apparent indifference altogether astonishing. ... Some of the Hindoos treated death almost as if it were a journey.'[145]

The conviction that helped them face death helped them also to fight for what they cherished. The things they cherished would not have appealed much to the men who were later destined to gather together in the Indian National Congress of 1885. The values of the mutineers were indeed repugnant to the men who were even then assembled in the British Indian Association, the Bombay Association, and the Madras Native Association. What a gulf lay between these alternative versions of patriotism! The Hindu pandits who served the Purbeah sepoys in Delhi used to sing what an English officer dismissed as 'wild rhapsodies', a description with which the nationalists in Calcutta, Bombay, and Madras would not have disagreed. Take this specimen:[146]

> No white face can move out
> Therefore advance your batteries without fear.
> The camp shall be destroyed like Lunka by fire;
> Increase the number of your guns.
> By the grace of Bulbhudder and Ramchander
> The Camp shall be annihilated
> Fight without intermission day and night;
> Protect from injury our mother and cow
> Offer sacrificial food to Joala Maee and Bhovanee
> And distribute it among the Brahmans
> Present daily an offering of fourteen cows.

The abstract concept of Mother India would shortly be formed by the English-educated Indians of the Presidency towns. However, mutineers of Hindustan, when referring to the Mother, thought more readily of the real animal that sustained life in their villages. In a fast-moving world that challenged them to look forward, they cast glances continually backward. Even so, there was something novel in their constructions, especially in one phrase repeated over and over again in the language of the Mutiny. This was the compound construction 'Hindus and Mussalmans of Hindustan', which was as much a political construct as the term 'Indian nation'. Even considered separately, these terms—Hindus and Muslims—were made-up categories, in view of the numerous divisions of tribe, caste, and region agglomerated in either community. Taken together, they were of course a more strikingly novel conglomerate.

In what sense were the Hindus and Muslims *both* entitled to the distinction of fidelity, as against '*kufr*' and '*shirk*'? Certainly in no doctrinal sense—there were far less serious differences among the People of the Book (Muslims, Christians, and Jews) than between these and the idolaters. The fidelity fusing the Hindus and Muslims as one confederate body was a concept born of the exigencies of political circumstances. They were linked together by the country to which they had a birthright: the country which the aliens had appropriated and were now threatening to destroy by undermining its characteristic social system.

In addresses meant for themselves and the people, the rebel leaders used the term 'Hindus and Muslims' unthinkingly. However, as soon as the sphere shifted to correspondence between themselves and the Nepal darbar, seeking to detach the latter from the British, the connotation of the term began to assume a clearer outline. The Nepal darbar, although Hindu, was understood to be outside the political system of Hindustan. Like the Kabul darbar, it was 'foreign'. It required correspondence with a foreign power to bring out the concealed national significance of the term, 'Hindus and Musalmans'. Thus, Birjis Qadr explained to the Maharaja of Nepal:

> The British some time ago, attempted to interfere with the faith of both the Hindoos and Mohammedans, by preparing cartridges with cow's grease for the Hindoos, and that of pigs for the Mohammedans, and ordering them to bite them with their teeth. The sepoys refused, and were ordered by the British to be blown away with guns, on the parade ground. This is the cause of the war breaking out, and you are probably acquainted with it.

The boy prince's ambassador, therefore, professed it 'astonishing that you should have sided with the impure infidels, who are tyrants and enemies of the religion, both of Hindoos and Mohammedans, and have fought against the army of the faithful.'

In his reply, acknowledging but rejecting the message from Awadh that 'the British are bent on the destruction of the society, religion and faith, of both Hindoos and Mohammedans,' the Jang Bahadur posed the question, 'What grounds can we have for connecting ourselves with the Hindoos and Mohammedans, of Hindustan?' and left the answer in no doubt: 'As the Hindoos and Mohammedans have been guilty of ingratitude and perfidy, neither the Nepaul government nor I can side with them.' Mindful of the fact that the Hindus and Musalmans of Hindustan were strangers despite sharing at least one religion with Nepal, the Jang Bahadur rejected Birjis Qadr's appeal that 'it is proper for us to band together in the cause of religion,' and harshly reminded the fugitive prince of Lucknow: 'Be it also known, that had I in any way been inclined to cultivate the friendship and intimacy of the Hindoo and Mohammedan tribes, should I have massacred nearly 5 (5000) or 6,000 of them on my way to Lucknow?'[147]

What emerges from the correspondence is an alternative conception of what the Congress were to conceive later as the political nation: the confederated body of the 'faithful', acknowledged in neighbouring countries as the Hindus and Muslims of Hindustan, and distinct, on the one hand, from Hindu Nepal and, on the other, from Muslim Afghanistan. In their own eyes, the men of the two distinct faiths were united in their opposition to the 'tyrants and enemies of religion'. The concept we have here is not 'the Indian Nation', but, in place of it, 'the Hindus and Musalmans of Hindustan'. These vague, half-articulate conceptions survived in the consciousness of the Indian population, fuelling the struggle for Gandhi's Ram Raj and the Ali Brothers' Khilafat movement three generations later. On that occasion, too, the two peoples joined together as one confederate nation. Here lay an alternative conception of the nation running through the history of India's struggle for freedom. The formation of these conceptions is, thus, of sufficient historical importance to try and trace in some detail.

In the common parlance of the day the Muslims were a '*qaum*' (people, race, community, or nation), and so, in their eyes, were the Hindus. Acutely aware of each other's separateness, yet compelled to reckon with their oneness, they had come to regard themselves as two peoples within one by the end of the eighteenth century. As late as that, many high-born Muslims of the country still regarded themselves, like the newly ascendant Englishmen, as conquerors from outside. However, the difference, as a Mughal nobleman and chronicler of keen insight put it, lay in the fact that the former had decided 'to fix the foot of residence and permanence' in the conquered country. 'Their immediate successors having learned the language of the country, behaved to its inhabitants as brothers of one mother and one language.' Writing in the twilight of the Mughal empire, under the shadow of Plassey and Buxar, Saiyid Ghulam Husain Khan observed, in well-chosen, justly celebrated words:[148]

> And although the Gentoos seem to be a generation apart and distinct from the rest of mankind, and they are swayed by such differences in religion, tenets, and rites, as will necessarily render all Mussalmans aliens and profane, in their eyes; and although they keep up a strangeness of ideas and practices, which beget a wide difference in customs and actions; yet in the process of time, they drew nearer and nearer, and as soon as fear and aversion had worn away, we see this dissimilarity and alienation have terminated in friendship and union, and the two nations have come to coalesce together into one whole, like milk and sugar that have received a simmering. In one word, we have seen them promote heartily each other's welfare, have common ideas, like brothers from one and the same mother, and feel for each other, as children of the same family.

Perhaps Saiyid Ghulam Husain Khan spoke a little too wishfully (although we may observe that his carefully chosen simile refers to one mother, the country, but not one father, the faith). However, the process of assimilation was certainly carried a stage further in his day by common subjection to the English.[149] The twin characteristics of the Englishmen that impressed themselves on his mind were the transitory character of their stay in the country and their single-minded devotion to 'scraping together as much money in this country as they can, and carrying it in immense sums to the kingdom of England.'[150]

A century of sharing the common experience of racial humiliation would certainly have blurred the psychological distinction Saiyid Ghulam Husain Khan drew in his day between the Muslims and the Hindus as the conquerors and the conquered. Folk memory, however, carried a residue of bitterness and distrust that exhibited itself in the trouble over Hanuman Garhi at 'Ayodhya' just two years prior to the Mutiny.[151] The year 1857 witnessed this antagonistic religious distinction being transcended by the dramatic redefinition of 'fidelity'. The term 'Hindus and Musalmans' suddenly emerged as a term of reference for the people of the country, fighting together for a diverse heritage of faith threatened from a single malignant quarter. Pronouncing two communities together meant speaking of the entire native population, minus the section that had lost fidelity (i.e. native Christians).

The 'other' of the 'infidels' formed an agglomerate not yet defined as the political nation, yet sufficiently formed in the consciousness of contemporaries for the *Risala' Fath-i-Islam* to urge: 'A proclamation should be issued both to the troops and people of Bengal if possible, or if otherwise, as far as possible at present, to the effect that the people of every city, whether Hindoos or Mahomedans, should be unanimous in attacking simultaneously this accursed nation (by the appointment of a leader in each city).'[152] The people of Hindustan were now a people at war, in a sense no less definite than the Hellenes, divided up in many a small polis, had been a people at war during the Persian invasion.[153] Consider the following proclamations by the Indian chiefs, using again and again the characteristic expression connoting the nation then in the process of being born:

[Khan Bahadur Khan]: Proclamation for the religious and faithful promulgated by authority.

Let it be known at present it is indispensable for both the Hindoos and Mahomedans to direct their united efforts to the extermination of the Christians—enemies of lives and faith.[154]

[Mirza Feroz Shah Shahzada]: To all Hindoos and Mahommedans of Hindoostan who are faithful to their religion know that sovereignty is one of God's chief boons, one which a deceitful tyrant is never allowed to retain. For several years the English have been committing all kinds of excesses and tyrannies being desirous of converting all men to Christianity by force, and of subverting and doing away with the religion of Hindoos and Mahommedans. When God saw this fact, He so altered the hearts of the inhabitants of Hindostan, that they have been doing their best to get rid of the English themselves; now the Feringhees have been destroyed, but still they overrun the country to its distraction, and persevere in their vain endeavours. Soon they will have been, by the grace of God, so utterly exterminated, that no traces of them will remain. Know that all Hindoos and Mussalmans have become so hateful to them, that they will not suffer any to live with honour.[155]

[Unnamed grandson of Bahadur Shah]: it is well known to all in this age the people of Hindustan, both Hindoos and Mohammedans, are being ruined under the tyranny and oppression of the infidel and treacherous English. It is therefore the bounden duty of all the wealthy people of India, especially those who have any sort of connection with any of the Mohammedan royal families, and are considered the pastors and masters of their people, to stake their lives and property for the well being of the public .... I who am the grandson of Abul Muzuffer Serajuddin Bahadur

Shah Ghazee, King of India, having in the course of circuit come here [Azamgarh] to extirpate the infidels residing in the eastern part of the country, and to liberate and protect the poor helpless people now groaning under their iron rule, have, by the aid of the Majahdeens, or religious fanatics, erected the standard of Mohammed, and persuaded the orthodox Hindoos who had been subject to my ancestors, and have been and are still accessories to the destruction of the English, to raise the standard of Mahavir.

Several of the Hindoo and Mussulman chiefs, who have long since quitted their homes for the preservation of their religion, and have been trying their best to root out the English in India, have presented themselves to me, and taken part in the reigning Indian crusade, and it is more than probable that I shall very shortly receive succours from the West.[156]

In characteristic Mutiny language, the loyalist Hindu Thakur of Kethyaree was thus addressed by a Muslim theologian: 'To Hurdeo Buksh of Kethyaree, Christian of Farruckabad.' He was admonished for 'your having deserted your kinsmen and brethren (both Hindoos Mahommedans)'. Upbraiding him for his 'shamelessness, worthlessness and dishonesty,' the man of God warned him: 'Even should victory smile on the cause of the English, you will be shunned by your brethren.'[157] The 'reigning Indian crusade' thus produced its own categories of patriots and traitors. Thus, the 'Peshwa' of the reborn Maratha confederacy, calling perdition upon the infidel chief of Charkhari, enjoined upon all officers, 'Soobadars, Sirdars and Sepoys' to consider him 'as an Englishman' and to 'send him to hell'.[158]

What was to be the basis of the patriotic alliance between the Hindus and Muslims,—or 'the reigning Indian crusade,' as the unnamed *shahzada* put it at Azamgarh? One popular argument, with intellectual precedents going back to the *Majma ul Bahrain* of Darah Shikoh[159] and the syncretistic cults of the medieval saints, was thus put in a secret letter from the mutinous 51st Native Infantry at Peshawar to two disaffected regiments stationed at Shubkudder on 15 May 1857: 'O brother! the religion of Hindoos and Mahomedans is all one—Therefore all you soldiers should know this.'[160] That this was not mere casuistry, but had genuine feeling behind it, is shown by the genuine regard the Muslim sepoys showed for the religion of the Hindu sepoys over the issue of the greased cartridge. As Khan Bahadur Khan's celebrated proclamation pointed out, 'The Musulman soldiers perceived that by this expedient the religion of the Brahmins and Hindoos alone was in danger, but nevertheless they also refused to bite them.'[161] The same mutual regard, intellectually based on the Indian dictum '*Svadharme nidhanaṁ Shreyah*', quoted time and again, formed the ground of the *Risala' Fath-i-Islam's* enunciation: 'The Hindoos will remain steadfast to their religion, while we will also retain ours. Aid and protection will be offered by us to each other.'[162]

That is all very well, a sceptic like Raja Man Singh of Shahganj (the commonly accepted protector of the so-called birthplace of Rama) might have asked, but what about the sharing of the realm? Maulvi Ahmadullah Shah's answer to this was not likely to satisfy him: 'The Hindoos should join the [appointed Muslim] chief ... inasmuch as formerly the Mahomedan Kings protected (as they felt it incumbent on them to do) the lives and property of the Hindoos with their children in the same manner as protected those of the Mahomedans, and all the Hindoos with heart and soul were obedient and loyal to the Mahomedan Kings.'[163] The assumption implicit here about the sharing of the realm: 'commonsense and a regard for faith point out that servitude under the Mahomedan Chiefs and such Rajahs as are dependents of the Mahomedan Kings is infinitely better than that under the infidel Victoria and the English'[164]—is unlikely to have appealed to a raja who only two years earlier was commonly believed to have declared, during the Hanumangarhi dispute, that but for the support the Nawab was sure to receive from the English, 'he would have marched to Lucknow, destroyed the Mahomedan dynasty, and established a Hindoo Government in its place'.[165] Only a month before he joined the mutineers at Lucknow with his levy, convinced by Havelock's precipitate retreat that the British were the losing side, the raja was writing in a letter to brother *taluqdars* of Awadh:[166]

> It is also surprising that people should aid and put into power those very Mussulmans who, on invading India, destroyed all our Hindoo temples, forcibly converted the natives to Mohamedanism, massacred whole cities, seized upon Hindoo females and made them concubines, prevented Brahmins from saying prayers, burnt their religious books, and levied taxes upon every Hindoo.
>
> They are those very Mussulmans who prided themselves on calling us infidels, and in subjecting us to all sorts of humiliation.
>
> If any person will reflect on their former deeds, it will make his hair stand on end, cause such disgust that the very sight even of a Mohamedan will be abhorrent.
>
> What is more surprising still, is that the people should consider it a religious deed to kill those very persons who permitted the establishment

of the decayed religion, and allowed all temples and places of worship to
be rebuilt, and all religious ceremonies to be performed without any
hindrance whatever.

We should consider how much we suffered in the time of the
Mahomedan kings of Oude.[167]

Man Singh voiced a part of the Hindi folk memory that
undoubtedly coexisted with fonder memories, such as the cherished
remembrance of the munificent Nawab Asafuddaulah of Lucknow in
whose name the Hindu shopkeeper of the city would intone as he took
his seat in his shop: '*Jis ko na de Maula, Tis ko de Asif-ud-Daulah*' (To
whom the Lord does not give, Asif-ud-Daulah will).[168] The rebel leaders
were acutely aware of the problem of Hindu–Muslim conflict and the
Muslim chiefs took particularly vigorous action to counteract it. A
compact banning cow slaughter, initiated by Emperor Bahadur Shah
during Bakr Id in Delhi,[169] was arrived at with the Hindu rajas and
sepoys:

> The slaughter of kine is regarded by the Hindoos as a great insult to their
> religion. To prevent this, a solemn compact and agreement has been entered
> into by all the Madommedan chiefs of Hindoostan, binding themselves,
> that if the Hindoos will come forward to slay the English, the
> Mahommedans will, from that very day put a stop to the slaughter of
> cows, and those of them who will not do so will be considered to have
> abjured the Kuran, and such of them as will eat beef will be regarded as
> though they had eaten pork; but if the Hindoos will not gird their loins
> to kill the English, but will try to save them, they will be as guilty in the
> sight of God as though they had committed the sins of killing cows ....[170]

The true extent of the concession under this national compact can
hardly be grasped unless we bear in mind the degree to which Indian
Islam had become symbolically and emotionally bound to the
ceremonial sacrifice of the cow over the centuries. How important the
compact was politically is briefly glimpsed in the communications from
the English officers besieging Delhi from the Ridge. As Id day
approached, Keith Young wrote expectantly on the basis of reports
received from spies:

> Some of the Mahomedan fanatics have declared their fixed intention of
> killing a cow as customary on that day at the Jumma Musjid. It is hoped
> that they will religiously adhere to their determination, and there is then
> sure to be a row between the Mahomedans and Hindoos.

A day after the Id, he wrote in a disappointed tone to his wife:

[O]ur hopes of a grand row in the city yesterday at the Eed Festival have
not, apparently, been fulfilled—at least the only newsletter received from
the city alludes to nothing of the kind. The king issued strict orders against
killing cows, or even goats, in the city, and this, if acted upon, must have
satisfied the Hindoos; and instead of fighting among themselves they all
joined together to make a vigorous attack to destroy us and utterly sweep
us from the face of the earth.[171]

Rohilkhand, where Khan Bahadur Khan scrupulously enforced the
compact, was tense with potential conflict. After a riot occurred at
night in Bareilly, the Nawab performed a special ceremony in the town:

He resolved to put up a large flag or holy dhvaj for the Hindus and a
Muhammadi Jhanda, i.e. holy flag, for the Muslims, and to call together
the principal Hindus and Musalmans under those flags. Having made
this resolve the Nawab proceeded through town that afternoon with some
Brahmans, Sobharam, Gokulanand, Newalanand, etc. and some Kayasthas,
Ganesh Rai, Harsukh Rai, etc. Needless to say the Hindus moved along
by their dhvaj; the Musalmans proceeded under the Muhammadi Jhanda.
The Nawab himself went round town with great pomp on an elephant.
The cry rose every now and then: 'Hindu Musalman ek'—'Ram Rahim
ek'—'Shrikrishna Allah ek', and it was proclaimed: 'Those who are strong
and adult among the Hindus, go to the Hindu dhvaj with arms, armed
Musalmans assemble under the Muhammadi Jhanda, and all swear to
extirpate the English'. Many spectators gathered round—such a crowd as
one could hardly make one's way through it. Amidst tumultuous sounds,
the holy *dhvaj* of the Hindus was planted on the bank of the Ramganga,
and on the same day the Muhammadi jhanda was planted in a garden
near town. Diwan Sobha Ram distributed food according to Hindu ritual:
luchis, sandesh, khir, on the bank of the Ramganga. Kalia, Kababs, Korma,
were being distributed in the garden.[172]

Earlier the same sort of ceremony had taken place under the aegis
of Nana Sahib in Cawnpore, where the green Muhammadi *jhanda* had
been set up, as well as a Mahavir *jhanda*, calling upon the people to
attack the entrenchment commanded by General Wheeler.[173]

The 'reigning Indian crusade', with battle cries of '*Deen Deen*' and
'*Har Har Mahadeo*' accompanying the unfurling of the green and white
flags of Muhammad and Mahavir, struck the *Hindoo Patriot*, an English
language paper which belonged squarely to a different and professedly
modern category of Indian patriotism, as a movement that, despite all
its limitations, reflected the 'national feelings', of 'martyrs to a holy

cause', who had been led to believe 'their national religion' to be in danger.[174] A proclamation from Charkhari some time later virtually echoed the same words: 'I am desirous to extirpate Infidel Christians and preserve the national religion.'[175] A Rajput Pardesee peon sentenced to death for fomenting mutiny in Satara cried to the spectators from the scaffold that his own countrymen had betrayed him to the English and hanged him. Now was the time to strike: 'If they were sons of Hindoos and Mussulmans they would rise, if the offsprings of Christians, they would remain quiet.'[176]

Interspersed with the continual exhortations to the 'Hindus and Musalmans', there are occasional references to the country and the countrymen; but they are incidental. In the absence of a clear political concept of the nation, the divisions within the population loomed large in the rebel language and consciousness. The written order of the Emperor to the chief police officer of Delhi, dated 6 September 1857, reads:

> You are directed to have proclaimed throughout the city by beat of drum that this is a religious war, and is being prosecuted on account of the faith, and that it behoves all Hindu and Mussulman residents of the imperial city, or of the villages out in the country, as well as those natives of Hindostan who are arrayed against us on the ridge, or anywhere employed on the side of the armies of the English, whether they be men of the eastern provinces [Purbeahs], or Sikhs, or foreigners,[177] or natives of the Himalays Hills, or Nepalese, to continue true to their faith and creeds, and to slay the English and their servants: and you are directed to have it further proclaimed that, those who are now present with the English force on the ridge, whether they be people of Hindustan, or foreigners or Hillmen,[178] or Sikhs,[179] or whatever country they may be natives of, or whether they be Mahomedans, or Hindus born in Hindustan, they are not to entertain any fears or dread of the enemy.[180]

These various categories stood sharply outlined in moments of fear: on 4 August there was a scare in town that the Pathans were coming from Swat, recruited by the English, to fight and kill the Purbeahs;[181] and the following day the Sikh sepoys in Delhi, annoyed with the Purbeahs for not receiving any assistance in their attacks on the English entrenchments, requested the Emperor that a regiment of Sikhs be formed amongst the sepoy regiments in Delhi to attack the English.[182] As for the citizens of Delhi, they looked upon the Purbeah soldiers as uncouth strangers,[183] and the latter were both disliked as an army of occupation and abused for cowardice in facing the British on the Ridge[184] (for fear of the advancing white soldiers lay like a pall on the town).

Fear, however, also psychically fused the people into one mass and knowledge of the common fate awaiting the Indians—Neill's savage, promiscuous butchery all the way from Allahabad to Cawnpore was known by this time—lent weight to the Emperor's exhortations to 'the people of Hindustan' to unite. Impelled by the subconscious mass conviction that the Hindus and Musalmans had become so 'hateful' to the English that 'they will not suffer any to live with honour', and that 'the padres and wise men amongst them, alarmed at the mutiny, the anarchy and the slaughter of the European', had concocted a secret, devious scheme for the extinction of the very identity of the people of Hindustan,[185] Shahzada Feroz Shah said, 'Oh Hindustanee Brethren! you have heard what measures they have resolved to carry out. You must now wash your hands, and becoming their enemies exert yourselves in exterminating them for the sake of your religion and your lives.'[186]

All at once, raw panic defined the opposed national identities in the words put into the mouth of the enemy: 'if all misconduct among the Hindustanis is punished, then the English rule will remain established for thousands of years'.[187] Voicing the same sort of mass panic and using the same coalesced expression of national identity, Nana Sahib circulated the following rumour:

> A traveller just arrived at Cawnpore from Calcutta states that before the cartridges were distributed a Council was held for the purpose of taking away the religion and rites of the people of Hindustan. The Members of the Council came to the conclusion that as the matter was one affecting religion seven or eight thousand Europeans would be required and it would cost the lives of fifty thousand Hindoostanis but that at this cost all the natives of Hindoostan would become Christians.[188]

With such unmistakable expressions of nationality—'O Hindustanee Brethren', 'the people of Hindustan,' 'the Hindustanis', 'the whole country of Hindustan'—now transforming the political climate in the country, it is no surprise that the language of patriotic war broke through even the crusading *maulvi's* rhetoric of jihad:

> Mussulmans of India being destitute of resources, having no ammunition, Guns, or Army, have been all along in a helpless condition, but the Gracious God who has strengthened the religion of Islam internally, has for the encouragement of weak creatures like ourselves, furnished us with the resources formerly enjoyed by the unsuccessful and unprincipled

Christians without any attempt being made by us. Our being backed by
a large Army of Infantry, Cavalry, and Artillery, our having obtained an
immense treasure, the arrival of the letter from the King of Delhi, the
bona fide ruler of Hindoostan who is the Shadow and representative of
God (May his Dominions ever extend!), the assistance given to us by the
Army of Birjees Kudur (May God bless him with prosperity!), our alliance
with the Rajah[s] of the Province of Oudh and the States adjacent to
Allahabad, and the union which prevails throughout Hindoostan,
notwithstanding the people are of different persuasions and tribes, are
clear proofs that the people are determined to extirpate these rebel
Christians now. O my Mussulman Brethren! as soon as you hear the above
glad tidings prepare yourselves for Jehad, come to Allahabad, subdue and
put to the sword the besieged Christians there, and try to expel the remnant
of their body from this country, and then rule the country according to
the laws and Institutions of Mohammed.[189]

The triumph and tragedy of Hindustani patriotism in 1857 are
summed up in these words. Liaqat Ali, weaver turned schoolteacher, is
wonder-struck by 'the union which prevails throughout Hindoostan,
notwithstanding the people are of different persuasions and tribes;' yet,
innocent of any notion of the political nation, deeply committed to
the '*deen*' that still encapsulates his universe in its totality, what can the
maulvi conceive as the outcome of the struggle but the Dar-ul-Islam?

However, surely if religion provides the ideological framework of
the Mutiny, the totality of the emotional experience goes beyond it.
Why is it that Bakht Khan explodes when the indispensable Bengali
commissariat clerk of the *risala* refused the offer of a thousand-rupees job
with the Bareilly mutineers: '*Nimakhārām! Beimān! Hazār rupaiyah
tankhā bhi kabul nehi kartā!*' ('Traitor! Disloyal man! You refuse to
serve even for a thousand rupee salary!') What '*nimak*' (salt) does he
refer to? What '*iman*' (loyalty) has he in mind? His own furious words
leave the meaning in no doubt: '*Angrez aur Bāngāli sab ek hai,
tumko nehi mālum hai, ki ham abhi tumhārā gardan kātne ka hukum
de sakte hai. ... Khub mālum hai ki Āngrezon ke sāth tumhari sāzish
hai*' (English and Bengalis are all the same, you don't understand that I
can order your head cut off right now. ... I know very well that you are
in cahoots with the English).[190]

The concept of 'salt' has, by now, undergone a dramatic turnaround
among the sepoys: '*Company ke nimak haram*' (the salt of the Company
is impure), cries the sentry on guard, and fires off his gun sounding off
the outbreak at Azamgarh.[191]

But for this reordering of loyalties, the fleeing Tantia Tope could scarcely have exclaimed: 'This is the country of grandfather and great grandfather, and yet no one gives me supplies. All the people of my country, Hindoos and Mussulmen, have become Christians.'[192] At the back of the new ordering of obligations in the rebel mind lies the feeling that the English are 'trespassers'—a feeling greatly intensified among the Purbeah sepoys since the takeover of their homeland Awadh.[193] Coming as it did as the climax to an alarming chain of annexations in violation of treaty obligations, the latest appropriation strengthened the impression that these 'accused vilaitis' were past masters in trickery ('dagabazi', as Nana Sahib puts it[194]) and would not leave anything to the princes and the people.[195]

Such were the perceptions that awakened the patriotic feelings lying dormant in the breasts of princes, noblemen, and people. The concept of the sovereign national state being unformed, the passionate attachment to hereditary possessions provided the focus to the expressions of patriotism. The Begam of Awadh exclaimed in her rejoinder to Queen Victoria:

> If our people were discontented with our royal predecessor, Wajid Ali Shah, how comes it they are content with us? And no ruler ever enjoyed such loyalty and devotion of goods and life as we have done. What, then is wanting that they do not restore our country? Further, it is written in the proclamation [of Queen Victoria], that they want no increase of territory, but yet they cannot refrain from annexation. If the Queen has assumed the government, why does not Her Majesty restore our country to us when our people wish it?[196]

Begam Hazrat Mahal's pronouncement on the loyalty of her subjects is echoed in their own voice, as will be evident, for instance, from the noble resolve of her faithful servant Muhammad Hasan Khan, the governor of Gorakhpur, 'hereafter to fight and die in the tenets of my faith and in the cause of my illustrious sovereign', adding:[197]

> The British have exceeded all bounds in their breaking of promises—this is notorious—(witness the treaties) between them and the Raja of Lahore, the Peishwa and other Princes too numerous to mention. My business is with the King of Oude. All the world knows of the binding engagements and treaties which existed between those two exalted Powers, the King of Oude and the English Government. ... The Kingdom has been wrested perfidiously from a dynasty which never opposed & and which always conciliated the English Govt., and all kinds of tyranny have been

perpetrated. No one now puts any trust in the British. I may sum up with the proverb 'who has not received the reward of his deeds?' The Princes and people of Hindostan, witnessing this perfidious oppression, took the opportunity of the revolt of the army (the result also of the English Govt.'s own conduct) and the outbreak took place, involving the slaughter and plunder of thousands of innocent servants of God.

What the Lucknow nobleman's words reflect is a sense of the country focused on but going beyond hereditary possession. The same range of obligations finds expression in Hanwant Singh's parting words to Mr Barrow. When the Englishman, having been conducted to safety, expresses the hope that the *taluqdar* would join in suppressing the revolt, the dispossessed chief stands erect and replies:

Sahib, your countrymen came into this country and drove out our king. You sent your officers round the districts to examine the titles to the estates. At one blow you took from me lands which from time immemorial have been in my family. I submitted. Suddenly misfortune fell upon you. You came to me whom you despoiled. I have saved you. But now,—now I march at the head of my retainers to Lakhnao to try and drive you from the country.[198]

The race of natives—that inchoate nation lacking the concept of the sovereign national state—is constrained to expressing its identity in the older and more familiar terms of realm[199] and religion.[200] Who can, however, mistake the spontaneous sense of identity that forms the bedrock? A party of Europeans fleeing from Fatehpur to Allahabad narrowly escape massacre by the cleverness of a lady who has the presence of mind to put out of her palanquin a fair hand on which she has taken care to put on choorees or Indian bangles. Seeing the ornament, *sawars* exclaim: 'O Bhaee! They are our own people; let them pass.'[201] Unshakeable commitments, passing through whatever ideological channel, must originate in spontaneous emotion. Compare the following statements, one by a Muslim bookbinder of Patna hanged by the British, the other by a Hindu prince from Bithoor driven to the pestilential terai of Nepal:

[Pir Ali, 'heavily fettered, his soiled garment deeply stained in blood', on being asked whether he had any information to give that might induce Government to spare his life]: There are some cases in which it is good to save life—others in which it is better to lose it. [He denounced the oppression of the British and added]: You may hang me, or such as me, every day but thousands will rise in my place, and your object will never be gained.[202]

[Nana Sahib, from his Nepal hideout, on being asked to surrender]: If you wish it, the thing can only be done in this way [by French mediation], and to this I consent If not, life must be given up some day. Why then should I die dishonoured? There will be war between me and you as long as I have life, whether I be killed or imprisoned or hanged, and whatever I do will be done with the sword only. [He was heard of no more.][203]

Faith or patriotism, the heartfelt emotion behind it is identical. The raw mass emotions that form the substance of nationalism must by their nature precede the intellectual concepts that give it definition. The emotions going into the making of Indian nationalism had a palpable presence in 1857, although still devoid of the conceptual form imparted by the modern political nation. What the people felt at the height of the mass movement in 1921—the raw feeling itself—was not perhaps so very different from the way they had felt earlier in 1857. Certainly there were echoes of emotions in the popular actions that took place during the Non-cooperation–Khilafat movements of 1920–2.[204]

The Inversion of Power

The Mutiny was a sudden inversion of dominion which occurred through the process of rumours. In analysing the oracles and rumours that brought about such a phenomenon it is necessary to bear in mind that they consist of two elements: one, the suppressed yearning, capable of bursting forth at the favourable moment, that the existing dominion should be overthrown in favour of those who have lost it, or have never had a share in it; the other, the sudden realization that the satisfaction of the desire, so long beyond anticipation, is at hand. The yearning and the anticipation may both be illustrated by means of two couplets Emperor Bahadur Shah, who sometimes used the pen name Nafar, composed for exhorting the rebel crowd of Delhi. The people's desire for the reversal of power was summed up by the Emperor in the following couplet: 'I, nuffer [servant], will seize London; for what is the distance from Hindustan?'[205] His more weighty reflection on how the desired objective had come into view was contained in the couplet:

Na Irān ne kiāyā, na Shāh Russ ne,—
Angrez ko tabāh kiyā kārtoosh (cartouche) ne.

'No [war with] Iran brought it about, nor the Czar of Russia. What overthrew the English was the [greased] cartridge.'[206]

As in France in 1787–88, so in India since 1856, the equations of power went through a series of sudden shifts and turns that whetted the desire, and sharpened the anticipation, of a total reversal. The annexation of Awadh, Anglo-Russian hostilities in the Crimea, the war with Persia, and Canning's announcement that the title of the Mughal sovereign would be terminated in due course were soon accompanied by a series of rumours about chapatis, impure flour, greased cartridges, and the hundredth anniversary of British rule; these rumours climaxed with the nightmare of the whites coming to kill, which, through its recoil, provoked the real white terror, and so realized the mortal fear. There was no grand high-level conspiracy to overturn British rule; the small conspiracies between a pair or more of the sepoy regiments would have to work upon these psychical processes, and manipulate these expectations and fears, if the plots were to get anywhere.

In 1849, Lord Dalhousie had urged upon the Court of Directors in London the expediency of abolishing, 'even in name, a rival in the person of a Sovereign whose ancestors once held the paramountcy we now possess'; and of removing the Mughal family from the Red Fort, 'a strong fortress in the heart of one of the principal cities of our Empire' and, he might have done well to add, the visible seat of sovereignty to the people of Hindustan. The Court, in a rare moment of perspicacity, had protested on that occasion: 'The traditional deference with which that memory is still regarded is altogether distinct from any hopes of its renewal. But it is a feeling which it is impolitic to wound. From mere hopelessness of resistance it may not immediately show itself, but may remain latent till other causes of public danger may bring it into action.'[207] Bit by bit, however, the marks of Mughal sovereignty had been wiped away amidst unexpressed anguish in the Red Fort: the *nazars* presented barefoot by the Governor-General's representative to the Emperor had been discontinued since 1842; the current coin of India had ceased to bear his name earlier in 1835 and the Governor-General had thrown out the seal bearing the sign of his vassalage to the Emperor, and prohibited the native princes from using one. In 1850, a promise was extracted from the then Crown Prince (destined to expire shortly) that on his father Bahadur Shah's death, he would leave Red Fort to reside near the Qutb Minar. Finally, in 1856, Lord Canning resolved that on the Emperor's death his heir would have to content himself with the title of Shahzada, an eventuality that would terminate the age-old Mughal sovereignty in Hindustan.[208]

The inmates of Red Fort realized with a pang that nothing could restore the good old days unless the realities of power were to change in an unforeseen manner. The wish was the father to the thought; and while the English clashed with Iran over the latter's investment of Herat, that very year a highly regarded fakir, physician, and soothsayer of Delhi reported a dream to the Emperor 'that he had seen a hurricane approaching from the West, which was followed by a great flood of water devastating the country; that it passed over, and that he noticed that the King suffered no inconvenience from it, but was borne up over the flood in his couch'. The way the *pirzada*, Hasan Askari, interpreted the dream was that 'the King of Persia with his army would annihilate the British power in the East, would restore the King to his ancient throne and reinstate him in his kingdom, and at the same time the infidels, meaning the British, would be all slaughtered'.[209]

The same man was instrumental in sending over the chief of the Abyssinian guard of the palace, Sidi Kambar, with some papers attested with the Emperor's seal, to the Shah of Iran.[210] According to the somewhat doubtful testimony of the Emperor's secretary, Mukund Lal, these papers included a letter from Bahadur Shah complaining to the Shah of Iran that the English had imprisoned him and 'had put a stop to all the marks of respect to which, as King, he was entitled', and had suspended the appointment of an heir-apparent. These circumstances were said to have induced him to express the hope to the Shah that a mutual understanding might be reached through an exchange of letters and visits.[211]

Popular rumour had it at the time that the Abyssinian chief guard, though ostensibly dispatched as a pilgrim to Mecca, had really gone to fetch the Russians. The wildest rumours had been rife about Russian moves since the outbreak of the Crimean War. 'This hot season', an Abyssinian guard told a Christian *risaladar* with some European blood in him, 'you will see the Russians all over the place.'[212]

The leading vernacular newspaper of Delhi, the *Sadiq-ul-Akhbar* (Authentic News), opined that the Russians were the hidden hand behind the clash between England and Persia over Herat; for 'using the Persians as a cloak, they intend to consummate their own designs by the conquest of Hindustan'.[213] The expected arrival of the Persians and Russians in the summer of 1857 was a topic of general conversation in Delhi on the eve of the Mutiny.[214] Every newspaper had at this time a correspondent in Kabul, and information flowed every week from the north.[215]

Excitement reached fever pitch when posters appeared on the walls of Delhi, intimating that the Shah of Iran was arriving shortly to 'sit on the throne of India', and make her Emperor and people happy.[216] Interestingly, however, the *Sadiq-ul-Akhbar* asked: '... what cause would the Hindus [sic, presumably a mis-spelling of the term Hindis] have were the King of Persia to exercise sway over India? From the proclamation it appears that he intends himself to occupy the throne of India. The Hindus [Hindis, i.e. Indians] would only then have cause to be pleased if the King of Persia, acting like Shah Abbas Safi, should enthrone our own King.'[217]

These rumours were the vehicle of an indirect expression of hostility to British rule, as were, indeed, the encomiums on the bravery of the Russians during the war in the Crimea. No other meaning can be attached to Azimullah Khan's joyful remark to war correspondent Russell while passing through Constantinople: 'I want to see this famous city [Sebastopal], and those great Roostums, the Russians, who have beaten French and English together.'[218] The direction of the rumours, however, changed significantly just on the eve of the outbreak of the Mutiny in Meerut, as news arrived of the discontent in the lines of the sepoys. It is on record that for four days or so before the arrival of the mutinous troopers from Meerut, Basant Ali Khan and the entire body of the Emperor's personal attendants, 'sitting about the entrance to his private apartments, used to converse among themselves, and say that very soon, almost immediately, the army would revolt and come to the palace, when the Government of the King would be re-established, and all old servants greatly promoted and advanced in positions and emoluments'.[219] The Emperor himself, persuaded by his eunuchs and the Begams, fully believed the popular rumour that 'the Commander-in-Chief had undertaken himself to Christianize the whole of India in two years'.[220] Indeed, ever since the news of the Barrackpore mutiny had arrived in Delhi, the *shahzadas* had been speculating that 'the native army would go over either to Nepal or Persia. But they had no idea that they would arrive themselves with the King, because he had neither money nor troops'.[221] This sudden eruption, neither from the direction of Iran nor from the Shah of Russ, but from the direction of the cartridge caught the higher echelons of the Red Fort by utter surprise.

Contemporaries were agreed that this rebellious spirit among the sepoys began with the annexation of Awadh and eventually exploded into mutiny over the cartridge issue. 'Oude was the birthplace of the

Purbeah race and these feelings of dissatisfaction affected the whole Purbeah race in the service of the British Government,'[222] in particular, those regiments used in the occupation of Lucknow. These were the 17th, 19th, and 34th Native Infantry. The 17th N.I. was reported by its English commander to have been in the habit of visiting the Red Fort, and making offerings to the *Badshah*, while posted in Delhi in 1853 and 1854. The regiment was thence ordered to march upon Lucknow. He came to learn after his troops mutinied that 'on the annexation of Oudh the 17th, 19th, and 34th Regiments offered their services to the King of Oudh'.[223]

According to the information of the first rebel *kotwal* of Delhi, the regiments stationed in Lucknow, after the annexation, had frequent consultations on the injustice of the measure,[224] and the aged Subedar Sitaram confirms in his memoirs that it was from this time that 'an undefined dislike and disquiet took possession of all of us'.[225] The 17th NI was subsequently posted at Azamgarh. As for the 34th and the 19th NIs, these two regiments were posted in close proximity at Barrackpore and Berhampore respectively. Both were seething with bitterness towards the government, and were enabled by their proximity to conduct constant secret correspondence with each other and other Purbeah regiments. They are said to have urged every Purbeah to withdraw his friendship from the foreigner. It was among these two regiments that the first isolated mutinies took place in March 1857.[226]

As the long summer descended on the dusty plain of Hindustan, there gradually began to take shape in the sepoy lines that rebellious mentality—of a resolve to do as others did—that was summed up in the peculiar contemporary phrase '*Fouj ke bheera*,' or 'general will of the army';[227] and rumours began to fly. Certain symptoms of the mentality are worthy of note: the sepoys' conviction 'that the imperial fabric rested on their shoulders alone: they had constructed it; they maintained it';[228] the mingled alarm and anger that the British, having extended their sway over all the soil, were now bent on invading the realm of the spirit: 'You have conquered and absorbed everything in Hindustan, you have no more foreign countries to take, and now you have determined upon a crusade against our religion and our faith',[229] the sudden hitting upon the truth that the salt of the Company was 'sinful' ('*Company ke neemak haram*'); the universal belief among the sepoys that the British were full of deceit ('*dagabazi*') and that their words were not to be trusted;[230] and the very vagueness of their fears, which no degree of reassurance would remove, all remedial measures coming up against the blank wall of the declaration that 'the regiment will become budnam if they fire any cartridges'; with the added proviso, a most significant one, that 'if all the regiments would take their cartridges, they would do so'.[231]

This was the perfect soil for the spread of rumours. These may be classified into three groups: first those prevalent in the cantonments, relating to the mixing of cows' and pigs' fat in the cartridge, which obviously affected only the sepoys in their lines, and not the town population; second, those relating to the bone dust in flour and sugar, which rose subsequent to the cartridge agitation, and spread through the bazaars from one town to another, drawing the town population into the vortex of vague fears;[232] third, the chapatis, the meaning of which nobody knew, circulating quite independently of the town and cantonment rumours, from village to village, through the agency of the village chaukidars.

The chapatis were the first in point of time, and the people concerned, including many future rebel leaders, wondered at the time as to 'what could be the object'. Some thought they might be the means of passing on some disease to other quarters, a propitiatory observance to avert an impending calamity; others, 'that they were circulated by the Government to signify that the population throughout the country would be compelled to use the same food as the Christians and thus be deprived of their religion'; yet others, again, that they portended some coming disturbance, 'implying an invitation to the whole population of the country to unite for some secret object afterwards to be disclosed'.[233] Whatever the interpretation put upon it, the mysterious event created a general alarm in the rural areas, which for the moment had no link with the panic in the lines and the bazaars.

The cartridge presented quite a different problem of interpretation. Many Englishmen, who suspected a conspiracy, and some intelligent Indians, whom the former pressed in that direction through leading questions, were inclined to believe that the cartridge was a smokescreen.[234] The prosecutor at the trial of Bahadur Shah argued:

> Even if we were to admit that all the cartridges were thoroughly saturated with pigs' and with cows' fat, still what real valid objection on the score of their religion could the *Muhammadan* sepoys have in using them? Their brothers and other relatives in the private service of officers never hesitate to handle or cook the dishes they are required to bring to our tables.

... That neither Mussulman nor Hindu had any objection to the use of any of the cartridges at Meerut or at Delhi, is sufficiently proved by the eagerness with which they sought possession of them, when their aim and object was the murder of their European Officers, or when, united under the banners of the Prisoner at your bar, they for months, constantly went forth to fight against the power to which they owed fealty and allegiance.[235]

The prosecutor had found a good trial argument: but in his anxiety to smell a conspiracy, he lacked the sensitivity to see that the cartridge was the perceived threat to the identity of the entire community, based on the sepoy's religion, for the defence of which he might turn the very weapon against the wielder.

Not bothered with marshalling arguments, the intelligence chief of the North-Western Provinces, who was concerned to get at the truth, wrote at the time from Agra:

... you will not fail to observe what Greathead says about the *cartouche* being the invariably assigned origin of the rebel movement, on all occasions of inquiry from deserters. ... A respectable native who was caught at Delhi by the outbreak, and was only able to get away lately, had full and constant opportunity of conversing with the sepoys on the subject, and says he could get no other assignable cause from them. He asserts that the Delhi people and sepoys were not prepared for the inroad of our mutineers from Meerut. But whatever may have been the views and machinations of some of the ringleaders, there can, I think, be little doubt that the fear of the cartridges as the supposed enemy of caste, was the motive that swayed the masses.[236]

A sensitive and sympathetic bystander, looking back on those times, had no difficulty in comprehending and conveying the meaning of the cartridge:

There is no doubt that twenty five years ago the status of Hindu dharma and people's reverence for it were very special indeed. And I have no hesitation to say that such a fearful rebellion (bhayamkara bamda) can never happen nowadays because of the cartridge alone ... But in those days people's respect for religion was so strong that they had more faith in the flow of the clarified butter of the sacrificial ceremony than they had in the sharpness of the sword.[237]

Exact records of the form and content of the rumours are hard to come by. However, the same source quoted above affords an unusually detailed glimpse of 'people's news' of the rebellion, reflecting their sense of the country, their eager waiting upon the native chiefs for an authoritative indication of the direction in which to proceed, and their inchoate comprehension of Indian nationality in terms of the Hindu–Muslim brotherhood. Near Mhow a fleeing Maharashtrian sepoy returning home to Goa gave Vishnubhat Godase an account of the rebellion in Hindustan. According to him, it broke out because the English had summoned all the rajas and nawabs to announce no less than 84 measures by which to take away the religion of the Hindus and Muslims.

The Raja of Banpur is represented in the story to have stood up and said:

> This is the Land of Hindu (Hindusthāna), the country of Bharata (Bhāratakhanda), the Island of Jambu (Jambudvīpa). It is called the Land of Deeds (Karmabhūmi). Attached to this island (dvīpa) are all the islands, such as Simhala (Ceylon). However, this is the principal land (mukhya bhūmi) of the Hindus. If the Hindu gods and goddesses vanish from amongst us, then only will this device (kāydā) of the Saheb Log be effective (lāgoa), otherwise no force will compel us to agree to all these devices. Even though the sovereign king (sārvabhauma rājā) imparts such impious (adharmāchyā) word and advice to his own subjects, all the subjects will not give their consent. If these eighty four clauses come into force, then a fight will break out over religion (dharma-sambandhi bakhedā).

A nawab then stood up and said: 'Here in Hindustan, Mussalmans and Hindus stay together in the same place (thikānā), nevertheless they do not cause trouble to each other over religion (dharma). The king who harms these two religions, will never obtain victory.'[238] The rajas and nawabs, having registered their united protest, returned to their respective places. Thereupon, according to the version received by Godase, the sepoys broke out in mutiny over the issue of the polluted cartridges.

Judging by the various Mutiny proclamations available in print, Godase would appear to have kept close to the oral news imparted to him by the fleeing Maharashtrian sepoy. The point of interest in his news is the notion of the indivisible nature of the land, and the united resolve of the Hindu and Muslim chiefs to defend their respective religions. Rumours, being by their nature oral, cannot be obtained in the raw form, except where they fortuitously take a written form, such as the news portions of the Mutiny proclamations, private vernacular letters (not many have been handed down from 1857),[239] and, in rare instances, the oracle. The widespread expectation that the centenary of Plassey would witness the destruction of British rule was based on purported prophecies made by the saints centuries prior to British rule. One prediction, in Persian verse, was attributed to a saint named Niamatullah in AH 570. It takes the typical form of the Indian Puranas, predicting the course of known historical events, the nature of events yet hidden to mankind, and the final coming of the Mahdi and the end of the world.[240] The importance of the oracle lies in the historical framework in which it places the Mutiny, affording a rare glimpse of the people's sense of the place of the event in history, and of their political and social conceptions. The Ode, in 29 verses, begins, significantly, with the ancestor of the Mughal dynasty, Timur:

> I tell the truth, an invincible hero will be born in the world
> And his name will be Taimur Shah.1.

The next four verses trace the line of descent from Timur to Babar Shah, 'born king in Kabul'. There follows, in seven verses a long and confused account of the struggle between Afghan and Mughal for the supremacy of 'Hindostan', till verse 14 establishes the triumphant return of Humayun to Hindostan and the final establishment of Mughal rule by Akbar:

> Thus Humayun reaches Hind and takes possession of it
> After which Akbar Shah, king of the world, is born.13.

There follows a brief mention of the splendid reigns of Jahangir and Shah Jahan, and then an interesting revelation of popular historical memory—the time of troubles that were perceived to have begun with Emperor Aurangzeb:

> The world is in astonishment as he appears,
> A jupiter from heaven is born scattering fire. 17.
> His name is Shah Alamgir and Aurangzeb;
> At his accession a commotion is spread through Hindostan. 18.[241]
> He imprisons his father, and becomes the murderer of his brothers
> For his oppressions the sounds of mercy and quarter will arise. 19
> Truth will decrease, lies and deceit will increase.
> Friends will become enemies and the good will be born then. 20

Verse 21, dwelling on the tyranny and schism (*jaur o bid'at*) following Aurangzeb's death, sums up the next forty years (an arithmetical mistake, fifty being the correct figure):

The nation of Sikhs (quam-i-Sikkhan) will gain the upper hand over the
Musalman
And for forty (years) this tyranny and schism will prevail. 21[242]

And then would come the Nazarenes (English) to conquer the
country and rule it for 100 years:

After that the Nisara will gain sovereignty over the whole country of
Hindostan (mulk e Hindostan tamam)
And for one century their rule will obtain in Hindostan. 22.[243]

At the lapse of the century the rule of the Christians would be
extinguished by a prince from the West (or alternatively, from Arabia):

When tyranny and schism (jaur e bid'at)
become the fashion during their dominion
The king of the West, the excellent rider, will
rise for their destruction. 23
Between them and him there will be great wars (jang e azim)
A great many people will without doubt
be killed in those wars. 24
The king of the west (Shah-i-Gharibistan)[244] will obtain the victory through
the sword of assiduity
And the sect of Jesus[245] (Qaum-i-Isa) will without a doubt sustain defeat. 25

Such is the prediction:[246] the rule of the 'nation of Jesus' is to come
to an end in *mulk e Hind* (or Hindustan) through a 'great war' at the
end of a hundred years. The rumour would appear to have been current
for at least a generation before the Mutiny, the exact course of which it
certainly does not anticipate. The next two verses bring the course of
events to the conventional predicted conclusion:

Islam will have the supremacy for 40 (years) in Hind (mulk e Hind)
After which Dajjal Tibti will be born in Isfahan. 26
For the subversion of Dajjal, this is what I say hear
Jesus comes, and Mahdi, the last of the world is born. 27

The Persian Ode, composed apparently in the so-called Wahabi
tradition, was later matched by a Hindu prophecy for the consumption
of the Purbeah sepoys in besieged Delhi. A spy brought news to the
Ridge: 'A Pundit rich in occult lore had made his appearance, and had
declared by his knowledge of the stars that the sepoys would rule this
year in India!' Tuesday, 21 July, the supposed date of the battle of Plassey,
was the day he fixed for the great attack: 'The horses' hoofs were to be

steeped in blood, and the action was to rival the great conflict of the Maha Bharat; after that the sepoys were to be dominant over India.'[247]

All these rumours—the polluted cartridge, bone-mixed flour, the hundred-year rule of the British coming to an end—were prevalent in Meerut and the country around it in the summer, and the chapatis had passed through the adjoining rural tract earlier in January and February, independently and without any connection with the bazaar rumours that followed.[248] In the final stage, stronger physical emotions were aroused by the new pieces of 'news'. First, there was the news that '2000 sets of irons were being made for the sepoys', and that 'the sepoys were to be deprived of the charge of their arms and ammunition'. This evoked strong feelings of dishonour, outrage, and bondage.[249] The sense of physical humiliation and emasculation, worked upon by women in the bazaar, brought to a boil the subconscious desire to invert the existing order. Then came the last explosive piece of news: the whites were coming to kill! This aroused that ultimate fear: of life itself. The news broke in the bazaar in the evening, and immediately the Mutiny broke out in the lines.

Was there a conspiracy behind these moves? If there was, then it was certainly not known to Bahadur Shah or other princes and chiefs, and must have been confined to small secret committees within the army—as Lieutenant-Colonel Buwoughs put it at the time, it was 'probably known to a select few only in each Regiment'.[250] It would appear, from the report of the conversation the Meerut mutineers had with Bahadur Shah when surrounding the palace, that some of them had discussed the idea that 'a revolt should break out on one and the same date all over India', should the British persist in their 'stringent measures' of punishment for disobedience. It was however also obvious from the same conversation that they had no such plan at hand to work upon.[251] The Mutiny outbreak in Meerut was in essence an outbreak of panic,[252] accompanied by a sense of dishonour—an assertion of manhood in front of women.

The Bengal Army was a bachelor army: sepoys did not stay with their wives and families, as was the custom in the Madras Army. Life in the lines was nonetheless intimately connected to the bazaar and the town, the meeting point being the houses of courtesans, a bolder, more independent, albeit much exploited section of the womanhood of Hindustan. Many courtesans had honoured places in the collective society of the *risala* (cavalry) and of the *paltan* (infantry), and individual bonds were often strongly emotional. In consequence, the courtesans loom large in the annals of the Mutiny, and there flash through its course prominent female figures, such as Azizan of Cawnpore, who was so popular among the sepoys there that she took a prominent part in their military arrangements. The emotional angle of sepoy life came into play in Meerut when Colonel Carmicheal Smyth sent 85 *sawars* of the 3rd Cavalry to jail on 9 May, all of them bound in chains like common criminals: their fault was their refusal of the cartridge on grounds of faith.

It was, as Kaye said,

> A piteous spectacle, and many there were moved with a great compassion, when they saw the despairing gestures of those wretched men, among whom were some of the very flower of the regiment—soldiers who had served the British Government in trying circumstances and strange places, and who had never before wavered in their allegiance. Lifting up their hands and lifting up their voices, the prisoners implored the General to have mercy upon them, and not to consign them to so ignominious a doom. Then, seeing that there was no other hope, they turned to their comrades and reproached them for quietly suffering this disgrace to descend upon them. There was not a Sepoy present who did not feel the rising indignation in his throat. But in the presence of those loaded field-guns and those grooved rifles, and the glittering sabres of the Dragoons, there could be not a thought of striking.'[253]

Meerut, in fact, was the last place for the 'conspirators' (if such there were)[254] to strike, for it was the one place in the whole of the North-Western Provinces where European troops equalled the native troops in number. At this stage, the women sprang into action.

While the troopers of the 3rd Cavalry were discussing the feasibility of appealing against the brutal sentence of the Court Martial, they 'were taunted by the disreputable inhabitants of the Sudder Bazar for allowing their brethren to suffer on account of religion and the cry of "Deen, Deen" was even early raised'. What tipped the scale, however, was the presence of those women in the crowd before whom the men of the *risala* were anxious to maintain their honour as brave troopers.[255] 'And now', says the Judge of Moradabad, 'the frail ones' taunts were heard far and wide, and the rest of the regiment was assailed with words like these: "Your brethren have been ornamented with these anklets and incarcerated; and for what? Because they would not swerve from their creed; and you, cowards as you are, sit still indifferent to their fate. If you have an atom of manhood in you, go and release them.'[256] Afterwards, the released prisoners themselves were said to have described the scene to Bahadur Shah in these terms:

> When we entered the gaol the Meerut Camp was in a state of great commotion. In every house there was a discussion about this. Particularly the ladies were most zealous and those whose men were sent to gaol were most vociferous. They mocked and jeered at the sepoys saying, 'Give us your arms: we shall fight and liberate the brave officers who have been confined to gaol. You can keep inside the home and can put on bangles'. Those taunts spurred all the sepoys and they decided to stake their lives on liberating the imprisoned officers.[257]

The address of the Meerut mutineers to Bahadur Shah is a construct left behind by a contemporary. It misses out on the last vital note in the overture to the outbreak. General Hewitt's report to headquarters the following day mentions the evening panic in the bazaar which spread to the lines and precipitated the immediate attack and the night flight to Delhi: 'I am led to think the outbreak was not premeditated, but the result of a rumour that a party was parading to seize their arms, which was strengthened by the fact of the 60th Rifles parading for evening church service.'[258] A cook boy of that white regiment ran up to the bazaar with the mistaken news, 'the Rifles and Artillery are coming to disarm all the Native Regiments'.[259] The sepoys, lounging about undressed and unarmed, ran helter skelter to their weapons. As the long summer day slowly gave way to twilight, the Mutiny began among the *paltan* and the *risala*, accompanied by the crowd from the bazaar. Among the latter, the butchers and the weighmen were the most prominent. They were joined at night by the Gujars from the surrounding country who poured excitedly into the town.[260]

The bazaar crowd was motivated by hatred of the whites, and the Gujars by motive of plunder. The key group, however, that is, the sepoys, were swayed by panic.[261] Showing no disposition to confront the white regiments, they fled 'in different and opposite directions', some towards Delhi across the Jumna, others on the Bulandshahr road leading to the Ganges, but 'all as disorganized mobs, with no acknowledged leader'. The move towards Delhi was almost instinctive, issuing from a collective memory long embedded in the popular mind. Fleeing for refuge, they hit subconsciously upon Delhi: 'Quick, brother, quick! Delhi, Delhi!' they all cried as they seized ammunition from the regimental magazine on their knees. The English captain who saw this confirmed after the publication of Kaye's book: 'That they were in a state of "scare", I could myself testify.'[262]

In the first blind impulse, fleeing without defined goal, the bulk of the sepoys met three miles out of town to debate where they should go. After debating the matter, they opted for the Red Fort.[263] A *sawar* from Meerut later explained to a Delhi sepoy that before the outbreak at Meerut they had no idea they were coming to Delhi. At the hurriedly gathered assembly in the village outside Meerut, there was at first some difference of opinion. A number of sepoys wanted to move towards Rohilkhand (a natural enough choice for many of the troopers who were Muslims and had their homes there), others towards Agra (presumably for the same sort of reason). However, after a heated debate, and a reasoned appeal that to move towards these places without guns would be dangerous, it was resolved to move rapidly on towards Delhi. The town, it was argued, could be easily taken. With possession of the magazine there and the person of the Emperor, they could hold out for months against the white soldiers who would surely pursue them.[264]

Under cover of night the sepoys sped on towards the hoped for refuge and shelter in mortal fear of their lives. As dawn broke, the *risala* of the 43rd Cavalry crossed the bridge of boats across the Jumna. The sepoys in Delhi were not expecting the visit,[265] but they joined the mutineers immediately as there was no European regiment there to restrain them. Gathering under the walls of the Saman Burj, they commenced calling out, '*Dohai Badshah!*' ('Help O King'),[266] cajoling and threatening Bahadur Shah by turns as he refused to entertain them: 'You are the King of both the worlds—terrestrial and spiritual. The whole of India is under your sway and every announcement is preceded by "God is Master of the Creation, order [sic, Country] belongs to the King and the Command is that of the Company". The English have been ruling on your behalf. We have come to you with our grievances. We expect justice from you. We are the servants of the English. It is we who have conquered the whole territory of 1400 *Kos* extending from Calcutta to Kabul for the English, because they did not bring any English army with them from England. Now when they have subjugated the whole of India, they have changed their mind and want to convert every one of us into Christians and thus meddle with our religion.'[267]

According to another source, however, their address was by no means so uniformly civil. 'We have already commenced a [Holy war] and have come to Delhi considering you the Muhammadan King, but it appears that you are in league with the Christians. You will see what will happen.'[268] Hakim Ahsanullah Khan accosted them on his master's behalf: 'You have long been accustomed under the English rule to regular pay. The King has no treasury. How can he pay you?' The officers replied, 'We will bring the revenue of the whole Empire to your treasury.'[269] As a reluctant Emperor was coerced into heading them, the Mutiny acquired a political dimension of incalculable proportions throughout the country. Thus was a government born in panic, coercion, reluctance, and foreboding.

In the mutinies that now broke out one after another right down to Banaras and Dinapore, the running thread was the great fear of the whites coming to kill: a fear all too real.[270] Early in the course of the revolt the Lieutenant-Governor of the North-Western Provinces was urged by an experienced officer of the Sepoy Army that no reference should be made to retribution upon the mutineers. If possible, a proclamation should be issued that the past had been forgiven. In recommending this line of action, the officer argued: 'For I have satisfied myself beyond all doubt that fear is the principal cause of all that is going on at present among the Native Army.'[271]

But it is only when one reads of events from the native point of view—even the accounts of the Bengalis then stranded in Hindustan who had no sympathy with the mutineers—that one appreciates the true psychic impact of the White Terror. These accounts make it clear that fear was indeed the key.

Take for instance Jadunath Sarbadhikari's Bengali *roznamcha* or diary, for the events of 4 June 1857 at Banaras. It differs vitally from the English account of the 'disarming parade' there.

> ... the generals at Varanasi ordered the native (desiya) infantry: 'A new order has come from Government, which we shall communicate in public. So stand at parade.' The meaning behind these words was this, the infantry of the voluntary corps [presumably the Irregular Infantry] are good fighters. But as their own fate induced them to oppose the cartridge (tota), they felt that the entreaties made humbly by the officers were a deception (kapat). Urged by the wicked men of the infantry, they made up their mind to kill the generals and government officers and to go off with the looted treasure .... The order for parade being subsequently issued on 4 June, they stood all at parade without arms—the Sikh infantry to their left, the sawars to their right, the voluntary infantry in the middle,—in short all infantry in the cantonment except two companies of the Paltan located at Ghazipur and Jaunpur. Thereupon the officers, armed and

accoutred, made a sign to the Gora infantry ordering them to kill the infantry by cannon fire.[272] The sign had been arranged before, so as soon as it was made the firing began. The battle field was thereby turned into the veritable field of the. Bharata war; the voluntary infantry were surrounded on all sides—as at the killing of Abhimanyu,—and were fired upon by the arrow-like cannon balls shot by fire guns. ... The Sikh soldiers had been obedient to the officers. The circular formation (chakravyuha) [i.e. the legendary formation that surrounded the boy Abhimanyu] had been arranged only for the death sentence of the contrary-minded infantry. Two hundred among the ill-fated voluntary infantry being thereby killed and the rest having fled, the field was plunged in darkness from the smoke of cannon as if enveloped by thick mist. But the Whites (Goras) did not desist from firing off the cannon. Nearly a hundred and fifty Sikh infantry were killed by these cannon balls. The Sikh infantry, seeing this, pondered in their mind,—'This is not merely blowing the voluntary infantry from the cannon—they will not let any black infantry (kala paltan) survive.' Having said this, ... they shot and killed the principal commander Major Guise, and went off. Seeing them go, five hundred among the one thousand armed cavalry that were there went off with them. ... Those troopers posted to guard the entrance of the formation (vyuha) remained in arms on the field for two days. The Sahibs intending to reward them said, '... you will each get ten rupees and a seer of sweets, Ungird yourselves and eat and rest'. The sawars replied, 'We shall not go unarmed to the parade ground after having ungirded ourselves. Because we are nothing but black soldiers and not white (*jehetu āmrā kālā sainya bhinna gorā nahi*). Since the voluntary infantry have objection to tota, we have the same objection ....' ... they went off with their arms and horses. Thus the army broke up.[273]

Durgadas Banerjee, the commissariat clerk of the *risala* at Bareilly, witnessed the same scenes of terror in Rohilkand: '*Bhai! Khabardar! Bai! Khabardar! Gore Aye,*' a warning cry at once echoed by a thousand terrified screams of '*Gore Aye, Gore Aye*' (the whites are coming, the whites are coming). While held captive by Bakht Khan, he heard these screams, '*Gore Aye, Gore Aye*', twice or thrice every day. 'I believe', he said later, 'that even while awake the sipahis had nightmares in which the white figures loomed large.'[274] The fear was not confined to the sepoys alone. At the other end of the country, there was a rumour among the Calcutta servants that the Sahib *logue* intended to shoot them at dinner. It actually induced one servant to take leave and provide a substitute for that night.[275] The belief was general that the whites had a master plan: convert or kill. Cringing native servants at Allahabad took Christian names to signify their non-resistance to the scheme.[276]

The long-delayed outbreak of the Gwalior Contingent on 14 June took place because of the same alarm, 'with loud shouts, tumult, and bugling in the lines, through which men rushed calling, "To arms", "the Europeans had come", the cry of that night'.[277] The *Risala Fath-i-Islam* outlined the master plan of the English in the form of the following 'news':

> Before the quarrel regarding the cartridges took place, these accursed English had written to the Impure Victoria thus: If your Majesty will permit us to kill 15 *moulvees* out of every hundred in India and the same number out of every hundred *pundits*, as well as five hundred thousand of Hindoos and Mahomedan sepoys and *Ryuts*, we will in a short time make all the people of India Christians. Then that ill-starred, polluted Bitch gave her consent to the spilling of this innocent blood. She did not reflect at all that she was not at liberty to permit the commission of the murder of the creatures of God. The accursed men, on the receipt of her permission, commenced committing general slaughter on the pretext of the cartridges. As no one was in a condition to oppose them, they would in a short time have killed every one who refused to become a Christian, had it not been that, by God's blessings, the bold sepoys butchered the English and put an end to all their power.

The pamphlet added significantly: 'They have weakened them in such a degree that it has been easy to kill or expel them.'[278] The message was that the time had arrived to turn the tables upon the white ruling élite. There was a show of strength by the Musalman population in Lucknow, 'who assembled in immense numbers at all mosques, and afterwards paraded about the city, to let us see, I imagine, that they mustered very strong'.[279] The idea that the realities of power had been decisively reversed was put forth in apocalyptic terms: 'Consider that formerly it was not in the power of even the Nawabs and the Rajas to kill even a common sepoy of the British, but now shoe-makers and sellers of spirituous liquors have destroyed British gentlemen of high dignity.'[280] The scheme of things, in other words, was perceived to be upside down. In this condition, one could even besmirch with impunity the name of the highest symbol of British power, 'the Impure Victoria', 'that ill-starred polluted bitch'.

Such notions about the altered scheme of things were common. When the British Deputy Collector reminded a Bundelkhand chief that the commissioner was still at Jubbulpore and would hold him responsible, the latter said derisively 'Where's the Sahib Commissioner now? He too has been killed or run away elsewhere and there is no longer any Sirkaree Umuldaree [Government rule].'[281]

The fleeing Mr Corridon had to suffer a more galling reversal of the accustomed marks of deference. Finding it difficult to obtain horse from a chaukidar, he threatened to report him to the agent for his 'misconduct'. 'He looked at me with a fixed stare and said—Ure jao, toomara ujunt juhunnum ko gaya' (Be off with you, your agent has gone to hell). Further down, he contacted a tahsildar whom he supposed to be obliged to him in many ways, but his bearing was now different. 'I was surprised to see the change which had come over the pliant and obsequious Rujjub Ali of former days; but as I was so entirely in his power, I was obliged to maintain a civil tongue.' He was wise in this. Only a short while earlier he had heard the crowd yelling: 'This is probably the Collector Saheb of Futtehpore; let us *mar* the *sala*.'[282]

The people had so long been held down by force, or rather by fear of superior force commanded by the ruling power. Once the sense of coercion lifted, the rage and suppressed violence burst forth in a terrifyingly direct urge to destroy the persons of the men, women, and children who shared that dominion. To destroy their bodies was to destroy the embodiments of the power that had the race of 'natives' in thrall. Hence the urge, born of the sense that power had fortuitously come into the latter's hands, to spare not one person. 'Hundreds of cannons and immense treasure have come to hand; it is therefore requisite that all who find it difficult to become Christians, all subjects, will unite cordially with the army, take courage and not leave the seed of these devils in any place.'[283]

Such single-minded violence did not incline to the one twist that Englishmen were mortally afraid of: the raping of their women. In the course of the first colonial century they had, by virtue of their dominance, privileged access to the women of the native race (a process resulting in the augmentation of that Eurasian breed of '*kala feringhees*' who were the object of the mutineers' wrath). The superior racial position that conferred this privilege upon the whites required that their own women should be rigidly denied to their racial inferiors and subordinates. A maddening, infuriating, secretly shameful fear seized them at the outset of the Mutiny. This was that the tables would now be turned upon them in this intimate respect, too.[284]

Even in the normal circumstances before the Mutiny, the faintest suggestion of English girls being appropriated in ever so slight a manner would have been repulsive. War correspondent Russell, recalling his strange encounter in Constantinople with Nana Sahib's bastard brother Azimullah Khan, recalled later:

'... I went down for a few days to Constantinople, and, while stopping at Misseri's Hotel, saw on several occasions, a handsome slim young man, of dark olive complexion, dressed in an Oriental costume which was new to me, and covered with rings and finery. He spoke French and English, dined at the *table d'hote*, and, as far as I could make out, was an Indian Prince, who was on the way back from the prosecution of an unsuccessful claim against the East India Company in London. In the course of his conversation he boasted a good deal of his success in London society, and used the names of people of rank very freely, which, combined with the tone of his remarks, induced me to regard him with suspicion, mingled, I confess, with dislike. He not only mentioned his *bonnes fortunes*, but expressed a very decided opinion that unless women were restrained, as they were in the East, 'like moths in candlelight, they will fly and get burned ...' When I came home that night I found he was asleep in my camp-bed, and my servant told me he had enjoyed my stores very freely.[285]

A year later, with his soul seared by the Mutiny, the Englishman's psychic vulnerability was exposed again on the same issue. Letters written to Azimullah Khan by English ladies of high rank were discovered at Nana Sahib's palace at Bithoor. The young soldier Roberts wrote indignantly to his sister on 31 December 1857:

While searching over the Nana's palaces at Bithur the other day, we found heaps of letters directed to that fiend "Azimullah Khan" by ladies in England, some from Lady —, ending '*Your affect*. Mother'. Others from a young girl at Brighton named —, written in the most lovable manner. Such rubbish I have never read, partly in French, which this scoundrel seems to have understood; how English ladies can be so infatuated. Miss— was going to marry Azimulla, and I have no doubt, would like to still, although he was the chief instigator in the Cawnpore massacres.[286]

The explosion of native lust for white women which Englishmen as a male race feared in 1857 did not occur.[287] The question was important enough for them to institute an official enquiry, which came up with the finding: 'The people, those who must know had there been cases of outraged honour and would have told us uniformly deny that such things were ever perpetrated or thought of.'[288] From the assertion that it was *not thought of*, one might perhaps conclude that even if some stray incidents did occur which escaped the official enquiry, a collective lust for the women of the dominant race was not one of the typical psychic forms of 1857. The force exerted by colonial rule in its first century had twisted the mentality of the subject race in many ways, but not in that direction.[289]

Muir, the intelligence chief put in charge of the rape enquiry by Lord Canning, was told by the Commissioner of Delhi:

> 'With reference to the enquiry which Lord Canning's Private Secretary has desired you to make, I would beg to state that I believe there is no reason whatsoever to suppose that the European ladies and girls massacred either at Meerut or Delhi were violated or outraged before death put an end to their sufferings. ... Every account which I have received confirms the fact that they were at once killed by the palace rabble and others, who rushed up into the quarters of the Palace Guards and there and then massacred the whole party assembled. ... I have spoken to Ramchunder on the subject, and he tells me that the only instance which came to his knowledge of any women having been ill-treated in any way at Delhi was when one of the 3rd cavalry troopers insultingly patted the cheeks of some poor creature at Durayogunge, on which her husband shot the man, and both husband and wife were immediately killed by the bystanders.[290]

The pattern of massacre of the women imprisoned in the Bibighar at Cawnpore was precisely the same. Slaughter occurred *en masse* without rape. The bloody deeds were seldom accompanied by the sort of incident recounted by Ramchandra in the Dariaganj quarter of Delhi. The humiliation to which the unfortunate women of Bibighar were subjected before their massacre had nothing to do with their chastity. They were taken out to grind wheat into flour by means of turning the grindstone—an occupation characteristic of the lowly village female known in Hindustan as the *pisanhari*. The symbolic act of turning the Mem Sahibs literally into *pisanharis* signalled their overthrow as members of the dominant race.[291]

Muir concluded from this inquiry that 'the object of the mutineers ... was not so much to disgrace our name, as to wipe out all traces of Europeans, and of everything connected with foreign rule.'[292] This is certainly true at one level. In the first blind, destructive urge, the mutineers at Cawnpore 'set fire to the records and to the building, and destroyed the collector's kutchery'.[293] A British officer marching to Cawnpore recalled later:

> Day by day as we marched along, we had ample evidence of the certainty with which the Asiatic had determined to tear us out of the land, root and branch; the untiring malignity which had, not content with murder

and mutilation, burned our bunglows and desecrated our churches as only an Asiatic can desecrate, we had witnessed, but we scarcely expected what we saw in passing along the road. There was satisfactory evidence that the genius of the revolt was to destroy everything that could possibly remind one of England or its civilization. The telegraph wires were cut up, strewing the ground, and in some instances carried off, the telegraph posts were dug out, the bungalows burnt, and the poor unoffending milestones so useful even to themselves, but still English, were defaced and in many instances destroyed.[294]

The same impulse drew thousands of natives to the Sati Chaura Ghat at Cawnpore to witness the ignominious departure, and possible destruction, of the British men, women, and children. The intent to massacre them seemed all too evident in the posting of sepoys all along the river on both sides with the cannon trained on the boats.[295] The meaning of the scene was not lost upon an Englishwoman who lived to describe it in terms tinged with the colour of her darkened mind: 'While we were endeavouring to embark the shore was linked with spectators, who were looking on and exulting like so many demons, as they undoubtedly were, over our distressing conditions, taunting and jeering at us for having at last fallen into their hands. The black devils grinned at us like so many apes, keeping up an incessant chatter in their monkey language.'[296]

The massacre at Satichaura Ghat was obviously due to the exercise of the collective will of the crowd. As far as the sepoys and the party of Nana Sahib were concerned this was war: the enemy was armed, the safe conduct to those perfidious deceivers and liars was not worth the paper it was written on, and in the confusion it was not even clear which side opened fire first.[297] It was however quite another matter as far as the massacre of the women and children in the Bibi Ghar is concerned—that cannot be regarded as the true assertion of a collective will. Sepoys could not be found to do the job, and butchers had to be hired to do the deed. The job was cold, cruel, and calculating, like the massacre of the women imprisoned in the Red Fort. The women of the Bibi Ghar, it must be recalled, were those who had been saved by Nana Sahib. He had stopped their massacre at the Satichaura Ghat and had ordered them to be imprisoned. The decision to kill them issued eventually from the men around the Nana, and not from the general will of the community. It was a calculated act of cruelty by a few who feared that the women would incriminate them if they lived to tell their tale.[298] In this it was of a piece with the massacre in the Delhi palace, which was carried out to incriminate Bahadur Shah and attach him firmly to the cause of the rebels.

The horrible deed, far from being an expression of the collective psyche, contradicted and damaged it. Shahzada Feroz Shah's proclamation to his 'Hindustanee brethren' issued the warning:

> The reason of the delay there has been in burying the English, is that the commands of God have been disregarded in as much as the soldiers have wickedly put women and children to death, and have, without the orders of their leaders, given themselves up to loot in such a way that they generally convert victory into defeat and the common people have been much oppressed. When you have rectified these faults, you will succeed as I have promised you.[299]

Raja Man Singh in his circular letter to brother *taluqdars* of Awadh said in harsher terms: 'We should indeed be surprised if any one was to say that we ought to take up the cause of our religion. The Telingas [sepoys] do not fight for religion. They do just the thing which religion prohibits. They plunder and murder women and children and no religion allows such deeds.' He added: 'People of this sort are called "chundals" or abominably wicked people, and no one who adheres to his religion admits of such deeds.'[300] Popular reaction to the deed may be judged from what Godase heard old men saying: 'We had thought that the Gore log would be obliged to go back to Vilayat and once again there would be Hindu and Musalman regime (Hindu–Musalmani rājya), but now the hope no longer remains. Because the killing of women and children is a great sin (mahāpātak) and the shastras do not assign the death sentence to women whatever be their crime. However, verily because of this wicked deed, victory would now be a far cry.[301]

Intimation of defeat had given rise to these dark prognostications. No less dastardly crimes lay upon the soul of the British soldiery, who killed women[302] and dishonoured them.[303] They were, however, quite convinced of the superior civilization and of their chivalrous treatment of women; and there was no damage to their psyche. Victory made all the difference in the world.

III
Counter-Government

That the people of Hindustan willed the destruction of British rule in 1857 is evident from the furious manner in which its marks were wiped out. No trace of it was left in the centres of rebellion.[304] What, however, did they want in its place? That surely is the clue to the more rational level of their self perception. Psychically, they needed an alternative to British rule in order to legitimize rebellion and massacre.[305] The question was important in practical terms too. The first manifestation of the Mutiny was an act of negation: negation of the power of the English, of their institutions, indeed of the race itself. However, even in the process of overturning British rule, they had to pose an alternative in order to make their act successful. This they achieved by that ultimate act of inversion: by declaring the British to be rebels before the sovereign Mughal throne. Translated into logical terms, their action consisted in setting right an overturn:[306] they cancelled the 'illegitimate' annexations of Dalhousie and restored the vanished supremacies of the eighteenth century. They inverted inversion itself.

There followed a series of political redefinitions. What the British called 'mutiny' was in their language 'firm attachment to the sarkar'; and those who were dubbed 'mutineers' now called themselves 'servants of the King of Delhi'.[307] By the extension of the same logic, slaying the English was defined as devotion to 'the Government cause';[308] and a petition from the officer commanding the Ali Ghol detailed his 'acts of devotion' to the Emperor 'as regards the slaughter and ruination of the accursed sect, the Nazarenes'.[309] The English were 'plunderers'[310] and 'disturbers of peace'.[311] They were 'rebels';[312] in the pregnant phrase of Maulvi Liaqat Ali of Allahabad, 'fraudulent and mutinous Christians' (*Taghee Baghee Nisaras*).[313] The people were asked to 'purify their hearts of loyalty to the Nazarenes' and to 'consider themselves subjects of the present Sultan (King)'.[314]

The Awadh rebel, Muhammad Hasan Khan, declared: 'We servants and dependants of the King of Oudh consider it essential to our prosperity in both worlds to display devotion in protecting the kingdom and opposing the efforts of invaders who seek to gain a footing in it. If we fail in doing so we are traitors and will have our faces blackened in both worlds.'[315] With such loyal servants behind him, Birjis Qadir expected confidently 'to exterminate the cruel, ill-behaved Kaffir

Feranghis from my hereditary dominions';[316] and Begam Hazrat Mahal, even in her hour of travail after being driven from Lucknow, could proudly refer to herself as 'we, the ever-abiding government, parents of the people of Oude', and to justly observe that 'no ruler ever experienced such loyalty and devotion of life and goods as we have done'.[317]

Under these definitions of loyalty, all helpers of the English were considered traitors and rebels.[318] The Raja of Ballabhgarh, whose loyalty to Bahadur Shah was for a moment suspect, was represented at the court to be 'professedly a servant of the state,' but 'in heart ... a friend to the English'. He was said to have collected stores of lead and powder 'with traitorous design'. Protesting his loyalty and condemning his ill-wishers, the Raja wrote to the imperial court:

> My ancestors and I have ever been the ancient and hereditary devoted slaves and servants of this exalted dynasty, and have never entertained an idea of disloyalty against you, who dispense mandates to the six cardinal points and the Seven Kingdoms of the world. For unalloyed gratitude and fidelity, I am as silver which has been thoroughly tried. If you test me a hundred times, I shall not fail in this test.[319]

The Jat raja was hanged by the British for his pains.

Certain zamindars of Buri Basari, we learn from Munshi Jivan Lal's diary, petitioned Bahadur Shah that the English were demanding revenue from them. 'If the king would only give the order they would not pay a single pie but would slaughter the English.'[320] It is striking that they did not offer to pay the revenue to the court instead. Yet the realization that they needed the name of the Emperor to defy the English shows that the blind impulse to mutiny, a Freudian id, had soon enough yielded to the voice of a rational calculating ego aware of the dangers that threatened the self with destruction. The collective self of the Mutiny, capable of appreciating the need to curb and discipline itself in order to survive, appeared in the attempt to construct an effective counter-authority. The town crier's drumbeat announcement, in the form of a well-known formula communicating official orders, changed significantly in the process. No longer would he cry: 'The universe belongs to God, the realm to the Emperor, the order to the Company.' Instead the beat was accompanied by the cry: 'The universe belongs to God, the realm to the Emperor, the order to ... [the local ruler].' The altered formula exhibited the rebels' ideas of government in the initial, spontaneous form. From the form of the drumbeat announcement, the notions of authority may be deduced as follows: (1) jurisdiction (*hukumat*) was invariably conceived in the form of the local principality—a realm from which the alien had been expelled;[321] (2) with a few exceptions, the authorities cropping up in this medley of jurisdictions were princely or baronial, government upon the whole being assumed to be monarchical; (3) the country (*mulk*) as a whole was thought to constitute the de jure sovereign domain of the Mughal Emperor, whose authority was regarded as derived from God.

All drumbeat announcements were highly conventionalized, consisting of three parts derived from long usage. These parts drew out the distinction between de facto and de jure power and derived the former from the latter and the latter from the heavenly jurisdiction over all creation. The gradation of these successive authorities was spelt out in terms of the space over which each held sway—God over the whole of Creation, the Emperor over the country at large, and the effective government over its own jurisdiction. Before the Mutiny, the greatest jurisdiction (*hukumat*) within the country (*mulk*) was that of the Company Bahadur. With the outbreak of the mutinies, it shattered into many fragments, but at the same time the rebellion maintained its integrity by conceiving each jurisdiction as part of the imperial territory (*Mulk-i-Padshah*).

Ideas of Authority

In the period before the Mutiny, when the rule of the Company went unchallenged, government orders proclaimed by the town crier were preceded, as a matter of course, by the drumbeat announcement:

[Persian]:   *Khalq-i-Khuda*
               Mulk-i-Padshah
               Hukm-i-Company Bahadur.

[Hindustani]: *Khalq Khuda ki*
               Mulk Badshah ki
               Hukum Company Bahadur ki.

That is to say, the Creation is God's, the country is the Emperor's, the order is that of the Company Bahadur. In a slightly modified form, the town crier might cry: *Khalq khuda ka, Mulk Badshah ka, Amal Ingraz Sarkar ka.*[322] Invariably, however—a point stressed by the Mutineers of

Meerut in their first address to the Emperor—the town crier's announcement specified that the sovereignty belonged to the Mughal *badshah*. The change that occurred in the form of the announcement in every town upon the outbreak of Mutiny is thus instanced by the Collector of Bijnaur: 'On the day of our departure Mahmood Khan proclaimed himself in the following terms:—"The people are God's, the country the Padshah's, and the order (or Government) Nawab Mahmood Khan's", in which his own name was substituted for the "Company", the usual proclamation running thus, "The people are God's, the country the Padshah's and the order (or Government) the Sirkar Company Buhadoor's ..."'.[323] It is in the vital third clause that the reversal takes place, deriving sanction from the constancy of the second. Such were the political conceptions in 1857: legalization of the overthrow of the existing government flowed from the implicit idea that no change had taken place in the legal framework of sovereign authority.

The very day on which the sepoys reached Delhi from Meerut, 20 guns were fired at midnight from the palace. 'Next day at about noon a proclamation was made by beat of drum that the country had reverted to the possession of the king.'[324] A more specific reference to the incident is made by the Emperor's secretary Mukund Lal: 'The same day proclamation was made by beat of drum throughout the city that God was the Ruler of the World, and that Bahadur Shah was Sovereign of the country, and had the supreme authority.'[325] A silver throne was brought out for the Emperor to enable him to hold audience. It had been removed and secreted in a recess of the palace since 1842 when the usual *nazar* from the Governor-General had been stopped.[326] There was no immediately recognized commander of the sepoys, hence the departure from the correct form of the third clause and the announcement of the *hukum* in the name of Bahadur Shah, though he was expected only to be a ceremonial figure. General Bakht Khan later arrived from Bareilly and was immediately conferred with the title of commander-in-chief, whereupon the town crier's call assumed a ceremonially correct form. The imperial order banning cow slaughter at Id was issued in the following form: 'The creation is God's and the Country is King's: Order of the highest officer of the army that any one who slaughter a cow, an ox or a calf (male or female), buffalo (male or female) openly or secretly, shall be considered an enemy of His Majesty and shall be punished with death.'[327] The Kotwal of Delhi quotes the order from memory in a slightly different form: 'The people are God's—the country is the King's—the decree is that of Bakht Khan,

Chief of the Army. If any man high or low sacrifice bullock or goat he shall suffer death.'[328]

The liberation of Delhi was the signal to the outbreak of a chain of mutinies. In the outstations, however, it was not always clear in whose name the '*hukum*' should be issued. The only fact which the people perceived with certainty was that the order of the Company Bahadur had ceased to be effective. Thus the Magistrate of Fatehpore, fleeing to Banda, had the mortification of being obliged to hear a conversation between two government peons who came and sat 'ostentatiously' near him. '"I say", cried one, "what would you give for this thing?" holding up his chaprass of brazen badge. "Four annas", his companion replied. "The brass is worth that—but the Government?" rejoined the first speaker with a sneer.'[329] Up to this time some sort of authority had adhered to the Magistrate and the little band of sahibs around him, and the behaviour of the people had been respectful. A body of irregular cavalry crossing the Jumna to the Banda side shortly afterwards raised the green flag in the village and had the proclamation announced by beat of drum:

> Khalk-i-Khuda
> Mulk-i-Padshah
> Hukum-i-Sipah.[330]

The issue of the order in the name of the sepoy army, however, was clearly a temporary expedient, until a suitable prince would be found to head the local government. The sepoys insisted on being the men to choose the ruler, but they had no thought of setting themselves up as the government. No sooner did the fleeing English party arrive from Fatehpore than Banda broke out in mutiny. All officers fled. On the night of the British officers' flight from town, the bungalows in the cantonment were plundered by the sepoys and burnt to the ground, and in town the ex-Nawab of Banda had himself proclaimed: 'Khalaq Khoda Ka Mooluk Badsha Ka Hookum Nawab Alli Bahadoor Ka.'[331] The following day the sepoys, incensed by the Nawab's unilateral assumption of power, proclaimed their own authority by the beat of a drum: 'Khulluk Khoda Mulk Badshah hukum Subhadar Sepoy Bahadur.'[332] The Nawab managed to appease their wrath by giving them a great dinner of sweetmeats and by acknowledging their authority to be final in all matters.

The sepoys then called the *amlah* (members of the subordinate staff) and told them grandly that they might return to their respective offices.

Muhammad Sardar Khan, deputy collector under the British, was appointed *Nazim* of Banda', with full powers of life and death. However, the slaughter of cows and bullocks was prohibited throughout town on the sepoys' own order. On 17 June the officers of the sepoys paid a state visit to Nawab Ali Bahadur and held a council of war. The Nawab's right was disputed by the Bundela chieftain of Ajaigarh, whose ancestors had held the country before the Nawab's forefather had been appointed by the Peshwa. It was resolved that the matter would be referred to Nana Sahib at Bithur and in the meanwhile the Nawab should hold charge of the country on the sepoys' departure. The sepoys left on the 19th with the money found in the treasury. Thereupon the Nawab proceeded to impose his own administration over the land.[333]

Rani Lakshmi Bai, too, experienced the same difficulty as the Nawab of Banda. On the evening of the massacre of the Europeans in Jhansi, the sepoys had a dispute with Rani Lakshmi Bai's delegates and, unable to come to terms, made the following announcement: 'The people are God's; the country is the King's (Padshah's); and the two religions govern.'[334] Here was a brief glimmering of the idea that popular sovereignty might be embodied in the two great communities of Hindustan. But the active search for a prince continued as the mutineers were apparently incapable of pushing their thought in that unfamiliar direction. A dispute had broken out between the widow Rani and her late husband's kinsman, Sadasheo Rao, as to who should succeed to the Jhansi Raj. The sepoys were in two minds regarding the claimant to whom the government of Jhansi should be made over. However, the Rani paid down a large sum and the sepoys before departing for Delhi had it proclaimed by beat of drum: 'Khalq khuda ka, mulk Badshah ka, amal Lakshmi Bai ka.'[335]

Clear embodiments of authority could not always be found, and in nearby Hamirpur the scene was one of utter confusion. Subadar Ali Bux of the sepoys proclaimed the Delhi dynasty, and himself its agent. Soon, however, troopers arrived from Nana Sahib to escort the sepoys to Cawnpore. The native deputy collector, Wahiduzzaman, received an order from the Nana to manage in his name. On 1 July the Bithur prince's name was proclaimed in Hamirpur.[336]

Nana Sahib had earlier proclaimed himself in Cawnpore with the support of the sepoys. There the bazaar had been ordered open to the beat of a tom-tom: 'Khuluk Khoda ka, Moolk Padsha Ka, hookm Nana Saheb and Fouj Bahadur ka, that whoever will not yield compliance to shall subject himself to severe punishment.' From Shepherd's account we learn that the troopers in Cawnpore took the lead in everything 'and openly declared that they did not care for the Nana. They even went to greater lengths in this usurpation of authority by causing every proclamation issued by beat of tom-tom to be accompanied with the words "hookoom sipah bahadoor ka (i.e. by order of the brave soldiery"'.[337]

As will be evident from the mention of the *fauj bahadur* or *sipah bahadur*, Nana Sahib's rule in Cawnpore was not too well assured. He was a stranger in town, his own residence being some miles off at Bithur. He therefore had no recognized claim to authority in the town or the country around it. The sepoys, often dissatisfied with his proceedings, toyed with the idea of placing a *rais* of the town, called the Nannhe Nawab, on the *gadi*.[338] This young man was the scion of a house which had made its pile in the service of the Nawabs of Lucknow. The family had since transferred its wealth and residence to British territory.[339] The 'little' nawab was a reluctant recruit to the cause of the Mutiny, and at first a prisoner of Nana Sahib on account of his suspected loyalty to the British. He made up with the Nana, obtained command of a battery which wrought havoc on General Wheeler's entrenchment, and was apparently promised by the Nana, who felt it politic to conciliate him, that in the administrative arrangements to be made after the expulsion of the British, he would be appointed Governor of Cawnpore.[340] Nana Sahib felt weak on the ground, his dynasty having never enjoyed authority here in the past. Further south, in Kalpi, where he asked Tantia Tope to set up a military base,[341] his authority had more assured recognition on account of the historical memory of the Peshwas having been the suzerains of the entire belt of Bundelkhand.

Jhansi having been formerly a subordinate *suba* of the Peshwa, Rani Lakshmi Bai acknowledged the authority of Kalpi, received help from Tantia Tope in the defence of her kingdom, and later figured as an important adviser in the Peshwa's moving council at Kalpi, Mahoba, and Gwalior.[342] The Nawab of Banda, a descendant and appointee of the Peshwa and an acknowledged relation of Nana Sahib, clearly spelt out the subordination of his government to the authority of the Peshwa Pant Pradhan and through him to the Badshah at Delhi, in his draft of rules for the administration of Banda.[343] The Rani of Jhansi, the Nawab of Banda, the Rajas of Shahgarh and Banpur, Tai Bai who set herself up as the Jalaun Rani for a time, and the various Bundela chiefs, all acted as confederates of the Kalpi centre in the military operations against the advance of General Hugh Rose from the south.[344] When the Bundela chief Deshpat, a local associate of Tantia Tope in his various operations, finally set himself up at Rath, the town crier proclaimed: 'Khalq khoda ka, Mulk Badshah ka, Raj Peshwa Ka, Hukm Despat Ka,'[345] clearly delineating the hierarchy of political authorities.

It appeared as if the whole intricate patchwork of eighteenth century regimes was being restored, but not quite. The sepoys were everywhere the decisive political voice at the beginning of each outbreak, and it was their will and conscious choice that determined the selection of chiefs, even in so obvious a matter as the reinstatement of the Nawab family of Awadh overthrown just a year earlier. There was nothing automatic about the 'restoration', as the Lucknow example goes to show. When the mutineers, with Maulvi Ahmadullah Shah of Faizabad as their *pir* and fellow fighter, entered Lucknow in triumph, looting and seizing people indiscriminately, they had no particular ruler in mind. They however saw the necessity of setting up a government when in error some members of the artillery were seized by other sepoys. The *maulvi*, who had been busy organizing *thanas* all over the city to protect the citizens from being plundered, expected to be acknowledged as the head of the government.[346] The sepoys, however, had other ideas. Their choice fell upon the boy Birjis Qadr after a long wrangle in which the only issue was the particular scion of the house of Lucknow who should ascend the throne.[347] The choice, however, was conditional upon the sanction of Bahadur Shah—an important condition in view of the fact that the Nawab Wazirs of Lucknow, prompted by the British, had earlier ceased to recognize the suzerainty of the Emperors of Delhi. The sepoys insisted upon the new '*Wali*' of Lucknow acknowledging the supreme authority of the emperor.[348] It was symptomatic of the realities of power that a paper was taken from the boy's mother, Hazrat Mahal, for the officers to sign, and that she retained this paper as a sort of *sanad*.[349] The sepoys having made their own terms, the announcement was made in the city: 'God's world, King of Delhi's Kingdom, Mirza Birjis Qadar orders that nobody shall plunder any more, otherwise he will be punished.'[350]

However, the revival of princely authority was not the only political idea in the air. The *maulvi* continued to maintain his own court in Tara Kothi,[351] and 'kept up a kingly state' there right until the British reoccupation.[352] After being driven from Lucknow in the midst of heavy fighting in which he distinguished himself, he was chosen as their chief by the army.[353] The *maulvi* then took a bolder step. On 15 March 1858 he crowned himself at Muhammadi and struck coins bearing the legend: 'The slave of Mehrab Shah [the *maulvi's pir*] struck his coins in the seven countries; a supporter of the faith of Muhammad is king Ahmadullah.'[354]

The idea of a saint setting himself up as the ruler was not entirely new. A year earlier, the same expedient had been tried in Allahabad, and around the same time the *Risala Fath-i-Islam* had mooted the idea of some 'Imam Akbar' being chosen by the people to lead them in a holy war against the English.[355] The idea could be put into practice in Allahabad because there British rule had wiped out all traces of the former ruling class and no prince could be found to head the rebellion. Leadership fell, by default, to a *maulvi* from a nearby village. 'This man, a weaver by caste, and by trade a schoolmaster,' the official account tells us, 'had gained some respect in his village by his excessive sanctity: and in the first spread of the rebellion, the Mahomedan Zemindars of pergunnah Chail, ready to follow any leader, placed this man at their head, and marched to the city, proclaiming him a governor of the district, in the name of the King of Delhi.'[356] A contemporary Bengali diary thus specified the proclamation in Allahabad: 'Badshahi Muluk, Mir and Maulvi Saheb's Hukum, arm yourselves to save the lives (dil) of Hindus and Musalmans and destroy the forces (dalbal) of the firingi.'[357] The Mir Sahib is unidentifiable, but the *Maulvi* is undoubtedly Liaqat Ali who in fact presided over the rebel court in Khusru Bagh.[358] The fakir's own account of the outbreak, related to the Emperor after his flight from Allahabad, provides an insight into the notions of power and sovereignty entertained by a lowly village pedagogue who had risen to sudden and temporary rulership of an entire town and district amidst the chaos of an overturned administration:

> The following is a detailed account of all that took place in the city of Allahabad during the troublous time when the wrath of God was visited upon the Nazarene race. The sepoys of the army murdered the English officers, and released the prisoners; and they took from the treasury (in which there was about twenty two lakhs) what was required by them; and plundering the rest, departed. On hearing this, your humble servant, who lived about 7 koss from the city, considering in his mind that, as the ancestors of the people had once lived under the ennobling auspices of this great [Mughal] Government, the fulfilment of the conditions of loyalty and the protection of the people was now incumbent upon him. He at

once, therefore, along with several champions of the faith, and a number of talookdars (viz., Sheikh Nizamut Ashruf and Gholam Ismael, and Muhammad Hossein and Chowdhri Meeran Buksh and others) went into the city to institute a religious war, and sent to hell the English who remained [in the Allahabad Fort], and with the intention, after sending a *congratulatory* address to Your invincible Highness, of assuming charge of the Zillah until receipt of further orders. The flag of Mahomet was placed in the chouk, and proclamation was made in the city to this effect: 'The Nazarene race is the enemy of the life and faith, both of Hindus and Mussulmans. This Fukeer having girded up his loins to protect the life and faith of the people of God, and to fulfil the conditions of loyalty to the ministers of the Kingly Government, it becomes you also to assist with all readiness the destruction of the English who remain'.[359]

This was a singular instance of a party of villagers—an obscure maulvi at the head of rustic Muslim zamindars and turbulent Mewati agriculturists—coming to town and setting up the government. No less surprising was the general recognition which a government of such lowly origins obtained in the town and district during the few weeks it worked before General Neill came and put it to flight. However, Agra, where also the Europeans were for some time incarcerated in the fort, experienced no such alternative authority for the town crier to proclaim. Here, too, the sepoys left for Delhi without setting up a government. Popular sentiments were as violent against the foreigners here as in Allahabad.[360] However, no alternative centre of authority could be located, and the insurgents left behind by the mutineers frittered away their energies in futile plunder and violence.

When news came to the fort from a native *tahsildar* that no sepoys were left in town, an attack by a force from the fort soon restored English authority without any effective opposition from the local insurgents.[361] The underlying difficulty they faced here was the same as in Allahabad, and indeed over large parts of Hindustan. Except in Awadh, and to some extent in Rohilkhand and Bundelkhand, British administration had over the years effectively dismantled the former ruling class, so that no traces of traditional authority could be found to supply ready materials for an alternative government.[362]

In the first flash of the Mutiny, therefore, British administration disappeared in many parts of the North-Western Provinces (Agra and Allahabad) with no former princely government springing up to replace it. The exigencies of the circumstances sometimes forced the local notables to proclaim novel political ideas to meet the vacuum. Thus, the closure of the bazaar in Jaunpur caused such hardship to the public that the 'pious and wealthy Qazi Sahib' of the town had his own men call out: 'Mulk-i-Padshah, Hukm-i-Panch[363] [lit., the Five, meaning the public], open up haats, bazaars and dukans as before for buying and selling. People must not do harm to one another. Whoever goes against this will be punished by the justice of the Panch, and will receive sentence from the person who becomes the owner of the realm.'[364] This arrangement did not last long. The Lucknow government appointed Beni Madho as *nazim* of Jaunpur and Azamgarh on the ground that these British districts were at one time parts of the kingdom of Awadh. A local landholder named Raja Iradat Jahan who got himself appointed as *naib nazim* held parts of Jaunpur and Azamgarh against the British forces for some time in the name of the Lucknow government.[365]

The republican ideas of the rule of the *panch*, the *hukm* of the *fauj Bahadur*, the governance of the two religions, or even the religious doctrine of the leadership of the Imam Akbar could not progress further among a people whose mentality was so historically conditioned to the hierarchical power of the nawabs, rajas and zamindars.[366] Topping all this in their minds was the sovereignty of the *Padshah* of Delhi. The remnants of traditional authority provided the *foci* of the alternative rebel order wherever such elements were found ready to hand. Whether these elements were the tribal chiefs of a few jungle *parganas*, as in Singhbhum, or the former Pathan rulers of an entire tract, as in Rohilkhand, the hold they had over the mind and imagination of the people provided a surer foundation of rebel government than the republican or saintly ideas.

It is not surprising then that the ex-Raja of Porhat in Singhbhum, Arjun Singh, should be the man to lead the Kol tribals to rebellion in Chaibasa. It was explained to the Kols and Mundas that the English had abandoned the country and that it had become the property of the Raja as before. Once the mutineers had left Chaibasa after plundering the treasury, the Raja who had helped them cross the river directed a proclamation being made through the Chaibasa bazaar: 'that everything belonged to God, that the country belonged to the King, and that the ruler thereof was Urjoon Singh.'[367]

The Rohilla chief at the other end of the mutinying country adopted the same formula as the jungle raja had employed at his own end. Habua, the town crier of Bareilly, was sent for on the day of the Mutiny at about one o'clock. Khan Bahadur Khan, sitting on the Kotwali terrace,

The Felt Community

directed the man 'to proclaim in the Bazar that the people are God's the country is the King's, the province Khan Bahadur Khan's sway.'[368]

The Rohilla prince could not, however, extend his sway to Moradabad district of Rohilkhand, which fell to the control of the pro-English Raja of Rampur. Before that, on the night the Bareilly Brigade marched out of Moradabad, Majjoo Khan, the man left in charge by General Bakht Khan, proclaimed by tom-tom 'that the people were God's, the country the King of Delhi's and Majjoo Khan was Viceroy of Moradabad, and that whoever shall fail to attend next day the durbar of the Viceroy, he shall be guilty of treason, and shall be blown away from a gun'.[369] So sudden a supremacy was not equipped to withstand the challenge from Rampur. It collapsed.

In the Doab, there were no strong remnants of traditional authority as in Awadh or Rohilkhand. There was, however, one exception. The Nawab of Farrukhabad, who had an easily recognized hereditary claim, initiated his rule with the cry at Fatehgarh on 16 June 1857: 'Khulck Ollah ka moolk Badshah ka hookm Nawab Raees Bahadur ka.'[370] The formula was the same everywhere;, and in most places the third clause mentioned a prince. The discerning observer could not have failed to detect a certain uniformity in the inchoate political ideas of 1857.

How was this patchwork of regimes to be consolidated into one political bloc against the English enemy? The rebels, as stated earlier, had no notion of the sovereign national state. They fell back on older ideas of union, not the integrated agrarian bureaucratic empire of the Great Mughals, but the loose, internally cleaved confederacies of the eighteenth century which popular memory could recall more immediately. The Late Mughal suzerainty of Shah Alam and the Maratha confederacy of the last Peshwa Baji Rao provided the models for federation. As Bahadur Shah felt the British stranglehold on Delhi closing, he sent desperate letters under his signature to the Rajput rajas of Jaipur, Bikaner, Jodhpur, and Alwar, 'that the King was in want of troops and was desirous of annihilating the English; but inasmuch as he had no reliable person to organize and administer the very important affairs of the empire at this juncture, he wished to form a Confederacy of States; and if the States now addresses with these letters would combine for the purpose he would willingly resign the imperial power into their hands'.[371] The Rajput rulers, however, proved to be confirmed allies of the British, and none replied to Bahadur Shah's message. However, so long as the court of Delhi survived there was an indisputable rallying point for the rebel regimes of Hindustan and Malwa, and embassies were sent from most rebel courts to Delhi for obtaining legal recognition or military assistance, as the case might be.

A party of sepoys came from Lucknow and—rescinding Awadh's earlier declaration of its independence of Delhi—told the Emperor that they had raised a son of Wajid Ali Shah to the *gaddi* on condition that he should, like his first ancestor, be the Wazir of the Badshah, and that the latter should sanction the appointment. Bahadur Shah ordered General Bakht Khan to reply to the petition conveying his sanction to the restoration of the old arrangement. Subsequently, Mirza Abbas Khan, *vakil* of the *wali* of Awadh, brought a *nazar* of gold *mohurs* as token of the latter's submission to the emperor.[372]

General Bakht Khan arrived from Bareilly with Khan Bahadur Khan's *vakil*, carrying the Rohilla chief's petition, together with his *nazar*—a horse with silver ornaments and 101 gold *mohurs*—as token of submission to the Emperor of Delhi.[373] Two months after the outbreak of the Mutiny, a confidential Maratha agent arrived from Nana Sahib and was introduced by Prince Mirza Mughal to the presence. A *shukka* was then addressed to Nana Sahib to come to Delhi, and the agent returned. Petitions were received from the neighbouring chiefs of Jhajjar, Ballabhgarh, Farrukhnagar, etc., all professing allegiance to the Emperor and excusing themselves from attendance on the ground that their absence would unsettle their respective lands.[374]

A petition was made by Maulvi Liaqat Ali of Allahabad, leader of the Mujahideen there, praying for military assistance for the recovery of the country from the advancing English forces. No reply was sent as the fleeing *maulvi* was himself expected to arrive shortly. When he came he was introduced to the Emperor by General Bakht Khan, and he retired with a patent appointing him Governor of Allahabad.[375]

The dispossessed Nawab Walidad Khan of Malagarh, father-in-law of Prince Jawan Bakht, was in Delhi at the time of the outbreak. He departed with a patent from his imperial master and matrimonial relation conferring on him the governorship of the Doab.[376] He was directed to suppress the depredations of the Gujars and to send in the rich revenues of the tract.[377] He was in fact the only appointee who actually obtained military assistance from the court of Delhi for the performance of his vital tasks.[378] He occupied Bulandshahr, and extended his hold over portions of the western Doab. Muhammad Ghaus Khan, zamindar of Sikandra Rao, became the *naib subah* on his behalf in

Aligarh,[379] and Chaudhuri Muhammad Ali Khan, zamindar of Suhawar, got himself appointed as his *nazim* in Etah.[380] The British military presence in Meerut, however, prevented Walidad Khan from consolidating Delhi's hold over the Doab.

The welcome address that greeted General Bakht Khan upon his arrival in Delhi expressed a resolve to dislodge the 'infidels' from the Ridge and then to proceed to occupy 'Meerut, Patiala, Hansi, Lucknow and Agra as a few Europeans still remain there'.[381] These plans never got beyond paper. The failure of the court of Delhi to create a liberated zone westwards into the Haryana tract or across the Jumna into the Doab eventually led to the triumph of the British on the Ridge.[382]

After the fall of Delhi, Nana Sahib renewed the idea of a confederacy of the Indian princely states. At one time his plans had been more grandiose, envisaging a *peshwai* of 25 *subas* worth a net revenue of Rs 25 crores payable to the centre: Gwalior, Agra, Delhi, Lahore, Kashmir, Amritsar, Lucknow, Murshidabad, Bengal, Calcutta, Bombay, Surat, Poona, Hyderabad, Aurangabad, Rangoputher (?), Nagpur, Nugger, Nugger-Jat (?), Furanan (?), Ahmadabad, Ujjain, Jodhpur, Jaipur, and Ratnagir.[383] The would-be Pant Pradhan had only an imperfect idea of the territories over which he claimed authority; and practical circumstances induced him quickly to moderate his ambitions. He recognized the suzerainty of the Emperor and the rights of the other princes, and a proclamation 'by Rao Punt Prudhan Peshwa' published under 'order' of 'Ullee Shan', 'Bundeegan', 'Ullee Huzoor' the Emperor of Delhi declared the former's wish 'to re-establish the Hindoo and Mahomedan kingdoms as formerly and to protect our country'.[384] Early in 1858, several months after Bahadur Shah's surrender, an agent of Nana Sahib in Kalpi assured the chiefs of Bundelkhand:

> The object which the Maharajah has in view to expel all the Christians from Hindoostan, is not to take possession of the territories and property of the Rajahs and Chiefs of India, or to assume the supreme command of the country, but on the other hand, it is his sole desire that after a victory shall be obtained over the enemy, all the chiefs may in peace enjoy the possession of the territories which they at present hold as well as those which they formerly possessed, and pass their days in the enjoyment of ease and happiness.[385]

The Framework of the Rebel Organization

All the same, the insistence of the sepoys that every prince and chief pay allegiance to the Emperor shows a conscious drive towards an integral framework of rebel organization. As the fighting force of the Mutiny, the sepoys appreciated the need for unity more than either the princes or the people. The presence of the sepoy army combated any atavistic throwback to the chaotic scene of the eighteenth century. Because the army was in control, there was no unqualified restoration of the pre-British conditions of Indian polity.

It must be borne in mind here that the primary instinct of the Mutiny was not to restore the older scheme of things. The Mutiny, in its primal impulse, was an act of negation of British power, and only secondarily an act of substitution of British power by the regimes that had preceded it. Yet, in the act of transcendence, that which negates retains within itself that which is negated. If the restoration was to survive in an altered world, it could not afford to scrap every innovation that British power had effected in the meanwhile, especially not the new procedures for the exercise of power. It had to reckon with the challenge of an organized enemy and it could only undertake the stern reckoning by turning that opponent's military instrument—the sepoy army—upon the erstwhile owner. There was an attempt, as far as possible, to preserve the military organization of the sepoy army, and to ensure a place for it in the new political set-up. Thus, there was no question of a total relapse, a regression to the eighteenth century. A complex, three-way process was at work, a negation of negation: the colonial rule of the English was negated; the old Mughal regime was restored; and certain English arrangements were preserved, especially those essential to the successful negation and the effective restoration. Under the circumstances, there was no going back to the same scheme of things as before.

The sepoy army, the organization of which remained partially intact, was the visible antithesis of those traditional supremacies that had been restored. The survival of the fragmented regimental parts of its organization was a fact of supreme importance in the progress of the Mutiny. Trapped by the old debate among British officials in 1857 whether they were facing an army revolt or a civil rebellion, some historians are still anxious to prove that the uprising was not a mere mutiny, but a popular, 'civil' rebellion. They have overlooked the fact that the mutiny of the sepoys was the most organized and in a way perhaps the most progressive part of the popular rebellion, without which it could not have spread as it did. Only a couple of years prior to the Mutiny, the Santhal insurrection had broken out on the western border of Bengal. Subedar Sitaram's account leaves one in no doubt that it was a very different kind of war, altogether smaller in scale than the Mutiny:

> In 1855 a small war broke out in Bengal with some jungle people called Santhals, and my regiment formed part of the force and was stationed near Raniganj, not far from Calcutta...
>
> The Santhals used bows, arrows, and large sharp axes, but they always dispersed when we fired on them. At first it was reported that they used poisoned arrows, and for this reason they were much feared, but we soon discovered that this was not the case. After a good deal of marching through thick jungle, and after guarding the main road by the Sone river through one hot weather, the rebellion was put down ... it was certainly a curious war.[386]

The old *subedar* learned that the grievances of the Santhals were 'all against the rich landlords and moneylenders, who had managed to get these simple folk into their clutches'. These complaints were the same as some of the agrarian grievances of 1857, yet the scale of the Santhal insurrection appeared to be altogether smaller in his vision. The revolt of the sepoy army linked together the tribal, clan, village, and dispossessed chiefs' rebellions into one simultaneous rising of the people, and the mutinying regiments alone helped maintain the linked character of the rebellion as it progressed.

The inchoate republican notions and practices in the sepoy army, the remnants of its unitary organization, its fixed resolve to be the decisive voice in the new political set up, all brought a novel and important dimension to the political organization of the rebellion. With the overthrow of the British officer corps, the higher command structure of the sepoy army crumbled. There were no native officers of the requisite rank to fill the vacuum. The Bengal Army thus ceased to be one fighting force, but the individual regiments sought to retain organization and unity of command. Many of the regiments dissolved;[387] most of those that remained degenerated in discipline and command.[388] The remnants, however, provided, for the first time, a general centre of resistance to the British dominance, and this was something that the Indian population, as the journalist and thinker Karl Marx noted at the time, had never had before.[389] In a few crucial instances, the fragments of the mutinous Bengal Army proved to be larger than the regimental units. The Bareilly and Neemuch Brigades and the Gwalior Contingent[390] were large conglomerates with a critical effect on the course and development of the 'reigning Indian crusade'. While no longer constituting a single operational army with a headquarters and a commander-in-chief, these[391] regiments, brigades, and contingents were individually intact fighting units which joined the rebellion under their respective colours. As Subedar Sitaram put it, 'All regiments took their Colours with them. They did not break their oath by deserting them. They left the service of the English and were supposed to have entered the service of another government.'[392] Discipline was no longer the same as before, but they maintained 'their English equipment and organization' and some sort of drill and parade.[393] In the areas where fighting was prolonged, the regiments often lost their distinct identity, but the princes and chiefs in turn raised their own levies, stiffening them with a leaven of sepoys,[394] or reforming the dissolved bands of mutineers into new regiments.[395] Invariably, the British regimental organization provided the model in forming these forces,[396] except in the case of the irregulars known as '*nujeebs*'.[397]

In one important respect, however, the sepoys could not maintain their English equipment and organization. This was the commissariat. Among the mutineers, as the commissariat clerk Durgadas Banerjee pointed out, there was a great source of disorder: the insufficiency of provisions.

> It is no easy matter [he observed with regard to Khan Bahadur Khan's army in Rohilkhand] to arrange the daily food supply for 16,000 men– 11,000 troops and no less than 5000 camp followers. The mutineers had no commissariat to speak of. The commander was also the man in charge of distributing provisions. To complicate matters, the commander of the cavalry did not pull together with the commander of the infantry. Suppose Nawab Khan Bahadur Khan had sent 100 cart loads of atta for the cavalry. The infantry had no atta at all on that day. The commander of the infantry would ask the commander of the cavalry for a loan of 50 cart loads of atta. The latter would reply, 'that can never be—this is my atta. If I give 50 cart loads of atta today, and no atta arrives tomorrow, what will my troops eat?' It was even reported that the cavalry and infantry had fought each other several times over the carts bringing atta and rice.[398]

According to Durgadas Banerjee, another major source of dissension in the camp was prostitutes:

> Pretty dance women were not rare in that hilly province. Just think—the soldiers had no work to do, except stuff themselves with edibles, sleep heavily in the afternoon, take a walk in the evening. The one piece of work they had was the morning parade—going to the parade ground to practise firing tumultuously. Apart from that, all they did was to consume bhang and hashish for 24 hours a day—to the accompaniment of obscene raillery, obscene jokes and obscene gestures.

The trouble was that there was no single commander-in-chief, only a commander for each regiment. The sepoys did not show their regimental commander proper respect, nor did that officer know how to exact obedience. He lived luxuriously, took his ease, ate well, and busied himself with his girls. True, there was no prostitutes' corner in the camp, but from time to time dance women were invited. 'When these dance women set their foot in camp, all hell broke loose. No sense of shame or respect for superiors was left there. ... It is against my religious principles to narrate such worm-eaten, infernal tales. Let me say briefly, the dance of destruction (bhairav-lila), with guns, swords and spears, would break out among the soldiery from time to time over these prostitutes. On both sides, ten or twelve would be killed.'[399]

It must be borne in mind that Durgadas Banerjee was deeply prejudiced and had refused to serve in the mutiny commissariat. Moreover, his description applies not to the Bareilly brigade which kept him prisoner for some time, but to the new levies raised by Khan Bahadur Khan after General Bakht Khan left for Delhi. All the evidence shows that the sepoys fought on desperately until the finality of defeat induced them to melt away as ordinary peasants. At this stage the fighting dissolved into the isolated jacqueries of the chiefs and their retainers in the jungles of the Terai and Bundelkhand. Unlike the princes and landed magnates, who sought to keep lines of communication open with the British, the hardened Purbeah sepoys knew that for them capture meant certain hanging on the gallows. They were, therefore, the most committed element in the fighting forces of the Mutiny.[400] Even in the last stages of the fighting, it was reported from Gorakhpur: 'The same feeling of despair is believed to exist among the regular sepoys; but Mr Wingfield's spies all represent them as still impressed with the full belief, that they have been fighting for their religion, and that they now have no alternative but to become Christians.'[401]

The remoulding of camp life to their own taste might have undermined discipline and unity of command, but they compensated partially for these gaps by a collective commitment to the cause[402] and a marked republicanism of spirit. The popular election of officers became the custom in the mutinous regiments, as the cross-examination of Subedar Bhondu Singh of the 17th NI clearly reveals:

> *Question*: If you had no hand in the mutiny, how is it that you were elected a General of the force?
> *Answer*: The sepoys elected me General for a few days but did not allow me to continue so. They nominated Dabeedeen as my successor, the sepoys had the power to do so.[403]

We are informed on one authority that panchayats were held in the sepoy lines every night.[404] Their function was to decide collectively the course the regiment should take. Jan Ali Khan, a minor functionary taken prisoner by the Indore mutineers marching to Gwalior, saw a well established panchayati system of administration among the rebels. All persons were treated on terms of equality. If anything was to be done, each company (the party consisted of 23rd Mhow Regiment Native Infantry, 3 troops of Cavalry, 7 guns and 2 companies of foot, one *risala* of Holkar's troops) sent one or two members to represent it at the panchayat and whatever was decided was done forthwith.[405] Descriptions of the functioning of the Gwalior Contingent makes it clear that the *panch* was an instrument of the ordinary soldiers, and that the general will of the army preponderated to an extraordinary degree:

> The rebels called to be their general Amanut Ali, Soobadar Major of the 1st Regiment, which, sparing officers, moved on Gwalior immediately after the revolt but the most violent sepoys in fact commanded. There troops spent their whole time in councils, *Panchayets*, courts, and deputations; and the Maharajah was compelled to receive daily, 'to report', one of the latter, composed of officers from every corps with privates delegated to watch them, bodies of from 80 or 40 to 100 men. They menaced, beseeched, dictated, wheedled, and insulted Scindia by turns, until they planted their Batteries against him .... .
> ... The Contingent now demanded peremptorily of the Maharaja his final plans, and to hear them their officers attended on the 7th with 300 men in his palace garden. Scindia asked what their wishes were. The officers began to reply, but the sepoys thrust them aside, and said that they had resolved immediately to take Agra, and destroy the Christians there when they would carry the Scindia's banner where he pleased. He replied, that they did not therefore await his orders; that their movement until after

the rains would be against his will, and they should receive from him neither pay nor supplies.

The sepoys declared indignantly that they had been betrayed, and returning to their camp planted a green flag for the Mahomedans, a white flag for the Hindus.[406]

The incident reflected two contradictory aspects of the sepoys' mentality: the strong republican spirit of the privates who sometimes thrust aside their officers to assert the collective will of the body, and their mental craving for the leadership of the princes or chiefs at the top of the social hierarchy. The Indore mutineers, to take another instance, had elected Saadat Khan, an officer of the Holkar's cavalry, as their chief. Not happy with this, they wanted the Holkar to lead them. As the prince would not comply, they searched around and took with them Nawab Warris Muhammad Khan, a relation of the Nawab of Bhopal then residing at the Residency Bazaar in Indore.[407] A curious manifestation of the same psyche was General Bakht Khan's claim, on his arrival in Delhi, that he was a descendant of the same family as the Emperor's. He insisted that Bahadur Shah satisfy himself on this point by an enquiry. Bahadur Shah replied diplomatically that there was no need, as a greater man than the general assuredly did not exist.[408] The sepoys had a sneaking feeling that their tumultuous proceedings were devoid of respectability, and, in hard military terms, not conducive to victory. Raja Man Singh, explaining the reasons to his fellow *taluqdars* why the Telingas could not possible win, wrote:

> 1st. Though they are well disciplined, and it is true that by their assistance the British conquered India, still, in reality, they were always kept like a machine which could move or fire a musket on the touch of a spring. They do not know how to fight, neither do they understand the art of war. The British officers kept this knowledge to themselves. Without these officers they are a machine without a spring, and in the time of need they will neither be able to move nor to fire.
>
> 2nd. There used to be twenty or twenty-five officers to every 1000 men, and these officers were subordinate to one single man, but now-a-days there are 1000 officers and 1000 kings among 1000 men, i.e. the men are officers and kings themselves, and when such is the case there are no soldiers to fight. Kings cannot fight alone.[409]

The notions of the society from which the sepoy army had sprung were hierarchical, though by instinct and practice the sepoy army was a republican body. They were, in consequence, bent on creating a political society which would conform, in ritual, to all the appearances of monarchy and aristocracy, but in which decision-making, in substance, would bear the imprint of their will. The mutinous troops in Delhi used to say among themselves, that 'they were the masters of the country' and that 'they would take different princes to different provinces of the country'. Hakim Ahsanullah learnt from Haidar Husain, who was familiar with the officers of the troops, that they spoke privately as follows: 'If we continue united together, we shall not be defeated by the Government troops, but shall become masters of the country.'[410] This shows that they were aware of the need to maintain unity among themselves. In their eagerness to evolve a single command structure for the regiments and to ensure a place for themselves in the realm, they hit upon a device which they called the 'court'—a sort of sepoy council destined to play a critical part in the process of military and political decision-making in Delhi and other centres of rebellion. The resultant structure was a curious mixture of royalty and republicanism.

Several sepoy councils sprang up during the course of the rebellion, first in Delhi and then in Lucknow, Cawnpore, Farrukhabad, etc. However, where the army moved off *en masse*, as happened in Bareilly and Jhansi, there was no sepoy council.[411] There the local potentates left behind by the sepoys, such as Khan Bahadur Khan of Rohilkhand and Rani Lakshmi Bai of Jhansi, raised their own troops and were able to set up civil councils properly subordinate to princely authority.[412] In the two principal centres of the Mutiny, however, that is, in Delhi and Lucknow, which were regarded as 'the first care' of the rebels 'inasmuch as these two places were the asylums of the sepoys and the people high and low',[413] the sepoy council was necessarily the key element in the construction of authority. Numerous regiments converged on these points from different directions. On a lesser scale this was also true of Farrukhabad, where a court of two sepoy officers, respectively representing the two regiments (41st NI and 10th Oude Locals) which had converged there, assumed plenary powers and acted as a court of appeal with the power to reverse the decision of any lower court.[414]

> Nawab Tuffuzool Hoosain Khan of Farruckabad was supposed to look down from his lofty throne, and watch and guide the proceedings of the various courts; but in truth he had very little power shortly after the commencement of his reign. He was a man of quiet habits, more given to painting and gilding, and the society of immoral characters than fitted to rule and direct a turbulent soldiery, and a rural population not over well inclined to his rule or to any system at all, except what their own wishes or ideas suggested.[415]

In Delhi and Lucknow too, the uproarious proceedings of the sepoys at the ceremonial restoration of the *Padshah* and the *Wali* exposed the tinsel in the glitter during the first tumultuous days.[416] On the day after the mutineers arrived from Meerut, Munshi Jivan Lal wrote in his diary:

> Towards evening a number of native regimental officers came and again represented the difficulty in getting rations. Forgetful of the lofty tone of the morning's order, and of the high-toned phraseology expressive of the King's dignity, they addressed him with such disrespectful terms as, 'I say, you King! I say, you old fellow!' ('*Āri, Bādshah! Āri, Buddha!*'). 'Listen', cried one, catching him by the hand. 'Listen to me,' said another, touching the old King's beard.[417]

In vain did Bahadur Shah threaten to don the red-ochred garb of the mendicant and proceed to Mecca. The sepoys heaped one humiliation after another on his old head, the ultimate insult being their demand to take Begam Zinat Mahal as a hostage on the ground (all too true) of her suspected complicity with the English. The aged Emperor later recalled:

> The officers of the army went so far as to require that I should make over the Queen Zinat Mahall to them that they might keep her a prisoner, saying she maintained friendly relations with the English .... The mutinous soldiery had established a court in which all matters were deliberated on, and such matters as, after deliberation, were sanctioned by this council, they adopted; but I never took part in these conferences .... In addition to all this, it is worthy of consideration that no person demands the wife of the *poorest* man, saying 'Give her to me, I will make her prisoner'.[418]

In Lucknow, on the day of the young boy Birjis Qadr's coronation, the sepoys crowded into the palace, 'creating the utmost consternation by their disregard of all decorum, and by their noisy comments on the person and appearance of the lad. Some likened him to a God; some admonished him not to abandon himself to wine, women, and fiddlers; and others loudly declared that he was too young and timid, as he stood trembling before the tumultuous crowd of armed men and started at the report of muskets discharged close around him in honour of the occasion'.[419] One sepoy, overcome by sentiment, embraced the boy and said, 'You are Kanhaiya'.

An attempt was made to restore discipline among the troops by appointing generals, brigadiers, colonels, majors, and captains. However, as the 'military council' in charge of the appointments was well paid by the rival candidates, 'this difficult duty was rather slowly performed, and the nominations sometimes resisted by the soldiery, who boasted of being the *Alpha* and the *Omega* of the whole administration'.[420]

As an institution the sepoy council was sufficiently novel and unfamiliar for the natives to refer to it by the foreign term '*kot*', a corruption of the English word 'court'.[421] The technical term by which the new institution came to be designated in Delhi was Jalsa-i-Intizam-i-Fauji-wa-Mulki (Assembly for the Arrangement of the Affairs of the Army and the Realm).[422] At the time when the mutineers arrived from Meerut, they had no formal collective organization. It would appear that the Emperor himself took the initiative towards formalizing any panchayat that they might have formed upon their arrival in Delhi. An order under the autograph cypher of the Emperor to his eldest son Mirza Mughal on 8 July 1857 runs as follows:

> Learn! that you, the light of our eyes, already know that a very small balance of cash remain in our Treasury. That there is no immediate prospect of revenue from any quarter, and that the little money which remains must of necessity be very soon expended. You are directed to call together, during the day or tonight, all the officers of the Regiments, which first arrived, in order that they may deliberate and decide on means to be adopted for raising funds to meet the daily necessary and emergent expenses. A meeting of this kind, in the language of the Soldiery, is called a 'court'.[423]

The aged Emperor had been distracted by scuffles between the Meerut and Delhi troops over the money in the treasury. With a view to restoring unity and discipline among them, he had appointed Prince Mirza Mughal as their commander, and, as new regiments began to arrive, he formalized what they referred to as the 'Court'. It then emerged as a regular institution of governance. In accordance with the Emperor's directive to Mirza Mughal, the Court assembled on 10 July and proposed:

> *Proposition First*—That money on loan at interest be obtained from some Merchant and that this loan, with interest, be paid off on the establishment of order.
> *Proposition Second*—That a force consisting of 15,000 Infantry, 500 Cavalry, and two Horse Artillery Guns be sent out into the Country to establish Police Stations, Revenue Offices, and Postal arrangements, so that it may become widely known that Your Majesty's rule has been established.

The petition was signed as 'The petition of the Slaves, the officers of the Court, Jiwaram Subadar Major Bahadur, Sheoram Misr Subadar

Major, Tahriyat Khan Subadar Major, Hetram Subadar Major, and Beniram Subadar Major'.[424] Accordingly, a loan was raised from the merchants at 1 per cent per mensem, those showing themselves reluctant to subscribe being detained by the troops at Red Fort.[425] The Court, however, did nothing much to give effect to the plans for bringing the surrounding country of Haryana and the Doab under a regular police and revenue administration. Bahadur Shah himself appointed no *tahsildars* for the collection of revenue, and the plan to send troops to bring in the revenue was not carried out. Later, Bakht Khan appointed *tahsildars* at Palwal, Hodal, and Shahdara and a Ziladar at Gurgaon, but no regular revenue machinery ever got going. In the city itself a *kotwal* or police chief was appointed: first Muin-ud-Din Hasan Khan, then Qazi Faizullah of Delhi, and finally Mubarak Shah, a Saiyid of Ilaka Rampur. Under the *kotwal*, *thanadars* were also appointed at Najafgarh, Mehrauli, Shahdara, Paharganj, and Bhadrapur.[426] Beyond the suburbs, however, chaos prevailed. As the third police chief of rebel Delhi, Saiyid Mubarak Shah, reminisced,

> Village attacked village. The strong preyed upon the weak—crime reigned supreme and weapons of every description were prepared in large quantities—14,000 battleaxes and 8,000 matchlocks (in these regions) in eleven days. ... Peace, confidence and safety deserted the land and a very different regime took their place. ... Those who had been ruined by the resumption of Jagirs (grants of land), or beggared by Civil Court decrees, or ousted by moneylenders, joined heart and soul in the disturbances so that large numbers were killed. The assailants were in their turn the victims of the rapacity of others. ... It must however be stated that the warlike preparations made by the people were not against the British Government but with a view to protect themselves from against their neighbours, with whom in most instances feuds of long standing were renewed—feuds which were not forgotten though they had for years been suppressed by the strong hand of the government. Moreover, a general plunder of moneylenders was set on foot and spread like fire in a forest. Great numbers of the Muhammadan population repaired to Delhi to take part in the war of extermination against the English.[427]

As Bahadur Shah pointed out in his bitter remonstrance when he threatened to go on pilgrimage to Mecca, it was the refusal of the army to implement its own plans and promises that had paralysed the Badshahi government financially and politically. The sepoys would not go out into the country to set up an administration, bring order out of chaos, and ensure the inflow of revenue.[428] An ironical couplet thus depicted the position of the puppet authorities of the palace: 'A fly was seated on a piece of straw floating in the urine of an ass, and thought himself conducting a ship.'[429] The Emperor himself wrote pathetically:

> The army surrounds me, I have no peace nor quiet.
> My life alone remains, and that they will soon destroy.[430]

Prince Mirza Mughal, appointed commander-in-chief by the Emperor on Hakim Ahsanullah Khan's advice, had formed an alliance with the sepoy council. This greatly displeased his father,[431] for the development destroyed the fond hopes of the youngest begam, Zinat Mahal, that her son Jawan Bakht would succeed to the throne.[432] Disheartened by the incompetence of the princes and the immobility of the sepoys,[433] the Emperor welcomed the arrival of Bakht Khan from Bareilly. He appointed him commander-in-chief. The people of Delhi were led to expect that discipline and control would now be restored among the soldiers, the administration would be set right, and the army would be induced to go out in battle marches in an orderly fashion, with provisions supplied by themselves.[434]

Bakht Khan was the only general of the sepoys with a grasp of large scale commissariat and military organization and he had made long and earnest preparations in Bareilly before setting out for Delhi with his forces. From the outbreak in Bareilly itself, his authority within the Bareilly Brigade—once Muhammad Shafi of the cavalry acknowledged the supremacy of the artillery commander—was assured and undisputed.[435] By means of careful planning and collection of supplies and treasure from Bareilly, Moradabad, Shahjahanpur, and Pilibhit,[436] he was able to transport to Delhi a large and well-equipped army. This at once raised him to the position of the greatest general of the Mutiny. He had 4 regiments of foot, 700 cavalry, 600 artillery guns, 3 field pieces, 14 elephants, 300 spare horses taken from the government stud at Hanpir, several thousand jehadis, treasure worth Rs 4 lakhs, a train of a thousand bullock-carts and camels laden with ammunition, shot, tents, supplies, etc., in all said to be 10,000 men of all arms, horse, foot, artillery, magazine.[437] General Bakht Khan, who had already distributed six months' pay in advance, assured the Emperor that he would not trouble him for supplies, and the grateful Emperor ordered all officers commanding detachments of troops to place themselves under the general.[438]

Bakht Khan's tactically mismanaged charge upon the British and his failure to dislodge them from the Ridge despite leading an attack with 10,000 men of both cavalry and infantry as well as the jehadis destroyed the hope that a unified authority would spring up under his direction.[439] The original mutineers of Meerut and Delhi, organized in the sepoy council, asked to be put under the command of Mirza Mughal.[440] Moreover, the newly arrived Neemuch Brigade, commanded by General Ghaus Muhammad Khan, refused to obey the Emperor's order to place themselves under the command of the Bareilly general. The Neemuch men made a separate and equally useless attack on the Ridge.[441] Devee Deen, a mutineer of the 3rd cavalry, was asked privately by Lieutenant-General Sir George MacMunn several years afterward:

> Who was Commander-in-chief in Delhi?
>   At first Mirza Mogul, King's son, then Subedar Bakht Khan, a Sheikh of the artillery of the Bareilly Brigade. He was fat and puffy. No one liked him, Sahib, and Ghaus Khan from the Nimach Brigade was made a general too. He was a Rohilla, and more alert than Bakht Khan, but not so clever.[442]

On 1 September a spy reported to the British: 'The state of affairs in Delhi is as follows: 'The Nusseerabad and Neemuch Brigade are supporters of Mirza Moghul, and the Bareilly Brigade is devoted to the King. The officers of the Bareilly force and Mirza are bitter enemies.'[443] The original sepoy council of the Meerut and Delhi mutineers, whose insubordinate conduct was commented upon by the Emperor himself,[444] aligned with Mirza Mughal in his confrontation with Bakht Khan.[445] The members of the military court—Het Lal Misr, Subadar Major, Tala Yar Khan, Subadar Major, Shio Buksh Misr, Subadar Major, Jewa Ram, Subadar Major, and Dhani Ram, Subadar Major, rebuked Bakht Khan for setting aside those officers 'who were the first to rush into this flame' and for not showing proper subordination to Prince Mirza Mughal who 'in every respect is your superior'.[446]

Till the arrival of the Bareilly Brigade, the members of the Jalsa-i-Intizam-i-Fauji-wa-Mulki decided, in mutual consultation at the residence of Mirza Mughal, which regiments would form the column that would attack the British troops on the ridge the following day. The troops as a body were offended when the title of governor-general (this appears to be the English translation of the term *Sahib-i-Alam* which occurs in the constitution of the *Jalsa*) was given to General Bakht Khan, empowering him to receive all reports from the *Jalsa*. The Meerut and Delhi officers pleaded with the Emperor that Bakht Khan was a mere artillery officer, in no way fit for such a high office, and that Mirza Mughal, already entrusted with full powers in military matters, was in every respect fit for the post of governor-general. A compromise formula was then worked out, at the suggestion, it would appear, of General Bakht Khan,[447] under which the army was to be divided in three sections: one composed of the infantry regiments of Delhi and Meerut, the second of troops commanded by Bakht Khan, the Neemuch Brigade and the Sirsa men, and a third division comprising the rest of the troops.[448] For some time Bakht Khan and the leading officers met in a tent pitched in front of the former military quarters to discuss and formalize all military matters. The majority, however, finding this unsatisfactory, shifted the *Jalsa* to premises near Delhi Gate. However, neither Bakht Khan nor Mirza Mughal would attend, though invited by the others to do so. The general was displeased at their having left the vicinity of the camp, and the prince considered it beneath his dignity to sit in any house in the city apart from his own.[449] Plagued by these disputes, the Emperor summoned 150 officers on 4 August and it was arranged that the army would be divided into three brigades, the Delhi and Meerut troops under Mirza Mughal, the Neemuch troops under Ghaus Muhammad Khan, and the Bareilly troops under Bakht Khan.[450]

Around the same time, the Emperor issued a constitution for the *Jalsa* to ensure unity of command and coordination of the war effort.[451] 'Where as to avoid disaster in the sections of administration of the military and civil departments it is absolutely necessary to form a constitution, and where as to work out the constitution it is necessary first to appoint a Court,' the Emperor announced that a 'Court of Administration' should be established, to be named 'Jalsa-i-Intizam-i-Fauji-wa-Mulki,' which would consist of ten members, six from military and four civilians. Of the military members, two should be elected by the infantry, two by the cavalry, and two by the artillery. From these ten men, one should be unanimously elected as Sadar-i-Jalsa (President), and another as Naib-Sadr-i-Jalsa (Vice-President). Five of these would form a quorum. No one, barring the Sahib-i-Alam Bahadur and His Majesty the shadow of God (Huzur Zille Subhani), would be entitled to be present in the assembled court. Clause VII of the constitution laid down the procedure of the *Jalsa*:

All the administrative matters shall be first reported for decision to the Court. After the decision of the same by a majority of votes it shall be submitted for the concurrence of the Sahib-i-Alam Bahadur to whom the Court shall be subordinate. After the concurrence of Sahib-i-Alam Bahadur the decisions shall be submitted for the information to His Majesty. No order regarding Military or Civil Administration shall be given effect to without the decision of the Court, concurrence of Sahib-i-Alam and the information of his Majesty. If Sahib-i-Alam does not concur in any decision of the Court it will be referred back to the latter for reconsideration. If again there is a difference of opinion between Sahib-i-Alam Bahadur and the decision of the Court, it shall be submitted to His Majesty whose orders shall be final.[452]

Regarding the formation of departments, Bahadur Shah laid down that those duly elected, from every section of the military, should be appointed managers and administrators of that section. Under their control there should be a committee of 4 men, and secretaries might be appointed to this committee as and when necessary. Whichever proposal was formally put up in that committee by a majority of votes would be presented to the court by those very officers of the committee. The same procedure would apply to the civil department.[453]

It does not appear that Muhammad Bakht Khan was able to consolidate his position as Sahib-i-Alam. He was, therefore, not in a position to give a unified and authoritative direction of the proceedings of the court. Distracted by the internecine disputes within the sepoy army and the anarchy let loose in the city, the Emperor told an assembly of 150 officers two days after promulgating the constitution that he had appointed both Mirza Mughal and Bakht Khan to command them. They were free to choose whoever they preferred of the two, but 'it was intolerable that residents in city should be harassed and threatened by the soldiers who had come with the avowed object of destroying the English and not their own countrymen'.[454]

With the position of the Sahib-i-Alam thus paralysed, Bahadur Shah 'issued orders to all the officers to obey neither the orders of Mirza Mogul nor any other General, inasmuch as His Majesty had appointed a Court of twelve members, six to be appointed by the King and six by the Army, for the future conduct of the siege. The Army was to obey all orders issued by the Court.'[455] The reconstituted court, according to a spy's report on 1 September, consisted of the following military members: Ghaus Muhammad, General of the Neemuch Brigade, Heera Singh, brigadier of the Neemuch Brigade, Muhammad Shafi, *risaladar* of the 8th Irregular Horse from Bareilly, Hyat Mohumed, *risaladar* of the 14th Irregulars, Qadir Buksh, *subadar* of 72nd NI, Hardutt, *subadar* of the 9th NI, the unnamed *subadar* of the Hariana Battalion, and the unnamed *subadars* of the 11th and the 54th NIs. According to the spy, the court also comprised 5 sepoys from every regiment and Maulvi Fazal Haq.[456]

As doom approached the city, the Emperor adopted the policy of referring all problems to the military court, which asserted its authority by expressing displeasure that the princes had taken several lakhs from the bankers and paid nothing to the army. The *Jalsa* issued a proclamation that in future no more money was to be paid to the princes.[457] The court, however, could not quite overcome its lack of self-confidence: 'There was a large gathering of officers at the Durbar to-day; they complained that there was no chief official to command or issue order. What should be done? For this there was "confusion worse confounded". The King replied: "You alone have the power to act. Whatever you think you are able to accomplish, that do."'[458] The military court was unable to mount a concerted assault on the Ridge to dislodge the British troops.[459] Tensions erupted spasmodically between the troops and the royal household,[460] between the troops and the city,[461] and among the troops themselves.[462] The enemy consolidated its stranglehold on the walled town and carried it by storm in mid-September.

Before the end, however, there were signs that the *Jalsa* was acquiring maturity and confidence, and the first signs of budding collective statesmanship were exhibited in the manner in which it sought to construct a regular system of war finance in place of the haphazard plunder of the bankers and traders by the princes and the sepoys. The military court arrested Mir Said Ali Khan, Dewan Mukund Lal, Bardar-u-Din Khan, Hakim Abdul Haq, with his sons, and Nawab Quli Khan, and put them in the palace guardroom till money was forthcoming for the defence of the city as shot after shot fell into it. The Emperor summoned the *Jalsa* and ordered them to release the high personages taken into custody. On their agreeing to raise the money by a self-imposed tax throughout the city for army pay, they were released. In accordance with imperial orders, the police proceeded to collect three months' rent from every shop and dwelling house to defray the pay of the sepoys.[463] These signs of the development of a more organized system of war finance and government were cut off by the British reoccupation of Delhi.

The inability of the revolutionary government of Delhi to survive longer stemmed from its failure to bring the surrounding Haryana country and the upper Doab under a consolidated police revenue administrative zone. In this, the Delhi administration fell markedly short of the achievement of its Lucknow counterpart. The latter succeeded in creating a liberated zone over the whole of Awadh, and proved eventually to be the longest-lasting of the Mutiny authorities. In sharp contrast, Delhi had no territory. When the son of Nawab Muhammad Mir Khan represented to the Emperor, on the part of several bankers, that twice the sepoys had extorted money from them, and were now demanding more, Bahadur Shah could only lament: 'If the Sepoys would only leave the city, and employ themselves in collecting the revenue, I should be in a position to pay them, and protect the lives and property of citizens.'[464] With the fall of Delhi, the scene shifted to Lucknow.

Initially the sepoy council played an equally critical part in the development of a revolutionary government in Lucknow, but as a nexus developed between the Begam's darbar and the great *taluqdars*, the retainers of the latter came to vastly outnumber the sepoys in the fighting with the British.[465] Therefore, the importance of the sepoy council diminished over time. Earlier, a united sepoy council had emerged in the interval between the sepoys' victory at Chinhat and their successful occupation of Lucknow. The exact circumstances stand out clearly from the proceedings of the trial of Raja Jai Lal Singh, a trusted servant of the royal house of Awadh. He struck up a friendship with the victorious officers of the battle of Chinhat by arranging for the supply of the sepoy army in Lucknow.[466] It would appear that the victors of Chinhat, infantry, cavalry, and artillery, acted separately for some time after arriving in triumph at Lucknow. The cavalry wished to set up the minor son of Malika-i-Ahad, and the infantry opted for Begam Hazrat Mahal's son, Birjis Qadr. The infantry, with Raja Jai Lal Singh as their ambassador to Begam Hazrat Mahal, ultimately prevailed.[467]

The decision came about as follows. In the chaos and looting that followed the sepoys' arrival at Lucknow, a dispute broke out between Captain Jahangir Baksh's artillery and a party of sepoys who had seized some gunners of his company. Raja Jai Lal then suggested to the officers that 'if a court was to be formed so that business be conducted according to the wishes of the army and every one agreed to obey it, all would go well'.[468] The officers, agreeing to the suggestion, placed Raja Jai Lal in charge of the city and asked him to organize a court and to select a head of government.[469] In the confabulations that now took place among the officers of the army, meeting in informal panchayat, Jai Lal Singh arranged with the infantry officers, Captain Raj Mand Tiwari of 22 NI

(Bole Regiment), Captain Umrao Singh of 6th Oude Locals (Barlow's Regiment), Captain Raghunath Singh of the Police Battalion (in whose house meetings used to take place for fixing the attacks on the Residency), etc. to establish Birjis Qadr on the throne.[470] The court, which would appear to have been as yet an informal assembly of officers, then appointed Sharif-ud-Daula as chief minister (*naib*) of the Begam, Mammu Khan as *darogha* of the Diwan Khana, and Jai Lal Singh as collector of the army.[471] At this stage the realization dawned on the officers that government could not be carried on without a court. It should represent the army to the government and direct the affairs of the former. About 8 to 10 days after placing Birjis Qadr on the throne they formed a court to which all branches of the army were to send delegates and which was also to include the chief civil officers of the government.[472]

The formally constituted military court now came to comprise the principal officers of the army, such as Barkat Ahmad, *risaladar* of the 12th Cavalry and architect of the victory of Chinhat, the infantry officers, Raj Mand Tiwari, Rajhunath Singh, Umrao Singh, etc., and the artillery officer, Captain Jahangir Khan. The principal government men, such as Sharif-ud-Daula, Mammu Khan, and Mir Kazim Ali (*darogha* of Magazine), were also members. Raja Jai Lal Singh was the superintendent of the whole court, and at his order the court assembled at specified hours. He was the medium of communication between the military court and the Begam of Awadh.[473] Sharifuddaulah formerly headed her civil executive, but the real power behind it was Mammu Khan, whom rumour had it was the paramour of the Begam.[474]

The deliberations of the court were submitted to Hazrat Mahal. She confirmed and forwarded them to Sharif-ud-Daula. The minister in turn sent the necessary orders to the *chakladars* of the districts, or referred matters close at hand to Mammu Khan, to be attended to in the respective departments. For instance, work relating to the magazine went to Mir Kazim Ali, army matters to Jai Lal Singh, duties of the city to Yusuf Khan. The court would assemble two or three times a week.[475] For work concerned with finance, administration of the town, distribution of troops, granting of commissions and civil matters, the full court assembled at the Begam's door or the minister's house, and then all the members of the government as well as the commandants attended. When the court assembled in the lines to discuss military matters, then Raja Jai Lal alone used to attend, and an assistant of

Mammu Khan might also be present.[476] The court was a formal body: verbal orders were never issued. Written orders were sent, to be circulated to those absent for their signatures, and were finally deposited in the Diwan khana. If the subject was top secret, Mammu Khan would keep the papers himself.[477]

As dissensions erupted between the Lucknow government and Maulvi Ahmadullah Shah, the court split and a section joined the latter at Tara Kothi. Unlike Bahadur Shah who was forced to rely completely on the sepoys, Begam Hazrat Mahal had alternative sources of support to rely on—the levies of the royal house and the more numerous retainers of the *taluqdars*. The Begam was a woman of great fortitude whose courage and determination shamed the sepoys as they melted away from Lucknow under the fierce British shelling.[478] Once the rebels were driven from Lucknow, the military court ceased to function. The brunt of the fighting was now being borne by the loyal *taluqdars* and their retainers. The habit of collective government had, however, become sufficiently well established for the Begam's government at Baundi to take the form of a council, albeit no longer a military one. This body, described as 'the Parliament' by an eyewitness detained there, still discussed and conducted all business, but it now consisted predominantly of *maulvis* and *taluqdars*. Even so, the military continued to be an important voice in the government at Baundi. Orders were issued in the name of Birjis Qadr, with Mammoo Khan acting as his agent; but the latter had a coadjutor in Bakht Khan, the *subadar* of the fleeing Bareilly force newly arrived from Delhi. There was keen rivalry between the Begam's camp and the sepoys under Bakht Khan's command, and in most matters the voice of the latter could not be ignored.[479] Until the remnants of the rebels were driven to the pestilential swamps of Nepal, the sepoys continued to be the essential link in the operations in the different theatres of the war.

The rebel drive towards a unitary framework of military–political organization was confined to the higher levels of command. At the bottom, the initiatives were local, and more often than not, autonomous.

Everywhere, petty rebel chiefships sprang into being. The jurisdictions were confined to small localities, even to a group of villages. There were, as we have seen, exceptions to this. Consolidated zones under centralized mutiny administration sprang up in some places: in Rohilkhand and Awadh north of the Ganges, in Farrukhabad mid-way up the Doab, and in Jhansi and Banda south of the Jumna. Larger stretches of territory were consolidated in these places under the authority of the princes and the sepoy councils. Elsewhere, however, the pattern that emerged was one of local and village chiefships that might or might not possess any connections with the Mutiny head-quarters.

Ancient memories of local autonomy were revived when the turbulent Gujars east of Meerut dug up the old and buried guns at Parikshitgarh last used when Nain Singh was 'Goojar King of Eastern Meerut' half a century earlier. They elected Kadam Singh as the new raja to head a Gujar government with a local levy of some 10,000 men drawn from the Gujar villages around Parikshitgarh town.[480] In a similar act of local usurpation, Debi Singh, at the head of the Jat zamindars around the *thana* of Raya in Mathura district, attacked and burned down the *thana*. Setting himself up as raja, he made a proclamation: 'the great Rajah Dayby Singh, monarch of the fourteen villages, victorious in war'. He set up his headquarters in the local school building, where he soon appointed 'a Board of Revenue, a supreme Court of Judicature, Commissioner, a Magistrate and a Superintendent of Police', before the British came and dispersed his government.[481]

Shah Mal, the rebel Jat landholder of Baraut astride the strategic highway from Meerut to Delhi, had much stronger connections with the Mutiny headquarters than either Kadam Singh of Parikshitgarh or Debi Singh of Taraf Raya. This was reflected in his decision not to assume regal sovereignty but to get himself appointed from Delhi as *subadar* of *pargana* Baraut.[482] Assuming command of a 5000 strong levy of Gujars, he destroyed the bridge over the Hindan, interrupting English lines of communication between the ridge at Delhi and the Meerut Cantonment.[483] The success enabled him to organize the Chaurasi Desh (a homeland constituted by eight-four villages) of the Saklain Jats (he belonged to the Mawi section of the Saklain *khap*) into a power base from which besieged Delhi drew its essential supplies: 'From every village vast quantities of supplies were poured into Delhi, the garrison of which but for the assistance would have been starved out.'[484]

Baraut, the *tahsil* town where the customary *khap* council meetings had been held from olden times to resist encroachments on the Jat clan-territory, became the seat of the government of Chaurasi Desh. A bungalow belonging to the deputy superintendent of the Eastern Jumna Canal was taken over by him as the hall of justice.[485] On the eve of his final encounter with the Khakee Ressalah from Meerut, his emissaries

went to 'every village of Chowrasee Des, calling all who could bear
arms to assist them and declaring that Shah Mall would meet the pale-
faced invaders of his territory on the morrow and annihilate the entire
party or die in the attempt'.[486] The Khakee Ressalah, having worsted
him in the battle, stuck his severed head on a pole to terrorize the
townsmen of Baraut, but were compelled to beat a precipitate retreat
from Chaurasi Desh when faced with the combined hostility of all the
inhabitants, Jats, Gujars, Rajputs, and Brahmans.[487] Shah Mal's nephew
and grandson assumed the leadership of the rebellion, and the retreating
English forces sent the hurried message: 'the whole country is against
us, 86 villages—it is said 10,000 attack us tonight, but with these jolly
Rifles we are equal to them, though the rascals fight desperately'.[488]

Despite the strong support of the other castes of the territory, the
Jat republic of the Chaurasi Desh was not destined to survive much
longer. Though narrow in scope and based squarely on clan and locality,
the combination of 'the 84 villages' was too dangerously close to the
Mutiny headquarters in Delhi to be permitted to carry on its activities.
Steady pressure from Meerut cantonment gradually brought the
Chaurasi Desh under British control. However, while the fight lasted,
'the excellence of the intelligence received by the rebels on all occasions'
proved them to have had 'many friends among those not committed to
the rebellion'.[489] The people of the district, according to the leader of
the Khakee Ressalah, were 'in a fever of excitement to know whether
"their Raj" or ours was to triumph'.[490] To the ordinary inhabitants of
the country, the distinction between 'we' and 'they' and between the
two kinds of 'raj' was clear enough.

Mutiny Administration

Where exactly did the difference lie between 'their' raj and 'our' raj?
Supposing the Mutiny had succeeded against the British, how would
its administrative institutions have differed from those of the colonial
regime? It is not possible to give a positive answer to a hypothetical
question. However, the record of the mutiny administration in those
areas where it functioned for some time may be suggestive. Unfortunately, we do not have a sufficient record of this but there is a detailed
record for one place: Farrukhabad. Alone among all the areas covered
in the voluminous British 'Narrative of Events', Farrukhabad has
detailed recording of administrative arrangements during the Mutiny.

This was drawn up by the incoming British officer who restored English rule. Magistrate C.R. Lindsay's account is not a view from within; but it is by far the most comprehensive report on the system of governance by the mutineers.

The rebel government of Farrukhabad originated in this manner. As soon as news of the outbreak of the Mutiny in Meerut arrived in Farrukhabad, the panicky Europeans left town to take shelter in the nearby fort of Fatehgarh. The exodus caused great excitement in town. The *kotwal* came to see the pensioned Nawab of the former Pathan ruling house. He apprehended that unless something was done quickly, looting would break out as many people of bad character had come into town from the neighbourhood. The Nawab sought to calm the excited crowd by having it proclaimed by the beat of tom-tom that the Europeans would return the following day, and that all disturbers of the peace would be severely punished. As the proclamation was made in the name of the English government, and was expressly mentioned as having been issued by their orders, it failed to have the necessary effect on those preparing themselves to loot. They said that the Europeans from whom the proclamation purportedly emanated had fled. Pressed by the respectable citizens who feared for their property, the Nawab, in consultation with his *naib*, then caused another proclamation to be issued to the same effect, but this time stating that it was by the orders of the Nawab *Raees Bahadur*.[491]

The *naib*, Wazir Ali, kept in touch with the English at the Nawab's behest during the next five days. Then the town was thrown into a fresh uproar by the arrival of a band of two thousand Mhow Pathans from the Shamsabad–Kaimganj–Mhow areas twelve miles to the west. The leader of the band was a Pathan war leader of Mhow named Ahmed Yar Khan. He used to enjoy a pension from the British on account of his father's services in Lord Lake's time. He was accompanied by his brother-in-law, Ushrut (Ishrat?) Khan, a native of Delhi, who similarly received a pension from the British, being related to the Bangash family.[492] Meanwhile, the 10th Native Infantry Regiment, which formed the garrison, were in touch with the 41st NI from Seetapore. The latter had arrived on the opposite bank of the Ganges, and were urging the 10th NI to murder their officers and seize the treasure. On the morning of 18 June, mutiny broke out: as the 41st NI and 10th Oudh Locals were crossing the Ganges on boats provided by a local *thanadar*, Ghulam Ali Khan,[493] the 10th NI seized the treasure, and their officers, carrying the colours of the regiment, besieged the Nawab in his house. The Nawab was roused from bed and compelled to give audience in his nightclothes. The native officers laid the colours of the regiment at his feet and took hold of his person.[494] The following conversation took place between him and the officers:

> *The officers*: 'Up to this day we have been servants of the Company, we are now servants of the King of Delhi. Your ancestors were formerly tributary to Delhi also. So we have come to place you in your old position on the Guddee as Nawab under the King of Delhi.'
>
> *The Nawab*: 'Leave me alone, I am content as I am. As you say you are servants of the King of Delhi you had better go to Delhi.'
>
> *The officers*: 'We are not to be got rid of in this way. If you do not do as we direct we well at once loot you and kill you.'[495]

Two officers then seized him each by the hand and led the hapless Nawab to a chair, while a third stood behind him with his sward drawn. The gun was fixed in salute to the new incumbent. The following day total chaos prevailed in the 10th NI lines as the incoming Seetapore mutineers wanted the garrison to share the treasure with them. To forestall their Seetapore compatriots, the sepoys started plundering the treasury and 'it was a regular rush to see who could get most'.[496] As soon as the scramble was over, the 10th NI dissolved into two main parties. The Purbeahs crossed over at once to Awadh to make for their homes and were relieved of their loot on the way by the villagers. Those whose homes were on this side of the Ganges went off by twos and threes to their homes, and the entire regiment vanished.[497] All that remained on the abandoned parade ground were the regiment's colours, its magazine, and 10 guns, of which the Seetapore men took possession.

About 100 sepoys of the 10th NI, who had announced their decision to enter the Nawab's service, posted themselves in the city gardens.[498] The deceived Seetapore men, enraged at being deprived of their share of the treasure, set fire to every bungalow, plundered the bazaar, and placed the 100 sepoys of the 10th NI under arrest. The sepoys from Seetapore, i.e. the 41st NI and the 10th Oudh Locals, wished the Nawab to compel the One Hundred to attack the fort in which the Englishmen had taken refuge. The remnants of the 10th NI did not like the idea, a severe fight ensued, and nearly all of them were killed. The Nawab ordered the rest out of town. The city gardens where they had encamped were taken over by the Mhow Pathans.[499]

The same evening the Nawab sent a messenger to the fort at Fatehgarh telling the English that he had done all he could and was now completely in the power of the rebels. Two or three days later the officers of the 41st and the 10th came with drawn swards, and the Nawab's *naib* was shot at. He barely escaped with his life, the cloth on his shoulder being singed by the fire. The officers stated that Wazir Ali, the *naib*, was a Christian, and to the best of their knowledge, the Nawab was one too.[500] The Nawab slipped quietly through the crowd into the zenana and sought to make his getaway to Agra. The sepoys, on learning this, posted a guard at the palace.[501]

The Nawab did not emerge for three days. At the end of this period Ahmed Yar Khan, the leader of the Mhow Pathans, went to the door of the zenana and persuaded him to come out on the basis of assurances that he would not be hurt. The next morning all the native officers of the Oudh regiments and the leaders of the Mhow Pathans had an audience with the Nawab. It was resolved at once to attack the English at Fatehgarh fort. An order proclaimed by tom-tom in the name of the officers of the army directed that whoever did not join them would be considered to be Christians and would be liable to expropriation and execution.[502] Determined attacks by the sepoys compelled the English at Fatehgarh to abandon the fort and most of them were killed on the way by crowds of villagers armed with swords, shields, and clubs, and by pursuing sepoys firing off their guns.[503]

On the day when the Seetapur mutineers ferried across the Ganges, the old *kotwal* fled town. Two days before the attack began on Fatehgarh, the officers of the 41st NI resolved that Ghulam Ali Khan, who had been of much help in crossing the river, should be appointed *kotwal*. The Nawab's servant, Turab Ali, was directed to draw up the letter of appointment, and the officers then made the nawab sign the *parwana*. This was the first paper of the Mutiny regime. He was to sign many more in the future. The signature happened to be in English. This caused much annoyance to the 'Doobye people', so called because presumably many of the men were of the Dube section of the Brahmans. They tore it up and made the Nawab sign a fresh one in Persian, saying 'there are no English here, you must sign in Persian'.[504]

The new *kotwal* energetically supplied the munitions with which the sepoys stormed Fatehgarh fort. The old *amlah* were then rounded up by Ahmad Yar Khan to get the administration going. The two leaders of the Mhow Pathans, namely Ahmad Yar Khan and Ushrut Khan, and the officers from Seetapore, among whom the most prominent man was Ganga Singh, began to attend the *cutcherry* daily to make the *amlah* work.[505]

In the evening all the papers were brought by Turab Ali to the Nawab for signature. He never read a single paper he signed, nor did he know their contents. The only reason why he was maintained in that ceremonious role was the mutual jealousy among the native officers of the different regiments. They could not agree to elect one of themselves to perform the duty, fearing that he would use the power of signature for his own ends.[506] No sooner had the *cutcherry* been got going than a dispute broke out between the Doobye officers of the Seetapore men and the band leaders of the Mhow Pathans. Both wanted power. Finally, Ahmad Yar Khan, having obtained the post of *nazim* of the western part of the district, departed with his men for Mhow. Ganga Singh and the Doobye officers continued to reside in the camp to transact the business in town. They were responsible for the massacre of the European ladies who had earlier found shelter in the Nawab's zenana.[507]

Having got hold of the town, the 'Doobye ke Pultun' sent an embassy to Delhi with a petition drawn up by the 41st NI, declaring loyalty to the Mughal Emperor and begging to be excused for not attending on His Majesty in person. The envoy returned with a *farman* from the Emperor confirming the masnad upon the Nawab of Farrukhabad and a directive to the 41st NI excusing them from attending in person and asking them to remain in their post to oppose the advance of the English. After the receipt of this communication, 'in which the Emperor highly praised the sepoys to whose bravery so much was due, the pride and haughtiness of the sepoys became greater than ever'.[508]

Thus commenced the administration of Nawab Tafazzul Husain of Farrukhabad, a regime of which he was no more than the ornamental figurehead.[509] The fact that a vigorous system of rebel administration kept going in Farrukhabad till the British occupation in January 1858 had a bearing on the overall military operations of the Mutiny. It acted as a barrier between the British forces from the Punjab besieging Delhi in the west, and Havelock's army from Calcutta operating on the Cawnpore and Lucknow front in the east. A section of the Grand Trunk Road ran from Cawnpore through Farrukhabad district towards Delhi, and this was well guarded by the government of the Nawab. Pickets and *thanas* were maintained all along this vital route,[510] preventing the junction of the two main British armies long after the fall of Delhi and the retaking of Cawnpore and Lucknow. As the larger formations of the rebels were driven back from the main centres of the Mutiny in Upper India, they all found refuge in Farrukhabad. It was a zone through which they could pass up and down to their respective retreats. Bakht Khan, Shahzada Ferozeshah, Nawab Walidad Khan of Malagarh, and a host of other leaders passed through this rebel-occupied territory in the Doab,[511] crossing and re-crossing the Grand Trunk Road and the Ganges as the British forces pressed in. None of this would have been possible but for the fact that the Farrukhabad administration remained so long in working order.

The details of the administration were recorded with close interest by C.R. Lindsay. As soon as the compromise was reached between the Pathan band and the sepoys by the assignment of the western part of Farrukhabad to Ahmad Yar Khan, the realm was divided into two great divisions, the east and the west. Mohsun Ali, zamindar of Sultanganj Khareta, was appointed *nazim* of the east. Ahmad Yar Khan, who had been offered the eastern division earlier and had vociferously objected to this arrangement, became *nazim* of the western division at his own insistence. Mohsun Ali was described by Lindsay as 'a habitual drunkard' and 'of a very common order of intellect'. Ahmad Yar Khan was made of sterner stuff. According to Lindsay, he caused great dissatisfaction by his ruthless acts and 'decisions utterly devoid of sense and justice'. Ushrut Khan apparently went back with his brother-in-law and his band of Pathans to the Afghan settlements of Shamsabad, Kaimganj, and Mhow, after having obtained charge of the western division.

Subsequently, however, we again find Ushrut Khan in Farrukhabad town as the Nawab's *mushir khas* (principal counsellor). There was apparently an attempt to form a semblance of civil government at the centre. The new minister and Nawab's wife, Bhigga Begam, gained influence, and they did what they liked in the affairs of the civil administration. However, the crucial decisions lay with the army, a council of two being set up to give effect to the will of the mutinous sepoys. The council, which had a judicial character, exercised plenary powers and had the power to reverse any decision by whatever court. It thus formed a kind of appellate court. The court was composed of Captain Ganga Singh, *subahdar* of 41st Native Infantry, and Sheo Ghulam Deechet, *subahdar* of the Sitapur local infantry. The latter had a pandit as his deputy, one Pitambar Doss, from whom he received an opinion in all cases connected with Hindu law.

There was also a city court, presided over by the Mufti. Ahmad Ali, who had been a record keeper under the British, Abdul Wahid, formerly a 'Koork Ameen' (clerk for attaching property under English rule), and Qazi Ahmed Yar Khan were the judges. These men, the civil and sessions judges of the city of Farrukhabad, received a salary of Rs 100 each, and in addition fees amounting to 10 per cent of the amount decreed in any suit. The bench, according to Lindsay, was 'not composed of men of any talent'. One alone, Ahmad Ali, was said to be of 'any average ability'.

So much for the government at the headquarters. With regard to the district administration, the division of it into 6 *tahsils* and 10 *thanas* remained as under the English administration. The pay of the *tahsildars* (the revenue collectors under the British) was the same as before the Mutiny: Rs 200 per month. The *barkandazes*, or police constables posted at the *thana*, received Rs 5 per month, and were now much greater in number than before.

On ascending the *masnad*, the Nawab issued a Code of Procedure for Criminal and Revenue Departments which closely resembled that in force under the British. Land revenue was fixed in 8 instalments (later reduced to 5). For the *kharif* crop, 4 monthly instalments were fixed from the 1st of Kuwar to the end of Poos. For the *rabi* crop, there were 4 monthly instalments from 1st Falgoon to the end of Jaet.

If the sums due were not paid into the *tahsildari* by the 15th of each month, the *tahsildar* would have summons (*dastak*) served by a footman (*piada*), the latter being quartered on the defaulter, at the rate of 2 annas a day. If the instalment still remained unpaid, he would issue, after the lapse of the month, another *dastak*, served this time by a rider (*sawar*), quartered at a charge of 8 annas a day. One quarter of this daily pay was credited when realized, to the government, the reminder was distributed among the men who served the summons. If the dues still remained unpaid, the *tahsildar* would then publicly proclaim that the defaulter must pay the dues within a week of the proclamation, failing which his movable and immovable properties, such as trees and gardens, but not his implements of cultivation nor his cattle for agricultural purposes, would be attached and sold. If the demand still remained unpaid, the *tahsildar* would have recourse to a second proclamation, this time to the effect that the landed property of the zamindar, or the share of the *pattidar*, would be farmed to the highest bidder for 3, 7, or 12 years.

The papers in the case, with a detailed account of receipts and balances, were then sent for approval to the Nawab. The *tahsildar* had it in his power, after having issued the two *dastaks*, to imprison the defaulter in the *tahsili*, rather than going to the length of attaching his property. The detention would be for 15 days in the first instance. If the zamindar did not learn his lesson even then, he might be sent to the Nawab for further imprisonment. This elaborate procedure was designed to mitigate the single feature of the British land administration that had made it universally disliked: the sale of land to realize unpaid revenue.

In the event of the tenants (*asamis*) not paying the rent to their zamindars, the *tahsildar* might go in person to the village in question. In the presence of the *patwari* or headman, he would then realize the government portion of the rent from each tenant separately. Summary *diwani* suits, too, were instituted, the procedure being the same as in the English courts except in one respect. In each case the *tahsildar* would give judgement and then send the proceedings to the Nawab. As an appeal was allowed, the *tahsildar* was not to execute any decree for a month. This was the time limit fixed for appeal to the Nawab. Petitions of all kinds were filed on plain paper, but a fee of 8 annas was charged by the court before which the petition was laid. Petitions for transfer of property (*kharij dakhil*) could be laid before the Nawab alone. The latter, having passed orders on such petitions, would send them to the *tahsildars* to be carried into effect.

So much for civil and revenue procedure. To turn to criminal procedure, a register of daily occurrences (*roznamcha*) was maintained in every *thana*, which was sent up by the *thanadar* to the *tahsildar* in the evening. Any person with a plaint had to initially enter a report in the *roznamcha*. He was then allowed to file his plaint. The *tahsildar* was empowered to pass final orders in minor cases. In cases of assault that did not result in deadly injury, he had powers to pass sentence for a year and impose fine up to Rs 100. The *thanadar* or head police officer could grant leave of absence to the chaukidars at his station for a month. Chaprasis, *barkandazes* and *jamadars*, whether in the police or in the revenue department, might obtain similar leave from the *tahsildar*. Such was the code of procedure ordered by the Nawab in criminal matters. There was no drastic departure from the English administration. Three out of six *tahsildars* under the British, six out of eleven *thanadars*, accepted service under the Nawab.

The new *nazims*—Mohsin Ali of the Eastern Division and Ahmad Yar Khan of the Western Division—gradually tightened their grip over the rural administration. The arrangements made by the Nawab for the administration of justice were soon upset by the severity of the *nazims*, despite the initial effort of the men around the Nawab to inculcate moderation and justice. 'Each man', according to Lindsay, 'ruled as he liked; the Tehseeldars under them became non-entities; police and Revenue matters they took into their own hands, and complete havoc they appear to have made.'

The bigger criminal and civil suits were brought before the Mufti's court. Its procedure was much the same as under the English administration. There was much paperwork: the *arzi-dawa* (petition of plaint), *jawab-dawa* (reply), *rud-jawab*, and so on, as in the English civil courts. A copy of the decree was given to the party in whose favour it was passed. In lieu of the stamp paper, the Muftis levied fees on the amount decreed by them at the rate of 10 per cent, and also one anna in the rupee when execution of the decree was served out. Many parts of their procedure seemed to Lindsay to be 'oriental in character'. His description of the state of justice deserves to be quoted as it affords glimpses of where a break had taken place with the former system:

> The civil suits instituted before the Mooftee were very few; criminal cases, other than petty thefts, and cases of ouster were numerous; for the stronger oppressed the weaker, and too frequently dispossessed him of his bit of land, of his shop or other property.
>
> The decision of this Court in those descriptions of cases appear to have given satisfaction, more particularly after the Nazims of the two divisions entered upon their functions.
>
> Many of the decisions of the latter were upset by the Mooftees, when this was once known to the people at large.

It would appear from this description that the Mufti's court performed a certain balancing role in the administration, ensuring justice against local oppression in the divisions and against the arbitrary rule of the *nazims*. Many of the latter's high-handed acts were remedied by the Muftis when the people in the divisions gathered the courage to appeal to headquarters. Lindsay's remark that the decisions given by the judges in cases of ouster and criminal matters gave satisfaction to the people is particularly significant.

Certain other changes took place in the criminal law and in its administration. It was now more severe than under the English, a sign of reversion to earlier times:

The decisions of this court in criminal cases were very severe; the punishment of theft was the loss of the right hand. Cases of theft were, however, very few; thieves appear to have found the times too hard for small thefts, and much more favourable for plunderings on a grand scale, which were rife on the great lines of road, and in the district. Kafilas were the order of the day,—single traveller or travellers in single bylees (a cart drawn by bullocks), seldom attempting a journey.

In a case where the bundle of little value of a traveller was stolen from one of the garees in the city, the offender lost his hand. The petty thieves consequently left the city.

As this was a time of trouble, there was widespread violence on highways, but thefts and private criminal acts were checked by the 'oriental' severity of criminal administration.

Gradually the judicial process fell under the influence of the sepoy army, a sign of the latter's ascendancy in the new political system. After the receipt of the Emperor's *farman*, in which he praised the sepoys for bravery, sepoys assumed a more direct role in the administration. In a case of murder in which a Muslim had been killed by a man of the Kurmi caste, the Mufti had delivered the judgment that the murderer was to give up his property to the plaintiff, or was to be killed by him. If neither sentence were carried into effect, then the Nawab was to have him blown from a gun. The friends of the accused, taking exception to the sentence, took up the matter with Ganga Singh and Sheoghoolam Deechet. The two sepoy commanders made a big stir over the matter, and the Kurmi murderer was let off. The captains had made their point: after this, the Nawab had it proclaimed that the officers of the 41st NI were to be obeyed in every respect, seeing that they had expelled the English.

Frequently, the sepoy commanders passed verbal orders on important matters. The sepoys of the 41st NI prevented the killing of cows and the lading of oxen with refuse. Such matter, they ordered, must be loaded and taken off on donkeys. These ritual symbols implied that the rule of the sepoys had become stronger than ever. Though formally the administration appeared to be Muslim at the top, the Nawab was a puppet in the hands of the Hindu sepoys from Sitapore.

The regulation of commerce, too, showed signs of reversion to indigenous modes of control in place of the laissez-faire economics of the English. As soon as the Europeans fled from the Fatehgarh fort, the Nawab established a system of 'octroi' on every article entering or leaving the city. The income from this source and from the *abkari* or excise of the town went to his own private purse. Every article of food and every marketed commodity were subjected to a certain duty. Wheat and ghee were taxed too, but as the sepoys objected to the tax on these two prized items of their diet, it was remitted. Even articles of small value, such as wood and peat, came under a certain rate, fixed at four cowries in the pice. Thus on a load worth a rupee, a duty of one anna was charged at the gate of the city. More valuable articles were taxed at the rate of 7 per cent. Despite these duties, the trade in iron from Chandosee, sugar and cotton from Khasganj, and Huldee (turmeric) from Shahjahanpur was brisk.

As the Mutiny continued, the prices of every article doubled and trebled, except wheat, the essential food article of the soldiery. Its export was prohibited. At the time when the town broke out in mutiny, it was estimated that twelve lakhs worth of cotton manufacture were waiting to be sold in the bazaar. Much of these goods were sold off at high prices in the district and the large traders made immense fortunes out of the business before the British returned and the influx of imported cotton manufacturers began anew.

The average income from the duties imposed on all articles of trade was estimated to be Rs 500 a day. This would have amounted to two lakhs of rupees a year. On some days the income might amount to as much as Rs 1700. Everything was taxed throughout the district to maintain the soldiery. The vegetable market in the city was farmed out for Rs 200 a year. The octroi of Kamalganj, a small town ten miles east of the city, was farmed out for Rs 700 a year. The contractor realized duties at the same rate levied on goods entering or leaving Farrukhabad city. The same rule obtained in every town throughout the district. It was the towns which had to pay for the waging of war against the British as land revenue from the country remained so uncertain.

The revenues from these various town and trade duties, except those of Farrukhabad and Kamalganj, went to the sepoys, who paid themselves arrears of pay from the source. The British system of taxation, based on the ruthlessly efficient collection of land revenue from the villages, thereby sparing the towns and permitting the free flow of long distance imports and exports, was quite different from the arrangements of the Mutiny administration.

As a system it was not at all unsuited to the habits and expectations of the population. Lindsay noted with a certain degree of surprise that the numerous duties on articles of trade appeared not to have caused the slightest vexation or annoyance to the people at large; 'in fact it was taken, as a matter of course, as the most, in fact the only, equitable tax that could be imposed: it was little felt by the people, and brought a large revenue to the Government'. The inevitable accompaniment of the process was the collapse of the colonial import–export trade. 'Trade with foreign parts,' with the exception of traffic with the neighbouring districts mentioned above, came practically to a standstill; still Lindsay found that the revenue from customs amounted to 'a large sum'. The concern with the imperial communications ceased. The ferry arrangements were no longer a matter of watchful supervision. The sepoys exercised their own will, and did what they liked with the ghats. 'As to the repairs of the roads, such a thing was not heard of.'

Rural administration during the Mutiny bore the unmistakable signs of the time of troubles. The *nazims* fished in troubled waters, but the occupation was by no means easy in such turbulent times. 'Mohsun Ali', according to Lindsay, 'was a great drunkard; he was a brave man in his way, but useless as a governor'. It soon became apparent that he was unable to cope with the business of collecting the revenue. Two magnates of the division of which he was in charge, the Rani of Tirwa and Chaudhuri Jaichand, refused to pay a penny. The mutiny administration of Farrukhabad consequently removed him. Thakur Pandey, a *subadar* of the 41st NI, was appointed in his place. The eastern division was made over to him and to his sepoys, to realize the accumulating dues as best they could.

Before Nazim Mohsin Ali was removed to make way for the sepoy captain, he (the *nazim*) had a pitched battle with Chaudhri Jaichand, in which the latter came off victorious. The fight took place on 15 October 1857, at Bishengarh, a strong fort belonging to the *chaudhuri*. Flushed with victory, the *chaudhuri* had a second fight near Sucunderpoor, on the Grand Trunk Road, with a party of sepoys returning from Delhi. He had heard that the party had much plunder with them and he wished to possess himself of it. He met with sterner stuff this time, and was defeated in the encounter; 'and by a wound he received in the fight lost all the fair fame he had enjoyed of invulnerability'. Thus did the tide of battle ebb and flow in the fight between the Mutiny administration and the turbulent rural population when Thakur Pandey arrived with his sepoys. What followed is described in an ironical vein by Lindsay:

Now comes on the scene: The Thakoor Collector Panday, an individual whose greatest forte was in drinking bhung, of which he took an immense quantity and in eating pehra (a native sweetmeat) ... .

It will be recollected that the 'collector' was placed in the room of Mohsun Ali Khan, at the desire of Captain Ganga Singh and Sheoghoolam Deechet, in order that the Eastern Division might be made to pay up its revenue. Well, the Collector determined to be severe; so he issued a new system and rates for dustucks (summons). If a man would not pay, then were to be issued upon him these kinds of summons:

	Rs
The dustuck of the Collector	100
The dustuck of a Sowar	10
Ditto of foot soldier	5

The city people began to fly: his tyranny was excessive, and he was an arrant knave, and a great fool.

In the western division, the *nazim's* rule was somewhat more successful, but things were still turbulent. Ahmad Yar Khan realized the revenues of his division at the cannon's mouth. 'One village Rohilla, in the Mahomedabad District, would not pay up; he accordingly proceeded there, and fired three shots into the village. This brought the zemindars to their senses, and they paid up; but in addition they paid a fine of Rupees 100 for each shot.'

According to Lindsay's information, collected after the occupation, the Nawab received little or nothing from his *nazims* by way of revenue. The latter either spent that of their divisions upon their troops, or nominally having done so, 'placed the proceeds in their private coffers'. All the same, it is clear from Lindsay's description that a system of land revenue administration did get going in Farrukhabad. This was more than could be said of the *badshahi* administration around Delhi, or even of the administration of Nawab Walidad Khan of Malagarh in his part of the Doab.

The principal expense of the mutiny administration was the army. Besides the Sitapore mutineers, a new levy of sepoys was raised under the name of the 10th Native Infantry, which, as we have seen had dissolved soon after the outbreak. The colours of this regiment, seized on that occasion by the mutineers coming in from Sitapore, were given to the new levy. Apart from the sepoy regiments, the Nawab had his own regular troops under a man named Agha Hossein. He raised six new levies and five new cavalry regiments. The pay of the Sitapore force was Rs 12.8 and of their *sawars* Rs 40 a month. Captain Ganga

Singh, Sheoghoolam Deechet, and Agha Hossein received Rs 400, Rs 1000, and Rs 500 month respectively. The nominal pay of the new levies was Rs 7 per month, but they seldom received full pay. The custom was to give them some money two or three times a month at the rate of 1 anna a day for current expenses. Their commandants were paid Rs 150 a month, captains Rs 30 a month, and *oolasdars* (a third grade of officers) Rs 15 a month.

The Sitapore force numbered about 2200 in all, foot and horse. Agha Hossein got together a considerable number of horse. The Sitapore troops kept up all the forms and customs established by the British. Sunday was always a holiday, and there was no parade on that day. They compelled the Nawab to pay them regularly according to the dates fixed for issue of pay under the English. When the Nawab happened to have no money, they paid themselves by imposing fines on this or that rich man or village. The Nawab's own levies were well armed, but the new levies were so badly paid and indisciplined that not a man would move out for a foray unless he got a certain sum as expenses. As to the magazine or commissariat, such a thing was not heard of. The exception to this was the Sitapore troops, who did maintain the old British arrangements when they moved out on a foray. The new levies and the artillery were constantly exercised on the parade by the officers of the Sitapore force. The force was divided into several parties: a section was located with each *nazim* and another in or about the city of Farrukhabad.

Regarding the overall quality of the Farrukhabad administration, Lindsay says in conclusion: 'In the commencement of the Nawab's reign, plunder, rapine, and every description of villainy was rife; but through the exertions of the Nawab, who appears to have done his best to rule well, and the severe punishment and exaction of the Nazirs, some sort of order was effected.' In June, there was a big battle between the Jhojhas (a Hindu community converted to Islam several centuries ago) and the Bhuttees (Pathans) on the one hand, and the Gailwars and Gour Thakurs on the other. The latter won in the fight and plundered and burned the villages of their opponents. About July, these rural wars were brought to an end. The skirmishes no longer took place on such a scale, but affrays and plundering on a small scale was rife throughout the Nawab's reign. Pokhur Singh, a great Thakur landlord, forcibly seized 64 villages. Still, some degree of stabilization had taken place. If the Nawab's administration had been given an opportunity to continue, a new political and social order might have emerged. Even in the course his short reign, there appeared striking differences with the preceding British rule.

In three essential respects, the mutiny administrations appear to have differed with the colonial set-up. First and most important of all, the transfer of lands in default of revenue or in execution of debt decrees came to a halt throughout the Mutiny administered areas. Secondly, criminal law returned to its earlier pre-British forms, including corporal punishments. The people on the whole appear to have had a sense of greater justice under the courts set up by the mutineers. Last but not least, the laissez-faire economics of the British was done away with under the new regime. Towns and trades were placed under levies. Grain and other trades were regulated in order to ensure military supplies and provision of the necessities of life. In all these respects, the mutiny administration looked back to earlier times. Yet the means of ensuring these ends were now notably more efficient. Everywhere the sepoy councils were keen on maintaining fragmented parts of the British military–administrative set-up in order to wage war successfully. The intervening colonial period had left its indelible mark.

IV
The Emotional Consequences of the Mutiny

When, upon reoccupying Delhi, the British soldiers turned the town into a graveyard inhabited only by ghouls (to use an Urdu metaphor of the times), the correspondent of *The Times* wrote home: 'No such scene has been witnessed in the city of Shah Jahan since the day that Nadir Shah, seated in the little mosque in Chandni Chouk, directed and superintended the massacre of its inhabitants.'[512] The experience was common to the rebellious towns of Hindustan, and whichever part of the country the occupying army happened to march through. 'Cawnpore was infested that summer by enormous swarms of flies, which blackened everything, settling upon each morsel of food as we lifted it to our mouths. Vultures, adjutants and others birds of prey, had found rich sustenance in the shambles of the neighbourhood; and guided by their wonderful instinct, they followed our column persistently, and were well rewarded for their pertinacity.'[513]

There was in the violence a calculated element that imparted to it an unnatural character. 'We had, to a man, been fearfully excited by the revolting spectacles which we had just seen with our own eyes, of the fate of our country-women and their poor children. And yet, I believe our feeling was not so much of revenge, as a desire to strike terror into the hearts of those natives who were in any way sympathizing with or had been aiding and abetting in these horrors. And there is no doubt that a terrible example was necessary ...'[514]

The cruel exercise could not but do damage to the psyche on both sides, tying the opposed black–white pair into an unnatural relationship. As far as the defeated were concerned, their violent physical and mental suppression put a lid on overt expressions. This made it difficult for future historians to probe the insult and the injury driven deep into the well of their collective psyche. One can do no more than seize upon ambiguous expressions. Even the loyalist poet Ghalib, hearing of the Queen's Proclamation which set the seal upon the fate of his country, gave vent to a cry from the soul: 'Allah! Allah! Allah!'[515]

Well might the helpless population call upon an unseen, and apparently unseeing, Almighty, in a piteous attempt to absorb and internalize the shocks so calculatedly administered to their collective psyche. For the psychological design on the part of the victors was all too remorselessly aimed to traumatize. 'Whenever', wrote General Neill from Cawnpore to a friend in Scotland,

> a rebel is caught he is immediately tried, and unless he can prove a defence he is sentenced to be hanged at once; but the chief rebels and ringleaders I make first clean up a certain portion of the pool of blood. To touch blood is most abhorrent to the high caste natives; they think that by doing so they doom their souls to perdition. Let them think so. My object is to inflict a fearful punishment for a revolting, cowardly, barbarous deed, and to strike terror into these rebels.

Neill then proceeded to explain in detail the measures he had taken to achieve this objective: 'The first I caught was a Subadar, or native officer, a high-caste Brahmin who tried to resist my order to clear up the very blood he had helped to shed; but I made the Provost-Marshal do his duty, and a few lashes soon made the miscreant accomplish his task. When done, he was taken out and immediately hung, and after death buried in a ditch at the roadside.'[516]

'*Let them think so.*' What Neill was trying to do was to condemn a whole race to 'perdition'. His purpose was to psychically fashion a subject race conditioned by the trauma of being born unfree. Such excess is bound to produce a recoil. Across the generations, the reverberations of Neill's unnatural act continued to make its impact. Not surprisingly, stories were circulated about this.

At the time of the occupation, he had, without proper trial, condemned to death a *dafadar* of the 2nd Light Cavalry whom he unjustly suspected of being the murderer of General Wheeler at Satichowra Ghat. Suffar Ali, the condemned man, was flogged by the sweepers, made to lick up a spot at the blood-stained floor of the Bibi-Ghar, and hanged. From the gallows, he asked every Muslim in the crowd to have a message sent to Rohtak, to his infant son. The child, Mazar Ali, was to be informed 'that his father had been unjustly defiled and flogged by the sweepers, by order of General Neill, before being hanged, and that his dying message to his infant son was, that he prayed God and the Prophet to spare him and strengthen his arm to avenge the death of his father on General Neill or any of his descendants'.[517]

Neill met his end on the march to Lucknow. The story went that the boy grew up to be *sawar* of the native cavalry. He was well past youth when, it is said, he shot Neill's son, Major A.H.S Neill, on the parade ground at Agra in 1887. The story thus ended with the avenging of the atrocious deed thirty years earlier at Cawnpore. The truth is that the sepoy who shot the major was wrongly identified as the son of the condemned man. It made a good story all the same.[518]

Such stories sought to dimly probe emotions that lived on after the Mutiny. The sense of injury might occasionally find expression in an isolated action, but no word was left for the historian to reconstruct the psychology. It was a member of the new class of intellectuals at the turn of the next century who gave cogent expression to the feelings that had been suppressed so long ago.

On the latter occasion, too, the British, ever on the watch to prevent the written word from reaching their native army, promptly suppressed what they saw as a well-calculated move to recall those emotions. The statement, originally composed by V.D. Savarkar in Marathi, was handed down in an English translation printed from Paris in 1909:

And who have the right of sitting in judgment on the people of Hindusthan for the offences they are alleged to have committed? The English? If there is anyone in this wide world who have the least right to condemn the conduct of the Revolutionaries, it is these English! Is it England that is to declare that Hindusthan was guilty of one or two massacres?—the England who produced Neill? Or the England which devastated by the sword and destroyed by the fire villages after villages with the women and children in them? Or the England which bound to the stakes, and burnt, actually burnt, those brave fellows with the spirit of Panday in them, fighting for their country—deeming hanging not a sufficient punishment? Or the England which seized the innocent Hindu villagers, sentenced them to be hanged, and then pierced them with bayonets, and then, Heavens! thrust beef dripping with blood—the blood of the cow—down their throats, at the point of the bayonet—a desecration to which they would have preferred being hanged and, even, being burnt alive? Or the England which ordered, under the very nose of the Commander-in-chief, that the body of the Nabob of Farrukhabad should be smeared all over with the fat of the pig? Or the England which advocated these and hundreds of other similar crimes as *justifiable revenge* on the 'mutineers'? Justifiable vengeance! Whose was the justifiable vengeance— that of the Panday party enraged and vowing vengeance because their mother—the country—was being ground down under oppression for a hundred years, or that Feringhee party which was guilty of that National oppression?[519]

These were the memories linking the succeeding generations to the experience of 1857. They fashioned in the area where the Mutiny had taken place a psyche that long afterwards impressed visiting Englishmen as palpably different. Edward Thomson writes in 1925:

> The mutiny, as I have said, means little in South India. Nor does it as yet mean a great deal in Bengal, though every year it is meaning more. Indeed, in some cases Bengalis in the North-Western Provinces perished with us, being killed as our supposed assistants. But from Bihar to the Border the Mutiny lives, it lives in the memory of Europeans and Indian alike. It overshadows the thought and the relations of both the races. A friend who visited the Mutiny Country after many years of residence in the South, told me with what a vivid shock this throbbing, tense existence to-day of the agonies of that time was brought home to him. Those memories have never slept, and now they are raising their heads as never before.[520]

It is significant that these words were written soon after the Non-Cooperation and Khilafat Movements of 1920–4. The deep-seated emotions aroused in the collective psyche of the people were destined to make their 'throbbing, tense existence' felt repeatedly in the course of the mass upheavals in the 'the Mutiny Country' during the twentieth century.

Notes and References

1. Celebrating Id at Jumma Masjid by sacrificing a sheep instead of a cow, Bahadur Shah composed the above verse, and sent it to General Bakht Khan, commander of the mutinying forces in Delhi. *Two Native Narratives of the Mutiny in Delhi*, translated from the originals by the late C.T. Metcalfe (London, 1898), Narrative of Munshi Jeewan Lal, diary of 2 Aug. 1857, p. 177.

2. The British arrested the pensioned Gond Raja Shankar Shah residing near Jabalpur for plotting with the sepoys and blew him from a gun. Part of the case against him rested on a Hindi prayer written by him on the back of a British proclamation calling upon the chiefs to be loyal. The relevant Hindi verse reads:

   सुद्घारका मार अंगरेज रेज कर देइ मात

   चंडी बचै नही वैरी —

   बाल बच्चे सुद्घारका संकर की रक्षा कर

   दास प्रतिपाल कर दीन की ।

   For the full text of the original poem and a translation by Commissioner W.C. Erskine of Jabalpur, see *Freedom Struggle in Uttar Pradesh: Source Material* (Publications Bureau, Uttar Pradesh, 1957; henceforth *FSUP*), vol. III, pp. 136–7. The translation above is mine as Erskine made some errors, in particular mistaking the Sanskrit '*deen*' (poor) for the Arabic '*deen*' (religion).

3. Mutinies occurred in Bengal (Barrackpore, Berhampur, etc.) and the Punjab (Ambala, Peshawar, etc.), but the sepoys of the Bengal Army were aliens among the population in both provinces. Among the Punjabis and Sikhs, the sepoys from Awadh were known as the 'Purbeahs', strangers from the east, who had fought for the English and had occupied their country. The Frontier tribesmen were frequently up in arms against the English, but so vast was the mental gap between these Afghan tribes and the Purbeahs, that despite an approach from the latter to the Akhund of Swat, the Pathans were convinced that the English were the winning side, and thus the British were able to replace the disaffected Purbeah garrison by Pathan recruits. In the Punjab plains the Jat and Sikh agriculturists exhibited a complete indifference to the rebel Hindustani sepoys, helping on occasion to round them up. To keep the civil population in check, the British found it sufficient to deport the 'disaffected Hindustanis', and in particular to round up the 'Hindustani fanatics' on the Frontier. Ludhiana seems to have been the one prominent town where the discontents of certain unstable

groups—Kabul refugees, Kashmiri artisans, and Muslim Gujars—coalesced with the rebellious mentality of the Hindustani garrison at the fort, causing an uprising in the town. In Bengal too, discontent among the indigo ryots against the planters broke out soon afterwards, but here there was no link at all with the rebellious mentality in Hindustan. The educated people and zamindars helped the ryots against the planters, but they had no sympathy with the mutineers. Their mind, profoundly influenced by the West, shrank from the obscurantism and violence of the Hindustani sepoys. See J.H. Kaye, *A History of the Great Revolt* (rpt Delhi, 1988), vol II, pp. 436, 472–80, 493–4, 506–7.

4. Hindustan, in the narrower sense, was the land of Hindi bounded by the Punjab to the west, Bengal to the east, the Vindhyas and the Deccan to the south. The Deccan, or '*Dakkan*' (South), was itself a term defined in relation to Hindustan. When the young Maratha Brahman, Vishnubhat Godase, set out from the Deccan on his journey to Hindustan on the eve of the Mutiny, his father lamented: 'Hindustan is very far away (*Hindusthāna phāra dūra āhe*). The road towards it is troublesome and full of dangers. The people there drink bhang and the women are bewitching. Moreover, you are not learned in the ways of the world. Because of these reasons, it is not my wish that you should go to Hindustan.' Vishnubhata Godase Varsaikar, *Mājhā Pravāsa*, ed. B.B.C.V. Vaidya (Marathi, Pune, 1st edn 1948, 2nd edn 1970), p. 5. At the same time, however, the term Hindustan was used in 1857 in the wider sense of the whole country (Hind). It was the latter sense in which Feroz Shah of the Mughal royal family used it when he issued the proclamation of 18 February 1858 from Bareilly: 'Be it known to all Hindoos and Mussulmans of Hindoostan, that power and domination are one of the greatest blessings of providence and that this blessing cannot long be enjoyed by a deceitful tyrant.' *FSUP*, vol. v, p. 376.

5. Sixty-five miles further up from Allahabad, W.H. Russell, *The Times* correspondent, saw a curious and revealing scene which he recorded in detail in his diary of 11 February 1858: 'Under a grove of trees, filled with green parrots, and vultures, and buzzards, were pitched a few tents, which represented the station …. A luxurious little baby was carried forth for a walk under the shade of the trees; it was borne in the arms of a fat ayah, beside whom walked a man, whose sole business it was gently to whisk away the flies which venture to disturb baby's slumbers. Another man wheeled a small carriage, in which lay another little lord of the Indian creation, asleep, likewise with his human flapper by his side, whilst two ayahs followed the procession in rear; through the open door of the tent could be seen the lady-mother reading for her husband;

a native servant fanned her with a handpunkah; two little terriers, chained to a tree, were under the care of a separate domestic. A cook was busy superintending several pots set upon fires in the open air, a second prepared the curry paste, a third was busy with plates, knives, and forks. In the rear of the servants' tents, which were two in number—making, with the master's, four—were two small tents for the syces, grass-cutters, and camel-men, or doodwallahs, behind which were picketed three horses, three camels, and a pair of bullocks, and ere we left, another servant drove in a few goats, which were used for milking. I was curious to know who this millionaire could be, and was astonished to learn that it was only Captain Smith, of the Mekawattee Irregulars, who was travelling down country, with the usual train of domestics and animals required under the circumstances.' William Howard Russell, *My Indian Mutiny Diary*, ed. Michael Edwards (London, 1957), pp. 26–7.

6. A little later Russell gives an example—a white ganger nearly beating railway coolies to death: 'There were a number of coolies sitting idly under the shadow of a wall: suddenly there came upon them, with a bound and a roar, a great British lion—his eyes flashing fire, a tawny mane of long locks floating from under his pith helmet, and a huge stick in his first—a veritable Thor in his anger. He rushed among the coolies, and they went down like grass, maimed and bleeding. I shouted out of the gharry, "Good Heavens, stop! Why, you'll kill those men!" One of them was holding up his arm as if it was broken.' Russell was not unaware of the fact that European rule could not have continued without native collaboration and that the whites would have been quite exterminated had the natives all been hostile: 'Our siege of Delhi would have been quite impossible, if the rajahs of Patiala and of Jind had not been our friends, and if the Sikhs had not recruited our battalions, and remained quiet in the Punjab. The Sikhs at Lucknow did good service; and in all cases our garrisons were helped, fed, and served by natives, as our armies were attended and strengthened by them in the field. Look at us all here in camp this moment! Our outposts are native troops—natives are cutting grass for and grooming our horses, feeding the elephants, managing the transport, supplying the Commissariat which feeds us, cooking our soldiers' food, cleaning their camp, pitching and carrying their tents, waiting on our officers, and even lending us money. The soldier who acts as my amanuensis declares his regiment could not live a week but for the regimental servants, dooly-bearers, hospital-men, and other dependents.' Yet Russell was keenly aware, unlike many Anglo-American historians today who look upon the British imperium as the outgrowth of the collaboration of natives, that the dividing line

between the rulers and the subjects was extremely sharp, and that force underlay the collaboration: 'I am deeply impressed by the difficulty of ruling India, as it is now governed by force, exercised by a few who are obliged to employ natives as the instruments of coercion.' Russell, *Diary,* pp. 37, 284–5, 150–1. After all, what was it that drove princes and the people to help the English in retaking the towns of Hindustan, and in slaughtering their kinsmen? For the princes, it was the knowledge that they would lose their patrimony if they did not back the winning side. For the people, it was, as Surendra Nath Sen points out, abject poverty and not avarice that induced them to serve the British in the lines at the risk of life: they risked their lives for 'a mess of pottage'. Surendra Nath Sen, *Eighteen Fifty-Seven* (New Delhi, 1957), p. 104. Coercion does not habitually operate through the actual exercise of brute force: the threat of it, or the need to earn the means of livelihood (engrossed and controlled by the coercive power), are sufficient to ensure 'collaboration'. The basic truth that British rule in India was a race regime based on naked force in relations with the governed has been obfuscated by the now defunct Cambridge School, and more recently by the *New Cambridge History of India.*

7. Extracts from a letter from Lucknow to Calcutta dated 29 May 1857 (a couple of days before the outbreak), published in the *Bengal Hurkaru and Indian Gazette, FSUP,* vol. II, p. 8.

8. Russell, *Diary,* pp. 29–30.

9. Letter from Lucknow, 29 May 1857, *FSUP,* vol. II, p. 8.

10. That is how the Mutineers referred to the British. Evidence of Hakim Ahsan Ullah, *The Trial of Muhammad Bahadur Shah,* ed. H.L.O. Garrett (Govt of Punjab, 1932), p. 264.

11. Referring to the support the British received from the Sikhs, Jawaharlal Nehru remarked that 'there was a lack of nationalist feeling which might have bound the people of India together'. Clearly, Nehru, in full awareness of the complexities of 1857, carefully chose the words 'a popular rebellion and a war of Indian independence'. Jawaharlal Nehru, *The Discovery of India* (Calcutta, 3rd edn 1947), pp. 268–7.

12. Susobhan Sarkar, 'Views on 1857', in Susobhan Sarkar, *On the Bengal Renaissance* (Calcutta, 1979), p. 119.

13. Rabindranath Tagore, 'Durasha' (1898), in *Rabindra Rachanavali* (1961 edn), vol. VII, p. 339. The point here is not about the unity and harmony between the two communities—there was much tension between them in 1857—but the groping expression of national identity through a religious formula.

14. Nehru, *Discovery*, pp. 268–9.

15. This is the most important argument in Eric Stokes's unfinished work, *The Peasant Armed: The Indian Rebellion of 1857* (Oxford, 1986), chaps. 1 and 2.

16. Ibid., p. 14.

17. Karl Marx, 'The Revolt in the Indian Army', *New York Daily Tribune*, 15 July 1857, reproduced in *The First Indian War of Independence* (Moscow, 1975), pp. 36–7.

18. Jawaharlal Nehru, while writing upon the Mutiny in jail with only Kaye's work as his source, does not seem to have been aware of the sepoy councils and their role in the Mutiny administration (a topic Kaye did not cover in his great unfinished work.) His information, limited at the time, led him to believe that the princes, chiefs, and their feudal retainers provided the only framework of organization during the popular rebellion, and hence he wrote that the revolt 'brought out all the inherent weakness of the old regime which was making its last despairing effort to drive out foreign rule. The feudal chiefs had the sympathy of the masses over large areas, but they were incapable, unorganized and with no constructive ideal or community of interest. They had played their role in history and there was no place for them in the future …. There was hardly any national and unifying sentiment among the leaders and a mere anti-foreign feeling, coupled with a desire to maintain their feudal privileges, was a poor substitute for this.' Nehru, *Discovery*, p. 269. With more information at our disposal now, it is possible to give an account of some of the more novel aspects of the Mutiny mentality and government. This will be attempted here, with a view to showing that the Mutiny, while certainly not 'modern', was not quite 'traditional' in the proper sense of the term.

19. Russell records in his *Diary*, 4 March 1858: 'Had a large party at mess, many of whom had been in recent 'dours', and I heard a good deal of "potting pandies", and "polishing-off niggers"', p. 67. 'Pandy' (Pandey): British nickname for sepoy.

20. At the beginning of the outbreak in Lucknow, 'Men were seen, here and there, with figures dressed up as European children; and much to the amusement of the mob, the heads of those dolls were struck off with sword cuts.' Captain Anderson, '*A Personal Narrative of the Siege of Lucknow*, *FSUP*, vol. II, p. 8. Interestingly, however, right from the beginning of the outbreak, the rebels identified the enemy not so much as the '*gora*' (white men) as the '*kafir*' (infidel), though the terms '*gora*' and '*feringhee*' were occasionally used. Thus, Feroz Shah refers repeatedly to 'Nazarenes' and 'Kaffirs', and only once to 'Feringhees',

in a proclamation dated 17 February 1858, *FSUP*, vol. I, pp. 459–63. Maulvi Liaqat Ali's proclamation proclaiming himself *imam* in Allahabad does not refer to *firangis* once, only to 'accursed Christians who have been awfully tyranizing over the whole country of Hindoostan'. *FUSP*, vol. I, pp. 445–6.

21. Conversation of Henry Lawrence with a Brahman sepoy on 9 May 1857: 'I ... was startled by the dogged persistence of the man ... in the belief that for ten years past Government has been engaged in measures for the forcible, or rather fraudulent conversion of all the Natives. His argument was, that as ... we had made our way through India, won Bhurtpore, Lahore &c., by fraud, so might it be possible that we mixed bone-dust with the grain sold to the Hindoos. When I told him of our power in Europe ... and that, therefore, we are not at the mercy of the Sepoys, he replied that he knew that we had plenty of men and money, but that Europeans are expensive and that, therefore, we wished to take Hindoos to sea to conquer the world for us. On my remarking that the Sepoy, though a good soldier on shore is a bad one at sea, by reason of his poor food. "That is just it", was the rejoinder. "You want us all to eat what you like that we may be stronger, and go everywhere." He often repeated, "I tell you what everybody says".' Record of conversation left in Lawrence's handwriting and his letter to Mr Colvin quoted in Kaye, *History*, vol. I, pp. 592–3.

22. Proclamation of jehad by Liaqat Ali, *FSUP*, vol. I, p. 447.

23. Nowadays the term '*ghadar*' is used in Northern India, and '*inqilab*' is heard of everywhere. At that time '*ghadar*' meant mutiny and smacked of trouble. '*Inqilab*' literally stood for topsy-turvy, turnover, though now it figures invariably in the slogan, 'Long live the revolution' (*inqilab* zindabad).

24. Thus Nana Sahib expressed his pleasure that Kalka Prasad, a Qanango of Awadh, had joined the 'Government troops' for 'slaying the English'. Apparently unaware of the irony in his words, he exhorted the latter: 'Persevere in your devotion to the Government cause.' Nana Sahib to Kalka Pershad, 9 July 1857, letter reproduced in Kaye, *History*, vol. II, p. 657.

25. Here was the ultimate in revolutionary inversion: the rebels were the government, the government were the rebels. Only a profoundly traditionalist rebellion could express, through the voice of the Maulvi, the thought that 'the people are determined to extirpate these rebel Christians now'. Proclamation for Jehad issued by 'the Imam named Leeaqut Ali of Allahabad, to both great and low men of Islam for massacring all the accursed Christians.' *FSUP*, vol. I, p. 447.

26. The mutinous *sawars* of 3rd cavalry rode through Meerut town crying: 'Babas, this war is in the cause of religion, whoever likes to join, come along with us.' Note that right from the outset the Mutineers are making war, not engaging in mutiny or rebellion. Deposition of Harnam Singh, Meerut mahajan, *Narrative of Events Regarding the Mutiny in India 1857–58 and the Restoration of Authority* (Calcutta, 1881; henceforth *NE*), vol. I, p. 337.

27. Both terms are used in Feroz Shah's proclamation of 17 February 1858, *FSUP*, vol. I, pp. 460–1.

28. Proclamation of Khan Bahadur Khan, trans. R. Temple, *FSUP*, vol. I, p. 443; *Risala Fath i Islam*, trans, Saiyid Zaheer Husain Jafri, 'The Profile of a Saintly Rebel—Ahmadullah Shah', Aligarh Seminar, 1989, p. 12n. English translations indiscriminately render '*dharma*' and '*deen*' as 'religion'. The terms have wider connotation than religious creed. *Dharma* means That which Holds Together: the moral law that binds the cosmos, the righteous social order. *Deen* is closer to the term religious creed, but in Islam the proper practice of the creed requires a self-governing Islamic community or realm (Dar ul Islam). Thus both *dharma* and *deen* stand for the entire community of righteous people, for a way of life. Indeed, they constitute the very basis of the community and its identity. Thus, fighting for *dharma* or for *deen* is not simply fighting for one's religious creed, but defending the collective identity of the entire community of people.

29. While the categories 'Hindu' and 'Muslim' were certainly traditional, the curious joint formula was not.

30. Drumbeat announcement of the sepoys in Jhansi 1857, *NE*, vol. I, p. 555.

31. Drumbeat announcement of the sepoys in Banda 1857: 'Khulluk Khoda Mulk Badshah hukum Subhadar Sepoy Bahadur,' *NE*, vol. I, p. 526.

32. Eric Stokes, *The Peasant and Raj: Studies in Agrarian Society and Peasant Rebellion in Colonial India* (New Delhi, 1978), p. 120.

33. Certainly the political world created by the Mutiny would have been unfamiliar to Shah Alam and Mahadaji Sindia, and it would have been totally unrecognizable to Aurangzeb and Shivaji. The sepoy army and its law-making council would not have fitted into their world.

34. Ranajit Guha, *Elementary Aspects of Peasant Insurgency in Colonial India* (Delhi, 1983), p. 29, quotes the Lucknow correspondent's remarks as one of several instances of 'turning things upside down', and 'turning the lowliest into highest.' Ideologically, however, the Mutiny aimed at a restoration of hierarchy rather than at its overthrow. What is interesting in this instance—a point missed by Guha—is the inversion within the inversion. The English had illegitimately inverted the right order. Now

their illegitimate order was inverted and the right order restored. This was not a simple case of the 'lowliest' becoming the 'highest'. Rather, the highest was restored to his rightful place, and the upstart overthrown.

35. *NE*, vol. I, p. 555.

36. Abdul Halim Sharar, *Lucknow: The Last Phase of an Oriental Culture*, trans. from Urdu by E.S. Harcourt and Fakhir Hussain (London, 1975), p. 66.

37. Capt. E.M. Martineau to Capt. S.H. Becher, 5 May 1857, quoted in J.A.B. Palmer, *The Mutiny Outbreak at Meerut in 1857* (Cambridge, 1966), pp. 32–3.

38. To cite some actual instead of fictional evidence on this point: '"By jove! Sir," exclaims the major, who has by this time got to the walnut stage of argument, to which he has arrived by gradations of sherry, port, ale and Madeira,—"By Jove!" he exclaims thickly and fiercely, with every vein in his forehead swollen like whipcord, "those niggers are such a confounded sensual lazy set, cramming themselves with ghee and sweetmeats, and smoking their cursed chillumjees all day and all night, that you might as well think to train pigs. Ho, You! Punkah chordo, or I'll knock—suppose we go up and have a cigar!"' Russell, *Diary*, p. 8.

39. Speech put into the month of Maulvi Sarfaraz Ali at Shahjahanpur by novelist J.F.F., *Mariam: A Story of the Indian Mutiny of 1857* (Benares, 1876), pp 11–17. Sarfaraz Ali, a *maulvi* from Jaunpur, was actually at the scene of the Shahjahanpur outbreak as a leader. J.F.F. was one of the survivors of the Shahjahanpur massacre and he bases his novel on the real adventures of an English mother and daughter, subsequently retold by Ruskin Bond in 'Flight of the Pigeons' and filmed by Shyam Benegal as *Junoon*. The novel, which shows a deeper insight into the native camp than the rest of the English Mutiny novels, purportedly made no attempt to 'touch up the facts', gathered at first hand from the English lady 'Mariam' whose daughter was wooed by a rebel leader. He gave them shelter and, to his honour, made no attempt to coerce the girl.

40. 'Is it not well-known to Government', asked Syed Ahmed Khan rhetorically, 'that even natives of the highest rank never come into the presence of officials, but with an inward fear and trembling?' Quoted by Sen, *Eighteen Fifty-Seven*, p. 30.

41. Thus, a British resident of the North-Western Provinces wrote: 'The sepoy is esteemed an inferior creature. He is sworn at. He is treated roughly. He is addressed as a "suar", or pig, an epithet most opprobrious to a respectable native, especially the Mussalman, and which cuts him

to the quick. The old men are less guilty as they sober down. But the younger men seem to regard it as an excellent joke, and as an evidence of spirit and a praiseworthy sense of superiority over the sepoy to treat him as an inferior animal,' Quoted in Ibid., p. 23.

42. A reader to the editor of the *Hindoo Patriot*, 30 April 1857: 'I am extremely sorry to confess that it would be very difficult to find out one single individual among our countrymen who does not hate Englishmen, at least inwardly.' *FSUP*, vol. I, p. 294.

43. Evidence of Mrs Fleming, *Trial of Muhammad Bahadur Shah*, p. 173. What the prince did not know was that the reversal of power he expected and hoped for would take quite another form, and that in less than a month it would be the sepoys who would be coming, not the Persians. Nor did he know then that he would have no power then to save anyone, including Mrs Scully, in whose murder he certainly had no hand. Ibid., p. 156. Nor did he foresee what terrible humiliation the victorious British would heap upon him in revenge, being bound by a promise not to kill him: that, shaking with fever on a charpoy in prison, he would have to sit up and salaam every Tom, Dick, and Mrs Harry who chose to visit him. Russell, *Diary*, p. 170.

44. 'All the Hindoos and Mahommedans are aware that four things are dear to every man; 1st. Religion, 2nd. Honor, 3rd. Life, 4th. Property. All these four things are safe under a native Government .... The English are the enemies of the four things above named.' Translation of a printed proclamation issued under the seal of Birjees Kudur Walee of Lucknow to all the Zemindars and Inhabitants of the country of Lucknow, *FSUP*, vol. I, p. 450. In the Mutiny proclamations, the four things most cherished by men are always mentioned in that order. Cf. Proclamation issued by Feroz Shah at Bareilly, 18 February 1858: '... it is certain that they [the English] will destroy the religion, honor, life and property of every one.' *FSUP*, vol. v, p. 376.

45. The editor of *Jam-i-Jamshed* got hold of the facts from an English journal in which he was an employee, and which had decided not to publish the news. He later became an aide-de-camp of the rebel leader Khan Bahadur Khan of Bareilly, *FSUP*, vol. I, pp. 409–12.

46. An attitude Russell heard his companions in the camp express unthinkingly when a native cooly bearer died of shell shot: 'Some of my friends in camp would deny he had any soul, or, as one of them put it, "If niggers have souls they're not the same as ours."' 'The blood', Russell entered in his diary, 'does not show so much on the dark skin as on the white.' Russell, *Diary*, 9 March 1858, p. 86.

47. Speaking of servants, Russell asked a friend in Cawnpore: 'Can you trust them, after all that has happened?' 'Well, I am going out alone— they carry my guns and everything, and I have 500 rupees also, but they won't do me any harm.' 'What is the difference between them and the sepoys?' 'Well, as to that, you know, they're all niggers alike, but I *can* trust my fellow.' Russell, *Diary*, 2 March 1859, p. 287.

48. 'India, be it observed, in English speech means Europeans in India.' Ibid., p. 285.

49. 'At the gateway of the bridge [across the Jumna leading to reoccupied Delhi] there is a guard-house, and Sikh sentries are on duty, who examine all natives, and force them to produce their passes; but on seeing my white face they present arms. My skin is the passport—it is a guarantee of my rank. In India I am at once one of the governing class—an aristocrat in virtue of birth—a peer of the realm; a being specially privileged and exempted from the ordinary laws of the State.' Ibid., 5 June 1858, p. 166.

50. The servants' term for European children was Baba Logue. Here is Sitaram's experience upon joining his regiment: 'My uncle made me stand up, and told me afterwards that it was bad manners to sit down in the presence of a *sahib*. After reading the note, the Doctor ordered me to strip, but I was so ashamed I could not move, for there was a *memsahib* in the room. She was sitting at a table covered with a sheet, and feeding the children with eggs—those unclean things! I began to regret having followed my uncle, and remembered the priest's warning about being defiled. However, I was ordered sharply to take off my clothes, and both the children began calling out—"Papa says you are to take your clothes off! Don't you understand? Donkey, pig, owl!"—and the Doctor joined in, saying I was a fool and an ignorant villager. Then the children cried out—'Oh, mamma, is he covered with hair?" I was so ashamed that I ran out into the verandah, but my uncle came out and told me not to be afraid.' *From Sepoy to Subedar, Being the Life and Adventures of Sita Ram, a Native Officer of the Bengal Army Written and Related by Himself*, trans. J.T. Norgate, ed. James Lunt (Delhi, 1970), p. 14.

51. Narrative given by one of the ladies who escaped from Sultanpoor: 'The ladies were dreadfully fatigued and endeavoured to get some rest. One of them, Miss O'Donel, fell asleep upon a couch in a room in which Lieutenant Grant had procured a native to pull the Punkah. Mrs Block was attending to her infant in an adjoining chamber, when she saw the native let go the rope of the punkah, and approach the couch on which Miss O'Donel was lying. He glared upon the sleeping girl with so fiendish an expression, that Mrs Block believed that she

was going to kill her, and screaming sprang into the room. Miss O'Donel awoke, and the native retired with slow steps, and resumed his pull at the punkah.' App. 4, M.R. Gubbins, *The Mutinies in Oudh* (Patna, 1978), p. 467. The hatred, in this case apparently unmixed with sexual attraction, was typical of the contemporary Indian response to European womanhood.

52. 'Much wearisome labour and drudgery fell on the ladies in those houses in which the servants had deserted. There they had to perform for themselves and husbands many menial offices .... I have since heard of cases where ladies have had to gather their own sticks, light their own fire, knead and make their own chuppatties, and cook with their own hands any other food which formed their meal.' Ibid., p. 206. On the basis of this catalogue of the ladies' sufferings and patient bravery, which would have been incomprehensible to the native women whom the white menfolk so often violated, Gubbins adds in all seriousness: 'To their honour be it said, that these hardships and privations were always patiently and cheerfully borne. Never probably, indeed, has the noble character of Englishwomen shone with more real brightness than during this memorable siege [of the Lucknow Residency].' Ibid., p. 206.

53. An English-educated Bengali intellectual searched the myths of oriental demonology in vain to find a metaphor for the white terror of 1857: 'The Martial law was an outlandish demon, the like of which had not been dreamt of in Oriental demonology. Rampant and ubiquitous, it stalked over the land devouring hundreds at a meal, and surpassed in devastation the rakhasi, or female carnival of Hindoo fables. It mattered little whom the red-coats killed; the innocent and the guilty, the loyal and the disloyal, the well-wisher and the traitor, were confounded in one promiscuous vengeance .... One's blood still runs cold to remember the soul-harrowing and blood-freezing scenes that were witnessed in those days .... For three months did eight dead-carts go their rounds from sunrise to sunset, to take down the corpses which hung at the cross-roads and market-places, poisoning the air of the city [Allahabad], and to throw their loathsome burdens into the Ganges. Bholanauth Chunder, *Travels of a Hindoo*, quoted in Kaye, *History*, vol. II, p. 669.

54. Russell, *Diary*, 2 March 1859, p. 286.

55. The 'horror of horrors', as Bholanath Chandra put it, can be grasped only when we recall that virtually the entire 100,000-strong sepoy army of Bengal became extinct in the war, one part of it melting away in the countryside, the remainder literally 'thrown to the jackals and the vultures', as no funeral rites were permitted. *From Sepoy to Subedar*, p. 168. It will be recalled that around 50,000 men died during the Reign of Terror in France.

56. Recalling the bloody suppression of an 'inferior race' in 1857, the historian will find nothing novel in Hitler's theories of race war, except that he applied it to Europe. At the time it was noted: 'I believe that we permit things to be done in India which we would not permit to be done in Europe, our Christian zeal in Exeter Hall will not atone for usurpation and annexation in Hindustan, or for violence and fraud in the upper Provinces of India.' Russell, *Diary*, 21 March 1858, p. 114.

57. Vengeance for the killing of women was undoubtedly a powerful motive in the soldier's behaviour, and Russell saw on the way to Cawnpore every bit of limewash upon walls covered with the writing of various marching detachments: 'Revenge your slaughtered countrymen! To— with the bloody sepoys', and rough sketches 'of men hanging from trees and gallows.' *Diary*, 8.2.1858, p. 21. There was a systematic character to the blood lust. The bloody action arose from the structure of psychological notions described above—especially the notion that niggers had no souls.

58. 'To "bag the nigger", had become the favourite phrase of the military sportsmen of the day. "Pea-fowls, partridges, and Pandies rose together, but the latter gave the best sport".' Bhulanath Chunder, *Travels*, quoted in Kaye, *History*, vol. II, p. 669.

59. *History of the Siege of Delhi, by One Who Served There*, quoted in Kaye, *History*, vol. II, p. 170n.

60. *Hindoo Patriot*, 7 Jan. 1858, *FSUP*, vol. V, p. 928.

61. Kaye, *History*, vol. II, pp. 373–4 n.

62. Papers presented to Parliament, 4 Feb. 1858: 'the aged, women and children are sacrificed, as well as those guilty of rebellion', *FSUP*, vol. IV, p. 665.

63. Reports of the *vakil* of the Sitamau at Indore 1857–58, printed in Raghubir Sinh (ed.), *Malwa ke Vidroh Kalin Abhilekh* (Jaipur, 1986), p. 186, quoted in B.L. Bhadani, 'The 1857 Revolt in the Indore Residency', Seminar on the Rebellion of 1857, Aligarh, 1988.

64. Letter from Mahommed Hussun Khan to Kyroodden, dt. 16 Rubee ool Sanee, full text in Sen, *Eighteen Fifty-Seven*, App. II. Cf. Russell, *Diary*, 16 March 1858, p. 110: 'An old fakir, whom we had saved from some Sikhs who had discovered his hiding place in a cellar, was lying with his brains out near the spot where we had, as we imagined, saved him .... After the Fusiliers had got to the gateway, a Kashmir boy came to the post, leading a blind and aged man, and throwing himself at the foot of an officer, asked for protection. That officer, I was informed by his comrades, drew his revolver, and snapped it at the wretched suppliant's head. The men cried 'shame' on him. Again he pulled the

trigger—again the cap missed; again he pulled, and once more the weapon refused its task. The fourth time—thrice had he time to relent—the gallant officer succeeded, and the boy's life-blood flowed at his feet, amid the indignation and the outcries of his men!'

65. 'Futteh Islam' (Pamphlet), *FSUP*, vol. II, p. 150.

66. 'In two days forty two men were hanged on the roadside, and a batch of twelve men were executed because their faces were "turned the wrong way" when they were met on the march. All the villages in his front were burned when he halted. These "severities" could not have been justified by the Cawnpore massacre, because they took place before that diabolical act.' Russell, Diary, 23 Feb. 1859, pp. 281–2. This was Renaud's advance column to Cawnpore. An officer remonstrated with Renuad, 'on the ground that if he persisted in this course it would empty the villages, and render it impossible to supply the army with provisions'. Ibid. The officer's fear was fully realized. Havelock's main army was delayed and the Cawnpore massacre took place before he could reach town. All along the line of Havelock's advance, as Sherer recalled later, 'the villages had been burnt by the wayside, and human beings were none to be seen …. The swamps on either side of the road; the blackened ruins of huts now further defaced by weather-stains and mould; the utter absence of all sound that could indicate the presence of human life, or the employment of human industry, such sounds being usurped by the croaking of frogs, the shrill pipe of the cicada, and the under-hum of the thousand winged insects engendered by the damp and heat; the offensive smell of neem-trees; the occasional taint in the air from suspended bodies, upon which, before our very eyes, the loathsome pig of the country was engaged in feasting;—all these things appealing to our different senses, combined to call up such images of desolation, and blackness, and woe, as few, I should think, who were present would ever forget.' Quoted in Kaye, *History*, vol. II, p. 368. Had Neill and Renaud not whiled away precious time turning Allahabad and the road to Cawnpore into the feeding ground of pigs, the Cawnpore massacre, which in fact was instigated by these horrific acts, need never have taken place. Sen, *Eighteen Fifty-Seven*, p. 150 ff.

67. The bitter race memory of this and other acts fuelled the later nationalist movement, which might have differed in its political concepts from the Mutiny, but was impelled by the same core of mass emotional responses. See Nehru, *Discovery*, p. 270.

68. *FSUP*, vol. II, p. 260. Cf. Russell, *Diary*, 9 March 1858, p. 87: '... Some of the sepoys were still alive, and they were mercifully killed; but for some reason or other which could not be explained, one of their number

was dragged out to the sandy plain outside the house, he was pulled by the legs to a convenient place, where he was held down, pricked in the face and body by the bayonets of some soldiery, whilst others collected fuel for a small pyre, and when all was ready the man was roasted alive!'

69. Russell, *Diary*, 7 March 1858, p. 77.

70. Vishnubhat Godase took no part in the struggle, but wherever the wandering mendicant met 'black sipahis' fighting the English 'for realm and life' his heart went out to them, if only because the British were a collective object of terror, the doom of all natives who happened to be in the way. *Majha Pravas*, pp. 33–4 and passim. Godase consciously made the mental distinction that he had nothing to fear from the sepoys and everything from the British (pp. 17–18), a significant pointer that the non-propertied classes identified mentally with the mutineers, and only people with property or those identified with the British had reason to regard the Mutiny as a fearsome development.

71. 'Memo of the Siege of Delhi', by E. Hare, Kaye MSS quoted by Sen, *Eighteen Fifty-Seven*, p. 111 n. The shooting of Bahadur Shah's sons in cold blood by Hodson near the Delhi Gate was an act of premeditated murder, disposing of Mirza Mughal, Mirza Khizr Sultan, and Mirza Abu Bakr in summary fashion for having been perceived in the popular imagination as heads of the Mutiny. Since then Indians have always known it as 'Khuni Darwaza' (The Gate of Blood).

72. Ghalib to Tufta, April 1861, quoted in Pavan K. Varma, *Ghalib: The Man, the Times* (New Delhi, 1989), p. 170. A letter written by Ghalib in 1858 has the following poem enclosed without comment:

'Each soldier of England is now a potentate
Men are mortally afraid to go into the bazaar,
The Chowk is the execution ground, the house dungeons,
Each speck of Delhi dust
Is thirsty for the Muslim blood ...' [Ibid., p. 162.]

The limitations of the political vocabulary of Ghalib's world constrained him to write 'Muslim blood' when in fact the blood that was being indiscriminately shed was Indian.

73. That is how the contemporary English documents render '*Deen*' and '*Dharma*', and for want of a better term the historian must perforce put it as such.

74. Charles Ball, *History of the Indian Mutiny* (London, n.d.), vol. 2, p. 242. It must be borne in mind that the sepoys said this when their death was certain and when they had nothing to gain from lying. Moreover, they met death with that extraordinary composure which only faith

could have inspired: 'The Mahomedans with hauteur and an angry kind of scorn; and the Hindoos with an apparent indifference altogether astonishing.' 'Some of the Hindoos treated death exactly as if it were a journey.' Lt Col. F.C. Maude, *Memories of the Mutiny: with which is incorporated the Personal Narrative of John Walter Sherer*, 2 vols (London, 1894), vol. 1, pp. 251–2.

75. Meerut depositions, statement of Bhagwan Das, resident of Sadar Bazar, *NE*, vol. I, p. 341.

76. Statement of Gunga Pershaud, *tahsildar* of Meerut, *NE*, vol. I, p. 308. Note the spontaneous resort to the joint formula, 'Brothers, Hindus and Musalmans', right at the start of the outbreak, illuminating the Mutiny's inarticulate and subconscious conceptions of the nation. The formula 'Hindus and Musalmans' stood for the people of Hind, conceived as a joint religious brotherhood.

77. State of Hurnam Singh, mahajan, *NE*, vol. I, p. 337. Sepoys, crowds, and chiefs alike repeated the same idea throughout the Mutiny, and the Begam of Awadh's rejoinder to Queen Victoria's proclamation of 1858 reiterated: 'The rebellion began with religion, and for it, millions of men have been killed.' *FSUP*, vol. II, p. 530.

78. Secret news from Lucknow, 2 Dec. 1857, *FSUP*, vol. II, p. 257.

79. Proclamation of Nana Sahib, 1 July 1857, *FSUP*, vol. IV, p. 602. In an earlier message to officers at Sitapur and Sikandra, dated 27 June 1857, Nana Sahib wrote: 'Here (Cawnpore) this day 4th Zikad (27th June), the white faces fought with us. The whole of them, by the grace of God, and the destroying fortune of the Jing, have entered hell.' Proclamations and correspondences of Nana Sahib, printed in Kaye, *History*, vol. II, p. 673.

80. Petition of Amir Ali Khan, son of the Nawab of Khurajpura, to the Emperor, 12 July 1857, *Trial of Muhammad Bahadur Shah*, p. 245.

81. Narrative of Mr Corridon, *NE*, vol. I, Allahabad, p. 20.

82. See, for instance, Liaqat Ali's proclamation of jihad against the English at Allahabad, never once mentioning them as Europeans, but invariably as 'Christians'. *FSUP*, vol. I, pp. 445–8. Some of the less complimentary expressions used by the *maulvi* against the English were 'Kufroh Fujruh Nisara (fraudulent Christian Infidels),' 'kooffar Nabukar Nisara Bad Utwar (useless and misconducting Christian Infidels)', and 'Taghee Baghee Nisaras (fraudulent and mutinous Christians).' Proclamation of Liakat Ali under seal of Birjis Qadar, *FSUP*, vol. IV, pp. 614–15. By far the two most common expressions of contempt for the English in the Mutiny proclamations are Kafirs and Nazarenes. Proclamation of

Feroz Shah, *FSUP*, vol. i, p. 462; Rana Beni Madho Bakhsh Singh's petition to the Vazier, 21 July 1856, *FSUP*, vol. ii, p. 454.

83. Deposition of John Fitchett, quoted by Rudrangshu Mukerjee, '"Satan Let Loose on Earth": The Massacres in Kanpur in the Revolt of 1857 in India,' unpublished paper. So strong was the identification of sin with the physical presence of the British in the mutineers' mind that the terms '*kufr*' and '*shirk*', denoting the abstract sin of lack of faith, was used by them to denote the English race. 'By God's grace *Kufr* and *Shirk* (the rule of the heathens) have been purged from Hindustan and Islam had been established' ran an imperial proclamation. *FUSP*, vol. v, p. 320.

84. Meerut Dispositions, statement of J.H. Jones, *NE*, vol. i, pp. 334–5.

85. Rudrangshu Mukherjee, *Awadh in Revolt 1857–1858: A Study of Popular Resistance* (Delhi, 1984), p. 67. Dīn is derived by Arabic philologists from *dāna li*—(submit to-), hence 'corpus of obligatory prescriptions', or more commonly, religion, in the sense of 'obligations which God imposes on His reasoning creatures'. *Encyclopedia of Islam* (new edn B. Lewis, Ch Pellat, J. Schacht, Leiden, 1965). The term *be-dharam*, a compound of the Persian negative '*be*' (Lacking) and the Sanskrit 'dharma' (that which holds together) is difficult to translate exactly: to render it as 'irreligious' would be to miss a subtle point. As *dharma* is, technically speaking, duty, understood in the context of social and religious prescriptions, *be-dharam* may be rendered as both undutiful and faithless.

86. *Majha Pravas*, pp. 17–18.

87. Proclamation of Feroz Shah, 18 Feb. 1858, *FSUP*, vol. v, p. 376.

88. Delhi Proclamation, May 1857, *FSUP*, vol. i, p. 438. Cf. Proclamation of the High Court of the Nawab, Ruler of the Province of Kutehur: 'To all high and low, be it manifest as the sun at noon day. That the English are the enemies of the life, the property, and the religion alike of the Moosulmans and Hindoos, and being puffed up with self conceit, forgetting themselves in their pride, have thought to make the people of God converts to the Christian religion. By the will of God, who abhors pride, whose displeasure they have incurred, these infidels have in many places been put to death, and sent down to hell .... Let all take notice of this Proclamation and so exert themselves that no trace of the unclean infidels be left in this province.' *FSUP*, vol. v, pp. 605–6.

89. Note the following words in the above proclamation: 'the Will of God, who abhors pride, whose displeasure they have incurred'; 'this [killing of Englishmen] will be an act of merit'; 'If any one in this religious

fight jehad, suffers Martyrdom he will to go heaven'; 'no trace of the unclean infidels be left'. A sense of doom, of ultimate sin, of God's wrath, of hubris and nemesis, of the duty and merit of meting out punishment, of jehad by the *ghazi*, of the attaining of heaven by the *shahid*, pervade the mentality behind the proclamation.

90. Kaye, *History*, vol. III, p. 213.

91. Letter from Isha Singh, Chatta Singh, Shumsere Khan, and Sheodeen Singh, Subadars and other officers in the Gwalior Contingent, to the Subadars and other officers in the service of the Raja of Churkuree, 31 Jan. 1858: 'It was not becoming in your master to oppose us in our recent outbreak being regardless of the next world.' *FSUP*, vol. III, p. 229.

92. In the English record of the event, General Neill, the butcher of Kanpur, is invariably portrayed as a man driven by a sense of religious duty. Curiously, in the indigenous Marathi record of the event, Nana Sahib, his counterpart, is also remembered in the same light, with the words '*Har, Har*' (invocation to Siva) on his lips, making the following resolve upon his defeat at Kanpur: 'All my endeavours till today for the sake of the Hindu religion (Hindudharmākaritān) have been in vain (vyartha jāun), but if it be the wish of Mother Ganga, I give up even the hope of life (jivitāchihi āshā āmhi sorali āhe).' *Majha Pravas*, p. 35. Apparently it does not occur to Nana Sahib to put in a word about the country, as distinct from religion. The conception of martyrdom for the country as such must, it seems, await the coming of Tilak and the Chapekars. Their predecessors of 1857, the patriotic Maratha Brahmans who issued a proclamation from Kalpi on 11 April 1858, are unable to conceive anything beyond faith: 'Formerly we served the Peishwa with great zeal and alacrity in the hope that we might obtain Jagheers and donations, but now if we all of us unite together in the present cause, we will please one deity "Maha Deo" and preserve our faith.' *FSUP*, vol. III, p. 356.

93. Consider the various Islamic calls for jihad in 1857. Thus Liaqat Ali: 'You all should act according to the following precept quoted from Kuran. "The real paradise lies beneath the strokes of swords." You will then obtain salvation and the honour of martyrdom, which is eternal life.' And Birjis Qadar: 'When death comes upon a man, who can save him? In every place and country, thousands of men die from Cholera, pestilence, and other diseases. No one knows whether they died in their senses or without their senses, nor can it be known whether they died with their faith firm or not. To die in battle with the English for the sake of religion is glorious, and he who falls thus is sure to become a martyr.' *FSUP*, vol. I, pp. 446, 447.

94. It is useful by way of analogy to bear in mind the importance of religion in fostering opposition to imperialism in the lands of Islam, and, in particular, in stoking Arab nationalism. India, of course, stands in a category by itself as Islam was a minority religion there. We shall have occasion to touch on the special issue posed by the coexistence of Islam and Hinduism for the articulation of a patriotic consciousness in Indian society.

95. Testimony of Mrs Aldwell, 1 Feb. 1858, *Trial of Muhammad Bahadur Shah*, p. 158. She was the one white woman, among the European prisoners of the palace, who escaped with her life. She pretended to be a Musalman woman from Kashmir, and took care to teach her children the Muslim prayer. During her stay in besieged Delhi she noticed that 'the Mahomedans always seemed glad that mutiny had taken place, and during the Muharram festival I heard the Mahomedan women praying, and teaching their children to pray, for the success of their faith ...'.

96. The *dharma* of the Hindus, after all, was never, like Islam, a defined creed, but was rather a righteous social order, and their grievances related instead to the fear of losing caste and the oppressive rule of the English. See n. 98.

97. Testimony of John Everett, *Trial of Muhammad Bahadur Shah*, p. 198:

Question: From what you know, were the Hindus in Delhi, or the Musalmans most averse to the Company's Government?
Answer: The Mussalmans.

The English had the same impression in Gwalior: 'With great exceptions and limitations, the Mahomedans co-operated with the revolt; the Hindus wished it well, but, having no religious grievance, while their civil grievances were inadequate to move them to arms unled by their chiefs, they did not rise, and protected the lives of defenceless Europeans.' Report of S.C. Macpherson, Political Agent, Gwalior, 10 Feb. 1858, *FSUP*, vol. III, p. 202.

98. The Gwalior darbar's view of the Hindu discontent, as conveyed to the Political Agent, was that the religious issue was inextricably mixed up in their case with other matters: 'As to the cause of the revolt, general hostility to our rule was ever broadly alleged; the cartridge grievance being declared to be merely its pretext, enquiry as to the sources of hostility producing reference only, first to the religious grievance, declared at once to have produced true panic amongst the troops, and to be their pretext for rebellion, and secondly, to the familiar causes of the unpopularity of our rule in the mouths of all. But the *durbar's*

views as to the relative force and precedence of the political and the religious element of the movement were, I thought, very confused, while I believed the latter to be the most important.' Machpherson's report, *FSUP*, vol. III, p 175. In point of fact, Macpherson himself would appear to have confused the Gwalior darbar by insisting on a rigid distinction between the religious and political discontent. The darbar would not have seen such a hard and fast distinction.

99. *FSUP*, vol. III, p. 175.

100. Birjis Qadar's proclamation to the Mahomedans of the Territory of Oudh, Kosheya Rampore, Moradabad, etc: 'The almighty God has enjoined thus in holy Koran, "O ye, the people who follow the religion! do not make the Jews and the Christians your friends. He who forms friendship with them becomes positively one of them, inasmuch as the friend of a Jew is a Jew and that of a Christian, a Christian. Certainly God doth not guide the tyrants, i.e. the infidels in the path of righteousness." This sacred text plainly shows that the forming of friendship with the Christians is an act of infidelity and that consequently he who is on friendly terms with them is not at all a Mahomedan.' *FSUP*, vol. II, p. 123.

101. *FSUP*, vol. I, p. 302. 'The Resuscitation of such dangerous and unauthorized Doctrines, not generally participated by respectable Mahomedans, however bigoted in India, was to some extent occasioned by feuds with Hindoos in Oudh regarding the site of a Temple at Awud ....' Significantly, the tract was translated in 1855, just after the 1854–5 disturbances at the so-called Ram Janam Bhumi near Fyzabad. A band of Muslims had gathered on that occasion under a *maulvi* to march on 'Ajodhya' and to take the place or die in the attempt. Raja Man Singh, later a rebel leader in 1857, had on the same occasion raised a large body of men to resist the march upon the Hanuman Gardhi temple. The British Resident persuaded the Nawab to prevent an encounter between the two forces. Gubbins, *Mutinies*, p. 292. The Mutiny obviously brought about a dramatic realignment of religious divisions by channelizing these forces in a new direction.

102. Russell, *Diary*, 5 May 1858, p. 146. Cf. the account by the police chief of rebel Delhi, Syed Mubarak Shah, prepared by the order of an English collector after his surrender: 'In this manner fully five thousand men from various quarters poured into Delhi as ghazis, the majority armed merely with [battleaxes]—dressed in blue tunics and green turbans .... Several of these fanatics engaged in hand to hand combat and great numbers were killed by Europeans.' Narrative of Syed Mubarak Shah, printed in Michael Edwardes, *Red Year, The Indian Rebellion of 1857*

(London, 1973), app. 5, pp. 220–1. Also see Gwalior Report of S.C. Macpherson, *FSUP*, vol. III, p. 184.

103. The Rajputs and the Hindu population would have fought the Muslims but for the fact that the Lucknow Nawab's troops came and dispersed the *maulvi's* rabble. Gubbins alleges that Man Singh, the leader of the Hindus, had declared his intention, before this, to march on Lucknow, destroy the Muslim dynasty, and install a Hindu government in its place. *The Mutinies in Oudh*, pp. 292–3.

104. Partial translation from the original by Saiyid Zahir Husain Jafri, 'The Profile of a Saintly Rebel—Ahmadullah Shah', Seminar on the Rebellion of 1857, Aligarh, 1988.

105. The outbreak of the predominantly Hindu Gwalior contingent is a case in point: 'He [the loyalist Maharaja of Gwalior who was trying to stem the tide] then, it is said, called for the Bodyguard, and it moved towards the left, I know not whither, but soon thereafter up to the rear. Scindia's right was carried by a single sepoy who ran up to it waving his sword and shouting "Dean". No one would fire at him. The mass of the rebels now came on. They and Scindia's men shouted "Dean" together, while many congratulated and embraced, and very many went off to eat water melons in the bed of Morar.' Gwalior report of Macpherson, *FSUP*, vol. III, p. 454.

106. *Delhi 1857: The Siege Assault and Capture As given in the Diary and Correspondence of the Late Colonel Keith Young, C.B., Judge Advocate-General, Bengal*, ed. General Sir Henry Wylie Norman and Mrs Keith Young (London, 1902), Colonel Young to wife, 21 July 1857, p. 143.

107. H.H. Greathead, *Letters Written during the Siege of Delhi*, ed. by his widow (London, 1858), letter dated 19 July 1857, p. 130.

108. Narrative of Syed Mubarak Shah, *Red Year*, p. 221. The narrative is inaccurate in one respect: the jehadin, as we learn from Greathead's letter, was not released, but sent prisoner to Amballa.

109. *Majha Pravas*, p. 95.

110. *Indian Antiquary*, vol. XL, 1911, Above translation by M. Edwardes, *Red Year*, p. 182.

111. *Majha Pravas*, p. 37. The striving for a Hindu realm was compatible, in Nana Sahib's view (as indeed in the view of his great ancestor Baji Rao), with the acceptance of Mughal sovereignty.

112. Liaqat Ali's proclamation for jihad, *FSUP*, vol. I, p. 447. Although Liaqat Ali spoke of a Dar-ul-Islam, he was fully convinced that this would accommodate the non-Muslim population of Hindustan and their interests. He specifically mentioned the services to the cause by the

Hindu rajas of Awadh and Allahabad and the unity of the people of different persuasions throughout Hindustan.

113. Meerut depositions, statement of Francis Shester, *FSUP*, vol. I, p. 301.

114. The Muslim rulers had long given up the thought of converting the Hindu population, and the Hindus would not convert non-Hindus any way. The social and political system was one that rested on the difference, permitting each sect to exercise its own concerns autonomously. Society was formed like a beehive.

115. Kaye, *History*, vol. I, p. 593.

116. Evidence of Cap. Martineau, *Trial of Muhammad Bahadur Shah*, p. 171. That is how the people around Ambala interpreted the mysterious circulation of the chapatis: a British plot to impose the same food and the same religion, i.e. Christianity, and no difference to remain between the various castes, and between Hindus and Muslims.

117. *FSUP*, vol. I, pp. 442–3. Cf. Rani of Jhansi's circular 'Victory of Religion', 14 Feb. 1858, *FSUP*, vol. III, p. 225, from which the next extract is given. Both proclamations were published by Maulvi Syud Kootub Shah at the Bahaduree Press in Bareilly.

118. The continuity of feeling that has gone into the formation of the modern Indian nation is reflected in the curious fact that Rabindranath Tagore, almost echoing Bahadur Shah's invocation to 'God', the Lord of the Nation', opened the national anthem of India with the line '*Jana-gana-mana–adhināyaka* ... *Bhārata–bhagya–bidhata*' (Lord of the hearts of the people ... arbiter of India's destiny, i.e. God).

119. We have already noted Jawaharlal's Nehru's judgement on the social and political notions of 1857 as backward-looking and 'feudal'. Vinayak Damodar Savarkar, whose views Nehru quoted, was instinctively closer to the notions of 1857: not a matter of surprise, considering that he was not a secular patriot like the writer of the *Discovery of India*. Savarkar grasped the mentality of the Mutiny far too closely for the comfort of the British government, which immediately proscribed the book (1909) in view of the impact it might have on Indian soldiers. Here is what Savarkar had to say: 'What were the real causes and motives of this revolution? ... These principles were Swadharma and Swaraj. In the thundering roar of "Din, Din", which rose to protect religion when there were evident signs of a cunning, dangerous, and destructive attack on religion dearer than life, and in the terrific blows dealt at the chain of slavery with the holy desire of acquiring Swaraj, when it was evident that chains of political slavery had been put round them and their God-given liberty wrested away by subtle tricks—in these two, lies the root principle of the Revolutionary War ... . But were these two

principles understood as different and exclusive of each other? At least, orientals have never had the ideas that Swadharma and Swaraj have no connection with each other.' Vinayak Damodar Savarkar, *The Indian War of Independence* (Bombay, n.d.), p. 8.

120. Queen Victoria's proclamation of 1858: 'Firmly relying ourselves on the truth of Christianity and acknowledging with gratitude the solace of religion, we disclaim alike the right and desire to impose our convictions on any of our subjects.' *FSUP*, vol. II, p. 526.

121. The Begam of Awadh's rejoinder to the above: 'In the proclamation it is written, that the Christian religion is true .... That religion is true which acknowledges one God and knows no other. Where there are three Gods in a religion, neither Mussulmans nor Hindoos–nay, not even Jews, Sun-worshippers, or Fire-Worshippers can believe it true.' *FSUP*, vol. II , p. 530.

122. *The Times*: 'The natives do not seem to resent or apprehend the results of individual conversion, nor to object, as far as we understand, to the probable influences of general education. Their alarms appear to have reference to Government alone—to its news, its decisions and its designs .... Under ordinary circumstances these apprehensions lie dormant and produce little or no effect, but at intervals they burst forth in paroxysms of terror, and then the smallest incident is magnified into a warrant for alarm and violence,' *FSUP*, vol. I, p. 350.

123. Delhi Proclamation, May 1857: 'In fact it is the absolute order of the Governor General to serve out cartridges made up with swine and beef fat: If there be ten thousand who resist this, to blow them up: if fifty thousand, to disband them.' *FSUP*, vol. I, p. 438.

124. For the expression 'holy warriors' (*ghazis*) being counterpoised to the expression 'kafirs and firangis', see *FSUP*, vol. v, p. 55. Walidad Khan to Bahadur Shah, 11 June 1857.

125. Although it was a technical term of the Islamic religion (derived from *kufr* or lack of faith), Nana Sahib and other Hindu leaders used it frequently. Nana Sahib to Dhiraj Singh, 14, May 1858, *FSUP*, vol. III, p. 374. The term became so common as to become a political term indicating lack of loyalty, as is clear from the fact that the loyalist Maharaja Ratan Singh used it against the rebel forces under Deshpat in Bundelkhand ('I lack in adequate means to enlist a force fit to oppose 20,000 Kafirs'). *FSUP*, vol. III, p. 625.

126. Proclamation for jihad by Liaqat Ali: 'Every Mussulman well knows and it is a notorious fact that the accursed Christians have been awfully tyrannising over the whole country of Hindoostan, especially over the District of Allahabad,' *FSUP*, vol. I, pp. 445–6.

127. Hukumnama of Birjis Qadar, 4 Aug. 1858, *FSUP*, vol. IV, p. 126. *Vilaitis* meant two different things in 1857: Afghan mercenaries in India, and foreigners (Englishmen).

128. Nana Sahib to the Officers of the Army, 7 July 1857, Kaye, *History*, vol. II, p. 674. Occasionally there is a more specific reference to race in Nana Sahib's letters: 'The European has been sent to hell, thus adding to my satisfaction.' Ibid., p. 675.

129. Kaye, *History*, vol. II, p. 314 n.

130. M.H. Court to G.F. Edmonstone, 21 July 1857, enclosing diary of events by the opium gomastah, *FSUP*, vol. IV, p. 507. C.f. 1921, p. 498, n 204.

131. 'The Rajah, Jeylal, ordered me to send all the Christians together with a list of their names with the Chobdar to Mummoo Khan. I picked out 15 individuals and on the 2nd day after this I heard that they had been murdered with the Sahib Logue, the day after they were sent.' '... the prisoners—Christians, half castes &c., were put into Golam Hussun's mukan under the latter.' 'The Rajah used to move about to collect loot, and to seize Govt. servants and Keranees.' *FSUP*, vol. II, pp. 94, 98, 100.

132. Dr Duff's letter, 6 Oct. 1857, *FSUP*, vol. I, p. 486 n.

133. Mutiny Narrative, Hamirpur, *FSUP*, vol. III, pp. 114–17. For the pattern of victimization in Allahabad, see Kaye, *History*, vol. II, p. 258. Here the Bengalis 'were soon eased of all their valuables, but were spared their lives on promise of allegiance to their (the Native) Government'. Bholanath Chunder, *The Travels of a Hindoo*, quoted in Ibid., p. 258 n.

134. Kaye, *History*, vol. III, p. 395 n.

135. Young to wife, 18 Aug. 1857, Delhi, 1857, p. 217.

136. Shepherd's report, 29 Aug. 1857, *FSUP*, vol. IV, p. 588. According to information of the Bengalis themselves, they were to be killed the following morning as several spies had been caught with letters in their possession, which, it was suspected, the babus had written to the English, providing them with information. *Hindoo Patriot*, Aug. 1857, *FSUP*, vol. IV, p. 684.

137. *FSUP*, vol. V, p. 127. 'Consequently *Mujahids* from the various villages and the countryside have collected here [Thana Bhawan]. For fear that the *Kafirs* might do harm to the villages and the countryside, their protection will be provided in two ways.'

138. The sepoys after mutinying in Farrukhabad resolved 'to proceed next morning to attack the English at the Futtehgurh fort and would consider any one that did not join them as Christians and would kill him and

loot their house.' The sepoy officers threatened to apply the label to the Nawab of Farrukhabad, who was vacillating at the time of the outbreak. *FSUP*, vol. v, p. 733.

139. Translation of the diary of the Nunna (the correct spelling *nannhe*, implies Young) Nawab, a native gentleman residing in Cawnpore, containing an account of the occurrences from June 5th to July 2nd 1857. Extracts given in App. A. *Selections from the Letters, Despatches and Other State Papers Preserved in the Military Department of the Government of India*. ed. G.W. Forrest, vol. III (Military Department Press, Calcutta, 1902), p. xi. The diary was written by the young nawab from memory during his captivity for trial by the British. At a less elevated plane of society, we have the example of three loyal sepoys who were captured in the Cawnpore entrenchment along with the Europeans by Nana Sahib's troops, who 'abused us; said we were Christians', and told them 'we ought to have been killed and not taken prisoners; we had become Christians'. Cawnpore depositions, statement of Gobind Singh, Sheik Elahee Buksh and Ghouse Mahomed, Forrest, *Selections*, vol. III, pp. cxiii–cxiv.

140. *Trial of Muhammad Bahadur Shah*, p. 49. It would appear, however, that apostacy was no certain means of saving one's life. Three Christian clerks brought from Bareilly to Delhi by General Bakht Khan were kept under guard by the *ghazis* and were killed in the fighting that took place when the English stormed the city—it is not known by which side, but presumed to be the British. Narrative of Syed Mubarak Shah, *Red Year*, p. 231, Kaye, *History*, vol. III, pp. 264–5.

141. Narrative of Syed Mubarak Shah, *Red Year*, p. 209. Syed Mubarak Shah was told by Bakht Khan that Mr Powell had been converted to Islam and that his life was not in danger. Ibid., pp. 222–3.

142. Narrative of Mainodin, *Two Narratives of the Mutiny in Delhi*, trans. C.T. Metcalfe (London, 1898), p. 60.

143. *The Freedom Struggle in Hyderabad (A Connected Account)*, vol. II (1857–1885), (Hyderabad State Committee, Hyderabad, 1956), p. 10. Text of Izaharnamah from MSS Central Record Officer, Hyderabad.

144. Nana Sahib to Raja of Rewa, 23 April 1858: 'Seeing the faith perishing I have girt my loins to defend it, and I have suffered much for it. But this is no man's doing. It is God's design; I have done my utmost; as I have already written to you the faith is the faith of us all, I have endeavoured to support and defend it; all chiefs, and monarchs, Hindoo or Mussulman who assist the English, the destroyers of the faith, destroy their religion with their own hands.' *FSUP*, vol. III, p. 367.

145. Lt Col. F.C. Maude, *Memories of the Mutiny: with which is incorporated the Personal Narrative of John Walter Sherer*, vol. 1, pp. 251–2.

146. Frederic Cooper, *Crisis in Punjab from the 10th of May until the Fall of Delhi* (1858, rept Delhi, 1977), p. 111.

147. The correspondence between the Oudh and Nepal darbars is printed in *FSUP*, vol. II, p. 444 ff.

148. Seid-Gholam Hossein Khan, *The Seir Mutaqherin* (around 1788, trans. rept Delhi, 1986), vol. III, pp. 188–9.

149. Ibid., pp. 161–2.

150. Ibid., p. 194.

151. See Raja Man Singh's letter to the Awadh *taluqdars*, 20 July 1857, referring bitterly to the Hanumangarhi incident at Ajodhya and many other past incidents over the centuries. Printed in McLeod Innes, *Lucknow and Oude in the Mutiny* (London, 1895), app. xii.

152. 'Futteh Islam', *FSUP*, vol. II, 156.

153. Cf. the illuminating discussion of Hellenic nationality in the opening chapter of Thucydides, *The History of Peloponnesian War*.

154. No date. *FSUP*, vol. V, p. 349.

155. No date. *FSUP*, vol. I, pp. 459–60.

156. Azamgarh Proclamation, 25 Aug. 1857. *FSUP*, vol. I, pp. 453–4.

157. Hokoom-namah addressed to Hurdeo Buksh by Shahunshah Mehral Shah Kubendur, 6 June 1857, *FSUP*, vol. I, pp. 439–40.

158. Proclamation by Peishwa, dated Charkhari 26 Feb. 1858, *FSUP*, vol. I, p. 464. The Peshwa of the proclamation was Nana Sahib's younger brother. Nana Sahib himself had assumed the title *pant pradhan*.

159. After enquiring into the doctrines of the Sufis and the Upanishads, Prince Dara Shikoh maintained that 'he did not find any difference, except verbal, in the way in which they sought and comprehended Truth'. Prince Muhammad Dara Shukoh, *Majma-ul-Bahrain* or *The Mingling of the Two Oceans*, trans. M. Mahfuz-ul-Haq (Calcutta, 1982), p. 38.

160. The letter, carried by a Brahman who was subsequently hanged was headed with 'obeisance' to Brahmins and 'salutation' to Mussulmans, *FSUP*, vol. I, pp. 353–4.

161. Ibid., p. 443. Evidence as to the ground of the Muslim objection to grease, rumoured to be mixed with pig fat, is somewhat conflicting. The speech of the sepoys before Bahadur Shah put the question, 'God only knows as to which were those animals whose fats were used. The Hindoos pleaded that they belonged to high castes—Brahmin and

Kshatriyas etc. and that they did not take meat at all. The Muslims also objected saying that they did not take the meat of those animals which were not killed in accordance with the Muslim religious rites.' *FSUP*, vol. I, p. 405. Capt. Martineau, posted in Ambala at the time, maintained in cross examination at the trial of Bahadur Shah: 'Yes, as far as the cartridge question went the Mahomedan sepoys laughed at it; it was only the Hindus that made the complaints in reference to losing caste.' *Trial of Muhammad Bahadur Shah*, p. 172.

162. *FSUP*, vol. I, pp. 155–6.

163. 'Futteh Islam', *FSUP*, vol. I, p. 155. The *Risala Fath-i-Islam* is recognized to be a work prepared under the aegis of Maulvi Ahmadullah Shah.

164. Ibid.

165. Gubbins, *Mutinies*, pp. 292–3.

166. Raja Maun Singh to the Talookdars, 20 July 1857, Innes, *Lucknow and Oude*, p. 336.

167. In this connection, Man Singh did not fail to remind the Hindu *taluqdars* about the recent incident at Ajodhya. The incident is thus narrated by Mr Gubbins: 'This is a place of great antiquity, and reputed to be of the highest sanctity among the Hindoos, and is distant from Fyzabad three miles, on the banks of the Ghogra. The Mahommedan aggression was secretly favoured by the bigoted and imbecile Court at Lucknow. A great convulsion appeared to be imminent; for the Mussulmans, with a fanatic molvee at their head, were marching on Adjooddea, resolved to enter the Hindoo shrine or die; while the Rajpoots and Hindoos of all the country around were flocking to defend their sanctuary. At this time Man Singh took the lead and placed themselves at their head, becoming the acknowledged leader of the Hindoo party. He raised a large body of men, with whom he too post at the Shiwala, or temple which he had built at his private cost, among the numerous convents and temples which crowd the deeply-shaded dells and ravines of Adjooddea. Fortunately the British resident's interposition prevented an encounter between the hostile parties. The King's troops attacked and dispersed the Mussulmans.' Gubbins, *Mutinies*, p. 292.

168. *FSUP*, vol. I, p. 636. Man Singh's own family, it may be noted, owed everything to the Nawabs of Awadh, in whose service they rose to power and wealth from obscure origins. Man Singh himself was an influential man at the Lucknow court prior to annexation and gave loyal service except upon the occasion mentioned. It should also be noted that the Nawab's troops came to his rescue at Ajodhya against the embattled Mujahideen—of course under the British resident's influence.

169. On Eed day Emperor Bahadur Shah sacrificed a sheep instead of cow at the Jumma Masjid, composing on the occasion the verse quoted under the title of this essay. Diary of Munshi Jiwan Lal, 2 Aug. 1857, *Two Narratives*, p. 176.

170. Proclamation of Khan Bahadur Khan, *FSUP*, vol. I, pp. 443–4.

171. Young, *Delhi 1857*, pp. 158, 171.

172. Durgadas Bandyopadhyay, Āmār Jivana-Charit (rpt in *Ātma–Kathā*, 3rd vol. Calcutta, 1985; first published in the magazine *Janmabhumi* in 1891–1896), pp. 344–5. This Bengali memoir was dictated by Babu Durgadas, who had been a clerk of the cavalry at Bareilly at the time of the Mutiny. He fled to Naini Tal, where the English had gone, after a precarious stay in town. The above news was brought to him by a native spy from Bareilly. The spy added caustically: 'Nawab Khan Bahadur came home after completing all this work at one prahar at night. But it does not seem as if it bore much fruit. I believe Hindu–Muslim cordiality did not increase one bit' (*āmār vishvās, Hindu–Musalmān sadbhāv ek karāo vriddhi hoila nā*).

173. Diary of Nunna Nawab, Forrest, *Selections*, vol. III, p. xi; Translation of Narrative of Events at Cawnpore by Nanakchand *mahajan* of Cawnpore, 7 June 1857; Ibid., p. ccc; Pratul Chandra Gupta, *Nana Sahib and the Rising at Cawnpore* (Oxford, 1963), p. 81. Azizan, a courtesan popular among the sepoys, was present at the scene and her evidence at court makes it clear that the people were cautious about the exhortations of the leaders asking them to attack the entrenchment. 'The sowars collected all the people, and took them to a house near the canal and they took me also. There were about 1,000 persons, men and women collected there. The Nana and Azeem Oollah [Nana Sahib's secretary, supposed to be his illegitimate Muslim half brother] ordered the people to attack the entrenchments. Maulvi Sulamut Oollah [who had been dragged there against his will] and the people said, "You first attack them, then we will". They then sent the people away and I also returned home.' Deposition of Azeezan, *FSUP*, vol. IV, p. 600.

174. *Hindoo Patriot*, 21 May 1857, *FSUP*, vol. I, p. 483.

175. Peshwa's proclamation, Chirkhari 26 Feb. 1858, *FSUP*, vol. I, p. 464. The original expression from which 'national religion' has been derived is not given in the translation. It should be borne in mind that the Indo-Aryan languages do not contain an exact equivalent to the word 'national' or 'nation'.

176. Magistrate of Satara of Bombay Govt., 7 July 1857, *FSUP*, vol. I, p. 363.

177. Original of the translated term 'foreigners' is not given in the text. If it was '*vilaitis*' (lit. men of the province or country), which meant either the British foreigners or the Afghan mercenaries from the Hindukush, then Bahadur Shah probably meant the Swat Pathans whom the English were rumoured in Delhi to have brought to the Ridge. Pathans from the Frontier or the Afghan country referred to their home as *vilait* and had come to be known in Hindustan and Malwa as the *vilaitis*. They were greatly prized as able and fierce fighters, and Rani Lakshmi Bai, who had such a corps devoted to her, had adopted their dress.

178. The joint expression 'foreigners or hillmen' makes it almost certain that Bahadur shah meant the Afghans—certainly he could not have meant by 'foreigners', the British. The specific reference to hillmen seems to distinguish the category from 'the people of Hindustan'. The latter expression was apparently used in a dual sense here: i.e. (1) the residents of the Ganges–Jumna valley up to the borders of Bengal, (2) the Hindustanis, or the Indians, among whom of course, the hillmen, too, would be counted but not the 'Nepalese', who are separately mentioned in the previous sentence.

179. Interestingly, 'Sikhs' are mentioned separately from 'People of Hindustan', and in the same breath they are associated with 'the Mahomedans, or Hindus born in Hindustan'. We are to understand then, that the Sikhs and the residents of the Hindi belt are separate peoples. At the same time, the Sikhs are an integral part of 'Mahomedans, or Hindus born in Hindustan', i.e. the nation at large. The Sikhs are associated with it, in the sense that they, too, would be part of 'the natives of Hindustan ... whether they be men of the eastern provinces, or Sikhs ...'.

180. *Trial of Muhammad Bahadur Shah*, pp. 248–9.

181. Munshi Jiwan Lal's diary, 4 Aug. 1857, *Two Narratives*, p. 180.

182. Ibid., 5 Aug. 1857, p. 183. The Emperor had no intention of acceding to the dangerous proposal, for the native troops fighting on the Ridge shoulder to shoulder with the English were Sikhs, and those in town might defect. He soothed the Sikh sepoys, encouraged them, told them not to despair of victory.

183. Note the way in which the police chief of rebel Delhi, Mainuddin Hasan Khan, refers in his memoirs to the sepoys, who might be aliens for all practical purposes: 'Oude was the birthplace of Purbeah race, and these feelings of dissatisfaction affected the whole Purbeah race in the service of the British Government' (the translated term, race, may however, unduly accentuate the sense of their foreign character). The

distinct character of the Purbeahs comes out elsewhere, too, in Mainuddin's narrative: '... this feeling was intensified on the annexation of the province of Oude. Thence first arose dissatisfaction among the native troops, most of whom were natives of that province.' Narrative of Mainodin, *Two Narratives*, pp. 37, 38.

184. Signs of the latent antagonism between the resident citizens and the stranger sepoys occur continually in Munshi Jivan Lal's diary. Thus on 30 May the Delhi Hindus, mostly traders, express joy at the sepoys' defeat at the Hindan river, for they had suffered much since their arrival. Again, on 9 June, the city people, who had anxiously mounted on the roofs of their houses to see the outcome of the battle of Badli Ke Sarai, pour volleys of abuse upon the returning mutineers, accusing them of cowardice (for they knew their own fate would be sealed if the British were to storm the town). *Two Narratives*, pp. 108, 118.

185. One part of the concocted plan to extinguish the identity of the Hindustanis was believed to be bribery and intimidation to get them to marry Europeans so 'that they may in a short time become the same as they'; another part, none but their doctors 'to be permitted to assist at the confinement of Hindoo and Mussulman women'. Proclamation of Feroz Shah, *FSUP*, vol. I, pp. 460–1.

186. Here again using the same form of address: 'O Hindustanee brethren! thus put on your guard against their subversive determinations, leave them to their folly, and all uniting break their head.' Ibid., pp. 460–1.

187. Ibid., p. 461. The pronouncement was attributed to 'their' wise men in secret conclave.

188. Proclamation by the Nana Dunder Punt, 6 July 1857, *FSUP*, vol. I, pp. 451–2.

189. Proclamation for Jehad by Leeaqut Ali, *FSUP*, vol. I, pp. 446–7.

190. Durgadas Bandyopadhyay, *Amar Jivan-Charit*, p. 86.

191. Statement of Quarter Master Sergeant Lewis, late of 17th Native Infantry, *FSUP*, vol. IV, p. 94.

192. Letter of Agent Governor-General for Central India, Indore, 24 Nov. 1858, *FSUP*, vol. III, p. 530. As Tantia Tope was in Mootye in Jabalpur territory when he said this, the reference to the 'country' is not to his native place, but to the country at large.

193. Narrative of Mainodin, *Two Narratives*, p. 31.

194. Nana Sahib's letter to the British from Nepal, 26 April 1859: 'Why should I join you knowing all the "dagabazi" perpetrated by you in Hindoostan?' Sen, *Eighteen Fifty-Seven*, app. III, pp. 395–6.

195. Rani Lakshmi Bai's circular letter, 'Victory of Religion', 14 Feb. 1858: 'These are the stratagems by which the Europeans deprive us of our thrones and wealth, for instance I refer to Nagpore and Lucknow.' *FSUP*, vol. III, p. 226. Her own heartfelt words in 1854, '*Mera Jhansi nahin dengee*', are now on every schoolchild's lips, magnified into a sense of the sovereign national republic of India. John Lang, *Wanderings in India* (London, 1859), extract pp. 84–96 in *FSUP*, vol. I, p. 64.

196. Begam of Awadh's proclamation, *FSUP*, vol. I, p. 466. That the Begam did not have in mind her own possession alone, but was impelled by a sense of English aggrandizement in the whole country, is clear from her preceding words: 'The Company has seized the whole of Hindoostan .... The company professed to treat the Chief of Bhurtpore as a son, and then took his territory; the Chief of Lahore was carried off to London, and it has not fallen to his lot to return; the Nawab Shamshoodeen Khan, on one side, they hanged, and, on the other side, they salaamed to him; the Peishwa they expelled from Poona Sitara, and imprisoned for life in Bithoor; their breach of faith with Sultan Tippoo is well known; the Raja of Benares they imprisoned in Agra. Under pretence of administering the country of the Chief of Gwalior, they introduced English customs; they have left no names or traces of the Chiefs of Behar, Orissa and Bengal; they gave the Rao of Farruckabad a small monthly allowance, and took his territory.

197. Mahommed Hussun Khan to Kyrooddeen, 16th Rubee ool Sanee, Sen, *Eighteen Fifty-Seven*, app. II, pp. 386–9.

198. G.B. Malleson, *History of the Indian Mutiny* (London, 1878), vol. I, pp. 407–8n.

199. Mahommed Hussun Khan to Kyrooddeen, 16th Rabee ool Sance: 'The meaning of all I have written is this. We servants and dependents of the King of Oudh consider it essential to our prosperity in both worlds to display devotion in protecting the Kingdom and opposing the efforts of invaders who seek a footing in it. If we fail in doing so we are traitors and will have our faces blackened in both worlds.' Sen, *Eighteen Fifty-Seven*, app. II, pp. 386–9.

200. Nana Sahib's exhortation to an unnamed (Possibly Rewa) rajah to act honourably, this being a religious warfare, in which 'antecedents or consequences are not to be considered'. Letter from Nana to Dhir Singh, 23 April 1858, *FSUP*, vol. III, p. 368; Feroz Shah's proclamation: 'Placing my trust in God; devoting myself solely to God's service; observing the precepts of religion; strengthening my determination; clothing myself in; my sword taken in my hand, the sword of religious zeal, I arise in the name of God.' *FSUP*, vol. I, p. 463.

201. *NE*, vol. I, Allahabad, p. 18.

202. Kaye, *History*, vol. III, pp. 85–86.

203. Nana Sahib's last letter, 26 April 1859, Sen, *Eighteen Fifty-Seven*, p. 396.

204. Thus, in a curious re-enacting of the scenes of 1857, the Bombay hartal of 17 November 1921, in protest against the jailing of the Ali brothers, pitted the Maharashtrian mill hands and the Muslims against Whites, Christians, Anglicized Parsees, and sometimes anyone in European clothes, Sumit Sarkar, *Modern India 1885–1947* (Delhi, 1984), p. 212. The objects on which mass anger focused instinctively did not alter. C.f. p. 377.

205. Frederic Cooper, Deputy Commissioner, Amritsar, *Crisis in Punjab from the 10th of May until the Fall of Delhi* (1858, rpt Chandigarh, 1977), pp. 110–11.

206. H.H. Greathead from the Ridge to Agra, 8 Aug. 1857, *FSUP*, vol. I, p. 329.

207. Kaye, *History*, vol. II, p. 20 n, 16–17. In 1850 a Civilian argued to the contrary that if indeed the Musalmans—'the most restless and discontented of our subjects'—had continued 'to look upon the representatives of the house of Timour as their natural head, and to count upon the palace of Delhi as a rallying point in the event of any outbreak amongst them', then it was sound policy, on the first favourable opportunity, 'to remove the head, and to put the projected rallying point into safe hands.' Ibid., pp. 25–6 n.

208. Ibid., pp. 9–33.

209. *Trial of Muhammad Bahadur Shah*, examination of Jat Mal, formerly news writer to the Lieutenant-Governor at Agra (he was frequently in the palace collecting news), p. 115.

210. Ibid., examination of Ahsanullah Khan, p. 112.

211. Ibid., evidence of Mukund Lal, pp. 162–3. Ahsanullah Khan, the king's confidante who was privy to his secret counsel, however, knew nothing about this alleged letter.

212. Ibid., evidence of John Everett, *risaladar*, p. 197. See also evidence of Theophilus Metcalfe, p. 133.

213. Ibid., Extract from the *Authentic News*, 26 Jan. 1857. This was a lithographed weekly paper with a circulation of 200, but with a wider readership and audience. The editor, Jamal-ud-Din, was hostile to the English, and published frequent articles on the activities of the Persians and the Russians. Examination of Chuni Lal, a news writer, ibid., p. 142.

214. Ibid., examination of John Everett, *risaladar*, p. 16.

215. The advance of the Persians upon Herat was much discussed among the natives, and frequently in connection with the idea of Russian designs upon India. Five or six weeks before the outbreak it was rumoured in the sepoy lines that 100,000 Russians were coming from the north to destroy the Company's government; 'in fact the idea of a Russian invasion was universally prevalent'. Ibid., examination of Theophilus Metcalfe, p. 134.

216. Extract from the *Authentic News*, 19 March 1857: 'Copies of a proclamation in the name of the King of Persia have been put up at the entrances of the streets and lanes of Delhi. One of my friends took an exact transcript of the copy which had been put up on the back of the Jama Masjid. The purport of it in a condensed form is, that people professing the true faith should, as a matter of duty, eschew assisting the Christians, and should, as being right and proper, exert themselves to the full extent of their ability to promote the welfare of the Mussulmans, that the true time is at hand, when God willing, we, the King of Persia, will sit on the throne of India, and will make the King and people of that country contented and happy. In the same measure as the English have done everything to make them destitute of the means of subsistence, we will exert ourselves to make them rich and affluent. We use no interference with any man's religion. Such is the substance of the proclamation. Moreover, a person of the name of Sadik Khan, by means of whom this proclamation has been made public, writes, that up to the 6th instant, 900 Persian soldiers, with some officers of high rank, had entered India, and 500 are staying in Delhi itself in various guises, and as an instance, he mentions himself as having reached Delhi on the 4th March, and circulated all the copies of the proclamation .... People say that this proclamation has been contrived merely to get up idle speculations, and being of the same opinion, I too would ask, what is the object of Muhammad Sadiq Khan's coming to Delhi? If his object is war, his coming in this way is absolute absurdity. If he has come as a spy, then his publishing his presence by a proclamation is a senseless inconsistency .... Setting all this aside, however, it may be asked what cause for rejoicing would the Hindus have were the King of Persia to exercise sway over India?' Ibid., pp. 209–210. Note that the term 'Hindu' here might also be understood as Hindi. This, according to the *Bahar-i-Ajam*, is an old usage.

217. The allusion, implying restoration of Mughal power in India, is to the help which the Safavid emperor Shah Abbas gave to the expelled Mughal emperor Humayun to recover the throne of Delhi, Ibid., p. 210.

218. Azimullah Khan, Nana Sahib's adviser, was returning to India via the Mediterranean after unsuccessfully prosecuting a suit for his master's pension and title in London, when news reached him at Malta that the Russians had inflicted a reverse on the English and French on 18 June. This so excited him that he made a detour and procured a pass to Balaklava to see the war with his own eyes. *FSUP*, vol. i, p. 308.

219. *Trial of Muhammad Bahadur Shah*, examination of Mukund Lal, Secretary to the Ex-King of Delhi, pp. 164–5. Bahadur Shah himself, however, and his confidential adviser, Hakim Ahsanullah Khan, were utterly taken by surprise when the troopers did ride down from Meerut to the gates of the palace, for, as the approver, Ahsanullah Khan, put it in his free and frank evidence, 'nothing had transpired immediately before their arrival which might have led us to expect them'. Evidence of Hakim Ahsan Ullah, late confidential physician to the Ex-King of Delhi, Ibid., p. 262.

220. Ibid., p. 261.

221. Ibid., p. 261.

222. Narrative of Mainodin, *Two Narratives*, p. 37.

223. Letter from F.W. Buwoughs, Lieut.-Col. Commanding 17th Regiment Native Infantry, 3 June 1857, *FSUP*, vol. i, p. 342.

224. Narrative of Mainodin, *Two Narratives*, p. 37.

225. Sitaram, *From Sepoy to Subedar*, p. 161.

226. Not much of this secret correspondence was recorded. According to Moinuddin Khan, the letters emphasized two main points: the growing displacement of the Purbeahs by the Sikhs and Punjabis in the Company service and the deposition of the ancient rulers of Hindustan. Narrative of Mainodin, pp. 37–8. Some letters of a *jamadar* of the 34th NI at Barrackpore obtained by Kaye expressed the sepoys' preference for leaving the service of the English and joining the Nawab of Awadh: 'We will go to our homes sooner than bite the blank ammunition.' 'The Feringhee Beteechoots are unequalled in their want of faith. The King of Lucknow put down his arms, and the Government have given him no allowance.' Kaye, *History*, vol. i, pp. 573–4 n.

227. '"We like our Colonel", said these men, "and will not allow him to be harmed; but if the whole army turns we must turn too!" There is great meaning in those words. The authority of the "Fouj ke Bheera", or "General will of the army", was, to individual men, or regiments almost irresistible,' Gubbins, *Mutinies*, p. 111. The word '*bheera*', in this sense, is, however, not to be found in the standard Hindustani dictionaries.

228. W. Muir to C. Beadon, 19 Aug. 1857, William Muir, *Records of the Intelligence Department of the Government of the North-Western Provinces of India during the Mutiny of 1857*, ed. W Colstream (1902), vol. II, pp. 130–1.

229. Troopers of 3rd Cavalry at Ambala to Captain Martineau, evidence of Martineau, *Trial of Muhammad Bahadur Shah*, p. 172. It is a notable fact that the *risala* men who said this remained loyal to the British. Rebel or loyalist, the sepoys to the last man thought that the British acted in bad faith.

230. Conversation between the Resident of Delhi and the sepoys: 'The Resident—Baba Log! listen to me. Give up the idea of killing us and fighting with us. On solemn oath, I promise to intercede for you and to save your life and honour, if you even now desist from further killing and fighting. I shall get all those punished who are responsible for playing false with you and your religion. His Majesty, the King also shares my opinion and advises you to stay back and remain peaceful.

Sepoys—Sir! We cannot trust you. You have often won victories through deceptive contrivances. Supposing we obey you, where is the guarantee that you will not hang us the other day? It is better to die fighting than to be hanged at the hands of a scavenger.'

Translated extract from Zahir Delhvi, *Dastan-i-Ghadar* (Urdu), *FSUP*, vol. I, p. 407. By 'Resident' is meant Captain Douglas, commandant of the palace guards, who argued with the mutineers from Meerut on behalf of the Emperor and was killed.

231. Capt. H.C. Craigie to Adj. of 3rd Cavalry, 23 April 1857. Forrest, *Selections*, vol. I, p. 228. ' ... they all refused to take them, saying they would get a bad name if they took them, but if all the regiments would take their cartridges they would do so,' Ibid. pp. 227–8. *The Friend of India*, 7 May 1857: 'No body knows of what it is that the sepoy complains, nor what course he proposes to take in securing a remedy, how it is intended to repress the existing signs of treason, nor how it is proposed to make mutiny less likely in the future.' *FSUP*, vol. I, p. 329.

232. See *FSUP*, vol. I, pp. 325, 329, *FSUP*, vol. III, pp. 129, 173. Mrs Young to her sister in London, 14 May 1857: 'Some months ago I was sending some whole wheat to a little mill on a stream a short distance from Simla to be ground, it makes such nice brown bread .... My *ayah*, when she heard that I was sending this wheat, asked me to send some for her also, as there was a report in the bazar that all the flour was mixed with the bones, finely ground, of cows and pigs. I laughed at her, and said "*Ayah*, what nonsense! Who says so?" She replied "It is quite true, all the bazar people say so."' Young, *Delhi 1857*, pp. 17–18.

233. See evidence of Jat Mal, Chuni the news writer, Hakim Ahsanullah, etc. in *Trial of Muhammad Bhadur Shah*, p. 121 and passim.

234. Lieut.-Col. Buwoughs asked a favourite sepoy regarding the cartridge: 'Then why is this objection made now?' Havildar Jagannath Tiwari replied, 'from villainy', and 'there he stopped short, not one word of information would he give'. *FSUP*, vol. I, p. 348. Maj. Macpherson, Political Agent at Gwalior, brought round the Gwalior darbar to his views over a month of intense questioning and extracted the following views from the darbar: ' ... the army were predisposed to revolt, by sharing with the people of Hindustan their feeling of dissatisfaction with our rule; thought success certain, from the smallness of our European force, and from popular aid; and made the cartridge grievance their pretext and occasion to rise.' Macpherson's Gwalior report, *FSUP*, vol. III, p. 202.

235. Judge Advocate-General's address to the Court, *Trial of Muhammad Bahadur Shah*, p. 234.

236. Muir to Tucker, 13 Aug. 1857, *FSUP*, vol. V, p. 894.

237. *Majha Pravas*, p. 30.

238. Ibid., pp. 15–16.

239. But see translation of a letter from Inayut-Oolah Goolaothee, of Bulandshahr, to his brother Fyzool Hussan, Extra Assistant, Rawal Pindi, Kaye, *History*, vol. I, pp. 641–3: ' ... The reason of my letters not reaching you is this: that on the 12th of Ramyanan, in Meerut "*Khas*", such a fight occurred between the Native and the European troops on a point of religion as cannot be described. The foundation of the quarrel was this: that thousands of mounds of atta was taken into every ressalah and regiment; and with this atta was mixed the ground bones of the cow and pig; and the cartridges were also made with the fat of the cow and pig. The shopkeepers in the city were ordered to purchase "atta" from Government and sell it in all the villages. It was ordered by beat of drum that atta be not ground in any village, and that in every district all the mills should be confiscated to Government. It was also ordered that ten maunds of atta be thrown into every well, kuchcha or pukka, in every village and town. The troops at every station with one accord said, that if the troops at Meerut should receive the atta and cartridges they would receive them without objection. A few European officers assembled at Meerut, and having collected the officers of the pultun and ressalah, ordered them to take the atta from the Government and to bite the cartridges with the mouth. A few Sirdars objected to do so; but two, one a Hindu and the other a Mussulman, bit the cartridge with the mouth. A reward of one hundred rupees was immediately

paid to both. The rest said that they would consult each other during the night, and intimate the result the next morning. There were about eighty four men. They were instantly sent to jail in irons. One among them, a Syud, who was fasting, struck his head on the ground and died. About two hours before sunset the troops girded up their loins and killed all the European soldiers and officers that were present ... from all sides the Native troops assembled at Delhi and desired the king to ascend the throne. His Majesty refused; but the sepoys said, "Do you ascend the throne, else we shall cut off your head and bury your body underneath the throne, and place one among ourselves on the throne." They then placed Shahzada Jewan Bakht on the throne ... . I have sent a man to Delhi to ascertain the course of events there; when he comes back the real state of things will be known. Traffic has ceased in several districts. The Jats and Goojurs have commenced plundering, and news arrives daily of the plundering of villages here and there. A revolution has occurred in the country ... .' It may be noted that Inayatullah's tone is distinctly hostile to the British: he calls the Saiyids of Abdullahpur 'scoundrels' for having handed over a detachment of the Meerut mutineers to the English.

240. 'J.F.F.', the novelist of *Mariam*, gives the Persian original with English translation in appendix III of the novel, and he says (1896): 'I first saw this ode in 1860, that is, just three years after the mutiny, in the hands of a leading Mussalman religious guide in Agra, and he assured me that it had come down in his family for generations.' *Mariam*, pp. 16–17 n.

241. The original Persian:
Shāh e Alamgīr bāshad nām u Aurangzeb
kaz julushash fitna dar Hindostān paidā shawad.

242. *Qaum-i–Sikkhān chire dastihā kunad bar Musalmīn*
Tā chihal in jaur o bid'at andarān paidā shawad.

243. *Bad azān gardad Nisārā mulk e Hindostān tamām*
Tā sadi hukmash miyān Hindostān paidā shawad.

244. The name Gharibistan in this couplet is doubtful. It might be read either as Gharibistan or as Arbistan. If the latter, it would be 'king of Arabia' instead of 'the West'. Kaye, referring to a native newspaper that cited it as the prophecy of the 'revered saint shah Mamat-ollah' (sic), gives the following translation of the newspaper version: 'After the fire-worshippers [a term of abuse for the faithless] and Christians shall have held sway over the whole of Hindostan for a hundred years, and when injustice and oppression will prevail in their Government,

an Arab prince shall be born, who will ride forth triumphantly to slay them'. Kaye, *History*, vol. II, pp. 36–7 n.

245. 'People of Isa' would be a more literal translation, or 'the nation of Jesus'.

246. *Chun shawad dar mulk e anhā jaur o bid'at rā riwāj*

Shāh e gharbi bahr e qatlash khush inān paidā shawad.

Darmiāne in o ān gardad basé jang e azim

Qatl e ālam bé shubah dar jang e ān paidā shawad.

Fath yābad shāh-i-Gharibistan bazor e tegh-i-Jehd

Qaum-i-Isā rā shakiste begumān paidā shawad.

247. Cooper, *Crisis in Punjab*, pp. 107–8. The Azamgarh proclamation refers to both Muslim and Hindu prophecies: '... and be it known to all, that the ancient works, both of the Hindoos and the Mohammedans, the writings of the miracle-workers, and the calculations of the astrologers, pundits, and rammals, all agree in asserting that the English will no longer have any footing in India or elsewhere.' *FSUP*, vol. I, 454.

248. Memorandum on the Mutiny and Outbreak in Meerut in May 1857 by Major Williams, Commissioner of the Police, N.W. Provinces, dt. Allahabad 15 Nov. 1858, *FSUP*, vol. V, p. 9.

249. Deposition of Mohur Singh, Deputy Collector, Meerut, *FSUP*, vol. I, pp. 392–3.

250. F.W. Buwoughs to Capt. J.H. Chamberlain, in response to letter no. 617 of 23 Jan. 1860, *FSUP*, vol. I, p. 347. Collating 'oral information' (unspecified) with 'facts as they occurred' (which, however, seem to point to the contrary), Cacroft Wilson, the judge of Moradabad at the time of the outbreak, formed the idea that Sunday, 31 May 1857, 'was the day fixed for mutiny throughout the Bengal Army; that there were committees of about three members in each regiment, which conducted the duties, if I may so speak, of the mutiny; that the sipahees, as a body, knew nothing of the plans arranged; and that the only compact entered into by regiments, as a body, was that their particular regiments would do as the other regiments did. The committee conducted the correspondence and arranged the plan of operations, viz. that on the 31st May, parties should be told off to murder all European functionaries, most of whom would be engaged at Church, seize the treasure, which would then be augmented by the first instalment of the rubbee harvest, and release the prisoners ...' From this combined and simultaneous massacre, the British were supposed to have been saved by the premature outbreak at Meerut on 10 May, which, according to Wilson, was a mistake that ultimately led to the failure of the Mutiny.

J.C. Wilson to G.F. Edmondstone, 24 Dec. 1858, *FSUP*, vol. I, pp. 403–4. The judge, it may be noted, did not produce a shred of evidence to back his theory of a simultaneous all-India uprising. Certainly the mutineers showed no capacity for such a high level of organization as events unfolded. Sitaram Bawa's evidence (*FSUP*, vol. I, pp. 372–6) paints an even grander conspiracy involving virtually every great native prince and even the Lucknow bankers, but it is full of elementary errors. For instance, he represents Baija Bai of the house of Sindhia, who threw in her lot with the British, as an arch conspirator.

251. Zahir Dehlvi, *Dastan-i-Ghadar, FSUP*, vol. I, p. 406.

252. J.A.B. Palmer argues that there was a deep-laid plot behind the Meerut outbreak, and that the panic in the bazaar was deliberately manufactured to provoke the sepoys. He says this on the basis of the fact that the telegraph line to Delhi was cut before the panic in the bazaar, and that a native officer told Lieut. Gough on the previous night that a mutiny would break out on the morrow. It is not, however, known for certain that it was near Meerut that the Delhi–Meerut line was cut on that fateful evening. All we know is that the line somehow ceased to operate, but not exactly where. The line to Agra was intact till after the outbreak, nor was the line to Ambala cut. In any case, cutting the wires or burning telegraph offices (the latter actually happened in Raniganj) was a recognized manner of registering protest in moments of tension and does not necessarily imply conspiracy. There circulated at the time many similar rumours of 'mutiny on the morrow', so there is nothing unique about Lieut. Gough's report. As regards any plotting behind the panic in the bazaar, there is no hard evidence. *Mutiny Outbreak in Meerut*, pp. 70–1, 96, 22.

253. Kaye, *History*, vol. II, pp. 51–2.

254. The only act even approaching conspiracy that came to light in the subsequent enquiries, was the following: 'Taking for granted that the statements of the men of the 3rd Light Cavalry are correct, it would appear that the first act of open and decided mutiny in their corps took place on 22nd of April 1857, when the men were sworn in, on the Ganges and the *Koran*, to refuse the cartridges, until the whole Bengal Army had consented to accept them.' Memorandum of Maj. Williams, 15 Nov. 1858, *FSUP*, vol. V, pp. 10–11.

255. Ibid., p. 11.

256. *NE*, vol. I, Moradabad, report of J.C. Wilson, 24 Dec. 1858, pp. 400–1.

257. The offensive imagery of inversion of the role of men and women was a psychological device to incite the former to assert their manhood. *Dastan-i-Ghadar, FSUP*, vol. I, p. 406. It would appear from the account

of the sepoys that the 'ladies' were not necessarily all courtesans. It is on record in the official report that some of the sepoys had their families living with them at the time: 'Another strong proof of there being no prearranged plan of action, is the fact of their wives and children being left totally unprovided for, who wandered about the city for some days, houseless and homeless, and at last scattered in various directions in search of food and shelter ... .' Memorandum of Maj. Williams, *FSUP*, vol. v, p. 12.

258. Maj.-Gen. W.H. Hewitt, commanding the Meerut Division, to Col. C. Chester, Adj.-Gen. of the Army, Simla, 11 May 1857, *FSUP*, vol. v, p. 8.

259. Memorandum of Maj. Williams, *FSUP*, vol. v, p. 13. On the day before the outbreak there was a rumour that the place where they were to assemble for receiving pay had been mined to blow them up, and in consequence they refused to attend. Ibid., p. 19.

260. Ibid., pp. 14, 16. As the country around went up in flames, the sturdy pastoral Hindu tribe of Gujars and the warlike Muslim agricultural tribe of Meos or Mewatis sprang to prominence in the rural violence, joined in by sections of the Jats. All along the Jumna valley, the violent outbreaks among the weighmen, the butchers, and the Mewatis were specially noted. 'These several classes, all Muhammadans, are generally well off. The Mewatis are thriving agriculturists, the *taulas* follow the profession of weighmen while the *qassabs* or butchers I am speaking of, are either wholesale or retain dealers in cattle or sheep. They purchase young stock and make it over to the *ahirs* or *gadarias*, and after they are grown, they drive them to long distances, even as far as Calcutta and Rangoon, where they sell them wholesale and realize handsome profits. As to the weighmen, at a period when the *balambha* or *Khari* salt [of Bharatpur state, made by solar evaporation] used to be manufactured, their profession was to weigh the salt before its removal from the *sars* or pits. Now that the manufacture of that species of salt has ceased, they pursue their trade as weighmen of cereals.' *Mariam*, p. 213. It would be obvious that urban insurgents, such as butchers and weighmen, had a roving rural ancestry.

261. Describing 'the impulse of a great fear', Kaye remarks, 'it is hard to believe that on that Sabbath evening a single Native soldier had discharged his piece without a belief, in his inmost heart, that he was going straight to martyrdom.' Kaye, *History*, vol. ii, p. 75.

262. H. Le Champion to John William Kaye, 27 Feb. 1871, Kaye, *History*, vol. iii, pp. 680–1.

263. The official report on the Meerut outbreak expresses wonder 'that after thus hastily releasing their comrades, doing all the injury they could

by the way, they should flee without an acknowledged head or guide, or any plan of operations; and then only (finding themselves unmolested) hold a hurried council to decide upon their future operations.' Memorandum of Maj. Williams, *FSUP*, vol. v, p. 23.

264. Munshi Mohan Lal, the famous explorer, overheard the *sawar* and recorded his remarks in *Memorandum on the causes of the Mutiny*, Kaye Papers, cited by Palmer, *Mutiny Outbreak*, p. 120.

265. Muir to Tucker, 13 Aug. 1857, *FSUP*, vol. v, p. 894.

266. Evidence of Gulab, messenger, and Ahsanullah Khan, *Trial of Muhammad Bahadur Shah*, pp. 88–9 and passim.

267. *Dastan-i-Ghadar*, *FSUP*, vol. i, p. 405.

268. Narrative of Syed Mubarak Shah, *Red Year*, p. 186. According to him, the white women and children who had taken shelter in the palace were ruthlessly massacred by Talyar Khan of the 3rd Cavalry from Meerut. The motive was to make the Emperor party to it. The latter wept and begged, 'Take care—for if you commit such a deed the vengeance and anger of God will fall on me—why kill the innocent? Ibid., p. 192.

269. Narrative of Munshi Jeewan Lal, *Two Narratives*, p. 83.

270. The white soldiers bayoneted the loyal sepoys who had stayed back after the Mutiny in Dinapore. Kaye, *History*, vol. iii, pp. 122–3.

271. Ibid., p. 231.

272. According to the English account, the parade, intended only to disarm the men, turned into a slaughter when some panic-stricken sepoys who believed that they would be shot down after being disarmed opened fire with one or two stray shots, which were met with the ruthless fire of the cannon. Kaye, *History*, vol. ii, p. 222.

273. Diary of 4 June, Jadunath Sarbadhikari, *Tirtha Bhraman* (Calcutta, BS 1322), pp. 465–8. He further recorded under the same date: 'At this place the Goras mad with lust of war are roaming here and there in search of the infantry. If an infantryman conceals himself for fear in any house and the householder does not turn him out, they at once burn the house down.' Ibid., p. 466.

274. *Amar Jivana-Charit*, pp. 93–8.

275. Kaye, *History*, vol. ii, p. 631 n.

276. *NE*, vol. i, Allahabad, p. 7.

277. Macpherson's Gwalior report *FSUP*, vol. iii, p. 182. The circumstances in which the Mutiny broke out earlier in Cawnpore are also instructive: 'An order was issued for the distribution of pay, and they were told to

lay down their arms before receiving it. This created a doubt in their minds, and thus the mutiny commenced. The sepoys declared that they had heard of what occurred in other stations with regiments that had been disarmed, and it remained to be seen what happened here.' Narrative of Events at Cawnpore by Nanakchand, Forrest, *Selections*, vol. III, pp. ccxciii–ccxciv.

278. *Futteh Islam, FSUP*, vol. II, p. 160.

279. Captain Anderson, *A Personal Journal of the Siege of Lucknow*, pp. 10–11, extract in *FSUP*, vol. II, p. 8.

280. '*Futteh Islam*', *FSUP*, vol. II, p. 151.

281. S. Thornton to W.C. Erskine, dated Samthar 21 August 1857, *FSUP*, vol. III, p. 12.

282. *NE*, vol. I, Allahabad, pp. 18–19.

283. Delhi Proclamation, May 1857, *FSUP*, vol. I, p. 438.

284. This is the underlying point in J.F.F.'s novel *Mariam*, by far the most sensitive and illuminating treatment of the secret theme. The examples of rape of white women in 1857 he cites are real historical instances, but to go by the official report on the subject which does not seem to have been available to him, those specific instances were false rumours and not real facts. On the other hand, the central relationship on which the novel turns, the relationship which he did know about straight from the girl's mother and from the girl's own lips, remained unconsummated and was untouched by coercion at any stage. *Mariam* (Benares, 1896). The novel was written after the mother's death, and published from Benares in 1896. The native people's shame, embodied in the 'Kala Feringhees', as Mrs Cooper heard them called, was on the contrary an accomplished fact—a further element in this complex of charged emotions. G.B. Malleson, *History of the Indian Mutiny*, (London, 1878), vol. I, p. 282 n.

285. *FSUP*, vol. I, p. 308.

286. Sen, *Eighteen Fifty-Seven*, pp. 127–8 n.

287. The one relationship during the Mutiny charged with an element of sexuality of which we possess a detailed account, portrayed by J.F.F. under the fictitious names of Mangal Khan, Miss Lavater, and Mariam (Miss Lavater's mother, half French, half Rampur Pathani), but keeping to facts as they really occurred, shows the Mutiny leader, a landholder of Shahjahanpur who captured mother and daughter, asking thrice for Miss Lavater's hand, and being thrice thwarted by Mrs Lavater with various excuses. Mangal Khan's 'fascination' for Miss Lavater (summed up by film director Shyam Benegal in the word *junoon*) may have been

partly due to the fact that she was at least a quarter Indian in blood. Her father, a massacred clerk of the Shahjahanpur Collectorate, was English. The first century of colonial rule does not seem to have produced a generation of Indians who secretly lusted for 'Mem Sahibs'. Mangal Khan's conduct was honourable throughout: when on their final parting he asked for a certificate from Mariam that no molestation had been offered to them, Miss Lavater signed the certificate, and willingly. Barring this exceptional instance, dislike rather than fascination seems to have characterized the Indian male response to the European female in 1857.

288. Memorandum containing the result of enquiries made by desire of the Governor General into the rumours of European females having been dishonoured during the late mutinies, Home Misc. no. 725 India Office Records, cited by Rudrangshu Mukherjee, '"Satan Let Loose Upon Earth": The Kanpur Massacres in India in the Revolt of 1857', *Past and Present*, no. 128, Aug. 1990, pp. 92–116; see also the circulated draft paper.

289. One reason suggested by Rudrangshu Mukherjee for the absence of rape in his paper cited above is that Europeans were considered polluting, so that the preservation of religious and caste purity would have ruled out contact with European females. This reasoning is based on a misconception of the process of ritual pollution. Physical contact with prostitutes, for instance, who have certainly lost caste, is not in itself considered polluting (many Brahman and Rajput sepoys certainly had physical relationships with prostitutes, including of course Muslim and untouchable females in 1857, but they would not accept 'water' from them). What is prohibited in any relationship with a polluted person is the acceptance of water: a prostitute is not, to use the characteristic expression, '*jal chal*' (water accepted). Similarly a European woman would not be '*jal chal*' either. That is the technical sense in which she would be 'untouchable'.

290. C.B. Saunders to W. Muir, 17 Dec. 1857, William Muir, *Records of the Intelligence Department*, vol. I, pp. 375–6.

291. Kaye, *History*, vol. II, p. 355.

292. Memorandum on European females dishonoured, op. cit.

293. *FSUP*, vol. IV, p. 513. When the British returned to Cawnpore they took over the rebel Nannhe Nawab's house to set up a collectorate. Francis Cornwallis Maude, *Memories of the Mutiny, with which is incorporated the Personal Narrative of John Walter Sherer*, 2 vols. (London, 1894), vol. II, p. 420.

294. Kaye, *History*, vol. II, pp. 368–9 n.

295. Maude, *Memories*, vol. I, pp. 109–110.

296. Rudrangshu Mukherjee, 'The Kanpur Massacres'.

297. Sen, *Eighteen Fifty-Seven*, p. 148 ff.

298. Ibid.

299. *FSUP*, vol. I, p. 463.

300. Rajah Maun Singh to the Talookdars, 20 July 1857, Innes, *Lucknow and Oude*, p. 336.

301. *Majha Pravas*, p. 33.

302. The sack of Jhansi by the victorious British: 'The whole city looked like a fiendish burial ground. Due to the dreadful conflagration in the city everything was clearly visible even in the darkness of the night ... Europeans used to set the grass on fire and compelled the persons in hiding to die in the same .... Eleven persons were killed in Agnihotri's house including him. His whole family perished .... They slaughtered people after hunting them from the dark corners of the houses and cells. Even the Dharmashalas and temples were resounding with slaughter and carnage of the great sinners. The most dreadful massacre took place at Koshthipur [weavers' quarter]. There even the poor ladies were put to the sword mercilessly.' *Majha Pravas*, trans. extract from Hindi version, *FSUP*, vol. III, pp. 338–41.

303. The sack of Delhi: 'A party of European soldiers more or less intoxicated entered the house of Ramji Das Mahajur [sic, Mahajan—this was the Gurwala family of bankers who financed the rebel court of Delhi] on pretence of protecting the women of the family but treated them in a shameful manner.' Narrative of Syed Mubarak Shah, *Red Year*, p. 234.

304. Banda on British reoccupation: 'Banda half deserted, no Omla, no clerks .... Station most wantonly destroyed, trees cut down and burnt, church roof taken off, and the building undermined, graveyard destroyed, and all tomb stones torn up and mashed into little bits. Every house entirely destroyed, except the large *pucca* house in which Judge usually resided, which has still a roof but no doors or frames, and the bungalows belonging to the Rajah of Jaloun and Mahomed Bada Khan late Deputy Collector. These two men are rebels and preserved their homes for their own use. Three rooms in the Collector's *cutcherries* have still roofs but there are no doors etc. Judge's *cutcherry* completely destroyed. The flag stones all torn up and removed in all the *cutcherries*. Jail destroyed.' Diary of F.O. Mayne, Magistrate and Collector of Banda, 29 April 1858, *FSUP*, vol. IV, p. 838.

305. There is a glimpse of the inner tension on the score in a conversation between Mangal Khan and his aunt overheard by the widowed prisoner 'Mariam'. His aunt said:

   "'I dont wish to run you down or the cause which you have made your own—the *rebel* cause I mean."

   "The *rebel* cause, the *rebel* cause! so you have always insinuated Chachi," burst he in evident vexation. "Rebels" against whom? Against aliens! Were not they kafirs, whom, with the blessing of the last prophet, we have expelled from the land. To fight with, and to kill them, was therefore not rebellion but a meritorious act surely."' *Mariam*, p. 369.

306. Emperor Bahadur Shah could not be expected to express the thought in terms of didactic logic, but with spontaneous significance he thanked for his exaltation 'that army which had rushed to his protection'. Jivan Lal's diary, 22 July 1857, *Two Narratives*, p. 161.

307. 'The men broke into open mutiny, saying, "We are servants of the King of Delhi ... ."' *FSUP*, vol. III, p. 109. 'It therefore behoves them [the zamindars] to put a speedy end to the infidels and thereby to exhibit their firm attachment to the *Sarkar*.' Lucknow proclamation, 25 Jan. 1858, *FSUP*, vol. II, p. 127.

308. Nana Sahib to Kalkapershed, Canungo, Oude, 9 July 1857: 'Your petition has been received, stating that seven boats containing Europeans were going down the river from Cawnpore, and that two parties of your men joined the Government troops and fired on them so unremittingly that they proceeded, slaying the English, as far as the villages of Abdool Azeez, when the horse artillery and yourself in person joined the rest, and sank six of the boats, the seventh escaping through the force of wind. You have performed a great deed and I am highly pleased with your conduct. Persevere in your devotion to the Government cause.' Kaye, *History*, vol. II, p. 675.

309. Petition from Muhammad Bakht Ali to the Emperor, 10 Aug. 1857, *Trial of Muhammad Bahadur Shah*, p. 109.

310. The Neemuch force reported to the Emperor 'an engagement with the plunderers (English) in which about two hundred men on both sides had fallen.' Jeevan Lal's Diary, 31 July 1857, *Two Narratives*, p. 175.

311. Hukumnamah of Birjis Qadar to Habibullah, 4 Aug. 1857: 'Ibadullah son of Mahammad Hasan Khan Taluqadar of Jalalpur pointing out in his petition the fact of some fugitive Nazarines having taken shelter at his residence, and knowledge of the same to the camel drivers of *Sarkar*, assures to send them with his *vakil* as and when they are called for. I have perused the petition and hence order him to send the accursed

disturbers of peace under the custody of his own men and escort camel drivers of the *Sarkar* to our presence. These enemies of religion and accursed *Vilaities* should be uprooted and driven out from wherever they can be traced out and your so doing will earn for you credit and fame. Consider this order as peremptory and act up to it.' *FSUP*, vol. II, pp. 125–6.

312. Nawab Walidad Khan to King of Delhi, 15 June 1857:

'Your Majesty—I beg to submit as follows:-

The application of the army posted at Bareilly soliciting the honour of kissing your feet reached the hands of this faithful. Hence I am sending you messenger, with every precaution (Bareilly army) should be ordered to stay here with me for the management of the country and the suppression of the Kafirs. The state of the country in the hands of the rebels is most straitened. The few Englishmen left at Meerut are instigating the rebels and malcontents to despoil the people and ruin the country. Although I have annihilated the Firangis stationed at Bulandshahr and have left no trace of them in the district still it is not possible to extirpate them and to carry on the revenue administration without the Royal army. Previously I have sent a number of applications to your Majesty requesting therein to despatch an army and these must have probably been perused by your Majesty. Now either out of your patronage and sympathy for the poor, your Majesty should kindly be so indulgent as to give orders to the above-mentioned army or despatch one platoon of Cavalry, one contingent of Infantry and one train of Artillery to me. May the sun of your glory and fortune ever remain constant'. *FSUP*, vol. v, p. 67.

Rani of Anupshahr to King of Delhi, 26 August 1857:

(Salutations)—Sir! The state of affairs here is this—Raja Ambey Rao, my (supporter) had ever been faithful and obedient to your *Sarkar* till his death. After his death I remained without any supporter at my place and entertained hope from you. I thank God that in spite of rebellion and the extirpation of the heathens, the management of Anupshahr is by God's grace in tact and there has been no plundering here uptil now. But the realisation of revenue has stopped. I, therefore implore your Majesty, the Shadow of God, that you will most graciously extend the grant of *Farman* of administration to my name so that I may realise the revenue from the *ilaqa* of Bulandshahr and send the same to you.

Submitted. May the sun of your prosperity and success over shine.' *FSUP*, vol. v, pp. 73–4.

313. 'The union of the Rajahs of Oudh and the surrounding Rajahs of Allahabad etc. and the aid given in men, ammunition and money by the Emperor of India and by Mirza Birjees Kudur, the Ruler of Lucknow, added to the assistance of the population of all creeds is (sic) sufficient proof of the will of the Almighty God in extirpating the "Taghee Baghee Nisaras" (fraudulent and mutinous Christians).' *FSUP*, vol. IV, p. 615. For an alternative translation see text over f.n. 189: '... the people are determined to extirpate these rebel Christians now'.

314. Proclamation at Thana Bhawan, Muzaffarnagar, *FSUP*, vol. V, p. 128.

315. Mahommed Hasan Khan to Kyrooddeen, 16th *Rubee ool sanee*, Sen, *Eighteen Fifty-Seven*, p. 389. Alternatively, take the case of the *taluqdar* Beni Madho, who was offered an opportunity to submit after being defeated. 'In the reply of the letter, he took high ground as a faithful subject of the king of Oude, and told the rajah, that one king was all he could serve, and that he had pledged his fealty to Birjies Kudr, and should not desert him or his cause.' *FSUP*, vol. II, p. 548. 'He proved his sincerity at heavy cost; for though offered his life, his lands, the redress of injuries, the full investigation of grievances—he rejected all, and became a homeless wanderer in the Terai, for the sake of the Begum and her son, to whom he had sworn fealty.' *FSUP*, vol. II, p. 627.

316. Proclamation of Mohd. Ramzan Ali Bahadur Birjees Kudr, 17 July 1857, *FSUP*, vol. I, p. 450.

317. Proclamation of Begum of Oudh, *FSUP*, vol. I, pp. 465–6.

318. Rana Beni Madho Bakhsh Bahadur to Ahmad Ullah Shah, 6 June 1858: 'Birndaban, the rebel, resident of Ghatampur who, by his ill luck, had joined the heathens, has been caught after a severe battle in which about 13 of our men were wounded.' *FSUP*, vol. I, p. 394.

319. Petition of Raja of Ballabhgarh, '"To the King!" "To the King!" Shelter of the World!' 31 July 1857, *Trial of Muhammad Bahadur Shah*, p. 55.

320. Jivan Lal's diary, 31 July 1857, *Two Narratives*, p. 176.

321. The idea occurs in the order of Bahadur Shah to the ruler of Kutch (Bhoj) expressing pleasure that 'you, ever faithful one, having put the whole of the infidels to the sword, have thoroughly cleansed and purified your domains of their unclean presence.' *Trial of Muhammad Bahadur Shah*, p. 107. The Emperor was misinformed, but for our purpose the notable feature is that the English were expected to be expelled not from one consolidated block of national or imperial territory, but from each princely dominion.

322. Maude, *Memories of the Mutiny*, vol. I, pp. 146, 202; *Majha Pravas*, p. 70.

323. A. Shakespeare to R. Alexander, Commissioner of Rohilkhand, 2 Aug. 1858, *FSUP*, vol. v, p. 331.

324. Evidence of Chuni Lal, pedlar, *Trial of Muhammad Bahadur Shah*, p. 146.

325. Evidence of Mukund Lal, ibid., p. 163.

326. Ibid.

327. Order to the Kotwal of the City, 28 July 1857, *FSUP*, vol. i, p 421.

328. Narrative of Syed Mubarak Shah, *Red Year*, p. 218.

329. Sherer's narrative, Maude, *Memories of the Mutiny*, vol. i, p. 141.

330. Ibid., p. 146.

331. *NE*, vol. i, p. 526; *FSUP*, vol. iv p, 566.

332. *NE*, vol. i, p. 526.

333. *NE*, vol. i, p. 526–8.

334. *NE*, vol. i, p. 555.

335. *Majha Pravas*, p. 62. Deposition of Madar Bux, Jamadar of Orderlies attached to Captain Gordon of Jhansi, 23 March 1858: 'After the *Sahibs* were killed, the Ranee proclaimed that, "The World is God's, the Country is the Padshah's, and the Raj is Ranee Luchmee Bai's". Before this the Teelungas had (also) proclaimed. The sepoys and the Ranee were in communication. The sepoys asked the Ranee to give them 125,000 Rupees for the Guddee which she agreed to do, and gave 15,000 but that night news came that the Gwalior Contingent was coming and the mutineers left Jhansee.' *FSUP*, vol. iii, pp. 38–9.

336. Mutiny Narrative, Hamirpur, *FSUP*, vol. iii, pp. 116, 118.

337. Translation of the diary of Nunna Nawab, Forrest, *Selections*, vol. iii, p. xii; W.J. Shepherd, *A Personal Narrative of the Outbreak and Massacre at Cawnpore During the Sepoy Revolt of 1857* (New Delhi, 1980 rpt, 1st pub. *Delhi Gazette* 1862), p. 85.

338. Nanak Chand's diary, 7 July 1857, ibid., p. cccxxxi.

339. Maude, *Memories of the Mutiny*, vol. ii, p. 420. 'A family who had made large sums of money at Lucknow in the old days, had got sufficiently over the border to secure their property by settling at Cawnpore, and lived there, enjoying their wealth, and the rank they received at the Oudh capital. There were three brothers, all Nawabs, and two of them undoubtedly joined the Nana; whilst with regard to the third, who was called the Nanha Nawab, or little Nawab, some believed his loyalty, and some did not.' Their house was confiscated as the new British Cutcherry, one brother was hanged, and Nanhe Nawab left India to live in Mecca a year or so after the Mutiny.

340. Kaye, *History*, vol. II, pp. 350–1.

341. The '*Rajya*' (realm) of Kalpi, worth Rs 56 lakhs according to Godase, became a revenue unit with a *tahsildari* office set up by Tayta Tope, from which authority was exercised over the military operations in the country south of the Jumna all the way to Gwalior and Bundelkhand. It was a strongly defended base of the Peshwai and the Gwalior Contingent, *Majha Pravas*, p. 63 ff.

342. *FSUP*, vol. I, p. 53; *FSUP*, vol. III, p. 347 ff.

343. Draft of Rules for the Government of Nawab Ali Bahadur found in the Nawab's private writing desk: 'Efforts should be made to establish terms of sincere friendship with Nana Sahib and complete submission and obedience should be shown to the Noble Emperor. An intelligent and learned person shall be appointed Wukeel and sent to Cawnpore through whom letters will be frequently forwarded to the Nana. Nothing important should be done without reference to him. Even the people of Ujoygarh are not to be expelled without consulting him. To secure the perpetuity of this Government prudent measures should be taken to procure a writing from the Nana or a firman from the Emperor giving permission to govern this country.' *FSUP*, vol. IV, p. 617.

344. *FSUP*, vol. III, 355–6, 369–70, 381–405, 446–7.

345. Tapti Roy, 'The Uprising of the Thakurs of Bundelkhand in 1857', Aligarh Seminar on Rebellion of 1857, p. 26.

346. Sarfaraz Begam to Jan-i-Jan Begam: 'Tilangas have thrown Lucknow into convulsion. Reaching from Fyzabad Maulvi Ahmed Ullah Shah has put a stop to these activities of pillage and plunder and has set up police posts. He has a considerable following of pigheaded persons.' *FSUP*, vol. II, p. 102. 'The people alarmed at the license of the troops, began to desert the place, and to remove their valuables in the dead of the night …. There seemed to be only one leader with the will to help and the Moulvi Ahmudoolla, always anxious to be acknowledged as the head of the Government, warned the troops that they must desist, and appointed police officers, with large rapacious retinues, to enforce his authority. He had it proclaimed that the citizens might put to death all persons attempting to plunder them, and taking up his abode in the beautiful building know as the Observatory, adopted all the airs and ceremonials of royalty. The party in the palace, annoyed at an impertinence that threatened to arrest their ambitious projects, incited the troops to resent the proclamation; and the Moulvi was robbed and ignominiously driven from the Observatory to which he was afterwards suffered to return only at the entreaty of the Mahomedan cavalry. He had not yet obtained the ascendancy over the Hindu troops that

subsequently gave so much trouble to the Begum and her supporters.'
T.H. Cavanagh, *How I Won the Victoria Cross* (London, 1860), extract
in *FSUP*, vol. ii, p. 139.

347. Statement of Mir Wajid Ali Darogah, 8 July 1859, *FSUP*, vol. ii, pp. 81–
3; Statement of Moonshi Wajid Ali, 29 June 1859, *FSUP*, vol. ii, p. 97.

348. *Qaisar-i-Tawarikh*, vol ii: 'The officers began to talk together. Some
said the boy was very young, others that he was handsome and delicate
and therefore could not be expected to do (hard) work; others accosted
him: "You should never become slothful and negligent. We make you
king:" Then they said, " We put you some questions and will make you
our ruler if you agree. The *first* is—we will submit a petition to the
King of Delhi and then you will become our ruler, in case, he agrees.
You will be called a King or Wazier just as the King of Delhi chooses,
and will have to make allegiance to him. *Secondly*, our pay should be
increased two-fold i.e. the *Tilangas* should now be given Rs. 12 and not
6 as before. *Thirdly*—All officers of the *Paltan* should be appointed by
our consent. Fourthly—The *Naib* and the *Diwan* will be appointed
and dismissed by us and nothing will be done except by the orders of
this Council or Court. Fifthly—All the arrears of pay we did not receive
from the British will be given to us now ... ." Thus a few minutes before
sunset the King was crowned and the astrologers predicted that his
reign would be short. Shihab Uddin and Barkat Ahmad, the *Risaladars*
of the *Risala* placed the crown on Birjis Qadr's head and offered
congratulations.' *FSUP*, vol. ii, pp. 87–8.

349. Written statement of Matta Deen, 5 July 1859, *FSUP*, vol. ii, p. 90.

350. Qaisar-ut-Tawarikh, extract, *FSUP*, vol. ii, p. 89.

351. Statement of Syed Eusuf then living in Ismail Gunge, darogah of
Shahinshah Mahal: 'They [the soldiery] therefore 8 or 10 days after
placing Birjis Kudr on the throne formed this Court ... . This Court
used to assemble in the Tara Kothee 2 or 3 times a week for deliberation.
But as soon as disputes arose between the Moulvi Ahmed Ola Shah
and Mummoo Khan [Begam's favourite] they [the sepoy officers of the
Court] divided, the majority joining the two latter and the few under
the Moulvee still remaining in the Tara Kothee.

'Nobody paid much attention to the Moulvee's Court, but
deliberations of the other one were submitted to the Begum, who on
confirming them forwarded them to Shruf-od-Dowla, who gave any
orders to the Chuckladars, himself sending others for execution to
Mummoo Khan, to be carried out in the different Departments ... .'
FSUP, vol. ii, 114.

352. *The Bengal Harkaru and India Gazette*, April 1858, *FSUP*, vol. ii, p. 145.

353. Lucknow news, 8 Dec. 1857, *FSUP*, vol. ii, p. 258.

354. Saiyid Zaheer Husain Jafri, 'The Profile of a Saintly Rebel—Ahmadullah Shah', Aligarh Seminar on Rebellion of 1857.

355. 'Futteh Islam', probably circulated at the instance of Maulvi Ahmadulla Shah, *FSUP*, vol. ii, pp. 154, 155–6. The *maulvi* objected to the sepoy's choice of Birjis Qadr on the ground that jihad could only be led by an Imam and that the creed of the Imam should be the same as that of the mujahids. Jihad, he maintained, was not obligatory on the Shias, and if Birjis Qadr, a Shia, were to be leader, the essential condition of jihad would not be fulfilled. The fight with the British would then no longer be a holy war, and the mujahids could not participate in such a war except in self defence. As they had taken the leading part in the fight, they should be allowed to be led by an Imam Akbar. The *maulvi* further maintained that he had arrived to fight at the behest of his *pir*, and the Imamate should legitimately be his. Fath Muhammad Taib, *Tawarikh-i-Ahmadi* (*masnavi* composed in 1863 by a disciple of the *maulvi*), cited in ibid. It should be noted however, that in *Risala Fath-i-Islam*, the *maulvi* recognized the suzerainty of the Mughal Emperor. *FSUP*, vol. ii, p. 156.

356. *NE*, vol. i, Allahabad, p. 12. The account adds: 'The insurgents consisted chiefly of the followers of the rebel zemindars of Chail and the bad characters of the city and the station, principally low-bred Mussulmans and others, who were induced to take up arms, in the hope of finding sufficient plunder in the station'. Jadunath Sarbadhikari's diary in Bengali is more specific: 'Having witnessed such power of the 6th Infantry over the officers, the inhabitants there, some eighteen hundred Prayagis, assembled and a Musalman named Mir Saheb with the thousand of his own caste and two thousand Mewatis joined the infantry, trying mightily to overthrow the Raj of the Company Bahadur.' *Tirtha-Bhraman*, p. 478.

357. Jadunath Sarbadhikari, *Tirtha-Bhraman*, p. 479. The diarist seems to have omitted the first clause, 'God's Creation'.

358. *NE*, vol. i, p. 12.

359. *NE*, vol. i, p. 12 ff.

360. Letter dated 19 Sept. 1857 in Rev. Alexander Duff, *The Indian Rebellion, Its Causes and Results*: 'An intelligent gentleman in Agra writing of the state of things when the British were obliged to abandon the city and retire into the fort, says,—"The populace was all in arms and there was nothing but plundering, most of the Hindustanies (i.e. country-Hindus) joined the Mohammedans. The Mohammedans to a man are against the British Government, and three-fourths of the Hindustanies."' *FSUP*, vol. v, p. 847.

361. *NE*, vol. II, pp. 64–5.

362. In the absence of other ideas, the Lucknow Government proclaimed the 'resumption' of its rule in Allahabad by 'appointing' its loyal servant, Mehndi Husain, as *nazim* of Allahabad. The measure was not totally impractical, for many *taluqdars* and *zamindars* of the *parganas* of the Allahabad district lying to the north of the Ganges joined the war operations of the Awadh authorities against the British. F.O. Mayne, Joint Magistrate of Gopeegunge, to the Commissioner of Allahabad, 24 Sept. 1857, *FSUP*, vol. IV, pp. 653–4. Similarly, Muhammad Hasan Khan, that other loyal servant of the throne of Awadh, was appointed *nazim* of Gorakhpur, for long a part of the British territory of the North-West Provinces, but at one time a dependency of Awadh. He declared proudly: '... I, with God's help, restored Gorakhpore to the Kingdom of Oude, to which it had been in former times attached ... .' Muhammad Hasan Khan to Khyrooddeen, 24 Oct. 1858, *FSUP*, vol. IV, p. 388.

363. The diary of Jadunath Sarbadhikari gives the words in Bengali: '*Muluk Patisahar, hukum panchajanar ... .*' I have taken the liberty to render it into what must, it appears to me, have been the original Hindustani words. It may be rendered *Mulk Padshah ki, hukum Panch ki.*' As before, the diarist omits mention of the first clause, Khalq khuda ki.

364. Jadunath Sarbadhikari, *Tirtha-Bhraman*, p. 447.

365. *FSUP*, vol. IV, p. 243 and passim.

366. With such idea in force among them, the rebels were in a quandary in those areas where the princes opposed their cause. Thus the opposition of the Scindia paralysed the Gwalior Contingent and prevented it at a crucial moment from joining the operations of the mutineers. Deprived of the backing of the prince to whom they naturally looked up for leadership, the sepoys at Gwalior eventually rallied under 'a green flag for the Mohammedans, a white flag for the Hindoos', instead of the 'Scindia's banner'. *FSUP*, vol. III, p. 192. Even so, they would not move against their master. The Scindia was finally driven from Gwalior only when the Peshwa, his own ancient master, moved in force against him. The Holkar similarly opposed the Mutiny in Indore, and the rebels, lacking an alternative plan, were reduced to proclaiming government in the name of the Holkar when they tore down the British flag. Bhadani, 'The 1857 Revolt in the Indore Residency'.

367. *NE*, vol. II, p. 183.

368. Deposition of Hubbooa Crier, trial of Khan Bahadur Khan, *FSUP*, vol. V, p. 599.

369. Mutiny Narrative, Moradabad, *FSUP*, vol. V, p. 329.

370. Deposition of Joseph Dore, 16 Feb. 1859, *FSUP*, vol. v, p. 752.

371. Jiwan Lal's diary, 4 Sept., *Two Narratives*, pp. 219–220.

372. Evidence of Hakim Ahsan Ulla, *Trial of Muhammad Bahadur Shah*, p. 268; Narrative of Mainodin, *Two Narratives*, p. 69.

373. Evidence of Hakim Ahsan Ulla, *Trial of Muhammad Bahadur Shah*, pp. 273–4; Narrative of Mainodin, p. 69. In strictly technical terms this was a departure from ancient historical tradition as Rohilkhand was a dependency of Awadh and as such not entitled to address the Emperor directly. In other respects the rebels clung to the ancient historical forms: thus the Nawab of Banda sent his Vakil to the Peshwa at Cawnpore. Quite correctly, he sent no embassy to Delhi; nor did Kunwar Singh, who paid his allegiance to his ancestral sovereign, the Nawab of Awadh. See Ahsanullah Khan's evidence, p. 3.

374. Evidence of Hakim Ahsan Ullah, pp. 273, 275.

375. Ibid., p. 275. This appointment ran contrary to Lucknow's resolve to re-annex the province of Allahabad by the appointment of Mehndie Husain as its *nazim*. As Delhi fell shortly and Liakat Ali himself became a fugitive in Awadh, conducting operations there and issuing proclamations under the seal of Birjis Qadr, there was of course no question of his asserting the claim. *FSUP*, vol. ii, pp. 160 n, 423–4, 428.

376. Evidence of Hakim Ahsan Ullah, *Trial of Muhammad Bahadur Shah*, p. 273.

377. Order to Walidad Khan, 16 May 1857, *Trial of Muhammad Bahadur Shah*, p. 182.

378. Diary of Jiwan Lal, 7 July 1857, *Two Narratives*, p. 142.

379. *FSUP*, vol. v, pp. 667–9.

380. Ibid., pp. 678, 683, 875–6.

381. N.K. Nigam, *Delhi in 1857* (New Delhi, 1957), p. 92.

382. Stokes, *Peasant Armed*, p. 117 and passim.

383. Pratul Chandra Gupta, *Nana Sahib and the Rising at Cawnpore* (Oxford, 1963), p. 86.

384. *FSUP*, vol. iv, pp. 589–90.

385. Circular letter to chiefs of Bundelcund by Mahomed Esak, 2 Jan. 1858.

386. *Sepoy to Subedar*, p. 160.

387. Stokes, *Peasant Armed*, p. 65. The Sixth Regiment in Allahabad, having plundered the treasury, disbanded itself. Each sepoy, weighed down with three or four bags of a thousand rupees each, set out for his village, and was relieved of his load by the people of the villages on the way. Kaye, *History*, vol. ii, p. 259. The diary of an opium *gumashtah* on leave

in Cawnpore also makes an indirect reference to the process of dissolution of the sepoy forces: 'Those sepoys who were returning to their homes, taking with them what plunder they had collected were in turn despoiled of their ill-gotten gains by the zemindars.' *FSUP*, vol. IV, p. 507. As against this, many regiments fought on till their final defeat. With regard to the Gwalior Contingent, it is no earlier than 9 June 1858 that news came 'that most of those who are natives of Oude have given up the cause as desperate and are slipping away to their homes, bent, if possible on seeing obscurity as agriculturist.' *FSUP*, vol. III, p. 428. Thus did a peasant army finally dissolve into the peasant mass, but only in gradual stages. Until that happened, the rebellion in the countryside did not dissolve into isolated locales. Significantly, the retainers of the chiefs began to preponderate over the sepoys among the fighting forces in Awadh and Bundelkhand, where the rebellion lasted longer than anywhere else in the last stages of the war. Consider the following Abstract of Intelligence, 26 March 1858; 'The Tantia has under him about 25,000 men, among these there are 2000 mutinous sepoys. The rest of the force is composed of the followers of the Chiefs of Shahgurh and Banpore, of Deisput, Adil Mahomud Khan and the Chief of Nurwur.' *FSUP*, vol. III, p. 305.

388. The mutinous sepoys of Cawnpore, in the initial act of negation, tore off the regimental colours and broke out from their lines and discipline was never quite restored again. 'The men', said three sepoys in their depositions in trial, 'did as they liked. No, they did not dress in uniform.' A native officer of the Bombay Army on leave in his village near Kanpur saw that 'the Native Officers were much bullied by the Sepoys who did as they liked ...' R. Mukherjee, 'The Cawnpore Massacres'.

389. There was a strong emphasis on maintaining collective identity in the regiments and contingents that had mutinied, which in turn helped in giving an integral character to the rebellion of the people. Macpherson's report, 10 February 1858, says with reference to the Gwalior Contingent: 'Against our rule the Contingent apparently acted as one man.' *FSUP*, vol. III, p. 183.

390. The Commissioner of Allahabad, anxious at the collective move of the Gwalior Contingent, wrote to the Government of India on 27 October 1857: 'The Contingent is a formidable body, unbroken as yet, well equipped, and numerous, with field guns, and a second class siege train.' *FSUP*, vol. IV, p. 434. Iqtidar Alam Khan observes in this connection: 'The rebel leaders of the Contingent appeared to be endeavouring from the very beginning to prevent its dissolution into small bands headed by individual native officers.' The device which

the rebel leaders adopted to keep the contingent intact was to take the unique step of electing a new commanding officer with the designation of general. Inayat Ali, till then subedar-major of the 1st Infantry Regiment, replaced the English general in that position. The Contingent subsequently inflicted a defeat on General Windham in the Battle of Cawnpore on 27 November 1857: 'the only occasion during the 1857 rebellion when rebel force was able to defeat an English army of a matching strength in an open battle'. Iqtidar Alam Khan, 'Gwalior Contingent in 1857–8. Organization and Ideology of the Sepoy Rebels', Aligarh Seminar on Rebellion of 1857.

391. The consequence of the lack of one commander-in-chief for all the fighting regiments was severe infighting, of which the most violent example occurred in Farrukhabad. The 10th Native Infantry, having mutinied at Farrukhabad, set up the ex-Nawab of Farrukhabad on the throne with a royal salute, and seized the money in the treasury. At this time two regiments that had mutinied in Sitapur, the 41st NI, and 10th Oude Locals, clashed with the 10th NI over the sharing of the treasure, and men were killed on both sides. An agreement was then reached between the contending regiments over the sharing of the spoils, but faithless to promise the 10th NI looted the treasure: 'it was a regular rush to see who could get most'. The sepoys with the loot dispersed here and there, the greater number crossing the Ganges. The 41st NI and the 10th Oude Locals, thus deceived by the 10 NI, plundered the bazaar in their rage. Two companies of the 10th NI imprudently remained behind, went to the Nawab and posted themselves in the city gardens. The 41st NI and the 10th Oude Locals wished the Nawab to compel the 10th NI to attack the fort in which the English had taken refuge. The 10th NI did not like the idea, a fight ensued, and nearly all the 10th were killed and the rest were ordered out of town by the Nawab. The 41st NI and the 10th Oude Locals were now urged by him to attack the fort, but they prevaricated. However, the fort was eventually taken and the Europeans fled, to be massacred on the way. *NE*, vol. II, pp. 129–33.

392. *From Sepoy to Subedar*, p. 174.

393. Maj.-Gen. Hugh Rose to Maj.-Gen. W.M. Mansfield, 22 June 1858, regarding forces at Kalpi: 'The rebel army was composed of the Gwalior Contingent, the finest men, best drilled and organized, Native Troops of all arms in India; other mutinous Bengal Infantry Regiments, such as the 52nd; Rebel Cavalry from Kotah; and a chosen band of *Valaitees*, the whole reinforced by the Force of all Arms of the Nawab of Banda, comprising a great deal of mutinous Bengal Cavalry, of which the 5th

Irregulars, dressed in their red uniforms, formed a part. All the Sepoy Regiments kept up, carefully, their English equipment and organization; the words of command for drill, grand rounds, etc., were given, as we could hear, at night, in English.' *FSUP*, vol. III, p. 388. This is not an isolated instance. Cf. Gubbins on the Lucknow scene during the siege of the Residency: 'We were continually insulted by the music of the mutineers. At early dawn their bugles regularly began sounding the assembly, and a variety of regiment calls; while the shrill horns and drums of the Rujwarra (a name used to designate the zemindarree forces) kept up loud and dissonant screams, which were again renewed every evening. Occasionally the bands paraded in our sight and played "God save the Queen", or other tunes which they had learned in our service.' *The Mutinies in Oudh*, p. 220.

394. Lieut.-Col. F.J. Wroughton's letter of 31 Oct. 1857 regarding Mehndie Husain's attacking forces from Awadh in the Banaras theatre of operations: 'There cannot be a doubt that the Nazim had a large number of mutineers, both Artillery and Infantry, attached to his force. The Artillery was manned by experienced gunners.' *FSUP*, vol. IV, p. 224. Narrative of Events for Gorakhpur: 'A large body of Bhojpore sepoys about 2000 in number, with 2 H.A. [Horse Artillery] guns of the troop which mutinied at Neemuch, have joined Kooer Singh at Azimgarh. The rest, all natives of Oudh, or our Eastern Provinces, about 1500 in number, with two iron guns, and two remaining guns of the Neemuch troop, have joined the Rajah of Gonda. These two latter bodies are probably mostly sepoys who have mutinied ....' *FSUP*, vol. IV, p. 321.

395. Sec., Central Provinces, to Sec., India, dated Banaras, 15 Oct 1857: 'On the next day news was received from Azimghur which tallied with that received from Jounpore, and the actual advance of what are called regiments of sepoys and *ressalahs* of cavalry are spoken of. Whatever these so-called regiments are *ressalahs* may be, the Lieutenant-Governor believes that they certainly are not any of our old organised regiments,' *FSUP*, vol. II, p. 216.

396. See proclamation proposing the organization of the troops, 6 July 1857 (Nana Sahib's blueprint): 'In every Regiment, whether of Infantry or of Cavalry there will be one Colonel as Commanding Officer, one Major as second in command under him; and one Adjutant .... The Officer who shall be appointed as Adjutant shall drill the Regiment and teach them manoeuvres and perform all other duties which from of old appertain to the post of Adjutant.' The blueprint also proposed to retain the Court Martial for trying army offenders. *FSUP*, vol. IV, pp. 605–7.

397. The sepoys had higher pay and status and the *nujeebs* were jealous of them. Lucknow news, 21 Dec. 1857: 'Today there was fight at the Begum's palace between the sepoys and *Nujeebs*, in which 10 men were killed, and it was with great difficulty that the Officers settled matters.' *FSUP*, vol. II, p. 259.

398. Bandyopadhyay, *Amar Jivan Charit*, p. 298.

399. Ibid., pp. 298–9.

400. News from Gwalior, up to 15 June 1858, *FSUP*, vol. III, p. 433.

401. Narrative of Events for Gorakhpur for the week ending 5 April 1858, *FSUP*, vol. IV, p. 321.

402. A new kind of unity was brought about through the process of mutual bargaining within the ranks, which of course contained many diverse elements. The Gwalior Contingent, for instance, contained Purbeahs, Gwalior men, and men from the north, such as Vilaitis and Rohilkhand Pathans. The men of the north and of Gwalior wanted to move on Delhi while the Purbeahs' instinct was to strike out for Cawnpore. Yet in the final analysis the Gwalior Contingent moved in one united mass. Macpherson's report, *FSUP*, vol. III, p. 190 ff.

403. Deposition of Bhondu Singh, *FSUP*, vol. IV, p. 100.

404. Charles Ball, *History of the Indian Mutiny* (London, n.d.), vol. 1, pp. 299–300.

405. Translation of Munshi Jan Ali Khan's Persian communication, 24 Jan. 1858, cited in Khushhalilal Srivastava, *The Revolt of 1857 in Central India-Malwa* (Bombay, 1966), p. 133.

406. Macpherson's report, *FSUP*, vol. III, pp. 189, 192.

407. Srivastava, *Revolt in Malwa*, p. 133.

408. Jivan Lal's diary, 2 July 1857, *Two Narratives*, p. 134. Bakht Khan was described by his own commanding officer, Captain Waddy, to have been 'sixty years of age; to have served the Company for forty years; his height about five feet ten inches; forty four inches round the chest; family of Hindu extraction, but converted under temptation of territorial acquisition; a very bad rider, owing to large stomach and round thighs, but clever, and a good drill.' Cooper, *Crisis in Punjab*, p. 108. Despite the stigma of Hindu origin in the camp, Bakht Khan was not deterred from pushing his claims to foreign Muslim extraction and on a second occasion he told the emperor that he was related to the royal family of Awadh and requested an enquiry to confirm this. Bahadur Shah said that there was no need as he was assuredly of noble family. Bakht Khan persisted: he wanted a formal inquiry because after expelling the English from Delhi, Meerut, and Agra, he would press

his claim to some mark of distinction. Obviously claims to leadership required the qualification of high birth in the eyes of the sepoys. Jivan Lal's diary, 11 July 1857, p. 146.

409. Rajah Maun Singh to the Talookdars, 20 July 1857, Innes, *Lucknow and Oude*, p. 335.

410. Evidence of Hakim Ahsan Ulla, *Trial of Muhammad Bahadur Shah*, p. 263.

411. Cawnpore was something of an exception. Here the sepoys, after an initial move towards Delhi, returned at Nana Sahib's persuasion, but never set up an organized council of their own. However, here, too, as the imprisoned W.J. Shepherd observed, the troopers 'took the lead in everything ... and openly declared that they did not care for the Nana. They even went to greater lengths in this usurpation of authority by causing every proclamation to be accompanied with the words "hookoom sipah Bahadur ka (i.e. by order of the brave soldiery)"'. Shepherd, *A Personal Narrative*, p. 85.

412. After the Bareilly Brigade left for Delhi, Khan Bahadur Khan called together a council composed of his Hindu *diwan* Sobha Ram and three Rohilla notables, Madar Ali Khan, Ahmad Shah Khan, and Mubarak Shah Khan, and after some discussion it was decided to appoint a committee for the trial of cases. The members, none of whom were sepoys, were Karamat Khan (descendant of the last Rohilla ruler Hafiz Rahmat Khan), Akbar Ali Khan (relative of Khan Bahadur Khan), Ghulam Hamza (*qazi* of Bareilly), Pundit Ojhar Tegh Nath (head pandit of the new ruler), Muzaffar Husain Khan (descendant of Hafiz Rahmat Khan), Jafar Ali Khan (a wealthy zamindar), Jaimal Singh (*thakur* of Keara), and Qalb Ali Shah (influential Muslim of the old city). This committee conducted business during the entire duration of Khan Bahadur Khan's reign, but real authority lay with him alone. Narrative of Occurrences by J.D. Inglis, dated Bareilly 30 Nov. 1858, *FSUP*, vol. v, pp. 285–6. For a list of the principal officers in the confidence of Rani Lakshmi Bai, both civil and military, see abstract of intelligence, Jhansi, 8 March 1858, *FSUP*, vol. iii, p. 285. The Rani's military officers were her own, not sepoy officers.

413. 'Futteh Islam,' *FSUP*, vol. ii, p. 152.

414. *NE*, vol. ii, Farrukhabad, p. 135.

415. Ibid.

416. Order from Emperor without seal or signature to Mirza Mughal, no date (apparently 21 May 1857): '... whenever the most distinguished officers of the highest ranks in the service of the British Government

visited the palace, they dismounted at the door of the Hall of Audience, and came thence on foot. These soldiery, however, used till recently, to come galloping up to the Hall of Audience on their horses, and as a last resort, both the gates were closed with a wicket only being left open; but they still ride up to the Hall of Audience, and Jalwa Khana, unsuitably dressed, and without their turbands in utter disregard to the forms of respect due to royalty. The officers of the army too make a practice of coming into court carelessly dressed, wearing caps instead of turbands and carrying their swords. Never during the British rule did any members of their profession behave in this way.' Bahadur Shah was so shocked that he expressed a resolve to don the garb of a fakir, proceed to the shrine of the Khwaja Sahib, 'and after making the necessary arrangements for the journey, to go eventually to Mecca'. *Trial of Muhammad Bahadur Shah*, pp. 220–3. No less shocking to contemporary sensitivities was the behaviour of the sepoys at the coronation of Birjis Qadr: 'It was so hot that Mirza Birjis Qadar had to leave his seat and come outside riding the *Tamjam*. The Tilangas began to fire cartridges in place of offering *salami*. Mirza Birjis Qadar entered the palace frightened and the firing of guns caused some consternation there. The *Tilangas* wanted to force entrance into the palace. Upon this, Qasim Khan *Naib Risaladar* set guards but nobody desisted.' *Qaisar-ut-Tawarikh*, extracts in *FSUP*, vol. II, pp. 87–9.

417. Jiwan Lal's diary, 12 May 1857, *Two Narratives*, p. 87.

418. Written defence of Bahadur Shah, *Trial of Muhammad Bahadur Shah*, p. 230.

419. T.H. Cavanagh, *How I Won the Victoria Cross* (London, 1860), extract in *FSUP*, vol. II, p. 140.

420. Ibid.

421. A spy of the British thus wrote from Delhi: 'The Kote (Court) also comprises five sepoys from every regiment and Maulvie Fuzul Huq.' Syed Moinul Haq, *The Great Revolution of 1857* (Pakistan Historical Society, Karachi, 1968), p. 128.

422. S.A.A. Razvi, *Swatantra Dilli* (Hindi, Publications Bureau, UP, 1957), p. 70; *FSUP*, vol. I, p. 419.

423. *Trial of Muhammad Bahadur Shah*, p. 64.

424. Ibid., pp. 64–5.

425. King to Mirza Mughal, 15 July 1857, Ibid., p. 66.

426. Hakim Ahsanullah Khan's evidence on King's administrative policy, ibid., p. 280 ff; King to Mirza Mughal, no date, ibid., pp. 99–100.

427. Narrative of Syed Mubarak Shah, *Red Year*, p. 192. Chaos was by no means unique to the country surrounding Delhi, as the NWP Police Commissioner Lieutenant-Colonel William's report on the Depositions of sixty-three Native and Half-caste Witnesses in Cawnpore makes abundantly clear: 'Such was the state of Cawnpore and its neighbourhood, under the brief reign of the arch-rebel Nana. Courts were formed, which shamelessly mocked at justice, wherein Baba Bhut, the Nana's elder brother, presided, seated on a billiard table .... The city was kept in continual alarm by reported intentions to plunder, being threatened alike by mutineers in search of wealth and insurgent Zemindars or landholders thirsting to be avenged on the commercial classes, who had bought estates when sold by the decree of the Civil Courts. Some wards of the city banded themselves together to check the mutineers, and even drove off a party of the 2nd Cavalry with brick-bats. The mutineers, when separated from their comrades, were disarmed and plundered by the insurgent population, so that it was only in large masses they dared to move through the country .... The state of the city and the surrounding districts, as described by eye-witnesses, gives the same features as elsewhere of rebel rule. The leaders exhibited no semblance of power or justice, and anarchy reigned predominant. The lawless seized the opportunity and revelled in rapine and plunder. Each avenged his real or imaginary wrongs. Every man's hand was against his fellow.' Cited in Maude, *Memories*, vol. I, pp. 115. Colonel Williams was of course profoundly prejudiced, though Mubarak Shah's evidence cannot be similarly indicted. What we must bear in mind is that the rebels were unable to create consolidated zones of administration around Delhi and Cawnpore. In Awadh, Rohilkhand, Farrukhabad, and Jhansi, where the country around the principal centre of rebel administration united with the city rebels in the expulsion of the British, signs of consolidation of rebel rule were visible amidst the chaos accompanying the collapse of the colonial administration. No such consolidations could take place in the Delhi country, the Upper Doab, Cawnpore, and Allahabad because of the early establishment of the British army of the Punjab on the Ridge, the continuing English military presence in Meerut on the Upper Doab, and the rapid advance of the army of Neill and Havelock from Banaras to Allahabad and Cawnpore. The presence of readily identifiable elements of traditional chiefship in Awadh, Rohilkhand, and Jhansi (to a lesser extent, Farrukhabad also) helped the rebels, too—such elements being absent in the Upper Doab, Cawnpore, and Allahabad.

428. Order from king, without signature, cypher or seal, to Mirza Mughal, no date: 'Again, notwithstanding that they have uselessly wasted the

whole of the magazine stores, and the money that was in the treasury, they now clamorously demand allowances daily, and above all, daily take allowances for more men than are present. Besides this, with oppression and violence they forcibly take away the wares of the shop-keepers in the city without paying for them, and commit, moreover, every variety of other excesses and aggressions imaginable. The state of things outside the city also demands notice. In consequence of no military troops going out to keep order, hundreds of people are being murdered, and the property of thousands is being plundered. As regards the civil administration of the country, in consequence of the insufficiency of the royal troops for the management of the whole of the provinces revenue and police officers cannot be established, and yet none of the military troops, whether cavalry or infantry, can be prevailed on to move out beyond the palace and the city. Under these circumstances, it is matter for distressingly serious reflection how supplies are to be procured from the country, and how the revenues of the state are to be realized .... Accordingly, nothing but total destruction of the city and the country can be expected as the inevitable end of this state of affairs. In addition to all that has been above noticed, the soldiery accusing the royal servants of entertaining views and feelings opposite to their own, subject them to indignities, and when they come to claim their daily allowances or ammunition, enforce their demands with unbecoming assumption of authority, notwithstanding that the royal servants, in consequence of orders to them to that effect, use nothing but entreaty and every other means of conciliation, and yet the soldiery will not be satisfied.' *Trial of Muhammad Bahadur Shah*, p. 221.

429. Rajab Ali, the British spy in Delhi, addressed the Emperor's chief councillor, Hakim Ahsanullah Khan, in terms which, if the letter fell into the hands of the sepoys, must infallibly lead them to presume treachery on the part of the hakim, and if not discovered by them, might divert his allegiance to the British. The couplet was introduced in the letter as being probably applicable to the hakim's position (and might also be taken to reflect that of his puppet master). Rajab Ali's letter was in fact discovered by the sepoys when they ransacked Hakim Ahsanullah Khan's house, and it served its purpose. The house was burnt down and the physician narrowly escaped by darting to the palace. Cooper, *Crisis in the Punjab*, p. 112.

430. Rev. J. Cave-Browne, *The Punjab and Delhi in 1857: Being a Narrative of the Measures by Which the Punjab was Saved and Delhi Recovered During the Indian Mutiny* (rpt Punjab Govt, 1970, 1st ed. 1861), vol. II, p. 37.

431. Bahadur Shah sent for his sons, Mirza Mughal, Mirza Abu Bakr, and Mirza Abdullah, and expressed his anger over their alliance with the sepoys, and warned them that they would be hanged as soon as the English entered the city. Jiwan Lal's diary, 31 May 1857, *Two Narratives*, p. 112. In the meanwhile the sepoys threatened to kill the Emperor's two chief councillors, his physician Ahsanullah Khan and his chief ennuch Mahbub Ali Khan, and also threatened to take away Begam Zinat Mahal as hostage for the Emperor's loyalty. 'There was a great uproar in the Palace, the sepoys on the hand and the King's household on the other, contending with violent language and harsh vociferations.' Jiwan Lal's diary, 16 May 1857, p. 93.

432. This was partly the reason why Zinat Mahal made repeated overtures to the British on the Ridge. The sepoys, who suspected it, did not know that Bahadur Shah himself also sent out feelers to the British. Rev. Cave-Browne, *The Punjab and Delhi*, vol. ii, p. 39.

433. 'The King addressed the sirdars of the sepoys, pointing out that they were destroying the Kingdom that had lasted for 500 years, and remarked sarcastically that when they went out to fight the English they returned "topsy turvy".' Jiwan Lal's diary, 25 June 1857, p. 128.

434. Extract from *Urdu Akhbar*, *FSUP*, vol. v, pp. 1002–3.

435. Durgadas Bandyopadhyay, *Amar Jivan-Charit*, pp. 81, 85.

436. Ibid., p. 86.

437. Ibid., pp. 151, 156; Jiwan Lal's diary, 2 July 1857, p. 135. Narrative of Syed Mubarak Shah, *Red Year*, p. 207.

438. Ibid. The crucial decision of the sepoys at Bareilly to elect Bakht Khan as their commander, which paved the way to his rise as the general of the Mutiny, would appear to have been due to the fact that he was the chief native officer of a famous field battery of artillery which had served at Jalalabad in the First Afghan War, and in which all the gunners happened to be natives. The battery had a mural crown as an honorary decoration on its guns. Bakht Khan had served at Jalalabad and was an experienced officer at the time of the Mutiny. *Two Narratives*, p. 133n.

439. Bakht Khan was himself partly responsible for this, for within a week of his arrival there were complaints that he had provided his own troops with supplies but had made no arrangements for the rest of the army. Jiwan Lal's diary, 6 July 1857, p. 140. Less than a month had elapsed after these complaints when he came to the darbar and complained that the soldiers no longer obeyed his orders. 'Tell them, then, to leave the city;' was the Emperor's unhelpful reply. Ibid., 3 Aug. 1857, p. 179.

440. Ibid., 7 July 1857, p. 142.

441. Ibid., 2 July, 31 July 1857, pp. 135, 150, 175.

442. Lieut.-Gen. Sir George MacMunn, 'Devee Deen, Mutineer,' *Blackwood Magazine*, 1928, extract in James Hewell (ed.), *Eye-Witnesses to the Indian Mutiny* (Reading, 1972), p. 27.

443. Syed Moinul Haq, *The Great Revolution of 1857*, p. 141. The reason for the close understanding between Bakht Khan and the Emperor, as Hakim Ahsanullah Khan explained it, was this: when he first arrived he advised Bahadur Shah not to entrust too much power to his sons, and suggested that all orders be communicated to him, in the event of which all would transpire as the Emperor desired. The Emperor, already dissatisfied with the insubordinate conduct of his sons, found Bakht Khan's advice to his taste and the general rose daily in his esteem. Evidence of Hakim Ahsan Ullah, *Trial of Muhammad Bahadur Shah*, p. 280 ff. However, Bakht Khan did not have it all his own way. Maulvi Sarfaraz Ali of Gorakhpur, the chief of the ghazis, met the Emperor at the advice of Bakht Khan, his disciple, and begged to be appointed prime minister. The Emperor replied enigmatically, 'We shall see about it'. Bakht Khan, conducting the affairs of state in conjunction with the *maulvi*, nominated Fazl Haq of Khairabad as governor of the Doab, but the Emperor, who was not consulted in this, objected that he had already appointed Nawab Walidad Khan of Malagarh to the post. The general and *maulvi* then obtained royal permission to nominate the governors of Banaras and Allahabad and appointed 'two illiterate mean-looking [men from Oudh] who during a durbar quarrelled and fought in the royal presence to the great scandal of the assembled nobles, calling for the sarcastic remarks of [one of the latter] who pointed them out as the distinguished individuals whom Bakht Khan & Co. had made nazims [governors].' Narrative of Syed Mubarak Shah, *Red Year*, pp. 210, 217. On another occasion, 'Mirza Abu Bakr, Mirza Rawas, and Mirza Abdulla were present at the Durbar. General Mahommed Bakht Khan rose from his seat, went behind the King, and whispered something in his ear. The princes, who were present, took objection to his doing so, and openly charged him with bad manners in thus violating the customs of good society, by whispering into the King's ear in their presence. The General apologised, and, after flattery from him to the Princes, the matter dropped.' Jiwan Lal's diary, 22 July 1857, *Two Narratives*, p. 161.

444. Ibid., 19 July 1857, p. 156.

445. According to Syed Mubarak Shah, the prince now began to plot with certain sepoys to waylay and kill the general, but the latter was

surrounded by too large a number of horse, foot, and artillery for the intention to be realized. *Red Year*, p. 211.

446. Quoted in Nigam, *Delhi in 1857*, p. 104.

447. Evidence of Hakim Ahsanullah Khan, *Trial of Muhammad Bahadur Shah*, p. 280 ff. However, according to the diary of Jivan Lal, 15 July 1857, Bakht Khan pleaded with the Emperor that three generals of divisions were not needed. *Two Narratives*, p. 152.

448. Bakht Khan made every effort to stay on the right side of Mirza Mughal in a vain endeavour to infuse unity among the troops. He paid a visit to Mirza Mughal and suggested a general parade of the army, in accordance with which Mirza Mughal and other princes reviewed the entire force outside the city wall. Orders from Bakht Khan, asking the troops to be sworn by oath to continue the fight against the English and the faint-hearted to return home, were read out. 'The unanimous answer of the army was that they would continue to fight the English to the bitter end.' Ibid., 22 July, pp. 161–3.

449. Narrative of Syed Mubarak Shah, *Red Year*, p. 212.

450. Jiwan Lal's diary, 4 Aug. 1857, p. 181.

451. The constitution was promulgated by Bahadur Shah in the *Sadiqul Akbar*, an Urdu newspaper, on 2 Aug. 1857. Translations are given in *FSUP*, vol. I, pp, 419–21 and in Mahdi Husain, *Bahadur Shah II and the War of 1857 in Delhi* (Delhi n.d.).

452. There is some uncertainty regarding the identity of the Sahib-i-Alam, the lord governor to whom the Court of Administration was bound to report. *The Freedom Struggle in UP* mentions that this personage was apparently Mirza Mughal (vol. I, p. 419 n), but Hakim Ahsanullah Khan is quite clear in his evidence that Bakht Khan was appointed governor-general notwithstanding the protests of Mirza Mughal's supporters.

453. *FSUP*, vol. I, p. 420.

454. Diary of Jiwan Lal, 4 Aug. 1857, p. 180.

455. Ibid., 23 Aug. 1857, p. 205.

456. Haq, *The Great Revolution*, pp. 127–8.

457. Diary of Jiwan Lal, 31 Aug., 1 Sept. 1857, pp. 215–16.

458. Ibid., 6 Sept. 1857, p. 223.

459. The long awaited concerted attack on the British position on the Ridge by enveloping it from two sides failed at the end of August when the Neemuch Brigade refused to join forces with the Bareilly Brigade, camped separately, and were suddenly attacked and put to flight by the

British troops. Bakht Khan who had earlier proposed joint action was forced to beat a precipitate retreat. After this there was no saving the city. Ibid., 26 and 27 Aug. 1857, pp. 207–9.

460. After a disastrous encounter with the British troops, the sepoys, suspecting treachery, surrounded the palace, demanding Hakim Ahsanullah Khan's head. Bahadur Shah summoned all his sons around him and told the princes to protect his life, whereupon the princes remained with him all night. 'There was a panic in the city; every shop was closed. The Mohammedans passed every hour in fear, and fully expected that the soldiers would kill the king and massacre the citizens.' Ibid., 7 Aug. 1857, p. 187.

461. 'Mirza Ziauddin and Mirza Aminuddin Khan called a meeting, and addressing it, said, "If there were any persons who preferred death to being plundered by the Sepoys, let them bind themselves to resist further exactions." The bankers of Lal Koti and Chandni Chowk were called on to sign a document to the same effect. When the Sepoys heard of this they determined to kill the originators, but finding the whole city against them, they thought better of it.' Ibid., 20 Aug. 1857, p. 202.

462. On 23 August the officers of the Neemuch Brigade accused Bakht Khan of negotiating with the English and withholding his soldiers from the fight. Bahadur Shah, who had been angered by Bakht Khan's refusal to march upon the rear of the English on the Ridge, was induced to issue an order that the general should not be admitted into the Imperial presence. The Neemuch officers then suggested that they should be allowed to disarm the Bareilly troops, and offered to do so with the 4 infantry and 1 cavalry regiments. The Emperor did not respond to the proposal but later in the day he transferred all powers from both Mirza Mughal and Bakht Khan to the *Jalsa*. Ibid., 23 Aug. 1857, p. 205.

463. Ibid., 7–8 Sept. 1857, pp. 225–6.

464. Ibid., 22 Aug. 1957, pp. 203–4.

465. In November the forces assembled in Lucknow numbered as follows: sepoys 7950, cavalry 7720 (?), Oudh regiments 5600, *taluqdar's* men 32080, total 53,350. *FSUP*, vol. II, p. 241.

466. Statement of Munshi Wajid Ali, trial of Raja Jai Lal Singh, *FSUP*, vol. II, p. 97.

467. Statement of Syed Eusuf, *darogah* of Shahinshah Mahal, *FSUP*, vol. II, p. 113; Decision in *Govt. vs Rajah Jy Lall Sing*, *FSUP*, vol. II, p. 647.

468. Statement of Munshi Wajid Ali, *FSUP*, vol. II, p. 97.

469. Ibid.; Statement of Mir Wajid Ali, *darogah*, *FSUP*, vol. II, p. 81.

470. Statement of Munshi Wajid Ali, *FSUP*, vol. II, p. 98; Statement of Matta Deen, *FSUP*, vol. II, p. 92.

471. Statement of Syed Eusuf, *FSUP*, vol. II, p. 113.

472. Ibid.

473. Statement of Mahmud Ali, Munshi of the court of officers of the army, *FSUP*, vol. II, pp. 110, 112.

474. *The Bengal Hurkaru and India Gazette*, 15 April 1858, *FSUP*, vol. II, 117.

475. Statement of Syed Eusuf, *FSUP*, vol. II, p. 114.

476. Statement of Matta Deen, *FSUP*, vol. II, p. 92.

477. Statement of Mahmud Ali, *FSUP*, vol. II, p. 112.

478. Lucknow news 18 Nov. 1857, *FSUP*, vol. II, p. 354.

479. Mukherjee, *Awadh in Revolt*, p. 143.

480. Robert Henry Wallace Dunlop, *Service and Adventure with the Khakee Ressalah; or Meerut Volunteer Horse during the Mutinies of 1857–58* (rept Allahabad 1974, 1st pub. 1858), pp. 57, 126; R.H. Dunlop, Magistrate of Meerut to Maj.-Gen. Hewett, 28 June 1857, *FSUP*, vol. v, p. 108.

481. Deposition of Dindar Khan, *barqandaz* of Thana Raya, *FSUP*, vol. v, pp. 695–6; Mark Thornhill, *The Personal Adventures and Experiences of a Magistrate during the Rise, Progress and Suppression of Indian Mutiny* (London, 1884), pp. 100–9. See also discussion by Gautam Bhadra, 'Four Rebels of Eighteen-Fifty Seven', in Ranajit Guha (ed.), *Subaltern Studies IV: Writings on South Asian History and Society* (Delhi, 1984), pp. 245–56.

482. Dunlop, *Service and Adventure*, p. 46. Despite his official position as *subadar*, he was called raja by his followers. He is described in the official English narrative as 'Governor of the purgannah of Barout with the title of Rajah'. Quoted in Bhadra, *Four Rebels*, p. 235.

483. Dunlop to Saunders, 24 June 1857, *FSUP*, vol. v, p. 108.

484. Meerut Confiscations Statement, quoted by Eric Stokes, *The Peasant Armed: The Indian Revolt of 1857* (Oxford, 1986), p. 164.

485. Dunlop, *Service and Adventure*, p. 107. For discussion, see Bhadra, *Four Rebels*, pp. 230–45.

486. Dunlop, *Service and Adventure*, p. 95.

487. Ibid., pp. 100–12.

488. Quoted by Stokes, *The Peasant Armed*, pp. 163–4.

489. Dunlop, *Service and Adventure*, pp. 116–19.

490. Ibid., pp. 97, 127.

491. Narrative of what occurred at Farrucabad during the outbreak, *FSUP*, vol. v, p. 729.

492. Narrative of occurrences by C.R. Lindsay, officiating Magistrate and Collector of Farrukhabad, 20 Dec. 1858, *NE*, vol. II, pp. 133–5.

493. Narrative of what occurred at Farrucabad during the outbreak, *FSUP*, vol. v, p. 761.

494. Ibid., pp. 730–1; Narrative of the Futteghur Mutiny by G.S. Jones, 13 Sept. 1857, *FSUP*, vol. v, p. 740.

495. Narrative of what occurred at Farrucabad during the outbreak, *FSUP*, vol. v, pp. 730–1.

496. Narrative of occurrences by C.R. Lindsay, *NE*, vol. II, p. 130.

497. Narrative of the Futteghur Mutiny by G.S. Jones, *FSUP*, vol. v, pp. 740, 741.

498. Lindsay's narrative, *NE*, vol. II, p. 130; Narrative of what occurred at Farrucabad during the outbreak, *FSUP*, vol. v, p. 732.

499. Ibid., pp. 732–3.

500. Ibid., p. 765.

501. Ibid., p. 733.

502. Deposition of David Churcher, *FSUP*, vol. v, p. 751.

503. Narrative of what occurred at Farrucabad during the outbreak, *FSUP*, vol. v, pp. 761–762.

504. Ibid., p. 762.

505. Ibid., pp. 763, 765.

506. Ibid., p. 763–4.

507. Ibid., p. 764–5.

508. Lindsay's narrative, *NE*, vol. II, p. 140.

509. The account that follows is based, except where otherwise stated, on the Narrative by C.R. Lindsay, officiating Magistrate and Collector, Farrukhabad, dated 20 Dec. 1858, *NE*, vol. II, pp. 129–44.

510. *The Friend of India*, 26 Nov. 1857, *FSUP*, vol. v, p. 927.

511. Lindsay's narrative.

512. Quoted in Edward Thomson, *The Other Side of the Medal* (3rd edn, London, 1930), p. 76.

513. Maude and Sherer, *Memories of the Mutiny*, vol. I, p. 67.

514. Ibid., p. 70.

515. Pavan K. Varma, *Ghalib. The Man, the Times* (New Delhi, 1989), p. 154.

516. Maude and Sherer, *Memories of the Mutiny*, vol. I, pp. 71–2.

517. Ibid., pp. 72–3.

518. Rudrangshu Mukherjee, *Spectre of Violence: The 1857 Kanpur Massacres* (New Delhi, 1998), p. 1.

519. Savarkar, *Indian War of Independence*, p. 280.

520. Thomson, *Other Side of the Medal*, p. 86.

5

Embedded Mentalities

The nation, in the sense in which the term is understood in political science, is a new kind of human community which grew out of the intellectual and institutional evolution of the modern world. But in the older medieval sense of the term, the nation is a community of sentiment and it has a prior emotional history. It is only in the narrow modern perspective that nations are re-imagined, reconstructed, reinvented. Essentialists amongst the earlier generation of historians of nationalism made a mistake in assuming that the nation was just there, naturally. The more perceptive historians of that generation could see that the nation had not always been there. Of late, some scholars have gone further and have made a distinct contribution by locating the invented element in nationalism. However, some of them write as if 'the Nation' was all of a sudden conjured into existence. There is obvious exaggeration in this constructionism. The real psychic element in this is as important as the invented intellectual and political component.

A longer-term view of history will reveal the pre-existing emotional building blocks that the 'inventors' utilized. The *populi*, the *nationes*, the *gentes*, the *qāums*, the *janas*, or, to use the modern terminology, the ethnic groups, religious communities, nationalities were all communities of emotion. When Firdausi wrote the *Shahnama* in 1010 CE, he thought of Iran and Turan as having been rival *qāums* since the beginning of creation. It is in that context that he placed the legendary fight of Rustam and his lost son Suhrab. This fight for an imagined Iran was placed in the epic hundreds of years before the birth of Zarathustra and the rise of the Achaemenid dynasty of Iran; indeed, before there was any such thing as Iran:

> Rustam tow'rds Turan's host now in the fight
> Turned as a panther with his prey in sight.

Suhrab tow'rds Iran's host then charged again
And to his swift-paced courser gave the rein.

Iran and Turan are conceived here as emotional communities. It is this notion that provided the narrative framework of Iran's national epic. Rustam still lives in Iran; but Afrasiyab, his great opponent who used Suhrab for Turan's battles, has vanished along with Turan. The process of transition from the community of emotion to the state-based political community called the nation was by no means 'given' at the start of 'modern' history: there were always several possibilities; alternate lines of development. This was so not merely because the modern inventors of nationalism sprang up with widely divergent interests to orchestrate, but also because many alternative loyalties and bonds of political sympathy existed in any situation for them to work upon. An individual is necessarily born with many affiliations, and emotional communities are interlocked in any person's existence. Any political space, inhabited by a number of people, is likely to be organized in terms of more than one exclusive emotional association. The communities of sentiment are as complex a welter as the processes of nationalist mobilization. To take a purely instrumentalist view of these processes is to betray ignorance of the realities of psychic and emotional existence.

Several communities of sentiment, existing within the same space, may form an overarching emotional community. The Indian subcontinent, an ancient graveyard of nationalities, evolved into a composite civilization rooted in a cellular social formation. That is not to deny a certain artificial element in the emergence of Indian nationalism. As Anil Seal has demonstrated, the nationalist movement was engineered by an English-educated élite of recent origin with very specific professional interests that suddenly budded in the colonial context of competition among themselves and collaboration with the rulers.[2] The degree of political engineering in colonial India, which the erstwhile 'Cambridge school' exposed in detailed local studies, shows how often the national identity was a mask for patron–client linkages in the localities. Established local interests thereby manufactured a new constituency for themselves in the broader political space created by the process of colonial governance.[3] The 'Subaltern school' exposed an equally wide variety of local and communal bonds at work below the wider processes of nationalist association and mobilization. Unlike the 'Cambridge' historians, these scholars emphasized the real emotions involved in the so-called 'subaltern' protests.[4] What is missing from both accounts is the wider community of emotion—the common inter-mixed culture and mentality—which eventually absorbed these instrumentations and counter-mobilizations.

Mentality had a long and complex history in India. Because it was 'real', insofar as any psychological phenomenon is real, the emergence of Indian nationalism is not, in the last resort, an invented, engineered, constructed thing, though it is that too in the shorter perspective. A longer view of history reveals the process by which this civilization effected its transition to nationhood. This involves the study of mentality in the wider and varied context of the subcontinent. The emergence of a common culture and mentality, and the accommodation of many cultures and mentalities within that felt community, is central to this process. The emotional and psychological element in this history constitutes the essential prior history of the nationalist movement. Tracing this element takes the historian a long way back. The starting point is not, therefore, the emergence of the Indian National Congress. Before that, there was 'the Reigning Indian Crusade' of 'the Hindus and Musalmans of Hindustan' in 1857, and even earlier there were the imperial Mughal campaigns against the usurpation of the East India Company in the later eighteenth century. In the first instance, however, the psychic antecedents of the story impelled us to explore the formation of the identities dubbed 'Hindu', 'Musalman', and 'Hindustan' in the seven centuries preceding these events.

Indeed, the story in a sense begins considerably earlier than that. The civilization of what we call India today found its first literary expression in the *Rik Samhita*, composed around 1500 BC in the land of the five rivers. Then, however, there was no India, in the sense of a commonalty embracing the entire subcontinent. The world of the Indo-Aryans who composed these early hymns was bound by the Indus plains called the Sapta Sindhu. We get the first glimpse of India in the proper sense in the surviving fragments of the lost book of Megasthenes, who was ambassador to the court of Sandrokottos in 302 BC. In the eyes of this Greek, the entire land from Palibothra to Pandaea was one. It is, however, in the inscriptions of Ashoka (273–232 BC), discovered as far south as the Karnataka country, that we have the first visible expression of one culture extending over the entire land. By this time the Indo-Aryan culture, now transformed by extension over the subcontinent and by interaction with Austric, Dravidian, and other languages, is a wider composite culture, expressed in the indigenous term Jambudvipa.

Every where in Jambudvipa, including those southernmost parts which lay beyond Ashoka's dominions, the people were one in their respect for Brahman priests and Buddhist monks, a feature which distinguished the country from other lands where these two groups did not exist. In due course, a common ancestor was conceived for them in the legendary Chakravarti king named Bharata: his offspring were Bhārati, and their land was Bhārata -Varsha.

In the early age of Islam, Indians were known as Hindus in both Arab (Arabic-speaking lands) and Ajam (non-Arabic lands of Islam), the term being derived from Sapta Sindhu (the seven Indus rivers) via the Iranian equivalent Hapta Hindu. The warriors of Ajam, belonging to both Iran (Iranian-speaking lands) and Turan (Turkic-speaking lands), knew of Hindustan (yet another Iranian term originally denoting the Sind province of the ancient Iranian empire) as a land of the infidel Hindus. The Turks of Khurasan (situated at the junction of Iran and Turan), having risen to military and political prominence in both Iran and Turan, extended their hold over Hindustan in the thirteenth century. The people of Hindustan, whom they called Hindus, knew them as Turashkas, Turaks, Turks. The Turkish conquerors themselves, however, or at any rate their learned religious literati (*ulama*) who chronicled the history of the Sultanat of Delhi, preferred the term Muslim, instead of Turk, in their chronicles. Meanwhile, a similar transition from an ethnic to a religious category began to take place in their use of the term Hindu. Originally, this meant, to the incoming 'Muslims' (i.e. Khurasani Turks), the indigenous Indian people over whom they had imposed their domination. Such Hindus might include, as indeed Al Biruni said explicitly, Indians of the Buddhist faith. Hindus were Indians irrespective of their religious affiliation. However, through a gradual shift, the confrontations between the warriors of the two lands, Khurasan and Hindustan, transmuted within Hindustan into a religious contra-distinction between the Muslims and the Hindus. Whether of Brahmanical or Buddhist persuasion, the Hindus were all infidels in the eyes of the Muslim.

The early chronicles of the Delhi Sultanat conceived the political universe in terms of three contending categories: Muslim, Hindu, and Mughal (Mongol). The Muslims were a community of faith who, irrespective of race (whether of Arab or Ajam, or of Iran or Turan), were divinely appointed to spread the message of Islam across the world. They had two principal opponents to reckon with in the early period of the Delhi Sultanat, the Hindus whom they had subjugated and the Mongols who threatened them in Khurasan as well as Hindustan. Both Hindu and Mughal were ethnic categories, as opposed to the religious category dubbed Muslim. The Mongols, despite having overwhelmed the Muslims in Khurasan, were themselves converted to Islam in the new generation. In the meanwhile, a community of Indian-born Muslims sprang up in the towns of northern India. They could not be called Hindus, though they were Indians, for the term Hindu was used in opposition to Muslim. Therefore, a new term was invented to describe Indians, as distinct from foreigners (generically referred to in India as Khurasani). This was 'Hindi', or alternately, 'Hindustani'.

The Hindi language, which is the official language of the Indian Union today, did not exist then. A 'Hindi' then meant an Indian, a native of Hind (or alternately, any native tongue of Hind, as opposed to Persian, the official language of the Delhi Sultanat). At that stage the term Hindu, by the implied exclusion of the Indian-born Muslim, became a religious category, indicating a particular community of faith. In consequence of this transition in the meaning of the term, it no longer embraced all Indians, as against the Turks. It obviously excluded the Indian-born Muslims. In course of time, the Rana of Mewar and the Raya of Vijayanagar described themselves as Hindu sultans, an indication that the Hindus had begun perceiving themselves self-consciously as a community of faith in the fourteenth and fifteenth centuries. The people of the Brahmanical faith had no collective denomination for themselves before they adopted the foreign (Muslim) term Hindu.

The binary opposition between Hindi/Khurasani and Hindu/ Muslim impeded the development of political commonalty in India, until the rule of Akbar and his successors fostered the notion of a legitimate *badshahi* in which these distinctions were effectively combined to create a new and inclusive sovereignty over Hindustan. Under the influence of this common imperial patriotism, even the Marathas who had rebelled against the Mughal sovereign rallied to the throne when Nadir Shah of Iran invaded India in 1739. When the Mughal army gave way, the people of Delhi, both Hindu and Muslim, rose in a body against the Iranian troopers in a popular patriotic insurrection reminiscent of an earlier occurrence in Delhi during the occupation of Timur three and a half centuries earlier. The course of Indian history had by this time defined three persistent ideas: (1) Hindustan and the

Hindian; (2) Hindu and Muslim; (3) the inalienable and indivisible sovereignty of the Mughals.[5] Even as the central Mughal power decayed after the sack of Delhi by Nadir Shah, the common Hindustani patriotism of the Hindus and Muslims, on the one hand, and the imperial Mughal legitimism of the officers and troopers, on the other, fused into a political commonalty which provided the only all-India basis for resistance to the colonial encroachments of the English.

The struggle that would determine the fate of India began in the form of a Mughal–English confrontation, the Mughals being then very much the ruling power, and the English thereby being cast in the role of rebels. As the tide of fortune turned, and it fell to the ruling English power to suppress opponents as rebels, those opponents, especially the rebels of 1857, clung tenaciously to the memory that the English were themselves the rebels, to be resisted on the ground that they were usurpers of the legitimate Mughal realm. There were visible shifts and underlying continuities in the language of resistance to colonial usurpation in the century between 1757 and 1857: expulsion of aliens and extirpation of rebels, which constituted the cause of the Mughals against the East India Company, continued as an idea in the changed context after the English occupation of the Red Fort (1803) in Delhi, when the inversion of the existing colonial order, and the return to the earlier Mughal order, constituted the new cause. The Mutiny, in that light, was not a mutiny, nor a simple inversion of authority: as the English had illegitimately inverted the rightful Mughal authority, the restoration of Bahadur Shah Zafar was by implication the cancellation of an usurpation, in other words, the reversal of an inverted order. What the later Indian nationalists revalued, in a profound break of ideas, as a popular rebellion, was, in the eyes of those much admired 'rebels' themselves, a legitimate restoration, an attempt to complete a task that had proved beyond the military capacity of the Mughal cavaliers at Buxar (1764).

To understand the series of prismatic permutations in the mentality of resistance to the English, it is necessary for a moment to refer back to Emperor Aurangzeb's imperious treatment of the East India Company in 1686. In that year, the English rebelled against the Mughal sovereign, and were promptly driven to the edge of the Sundarbans. Pardoned subsequently by the Emperor for this inconsequential misdemeanour, they were somehow allowed, after his death, to offer shelter to fleeing Mughal subjects in their new settlement (Calcutta), to strengthen their fort (Fort William) on the pretext of hostilities with the French, and to push their private commercial ventures without paying a pie to the Mughal government. These usurpations, which created an extra-territorial jurisdiction where the Mughal writ did not run, impelled Nawab Sirajuddaulah to invest Fort William in 1756. As imperiously as the old Emperor, the young Governor drove the rebels out, brought Calcutta under Mughal jurisdiction, and renamed it Alinagar to the beat of tom-tom: The creation belongs to God, the realm belongs to the Emperor, the executive belongs to Nawab Mansur-ul-Mulk Shah Quli Khan Sirajuddaulah Bahadur Haibat Jang. However, the altered equations of power within the Mughal realm enabled the English to effect what the Mughal poets and chroniclers described as a melancholy revolution (*inqilab*). By exploiting the internal alignments of the Mughal nobility, the usurpers set up a new Mughal governor (Mir Jafar) and then replaced him with yet another one (Mir Qasim).

Driven to the wall, the imperial officer class in Bengal rallied under their Governor Mir Qasim. Adapting the language of Emperor Aurangzeb and Nawab Sirajuddaulah to the changed political context, they made an authoritative pronouncement of war against rebels and aliens, but also spoke of 'the poor' who had been 'deprived of their daily bread' by the English agents and *gumashtah*s. 'So my country is to go to ruin', exclaimed Mir Qasim. A whole range of Mughal subjects, injured by the illegal extension of private English inland trade since 1757, urged the Mughal administration 'to put oppression and injustice to flight'. Both *zamindar*s and *raiyats* solidly backed the Mughal officials in the districts as the latter drifted into an undeclared war with the English factors in remote corners. The Mughal nobility of upper India, headed by the Nawab Wazir of Awadh and Emperor Shah Alam himself, joined the war to expel the aliens from the Mughal realm, galvanized by the fear of the latter's 'wicked design of seizing the country for [themselves]'. A united Mughal ruling class swore that 'the heads of disturbers' would be devoured 'by the swords of justice'. They were aware that this was a war in which 'the fate of all Hindostan' was at stake. At Buxar, English firepower finally prevailed over Mughal horse. The Emperor was obliged to legalize the Company's position in Bengal in return for the promise that they would govern the *suba* 'agreeable to the law of the Empire'.

Talk of 'extermination of the traitors of this realm' (i.e. the English usurpers) still continued in scattered pockets to the accompaniment of poetic lamentations over the *inqilab* that had taken place. This talk did not die down until General Lake's troops occupied Delhi in 1803, to the beat of tom-tom: the creation belongs to God, the realm belongs to the Emperor, the executive belongs to the Sarkar Company Bahadur. But the language of Mughal resistance was not lost from popular memory. The attempt to overthrow the Company in 1857 was accompanied by cries of 'The creation belongs to God, the realm belongs to the Emperor, the executive belongs to [the *Wali* of Awadh/the *Rani* of Jhansi, etc.].' This implied the cancellation of the usurpation of the East India Company, and the restoration of the various intertwined jurisdictions of late Mughal India. And yet, the presence of the sepoy army at the centre of the fight against the Company lent to the war a wider republican character which had been absent from the earlier resistance by the eighteenth-century Indian powers.

This raises certain questions regarding the political scope of the early opposition to the Company. Indian resistance to colonial penetration did not display the commonalty which was to make the sepoy war so formidable an affair. The early wars against the Company, with the exception of the Mughal campaign culminating at Buxar, were waged on the basis of a specific region or a particular religion, as for instance, the Khudadad Sarkar of Mysore, the Swarajya of the Marathas, or the Khalsa of the Sikhs. Religion was also central to the Sepoy War, but this time the Hindus and Muslims waged a joint 'Indian crusade', and a myriad local political formations were sucked into the process of resistance. This was because, during the intervening period, the British had laid the basis for commonalty of political action by imposing their alien domination over every 'native' chief, and every 'native' community of people. This had not been so when the Company embarked on its career of conquests. Its domination was imposed serially over one political formation after another, each with its own separate sphere, forming a self-contained world of lordship and community. The one exception to this was the imperial bond of the Mughal ruling class, the only all-India class before the emergence of the English-educated middle-class of lawyers and civil servants. However, the Mughal cavaliers were no longer capable of militarily holding their own, fated as they were to the regency, first, of the Marathas, and then, in turn, of the English.

In 1780, a confederacy of India princes made another effort to resist the Company on an all-India basis. Militarily, the balance was more even this time, for Mysore, Hyderabad, and the Marathas had by then integrated firepower more efficiently to movements of cavalry. In any case, the light Maratha horse were not so vulnerable to the muskets of the redcoats as were the heavy Mughal horse accustomed to *en masse* frontal assaults upon the enemy. However, the confederacy of the Indian princes disintegrated no sooner than it was put together, for it lacked the ideological cohesion of the Mughal legitimate cause defeated in 1764.

The Sepoy war of 1857 issued from three principal quarters: (1) the Mutiny of the sepoys at Meerut and other cantonments; (2) the discontent that blazed into 'the reigning India crusade' at the Red Fort in Delhi; and (3) the post-pacification revolt in Awadh that drew every *taluqdar* out of his own domain to Lucknow in common defence of the throne and common rejection of alien rule. The political concept of the nation had appeared in the Presidency towns of the East India Company by then, but was absent in northern India. Resistance to alien domination was inspired by other causes: the defence of religion, the recovery of patrimony, and a general sense of patriotism that inspired the corporate body defined as 'the Hindus and Musalmans of Hindustan'.[6] The British had created the basis for this commonalty by subjecting all blacks to white domination. In course of time this universal domination would provoke the resistance of 'the Indian Nation'. At the moment the commonalty could find no formula to express itself other than 'the Hindus and Musalmans of Hindustan'.

We are back at the question: what was the state of nationality in India before the emergence of nationalism? This is the central question that this work has so far addressed. Added to this, is the further question: what relationship did this earlier political commonalty bear to the later ideology and thinking of the nationalist movement?

The missionary and historian, F.W. Buckler, spoke perceptively of the political theory of the Indian Mutiny many years ago.[7] Theory may not be exactly the right word in this context: the mutineers had neither the time nor the intellectual inclination to develop one. They did, however, have ideas deriving from the past and relevant to the future. The intellectual world of late Mughal India, in which there was a notion that the Hindus and Muslims of the Mughal empire were brothers from a single mother, was not entirely lost to them. Nor, on the other hand, was their mental world, which was groping towards a conjoined Indian nationality of Hindus and Muslims, wholly alien to the later conceptualisations of Indian commonalty by Mohandas Karamchand Gandhi and Mohamed Ali, who jointly harnessed the Indian struggle of 1920–2 to the combined visions of Ram Raj and Khilafat. The imperfectly articulated ideas of 1857 may be placed mid-stream in a flow of notions that go back to the Mughals and move on to the Mahatma. Scores of Mutiny proclamations, orders, and leaflets were translated by the British during and after 1857. These translations, which have been quoted at some length in this work, hint at several inchoate ideas, hardly amounting to a political theory as such. Upon closer observation, however, they seem to fit into an identifiable view of the country and the people, expressed in a specific political language. Fortunately, the records of the then Government of India also include some specimens of these proclamations in their Hindustani original: one or two instances may be cited here[8] for a closer glimpse of the language and mentality of 'the reigning Indian Crusade', as the men of 1857 viewed their own struggle.

> All the Hindus and Musalmans (*sab* Hindu *aur* Musalman) know that four things are dear to all human beings. First, *Deen* and *Dharma*, second, honour (*izzat*) and respect (*abru*), third, one's own life and the life of one's [dear ones], and fourth, wealth (*mal*) and goods (*asbab*). These four things are safe under Hindustan regime (*amaldari* Hindustan). Under this regime, no one interferes with *Deen* and *Dharma*. All human beings remain with their own *Deen* and *Dharma* ... And English people (*Angrez log*) are enemies of these four things. *Deen* and *Dharma*—which Hindus and Muslims (Hindu Musalman) do not wish to lose—they want all men should be Christians and should become *Nazarenes* (*Nasarani*). Under their jurisdiction (*amaldari*) thousands of people have become and are becoming Christians ... So all Hindus and Musalmans (*sab* Hindu Musalman) are warned, that those who wish to save *Deen* and *Dharma*, and honour and respect, and the lives of oneself and of one's own people, and wealth and goods, should join the forces of this government (*Sarkar*) to fight the English (*angrezon*) unitedly (*bettafaq*).[9]

The repeated use of the term Hindu and Musalman is linked here to the two religions (*deen* and *dharma*), but it is also joined to the pregnant expression *amaldari* Hindustan (i.e. Indian, as opposed to alien, regime). Similarly, Emperor Bahadur Shah's celebrated address to the Hindu zamindars proclaimed:

> Were you and we of the same mind then we might easily succeed in saving our country and faith (*apne mulk aur iman*) by destroying the English (*Angrezon*). For, the good of Hindus and Musalmans (Hindu Musalman *bahtari*) is the aim of you all and the English are the enemy of both communities (*angrez dono firguon ke dushman hai*).

The same proclamation set apart 'the nation of Hindus' (*ahl-i-Hindu*) and 'the nation of Islam' (*ahl-i-Islam*) from 'the nation of the firangi' (*ahl-i-firang*), who were further defined as 'Christians and Europeans' (*Isaiyan aur firangiyan*). At the same time 'the Hindustanis' (*Hindustaniyon*) were set apart from 'the English' (*Angrez*). 'Some people of our country' (*hamare mulk*), regretted Bahadur Shah, 'have joined the English.' It should, however, be clear as daylight to 'the high and low of Hindustan' (*garib aur amir-i-Hind*) that deceit was the inborn instinct of the English. 'It is my conviction', said the Emperor, 'that if the English today [are allowed to] remain in the country of Hindustan (*mulk Hindustan*), then tomorrow they will kill the population of this country (*is mulk ke admiyon*).'[10]

This is an ethnic and religious patriotism, far removed in spirit from the civic and political nationalism of the last quarter of the nineteenth century. Even so, the ancient terms, '*ahl-i-Hindu*' and '*ahl-i-Islam*', occurring along with the newly construed '*Sab Hindu aur Musalman*', were as capable of producing modern political consequences as the idea of 'Bosnian Muslims', or 'the Nation of Islam'[11] (an American term that came to represent a new collectivity among the Black Muslims of the United States in the 1950s). In the correspondence between the rebel government of Lucknow and the Nepal durbar, the expression 'Hindus and Musalmans of Hindustan' occurred as a political term. It was not used here in the loose sense of common parlance, meaning the two major communities of the Indian subcontinent. It was, on the contrary, a construed entity, like the United States of America in the Declaration of Independence, or the People of India in the Constitution of the Indian Union.

The idea conveyed thereby was not the simple idea of communal amity, for in fact there was a good deal of disharmony among Hindus and Muslims in 1857. It was something more than that, or rather, something other than that. It signified a confederation of two separate peoples bound together as one political unit by the shared perception of Hindustan as one land. The correspondents of Lucknow and Kathmandu were aware that there were Hindus in Nepal, just as there were Muslims in Afghanistan. However, neither could be said to be part of the political community spelt out in the correspondence between the Nepal durbar and the mutineers as 'the Hindus and Musalmans of Hindustan'. The Nepal durbar were aware that the mutineers of Hindustan were using the formula as a specific political category. The

Nepal authorities used the term in the same sense, conveying their perception of the population of Hindustan as one category of people. Several things were implied in the use of the term 'Hindus and Musalmans of Hindustan':

(1) The Hindus and Musalmans each constitute a people (*qaum/ ahl*) based on their respective creeds (*dharma/deen*); (2) they are co-sharers of the realm (*mulk*) of Hindustan, and as such are one people, and two peoples, at one and the same time; (3) there is, as yet, no conception of a single national community of Indians, bonded together by secular political loyalties alone; (4) on the contrary, they are bonded together by a united struggle for the *deen* of the Muslims and the *dharma* of the Hindus; (5) the basis of this unity is the alien and aggressive British presence which threatens the *ahl-e-Hindu* and the *ahl-e-Islam* equally; (6) what distinguishes these two peoples from other *qaums*, including those external ones belonging to one or the other creed, is the land itself; (7) in the cultural and social perception, the land is one; (8) the Hindus and Musalmans of Hindustan is a term taken by the mutineers, in a political sense, to embrace its population as a whole.[12]

These ideas were not the same as the idea of the Indian nation propagated twenty-eight years later by the Indian National Congress. Though the margin of time is so short, this is a different mental universe. The religions (*mazhabs*) of India, *deen* and *dharma*, were to be the joint basis of a whole reconstruction of the political world; one in which the land would be purged of the alien race threatening the spiritual identity of the population of India. The basic sentiments behind this mental reconstruction were those of race (*ahl-e-Hind*), religion (*deen* and *dharma*), and realm (*mulk-i-Padshah*). Closely intertwined, they were the constituents of an ethnic–religious consciousness that charged and activated the mass. Racial humiliation, in a crude physical form, was bound up with an equally violent fear of spiritual enslavement. This was the fear of conversion to the religion (*mazhab*) of the alien race (*ahl-e-firang*) and the loss of cherished beliefs and practices.

Associated with all this was a sense of the land being lost and at all levels. This sense of loss ranged from the loss of the hereditary possession of the peasant, the zamindar, and the prince to the alienation of the indivisible sovereign realm of Hindustan, which belonged right-fully to 'the King of Delhi, the bona fide ruler of Hindoostan who is the shadow and representative of God'. The Mutiny was in essence an outburst of anger: a defensive and punitive reaction against the fear, and reality, of outrageous aggression at all levels, physical, spiritual, and material, by the white intruders. The mass that rose was one. In its violent suppression, too, it was branded as one. Bowing before irresistible aggression, Emperor Bahadur Shah, before his final exile to Rangoon, is said to have uttered the following lament for his defeated people:

> *Yeh riāyā Hind hui tabāh*
> *Kaho kyā na inpe hui jafā.*
>
> (This people of India is ruined, say what oppression has not been practised on them?)[13]

Emotionally, the subjects of India (*Riaiya Hind*) were now as sharply distinguished as ever from the conquerors. The English-educated Indians of the time felt this emotional difference as keenly as the rest of the population. A native, wrote a former graduate of Hindu College three years after the Mutiny, might read Bacon and Shakespeare, but he would never be an Englishman in his inner core. 'Morally and intellectually he can easily Anglicise himself. Politically, he may, sooner or later, be raised to an equality. But socially, in thought, habit, action, feelings, and views of life, he must long measure the distance that exists geographically between him and the Englishman.'[14] What he spoke of was a psychological distinction, an emotional difference. Its duration was altogether more lasting than the changing political ideas on the subcontinent.

The emotions that subsequently went into the making of Indian nationalism, the raw materials without which it could not be formed, were visible in the expressions of antagonism to the aliens in 1857. The inchoate sense of nationality—Bahadur Shah's much lamented 'subjects of Hindustan'—was yet to take shape in a modern political nation. Nonetheless, what the emotionally charged collectivity felt in the struggle led by the Indian National Congress and the All-India Khilafat Committee—the vague yearnings for Ram Raj and Khilafat as also the raw antagonistic impulse itself—would appear to bear a certain generic resemblance to the sentiments expressed in the Mutiny. These sentiments are unmistakable: the singling out of the members of the ruling race as well as those mentally associated with them by the people, the waging of a combined war in support of the mutually acknowledged claims of the Muslims and Hindus to establish their sacred realms upon the soil of Hindustan, and above all the vocalizing of the two-in-one formula of 'the Hindus and Musalmans of Hindustan', two *qaums* based on two different faiths, but constituting a confederate people bent upon purging the shared land of an alien and impure presence. '[A] nation of Hindus and Muslims is being created before you today', declared Mohamed Ali after the Jallianwala Bagh massacre.[15] In a notable repetition of the occurrences of 1857, Bombay witnessed a hartal on 17 November 1921. In furious protest against the jailing of the Ali brothers, the Maharashtrian millhands and Muslim townsmen attacked whites, Christians, anglicized Parsees, and indeed any one wearing Western clothes.[16] The targets of hostility, an unfailing indicator of mass emotions, were the very same.

However, if the emotions were the same, the concepts were not, for in the meantime a civil society had sprung up, along with public opinion. A civil society is a society in which everyone is equal in the eyes of the law, and one in which the law rules, even over the government which has promulgated the regulations. The life and property of the individual is guaranteed by law in this individualistic formation. The law operates irresistibly ('the rule of law'), and is no respecter of persons ('equality in the eye of the law'). Since everyone enjoys the same rights, no differentiation of status is possible on the basis of birth, or the custom of the community in which a person may be born. There is a transition from status to contract. Members of a civil society, when they form associations, do so voluntarily. One is not born into an association, as one is born into a caste or a religious community. Free choice distinguishes *gesellschaft* (association) from *gemeinschaft* (community). Arbitrary government or hierarchical society are inconsistent with a social formation based on individual rights and voluntary associations.

The growth of a civil society was fostered in India by the consolidation of British rule and the emergence of public opinion. The Indo–Persian literati had earlier formed some sort of a public.[17] Ideas were interchanged in salons where poetry and music and the issues of life and death were discussed in free company which included public women. However, because the Mughal government did not act by fixed rules, the state did not coexist with a society possessing civil rights. The rules promulgated by Lord Cornwallis in 1793 guaranteed landed property under the Permanent Settlement and set up courts to administer the new land rules. His regulations laid down the foundations of a civil society; one in which the rule of the law would prevail. The regulations were printed and promulgated for 'the public' by a government press set up for the purpose. Subsequently the Baptist

Mission set up a press for the information of the public. Newspapers began to circulate among the native citizens of Calcutta. The formation of voluntary associations, of which the first was the Atmiya Sabha formed by Rajah Rammohun Roy, indicated the crystallization of a public in Calcutta around 1815.

The Atmiya Sabha was a religious body, not a political one. The Landholders' Society (1837) and the British Indian Society (1843) of Calcutta, followed by the British Indian Association (1851), the Bombay Association (1852), and the Madras Native Association (1852), were the first voluntary political associations. In course of time, the political associations speaking the new language of rights cut across the provincial boundaries to which they were initially confined. The process culminated in the Indian National Conference of 1883 and the Indian National Congress of 1885. The Indian public which these new bodies claimed to represent was at first confined to the smaller gentry with guaranteed landed rights, who supplemented the rents from their land with salaries in government service and earnings from the new professions of law, education, journalism, and Western medicine. They called themselves the Indian middle class.[18] This class was the core around which civil society coalesced in the course of the nineteenth century, for they had access to new institutional opportunities and were integrated by a liberal enlightened ideology. Political society, fractured and fragmented at the time, was larger than this civil society; it included the stirrings among numerous castes and communities which sought access to the same opportunities. Moved by a sense of discrimination, these hereditary units of traditional society formed no part of the integrated new individualistic civil society either morally or emotionally. But they too spoke the same language of rights.

The British government in India encouraged the involvement of these hereditary groups in the political process by building a system of communal representation into the processes of government after the Mutiny. The Indian Councils Act of 1861, the Indian Councils Act of 1891, the Morley–Minto reforms of 1909, the Montague–Chelmsford reforms of 1919, and the Government of India Act of 1935 laid down the foundations of a future representative democracy. The system involved an increasing number of voters, but defined the constituencies largely in hereditary, communal terms. The growth of the representative system encouraged the extension of civil society, but at the same time it confirmed the distinctions within the fragmented political society. In a parallel development which forced the pace of constitutional reform, the Swadeshi Samitis in Bengal (1905–8), the Home Rule Leagues (1915–17), the Satyagraha Sabhas and Khilafat Committees (1919), and finally the Indian National Congress under Gandhi (1920–42) and the All-India Muslim League under Jinnah (1940–6) involved an increasing number of people in the struggle for political freedom. The appeals to the people by Gandhi and the Ali brothers were couched in religious terms that reflected a profound awareness of the time-honoured categories of Indian society at large. Thus, political mobilization reinforced constitutional categorization in terms of the older units of society at the same time that it extended the influence of the middle class.

The mass political society thus called into existence by the Raj, the Congress, and the League absorbed a wide variety of castes and communities in the elections and agitations of the twentieth century. Their growing involvement in politics ran counter in some ways to the civil society from which the early Congress had emerged. This was so because the castes and communities newly drawn into politics were still outside the scope of the limited and imperfect civil society which had coalesced around the Indian middle class. It is important to add that the communal constituencies were no longer encapsulated in the old hierarchical bonds of the cellular structure of Indian society. They were reified blocs that operated *en masse* in electoral and militant politics. The new mass political society was potentially a threat to the fragile civil society seeking expression through modern political nationhood.

The Indian National Congress embodied this modern national identity, and sprang out of this civil society. It sought to occupy the political space created by the colonial state, as did the All-India Muslim League and the Hindu Mahasabha. As the political space had not been available earlier, the emergence of national blocs, dubbed 'India', 'Muslims', and 'Hindus', meant a profound break with the past, both intellectually and politically. 'Politics', with the novel link between 'people' and 'politicians', was a distinct new sphere. Socially and emotionally, however, the break with the past was by no means as sharp. The power of the Raj integrated the political space, but mentality and culture shaped the multifarious, richly divergent forms which the struggle for freedom by the nationalities of the subcontinent assumed as time went on.

The Congress, the League, the revolutionaries, the Satyagraha Sabha of Gandhi, and the Azad Hind Fauj of Subhas Bose used various techniques. Constitutional agitation, revolutionary conspiracy, passive resistance, open war, and 'Direct Action' were all means to obtain freedom in the political space which had been created by the Raj. This space had not existed before. The mental landscape was another matter. The emotional, psychical, and cultural roots of the struggle went back a long way into the past. Memories transmitted over the generations had fostered a culture and mentality in the very space which the Raj had appropriated and integrated, and which it was destined to divide and hand over.

It is a mystery how these emotional communities are formed, but once formed they endure. No magician can conjure them into existence, nor can he cause them to vanish. The felt community is not amenable to construal. It evolves, develops, changes, disintegrates, and is quite unlike an imagined community. The Raj, the Congress, the League, and the Mahasabha battled for the newly created space, but could hardly have manufactured the feelings behind the struggle. The emotions were already present. Of course, such sentiments might be manipulated this way or that, but they were there. They exerted a force which no mere manipulator could direct at will.

Furthermore, behind the persistent plurality lay a no less persistent commonalty. Indian nationhood as it evolved in the nineteenth and twentieth centuries in the integrated political space created by the colonial state contained a multiplicity of nationalities, all capable of flowing into one, two, or more nation states. Thus, Rabindranath Tagore who sang of partitioned Bengal's unity in 1905 ('May brothers and sisters of all Bengali homes be one, O Lord') placed the same song in the service of 'the great nation' (*mahajati*) of India at the foundation of the Mahajati Sadan building of Calcutta in 1939, and added, after the last line quoted above, '. . . may Bengal's message make India's message come true'.[19] Similarly, Muslim religious leaders stressed the Muslim identity, and placed it too at the service of Indian nationhood. Maulana Mohamed Ali, in his presidential address at the Congress in 1923, stressed his acceptance of separate electorates, which in his view was 'the consequence and *not* the cause of the separation between Muslims and their more numerous Hindu brethren'. He added in the same breath that India's hope for the future lay in becoming 'a federation of faiths', and not in 'a misleading unity of opposition'.[20] This was but an echo of the sepoy's call in 1857 to liberate 'the Hindus and Musalmans of Hindustan', who constituted two nations in one. At the Round Table Conference in London, Mohamed Ali said on 19 November 1930:

> I have a culture, a polity, an outlook on life—a complete synthesis which is Islam. Where God commands I am a Muslim first, a Muslim second, and a Muslim last, and nothing but a Muslim ... But where India is concerned, where India's freedom is concerned, I am an Indian first, and Indian second, and nothing but an Indian ... I belong to two circles of equal size, but which are not concentric. One is India and the other is the Muslim world. ... We as Indian Muslims ... belong to these two circles ... and can leave neither.[21]

When Saiyid Ghulam Husain Khan had earlier spoken of Hindus and Muslims as brothers from the same mother (and by implication, not the same father), he had in mind the same sort of idea. This was syncretic and not secular patriotism, embedded in the cellular structure of Indian society, and with an extension into the Islamic world to the west. Muhammad Ali Jinnah was a secular man, unlike Maulana Mohamed Ali, who was a religious person. However, he endorsed the same idea of two nations within one country when he lent his qualified and hesitant support to the Cabinet Mission's plan for an Indian confederation, hedging his support with the qualification that Congress must do the same. As it happened, Congress baulked, for Jawaharlal Nehru wanted Indian to be a secular state. He envisaged a civil society in which there would be no communal cells, only individuals equal in the eye of the law.

That the confederation envisaged in the Cabinet Mission Plan did not materialize was due paradoxically to the Nehruvian Congress's unitary vision of a secular, socialist, democratic nation. Nehru, not Gandhi, insisted that this vision be untrammelled by the Muslim League's 'reactionary' presence. Congress, despite Gandhi's intervention, had remained what it was: the replica of an individualistic and egalitarian civil society and not of the communitarian Hind Swaraj.[22] The addition of socialism by Jawaharlal Nehru and Subhas Chandra Bose to the earlier vision of democracy and secularism had taken Congress even further away from the visions of Mohamed Ali and Gandhi.

It will be recalled that the ulama of the Delhi Sultanate had at one time advocated the unitary model of the Islamic state and community. This was their substitute for the beehive formation of Indian society. They had confronted Sultan Iltutmish with this model, but in vain.

Since the ulama did not succeed in converting the population of Hindustan, as had been done earlier in Iran, Islam had to come to terms with India. In the process, Islam enriched the cellular structure of Indian society by adding new cells to the beehive. When this social formation met the challenge of the *Firangi* race and the *Nasri* doctrine, the perceived threat galvanized the Hindus and Musalmans of Hindustan. Thus, two nationalities in one people, one *mulk* with two *qaums*, were evident in 1857. Gandhi and Mohamed Ali instinctively followed the logic of the same struggle. They realized how deeply plurality was embedded in India's age-old social structure. When in the 1930s and 1940s the Congress adopted democracy, secularism, and socialism as the basis of an integrated nation state, a new unitary model began to run counter to this beehive formation. There was no room in this unitary vision for the United States of Southern Asia spoken of by the Agha Khan and implicitly endorsed by Muhammad Ali Jinnah.

As Ayesha Jalal has established with a wealth of documentation, the famous Lahore resolution of the Muslim League in 1940 did not envisage Partition, nor indeed even mention Pakistan.[23] Jinnah was willing to accommodate his vision of Pakistan within the confederation proposed by the Cabinet Mission. In a sense, the Muslim League stood for the beehive formation; and in strong contrast the Congress stood for the unitary state and society. It will be recalled how profoundly the unitary model of Islam strained the cellular structure of Indian society at one time; this time there was another, equally powerful unitary model: the secular democratic socialist state of the Congress High Command. Congress radicalism would not brook the conservative plurality of the beehive formation. Because of the mutual suspicions which this stand generated, the confederation proposed by the Cabinet Mission—the only rational solution to the problems of the subcontinent in the circumstances—did not materialize. Hence partition, and the continuation of an age-old tension: a perennial civil war between two embattled sovereign national states of the same population. Nonetheless, in the longer logic of history, the proposed confederation was, and is, a viable solution to the contradictions in the subcontinent.

A series of contradictions were transmitted and re-transmuted by the dialectics of Indian history. Viewed from a distance, the spatial confrontation between Khurasan and Hindustan was transformed in course of time, and there appeared the religious contradistinction between the Muslims and the Hindus of Hindustan. The historian

impervious to these longer-term dialectics will at his peril dismiss
the religious dichotomy that subsequently transfused into the tension
between the two national states in the subcontinent, Pakistan and the
Indian Union. In its remote origin, the Hindu–Muslim dialectic started
off as a war between two lands: attacks from Khurasan upon Hindustan.
The war then narrowed and sublated in the fifteenth century into a
new communal distinction between Hindu and Muslim as the Khurasani
invaders became part of the social and political formation of Hindustan.
The growing body of Hindustani Muslims turned Muslim political
power into a durable social presence. When the fault line within the
formation produced two national states in the unforeseen and novel
political circumstances of 1947, the older communal divide unexpectedly
transmuted again into a civil war between two neighbouring countries
within the subcontinent. Even so, in the meanwhile, a no less persistent
tradition of syncretism had fashioned a composite social and cultural
system that represented at a broader level what can be recognized as the
idea of India.

Through all these transmutations, al-Hind as an entity persisted: a
civilization of many nations. That is the wider picture which an exclusive
vision might miss out. In a striking instance of sublation of the
contradictions, the Hindus and Muslims of Hind formed a commonalty
ranged against any new invader from Khurasan, be he Timur Lang of
Turan or Nadir Shah of Iran. The commonalty persisted in the Reigning
Indian Crusade of 'the Hindu and Musalmans of Hindustan' against
the Baghi Nisara from Firangistan in 1857, and later still it provided the
basis of the joint struggle for Ram Raj and Khilafat by 'a nation of
Hindus and Muslims' in 1920.

All commonalties which have persisted for any length of time are
necessarily grounded in emotional and psychic realities. Cultural
identities then become part of the submerged collective consciousness.
The ancient contest between Iran and Turan celebrated by Firdausi bears
testimony to this. The mentality of a people grows out of history, and
out of the myths and legends through which the people interpret and
understand the past. The mentality of the Hindus, who had no recorded
history but a plethora of myths, was evident to Al Biruni in all its
psychic and cultural manifestations. Again, the mentality of the people
of Hindustan, with all its collective psychic drives which manifested in
the Mutiny, was no less evident to the contemporary historian J.W. Kaye.
This mentality, which went through profound transformations even as

its contours become historically discernible, supplied the emotional basis for the subsequent struggles for freedom which culminated in the emergence of Pakistan on 14 August 1947 and of the Indian Union on the midnight that followed.

The subcontinent is capable of producing more national states. The emergence of Bangladesh in 1971, and the ongoing struggle for freedom in Kashmir, bear testimony to this. Nonetheless, the subcontinent was and is one, in a far deeper sense than the mere presence of the South Asian Association for Regional Cooperation (SAARC) would suggest at first sight. Historically, this society is a cellular formation capable of accommodating all these nations and more. It exhibits variety in commonalty, and commonalty in variety.

The seers of early twentieth century India were aware of this. Rabindranath Tagore and Mohandas Karamchand Gandhi were both of the view, in their youth, that the sovereign national state was not the true form of emancipation for the people of India. They shared the conviction that the essence of Indian civilization lay in the self-regulating character of society. This social autonomy was rendered feasible by the peripheral existence of the state insofar as the inner life of the community was concerned. For centuries, the various communities and the villages had lived in their demarcated spheres, secure in the autonomy of their local and communal concerns from the interference of the central Muslim realm of Delhi. However, as Tagore and Gandhi saw in their childhood, the self-regulating units of society were forced into dependence as an alien government broke into concerns hitherto regulated within the village and the community. The British made state power central to the life of the people, and thereby profoundly disturbed the balance between the various cells that had constituted the beehive. To both these men, the vision of bypassing the state and of restoring to society the autonomy it had lost in their childhood came naturally. Tagore's concept of 'self strength' ('*Atmashakti*') and Gandhi's notion of 'self rule' ('*Swaraj*') were both anti-state in tendency, one stressing the autonomy of the community, and the other the self-sufficiency of the village. Neither of these prophets of Indian regeneration gave primacy to the political movement in their doctrine of self-help. The aim was to make society self-sufficient again, so as to render the state irrelevant. Ironically, Gandhi saw at the end of his life (Tagore was dead by then) how his very life work had enabled the state to threaten the community on a wider front. The process of transfer of power menaced the groups constituting the composite society with the danger that one or other of them would capture state power and use it to subordinate the others. In a smoother transition from his youthful communalism, Tagore graduated to a universal humanism. The India of his childhood was once again the inspiration of his mature internationalism:

> No one can tell whence
> At whose mysterious call
> Streams of humanity, countless, irresistible,
> Flowed hither to be lost in the ocean.[22]

In course of time, Indian civilization had accommodated many races, tribes, languages, and religions, and its caste society had assigned each new group a place in the hierarchy, free to regulate its own concerns. A poet of enlightened modern outlook, Tagore deprecated the inequality but valued the multiplicity. He knew that the sovereign national state, the alter ego of the British colonial state, would not brook the autonomous regulation of society. However, he did not live to see how full of anxiety this would be for minorities and small communities.

Nevertheless, as early as 1891, he pointed out perspicaciously, 'The very word nation is missing in our language, and is not to be found in our country. We have learnt recently to give an excessive importance to national greatness under the influences of Western education. Nation formation has no primacy either in our history, or in our divine law, or in our social and household constitution.'[25] On this view, India was a culture, a civilization; to put it in the words of Max Weber, a community of sentiment but not a nation, at least not in the modern sense. In entitling his autobiography *A Nation in Making*, Tagore's contemporary, Surendranath Banerjea, had the same idea: there was no nation before his time.

He might have added that there was no certainty as to the future shape of the nation(s) in making. As late as the arrival of Mountbatten, there was indeed no telling which way the tide would turn. The British had three contingency plans, and were willing to give each a try. They would like to transfer power to the duly constituted government of a united India; they would, if necessary, devolve authority to two successor governments in Hindustan and Pakistan; and they might, at a pinch, proceed under 'Plan Balkan' to hand over power to a separate government in each province. While Gandhi pleaded for a united India, and Nehru and Patel manoeuvred to hand Jinnah a moth-eaten Pakistan, there were takers for bits of Plan Balkan, too: H.S. Suhrawardy and Sarat Chandra

Bose set a move afoot for United Bengal, and Khan Abdul Ghaffar Khan pleaded desperately that if the country were to be divided after all, then the North-West Frontier Province should be allowed to go its own free and separate way as Pathanistan.[26] For one brief and tantalizing moment in 1946, the Cabinet Mission held out the plan of an alternative to the nation state(s) in the form of a multinational confederation: Hindustan, Pakistan (consisting of the Muslim majority provinces of the north-west), and perhaps United Bengal, each ruled by an autonomous government with a say at a confederate centre which would discharge the barest minimum function of common defence and conduct of foreign affairs.

Half a century after Partition, and especially after the bloody birth of Bangladesh and the violent stirrings of Kashmir and Khalistan, no uprooted inhabitant of the troubled subcontinent can look back to the multinational confederation of the Cabinet Mission Plan without a sense of nostalgia. Nothing was preordained. The state-based nation was not the natural political form of this community of emotion, given the mixture of its peoples, the self-regulating character of its society and the long-cherished autonomy of its localities and communities. The subcontinent, now divided into the three nation states of India, Pakistan, and Bangladesh, is torn by the frustrations of even smaller fragments: the tribal particularisms of the Chittagong Hill Tracts (the Chakmas), the north-eastern hill states (the Nagas, Mizos, *et al.*), and the North Western Frontier (the Pathan and Baluch tribes); the unfulfilled Khalistani, Sindhi, and Kashmiri visions in the north-west; the tangled aspirations of the Assamese and Bengali Muslims in the north-east; and the crushed minority demands of the Biharis in Bangladesh and the Pandits in the vale of Kashmir. The civil war across the Palk Straits, with the Tamils agitating against Sri Lanka and the Tamil Muslims up in arms against Tamil Eelam, belongs to the same pattern of nationalities in the crushing grip of nationalism.

In the wider perspective, the tribes of black Africa, the ethnic communities of South-east Asia, and the castes, linguistic groups, and religious communities of South Asia, were all forced into the political system of sovereign national states at a time when the social formation did not organically fit into it. The process of nation forming began in these colonized societies in reaction to European hegemony; yet nothing revealed the pervasive character of the hegemony more than the adoption of the forms of European political organization by the emerging nations of Africa and Asia. The sovereign nation-state did not evolve here as it had in Europe, as part of an organic social process. It was something of an alien imposition, and has remained so to this day—a source of anxiety to small, localized, self-sufficient communities subjected to an increasingly thorough and harsh agglomeration, at first by contending imperialisms, then by successor nationalisms. What was lacking here was the fit between civil society and the state. Nationalism, the antithesis of imperialism, retained within itself the older imperial contradiction between state and society, but in a transmuted form.

The Indian National Congress grew out of a contradiction between the colonial state and the civil society which colonial rule had fostered. There was, however, a longer-term contradiction between the modern state and the traditional or not so traditional society. On the one side of this divide lay civil society and the colonial and national states; on the other side, the autonomous localities and self-regulating communities of the ancient subcontinent, and the reified caste, communal, and regional blocs which electoral and agitational politics had brought into play in the new political society. The resultant political configuration of castes, communities, and regional/linguistic blocs, a substitute for the older beehive formation, ran counter to civil society even as it supplemented the latter.

The beehive formation, the civil society, and the new political society were related to one another in complex ways in the emergence of Indian nationalism after the Mutiny. The year 1857 witnessed the outburst of a cellular society profoundly strained by the colonial state. Thus, the proclamation of Mirza Muhammad Ramzan Ali Bahadur Birjis Kadar of Awadh appealed against the British to the landlords (*zamindarano*) as well as the common people (*muman*); to all the Hindus and Musalmans (*sab Hindu aur Musalman*); and to the high born (*ashraf*) of whatever group (*qaum*) as well as to the low born (*paji*). He appealed by name to the Saiyid, Shaikh, Mughal, and Pathan among the high-born Muslims, and the Brahman, Kshatriya, Vaish, and Kayasth among the high caste Hindus; he appealed also to the low-born sweeper, Chamar, Dhanak, and Pasi castes.[27] The success of this appeal to hereditary relationships between high and low exposed how marginal the civil society was in the hierarchical political world of India in 1857.

The process of administrative integration and political representation which the colonial state initiated after the suppression of the revolt aided the extension of civil society, but special constituencies and separate electorates encouraged the reification of the hierarchical units of the beehive formation as political blocs at the same time. As Louis Dumont has pointed out, the caste blocs of this politicized society were in no way comparable to the strong vertical relationships between high and low castes which had earlier integrated the hierarchical society.[28]

The increased British administrative presence in the locality, the expansion of the functions of government, the integration of various levels of government, the new system of municipal and local self-government, the introduction of the legislative councils, together with other constitutional and administrative measures created an apparently uniform and flat political surface. This in turn led to the emergence of a politically active all-India public for the first time. Because of the closer presence of government in the life of the people in every locality, there was now no alternative but to be involved in the wider political arena thus created. Local and communal concerns could no longer be self-regulated; demands would have to be asserted in a modern political fashion.[29] The emergence of this new arena, a formation in which individuals were equal under a growing body of laws and regulations, encouraged the growth of a unified nation within a single civil society. Equally, however, it provided a platform, increasingly tailored by government to the purpose of counteracting this process, whereby various castes, communities, and regions could assert more particular and often conflicting demands through special constituencies and separate electorates.

The ground then was not so flat. The political surface was broken intermittently by the debris of the beehive society and the erection of new blocs. Nationalism had to negotiate with a plural society, old in origin, new in part. The introduction of English education and Western enlightenment fostered the growth of reason, modernity, and civil society; at the same time the institutional and job opportunities associated with the new education quickened the rivalries within the crumbling beehive. As Anil Seal has pointed out, the emergence of an English-educated élite in the Presidency towns of Calcutta, Bombay, and Madras, speaking a common language (i.e. English) and sharing a common political vocabulary (i.e. the modern language of nationalism), was part of the same process that fostered growing competition between various castes, communities, and regions, all seeking a share in English education and its rewards.[30] Thus, the English-educated, Congress-led nationalism that emerged in the later nineteenth century was threatened by subnationalisms from below of all sorts.

This was the new political society. It jostled with civil society in the same space: an arena of public activity which British administrative measures and constitutional reforms had defined after the Mutiny. Before the colonial state created this new framework of rules, and thus fashioned a public as distinct from the government, society was compartmentalized in localities, and was hierarchically organized in each locality. The basis of the earlier resistance to the British ascendancy was therefore radically different. Princes and peasants, linked together by vertical ties of mutual dependence characteristic of the hierarchical old society, alike participated in armed uprisings. Of these attempts at violent overthrow of alien rule, the Mutiny was the greatest by virtue of its appeal to the broadest communities of emotion encapsulated within the lineaments of the beehive: Hindus, Musalmans, and Hindustan. After its violent suppression by the British, however, it was evident that society would have to devise new methods of tackling the state. It was then that the emerging civil society set out to systematically manipulate the rules of the colonial state to gain positions of advantage within the system.

These tactics were efficacious because the new system of governance devised by the British to secure their power was one that operated more than ever by rules. As this realization dawned upon the new generation of educated Indian leaders who understood the mechanics of the system, they manipulated it with growing skill, forcing the British, inch by inch, to give way inside the framework. This was the achievement of an intellectually aware and organizationally adept, educated middle class which successfully established the claim to represent what they self-consciously called the 'public'. The concept was new: a social formation of individuals equal in the eye of the law, with their persons and properties guaranteed by rules obliging the government to respect civil, if not political, rights. The existence of a public had been demonstrated even before the Mutiny by the agitation preceding the revision of the Company's Charter in 1853. On that occasion, the British Indian Association, the Madras Native Association, and the Bombay Association had voiced the demand that political rights be given to the Indians. Based on cooperation between rich notables and dependent professionals, these associations were timid at the time. After the Mutiny, more assertive associations run by professional men came to the fore. The Poona Sarvajanik Sabha (1870), the Indian Association of Calcutta

(1876), the Madras Mahajana Sabha (1884), and the Bombay Presidency Association (1885) represented a vocal public.

As civil society extended its hold, and the Indian middle class coalesced as a body, these associations federated in 1885 and 1886 to form the Indian National Congress. In doing so, they represented a new principle in Indian society: the voluntary association of individuals for a public objective. The Mutiny had appealed to castes, communities, and hierarchic ties between princes, landlords, and peasants. Instead of these hereditary ties, the public political association, conference, or congress represented a voluntary tie between individual members of the public to secure political rights, either for the entire nation or for a more specific group. A gradual displacement of the British within their own system, rather than its violent overthrow, was the ruling spirit of modern politics in India. By a natural extension of the principles of agitation and accommodation (i.e. pressure and compromise), the new political strategy incorporated non-cooperation and civil disobedience under Gandhi's leadership. The revolutionary societies and the Indian National Army of Subhas Chandra Bose too aimed at acquiring a hold over the modern state. There was no question of replacing it with an earlier regime.

Did the traditional resistance movements give way to the new strategy without leaving a trace on the emerging nation? Not so at all. At the factual level, it is observable that tribal insurrections, religious crusades, sectarian uprisings, and peasant rebellions created serious local crises for the colonial state at various places long after the Mutiny and well into the twentieth century. At the theoretical level, Eric Stokes has demonstrated that the traditional resistance movements reflected inchoate popular aspirations that could not find vent in the modern constitutional politics of the English-educated groups organized in public associations. In the longer run, however, these two distinct levels in politics, the élite and popular, did link up. As Stokes formulated it, a groundswell of millennial popular aspirations linked up, after the First World War, with the downward spiral of élite competition to give the Congress its mass character under Gandhi's leadership.[31]

Even after the link-up, however, the politics of the lower orders of the population remained in some respects visibly different from the politics of the modern and articulate political parties. Militant popular movements, as Ranajit Guha has shown, aimed typically at turning the existing hierarchy upside down. Confined within the narrow horizons of the older mentality, the insurgents were unable to proceed further than inversion and were, therefore, incapable of moving into a brave new world.[32] Primordial ties of caste and community were critical factors in the organization of the rural rebellions, which tended to be spatially confined to particular localities. The so-called 'subaltern' militancy, when on its own, had no prospect of growing into a wider and transforming force. Modern political organizations which had sprung out of civil society were needed to link up dispersed popular movements in cut-off localities into a coherent mass upsurge. Congress under Gandhi did this in the Non-Cooperation movement of 1920–2 and again in the Civil Disobedience movement of 1930–4 and the Quit India movement of 1942–4. The Muslim League under Jinnah did this too in the Pakistan movement of 1940–7. As the consciousness of the people was still rooted in older cultural, religious, and social conceptions, Congress and Muslim politicians who had essentially modern political objectives had to evoke visions of Ram Raj and Khilafat, manipulate caste and community ties, employ sadhus and ulama, and appeal to felt communities rooted in the past. There was a hiatus between the objectives of the modern political organizations and the aspirations and conceptions of the illiterate crowds.

Gandhi's strategy of getting a popular movement going by mobilizing the older units of the beehive formation was a critical departure from the Congress's earlier moorings in the Anglicized civil society. As Ravinder Kumar has pointed out, his *satyagraha* brought the masses into the national mainstream, and at the same time it accentuated the older solidarities of caste and community.[33] In a moment of inspiration he formed an alliance with the leaders of the Central Khilafat Committee. Congress obtained unprecedented Muslim support as the ulama brought the mass of the Muslim population into the Khilafat movement. They mobilized the dispersed Muslim community of the subcontinent around the common religious symbols of the Kaaba and the Khilafat, and forged new bonds of political solidarity among them.[34] Later, sections of the same ulama supported the Muslim League's demand for Pakistan, and brought Jinnah essential popular support which enabled the League to deal on equal terms with the Raj and the Congress. Psyche and intellect, old emotions and modern conceptions, *Gemeinschaft* and *Gesellschaft*, were woven into this tense, complex pattern. Jinnah constructed a new nationalist movement, and pressed the demand for Pakistan, by mobilizing an old felt community: the Muslims of Hind.

The local and communal concerns of the popular psyche thus impacted hard upon the intellectual articulation of modern nationalism in the subcontinent. Socially, a locality, caste, or community is rather like a pyramid, a few people at the top, many more in the middle, and a broad mass at the bottom. Together, they form a community of emotion. The Congress of Gandhi and the Muslim League of Jinnah were able to mobilize these hierarchical units of traditional society, because the communities could not afford to stay aloof from modern politics in view of the expanded power of the state and the increased importance of constitutional representation. The Congress and the League both forged continental alliances between many different blocs, and their political strategies were based on accommodation of diverse communities and regions. The limits of civil society were exposed in the process. The individualistic society of citizens equal in their rights was still too weak to absorb and digest the mobilizing units of the new political society. The polarization of the various hierarchical pyramids impeded the expansion of the circle of enlightened citizens. The politics of mass mobilization, instead of supplementing and buttressing a voluntary assembly of equal individuals, began to run counter to it. The result was Partition. The interwoven communities of the beehive turned overnight into beleaguered minorities in one or the other of the two new sovereign national states on 15 August 1947.

When Partition fashioned the world's largest minority on that midnight, the Muslims stranded in the Indian Union by the emergence of 'the Consecrated Land' on the other side of the border faced the agonizing question:

> Say what is Pakistan? Where are we asked to live?
> What do they mean by it?
> Do we live in an unconsecrated land?
> The pillars of our faith, do they rest on polluted soil?
> Scorpion spare! The heart of Chishti bleeds!
> Is the ground of Ajmer profane?[35]

The crowds of the subcontinent provided answers of a sort to the poet's question. The *urs* celebration at Ajmer (Rajasthan, India), Nizamuddin (New Delhi, India), and Ajodhan/Pak Pattan (Punjab, Pakistan) still draw pilgrims from all over India, Pakistan, and Bangladesh. The shrines of Shaikh Muinuddin Chishti, Hazrat Nizamuddin Auliya, and Baba Farid attracted both Muslims and Hindus through seven centuries as empires and nations rose and fell. Viewed from this perspective, the whole of the subcontinent is Pakistan; and the whole of its population is Hindi. Hindus at one time, Hindis afterwards, Pakistanis and Indians and Bangladeshis now, this community is one in their range of emotions. The felt community, once born, reproduces itself in various form. The riots across India, Pakistan, and Bangladesh following upon the Babri Masjid/Ram Janambhoomi events of 1992 exposed this underlying community of emotion. Ambiguous encounters at close quarters derive their proximity from the running conflict. No 'lion's mosque' demolished, no temple erected to 'the one who delights', can erase the psychic oneness in this conflict of emotions. If the mingling of the seas (*Majma-ul-bahrain*) conceived by Dara Shikoh produced a profound churning, the ocean of humanity (*mahamanaber sagar*) celebrated by Rabindranath Tagore still surges on. As civil society continues to extend the hold of reason and equal rights over this community of surging emotions, it may yet break across the barriers, reproduce the felt community, and mingle it with humanity at large.

Notes and References

1. *The Shah-Namah of Fardusi*, Trans. Alexander Rogers (New Delhi, 1989, 1st pub. 1970), p. 171.

2. Anil Seal, *The Emergence of Indian Nationalism: Competition and Collaboration in the Later Nineteenth Century* (Cambridge, 1971).

3. John Gallagher, Gordon Johnson, and Anil Seal (eds), *Locality, Province and Nation: Essays on Indian Politics 1870 to 1940* (Cambridge, 1973).

4. Ranajit Guha (ed.), *Subaltern Studies I: Writings on South Asian History and Society* (Delhi, 1982).

5. For a recent discussion of the development of these ideas, including the emergence of the term 'Hindian', before and during the reign of Akbar, see M. Athar Ali, 'The Perception of India in Akbar and Abul Fazl', in Irfan Habib (ed.), *Akbar and His India* (Delhi, 1997), pp. 215–24.

6. See Iqbal Husain, 'Awadh Rebel Proclamations during 1857–58', Indian History Congress, Bangalore 1997. Husain cites from *Zafar Nama Waqa-i-Ghadar: 'Deen to doi deen, Hindu ka dharam, Musalman ka iman. Ek*

pita ke dooi putra, ek Hindu ek Turk ...' ('Faith is but twin religions—the *dharma* of the Hindu and the *iman* of the Musalman. Born of one father, one is a Hindu and the other is a Turk').

7. F.W. Buckler, 'The Political Theory of the Indian Mutiny', reprinted in A.T. Embree (ed.), *1857 in India* (Boston, 1963).

8. Professor Iqbal Husain of Aligarh Muslim University kindly provided me with the Hindustani originals from the National Archives.

9. National Archives of India, Foreign Department (Secret), nos. 68–9, 25 June 1858. The file contains an English translation. I have, however, made a literal translation from the original, and it differs in certain material respects from the official version.

10. Copy of Hindustani text from NAI, courtesy Professor Iqbal Husain. My translation being more literal, differs materially from the official translation in Foreign Secret Consultations, 30 April 1858, nos. 21–3 (Hindustani original is numbered 259–60).

11. *The Autobiography of Malcolm X*, with the assistance of Alex Haley (New York, 1992), p. 238.

12. The 'Hindus' stood for all non-Muslims, including Jains, Buddhists, and animists, but not Christian converts.

13. J.F.F., *Mariam: A Story of the Indian Mutiny* (Benares, 1896), app. XXIX.

14. Bholanauth Chunder, *The Travels of a Hindoo to Various Parts of Bengal and Upper India*, 2 vols (London, 1869), vol. I, pp. 165–6.

15. Mushirul Hasan (ed.), *Mohamed Ali in Indian Politics: Select Writings*, vol. II (New Delhi, 1983), p. 299. For a recent discussion, see Bimal Prasad, *Pathway to India's Partition, Vol. II: A Nation within a Nation 1877–1937* (New Delhi, 2000), pp. 7–8, 154 and passim.

16. Sumit Sarkar, *Modern India 1885–1947* (Delhi, 1984), p. 212. C.f. p. 377.

17. For the elements of a public in precolonial India, see C.A. Bayly, *Empire and Information: Intelligence Gathering and Social Communication in India, 1780–1870* (Cambridge 1999), pp. 180–211; for civil society in its international and Indian contexts, see Sudipta Kaviraj and Sunil Khilnani (eds), *Civil Society, History and Possibilities* (Cambridge, 2001).

18. I have dealt with the material and social basis of this class at some length in 'Evolution of the Professional Structure in Modern India: Older and New Professions in a Changing Society', *The Indian Historical Review*, July 1982–Jan. 1983, vol. IX, nos. 1–2, pp. 121–92.

19. Sugata Bose, 'Nation as Mother: Representations and Contestations of "India" in Bengali Literature and Culture', in Sugata Bose and Ayesha Jalal (eds), *Nationalism, Democracy and Development: State and Politics in India* (Delhi, 1997), p. 69.

20. Ayesha Jalal, 'Exploding Communalism: The Politics of Muslim Identity in South Asia', in Bose and Jalal (eds), *Nationalism, Democracy and Development*, pp. 87–8.

21. Gail Minault, *The Khilafat Movement: Religious Symbolism and Political Mobilisation in India* (Delhi, 1982), p. 237, n. 92.

22. The young Subhas Chandra Bose said in 1928: 'Privileges based on birth, caste or creed should go, and equal opportunities should be thrown open to all irrespective of caste, creed or religion.' Sisir Kumar Bose and Sugata Bose (eds), *The Essential Writings of Netaji Subhas Chandra Bose* (Calcutta, 1997), p. 86.

23. Ayesha Jalal, *The Sole Spokesman: Jinnah, the Muslim League and the Demand for Pakistan* (Cambridge, 1985), pp. 52n, 58, and passim.

24. Government of West Bengal, *Rabindra Rachanavali* (new ed.), vol. 4 (Calcutta, 1987), song no. 756 dated 18 Asharh BS 1317 (1910), p. 320, Translation mine.

25. Rabindranath Tagore, 'Eastern and Western Civilisation' (1891), *Rabindra Rachanavali* (birth centenary edition), vol. 12, pp. 1060–1.

26. See A.K. Gupta, *North West Frontier Province Legislature and the Freedom Struggle* (New Delhi, 1976); and Joya Chatterji, *Bengal Divided: Hindu Communalism and Partition 1932–1947* (Cambridge, 1995).

27. NAI, Foreign Secret, 25 June 1858, nos. 68–9 (see n. 9).

28. See his modern sociological classic, *Homo Hierarchicus: The Caste System and Its Implications* (London, 1972). In his view of the caste system in its true form, vertical interdependence between superior and inferior castes constituted the substance of the system, and lateral ties between fellows of the same caste were in earlier times confined to the immediate locality.

29. Gallagher, Johnson, and Seal, *Locality, Province and Nation*, passim.

30. Seal, *The Emergence of Indian Nationalism*, passim.

31. Eric Stokes, *The Peasant and the Raj: Studies in Agrarian Society and Peasant Rebellion in Colonial India* (Cambridge, 1978).

32. Ranajit Guha (ed.), *Subaltern Studies*, vols. I, II, and III (New Delhi, 1982–4); Ranajit Guha, *Elementary Aspects of Peasant Insurgency in Colonial India* (Delhi, 1983).

33. Ravinder Kumar (ed.), *Essays on Gandhian Politics: The Rowlatt Satyagraha of 1919* (Oxford, 1971), 'Introduction'.

34. Gail Minault, *The Khilafat Movement: Religious Symbolism and Political Mobilisation in India* (Oxford, 1982), passim.

35. Urdu poem by Shamim Kashani, trans. S.M.A. Husaini, *The Guardian*, Madras, 17 Jan. 1946, rpt in Mushirul Hasan (ed.), *India Partitioned: The Other Face of Freedom*, 2 vols. (New Delhi, 1995), vol. I, p. 81.

Index